I Am is The Way

1966 Lectures

NEVILLE

Order this book online at www.trafford.com
or email orders@trafford.com

Most Trafford titles are also available at major online book retailers.

Scripture quotations marked KJV are from the Holy Bible, *King James Version*
(Authorized Version). First published in 1611. Quoted from the KJV Classic
Reference Bible, Copyright © 1983 by The Zondervan Corporation.

Scripture quotations marked RSV are taken from the *Revised Standard Version of the
Bible*, copyright © 1946, 1952, 1971 by the Division of Christian Education of the
National Council of the Churches of Christ in the USA. Used by permission.

(1966 lectures unabridged, verbatim, and all transcribed from tapes recorded in live
audiences in Los Angeles, CA. Transcriptions and books compiled by Natalie.)

Print information available on the last page.

ISBN: 978-1-4907-7333-9 (sc)
ISBN: 978-1-4907-7334-6 (e)

Library of Congress Control Number: 2016907490

Trafford rev. 05/11/2016

 www.trafford.com

North America & international
toll-free: 1 888 232 4444 (USA & Canada)
fax: 812 355 4082

OTHER WORKS BY NEVILLE

Your Faith Is Your Fortune
The Search
Awakened Imagination
He Breaks the Shell
The Neville Reader (reissue of Neville or Resurrection containing):

> *Out of This World*
> *Freedom for All*
> *Feeling is the Secret*
> *Prayer—the Art of Believing*
> *Seedtime and Harvest*
> *The Law and the Promise*
> *Resurrection*

The Awakening: 1963 Lectures
Imagining and the Transformation of Man: 1964 Lectures
The Wonder Working Power of Imagination: 1965 Lectures

CONTENTS

NOTE FROM AUTHOR

(This is Neville's last piece of writing, given to me by Mrs. Goddard after his death in 1972. Neville felt "that the chapter Resurrection needed something to lead into it.") Natalie

Introduction to *Resurrection*

If I tell you what I know and how I came to know about it, I may give hope to those who would gladly believe the Bible but who do not understand it or who may have thought that the ancient scriptures are but a record of extravagant claims. Therefore, the reason for this report from me, rather than from another whose scholarly knowledge of the scriptures is more erudite, is that I am speaking from experience. I am not speculating about the Bible, trusting that my guesses about its meaning are not too wide of the mark. I will tell you what I have experienced that I should convey more of God's plan than the opinions of those who may know the Bible so intimately that they could recite it from end to end, although they have not experienced it.

He who knows something out of his own experience knows something that makes the finest and wisest opinion look shadowy. True knowledge is experience. I bear witness to what I have experienced. Looking back, I do not know of anything that I heard or read to call forth this knowledge. I did not receive it from man, nor was I taught it, but it came through a series of supernatural experiences in which God revealed himself in action for my salvation.

He unveiled me. And I am he. We mature only as we become our own Father.

I do not honestly expect the world to believe it, and I know all the varieties of explanation I myself should give for such a belief had I not experienced it. But I cannot unknow that which I have experienced. When it occurred it was the most amazing thing that every happened to me. I could not explain it with my intelligence. But God's plan of redemption unfolded within me with such undeniable insistence that finally it became both a mystery and a burden laid upon me. I literally did not know what to do with what I knew. I tried to explain it to friends, and I know that with all good will they could only think, "Poor Neville, he has evidently had a very bad time."

From the first experience, I felt commissioned. I could not unknow it, and I am burdened with that knowledge. The warnings of my friends could make no difference to the truth I had experienced. That truth remained. Whether I could be a living instrument of it or not, I could not say at all. But until I put it into words so that others could read it, I did not feel that I had accomplished the work I was sent to do.

Now that I have written it, I feel that I have finished what I came to do. And that is to reveal the true identity of Jesus Christ. Jesus is the I AM of everyone. He is the Lord, the one God and Father of us all, who is above all and through and in all. Therefore, if the words *Lord, God, Jesus* convey the sense of an existent someone outside of man, he has a false God. Christ is the Son of God. The Son of God is David, the sweet psalmist of Israel.

It's the Father's purpose to give himself to all of us, to each of us. And it is his Son, David, calling us Father, who reveals the Father's gift to us. The Father's gift of himself to us is not discovered until the very end. And all discovery implies suffering to be endured in the process of discovery.

The Father became as we are that we may be as he is. He is never so far off as even to be near, for nearness implies separation. He suffers as us, but we know it not. God as Father is made known only through his Son, David. The core and essence of David's work is his revelation of the Father. Can one come to an identity of oneself with the Father without the Son's revelation of him? Personally, I feel quite sure the answer is no, one cannot. "No one knows the Son except the Father, and no one knows the Father except the Son and anyone to whom the Son chooses to reveal him."

If two different witnesses agree in testimony, it is conclusive. I now present my two witnesses: the internal witness of the Spirit, my experience, and the external witness of scripture, the written Word of God.

Neville
September 1972

FOREWORD

(to 1966 book)

Welcome to the world of practical imagining, of visionary and mystical experiences, of a deeper appreciation of the meaning of life, the inward journey, and the eternal ancient wisdom revisited.

We are led to the truth when we are ready for it. I was led to Neville when answers had to be found, where changes in thinking had to take place in order to expand spiritual awareness. The first most compelling concept encountered was that a change in attitude begets a change in the outer world, stated by Neville as "imagining creates reality." It followed that one's world is a reflection of one's inner thinking plus the attendant emotions; and that to dwell on anything you desire, feeling the possession of it in the present moment, remaining faithful to that feeling of having it now, believing it wholeheartedly, produces that result.

I tried it and it worked. To my joy, a three-and-a-half-month trip to Europe, all expenses paid, came in within about a month after doing an imaginal act of feeling myself flying in a jet over the ocean and then seeing through the window well-known landmarks of Europe below. I did not lift a finger to make it so, told no one about it, and it came out of the blue. This is the pragmatic and provable law that everyone can test endlessly to their satisfaction. It's truly the way to everything in the world; and it's being done by every person every moment of time, either wittingly or unwittingly. It's a magical overcoming of limitation when done deliberately. And it is, you learn, God the I AM, your "I am," in action.

Neville taught from his own visions, mystical experiences, discernment (not speculation) and Bible study, not only that imagining creates reality but that every soul is destined to spiritually awaken eventually as God, yet retaining one's individual identity. He never claimed to be more than the messenger of this eternal story that all will one day experience…a gift which can't be conjured or earned. This book of 1966 talks (the fourth in a series) chronicles a continuing growth in understanding of his six major visions that began in 1959 with the last one occurring after three-and-a-half years. Through extensive study and insight, he found these visions paralleled those in the Bible, the story of Christ; and they proved to be the keys to explaining the hidden mysteries of the prophetic Old Testament and their fulfillment in the New Testament. Perhaps an appropriate analogy would be the Rosetta stone and what it did for the Egyptian hieroglyphics. Once understood and accepted, the larger picture emerges. The questions "Who am I? What am I doing here? Where did I come from? What is the purpose of life?" are all answered in this new at the same time ancient revelation. A sense of power is returned to the individual, plus a great sense of peace comes knowing life really does have a glorious meaning…in spite of the seeming chaos and horrors of the world.

As Browning said in his *Paracelsus,* "Truth is within ourselves; it takes no rise in outward things…There is an inmost center in us all where truth abides in fullness…and to know rather consists in opening out a way whence the imprisoned splendor may escape, than in effecting entry for a light supposed to be without." Neville's teaching gives us the way to that center and how to help open out the way so that the imprisoned splendor may escape. So the story needs time to be understood, to be heard repeatedly, and to be internalized by the seeker. And that is why the eleven years of his lectures are so precious and unique, gradually leading one through the process that culminates in an awakened individual.

Study of this higher level of being helps stir the sleeping giant in all who have been made by their Inner Being into the good soil, that is, made ready to awaken. To awaken is to personally experience those same six visions. These are the signs that the transformation has been completed, and that our divine heritage has been returned. (As encouragement to all, this writer can also bear witness to experiencing the last of the six visions.) Then we can go back to eternity expanded and triumphant having overcome death and the illusion of this world.

Natalie 5/02/2016

ACKNOWLEDGMENTS

Deepest thanks to Neville for being the source of these wonderful insights. The inspiration they will forever engender in readers of his work is undeniable and it is that which is the incentive to preserve his lectures for posterity.

In memory and thanks to William Machgan for his love of Neville's teachings which led him to lend support to this project.

To all who will find help in these volumes, grateful thanks for your interest and for helping spread the good news.

N.

YOUR FUTURE

1/04/66

Tonight my subject is "Your Future." This is open season for prophesying—astrologists, numerologists, teacup leaves, monkey bones—using all these to tell the future. Well, we will confine ourselves to the Bible, and tonight you will find it the most practical right down here in the world of Caesar. The Bible does not tell any man that he has a predetermined future in the world of Caesar. Everything here is conditioned. The Bible teaches that you have an ultimate future which is to awaken as God; that's your real future that's unconditional, unearned. You don't earn it, it's a gift. It's called in the Bible "grace." So everyone is destined to succeed because God is playing the part, playing all the parts; and in the end he awakens and you are he. On this level everything is conditioned.

Now we turn to the Book of Matthew, the 21ˢᵗ chapter, the 22ⁿᵈ verse: Whatever you ask in prayer you will receive if you have faith. It doesn't say that you ask for things that are good for you…"whatever" is all inclusive. *Whatever* you ask in prayer you will receive *if* you have faith.

Now prophets, as Blake told the Bishop Rexford, in the modern sense of the word have never existed. Jonah was no prophet in the modern sense for his prophecy of Nineveh failed. Every honest man is a prophet. We value his opinion both private and public in this way: if you go so, the result is so. He shall never say so-and-so shall happen let you do what you will. He will never say that, for he is a seer, not an arbitrary dictator. You go to a medium and they will tell you so-and-so is going to happen to you, allowing you to be anything you want to be in the meanwhile. It's not true, it's a lie. The only way it would come true or could come true is if on departure you *believe* what you heard. If you believed it and completely convinced yourself of the truth of what he or she said, whether they use tea leaves or coffee grounds or stars or anything else, your future is in your hands. You cannot be in one state of consciousness and not suffer the consequences of not being in another state of consciousness. You cannot change the course of your future life so long as your present state remains the same. A change of state is a change of your world. This whole vast world is infinite response. It's response to you; you are the operant power.

Listen to the words of scripture, "We love *because* he first loved us" (1 John 4:19). We love because *he* first loved us. What "he"? He's speaking of God. Something out there? No, God is *in* man as man's own wonderful human Imagination. So I will now have the world respond? Well, then I must be the operant power and ___(??) it. What would I do? Well, I'd make a selection, single out what I want to be this year 1966; assume that I am it; persuade myself that I am it *now*, though not a thing in this world suggests that I am it or could even become it; and to the degree that I am self-persuaded the world will respond. It *has* to! The little word "because" implies causation: Because he first loved us. You dwell upon it.

Let me tell you a story...you may go out on a limb and tell it. You need not wait until it happens and hope that they will believe you. You can tell it before it takes place *if* you have faith. A few weeks ago I told you the stories of a lady who came here with her husband. He is her minister. She took eleven case histories...nine had come to pass. She wrote of eleven—two were prophetic in the sense they had not yet been realized. You who were here that night will recall the stories. This is one not yet realized. The day was July 27th of last year. She said to her husband Daniel, the minister, "I want you to play this record back for me in your mind...not audibly. Sit quietly and listen to my voice and this is what you're going to hear, 'Danny, I am so happy that you have sold your song and have your 100,000-a-year-plus income.' You play it over and over until my voice becomes as natural to you in this imaginary state as it is when I'm talking to you now." One month later, on the 29th of August...now I do not know these people in the theatrical world. I've been out of it for years and years. I do not know the terminology of the musical world. But she said this lady and she called her by name (she did not confine me to secrecy), the name is Gloria Wood, whoever she is, never heard of her. She said that she has nine gold star records (whatever that means). She is a commercial artist and receives as high as $50,000 for one commercial jingle that only goes a half-minute. She likes Danny's voice, likes his songs, and said to him after the service that she would like to help him. Then, said she, at the very end of her note to me, "This is prophetic. I am sure this will be as real as the nine that I have told you that are already behind us."

On Christmas week, Danny calls up and he tell us—my wife answered the phone—'I know that my wife told you of my hope to put my songs over in an album, well, (calling this same lady by name), she has the reputation'—her name associated with his is an instantaneous sale—'we've made the album. It's distributed by the company who has promoted her to the tune of nine gold records!' Now, $100,000…it just started. But her name was identified with his name on the records in his album, using only his songs, and he plays piano. In fact, he's a one-man-show: plays the organ, he's his own chorus, he's the minister, and he does everything but take up the collection. You've seen him here…big strapping fellow. Well that's one.

Now, to come back to our theme tonight, your future is in your hands, as based upon that verse in the 21st chapter, the 22nd verse of Matthew: "Whatever you ask in prayer, you will receive if you have"… First of all, when you read it you will think…you've been taught by your ministers to pray audibly, get down on your knees and say the words. You go to these churches…over the weekend if you like the ballgames as I do, each started with a huge big prayer. One hundred thousand on the outside and one man is leading them in prayer. He couldn't possibly begin to believe what I want. You if you were present, how could he possibly lead you in prayer? Prayer is a very individual thing. No two tonight in this room desire the same thing and he's leading 100,000 in prayer, in this audible prayer. You don't do it that way. The word prayer as used in the Bible means "motion towards, accession to, nearness at, at or in the vicinity of." That's the meaning of the word prayer. So I have a desire. How am I going to move towards the fulfillment of it? How will I get near? Suppose my desire this night would take me to the East, how would I get near 3,000 miles away? Because I am all Imagination, it's easy. "Man is all Imagination and God is Man and exists in us and we in him. The eternal body of Man is the Imagination, and that is God himself" (Blake, *Annotations to Berkeley)*. All things are possible to God. Is there something you can't imagine? You may not believe it, but don't tell me you can't imagine it!

So now here is the story. In one of my books—I can't recall the title of the book.—if you are familiar with my books, you'll know it. But I'm quite sure that the majority here have never read it or heard this story. The lady to whom it happened did not confine me or in any way swear me to secrecy. She's a gracious, wonderful lady, and so I'm going to use her name. Not to drop names but to let you know who she is, and that with all of her background, tremendous background, she didn't know how to pray. She's a pillar of the Episcopal Church in New York City, a pillar of the church. Her name is Mrs. Archibald Roosevelt, the daughter-in-law of our late Teddy Roosevelt. She came to me, in fact she came once a month, at least once a month, for a period of years. She said, "Neville, every year I have rented my town home, and with that rental paid in advance I've been able to open my country home in Long Island. This year for the first time in over twenty years no one has shown any interest. We have the same real estate agent in the same social world that he caters to, but this year the season's slipping by and rentals will be at an end, for it's only for the summer. Not one person has shown any interest in taking my apartment, and unless I rent it, I cannot open my home in Long Island.

"We have a social position and a political position, but we're not people of means. My husband works for a salary. We are not wealthy Roosevelts. We are Roosevelts and the name is powerful in the political world and in the social world. The demands on me and my husband are so great because of our name at the end of the year we don't know where the next is coming from to give to charity as is expected of us. We have many children and like all mothers the world over, all parents, there's always need and so they come first. So there is always need from one or the other of the five that we have. So, what must I do?" I said, you've been coming here over the years now. You know about me ___(??) from the past. I'll tell it all over again. If you rented your place today, where would you sleep tonight? She said, "Where I slept last night." I said, "Where was that?" "In my New York apartment." I said, "No you rented it. You aren't taking in boarders, you rented the place." "Oh, but" she said, "in the past I always had grace...three, four, five days to get ready and then they would come in after I moved." I said, no, this is an emergency. They rented it, made your payment in advance, and they want to occupy today. She said, "Well, under such circumstances I wouldn't waste the money by going to a hotel, I would go straight to my home in Long Island, even though it's not ready to receive the family." I said, *that's* where you sleep tonight! "Oh," she said, "that isn't practical."

I said, I am not telling you you are going to sleep there physically; you are going to sleep there in your Imagination. Your Imagination is the *real* you, Mrs. Roosevelt. I'm looking at a mask. If I could tear it away, I would see God unmasked. But here, I'm looking at a woman who in the world of Caesar is prominent. I'm speaking now to the *God* in this woman, to your own wonderful human Imagination. And in your Imagination you sleep this night in your home in Long Island. To prove that you *are* there, you must think *of* this apartment, and you cannot see it under you, around you and over you. You must see it across the East River in Manhattan, and you must feel the naturalness of your home in Long Island. She said to me, "*If* this works, I'll call you." I said, the only "if" about it is *if* you do it. If you do it, you'll call me. But you know, you're one of nine in the Bible. He said, were there not ten or you and only one returned to give thanks, and the one that returned was a stranger, a Samaritan. The other nine got the same results, but they didn't return. You've been coming here over the years and often I've read of the answer to your request in this group in the newspapers...I never got it from you. But let it not work, you're on the phone to tell me, like all the others. Let it work…he should know anyway…and so I've grown indifferent to the working or not working. I know the law cannot fail. I have taken it from scripture and the Word of God is true, everlastingly true, and that sentence is true. So tonight, you sleep in your Imagination in your home in Long Island.

This was on Thursday. She went to bed early that night, about nine. She said to her husband and family, "I do not wish to be disturbed unless there is an emergency. Do not call me for any other reason." At nine she retired and to prove she was in the home in Long Island, she thought of her home in Manhattan, and saw it across the East River in Manhattan. She got off the bed in her Imagination and walked through the door into an adjacent room that could only be entered were she in the home in Long Island. She did these many little things and gave this imaginal state all the sensory vividness and all the tones of reality that she could possibly muster. Then she slipped into the deep. In other words, if I were to define faith for you, faith is a simple surrender of self to the Spirit of God. God is your own wonderful I-am-ness, is he not? That's my name forever. "So I'm on my bed…I've just done things that would prove to me I am in my home in Long Island. And the reason why I'm here, my place rented, and I'm very happy about the tenant." This was on Thursday.

On Friday noon or there about, the phone rang and the agent called her, "I have someone interested in your apartment, may I bring him?" "Certainly!" A man came up, he had all the necessary references, he had all the qualifications, and he offered her a check without any argument in advance for the entire summer months. But one condition he imposed upon her: He wanted immediate occupancy that day, which is now Friday. "If you could get out today, I'll take it…but only on condition you move today." She said, "This has never happened to me before, but if this is your condition I will get out." She called her husband about what happened and he said, "It's perfectly alright. Get your things together as quickly as you can. I will take off and I will come and help and we'll move to the home in Long Island." This was on Friday. On Saturday morning at nine, Mrs. Roosevelt is on the telephone and she said, "Neville, this is Mrs. Roosevelt." I said, "Yes?" She said, "I slept in my home in Long Island last night." She expected me to be thrilled. I said I'm not surprised. If you did what I told you to do, you *had* to sleep there last night! Well, she was a little bit taken aback, because she thought now this is a miracle and I should rejoice. All others are miracles too, but she never called me until I put my foot down and said you're just like the other nine that never come back and say thank you.

And so that was the story of "motion towards." In what way—in your Imagination— "accession to; at or in the vicinity of"—at the house, in the house, right in the vicinity of the house. And she did it. To locate herself and make it seem natural she thought of her home across the river and saw it away in the distance in her Imagination, but *not* under her and *not* around her and certainly not over her. That story, as I've told you, I could just add all the little places to it to make it all the more beautiful as it actually happened.

So I tell you, your future is not in the stars, not in teacup leaves, not in anything outside of your own state of consciousness. Everything is here for the taking. You appropriate it, you live in it, and you conquer it in the world. Listen to these words, "By faith he understands that the world was created by the Word of God, so that what is seen was made out of things which do not appear" (Heb.11:3). Did anything appear outside of her own Imagination? What did she do with visible things? Nothing! If anyone had entered her room in Manhattan that night, they would have seen, if it was a child, their mother—if her husband entered, his wife—seemingly asleep. She was asleep to the world. She had shut out the obvious. As you're told, "When you pray, go within and close the door; and your Father who sees in secret will reward you openly" (Mat. 6:6). What was he seeing in secret? He saw her living in her home in Long Island. He saw her happy because she had rented the New York place. It hadn't burned down…she was happy about it. But who could have looked to that woman and seen any visible things that she used to construct this scene? So here it is, what is seen is made out of things which do not appear. Now isn't that clear? So where is my future? It's within me.

Religion always needs tests. Without it, all religions become distorted into creeds, into some ritual, yes, even into self-centered ___(??). So religion does not ___(??) when it appeals to personal experience despite the risk involved. And I say that advisedly, because many will come here—which will shock you—you think if they heard it on the wing and they were not exposed to it as you are—but many will come here in a meeting like this and I will say over and over always use your Imagination *lovingly* on behalf of others, never use it in any hateful manner. There is no *other*; you're only going to hurt yourself. *Always* use it lovingly on behalf of others. Yet there are those who will gloat over the hurt of another, and gloat in the presence of others and tell them, "I want to see him dead…and he is dying before my face…and hurt these, too, because they don't want the speaker dead"…just actually feel it… then you're taking this fabulous law that could set *you* free and bind yourself all the more.

So I will say to you who has done it, you cannot cause me to depart before my time. No one multiplied by all the people of the world has the power to cause my departure one second before my time. You can't hasten it and you can't delay it. And it would be better if a millstone were tied around your neck and be cast into the sea than to dare to put your finger on one whom he has called to tell his story! If you saw tonight's TV, here is Mike Quinn, head of the Transport Union. He incited the entire city of New York. He was brought before cameras and these are his words...there he is before the cameras and he's saying, speaking of the judge who sent him to jail, he said, "I'm waiting for the sheriff to come and he will take nine of us...and let the judge drop dead and rot in his black robes. I will not" said he "call back this strike." Alright, the sheriff came through the door and picked him up, put him in the wagon, and off to the city jail. He was there two hours and *he* came down with a heart attack. Here came the ambulance, they wrapped him up in his blankets, and rolled him out to the waiting ambulance to take him to Belvue. What he wanted for the judge arrived within two hours and happened to him. There is no "other." So I tell you, use your Imagination *lovingly* on behalf of all because there is no other—it's yourself pushed out. This whole vast world is yourself pushed out.

Your future is really in your hands here in the world of Caesar. But because you don't use it lovingly...I could never tell you how long, how vast, how severe the anguish before you are brought forth from the furnaces. For you aren't going to be brought forth from the furnaces and enter the world called "the kingdom of God" until you are perfect as your Father in heaven is perfect. So do unto others as you would have them do unto you, that's the eternal code. And never accept a feeling of getting even or hurting unless you want the same thing done to you.

So I tell you, the story is true. Whatever, as vast as eternity, you ask in prayer—remember what prayer is, motion towards the fulfillment of the wish fulfilled, that's motion towards...all in your Imagination. You will receive it, that's a promise, *if* you have faith. So take tonight's definition of faith, which I'll give you, which is "a simple, simple surrender of self to the Spirit of God." You put yourself in the state and sleep, you surrender your Spirit: "Into thy hands I commit my Spirit." After having occupied the state, simply relax in that state and God sees the state you're in, and that's like a ___(??) and the whole vast world responds to what you have done. You don't have to ask them anything. Mrs. Roosevelt didn't go out and come up to a person saying "You've always over the years rented my place, what's wrong?" She didn't complain. She simply went home, she believed what I told here, and she applied it. The very next day it's rented and she has her check for months in advance. With that she could open her place and have a wonderful, wonderful summer.

So let no one put any wet blanket upon you by telling you that the future is already written for you and it's in the stars. Those wonderful words of Cassius to Brutus, "The fault, dear Brutus, is not in the stars but in ourselves that we are underlings." Not in the stars! Look there if you want to, but you won't find them there at all. I'll tell you a story concerning one who is now gone from this world. Last fall in New York City, I learned that she had just recently before my arrival made her exit. She was a teacher in a high school in

Scranton, Pennsylvania. She came to New York City, she was a widow, she had a widow's pension from the railway—she could always travel on the railway without paying anything—but she wanted to live in New York City. She had a nice pension from the school and from the railway; it was adequate, not big. She wanted to do something in the City. Well, my old friend Abdullah...I took her to Abdullah...and she couldn't quite get the feeling of what Abdullah was trying to get over, but she could believe in astrology.

Well, I think I know how to erect a chart and regress a chart, and so I taught her. I told her, it isn't there at all, it's all *in you*; but if it takes you to persuade you of something nice to tell someone, then use it. But, eventually, you'll take it like a crutch and throw it away. Well, one day I called on her and she was in tears, actual tears. I said, Norma, what's wrong? She said, "A man came in here, very highly recommended, a good business man, successful, and I read his chart. I told him that he will send me the $100 he promised me he would. In fact, I'm so convinced that it's true, I said to him, "Don't wait, give it to me now!" He said, "No, if it works today as you tell me, well, then I will send you the money." I said, well, what's wrong with that, Norma? She said, "The chart wasn't his chart. I was sitting at the open window and the wind blew over the Ephemerides." They were bound...she had about 100 years of these all bound in one volume, and while sitting at a window she was distracted and she came back, not checking, and drew a chart from what she saw there, not knowing the wind had turned over the pages and she's now drawing a chart of one who wasn't born until ten years later. But she said, "Neville, I drew a chart of a man who was ten years not yet in this world." And what's wrong with that? Did you convince him? She said, "I think I did, for I said in all seriousness give me the $100 now. If you're going to send it to me after it works, give it to me now. That seemed to convince him all the more, Neville." I said, it's done! Forget it! She still couldn't stop her tears.

That night after dinner I called on her again. I was in her suite of rooms at this Knott (?)

Hotel, at 72nd and Broadway—it's gone now, of the old Knott chain—when the doorbell rang, it's a messenger from Western Union. It's a hundred dollar check, a Western Union check. And she drew a chart of a man who wasn't born! But she was convinced when she spoke to him—and he didn't see her tears and our conversation didn't hear that—so he went away convinced of the reality of her abracadabra. He's a big business man. You see, it comes in all walks of life. They tell me that Hitler wouldn't make a move without consulting his astrologer...so they tell me. Where did it get him? Where did it get him finally? And so all this business of something on the outside...she got that $100 and I was in her room when that Western Union boy delivered that Western Union check.

Yes, you can persuade yourself if you want these things, but don't, don't resort to anything but God, and God is your own wonderful human Imagination. If God is the only creator, he is the only receiver as well. So you think of your home right now, who's doing it? If I said, what are you doing? "I"—right away you said God—"I am" and then you name it. Well, who's doing it? You said, "Well, I'm doing it." Well, that's God. He is the only receiver. But if you don't know that, you aren't going to believe in the reality of what you're doing. So you imagine something now, that's God doing it, that's God in action. So when this chap, Danny, imagined his wife's voice saying, "Danny, I'm so happy that you sold your songs and you have a 100,000-plus in income a year," it's only just on the market this past month of December, but at least it's in an album. How many people today who have written songs would give anything to make one record of it! And here a woman comes off the street, comes into his little church here on Wilton Place, I think it's 801 Wilton, and likes the man's voice, likes what he's singing, and ___(??) so that right after the meeting she goes up and tells him what she thinks of the songs. Well, that's just what Danny wanted, and he puts on a whole show for her; and then she said, "I want to help you." So she, because she has nine gold star records, she wants to associate her name to help his name, and does it. I think it's called "My Pastor and I"…I think it is. He called up and told this story to my wife.

Well, I tell you, your future is not outside your ability to imagine that you are the one that you want to be. Just imagine that you are now the one that you want to be, and forget all these things round about you. *If* you are faithful to it, surrendering yourself to the Spirit of God, all things being possible to God, it will come to pass in your world. Everything in your world is conditioned. The only unconditioned is God's ultimate promise to himself which is man that in the end he will awaken and he will be Jesus Christ. You will know there is only Jesus Christ. *Everyone* will know he is Jesus Christ and yet no loss of identity; although a radical discontinuity of form, for your form will be the glorious risen form of the risen Christ!

Now let us go into the Silence.

*   *   *

Q: (inaudible)

A: I find that many of us try to hold a thought…just identify yourself with a state, and if you are in a state, to prove you're in it, ___(??) take the presence of your friends, an event. If they see you as they've always seen you, then you haven't changed your state. Because they can't see you as you were if you change, so let them see the change. ___(??) Don't carry on a conversation; just allow them to become aware of your new state. Eavesdrop as it were. Hear *their* conversation.

Q: In the healing miracle, Jesus says, go forth and tell the ___(??). What's the reason for that?

A: Those who have little faith…he said, "I tell you before it takes place, that when it does take place, you may believe." Read that in the 14th chapter of the Book of John (verse 29). I tell you before it takes place…and they didn't understand it. I'll tell you all these things before and when it does take place *in you* you'll believe. You have the courage to know that in everyone the thing is going to happen, he tells them. I tell you that God's plan of salvation must be experienced in everyone, therefore, in everyone individually. So I tell you before it takes place that when it does take place, you'll believe all that I've told you is true.

Q: "And I, if I be lifted up from the earth, I will draw all men unto me."

A: That interpretation? Well, first of all, it's an actual true story. You'll find the interpretation of that in the 3rd chapter of John. He's speaking of the Son of man. The Son of man is the Son of God; the Son of God is the resurrected one. These three are not three persons but one being, designated the Son of God through his resurrection from the dead. And what does he say of the Son of man? He's asking the Son of man, he identifies him with the Christ, he said, "What think ye of the Son of man? What will people say of the Son of man?" as you read it in the 16th of Matthew. Some answered, "John the Baptist, some say Elijah come again, others say Jeremiah or one of the prophets" (verse 13). He doesn't respond, he said, "Well, what do *you* say that I am?" So he identifies himself with the Son of man. "But what do you say, who do you say that I am?" Then Peter answered, "Thou art the Christ." He accepts that; therefore, the Son of man he calls himself and then he allows him to be called the Christ. In the 3rd of John, "As Moses lifted up the serpent in the wilderness, so must the Son of man"—which is I AM which is Christ—"be lifted up." And that's an actual true experience. The day will come that some bolt of lightning will split you from top to bottom. Not physically, yet to you it will appear to be a physical act; for you will see your body—but it can't be this [pointing to body] one, and yet it is a body—split right down the entire spinal column. Every little niche split right in half to the base of your spine. And you will see at the base golden, living, liquid, light. As you look at it, you know it is yourself, and know that "It is myself,

O my Divine Creator and Redeemer." Then you will fuse with it, you the perceiver, and you'll go up that spine of yours in a serpentine form just like the Seraphim right into Zion. "I, if I be lifted up, I will raise all men unto me."

Q: (inaudible)

A: A negative is just as powerful, because there's steam behind it. When Mike Quinn tonight said, "Let him drop dead in his black robes and rot," he had all the feeling that that sixty-year-old body could muster. He's been a revolutionary all his life. That's perfectly alright. He's done great things for the Transport Union. He's taken them from starvation-wages up. But you must consider eight million people who live in New York City. It's costing the city a hundred million dollars a day. Every day that the strike is on, 100 million dollars is lost to the city. He doesn't care. There must be some way of getting together, and get the men a living wage, whatever they're asking for. Their present request would take the fifteen cent fare and make it forty-five. Well, a round trip fare on a subway or a bus is up to ninety cents a day. He said, "But the city will pay." The city can't pay anything, you and I will pay. Every increase in taxes must be paid by us. So tonight we have a new budget—110, maybe 115 billion. We were promised only a year ago there would be no increase. It was under 100 billion. So all of sudden you get, well, what does it matter, fifteen billion more, another so-and-so billion more? And then who's going to pay it? *We* have to pay it. They say Uncle Sam! He doesn't exist. The federal government will pay it, with what? They can't give me one penny until they first take it from me. Take it from me and then give it back to me and say it's from Uncle Sam…can't do it.

We go blindly on believing that the other fella's going to do it. There must be something that is wrong. If the rate isn't equal to the inflation, the man must get more even though we have to pay. But don't jump from fifteen cents, thirty cents a day, up to ninety cents. Give him something… maybe up it another twenty cents, fifteen cents. But he said, no, he would not call back his strike. ___(??) dictator. And he was shocked when they said go to jail, because, in the past when Lewis defied the court order they crippled him with the first fine and the union as well. They paid it, Lewis paid it, and the union paid it, but they didn't send him to jail. Well, tonight when this man has to go to jail with eight other officials of the union, it was an awful blow to one who was so prideful anyway as Quinn is. I'm a great admirer of the Irish. Sometimes I think we are all Irish. He came to this country as a boy, very small boy, and there's no ___(??). He has contemplated what he thinks America expects an Irishman to sound like. Puts on this brogue that no Irishman speaks that way, carries a shillelagh. But he was cut out for the kind of a person he is. When we came here, someone said tonight that "I knew him from the time he was a boy. He came in as a rebel, a raging rebel. What he was looking for 'something to fight and Englishmen to eat.'" That was his diet. What I'm getting at, he can no more pronounce this thing of death on the judge than he ___(??).

Q: Neville, I'm puzzled over these problems of good and evil. Are not these largely human concepts? Do they have any absolute value?

A: You're told that only two things displease God, so the Bible teaches. One is eating of the tree of the knowledge of good and evil, and the other is the lack of faith in I AM he. These are the only two things that displease God. "Unless you believe I am he, you die in your sins" (John 8:24) and then the other is eating of the tree that bears good and evil. Look into the world tonight. We're going to spend and have been spending billions in Vietnam, Southeast Asia. Everyone who is fighting against us thinks they are doing good and we are thinking we are doing good. Well now, who's doing good? We know we're doing good, and they know with equal strength they're doing good. They know we're doing evil and we know they're doing evil. And so, when the last war came to an end I was on jury duty, and so the judge said, "Don't ___(??) today." Nothing came very early ___(??) the news early, and so at that moment every German either openly or inwardly wept. They thought they were doing the right thing and we knew we were doing the right thing…every German, every Italian, and every Japanese because they knew it was coming to an end. They knew it couldn't be far delayed. I'm told, though I don't know, that something like 80,000 Japanese committed suicide the day that they signed the peace treaty. 80,000 of them because they thought that their good went unnoticed. So good and evil are all relative terms. We have one wonderful code: Do unto others as you would have them do unto you. You can't go wrong if that is your code. Would I want it done to me? Well then, don't do it to the other fellow. And with that as your code you can't go wrong.

Q: I would like to move next weekend and I'd like to know how I can ___(??).

A: You'd like to move?

Q: Yes, I have the house all picked out and everything.

A: Well, sleep in it mentally.

Q: I've been doing that and it seems that it's at a standstill, but I wondered if perhaps I started packing or something it might help?

A: You don't have to aid God.

Q: I see...

A: No, she doesn't have to aid God. I have done these things in idle moments to find that I regretted that I had, because it works. For instance, my wife and I sent off our check to Maine in the year 1941 for a vacation. ___(??) in New York City, when it came to the hot months, people take off July and August and return after Labor Day. So we thought we'd just take our clothes and take off for the month of August and go to Maine, sent our reservations and our check. That very year...it was a cold beastly night in February, and a very small crowd came, about 150-175 and I used to get 750-1,000 people, three times a week in an old church right off Times Square. But the snow was twelve inches on the ground by 6:30 in the evening and it was still coming, so I knew they wouldn't come out. It was the first night I brought out my book *Your Faith is Your Fortune*. So naturally, there were just a few people that I could expose the book to. So I went home a little bit disappointed and I slept in the assumption that I was in Barbados in that wonderful warm climate. I could hear the coconut leaves on the top of the shingled roof and smell the tropical odors. I did all the things that were natural ___(??).

Next morning when I woke there weren't twelve inches; there were twenty inches on the ground. I was still in New York City. But the deep of my being, the soul, did not forget and when I planned a vacation in the month of August in Maine, what I had planted in the month of February was maturing. I got a cable from home saying that mother is in a terminal state and if you want to see her ___(??) come. This was on a Thursday and we ran around getting papers and sailed on Friday night without our papers. 1941submarines were sinking ships left and right, but we went on an American ship with a huge, big flag painted on it, and lights burning all through the day and night. We had escorts taking us through the night. ___(??) huge, big passenger ship and that was the last time she sailed, because we were at war two months later in December.

You see, I planned idly. I slept in Barbados because I was disappointed with the snow and to get away from it all, I actually planted the seed and it came into fruition in the month of August. My wife and I sailed the last of August and spent the month of September and got back here in October. Then Pearl Harbor came in December. You see, don't do it idly…(tape ends).

BELIEVE IT IN

1/07/66

Tonight's subject or title is really "Believe It In." But the paper didn't believe that I meant that and so they rearranged it, without my permission, and called it "Believe In It." So when they sent the proofs back, it was so late I had no time to correct it because they had gone to press. Well, they did no more than our scholars do to the Bible. We have a passage in the Bible that "woman is saved by the bearing of children (1Tim.2:15RSV). They give you a footnote that the real passage reads "woman is saved by the birth of *the* child." It's all the difference in the world. And through the Bible you'll find when it does not make sense, our scholars *give* it sense…and it isn't so at all. In the Book of Jeremiah, we're told that man draws himself out of himself, and he begins the drawing when he reaches the hips. He actually comes out of himself, and then he uses his hands to draw the remaining portion. Well, the scholars could not believe that and so they say "Why do I see every man with his hands on his hips just like a woman in labor? (30:6)"

So I did not intend the title they gave me. The title is "Believe It In." The late Robert Frost, oh, maybe two or three years before he died, some reporter from *Life* magazine interviewed him, and he said—and it startled the readers of *Life*—that "our Founding Fathers did not believe in the future, they believed it in; we are always believing ahead of our evidence." He said, "What evidence had I that I could write a poem? I just believed it." He said, "The most creative thing in us is to believe a thing in." The Bible teaches that "*all* things are possible to him who believes" (Mk 9:23)—not a few, not *if* the wise men say that it is possible, if you can believe, all things are possible to him who believes. If this is true, you and I should devote all of our lives, really, to the mastery of the art of believing.

How to believe when reason denies it, my senses deny it, everything denies it? Yet I am haunted with the statement of scripture, "All things are possible to him who believes." So how do I do it? Fawcett said—using the word Imagination, but really you can take the word belief in the same way— he said "The secret of imagining is the greatest of all problems to the solution of which the mystic aspires, for supreme power, supreme wisdom and supreme delight lie in the far off solution of this mystery." Well, if that is true, I should devote all of my energies to the mastery of this art of believing and the art of imagining. For Imagination and believing are the stuff out of which we fashion our worlds…every one of us. There isn't a thing in this world that comes suddenly upon us that really did not have its cause in some invisible imaginal state where we believed it. We forgot it, yes, went about our business, things are active, and suddenly it confronts us, and we don't really recognize our own harvest. But everything comes by reason of the law, and we plant it by believing. We were told the story and we believed it. Others rejected it; we believed it.

Or we can tell ourselves a story. Let me tell you a story that I know intimately, because it's part of my family's world. You can't conceive of anything poorer than to be born on a little island say like Barbados where I was born, and born with a light skin and be poor. If you were born with dark skin, you have a chance. If you were born with a white skin and you have money, tremendous chance. But to be born with white skin and poor, you're behind the eight-ball at birth. Well, both my father and mother were born in these situations, poor and white. The highest education we had on the island would be what we could call high school, but not the standard we have today or certainly not the standard when my father went to school that we had then in this country. He went as far as he could go and he had to get a job, his first job in the city, paying five shillings a week. A shilling, call it a quarter, it was really twenty-four cents, but call it a quarter. There was no transportation and he lived ten miles in the country from the city. He had to be on the job at six in the morning and he had to walk it. It was six days a week and he walked back when the store closed at six, walked back another ten miles for his five shillings a week.

There was a huge big building judged by other standards on the main street. It was called C. F. Harrison & Company, a department store. They also had a commercial agency in the store. Some nights when he was beastly tired and to compensate he used to play the little game of believing, and to comfort himself he would believe that he owned that store. Well, he was as far from ownership as possible…well, how would I even compare it to something else… my being near the White House. That's already been ruled out by human law, because I was born outside of continental America, so I would be as far removed, as my father, from owning this building. It occupied a whole block on the main street, a wonderful wide side street to the second street, a whole block. It was owned almost 100 years by the same family, but they lived in England; they never saw it. They hired local men and occasionally they sent a man out from England to take over management. But he played this game and it helped him, it compensated him when he was beastly tired, walking home in the belief he owned C. F. Harrison & Company.

Now, the Bible teaches that "every vision has its own appointed hour, it ripens, it will flower. If it be long, wait, for it is sure and it will not be late" (Hab.2:3). No two seeds have the same time interval to sprout. Some will take years, some will come overnight like a mushroom, but they all come in different time periods. Well, in 1942 the War is on, a 2nd World War. My father in the meanwhile…this goes back into the 19th Century, 1894, 1895, when he was playing this little game of believing. Then he got married and raised ten children. Through hard work, he was given a junior partnership in a small little grocery venture. They carried groceries, liquor, meat, and so on. 1919, for reasons that need not be explained, for they're still unexplained, he was eased out of his partnership. They wanted it for themselves, and five men got together and eased him out. He had no choice in the matter. He was eased out with ten children, unschooled…where to turn? No equity, really, in that little junior partnership.

It all adds up. With borrowed money he started a little grocery store, that's all that he knew, and one of my brothers with him. In 1942, a man came by… he was standing at the front of his store looking at this big building, and this friend said, "Mr. Joe, what are you doing?" "Oh," he said, "I'm just looking over at this building. I've always liked it." He said, "Would you like to own it?" "Huh!" he smiled. He said, "If any man who owns this building were ever to entertain the thought of selling it, he should have his head fixed. This is a gold mine. It's owned by an Englishman who is ninety-two years old. He has two sons—one is a priest who doesn't want any part of the commercial world, and the other has been a playboy all of his life. He has all the money in the world and would have not a thing to do with overseas properties. He has all that he needs in London plus this. This is his, too." "Well," he said, "I'm just asking" said this man to my father. He said, "Where is Vic?"…Vic is my brother. "Oh," he said, "he's somewhere around. I saw him here recently." He said, "I want to see Vic." So when Vic came by, he said, "I want to see you alone." Took him upstairs to the office and he said, "Vic, read this letter. It came from the old man who owns the building, trusting me as an honored friend, a trusted friend, to sell it to some local family who has the island's interests at heart, who has worked hard and proven by their efforts that they're really good hard workers and a local family." Vic read the letter and he could hardly believe his eyes. In the letter he said "All I want is a good value, no great profit. Value the building, take an inventory of the stock, and then that's all that I want. But I want whoever buys it to take over the obligations of the insurance policies for my employees." He employed about, oh, maybe seventy people and all were insured against retirement.

So here was the figure when he'd taken inventory. The building is worth… and he quoted a figure. He said, "Now let me call my father." Daddy read the letter and then he said, "All right, let's go straight to the bank. I'll take it, have no money, but I'll take it." Went to the bank and then he said to the bankers, "I need so much, but I can't tell you why. If you want to know why, I can't tell you. Cable headquarters in Toronto," and then he made a promise, "and tell them we want to borrow a certain sum of money which is in excess of our present loan, but we can't tell them why we want it." The bank sent back, "This is the most unusual request, but we've dealt with the Goddards now for twenty-odd years and so we will say yes to this request." Then he wrote a letter, went to the head censor, the War was on, this man's name was Johnny Walker, a descendant of the Scotch family, he was the head censor, and he said "Now Mr. Walker, I want you to read this letter and you will see in this letter that we have said nothing to in any way affect the War effort, no secrets. We are just simply accepting an offer and making an offer." The man read it, he said, "Now I want you to seal it in my presence so these 275 girls and boys will not read it after you've sealed it. You read it and seal it, and let me see you mail it." For in those days our ships were going down left and right by the subs, so we had no assurance the letter would ever reach England; for we had no other means other than water transportation. Time went by…three months later came a cable, "Accept Goddard's offer." By then the Bank of France wrote the money, the whole thing was done, and it broke in the papers the next day. Every merchant in the island rushed in to buy a piece of it. My father said "No, it's just for the family, just the ten of us, nine brothers and a sister, and my father and mother, that's all." In fact, mother had just gone, for she left us in 1941.

What I'm getting at is this. The old man was right, Robert Frost: "We're always believing *ahead* of our evidence." In the meanwhile he worked, they all worked hard, and then came the evidence of what was no idle daydream, which he indulged in only to help him walk ten miles after being tired all day and walking home to his little hut in the country. That building today with its present rate of business, I don't think anyone could come for it under, say, eight million dollars. I don't think anyone…and it's not for sale because business is too good. The very commercial agencies that we have are in themselves a fantastic business, aside from the actual business that is conducted there. First thing my brother did, he brought in an English architect, disemboweled the place and modernized it, and used every square inch that he could use as against the old concept…like the Emporium in San Francisco. Just disemboweled the center so as to give it air or to watch the people below, something, and all that space is wasted. We had something similar. He put in elevators, put in escalators, and covered the entire four floors, occupying every square foot of the space. And today, it is the most valuable piece of property…all based upon my father's believing.

The art of believing…he used to practice this every day of his life. He would come home for breakfast. We call breakfast at home the first heavy meal around ten, ten-thirty. Early in the morning it's really breaking the fast but you do that with a cup of tea or a cup of coffee, and then you go off and return around ten, ten-thirty for a substantial meal which we call breakfast. So after this substantial meal he would sit in a chair, and with his eyes partly closed, he would see what he wanted to see. He would imagine what he wanted to imagine, and carry on mental conversations with imaginary people from premises of his fulfilled desire.

So he started from scratch, behind the eight-ball, but if all things are possible to the one who believes, well then, he's proved it. He had not a thing in this world to support the claim that believing he had it that he would have it. And look at the things that happened in the interval. One became a priest…he wasn't even born when my father began to do this. The old man who was then ninety-two, if you take off the almost fifty years, well then, he was in his forties, early forties. And if the one who is the priest was born, he was a young man; the other who became a businessman but really a playboy. They never saw their overseas properties; then came two world wars while this little thing is maturing and germinating. So his vision, his belief was in keeping with Habakkuk, "The vision has its own appointed hour. It ripens, it will flower. If it be long, wait, for it is sure and it will not be late." That's the 2nd chapter of Habakkuk (verse 3).

So here, the whole vision is for man. You are as free as the wind *if* you believe these principles in scripture, not based upon anything on the outside at all, all based upon you. Can you believe? And this story is told after the disciples failed to cure a certain lad and they asked, "Why did we fail?" He said, "Because of your unbelief, you faithless generation. How long must I be with you?" And then he explained and the father said, "I believe you; help my unbelief" (Mark 9:24). So that's what we're here for, to help each other's unbelief. You say, I have a certain goal, but so far I haven't realized it. Well, that's the purpose of the platform: it's to help. What are you doing? I find the great fallacy of the whole world in this art of believing is perpetual construction and deferred occupancy. Occupancy is incubating the dream. What do I mean by occupancy? I mean thinking *from* instead of thinking *of.*

I can stand here and think of for the rest of my days, think of owning that, owning this, or I can think of something I'd like to do; but until I actually occupy it, dwell in it, and look at the world from it, I haven't incubated it, I haven't fertilized it. I can take an egg, ___(??) egg, until that sperm enters it isn't fertilized. How does the sperm enter the egg? It's still a mystery to our scientists. Well, here a sperm enters the egg from the outside and yet there are no holes on the outside of that egg either before or after fertilization. How did he do it?

Well, you can do it because you are the sperm of God; you are the creative *power* of God. How do I do it—by Imagination. I can stand here and no power in this world can stop me from imagining that I am where I would like to be. They can't stop me. I can stand here, you can bind me, you can do anything, but you can't stop me from imagining that I am, say, in San Francisco. You will say what does that matter? Well, if I desire to go to San Francisco and I haven't the time or the means, I will go to San Francisco in my Imagination, and things will reshuffle themselves to give me the time and the means. Then I'll be compelled to move across a bridge of incidents that will lead me from here to where I am in Imagination, and I'll go to San Francisco. I have done it time and time and time again. So when you know what you want, occupy it. Occupy any state in this world. Occupancy is fertilization, and the egg is not fertilized until you occupy it. When that sperm enters, it doesn't break the shell. You need no door to open the door; you go in and occupy it.

Now, we are told that God speaks to man in a vision or rather he makes himself known in a vision and speaks to him in a dream. A few years ago, I think it was Christmas night, about two or three years ago, I had this vivid, vivid dream. It as more than a dream, it was like a waking dream, a waking state. But I found myself in New York City on Fifth Avenue in one of the huge, big mansions that dotted the avenue at the turn of the century. These were enormous mansions, sixty to eighty rooms to a mansion, where people occupied them, one family, but they had maybe twenty-five guest rooms. They had their stables on the west side where the servants lived above where the horses were kept. But these enormous things...I saw them when I came to this country in 1922. They had just begun to demolish them, and the big buildings were going up then. But in my vision I found myself on the inside of this fabulous mansion and there were three generations present. One was invisible; he was spoken of as grandfather. Then there were two visible, the second and third generations, and the second was telling the third that grandfather used to say while standing on an empty lot, "I remember when this was an empty lot." He's standing on it, and he would tell them, "I remember when it was an empty lot." Then he would paint a word picture of his desire for that lot, and paint it so graphically they could see it as though it were fact and objective to vision.

I woke on my bed in Los Angeles and the whole thing was so vivid, I got out of bed, it was early, 3:30, and I wrote the whole thing down, the entire vision. It was too early to get up and remain up, so I went back to bed and re-dreamed the dream, only with a slight change. Now I'm in the mansion, the same mansion, and there are three generations but I am grandfather. I didn't speak *of* grandfather; I was grandfather. I heard the story in my vision and I had so absorbed the power of faith, the power of belief that now in telling the story, I told them…"I would stand on an empty lot and I would say to those who were with me, 'I remember when this was an empty lot.'" Then I painted the word picture of my desire for that lot and did it so well and so vividly that they all saw it.

Now the Bible teaches that the doubling of the dream means that God has fixed the thing and God will shortly bring it to pass. You read that in the 41st chapter of the Book of Genesis (verse 32)…the doubling of a dream, the thing should come to pass, for God has fixed it. Now, who is the God that's spoken of? It's your own wonderful I-am-ness, that's God. "That's my name forever. By this name I am known and will be known throughout all generations" (Ex.3:14). Well, who had the experience? I did. And when you woke and wrote it down and went back to bed who had the second one? I did. Therefore, the whole thing came from the depths of my own soul.

Now, have a wonderful, wonderful experience in your Imagination and make it real. Give it all the sensory vividness, all the tones of reality, and when it seems real to you and you're thinking *from* it, it's done. In a little while, do it again, double the vision, the dream. For you're told, if it's double then it's fixed and God shall shortly bring it to pass. So, take the Bible at its word and double it, and see how this thing comes in this world. You bring things in by believing. You are always believing ahead of your evidence. The most creative thing in man is to believe a thing in.

May I tell you, it's not difficult. Not only it's not difficult, there is no strain, because if you believe a thing, there certainly is no strain to it. If you have faith, there's no strain to it. Faith is only loyalty to unseen reality. You're told in scripture, he calls a thing that does not exist and he calls it into existence. Read it in the 4th chapter, the 17th verse of Romans. The Catholic Bible translates that passage "He calls a thing that is not seen as though it were, and the unseen becomes seen." Well, no one saw my father owning that place, and he didn't share his little story with anyone else. So he was calling a thing that was not seen by another as though it were seen by the world… and then the unseen, in time, became a fact. So here, you call a thing that is not seen just as though it were and the unseen will become seen. You do it with anything in this world. You are the operant power and you have to make the choice. There's always risk in your choice, because you may not always choose lovingly. If you don't choose lovingly, well, you will still get it, only you will find it was an unwise choice. Time will prove it, because in the end you'll discover there is no "other" but really no other just yourself. So if you choose something that is to another's disadvantage, you'll prove, time will prove it to you that you made an unwise choice. Yet you are free to do it, because the story is *all* things, not a few things, "All things are possible to him who believes."

Now, here is the secret in this little story of believing: You always start at the end. The end is where I begin. In my end is my beginning. You go to the very end, the thing accomplished, you start there. And then you bounce back here...and then you move across this series of events that lead you to that end that you had already predetermined. Here is something that...of course I don't like to use science to support anything in scripture, because scripture is so far *beyond* anything in science. It doesn't appeal to the rational mind as science does. It belongs to a depth so deep that reason can't reach it, that's why it still remains undisturbed by all the arguments, all the intellectual criticisms that you can throw at it. It still remains undisturbed, but sometimes some fantastic thing comes out which, well, it's so funny the scientists have said it. In fact, right now, or it just happened in—is it Norway where they give these prizes out?—well, this wonderful prize to Mr. Feynman, Professor Feynman, he's now at Cal Tech. But they're giving it to him today for something that he stumbled upon in 1949 (because I have his scientific paper at home, the Nov. 15th or Oct. 15th issue of *The Science News Letter*). And he said what they're giving him today is for something he discovered a way back in 1949. He said, "It's no earthly good from a practical point of view, but you can't discount it, you can't rub it out, there it is." This is what he said concerning a little particle discovered in atomic disintegration, something known to scientists as the positron. Now he said, "The positron is a wrong-way electron. It starts from where it hasn't been and it speeds to where it was an instant ago. Arriving there, it is bounced so hard its time sense is reversed and then it speeds back to where it hasn't been." He's getting a prize for that...this is Professor Richard Feynman of Cal Tech.

Now the physics of the mind cannot differ really in any respect from the physics of the rest of nature, for God is one, there's a unity here. Alright, how could I relate that to this statement now from the 14th of John: "In my Father's house are many mansions; were it not so would I have told you? And now I go and prepare a place for you. When I go and prepare a place for you, I will come again and receive you unto myself, that where I am there ye shall be also" (verse 2). Now look upon it as a conversation taking place within one man. The outer man can't do it, he's helpless…he has no money, no position, he has nothing…but he has a desire. He has to turn that desire over to the depths of his own soul who is God, his own wonderful human Imagination, that's God, so all things are possible to God.

The outer man can't do it, so he puts him on a chair, puts him on a bed, leaves him just where he is, he's helpless. Now in Imagination I go and prepare the place for him, wherever I would like to take him. But he has voiced the request, his desire, so I go into a state named by him. I occupy the state, it seems so real, and then I break it and speed quickly back to where I left the garment one second before. Now, to the outer mortal eye no one saw me go any place and no one saw me speed back, but I know what I did. I went into an unseen state based upon the mortal eye, and when I broke the spell I sped back to where I was physically. And I'm bounced so hard by the realities of things round about me that my time sense is reversed; and now I move across this series of events, this bridge of incidents that takes me from where I am physically to where I really am in Imagination.

So I move forward across this ladder of events and so he said, "It speeds from where it was not and comes back to where it was an instant ago; arriving there, it is bounced so hard the time sense is reversed, and now it goes back to where it hasn't been." All right, I can see that. I'm going back to where I haven't been physically, not as yet, but I *was* there spiritually. So I go in spirit to prepare it and start back to where I was physically; we coincide once more; then I go forward to where I am in spirit and take with me this garment that I had left behind.

Now, said he, having seen this peculiar behavior of the little particle, man's entire concept of the world has changed. He can no longer believe that the future slowly unfolds out of the past. Now he has to see the entire space-time history of the world laid out and we only become aware of increasing portions of it successively. The whole thing is finished and I simply become aware of portions of it. He said, the direction that it takes is irrelevant.

For that he's getting $50,000. If I told you that story without prefacing my remarks by telling you a very honored man is this night receiving a great honor for that discovery and led you to believe that I said it, if you're here for the first time, I prophesy you're here for the last time. But it's Professor Feynman and all scientists today are way up in the minds of men. Because he said it and he's being honored for it, oh, isn't that marvelous…tell us something else equally crazy and try to relate it to the Bible.

Well, everything is equally crazy if you come into the Bible. For the story of the Bible is the most incredible story in the world, and yet it's true. It cannot be proven to the rational mind on this level. You can't for one moment prove it. You have to wait for it; and then the whole drama of Jesus Christ unfolds in man, but the whole drama. Everything said of him you are going to experience: that the great sacred history of Israel came to its climax and fulfillment in the story of Jesus Christ. Not only came, it came and comes, because it's taking place in everyone in the world. The day will come and you will have the experience of being the one you always thought was unique and different that lived 2,000 years ago, that you are he and the whole story is your story.

Now I asked before I closed to share with me your experiences. Not only of things here in the world of Caesar—how you get a home, a better job, more money and all these things, they are important—but I also asked you to share with me your dreams, your visions. For if they are in any way foretold in scripture, they are important. Well, next Tuesday I shall take four from the same lady who said they happened to her between closing December the 17th and my reopening January the 4th. They are perfectly beautiful, and I can tell her now, they're all in scripture. They're *all* in scripture—maybe she doesn't have a concordance—everything she told me. I found this letter and read it over...everything is there in scripture. Not everything recorded in scripture completes the vision. As you're told in the end of John, there are many other things that he did that are not written in this book, but these are written that you may believe (21:25). The important eschatological story *is* written, that great finishing drama when it's come to its climax, its end; but so many of the visions are not written. These four of hers are all in scripture.

So we'll take them and weave them into the story which we'll give to you on Tuesday. This is prompted not only by her four stories but by an article that my friend (who is here tonight) sent me last Tuesday. It's in the current issue of *Harper's Bazaar* and is about dreams. This practicing psychiatrist has been one for twenty years, but he wouldn't give the Bible credit for anything. He quotes J. W. Dunne, Freud, Jung, Adler, and all the so-called authorities on dream, and only vaguely mentions in the very end this trinity in man, which he calls the self, the rational mind or ego, and then what he speaks of as the Holy Spirit as a reflection of the great trinity. That's all that he would mention of scripture; and the Bible, from beginning to end, mentions the importance of dreams.

It also tells us we are past masters at misinterpreting dreams. If it's a simple, simple little dream, all well and good, but when it comes in symbolism you need a professional interpreter...and I don't mean Freud. He'd put it right down into the loins. No matter what the vision is he takes it right into the loins...and that's not the story. So on Tuesday we will take that. And strangely enough, someone gave me for Christmas the Sunday issue of the *New York Times* that will come through the year, and in the book section, the first book reviewed is on dreams, something new. He, too, mentions these same "authorities" but not scripture. So on Tuesday, it will be that to show you what scripture teaches concerning this activity in the depths of the soul of man; and the four that she gave me last, well, I got it in the mail this week, are perfectly marvelous. I will tell her to read the 10th chapter, the 20th verse of Ecclesiastes tonight, and, I think, the 31st of Jeremiah, the 5th verse.

Well, let us go into the Silence.

*   *   *

Q: (inaudible)

A: The churches teach the three persons of the Trinity. They speak of God the Father, and God the Son, and God the Holy Spirit. You'll never understand it if you connect them with "and." You must connect the three persons of the Trinity with "or's." "When you see me you see the Father." If you've had the experience of being a father, you may think you're a better man, but you've seen the Father. The Father or the Son or the Holy Spirit, and the three are one, not three persons. Dwell upon it. Connect the Trinity, the three persons of the Trinity with "or's" not "ands" and it will come to you.

Q: When your father sat in the armchair and used his Imagination, was that a deliberate act or was it just unconsciously thought?

A: Deliberate! His morning meditations were deliberate with my father. This that I spoke of earlier was the one of a big building. That was an escape, but it worked. He did it because it would compensate—to get five shillings, one dollar and twenty-five cents for a six-day week and a twelve-hour day, and you walked ten miles in and ten miles back.

That's how he started life and raised a family of ten.

Q: What was the significance of your dream of where you were standing on an empty lot?

A: Well, the significance of that is I stood on an empty lot and yet I would say "I remember when"…that would imply it's not empty any more, that whatever I wanted for it had already come to pass. You can say of someone, I remember when she was a spinster. Well, you're implying right away she's not one now. You can say, I remember when he was poor, when he was unwanted, when all shunned him. If you remember when that was so, it's not so now.

Q: (inaudible)

A: Oh, my dear, I do it daily, not only for myself but for others. If someone writes me that they would like a raise in their position, either in money or in position, well then, I can't deny that their very request tells me where they are financially and where they are in the position. If I could say now "I remember when they held only that position, or I remember when he had only so much." Don't take this lightly because it works!

A friend of mine called me last night. He had gone to see...the night before he had gone off to Pasadena to hear ___(??), the great pianist, and he loved it. He said he came home, they were discussing the concert, he put the dogs to bed, his father to bed, and he and his friend were discussing and pouring a little drink. Then one went to bed. He thought it too early so he sat in his place, he lives in Eagle Rock, and looked out on the lights of far off Colorado Boulevard, and said to himself, "Wouldn't it be wonderful if I had just a little bit more money coming in to do that much more." He loves the concerts and he gets the best seats. Just a little bit more, said he. They both are bachelors. So he said, "I sat there just drinking it in, the feeling of, well, almost giving thanks for it as something accomplished." He said, "I went to work the next morning and here my boss said to me just like ___(??), "Bob, I have news for you, as of now you get twenty-five a month more." It's not an enormous jump, but twenty-five a month more.

That same Bob worked for RCA with his friend, who also worked in another division of RCA, so they pooled their cars, and one would drive one car one week, the other would drive the other car the next week. But, it was bumper to bumper where they had to go to this RCA display area. One had the Whirlpool division; the other had the color TV sets. So the one who had the Whirlpool division, he got so tired of this bumper-to-bumper ride every morning that when he wasn't driving he would close his eyes and imagine that he was going downtown where he had worked for almost thirteen years, knew all the fellas, all the restaurants, knew the area, and he would lose himself in this controlled daydream while his friend drove the car. Right before Christmas when the sales were open now, one person is fired in the entire building. Who is it?—my friend Bob. All right, he dreamed himself out of a job. He was so shocked. All the papers said they made more money than ever before...RCA...they made millions and millions and millions. Chicago goes through a list, or they put it through a machine—this department has one man too many. Regardless of his name, regardless of his sales effort, because of what he's done, the computer said one man must go. So the one man had to go and he was the one man. So when he told me this story I said, "Bob, have you forgotten how you would sit next to Mort and when Mort drove for the week you would dream you were going downtown?" Well, where do you think he's working, downtown within two blocks of where he worked for almost thirteen years. That's where you ___(??) there. He fired himself. At first it was a shock...how can they fire me?

So my father, on reflection, so he was fired out of this tiny, little junior partnership. If he hadn't been fired in 1919 and though put together it seemed like such a horrible thing to have done to that man with a large family, no money; but on reflection it was the blessing of blessings that day, for these had no vision. When two of my brothers went to one of these partners, who looked upon us as nephews, in fact, my oldest brother was named after one of them. His name was Walter Cecil and my oldest brother is called Cecil. So he and my brother Lawrence went down to ask what happened, "What did Daddy do?" You know what satisfaction he gave my two brothers? He said to my brother, "You Goddards try to hang your hat too high." So they kept on putting theirs in the gutter and that's where they all died. So when my father died at the age of eighty-five, he hung his so high he could leave a family of ten financially independent, when all the others went across the veil holding their hats so low they were in the gutter. Don't hang it low, hang it high!

Q: Neville, in the 5th chapter of 2nd Kings, Elisha's messenger sends Naaman to wash seven times in the Jordan to be as clean as a little child. Would you explain that passage?

A: Well, seven is the Christ number on this level; eight is the true Christ number in the new age. So numbers are tremendously significant in scripture. Every letter in the Hebrew alphabet has not only a numerical value, also a symbolical value. Seven, which is Zayin, is the sword; but that seven is the number of Christ, the 7th eye of God. The Bible speaks of the seven...Blake names the seven and gives the 7th eye that of Jesus. There was an eighth; the eighth was called but he would not come. He couldn't come; you can't call him into this dimension at all. You accept the story on faith. You can't call the eighth; he belongs to an entirely new age, the world of resurrection. So this cleaning was just at the end of this journey.

Q: The Jordan...am I in error that you had interpreted previously the Jordan as being a challenge or a problem?

A: It is a challenge. You go down to the Jordan, it's the lowest, you go down to the very lowest. You've got to look beyond the Jordan, beyond where your senses take you. You must lift them and look beyond the Jordan as told us in Joshua.

Now the time is up. We're here every Tuesday and every Friday. I can't tell you when we're going to close, but until…(tape ran out).

BEHOLD THE DREAMER

1/11/66

Tonight's title is "Behold the Dreamer." I am told that a great interest has been revived in scientific circles concerning the Dreamer in man and his dreams, but they do not turn to the Bible for any light whatsoever. They're experimenting, trying to find out who or what the Dreamer within us is, and of whom is this Dreamer talking. We would turn to the book of books, the Bible. The Bible teaches, from beginning to end, all about this Dreamer: that God speaks to man in a dream and makes himself known in vision (Num. 12:6).

Tonight I have four stories that this artist brought me, or rather sent me this past week. Now, if I ask you to share with me your dreams, your visions, I do it for a purpose: I want to see how near we are getting to scripture. For the whole thing is contained in us and when we begin to awake, the entire book begins to unfold *in* us and it comes in the form of a dream, it comes in vision. Paul made no doubt about this Dreamer. He didn't say what the Dreamer within us is, he said, "I know *whom* I believe." Not what I believe, whom. I make you a promise, you too will find him. You will find the Dreamer. When you find him, you will find God. When you find God, you find yourself. The day will come—may it be tonight—if you are near the end where you have only one God. You can't find him while there are two gods. You can only find him when you really only serve one God.

Now this one God was revealed, we are told, to Moses. Well, Moses is not *a* man any more than Abraham, Isaac, and Jacob. These are the eternal states of the soul through which the immortal you *must* pass to awaken as God. So the word Moses has a great significance...all the words, all the names of scripture. The word Moses is the old perfective, that is "tending towards" or "tending to make perfect" of the Egyptian verb "to be born." There is something to be born from man that must be perfect as God is perfect. No imperfection, just pure. That's the prototype of the one we speak of in scripture as Jesus Christ. It's something to be born. We're told in scripture, And the Lord said unto Moses, behold, you are about to sleep with your fathers. That's a nice way of saying die. When you die, this people will rise and play the harlot after the strange gods in the land where they go to be among them, and surely I will hide my face in that day on account of all the evil which they have done. I'll tell you why: because they have turned to other gods (Deut.31:16).

He equates the evil of man with turning to another God. He equates these two with harlotry, he equates them with idolatry. The only idolatry recognized is turning to another God. This he calls playing the part of the harlot. They'll rise and play the part of the harlot. Hasn't a thing to do with what the world calls the harlot in this world, not a thing to do with sex as you and I understand sex; it is all to do with turning to a strange God. Yet man can't help it, for he foresaw that when this sleeps in man and is not there to guide man, then man will look out on a world that seems so vast, so great he'll be dwarfed by it, and he will not know who brought it into being and for what purpose. He will make strange gods. So you can't blame man.

So here we are told that the divine name Jehovah, which is Yod He Vau He, which we translate as I AM was not known prior to its disclosure to Moses. Jehovah was, yes. The same God who appeared to the patriarchs— these eternal states from Abraham, Isaac, Jacob—but they knew him by a different name. As we're told in the 6th chapter of the Book of Exodus: "I am the Lord" said he to Moses, "I am the Lord" (verse 2). In other words, the word translated Lord is I AM. I am the I AM. I appeared to Abraham, to Isaac, to Jacob as God Almighty, El Shaddai, but by my name the Lord I did not make myself known unto them. So in these states you were not told who the true God was. You saw him only as God Almighty. You saw him in the thunder, in the lightning, in all manifestations of power, but you didn't know the real God. He was not revealed to man prior to the disclosure as made to Moses, the state called Moses. That's the most difficult thing in the world for man to keep…and the *only* God is I AM…he finds it so difficult.

Here, let me give you a series of pictures, a series unfolding by this artist. It happened between December the 17th when I closed and my re-opening day on January the 4th. "The first one is a dream and in this dream I found myself in a dim light observing a figure. Here before me stood a slender, beautiful lady in a wonderful dim light. As I looked closer, I am looking at myself; as I looked closer here my very self stands before me." She said "That's all, that's the first dream." "The second, I find myself standing in a grove of trees. They are separate, maybe say ten, twelve feet apart. The trunks are perfectly straight and very smooth. I didn't look up but I sensed the foliage, the beautiful foliage above. Then I wound my way among, in and around the trees, like a procession of one. And then I heard this divine voice and it spoke so clearly and it spoke as though it spoke in a chant. It said "Impollinate, impollinate, impollinate the child yourself." It repeated it, "Impollinate, impollinate, impollinate the child yourself." She said, "I know of no such word impollinate. That's all. The vision broke into speech in the form of a chant and I do not know the meaning of the word impollinate. Pollinate yes, but not impollinate."

Now she said, "The other two are not dreams, these are experiences. Quite often when I wake in the morning my head is filled with a golden light, and in this light if I draw up a name or a face or something, eventually I will hear good news, wonderful news, exciting, productive news about another person. But the morning that I write of this experience, I was thinking only of the presence of God. All I'm thinking is the presence of God, and here I heard the chirping of a bird. I turned to my right, at my window, and between the window glass and the screen is a little bird. There he is looking at me and chirping urgently. I said to myself, well, the screen must be torn, because reason dictated that. She said, "I knew it wasn't torn, yet reason said it must be torn, there's a hole somewhere. How could a bird get between the screen and the window? I was about to get up to investigate, and then set the bird free into the room, when he made several circles around the inside of the window, and looking directly at me, he turned and disappeared through the screen. Was his message to me to tell me to follow him? That nothing, but nothing really finds us in this world? What was his message to me? There he was a little bird. I got out of bed and examined the screen thoroughly. There wasn't a tear, there wasn't a hole, the screen was in perfect order, and fitted perfectly.

"A week later as I woke, the same wonderful light and then this similar voice of the bird, I turned and there is the bird, the little bird between the screen and the window. As I looked, he didn't circle the screen as he did the first time, he remained at the top, and he chirped so urgently, looking at me intently. Then he departed as he did the first time, right straight through the screen. Now that's all…is it in scripture?" Yes, it's in scripture. You'll find it in the 10th chapter, the 20th verse of Ecclesiastes: "Even in your thought, do not curse the king, nor in your bedchamber curse the rich; for a bird of the air will carry your voice, or some winged creature tell the matter." We think we are alone because we are in our bedchamber and we think that no one sees what I'm thinking. Just as it will carry the curse, my curse of the important relative to me, the rich, the king, it will carry the blessing as well. All of this is imagery, yes, beautiful imagery, but these are the eternal images that you will find in the soul of man. It comes *after*, in her case, after she found herself. She actually looked right into this slender, beautiful lady's face and saw that she was looking at herself. That's when man really knows "I am He."

I can tell you from now to the ends of time that your wonderful I-am-ness is God. I can't persuade you to the point of belief or conviction until you drop all other gods, when you have no other God beside me. As we are told, "I am the Lord who brought you out of the land of Egypt, out of the house of bondage" (Ex.20:2). "You shall have no other gods besides me. I, even I, am He...and there is no god beside me" (Is.43:11). "I kill, I make alive; I wound, I heal; and none can deliver out of my hand" (Deut.32:39). That's the being in you—it kills, it makes alive; it wounds, it heals. So, "If anyone should ever say to you, 'Look, here is the Christ!' or 'Look, there he is!' do not believe it" (Mat.24:23). Do not believe it! For take heed, I've told you all things beforehand...before I disappeared in you as your own being, I told you all things. "It may not yet appear what we shall be, but we know when he appears we shall be like him, and see him as he is. Therefore, the man who thus hopes in him purifies himself as he is pure" (1Jn.3:2).

I purify myself as he is pure...well, how do I do it? Change my diet? No. Change the things of the world? No. Purification comes only in one way: giving up false gods. I can eat all the meat in the world, drink all the liquor in the world, if I can hold it, do anything; that doesn't make me impure. Impurity comes with going after strange gods. "Blessed are the pure in heart, for they shall *see* God." The man who hasn't seen *himself as* God is not yet pure in heart. He is not yet free of the false gods of the world. He turns to all kinds of gods on the outside. Call them numerology, call them astrology, call them teacup leaves, call them entrails of fish, entrails of birds—yes, they look at all these things and call that God—to tell them the future. Yet we're told so clearly in the book of Daniel, the 2nd chapter: There is a God in heaven that reveals secrets...and makes known unto you what shall be in the latter days. Your dream and the visions of your head as you lay in bed are these (verse 28). Sitting alone or maybe in a crowd but you are alone to yourself, all the thoughts you entertain—these shall be in the latter days; for the bird of the air will carry your voice or some winged creature will tell the matter. And just as you entertain it it comes back, bringing itself an hundredfold, and there is your harvest.

But no man is free until he finds the one God, the *only* God. For in that day when you find the only God, you have found the one spoken of in scripture as Jehovah, and he is your very being. God became man that man may become God. As you walk the earth, little as you think you are, that's God walking the earth. If you can turn to any other god, you still have one to overcome, and you must overcome and overcome until there's only *one* God. That one God isn't on the outside. You can't turn to anyone on the outside. So no matter how wise the man appears to be or wonderful he appears to be, don't look there. So there isn't a figure on the wall that you worship. When you go to church you have all these icons, go into these homes and you see all these pictures of what they consider Jesus to be like. Is he like you? If he's not *just like* you, he's a false god. I could take you to the library in New York City and show you at least forty-six beautiful paintings of the great artists, each claiming that this is the true likeness of Jesus Christ.

I've gone on panels on TV where these men are trying to persuade me that this little shroud that they have is simply the impression of Jesus Christ as he lay in this tomb. So I asked this archaeologist, "Does he look like you?" and he wondered, "Why do you ask me a question of that nature?" If he doesn't look like you, then you're worshipping a false god. He is so unlike what you could ever be, therefore, that's not Jesus Christ. Don't you know scripture? When I was on radio back east when there were twenty-six states tuned in, these wires would come through and they pinpointed the 13th chapter, the 21st verse of Mark. I could almost wait for it. The telephone would ring, some lady or some gentleman would say I'm setting myself up as Jesus Christ, ask me to go and read that passage. Well, I would give it backwards...I would tell her to go and read the 1st epistle of John, the 3rd chapter. And if you don't know what you look like, may I tell you, you'll know him when he appears because you will be like him (verse 2). And if now the God that you hold in your mind's eye isn't like you, well then, you haven't found him.

Keep on bringing all of these gods into your world and they'll die. Man is purified by the death of his delusions. So every god dies, one after the other, and finally there's only one left, and you are he. Your own wonderful human Imagination, that's God. Your own wonderful I-am-ness, that's God. Yes, you pass through al the furnaces; you did it purposely. You entered these furnaces for a purpose and limited yourself to this called man. When you begin to expand, you break through, and you're infinitely greater than you were prior to the great journey that you yourself initiated.

As we are told in scripture, "God has consigned all men to disobedience, that he may have mercy upon all" (Rom.11:32). Here is...Bible is teaching that...in the Bible? Yes, God has consigned all men to disobedience, that he may have mercy upon all. For if Moses did not sleep—and listen to the story carefully—and Moses died, God buried him; and to this day no one knows the burial place of Moses, for he only comes out of that burial place as Jesus Christ; comes out of *you* when you're perfect. He's the old perfective of the Egyptian verb "to be born." It must be perfect before it can be born. It can't be perfect with two gods, there's only one God: "Hear, O Israel: The Lord our God is one Lord" (Deut.6:4). This wonderful compound unity! So here, if I put it into this language of ours it is, "Hear, O Israel"—we are Israel, the man of God—"the Lord, the I AM, our I AMs is one I AM." No loss of identity, no loss of individuality, and yet *one* God.

The question is asked, "Who established all the ends of the earth? What is his name and what is his son's name? Surely you know" (Prvb.30:4). Well, when he asked what was his son's name he revealed the name of he first question. He has a son, so he is a father. So whoever created the end of the earth and established the heavens is a father. And what is his *son's* name? That is the great problem. It comes only by revelation. You can sit down and read that book from beginning to end, and trained as you and I were trained— most of us were trained in the Christian faith—and trained in the Christian faith I was trained that the son is Jesus Christ. My mother taught me that, the priest taught me that, my school teachers taught me that, and so having been conditioned that way I saw no other but Jesus Christ the Son of God. I didn't know that Jesus Christ was God the Father.

I did not know until revelation possessed me and it was revealed to me that the only begotten son that bears witness to the Father is David. It is David who showed me the fatherhood of God, that I am the Father. The same David will one day appear before you. No doubt in your mind when he appears who he is and the relationship between you and David: You are the Father. And if everyone that walks the face of the earth has and must have this experience and *all* are revealed as the father of David, then the question is answered in the Book of Proverbs, "Who established all the ends of the earth? What is his name and what is his *son's* name? Surely you know." Well, David's father's name in scripture is I AM. The word is Jesse and Jesse is any form of the verb "to be."

If you take it as it really is recorded in the early manuscripts, there is no parent of Jesse, none. The most scholarly criticism of the Bible in the world today is the *Encyclopedia Biblica.* One hundred fifty scholars *worked* on it for years and years, and here they will show you there is *no* early manuscript support for the claims made in the Book of Ruth and the claims made in the genealogy of Matthew and Luke (4:17). Some scribe inserted that to make it a natural birth. But I am not dealing with a natural birth; I am not dealing with a natural man. Jesus Christ the perfect in man that is coming out is a wholly supernatural being. He is God the Father. God the Father became man that man may become God the Father. God the Father has the sum total of all the generations of men fused into a single being, called in scripture "eternity," the eternal youth, and it's David.

David stands before you and calls *you* Father. You know it, no doubt whatsoever. I have two children. I firmly believe that I sired these two children. I have never doubted for one moment I'm the father of these two children on this level. But there is never any uncertainty when David appears. There are no doubts whatsoever when he appears before you and calls you Father. You know that more certainly, more surely, than you know anything else in this world. So *that* is hid in man, that eternal being called "eternity" or called "the word" in scripture. The word is Olem; it means "eternity." But eternity is personified as a youth, not an old man as our...I wouldn't call them blind, they have partial sight but not true sight...and our Greek scholars personified eternity as an old man with a scythe; but they didn't know David.

So I can speak from experience that you are the Father spoken of in the Bible as Jehovah. Jesus Christ tells you, I am the Father...when you see me you see the Father. "How then do you say, 'Show us the Father'?" Philip said, "Show us the Father, and we will be satisfied." Jesus said, "I've been so long with you and you do not know the Father? He who sees me sees the Father; how then can you say, 'Show us the Father'" (John 14:8). Then he brings up the most wonderful thought that no one asked, he said, "What think ye of the Christ? Whose *son* is he?" because they're talking about Christ being the son. Whose son is he? They answered, "The son of David." He said, "Why then did David in the Spirit call him Lord?" (Mat.22:42). That's the word used by a son of his father. Why did David call him Father if he is David's son? Yet in a way he is, because he comes out of man. He was buried in man for a purpose and when he rises, he rises out of man. So man in some way was his father. When he comes out of man and then the son of man—all the generations of men and all their experiences fused into a single being in David—and that calls *him* now Father. So man matures when he becomes his own father's father.

So here, this lady, this artist, the sequence is perfect. It started with seeing herself. And you can't conjure it, it comes when these gods die; when they all die leaving only one God. And that God is your own wonderful I-am-ness, your wonderful human Imagination. Then you know that "Man is all Imagination and God is man, and exists in us and we in him. The eternal body of man is the Imagination, and that is God himself" (Blake, *An. to Berkeley*). So when you know it you don't turn to any other god...they all die. Then you come out of Egypt. You're told in scripture, "He brings us out of Egypt with signs and wonders" (Jer.32:21). Only signs and wonders bring it out. You see these fantastic things in the depths of our soul, and everything recorded in scripture is happening in you, and you are the center, the star of the drama. You come out and you are he.

But you don't tell anyone that "Here is the Christ!" for that's a lie. Christ is buried in everyone in the world. Christ is the reality of every being in the world, and Christ is being formed into that perfection foretold in the story of Moses. But you cannot enter the Promised Land. Who's going to enter the Promised Land?—Joshua. Well, the word Joshua is the Hebraic form of the anglicized word "Jesus," same thing. You spell it the same way. So Moses cannot go into the Promised Land, but Joshua does, and Joshua means Jesus. So Jesus and Jesus only in the end comes out of man, and he then becomes the Father…the promise that was made in the beginning. Because of this, no one can fail. There can't be one failure in the world, not really.

So here, today they study the Dreamer and they wouldn't turn to the Bible. You take the story of Jung, the great Carl Jung. He had this vision in 1944, but he would not allow it to be printed until he died. So in the '60s the book came out, giving the vision of Jung. He was ashamed to admit that he, the great teacher, also had dreams, also had visions. But he recorded this in 1944…and in a dream—which to him was more than a dream; it was so clear it was almost bordering on vision—he found himself walking on a country road and here was a little chapel. He thought it would be a Christian chapel. The door was ajar, so he stepped through the door, walked up the aisle to the altar; and to his surprise there was no picture of the Virgin Mary, no crucifix, but in the place of these a wonderful arrangement of flowers ___(??). Looking down he noticed a Yogi in the lotus posture, looking closer it had *his* face. He was looking at it and he saw it was his face and it scared him almost to death. He woke startled. He said to himself, "So, aha, you are the one who is dreaming me. You have a dream and I am it, and when you awake I will no longer be."

Well, he's right. But Jung had not yet awakened or he wouldn't be frightened. He's David going into the deep. He calls it the "unconscious mind, the collective unconscious" where man is actually going deeper and deeper into himself, but he calls it the unconscious. I don't like the use of the word, because it means the absence of psychical activity. Yet all that he recorded was the result of a psychical activity. How could it be the unconscious or the absence of consciousness? And it's a person…and he doesn't want to believe that God is a person. He doesn't want to believe that the real self has form. I tell you, you are a person; God is a person. He doesn't differ from you at all. Only when you see yourself, if you're ever startled you're startled only because you can't believe that you could be so beautiful, that you could be so perfect…a face with such majesty, such strength of character, such wisdom, everything embodied in that one face…and you know it is yourself. You don't believe eternity is long enough to achieve that goal, but you're perfect. You look right into your face and it's perfect! There you are glowing like the sun.

When you only have one God, well then, it doesn't frighten you at all. You simply come back from it and there you are cognizant of the fact that the Bible is true. Go and tell them to "Be still and know that I am God" (Ps.46:10). Go and tell them I am he. Also tell them "Except they believe that I am he, they'll die in their sins" (John 8:24). So you want to be healthy, wealthy, this, that and the other? Unless you believe I am, and you name it, you remain where you are. You have to actually claim it and let it come from the depths of your soul and wear it as you would a suit. This is the teaching of the scripture. There's no one to whom you turn. Yes, you can turn to a friend and say, "I'm too close to the picture; hear for me that I have achieved a certain goal." Because he knows there is no other, he's actually doing it for himself. Because, really, there is no other, for if I am the father of your son and you are the father of my son, are we not the same father? Here is a tremendous diversity as told us in the very word itself—a compound unity, one made up of others. The whole vast world pushed out is the one God…and you are that one God. And the day will come, this series, this fantastic series will unfold within you, and you will know who you are.

What I want to convince you of tonight is that the Dreamer that our scientists are trying to find is your very reality…it's Jesus Christ. He's housed *in* you. He is uniquely and profoundly related to that inner being of every man in every age. He's the one rising to the surface. And when he comes to the surface, and he's only one God and he is it, you turn from all other gods; then what was foretold and foreshadowed in the story of Moses has come to fruition in Jesus Christ. That which was tending towards perfection has become the perfect; and then you see God. "Blessed are the pure in heart for *they* shall see God." No one but the pure in heart can see God. The pure in heart doesn't mean a thing about purity as the world sees purity. It means "those who are not going after strange gods." For they are called the harlots of the world. "I will hide my face from them on account of all the evil they've done, because they have turned to strange gods, to other gods" (Deut.31:16). And there is no God besides me.

So as long as you can believe in some god other than the *only* God, and that God is your own very being, you won't see God. I have had people say, "I wish I could see God. I expect to see someone else" and you can't persuade them that they aren't going to see another. When all the gods die they will see God; see themselves as they never dreamed they could ever be so perfect, and that's the God. Everyone, one after the other, will be gathered into this one God. As you're told, "In that day the Lord will be one and his name one" (Zec.14:9). Well, can you say I AM and mean two? The Lord will be one. What's your name?—I AM. "Go tell them I AM sent you. If they ask any more, just say I AM…that's my name forever…and by this name I shall be known throughout all generations" (Ex.3:14). I did not always reveal myself by this name. To your forefathers Abraham, Isaac and Jacob I was known to them, by them as God Almighty; but to *you* I reveal my true name. My name is I AM. So whenever you read the word "the Lord" in capital letters in scripture, it is I AM. But the translators quote as the Lord, Adonai; they do not like to use the name I AM. They use it in the 3rd of Exodus and they will use it in the Psalms and certain portions of the Old Testament, but the Book of John is filled with it. It's the grand declaration of I AM, the very end.

The day till come you will know you are the very being spoken of in scripture as Christ Jesus. Don't tell anyone. There's no reason to tell anyone. You're telling the story, and the story unfolds within man. So we'll show you on Friday how the story begins and through what medium it comes to man. Can't come through the greater revelation…that's the end; it comes through the lesser. We'll show that from the beginning to the end it's the appeal to this lesser which has to be accepted, only on faith. When it comes through the greater, you are at the end; you don't need faith, you have the experience. It comes first through the lesser revelation. Man has to hear it and believe what he's heard; then it unfold within man and comes to the surface.

Now let us go into the Silence.

*   *   *

Are there any questions?

Q: Where is the quote where Christ says, "How long have I been with you…?"

A: The 14th chapter of John.

Q: These dreams that you speak of, do you mean dreams like those that occur when you're asleep or while you're awake or…?

A: Every dream has significance. The Bible only recognizes one source of dream: all dreams proceed from God. Even the most disturbed dream has meaning. But the dreams that I speak of that are scattered in scripture, these are the eternal pictures…like the lady's bird.

We're told he was crucified upon a tree. She found herself in a grove of trees. The word tree defined in scripture means "the spine, the backbone of man." It also means "the carpenter"; it means "the gallows." So where is this tree that the scientists are looking for, the tree of life? They think they're going to find it in the laboratory in some little vial. Every week they come out saying they're closer and closer to making life. They'll never find it. As Blake put it so beautifully: "The gods of the earth and sea sought through Nature to find this tree. But their search was all in vain; there grows one in the human brain." It's this [pointing to the body] tree where God is crucified, and he has to rise from this.

Q: Was she awake when the bird left or was she still in a trance or a dream?

A: I can only take the lady's word. She said this was not a dream. "I was in my own room, looking at my own window, my own pane, a screen, my bed, the window, and it ought to be relative to my head on the bed. So

I was in my own room and fully aware of the fact I'm in my own room, entertaining the thought that that screen must be torn, because how could that little bird be between the screen and the windowpane?" As she's about to get up, the bird was so pretty she kept on looking at it, when it departed. Then she got up and examined the screen thoroughly. She didn't return from a dream…this was an experience right in her room.

Q: Neville, maybe I'm clear off the track, but is this…how is this analogous to your belief always ___(??)?

A: No.

Q: No? This is something different? Because that was something you found you were able to do yourself, is that the idea?

A: The leaves?

Q: No, the bird flying by…

A: Yeah, no this differs from that. This is the perfect, perfect experience. What was the message of the bird? First of all, the word called "impollinate" is not in my dictionary.

The prefix "im" before a "p" or a "b" they say adds intensity. So she has to impollinate the child herself. Now she has to dwell upon that. It's to her this thing came. The divine voice spoke to her, using a word that's not in the dictionary. But the prefix—you can look up—when it appears before a "p" or a "b" it intensifies. So in her case, there is an intensity here that she has to match.

Q: Then Divine Imagination and human Imagination, the only difference would be intensity?

A: Intensity! I'm glad you are here, Art. Congratulations!

Art: I'm glad to be here, Neville.

Neville: You wrote a marvelous letter, where you moved from scratch to a considerable sum weekly—unfortunately, he's now in another city and comes all the way from Long Beach—but his jump is a considerable jump in the financial world. From nothing, behind the eight-ball, two eight-balls! So let me congratulate you. I see Bill here tonight.

Tell him for me that that's enough. I got the call last night from New York. You can tell him.

Q: It seems that so much of Blake's description is about fire and thunder and black pits. Do you believe that these were states that actually exist that he envisioned, or is this just symbolism?

A: It's all symbolism. But may I tell you, all those symbols are true, they're really true…all the hell through which man has passed to awaken as God.

But as Paul said, "I do not consider that the sufferings of this age (this time) can be compared with the glory to be revealed to us," that which comes as a result of having gone through the furnaces. Then you forget the furnaces. Like a woman in labor, she doesn't remember after the birth of the child.

Q: It certainly isn't that this exemplifies a highly artistic state. I don't know whether I would strive for seeing all these things.

A: You were shown everything before you started. Then you were told that you would forget and in forgetting the one God who's playing all the parts, that you would go after strange gods. You were told that. So you see, in the end there can't be any condemnation. "Father, forgive them; they know not what they do" (Luke23:34).

Speaking of dreams, are we not told in the 27th of Matthew that Pilate's wife sent a message to him saying, "Have nothing to do with this righteous man, for I have suffered greatly because of him today in a dream" (verse 19). But he didn't listen to it; he played his part. But man ignores the dream, this little dream, it's just a dream meaning nothing.

And yet a day dream …what is anything in the world that is now an accomplished fact but what it was once only a day dream? There isn't a thing in the world that didn't begin as a dream. There isn't a marriage that he entertained the thought ___(??) she'll be my wife, or she entertained it, he'll be my husband. And before the union they entertain these thoughts…they day dream.

Q: Neville, what do you do with your dreams that are not scriptural, or if you have any?

A: Well, I'll tell you, not everything is written in the scriptures that he had in dream, but what is there is enough. We have many a ___(??). For instance, the stopping of the leaves and the stopping of the bird in flight, that's not in scripture, but it is in the Apocryphal scripture of the gospels, the Gospel of James. But it's not considered something to be included in what we call the canon of scripture; but it is in scripture if you take the Apocryphal books into consideration.

Q: You don't consider a dream as a reproach at any time, like…

A: It's a self-revelation. It's telling you what you're doing; you're cursing or you're blessing.

"I set before you this day life and death, good and evil. Choose life." But the choice is yours…you don't have to choose life.

Q: Then the word to describe what a dream is telling you is your progress on
the path.

A: Your progress on the way. When you meet yourself, you are out of Egypt.
He brings us out of Egypt with signs and wonders. And only one God
can bring you out of Egypt; two gods leaves you there. We have multiple
gods and you are in Egypt, the land of darkness, the land of slavery, until
you find the *one* God, and that one God is yourself.

It frightens the priesthoods of the world. I sent my book…he asked
for it in the Army…gave him *Your Faith is Your Fortune*. Well, that whole
book is based upon I AM.

A priest came by and asked what he was reading, he showed it to
him. Priest said, "May I have it for a little while?" The next day when he
met the father, the father told him that's not the kind of literature to read
and then he confiscated it. He must not only not read it but not ___(??)
be in the Army. The father had multiple gods, filled with devils—he
didn't know it—praying to this saint, that saint, the other saint. If this
one didn't answer, he prayed to the other one. That's what they do. Give
him just so long to answer my prayer. If you don't answer my prayer, you
piece of stone, well then, you're no good, so he turned to another one.

We are told to be still and know that I AM God! (Ps.46:10)…can't
get it any clearer.

Man looks up and sees the mask that God wears and he thinks that is
God. He knows he can't accept that. No man has seen him, why? When
you resurrect in your tomb in your skull, you don't *see* yourself; you know
you are, you're perfect, and here is the presence of God. You see all the
symbolism when you go out and you're born from above. But you don't see
you because no man can see God. So the witnesses can't see God…they
see the sign, the little infant; that's the *sign* of your birth, but they can't
see God. So you know you are more than you've ever known yourself to
be, but you don't see yourself. You see your Son and the Son reveals you.
But even then when the Son looks at you, you know that you are, and you
say of yourself, I am, but you don't see yourself. He looks at you and calls
you Father. The Son and only the Son knows the Father, for God is Spirit.

Until Friday. Thank you.

THE BIBLE IS ALL ABOUT YOU

1/14/66

Tonight's subject, as always—but tonight it will be more potent than ever—is all about you and you individually. You may not know it but the greatest book in the world is written about you. People spend fortunes having ghost writers write some biography for them. They spend millions renaming cities and rivers and mountains after themselves. Now, according to a rabbinical principle, what is not written in scripture is non-existent. The principle of Jesus or the drama of Jesus follows this principle. You may not know it; I will try to persuade you tonight that *you* are Jesus Christ. Everyone must experience scripture for himself before he can begin to know how wonderful it really is. That is why no account was given in scripture of the personal appearance of Jesus. It couldn't be. Yet men insist on making pictures of this central figure called Jesus Christ.

My task is not the easiest, for there is no, I would say, heavier weight than that which is required to change man's misconception of Jesus and scripture. We speak of dead-weights, but what weight could be heavier than to try to change a man's fixed opinion when he was conditioned in the cradle, whether he be Christian or Jew. So he was conditioned as a child before he began to think and he believes scripture to be a book of history; and there is no secular history in the Bible. The Bible is *sacred* history and this history must be fulfilled in us.

Let us turn to scripture. The Bible is called the Word of God. We're told in the Bible, "And his name shall be called The Word of God" (Rev. 19:13). So he, speaking of him as a "he," is scripture. We're told, "And my word that goes forth from my mouth shall not return unto me empty, but it must accomplish that which I purposed and prosper in the thing for which I sent it" (Is. 55:11). Now what is this Word? He's called "the Word." He said, "I came out from the

Father and I've come into the world; again, I leave the world and return to the Father" (John 16:28)...but not until I accomplish the work he sent me to do.

Now are these two? The Word of God is called Jesus Christ and the Word of God is called scripture. Now, you follow this closely: "In the beginning was the Word, and the Word was with God, and the Word was God" (John 1:1). Suddenly this plan of salvation—for the word is logos which means "plan of salvation," which means "meaning"; it's a thought with a plan, with a purpose—suddenly it becomes a person. "He was in the beginning with God." Now if the Word is God and suddenly now the Word is a person, is God not a person? Are you a person? You're a person. Tonight I will show you from experience that you really are Jesus Christ.

You have to awake to it and become the Word awake or "The Word of God." Now if scripture is his Word and the name by which Jesus Christ is called is "The Word of God" and we have just heard that he comes and all of a sudden this plan takes on the form of a person, yet no description is given us of this person...well, where is this Word sent, into the world? We're told that not a thing out there will last, it will all vanish—the cities, the mountains, the trees, the very lands themselves will be submerged—but the Word will stand forever. It will never cease to be. It has to fulfill itself wherever it is sent. And sent where? Sent into man...and there it is buried in man, it unfolds in man and when it unfolds, that man knows from his own experience he is Jesus Christ. Everything recorded in scripture concerning this Jesus Christ *he* experiences...without loss of identity, without any change of individuality, just a complete radical change in his form that no mortal eye can see. He wears now an entirely different form that no man on earth can see.

Now does he first come into the world? I have heard people say, "Oh, wouldn't it have been marvelous if I lived when he walked the earth." What a misconception! "If I had only lived when he walked, even if I didn't understand it, to say I actually walked when he walked"...as though he were another. They would give anything to have walked when he walked as something other than themselves. This is the first appearance of Jesus when you hear the message of salvation. It comes through the lesser revelation to the ear, the 42nd chapter of Job, "I have heard of thee with the hearing of the ear" (verse 5). And then we find it in the 10th of Romans, "And faith comes through hearing and hearing comes by the preaching of Christ" (verse 17). Then we read it, almost as a criticism, in the 3rd chapter of Galatians, "So let me ask you only this: Did you receive the Spirit by the works of the law, or by hearing with faith? Are you so foolish? Having heard the Spirit and received the Spirit through hearing by faith, are you now going to follow the flesh? And turn to a man of flesh and blood (verse 2)?" "Flesh and blood cannot inherit the kingdom of God" (1Cor. 15:50).

So you heard it first and you accepted it. The acceptance of the plan of salvation was his first appearance through the lesser revelation to the ear. And so, it was dramatized as though I took a book and read through the plan of God's salvation. Of whom? Of himself. God prepared the way for himself to return; for when you experience scripture, it's not another, it's yourself. All that is said in scripture of the Word of God unfolds in you as a personal experience. Therefore, who was experiencing it when God and the Word are one? Is it not God? Well, if you're saved in this manner, is it not saving himself? Are you not then that self that he saves? There is only God.

So the lesser comes from the ear and to the ear. I'll take the story and tell you, not as you heard it in the cradle, as I have experienced it. You hear it either with acceptance, or you reject it, it's entirely up to you, and continue the sleep, the deep, deep sleep in the grave. Then the second appearance, the second coming, is when the Word is experienced in you and by you. Then you can say scripture must be fulfilled in me (Luke 22:37). And beginning with Moses in the law and all the prophets and the psalms, you will interpret to all all the things concerning yourself. So when he comes, that second coming is simply the fulfillment in you of what you heard and accepted with faith. I can take that story as told in Galatians, "O foolish Galatians! Who has bewitched you, before whose eyes Jesus Christ was publicly *portrayed* as crucified?" Who bewitched you? He was portrayed as crucified. "Now let me ask you only this, did you receive the Spirit by works of the law"—external ceremony, ritual, and all these things—"or by hearing with faith?" When the drama was told you, you saw it mentally; you heard it and you believed it. Now, having accepted it, are you going to turn back to the flesh and see now a man of flesh and blood? Then he tells them, even though my thought was once absorbed with the human Christ, I see him so no longer (2Cor. 5:16). He experienced scripture; having experienced it, he couldn't turn to any outside man. See, there is only God in the world. The word Jesus means Jehovah. It means "Jehovah is salvation." Scripture recognizes only one Savior, that is, Jehovah. "I am the Lord your God, the Holy One of Israel, your Savior... and besides me there is no savior...I know not any." Read it in the 43rd and 45th of Isaiah (verses 3, 2, respectively). So the only God is the God who is actually buried in man.

Now, this whole drama begins with the resurrection. Man is redeemed. For man is born again into an entirely different world, differently formed, through the resurrection of Jesus Christ from the dead. So when *you* experience the resurrection, there is no other. If you had any doubts in your mind as to who you are, and if only Jesus Christ is resurrected, and by his resurrection I am reborn (1Pet.1:3). I know I was born on the heels of the resurrection— but *I* was the resurrected. So if I am the resurrected and *only* Jesus Christ is resurrected, well, I know who he is. So go and tell it, go and preach the story of salvation. We've all heard it incorrectly. Priests will circumnavigate the world to make one proselyte and bar him from going in, because they themselves have lost the key. They're so completely concerned with ritual and outside paraphernalia they know nothing of the kingdom of God within them. And this whole drama must unfold within us.

So the pathway of salvation is so very short, really. When the first bud appears, the tree falls into bloom in just three and a half years…just completely falls into full bloom in three and a half years. No one can see the bloom, no mortal eye can see the flowers, no mortal eye sees that Tree of Life in full bloom. There are those who have experienced scripture. So you walk the earth completely unknown, for you are the lit Tree of Life, and no one sees the tree in bloom. But I tell you from experience, when the first flower appears which is the resurrection on the heels comes the birth. Then the others quickly unfold and it takes three and a half years as told us in the end of Daniel (12:4). Seal it; no one can break the seal until he comes ___(??). It's broken *in him*. And no one walking this earth could ever have foretold the manner in which the flowers will appear. Judging the world only through mortal eyes, how could you ever conceive of the resurrection in the way that it actually happens? How could you ever have foreseen it? But it comes not at the end of history but within history. While you're walking this earth it happens within history.

You tell it to those who have been misled and you hear nothing but deaf ears. They blind their eyes…they don't want to see it. Your most intimate friends don't want to see it. It's not the way they heard it. And there is no dead-lift so heavy, but really none, as that which requires this to change man's misconception, no greater. You name one…where your most intimate friend turns his back and pities. When your brothers and your sisters and those who truly love you, and have proven it by their gifts and their actions towards you, if you raise one finger to change the course of their fixation, they'll have no part. Again, scripture…and his brothers did not believe him. If they believed you, it would not be the fulfillment of scripture…just as though they *had* to start with a misconception and hear the Word along the way; and some toy with it and wonder if it is true as they go their way, if the time is right. For it cannot happen before its time.

The prophets who prophesied of this grace that was to be yours, they searched and inquired about this salvation. They inquired what person or time was indicated by the spirit of prophecy within them, the spirit of Christ within them, when predicting the sufferings of Christ and the subsequent glory. It was revealed to them that they were serving not themselves but *you* (1Pet.1:10). The time had not yet come. But when the time had fully come so that one could burst, he broke it by beginning in the grave. The Book of Acts associates the grave with rising from the dead, and it is said they laid him in a tomb and God raised him from the dead. The tomb is present right here. Don't be disturbed if you should drop this night. And what I will now call the tomb…I will speak of this…but, really, it isn't this little physical skull; it is an eternal skull, really, in a way where God is buried, where no man has ever yet been buried. It's a skull…it's your skull.

One day he breathes upon it, he breathes upon himself, and that breath is called "a wind, the sound of a trumpet." The word sound is simply a vibration or a reverberation or a tone like striking a tone on the piano. And all tones in sympathy with it begin to sing. So when your tone is called, and not before—he calls him according to his purpose—and when all are called, we are a tone unlike any tone in the world. You can't resist it. When that tone is sounded by God to God (for you are God) and when he sounds *that* tone, you begin to stir, and you can't stop it. You begin to awake and awake and awake, and finally you are awake as you have never been awake before. And where are you?—in your skull. You know it to be a sepulcher and you know that someone placed you there because they thought you dead. So you understand the words, "God himself enters death's door with those who enter and lays down in the grave with them, and shares with them their visions of eternity until they awaken" (Blake, *Milton*, Plt.32).

So this whole vast nightmare he shares it with us; for he is my very being, he's not another. And when he awakes, I am he. I didn't know it until that moment when there was no one but myself, yet I am in the sepulcher, I am in Golgotha. And there isn't the slightest little opening, not a hole, nothing leads out, and I'm sealed as an egg. Yet I know that if I could but push the base of this skull, I would get out. And so I push and out I begin to come, like one being born. So it is said truly that I am reborn by the resurrection of Jesus Christ from the dead. It's out you come, and you don't see yourself… no one sees you, for you're not clothed in this garment. You see this garment on the bed. You see the garment out of which you've just emerged, but you don't see yourself. You are God and God is Spirit. Therefore, no one can see the Father at any time but the Son, and anyone to whom the Son chooses to reveal him (Mat. 11:27). So your next step is going to be the revelation coming from the Son.

Strangely enough, all of these experiences save the one with the Father take you by surprise. You cannot say I did this before. You cannot say that you have any memory of this. The only memory is God's written Word. If you're familiar with it, you can go back and find out the witness that was recorded in the written Word. When it comes to the Son revealing you, memory returns. It doesn't seem to have any beginning. It's something you've always been, the Father. You didn't know it until that moment, because memory hadn't returned. But this is the one event of the unfolding four where memory plays the part, and suddenly you know. There is no uncertainty in you concerning this relationship between you and God's only begotten Son (Ps.2:7)...and you know who you are. You know you are the being spoken of in scripture as Jehovah, called Jesus Christ; for both are one, and that one is the Father of this Son [David].

The others, they take you suddenly and by surprise, but you cannot honestly say you played the part before. All these other events are new. They were foretold you by yourself, and you believed it, and became subject unto death, even death upon the cross (Phil. 2:7). To do it, you had to empty yourself of all that you are and you are God. So you emptied yourself of being God and took the form of death called man. Only one of the events is memory, all the others were foretold you. So when he comes he tells you, I will bring to your remembrance all that I said unto you. But this concerning the Father is something that everyone has as memory, but memory has vanished. It's like being in a deep, deep coma. And you know the party well, you can scream at him and tell him you know all about him and tell him...but he can't remember. So I can tell you from now to the ends of time about David and his relationship to you, but not until memory returns do you fully understand this relationship and how you've always known it. You were *always* his Father.

Now listen to the words, we're told the Word cannot return void; it must accomplish that which I purposed and prosper in the thing for which I sent it (Is. 55:11). Now, he said, "I've glorified thee on earth" (John 17:4). Glorification is equated with lifting up the Son of man. He said, my hour has come, the hour for the Son of man to be glorified. I've glorified thee on earth, now "Father, return unto me the glory that *is* mine, the glory that I had with thee before that the world was made" (John 17:5). I'm not asking for anything that was not mine. He glorifies me with himself, and the self is Father. Now return, return that memory which I willingly gave up to do a work that I was sent to do. You and I are one; now return this unity by bringing back this memory of my fatherhood. And only the Son can bring back the memory of the fatherhood, so if the Son appears and calls you Father, then you know it. So when this rises *in* man, there is conferred upon the risen Christ in the experience of men the divine name of Lord. And what is "the Lord"?—Jehovah. He confers not only his name but all that the name implies, for the Lord is father. So the memory returns and you are the Father. Then you mark the little time trying to correct the misconception, trying to show them the truth concerning God's Word. And no matter how many hear it, if just a handful, tell it, because in the end not a thing will last but his Word.

Now this will not take from you a plan of all he gave you after he read you that message of salvation. He knew the horrors that would befall you, he knew the pitfalls. He knew everything, and he gave you a law, a law that would enable you to go through this horrible scene and be the man, the woman that you want to be...even though you know in your heart it's all vanity...it's all going to pass away. Yet until it passes away you can have it. Take it all! Indulge yourself! Realize all your dreams though every dream will pass away. Man not knowing that, he builds his monuments and hopes to perpetuate his little name, and that's not the name at all. None of these names will last, for that's not the name. For, in that day the Lord is one and his name one (Zech. 14:9).

What's that name?—Father. Just one...you are the Father and I am the Father, there's only one Father. But we can speak of fathers, because the book allows it. It uses the plural word Elohim. It was the Elohim who made the decision to create this scene. And the word is true, so we are the fathers, the Elohim. Put them all together, for it's a compound unity. It's only one Father, for all have the same Son. Having the same Son...must be the same Father... not one greater than the other. So in the very end, you will say, yes, "I heard of thee with the hearing of the ear, but now my eye sees thee." To see and to know are the same in scripture, same word in Greek; to know it is to see it, to experience it. So he knows now that he has experienced all that he accepted only in faith. And this is the one whose life is the life of every person in the world...Job. This comes at the very end, the 42nd chapter (verse 5).

Then we are told in the end of Job, all those who left him—his brothers, his sisters, friends, all left him—they came back and ate with him to comfort him for the evil that the Lord had brought about. Here was the most cruel experiment ever to be seen. But he brought it upon himself for he played the part.; he didn't put it upon a man called Job. The word Job, the meaning is "Where is my Father?" That's the true meaning of Job, "Where is my Father?" If he could only find the Father, he'd find himself. And finding himself, he finds the reason behind his suffering: for only through suffering would he come to the end, more brilliant, more wonderful, more expansive, more translucent than he was when he started the journey.

So don't think for one second he did anything that was wrong. Read the story of Job. He did nothing that was wrong...any more than you did. To justify inequalities in this world they bring in reincarnation, karma, and all these irrelevant things, hasn't a thing to do with it. You're not playing the part you're playing because of anything you did in the past. You're doing it because it is the will of God. "Master, who sinned, this man or his parents, that he is born blind?" "Neither the man, nor his parents, but that the works of God may be made manifest" (John 9:2). You play all the parts...or you will. And in the end, having played all the parts you'll forgive all, forgive every part in the world, for the same actor plays all the parts. "God only acts and is in existing beings or men" (Blake, *Mar. of Heaven and Hell*).

So the story of the gospel is your biography. No ghost-writer wrote it for you. It's not of human composition. No man could sit down and compose the gospels; it's all revelation, it's eternally true and it's your biography. So tomorrow, dwell upon it; dwell upon it as much as you can from now on. Try to correct your misconception. Well, how will I know that I am correcting it? Well, I can't avoid in this land of ours seeing or hearing the name Jesus, can I?

It's so much a part of our society. Well, when you hear it just watch your reaction…do you think of another? Then you haven't yet corrected it. If you go to church and someone says, "And Jesus said" and you think of another, you haven't corrected it. When you hear the word Jehovah and "the Lord God," and you see a being on the outside creating, you haven't corrected it. "In the beginning was the Word"—the plan of salvation—"and the Word was with God, and the Word was God" (John 1:1). He was in the beginning with God. Here we find a person and *you* are that person. For God being a person, his wisdom and his power are personified. It's his wisdom, his power buried in you as a plan of salvation revealing his own power, his own wisdom, but enhancing it as you come back.

So, when the whole thing unfolds within you, the last flower appears. Then you simply tell it and tell it and tell it. Whether they listen or not you tell it. Not a thing else to tell but Christ. As we are told in the 10th of Romans: "And faith comes by hearing, and hearing comes by the preaching of Christ." What else to preach? Yes, I can tell you how to make money and I will. I'll tell you how to get a home…yes a home. You may want one in the flood area. There are thousands of them. Down in Brazil tonight thousands of homes are gone. They thought they had it forever. Year after year we have it too, all the plots and plans of men, but it all vanishes; everything vanishes but the Word of God.

So get the Word correctly, get it just as it was intended, and get it from one who has had the experience. In the 10th chapter of Romans he then qualifies it: "And how can they believe in him of whom they've never heard? And how can they hear of him without a preacher? And how can there be a preacher unless he's sent? (verse 14)." Can't send yourself…not on this level. You are called and sent, and you are sent to preach the experiences that are about to unfold within yourself, to preach Christ, the true Christ…who he really is. So no man can ordain you to send you. And those who hear the story and believe it, yes, they can tell what they have heard from the one who experienced it. That's good, very good, but the one he sends, he knows the ripeness of that tree and it's just about to burst into flower. So he calls him in advance and sends him. And the one command ringing in his ear is "Time to act!" Don't postpone it, don't keep putting it off…time to act. You'll always feel as Paul felt unqualified. He said, I'm not a voice. I have a thorn in my side. They laugh at my physical limitations. Moses did not volunteer; he was drafted. So, when no one volunteers for the job, you are called, you're drafted, and then you're sent.

When you are sent, you flounder because you always feel unqualified. Your background doesn't qualify you. But he knows best, because no scholar can arrive at these conclusions. You're not a scholar. He didn't ask you if you wanted it, he said, "My grace is sufficient for you." Three times he prayed to take it from him. My grace is sufficient...I will be your voice. I'll speak, I'll put you aside and I'll speak, but you'll be the instrument through which I'll speak. For in this instrument I'll unfold the flowers and bring to completion my plan which is my Word. When they're completed...no one knows the time, and you don't have to ask when. The tree is in full bloom any moment of time you call him into an entirely different world, clothed in the one form, the form of the risen Christ. Completely transformed into the one body, that of the risen Christ.

Now let us go into the Silence.

*   *   *

Don't let it shock you, don't be disturbed when I tell you how great you are. This is not to flatter you, because no mortal tongue could tell you how truly great you really are. When I talk to you I'm talking to God! I'm talking to God who *deliberately* imposed this restriction upon himself. And before he did it, he had a plan, a plan to bring himself back to where he was but enhanced and expanded beyond the wildest dreams.

Q: (Inaudible)

A: No, my dear. The times are all like a play. We enter and exit on cue. You're told in the 3rd chapter of Ecclesiastes, there's a time to be born and a time to die. Man will not believe it. Today we believe, that is, our doctors do and our scientists that they can prolong life by proper eating habits, by certain chemicals. I read the obituaries in the morning and there are just as many doctors who are dying in their fifties, forties and sixties as others who never could afford to go to a doctor. Then there are those who live to be 108, 111. You ask them to what they attribute this longevity: Starting at 3:30 with a huge, big hooker of Bourbon! That's poison to the doctors' concepts. But this book, or rather, this magazine that my friend gave me concerning the dream, it speaks of the fashions we have in this world. You and I when we think of fashion we think only of ladies' apparel, but there fashions in everything. One of the biggest industries in the world is simply industrial design. We change the bottle of perfume and we mark it up from a dollar, where they're making ninety cents profit anyway, to twenty-five dollars for the package. They simply made it more beautiful and more attractive, and they change from year to year. But they said the most rapid and the most radical of all changes in fashion we find in medical opinion. I'm sixty-one and I recall in my short span, well, if you didn't have your appendix out, you weren't in it. It wasn't fashionable to ___(??) and your tonsils had to come out. You mean that you didn't take this little boy's tonsils out? They should all come out; they're nothing, they're not used. And they all had these opinions.

I know in Barbados there was a cholera epidemic years and years before I was born. They still have the burial place, or they had it, but man realized that the whole thing was stupid, so they simply plowed the whole thing up, and now a huge, big lumber factory is there. But no one would touch it for years. It just remained as it was, the burial ground of the dead of the cholera. And it was fashionable not to give them water. The one thing they wanted more than anything else was water. Those who defied the order and could crawl out of their beds and go to some water jar and drink 'til it came through their ears, they survived. All the others who had the opinions of doctors they died.

So they changed their opinions radically, and more often than any other profession. Yet they're honored. You tell a doctor you're not going to keep me here one second beyond my time, well, first of all he's annoyed with you because you don't treat him as a god. Oh, yes, they have many wonderful things to help you, wonderful things, and they can be a tremendous help to these little garments of flesh and blood; but don't think for one moment they know it all and that in any strange way they are endowed with the power to extend life. Scripture will not be broken. We come and we go.

My father broke every eating rule in the world and drinking rule… he and Churchill. When Churchill came home, he always wanted my father, right away. ___(??), he's the only one who could keep up with him. ___(??) drink me under the table. My father could hold his own with anyone…lived to the eighty-five. I still get the question, why did he die? They still want me to confess he drank too much. Mother never drank in her life and she died at sixty-two…never smoked in her life… lived a very quiet life, sixty-two. So they don't bring that up. Those who just don't like liquor—for millions of reasons they don't like it—alright, don't take it! You don't have to take it. Some just don't care for it; others can't take it, it's like poison. Alright, don't take it. But don't tell me that it affects everyone the same way, because it doesn't.

I come from very big family. I took one man home back in the thirties. He and his father had had a fight. The father fought with all the children—he had four boys and a girl, he had lots of money, and he fought with one after the other, and then they all pulled out. He regretted it, but it was too late. He asked my father to find this fella in New York City and bring him home. We found him in the gutter, a real alcoholic. These were Prohibition days, before Prohibition went out. He would drink anything, drink it out of automobiles. Well, we found Ken and it was my duty to get him aboard the boat. Oh, what a ride! Picked him up near Coney Island, got him in the cab…he knew every speakeasy all the way down. He said, "Nev, I can't go any further, got to stop." Go in with him, they all knew him. Ken got his little bottle, a flask, out again. He drank it like water. Where he hid these things, I don't know, but he had them all over. When we got him aboard the boat, I thought he would never survive the ten days at sea. He did. He's still in Barbados and all the others he buried, all the doctors, all the people who felt sorry for hm. There goes Ken. Once in a while he goes on a binge, just once in a while. But he gave it up…not right away. And the old man when he died left him, oh, maybe a quarter of a million dollars well invested, so Ken just clips the little dividends. Has a couple of servants who'll cook for him and take care of him and here is Ken, vegetating, that's all he's doing. But alcohol didn't kill him, it preserved him.

Q: (inaudible)

A: What does it mean in scripture when Jesus cursed the fig tree? Every parable has one central jet of truth. When man is redeemed, he's God. Everything is subject to his command, for that man is God. There is no such thing as "out of season." So when something is not bearing when *I* want it ___(??). You couldn't conceive of the infinite love cursing a tree. It's to tell a truth. It's to tell us something: Don't accept no for an answer! When you begin to exercise this power, everything is against you, and they will give you reasons why you shouldn't have it now, because it's not in season, don't accept it!

Until Tuesday.

THE HUMAN IMAGINATION

1/21/66

Tonight's subject I will call it "The Human Imagination." I could call it, maybe you will, by many other titles. The human Imagination is the true vine of eternity, the eternal body of God. So let us turn to the works of Paul and see what light he throws on it. You will see that there is nothing impossible to your wonderful human Imagination, but man will not accept it. He turns out to other gods, gods that do not exist. In the writings of Paul no trace can be found of an historical Christ as we today use the term. And yet that is all that Paul preached. He only preached Christ crucified, and yet there's not the slightest trace of an historical Christ in the letters of Paul. He said, "From now on we regard no one from the human point of view; even though we once regarded Christ from the human point of view, we regard him thus no longer" (2Cor. 5:16).

Now let us see what he has to say about Christ. He said, "Since, in the wisdom of God, the world did not know God through wisdom, it please God through the folly that we preach to save those who believe" (1Cor.1:21). Well, what did he preach? He preached "Christ crucified, a stumbling block to the Jews and folly to the Greeks. Christ is the power of God and the wisdom of God" (1Cor.1:23; 1:24). That's what Christ meant to him: the power of God and the wisdom of God. As you read his letters you can come to only one conclusion…that he is speaking of your own wonderful human Imagination…that's Christ.

He said, "The wisdom of man is foolishness in the eyes of God. The foolishness of God is wiser than men and the weakness of God is stronger than men" (1Cor.1:25). He looked upon the crucified Christ as God keyed low, the very lowest point. To him he was impotency of the creative power; and yet that impotency that appeared dead was to him more creative and more wise than the power of man and the wisdom of man. So when he speaks of "bearing on his body the death of Christ that he may also manifest the life of Christ in his body," the word translated death is defined in scripture as "impotency." It's keyed so low it appears to be dead; and yet, in spite of the appearance of death, it is wiser than the wisdom of man and stronger, the seeming weakness, than the strength of men.

You can try it and put him to the test. He said, "Come test *yourselves* and see. Do you not realize that Jesus Christ is in you?—unless of course you fail to meet the test" (2Cor.13:5). Well, if he's my human Imagination and all things were made by him and without him there's nothing made that is made, I certainly can test him if he's my human Imagination. You see, he has the wisdom to devise the means. I don't have to consciously devise the means. He has the power to execute the imaginal assumption. So I dare to assume that I am what reason denies, what my senses deny, knowing that the being that is assuming it is Christ Jesus, and it has this wisdom, though weak. For what is weaker than a mere assumption that a thing is so, though reason tells me that it is not so? When my senses deny it and every person around me ___(??) wise persons forbidding it if I confided what I had done? But here I am behind the eight-ball and I dare to assume that I am now what everything denies that I am, does that assumption have the power and wisdom to execute itself? I am told it has if I will accept it. But I'm also told that man will not accept it...very few will.

Samuel Brothers was writing about the cross said, "He that takes up that bitter tree and carries it cannily"—in other words, carries it quietly, don't discuss it, just carry it quietly—"will find it such a burden as wings are to a bird or sails are to a boat." If you dare to carry that bitter tree, you'll find it that kind of a burden. Is that a burden? We understand the words "Take my yoke upon you and learn from me. For my yoke is easy, and my burden is light" (Mat.11:29). Is there any burden to that, to carry that kind of a cross? Where could you go that you cannot imagine? Where could you go where you're devoid of the capacity to imagine? Put you in a dungeon, I can't stop you from imagining. I don't care where I put you, I can't take from you...if I knocked you unconscious I can't take from you your capacity to imagine. Well, is that a burden? He said, my burden is light and my yoke, if you accept it, is easy. He offers *his* yoke which is his knowledge based upon experience, his knowledge of scripture for yours based upon speculation, based upon theory, based upon your misconceptions as taught you in the cradle.

So he offers you what he personally has experienced. I'm speaking now of Paul...he offers this entire picture...for he went out to persecute all those who believed in "The Way." Christ said, "I am the way, I am the truth, I am the life" (John14:6). Well, what's true about an assumption that reason denies? Is that a true judgment? If I now wrote out exactly what I *want* to be and wrote it out as though I had it, well, that's not a true judgment if truth must conform to the external fact to which it relates. So I write out exactly what I want to be, but I don't write it in that manner, I write it as though I am it. Well, if I present that and can't present the evidence, well, then that's a lie. And so, he said, "I am the truth." Well, if he's my Imagination and all things are possible to him, I can write it in that manner, knowing I contain within myself the power and the wisdom to make it so. I need not try to break a blood vessel to devise the means to make it so. I simply assume that Christ Jesus is the eternal vine, the eternal body of God, and this is my own wonderful human Imagination. If this is true, and all things are possible to him, and without him there's not a thing made that is made, well, then I start to assume that I am now what I would like to be. So I stop wanting to be it because I am it, and wait confidently for it to externalize itself upon the screen of space.

Let us turn to a little passage in scripture. You see, the book is a mystery. Paul uses the word mystery no less than twenty times. We think it's simply history, secular history. Hasn't a thing to do with anything in the world we call historic. You'll never find these characters in any part of the ___(??). Never will you find them by digging up the earth and looking for them; they're all in the human Imagination. So let us see tonight if you are not Simon. I hope you are. Your name may be Ann, may be Mary, may be some other name, but I hope you can say that you're Simon. Simon appears in the beginning of the story and at the end of the story. But we are told to reverse the story: The first shall be last and the last first. So if you take his last appearance…and they're leading him to the cross, and they seized one called Simon and made him carry the cross. So, they laid on him the cross, and when they came to the place called "the skull" there they crucified him…the skull. The word Simon means "to hear." It's Shema, the first great word of the confession of the Jew as to his faith: "Hear, O Israel"—that is Shema, that's Simon—"Hear, O Israel: The Lord our God is one Lord" (Deut.6:4). Can't get away from it, can't find two Gods, only one, and his name is I AM (Ex.3:13-15). When I say "I am," I don't mean two. It's just so much the core of my being…I am.

So his name is Simon. It means "to hear intelligently, to understand," but "to consent, to obey." I can hear intelligently and turn my back on what I've heard, understanding every word you said, but I don't agree with you so I turn my back. If I hear with understanding and *consent* to it and then obey… he said, "Why call me Lord, and do not do the things I say?" So you heard it now, well, will you consent to it? Well, now obey. So here is Simon carrying the cross. He tells him, my cross, this burden is light. He who will take upon himself this bitter tree and just carry it, carry it cannily, quietly, he'll find it such a burden as wings are to a bird, as sails are to a boat, no place where I can't quickly and easily go...if I accept it.

Now we turn to the first use of the word Simon, and we find that he comes in spirit, not in the flesh. This whole drama takes place in the supernatural being. For this being called your own wonderful human Imagination, personified as Messiah, personified as Christ Jesus, is a wholly supernatural being. So he comes in the spirit into the temple. What temple? Are we not told, "You are the temple of the living God and the Spirit of God dwells in you" (2Cor. 6:16). If I come into the temple, the drama is going to unfold within me. So Simon comes into the temple and here is the Christ child being presented according to the law. He takes him up in his arms, and then he said, "Lord, now let thy servant depart in peace, according to thy word." This is from the 52nd chapter of Isaiah (Luke 2:29). For God's promise to Israel, to the whole vast world, was that you would see God's salvation. He calls it a sign. He takes up the infant child; but he calls the child a sign for the whole vast world to see. He takes the child in his arms, and asks now for permission to depart; for he is the beginning of God's redemptive power.

A complete reversal now takes place, and that power that was keyed low to human Imagination is now reversed; and from generation—creating on a divided image, male-female, it now turns up, and moves above the organization of sex where it doesn't need a dual image to create. It is God creating in himself now. No divided image; above, completely above the organization of sex. A reversal of the great powers that were keyed low, called in scripture, "the fall." And yet, the verb He Vau He in the great name of God, Yod He Vau He, its primary meaning is "to fall" or "the one who causes to fall"; or it means "to blow" or "the one who causes the wind to blow." So we take it in its primary meaning, and so who fell? God and his creative power can't be separated. So when we speak of the fall of man, it is the fall of God, his creative power, his wisdom, keyed low. And it reaches the limit of contraction called man, the limit of opacity called man.

And then after this frightful journey through the wilderness—this is the wilderness—he reaches that moment in time which was all predetermined, where the individual having gone through the furnaces of affliction called experience, now the forces are turned around. It now not only returns to where it was but returns expanded. The whole thing is expanded beyond what it was. The wisdom has increased beyond what it was. There is no limit to expansion; there was only a limit set to contraction. There is no limit to translucency, only a limit set to opacity. So when that limit was reached and the journey began, in spite of that reduced power right down to the very lowest key, it was still wiser than the wisdom of man. It was still stronger than all the strength of man...though it was God at his weakest point, when he simply took upon himself the garment called man.

So here, the Christ spoken of in scripture through the eyes of Paul, the one who carried the message beyond all, he finds no human Christ, no historical Christ; only the power of God and the wisdom of God, and it's keyed low, and it's human Imagination. So he said, "I preach only Christ crucified." Well, he's crucified—this [body] is the cross that he bears, this is the Tree of Life. The wise men seek for this tree in the laboratories of the world, but he said, "There grows one in the human brain." It's all turned down, like the inverted tree, as told us in the Book of Daniel. It was felled and the tree fell, but the roots remained in tact. Don't touch it, leave it as it is. It will once more be watered with the dew of heaven, and it will grow, this time beyond where it was; this time being the shelter for all and supply the food for all. This is the great tree. "So the gods of the earth and the sea they sought through nature to find this tree; but their search was all in vain, there grows one in the human brain" (Blake, *Songs of Experience*).

So the whole thing is here as we're seated here. Could you say to what you've just heard, "I am Simon. I'll carry the cross. I will not only hear what you said, I will consent to it; I will obey." So when I hear all the discussions and no one comes up with a solution, there's always a solution present: What do you want in place of what you have? Well, *that's* the solution. But you say, "It can't be obtained, can't be had." Doesn't matter what they say, it's what *you* want. All things are possible to God, even when he's keyed so low that it's only human Imagination. But human Imagination and divine Imagination are one. The difference is simply a degree of intensity. And so, when keyed low, it seems dead, it seems impotent.

But when you become a Simon knowing now...as the poet Francis Thompson said, "For birth has in itself the germ of death, but death has in itself the germ of birth." So it begins now with the cross, leading towards the skull where they crucify him. But that death carries in itself the germ of birth. Reverse the story. He first appears holding the birth, the sign of God's promise to man, the sign that he promised Abraham: "I will give you a son" (Gen.17:15), the prototype of this child. There is something born when someone couldn't bear a child, when someone couldn't sire a child; therefore, he's not to be thought of as a child born of woman. It is to be thought of as God begetting himself, actually begetting himself. So here is this child...it's an actual child when you encounter the story, when you have the experience; it all takes place in you. You *do* see the child, you *do* hold the child, and you pick it up. And the word Isaac means "he laughs"...the child does laugh; it breaks into the most heavenly smile when you hold it in your own hands. At that moment you are Simon. Yes, they call you Neville in the world of Caesar, but you are playing the part of Simon in the drama.

To have played the part of Simon holding the child you must have carried the cross. And so they gave it to Simon and he carried the cross to the place called The Skull; there they crucified him. Crucified whom?—the power and the wisdom of God. Now it's personified in scripture. Well, certainly it's personified, aren't you a person? You're a person, I am a person. So the power is personified, for the power needs man as an agent to express itself. And so here I stand as a man, but I know the power, the power is my own wonderful human Imagination, and that's Christ Jesus. There never was another, there never will be another… just your own wonderful human Imagination. And so, test it and see. So if I dare to test him, I should prove him in performance. And so I will take the challenge. You do it not only for yourself, you do it for another.

Now, many used to come here when I had the theater filled to overflowing, but it was a social gathering. Night after night when I would come out from twenty-one lectures, we'd go back to the hotel, and it was simply a raft, all having fun. Not one word I said was ever heard. As long as you'd keep it going on a social pattern, wonderful, but when I called a stop to that, we'd meet at odd intervals, still friends, but they never understood one word. There's a couple who I call friends, they're really dear friends of mine, they never come…but twenty years ago when we met he represented a very small, little pharmaceutical manufacturer back East. He graduated from Princeton, came back, married, bought a little home where there were only two homes on the street. Naturally, with inflation all things have grown, the house is now worth many, many times what he paid for it, but it's still a little home, a little tiny home. The lot's small, but the value because of inflation has gone up.

She said to me one day, about fifteen years ago, "Oh, I do wish that he could just get more…be more important. Here is this man from ___(??), Princeton, and all these things, and look what he's making." I said, "You want him to really make more?" "Yes." "Alright!" Turning to the only power that I know of, my own wonderful human Imagination, I carried on with her a conversation from the premise that he *was* making more. I didn't outline the means that would be employed for him to make more, I just simply imagined that he was making more, and that it came from her. Finally, his little firm was absorbed by a larger firm, and so a reorganization. He was kept, he knew the doctors, knew the druggists, knew the territory. But then they enlarged his territory. They gave him the whole state and they gave him all up to Washington, and all these states, Utah, Nevada, into, well, Arizona, which meant he had to be away seeing his sales force. He then began to take on a sales force, and he employed, oh, six or seven. He was always letting one go and getting another. Then she began to complain: "He's making more, he's important, he's actually employing now six, seven people. He can fire them and hire them as he feels." "But didn't you ask for it?" "But he's not at home." So we got together. She still wanted the feeling of power that such a job gave him; so then another firm, bigger than the two together, absorbed the two. They kept him on, raised him in salary, and then gave him a commission on the sales efforts of his four to twelve now. And then the fire began. I said he has a small home…he has spent in that home to satisfy her, without avail, the value of the house many times over. In the fifteen years since, he's completely re-carpeted it, completely refurnished it. I've seen them bringing the furniture in. She has the money, she picked it out—he didn't send it home—picked it out and one week later a new set. Carpets, take it back after a week; wallpaper, tear it off and put on some more. For what he has spent on it he'll never get out of it…all to pacify her. She can't be pacified.

She doesn't know one word of the story of Christ Jesus, yet she calls herself a Christian. Well, multiply her by all the Christians of the world, because there are so few who understand the mystery of Christ. You might say that 500 million do not know the mystery of Christ. They stick him on the wall, made out of plastic or something, monstrous artists… ___(??) all the artists that made them. All these little indulgences, and there they are, and they call that a Lord, making and violating the second Commandment: "Make no graven image after me"…none. How can I make a graven image and fall down and worship the works of my own hands? I'm creating out of my own wonderful Imagination. That's Christ, that's the power and the wisdom of God. To personify it I must see myself. And the day will come you *will* see yourself in the depths of your soul; and you've never seen such beauty you've never seen such character, such majesty as yourself in depth. And there he is, meditating you, this surface thing that is flesh and blood.

When you accept this, really accept it, to the point where you consent to it, and you obey it, then you can't turn to the left or to the right. In the midst of hell you will still call upon this power. No matter where you are call upon the power. I am not saying the body will not decay. As Paul said it so clearly, he said, "Our hearts are not cast down. Though our outer nature is wasting away, but our inner nature is renewed every day. And this temporary affliction is preparing for us an eternal weight of glory beyond comparison" (2Cor. 4:16). So to his very end the body was fading, before his eyes the body was wearing out, wasting away; but he still taught it from morning to night. And when they ___(??), but look at yourself, "Physician, heal thyself," he still taught that the *only* Christ was your own wonderful human Imagination.

Knowing that this outer garment more…it begins in time, ends in time…and though they may live to 120 they make their exit too. If they live that long, the chances are they'll have not one around them who truly call themselves lucky. They may be senile, dependent upon everything other than themselves, doing nothing for self. Paul didn't care, for he knew there is a time for everything in this world, a time to be born and a time to die. He wasn't going to hasten it. He knew that no one could delay it, but it would waste away…and he would continue to preach forever Christ crucified. As if infinite power was reduced to the little tiny human Imagination, and yet it was wiser and yet it was more powerful than the wisdom of man and the power of man.

Yesterday, we were confronted with a picture. The mightiest land in the world, America, our production exceeds the production of the world put all together. If you take real production, we have the mightiest machine ___(??), 190-odd million of us, higher standard of education; and here a little country of seventeen million, they have no productive power, no know-how as we understand the word, and we are tied down? This mighty machine and it's tied down? And nothing will get us out of debt? Did you hear our Secretary of State ___(??). He said not a thing that you hadn't read a year ago in the paper, not a thing. I rushed through my shower to hear it. I should have remained under the shower. There wasn't one word he said I hadn't read it in the papers that go back for months, and magazines, and commentaries, all double talk.

They say they really want the solution. Well, the solution that you really want, peace, as we understand it. So the government decides for itself. And let's not have some outside force impose its will. Then let them really believe, because all are going to suffer, and with few exceptions they are Christians. This is the land where most everyone in it calls himself a Christian, you find ___(??) a Jew, but a 190-odd million Americans. We have others that call a different…we have a few Buddhists, a few of the Hindu faith, but even if you take the atheists away and the agnostics away, we would still have well in excess of 100-odd million who call themselves Christians.

Not one of them seems to know the power of Christ and the wisdom of Christ. Tomorrow they'll go to church and pray to an unknown God, and go through all the outer palaver, all rituals. If there was one thing that Paul was dead set against, all institutions, all authorities, all customs, all laws that interfered with the direct access of the individual to his God. Anything in this world that in any way turned him aside from a direct access to his God Paul was against it. And so that God is *in* man, man's own wonderful human Imagination. It is the power, the creative power of God, the wisdom of God, and you can't separate a man's creative power from his Imagination which is imagining from Imagination itself. Imagining is Imagination in action, but you can't separate them. So Christ is God in action. So you say he's imagining and God is all Imagination. So "Man is all Imagination and God is man, and exists in us and we in him. The eternal body of man is the Imagination, and that is God himself" (Blake, *Berkeley; Laocoon*). Man turns to the outside in the hope that some little thing is going to intercede and help him. He'll look in vain; he has a false god.

So this is what he meant by "I preach Christ and Christ crucified, a stumbling block to the Jews" (1Cor.1:23). He didn't mean people who accept the Jewish faith, for that's the foundation of Christianity. He means those who look for signs and who believe in external worship, whether it be a dietary law, whether it be some other kind of outside worship. "And it is foolishness to the Greek." The Greek was called "the scholar of the world" and if you couldn't bring it out of the laboratory and prove it and show them the evidence, well, then it isn't. But not to Paul; for he found him not as a man, he found him in himself, and was quite willing to teach it, even though before the eyes of those he taught he faded. And he said, "My heart is not cast down. Though my outer nature is passing away, is fading, my inner is being renewed every day. And this temporary affliction is preparing for me this weight of glory."

It's an eternal weight of glory beyond comparison. There's not a thing in the visible world that you can use to compare to the glory that is man's when he begins to rise within himself. When that something turned around in man, the creative power, and it starts up, there's not a thing in the world that is as luminous, not a thing in the world that is as powerful, not a thing in the world that is as beautiful. So he couldn't find anything in the outer world to compare to this weight of glory that was simply rising from within. And he knew at the very end he would do what everyone has to do, take it off. And in his case there was no return.

He knew those who did not accept it, and dared not to the point of holding that child, would be restored at what we call death only to die again. But everyone at death is restored to life only to die again. And only those who hold the child that is the promise of God to man…where the whole thing has been completed…for birth has in itself the germ of death, but death has in itself the germ of birth. So when I carry the cross___(??) self, I am carrying it right into death; but the germ of birth is in death, and so I will now hold the child in my hand and say, "Let me depart, according to your word" (Luke 2:29). And your word was that the whole vast world of flesh would see your salvation, and here is your salvation. So everyone who holds him departs, never to return…he can die no more.

Now let us go into the Silence.

*   *   *

Now are there any questions, please?

Q: (inaudible)

A: This world that you see as so real...you're seated there, I am standing
here...I have gone into worlds just as real as this without moving more
than two inches...it's all here. There are worlds within worlds within
worlds and all equally solidly real, peopled as this world is peopled.
You're told that in the 20th chapter of the Book of Luke when those who
were called not agnostics, they were really the atheists of the day called
Sadducees. The Pharisees believed the law, believed the resurrection, but
not as taught by those who came saying "this is how it happened."

So the Sadducee asked a very simple question to trip him, for if you
are a student of the Bible, you must know the law of Moses. So he said,
"Teacher, Moses in the law said that if a man marries and dies leaving
no offspring and he has brothers, the brothers should take the wife and
marry her to raise up seed for his brother. Well, there were seven brothers.
The first married and died leaving no offspring; and the second married
her and he died leaving no offspring; and finally the third, the fourth,
the fifth, the sixth, the seventh all married her, and finally she died, and
there was no offspring. In the resurrection, whose wife is the woman? For
she had seven husbands" (Luke 20: 27-33). They said this to trip him.
And this is his answer: "The children of this age marry and are given in
marriage." One translation of that Greek passage for ___(??) to read it, but
it means that we beget on a divided image. "But those who are accounted
worthy to attain to *that* age"—now he divides the ages, this age and that
age—"and those who are accounted worthy to attain to that age neither
marry nor are they given in marriage, for they cannot die any more; they
are sons of the resurrection, sons of God" (verse 34). His creative power
personified as a son has entered a new age by being resurrected from this
age; and this age in scripture is called "the age of death," where the power
is keyed so low it is as though it died. When it's turned around and man
is raised from this level, then he cannot return. He continues into the new
age, therefore, he cannot die any more. If I said he cannot die any more,
I imply those who are not as he is they must die. So at death, as we call
death, a man is restored to life, only to die again.

And so, the journey is on. But because God is playing all the parts, no
one is going to fail. In the end, everyone must be resurrected or a portion
of his infinite creative power is missing, and that can't be. So he implies
that your marriage here may be blissful, may be happy, it doesn't mean
that you'd be mated there to the same one. It doesn't mean that you'll

play the part that you're playing now. He implies there will be no loss of identity, no change of individuality; the actor remains the same but the part differs. And you learn to accept the cross, and live by it, consent to it, that you may know how to resolve every problem in the world, even though keyed low; that you trust the power of God and the wisdom of God, and not necessarily the wisdom of man.

So where you start in life...if you know Christ crucified...it doesn't really matter. You don't have to be on the right side of the street, born to the right family as they consider it. That does not mean that you're nearer the new age. So he implies, in fact he states, spells it out: "Those who are accounted worthy to be of the resurrection"...well, the whole drama begins, really with the resurrection, the new age. The drama, the overall drama begins with the crucifixion, that's over. Crucifixion is over for all of us. Everyone has been crucified with God, for everyone is alive, and that Imagination of man is keyed low...that's the crucifixion. So the crucifixion is over for every child born of woman. Will he now, while crucified, hear the story and consent to it and live by it? Then it leads him towards that birth, the birth of the child, where he holds it in his own arms, and asks that God keep his promise: "Let me depart in peace, according to your word." Everyone will hold him.

Any questions?

Q: (inaudible)

A: What about those who believe in karma? Well, karma is about cause and effect. The Bible does not say it isn't a world of cause and effect. So let man not be deceived, for as you sow so shall you reap. If I plant corn, I'll reap corn. "See yonder fields, the sesamum was sesamum, the corn was corn; the silence and the darkness knew and so was man's fate born." We always reveal what we are sowing...all imaginal acts. But he also teaches that when a person comes into this world maimed—he uses the story of the blind man—not because of some previous experience on earth that he takes the sight of another, blinded the other, therefore he has to now repent, no. He said: "That the works of God be made manifest." You will play *all* the parts in the world or you have played them.

But here, be careful what you're planting, your imaginal acts. And if the whole vast world believes in karma, meaning reincarnation, the Bible doesn't teach that. It doesn't teach any loss of identity. I couldn't meet those that have gone beyond, as I do, and have loss of identity. My mother died at sixty-two, sixty-three, a painful death. She looked, oh, many, many years older than that. Yet the moment she died, 2,000 miles away from where I was, she appeared this beautiful, glamorous woman about twenty, nineteen, twenty, twenty-one, just brushing her lovely long blonde hair. She was very blonde, China-blue eyes. Wouldn't talk to me, but there she stood, and just simply brushed her hair and smiled. So here she dropped off at least sixty years from her appearance. She preceded my father in death by twenty years. And so, what part she plays now I don't know, but she's playing the part best suited to awaken. For the purpose is to awaken and turn around. And we did nothing to cause the fall. The fall was self-imposed by God for a creative purpose: Only by restricting himself could he expand himself. So no one is to blame.

Any other questions, please? Test Christ, your own Imagination, test it. Put it to the test. You should prove it in the testing. If he's your Imagination, you should prove it. Don't just have someone else do it for you. This friend of mine who is still a friend, a dear friend, she hasn't one thought concerning Christ, yet she has her prayer answered. She herself knows she did nothing, but she didn't like the way it was answered. So she doesn't see him, save on a weekend. Maybe that was his prayer too. He comes home on Friday night, goes off on Sunday, and, personally, I think that he's never been happier. For not a thing that money could buy can make her happy. And so, we get together now at very long intervals... never discuss this. We discuss personalities that a long gone from this world, long, long gone. She had some relative in the theater before the turn of the century, had a name, the old days of Vaudeville, and she's still living in that ancient dream. Why spoil the evening? Go along with it, and just pick it up and talk about ___(??). The same...put the record on, over and over and over. But to bring this up, it's like talking Greek... doesn't know what you're talking about.

Q: Now, just want to get one thing clear. If we, as you were talking about, are born into a situation that we are born into because we play our part... okay, so if we do that then you said that we just watch the part that we're playing with our human Imagination because as we sow we reap. But yet, if we are going to play all the parts, then we still are in command of our lives here now? I mean, like you said, there's no unconditioned future for us right now in this level?

A: All right, if I understand your question. Finding yourself here clothed in a garment that is mortal and weak, and needs to be fed and clothed and watered every day, and so here we have something that's a burden, carrying it with you, but could you honestly admit that you had anything to do with it? Would you not admit that you were born physically by the actions of powers not your own? You found yourself clothed in a garment of flesh and blood and you make the most of it. Along the way you hear of a power that you possess, it is your own being, and you either believe it or you do not believe it. If you believe it, you consent to it, obey it, live by it. Well, just as you were born physically by the actions of a power not your own, let me assure you you will be born spiritually by the actions of a power beyond yours.

When that time comes and you are awakened—for that's what the verb means "to be awakened"—for although he appears dead, he isn't dead. The crucifixion is not death as we understand death. It is keyed so low it's impotent, and it seems that the entire creative power of God is now dead. Yet, at its weakest point it's stronger than the strength of man; at its most foolish point it is wiser than the wisdom of man. So we accept it, and one day we will be awakened. And that same little tiny power, called in scripture Jacob—"Jacob, he is so little, how could Jacob stand?" And the Lord regretted that he had done this and said, "It shall not be" and then the prophet repeats it, "Oh, but Jacob is so little, he's so small. How can Jacob stand?" (Amos 7:2,5). Well, he does! The word Jacob in the true sense of the word means "to augment, to expand, to increase." So here is Jacob increasing the twelve tribes, all coming out of him, an expansion has taken place. Yet he is so little. And so here, you reach that little point and then you awaken. You're turned around and expansion begins. And there's no limit to expansion back beyond where you were as the creative power of God...and personified, yes a person.

Until Tuesday.

EVERYONE HAS THE
PLAN IN HIM

1/24/66

___(??) the Bible is. I'll let you decide from what you will hear. For what would I call it? I presume that everyone here has a plan, has a purpose. We find it in business, we find it in government; and we wonder, if we believe in God, well, does he have a plan, does he have a purpose? Is there a plan for the overall picture? We're told in scripture there is a plan; "As I have planned, so shall it be; as I have purposed, so shall it stand. And the anger of the Lord will not turn back until he has executed and accomplished the intents of his mind. In the latter days you will understand it clearly" (Is.14:24; Jer.23:20). The word translated anger in our biblical concordance (Strong's) is "to breathe hard." He used the word with emphasis on breath. Well, breath, wind and Spirit are the same in both Greek and Hebrew. It could be the Spirit of the Lord, which could be the Lord himself. They give another definition, "to know," therefore the face, therefore the person himself. So you may read it: "The Lord will not turn back until he has executed and accomplished the intents of his mind. In the latter days you will understand it clearly."

It is not what man was looking for. No man by the revelation in the Old Testament could have discovered his plan, could have discovered his purpose. The New Testament interprets the Old; it's not the other way around. And when it came to the surface after the fullness of time, man could not accept it. He didn't accept it then and he doesn't accept it today. The hundreds of millions who *think* they have accepted it by calling themselves Christians are as far from the truth as they were when it was first revealed. So from time to time he sends one, as he sent Paul, and he sends him not because Paul was wise, articulate, a big strong man. No one sent seems to feel qualified, and they aren't qualified in their own eyes. But he who sends him by the very act of seeing him qualifies him. That one qualification is the consequence, not the result of anything that we did but the consequence of seeing God. When you see him you are qualified; not because you've earned the right to see him. What he saw in you, you didn't see, and no one on earth saw. But he sends you.

So Paul in his letters, or his one letter to the Ephesians, he speaks of "the mystery of the will of God, according to his purpose, which he set forth in Christ as a *plan* for the fullness of time" (1:9). And then he goes on in the same letter and he said: "This mystery was made known unto me by revelation. When you have read it you will perceive my insight into the mystery of Christ" (Eph.3:3)...when you read it. Now he goes on and makes the statement, and you will see from the statement he now makes, that the mysteries of God are not matters to be kept secret, they are truths which are mysterious in character, truths so fantastic that man denies them. They are not to be kept secret and that's why the prophets of the Old could say: "If I say, 'I will not mention it or speak anymore in his name, then there is in my heart as it were a burning fire shut up in my bones, and I am weary with holding it in, and I cannot'" (Jer. 20:9). You can't restrain it, though in the eyes of others you are a laughing stock. You are sent to tell it...God's plan of salvation.

Today we think by historical research we will find religious certainty. Historical research cannot give us religious certainty. You may dig from now to the ends of time, find all the old manuscripts that even predate what we have, but you will not have that inner certainty by anything save through revelation. And this one he makes now as ___(??), he said, "To me this grace was given to preach...and to make all men see what is the *plan* of his mystery hidden for ages in God" (Eph. 3:8). And I am convinced that you may do whatever you think you should do for ___(??), but you cannot hasten the time. It's like a birth and it's coming into fulfillment in its own good time. When that time has reached fullness you will experience these signs.

They are signs spoken of especially in the gospel of John. But the signs were not the signs which man was looking for. He denied them when they came; he denies them now. Because the one who brings it, the message, the message of salvation, cannot produce the witnesses, he cannot produce the sign. All you can do is tell them about it. He can talk about it, but he cannot produce the sign. And no man can throw himself into a state deep enough to experience that sign. He has to wait for it to come. But when purpose is known, all things fall in to place. So, "Go and preach." Preach what? Preach his purpose, tell of his plan. For he's not concerned with this outer man; this outer man is a shell and he's given the outer man a law by which he can cushion the blow as it must come, inevitably comes to every man as he turns from hearing the story to its fulfillment. It's called a four-hundred-year journey. Not any 400 years…that too is a mystery. 400 is the numerical value of the 22nd which is the last letter of the Hebrew alphabet. Its symbol is that of a cross. And so, I will bear my cross in a land where I will be enslaved, ill-treated, beaten, set upon; I will lose everything and be a stranger in that land. Then will come the fullness of time and he will bring me out with signs and wonders.

You tell them of the signs, to look and expect. They will come, every one of them will come. There aren't many. When the first one appears, the last isn't far behind. It will all happen here in this section of history. And the millions who think it happened and now hope in some strange way to have the promise of his coming again fulfilled, are looking in vain. The true return of Jesus Christ is when the individual experiences these signs of Christ within himself. That is his only return. Then you stand amazed at this peculiar thing, that God who planned it all is the *only* one. He planned it all, and the God of the entire drama being one, the end has an ultimate unity. You are that being who planned it all and I am that being who planned it all, and we aren't two. Yet we do not lose our distinctive individuality, we do not lose our identity, and yet we are one. He plotted it and planned it in a way that no man could ever have guessed. No man is wise enough to work it out; he had to reveal it. So Paul said, it was given to him by revelation, and when you read it you will discern my insight into the mystery that was hidden for ages in God. It could not be revealed until the end. And they called the one who in his own mind's eye called himself least qualified.

Now what are the signs? They will come… I tell you this from experience. I have friends in all walks of life. Last night, my wife said to me, speaking of two close friends here in the city, and every time we get together he brings up religion. They are pillars of the church in Beverly Hills, pillars of the church; give generously not only of money but of their time. And I wondered if they would be present at a certain party. Well, he didn't know, because they're going off to Denver to Billy Graham's gathering, this enormous crowd. And he had the ___(??) come in to ask me when he was home the last time, about a month ago, looking at his brother, he said, "Do you think"—calling him by name—"that he could understand the Christian mystery?" Well, I was raised in a nice family not to offend my guests, but I thought, "Do you?" He's pointing to his brother. He's as far removed from understanding this mystery and to him it is not a mystery, in spite of scripture. "Great indeed" said Paul to Timothy "is the mystery of our religion." He tells us it's a mystery and it can only be known by revelation. It can't be known by any philosophic contemplation…can't be known that way. Yet he thinks he knows this, he's going off to Billy, and both will be as blind as bats walking right straight towards the inevitable pit, and that's where they fall. But they don't know these signs that all men have rejected.

Let me now share with you from experience the signs. Again, let me repeat, I have no knowledge of having earned them, none. I cannot brag, for I have no memory of this long, long journey that would lead me to believe that the suffering that I *must* have gone through—for all pass through the afflictions as told us in scripture—qualified me to receive the signs. So I do not claim that I have any memory that in any way would qualify me to have received them, but I've received them. Therefore, I would say to all, don't try to earn it; don't try to acquire merit that you may earn it. You want to acquire merit, do it if you want to appear big and wonderful in the eyes of men, yes, if that's what you want; but in the eyes of God no—no, because it's not by anything known to man here.

So here, when you least expect it…and I tell you it will happen…you'll be so awed, so surprised you can hardly believe. You know the population, three and a half billion, and you, how could it be? Yet you can't deny the experience. And you too will be moved in a way that if you didn't tell it, you too would feel the fires burning in your bones; and you'll *have* to tell it, and tell it from morning to night until you close your eyes in this sphere for the last time. You will tell it. Until you actually have the experience, I can only plead with you to believe it. It has been my privilege to speak to tens and hundreds of thousands of people. What percentage believed it, I don't know. I've been promised in scripture there always will be a remnant. Don't run, he said to Elijah, go back. I have prepared a remnant for you, go back. He thought he was alone and he ran from the horror that he saw in the city.

But there will always be a remnant. It need not be the 100,000 that you're told are listening or viewing you on TV, or maybe the two million who tune in on radio. Maybe one nth part of one percent may be arrested for a moment and actually begin to dwell upon it. They can't conjure it, but they could dwell upon it and let it lodge within them. For we are told, you and I in the loins of Abraham were given a preview of the gospel, as we're told in the 3rd chapter, the 8th verse of the Book of Galatians. Paul takes scripture and personifies it and said, "Scripture, foreseeing that God would justify the Gentiles by faith,"___(??) showed him, revealed to him the mystery of the gospel. So here, one, 2,000 years B.C., if you take it chronologically, was given and granted that privilege of actually having a preview of the gospel. And he saw it, and "rejoiced that he was to see my day," saw the whole plan as concealed in Christ and Christ as in man. Christ is God *in* man. Christ is a wholly supernatural being. Hasn't a thing to do with some little being born as we are told he was born. He is in every child born of woman. He is your own wonderful human Imagination, that's Christ; one with his Father who sent him, who is all

Imagination. And he comes down to the very limit and takes upon himself the limit of the cross, called this [body], and becomes obedient unto death, the death upon the cross. To do it, he emptied himself of his unity with his Father, and he is the Father...God in action now. God's creative power keyed to the lowest point, brought down to the lowest point of opacity; and he it is Christ in man, your own wonderful human Imagination.

He's not devoid of a law by which he could struggle in this outer world while he bears the cross. But he carries within him the plan of salvation. Therefore, I can't teach you and bring it out; it's buried in you. But I'll tell you the plan, for it has unfolded in me; it's the same plan, the same Christ, the same God. You're not another little Christ, same Christ, only one. Not another little god, there's only one God. "I tell you this that you may know and believe that I am he...and besides me there is no God. No God was formed before me nor shall there be any after me. I, I am the Lord...and besides me there is no God" (Is. 45:5). One God, the same God that is in you as your own wonderful human Imagination.

Now this is what happens and I can't tell you the surprise, the awe, well, it's almost one of fear and yet not fear...I struggle for a word to describe the emotion that possesses you when it happens. You find that you thought all along that you were awake. For fifty-odd years you woke at least once a day—when you were a child, oh, maybe many times a day—but every time you woke into this familiar environment you thought you had slept and this was waking. You carried that forward through the years. And you're in your fifties and always believed that when you are in this world that's when you were awake, and when you slept and lost consciousness in this world, that's when you slept.

Then this moment happens, and the wind, the anger of the Lord God himself is possessing you. All you can see is this vibration, and you know you're waking. It's the only thing that entertains the mind, you're waking. You expect the same kind of waking that you've done for fifty-odd years, you expect it. But you wonder why this strange vibration, because if it goes any further than it is now you'll die. You feel, one more intensity, one little bit more, and you're going to split. You feel some massive hemorrhage will simply put you out of this world. But you don't have any massive hemorrhage, you wake. You become completely awake as you were never awake before. You've never known such clarity of thought, never known such waking.

And there you are, you're sealed in a tomb and the tomb is your skull. You know it is a sepulcher, and you know you can't remember walking in there. Someone must have put you there thinking you dead, for only the dead are buried. And sometime, somewhere you were thought dead and you were buried, buried in your own skull. You know beyond all doubt this is your tomb, but now you're awake. And you are awake as you have never been awake before, never, something entirely different...and yet you're sealed. Then memory returns and you know the one point in the entire sealed sepulcher that would give if you pushed it, the base of the skull. You push it and something gives. It rolls away...and you come out your head first.

You know what to do. You're pushing and pushing and pushing, and when you are just about here, down below the hips, you then take them and you pull, and pull the remaining portion of you right out of the skull. There on the floor you remain for just a matter of moments and then you rise. Now strangely enough there's no sepulcher...it's an interior, but you see the body out of which you've just emerged and you wonder at the ghastly paleness of it. It seems so white, so much like death. As you look at it, the wind seems to increase, only now it's divided. It's still in your head, but it's over in the corner. For a moment you're distracted because of it and you wonder, what is it, a hurricane, a cyclone? It's far greater than any wind you've heard.

And so, as you look over, once more you turn back and here this thing, this garment, the body isn't there. But in its place you find three men, one where the head was and two where the feet were. You look...they can't see you. You're more powerful, you're more wise, and you are invisible. You can discern every thought that they entertain, and their thoughts, not expressed, are audible to you and objective to you...you see them. Their every thought becomes an objective picture to your sight. You look at them. They're seated and they are disturbed by the same wind. One seems more disturbed than the others, so he goes in the same direction. As he moves in that direction, he hasn't gone more than a foot before he's attracted to the floor. He looks down and there before his eyes...he makes an announcement and he calls you by name.

You haven't lost your identity. Whoever you are now, whether your name is Benny, he will call you Benny, if your name is Mary, he'll call you Mary; and he'll speak of you as one he knows (I knew these three), and he will say, calling you by name, it's your baby. If you are as I am a male, these other two are incredulous as they were in my case, "How can Neville have a baby?" He doesn't argue the point, he presents the evidence. He lifts this little infant wrapped in cloth and just puts it on the bed. Then you will bend over and take up that little body; and when you raise it, you will look into its face and speak in the most endearing manner to it. I said, "How is my sweetheart?" He looked right into my eyes and broke into a smile, the most heavenly smile. Then the whole scene dissolved and I'm in my inn, my hotel room in San Francisco.

There is a combination; two scenes in one. The waking from a long, long sleep, for that's what resurrection is, "to rouse from sleep." Look it up in the concordance. "To rouse from sleep" is the definition given in Strong's Concordance. And we think it means to reassemble the dust and the bones of the dead, hasn't a thing to do with that. There is one in you that cannot die. It *can't* die, for it is God. It was God who imposed upon himself this self-limitation. It never dies. It was never really born. It simply imposed upon itself the limitations, and then in you it dreams the dream of life. Then must come *that* moment, the first sign, as revealed to everyone to whom he sends. So here is the sign. "You must be born from above. Except you be born from above you cannot in any way inherit or enter the kingdom of God" (John 3:3). You cannot. It takes a new form; it takes the awakened Christ in you to enter the kingdom of God. There's no other route. You're in a new body and yet no loss of identity. But you must be clothed in the Christ body.

Now everything I've told you has scriptural support in the Old Testament. You will read the pulling out of one's self in the 30th chapter of the Book of Jeremiah, word for word. But no one understood it. The question is asked, how could man do it? For the question is asked, "Can a man bear a child?" The obvious answer is no, can't do it. Then why do I see man just like a woman in labor? Why do I see—the word is shallots—"Why do I see him with his hands pulling himself out of himself just like a woman in labor?" If I see it, and every man is doing it, why isn't he bearing a child? I see him as though he were bearing children, or rather, a child. That is the 30th chapter of Jeremiah (verse 6).

And here is the grand awakening. He takes it out of man. Takes what out of man? He takes Christ out of man. Did he not tell him in the 7th chapter of 2nd Samuel: "And when you are gathered with your fathers"—meaning when you are dead; this [world] is the death spoken of—"I will raise up your son after you, who shall come forth from your body. I the Lord will be his father and he shall be my son" (verse 12). They're waiting for that to happen, and they don't know the mystery of it all. He brings forth himself, for the father and the son are one in this case. So he brings forth himself.

Now comes the crux although it's only the second of the four signs. I call it the crux because it's the universal fatherhood, which is the ultimate revelation: to know the unity of God in spite of the seeming diversity. That to me is the greatest of them all. Others do not agree, but I can't see anything in the scripture comparable to the revelation of the unity of God in diversity. And this is when we're told, "God so loved the world he gave his only son" (John 3:16). He didn't give me his son as a companion. He didn't give me his son as a mentor. He didn't give me his son as someone who would walk the street with me. He gave me *his* son, and in doing so he gave he *himself.* If I have a son, I can say as people say in marriage, I gained a son…he married my daughter. It's a lovely way of expressing it. And maybe he will be to me a wonderful son. He married my daughter and maybe I couldn't have a son that would be as kind and considerate as he. But still I am not his father. When God gives you his son, he gives you himself. He doesn't share him with you; he gives you himself. And when you see God's *only* son, he fulfills the 89th Psalm: "I have found David. He has cried unto me, 'Thou art my Father, my God, and the Rock of my salvation'" (verse 26). That's exactly what he calls out: "My Father, my lord." And you know he is your son and he knows you are his father. You not only know it, but you know that every child born of woman contains him; and one day he's going to call everyone "Father."

And because there's only one David and David's father is I AM, that's called in scripture Jesse, and Jesse is I AM, so he calls him I AM. Some scribe along the way to give sense to the genealogy gave Jesse a father and a mother. You read it in the Book of Ruth (4:17). The most ancient manuscripts that we have on record show no father of Jesse. You will find that in the most critical of all scholarly criticisms of the Bible and that is *The Encyclopedia Biblica*. They say there is no ancient manuscript that mentions any background of Jesse. As though he were like Melchizedek, without father, without mother. As we're told in the New Testament, of Hebrews, and he became a member of the order of Melchizedek, no father, no mother, no beginning, no end. And when you are God, because his son is your son, you're Melchizedek, no father, no mother. What father would God have? What mother would he have? What origin would he have when he is the origin of all?

And so, here in this is the apex of all the revelation: The universal fatherhood is you, and you are God the Father; and there is no way in eternity that it could ever be revealed save through the Son. "No one has seen God; but the Son, the only Son, who is in the bosom of the Father, he has made him known" (John 1:18). Why haven't you seen God? For we are told in the 33rd of Exodus: "You cannot see my face. For no one can see me and live" (verse 20). Right, you die to everything you've ever believed concerning God. There is no other God, and so you completely die to everything in this world when you see the Son, and know that son is God's only begotten son, and he's *your* son.

So how could you now have a God on the outside? To whom would you turn? "Before me there was no God, nor shall there be any after me. I, I am the Lord, your Savior." That's what we are told in the 43rd chapter in the Book of Isaiah (verse 11). So believe it, said he, that I am he. Believe it now; tomorrow you'll know it. You'll know it by revelation when he gives you himself. To give you himself, if he is a father, you too must be a father. If you are a father, where is my honor, where is my son? So the last book of the Old Testament, the Book of Malachi, ends on the note: "A son honors his father. If then I be a father, where is my honor" (verse 6)? It wasn't answered in the Old Testament. It's promised but not answered; in the New, it is answered. So he comes in, and

David calls him "Adonay, my Lord, my Father." So here, that's the limit, the apex of all revelations, when you are revealed to yourself who you really are.

Now the third one is a sign—they're all signs, signs taking place in the grand supernatural you—and that is when the temple of your body must be split to reveal your sacrificial blood that made it all possible; for life was in the blood. And now you're going to redeem it, and so your whole body is split from top to bottom, revealing blood…but the blood is living, golden, liquid light. As you look at it, you not only know it is yourself, but you know it is the Creator and Redeemer…and yet you know it is yourself (Blake, *Jer.*, Plt.96). So who is the Creator and who is the Redeemer? You're told: "I am the Lord your God the Holy One of Israel, your Savior." Yes, your Savior, your Maker. If I am your Maker, I am your Creator. And as you look at it, you know it's not only yourself, it is the Creator, it is the Redeemer, and you fuse with it. Then as you're told in the 3rd chapter of John: "As Moses lifted up the serpent in the wilderness, so must the Son of man be lifted up" (verse 14). And so that's how you are lifted up, right back where you came from, this time completely awake.

And the fourth one, which is a glorious one, but to me although it comes last and should be the greatest, it is only confirmation of all the promises, where he's satisfied with his work. And that is when the Holy Spirit takes the form, the symbol, of a dove and descends upon you, and smothers you in love, smothers you in affection. When you are all completely smothered and this world becomes infinitely transparent, there is no circumference. And where is it taking place?—within. And then you will understand these strange words of Blake: "The circumference is within you; it's the selfish center that is without." The circumference is within, ever expanding in the bosom of God, and you've found God. So from now on the whole thing is translucent. There is no circumference, you can't see it; it's ever expanding. You've never seen such clarity. There is no boundary. And here you are expanding, expanding, expanding. Where? All within, the whole thing is within you.

Now in that day when everyone has this series of events unfolding within him, and you and I meet in that union, can you conceive of the joy of the return of all of us to form one? So he said, then you will know, "Hear, O Israel: The Lord our God is one God." This multiple, infinite series, this divided, fragmented being forms one, one made up of others, and no loss of identity; and all returned, and all the same Father, the same Son. Can you conceive of the joy, can you conceive of such love, when the whole thing is done?

So I ask you to name it. I couldn't name it when I thought of what I would tell you tonight. But I know as I stand before you, the name is called Neville, but Paul did not have any commission other than the one given me. I, too, stood in the presence of the risen Christ. I answered in the words of Paul, yes, but the words of Paul are revealed words dictated by the risen Christ. He is the Spirit that moved the prophets. He is the Spirit that moved Paul. So when I was asked, "What is the greatest thing in the world?" my automatic answer—as though I was divinely prompted, I didn't stop for one second to answer—"Faith, hope and love, these three; but the greatest of these is love" (1Cor.13:13). And then infinite love embraced me and incorporated me into his body, never to be separated again. His body became my body, and yet, in some strange way, sent into this little body. But I could say with the central figure of scripture, "He who sent me is with me"…never left me. You don't see him, but he hasn't left me, because I can't ever again be separated. I can't be, having once been incorporated into the body of love.

So everyone will be incorporated into that body of love and you will know the statement in Isaiah: "I will gather you one by one, O people of Israel." Yes, one by one…you're so unique. You can't bring a friend, you can't bring a wife, a husband, a child…one by one. You can't be replaced; no one can take your part. Therefore you can't be lost, because if one were lost the temple would be incomplete, and that's unthinkable. But everyone will be gathered one by one to unite into a single being who is God, and that one being is made up of all. And the rejoicing that takes place when the drama is over! So God has a plan, he has a purpose. He reveals it to his servant and his servant is sent to tell it. And it's not the servant's concern who hears it, for he's planned who's going to hear it. He has a purpose, and no one can force it upon himself and say I'll make the effort to be. This is a plan for the fullness of time.

Here, I got a letter today from my daughter-in-law in New York City. My first wife was born and raised a Catholic, now she's a Jehovah's Witness. He was married twice before he married this girl. This girl was born and raised a Catholic, but they wouldn't marry them in a Catholic church because she is the third. He did give his marriage enough…but marriage was in order, and so they got married in a small, little church and came to New York City. Now I've learned today from her letter that she's going to St. Bartholomew and taking lessons to prepare herself for conversion. Now, she knows my books, I'm her father-in-law…she has them. She's heard me speak, not often, but she's heard me…but the fullness of time has not come. She has to hear all these things and go through all the blind alleys, and believe all these things told by the blind leaders of the blind, until one day in eternity the fullness of time has come and she will hear it as you're hearing it.

But the ancients did not recognize the signs, for they were not the signs they were looking for. They thought he would come in the same manner that you and I came, and conquer the enemy of Israel, and establish a new Israel that would simply dominate the world. That's what they wanted…not the kind that one could ___(??). He comes quietly. Dramatically yes and suddenly, but comes in a way that no one but the one to whom he comes can see. When he comes it's simply repeated in the one to whom he comes, his story as recorded in scripture. The one is amazed that the whole thing is taking place in him. He had no idea the story that's written in the gospel was all about him. He thought it was all about someone else—he was taught that—and suddenly the whole thing is all about hm. He can say with the psalmist: "In the volume of the book it is all about me...and I have come to do thy will, Lord." That's all I'm going to do, fulfill the will of God; and to fulfill the will of God is to fulfill scripture. That's all.

So tonight, we're all plotting and planning what we're going to do as a nation, as a family, as a business, and chances are in our own eyes it is good. And if we apply God's law wisely, the chances are we'll realize our objective... if we apply it wisely. That's the law. All the ways of men are good and pure in their own eyes, but the Lord sees the heart and he's not getting off his prearranged plan. His prearranged plan is to redeem himself that is buried in us. That's his prearranged plan, and he brings it all back. I tell you this tonight because, as I told you earlier, I am planning to go to Barbados and I'm just waiting for one little answer to some request I made. It's still crowded there...can't get on the beach it's so crowded. But I am led to believe maybe the first week of March they'll begin to disappear and go back to their homes in Canada and England. Then, of course, if that is true, Bill and I will fly off the first week of March. And so, I will be planning to close here approximately the 25th of February...that gives me just four weeks.

And if I am sent to preach, it's not really to tell you every night how to get another house, and how to get more money, and how to get the things of the world. You know it. I will come back to it time and time again. But what I was sent to tell you'll find in the signs in the life of Jesus Christ. That's what it is. And these signs are not the signs for which man was looking, they're not. So having received the signs, having experienced them I must tell you. Even though I have told you this time and time again, I still must tell it to those who may not have been here before or maybe they haven't heard it, or haven't heard it in the way it was told tonight. For these are the signs and they will come to everyone in the world, so don't despair, and don't try in any way to hasten it, just believe it and let it happen. They will not delay one second, not one moment, and they will not change. The signs are recorded in scripture and there they remain forever. They will not change.

And you will go back into the ancient witness called scripture, and it will dovetail with your internal witness. And when we come into the court we must have two witnesses. If two different witnesses agree in testimony, it's conclusive. We all have the witness of God's word as recorded in scripture; we have to bring the living internal witness that we experience scripture, and when the two parallel and agree in their testimony then it's conclusive. And we are told, "You are my witnesses, my chosen servant, the ones that I have chosen that you would hear me and understand that I am he." And so, everyone will be a witness, and the witness you bring is your own internal testimony to the truth of God's word. The second witness is already recorded; it is the Bible... that's God's word. And so you have the witness there, but you have to come with the second witness. For the testimony of one man is not sufficient. You cannot bring yourself as the only witness. And no one can go into court with himself as the only witness. He must have two minimum; three, all the better.

Tonight, I am fortunate. I have a third witness who has the internal testimony of scripture, and so he is a witness to the truth of God's word. And so, I can present three of us...the Bible and the two of us. But if I can present two—the Bible we can all present, and then yourself—and stand unashamed, unafraid, for it has happened, and no power in the world can deny to you that it has happened; and so you stand as a witness. And you don't need mortal eyes to see it. When you are brought into the divine assemblage, they know from your appearance whether you are the witness or not. For you are the living book, and you witness to the external witness that God gave to man through his servants the prophets, and you experience within yourself as you come now. And that's your only judgment, really, no harsh judgment...you're the witness.

So when you take off the garment here after witnessing these signs, you go as witness into the divine assemblage and you're one with them all, not less than. For all you have to do is to fulfill scripture. He said: "Scripture must be fulfilled in me" (Luke 22:37). "And beginning with the law of Moses and all the prophets and all the psalms, he interpreted to them in all the scriptures the things concerning himself" (Luke 24:27). And so he brought himself as the fulfillment of all that they had foreseen, and he was the living, living witness. And the book is a living witness...it's forever.

Now let us go into the Silence.

*   *   *

Are there any questions, please?

Q: ___(??) wondering if I might have your comment. "Resist not evil" is the sentence.

A: "Resist not evil but turn the other cheek." In other words, another face: look at it differently. Practice the art of forgiveness as taught in the Bible, called repentance, or called by my terminology just simply revision. You see, what to do with evil, what to you is evil, alright, revise it. See it as you would like to see it. But again, let me quote scripture, he said, "I know and I am persuaded by the Lord Christ Jesus that there is nothing unclean in itself; but any man who sees anything to be unclean, to him it is unclean" (Rom. 14:14).

If we take our code today and compare it against the code of our forefathers, they wouldn't gel. Tonight, the world is divided in this conflict. At six o'clock tonight I turned on the news and some very hush-hush meeting is taking place in Washington, all the cabinet members, the war staff, our president, and some great decision, which may still be hush-hush tomorrow, but they're called upon to make a decision tonight. He has to make it and he has to have the confidence of those that would execute it. 290-odd million Americans will be told eventually after it's done, for they think they are doing right. Maybe they are…but all these things are relative.

I must stress, stick to the signs of the end. Let them become your guide, so that no matter what happens, you know these signs are forever. They will happen; because he in you can't die, cannot die. He is subjected to this dream of life and he'll dream it, but he cannot die. In the end, he never really was in you, because he can't show he's in you. He's perfect, the one of whom I speak. And so, if that guides you, even though they make the decision tonight that might ___(??), doesn't really matter. But these things are relative. One's good fortune may be another's misfortune. Tonight, and this seems a bit sordid, but I don't mean it that way, but it's a graphic picture. Some family must think…you'll find them weeping and they mean it, they're all tears at the loss of a loved one; and some mortician is rejoicing, business is good. So that's relative. It's a graphic picture, not a pleasant one, but it's a true picture, true on this level.

Tomorrow, you watch the market. The market's been going this way. In New York City, oh, about a year ago, the headline came out someone… there's a rumor of a possible peace. What do you think the headline was? "Peace Scare" and the market went that way. Peace scare. So if people talk of peace, do you think they really mean it? So why can't we have peace? And you say the ___(??) can be stopped? And they will say, if they have it, yes. Well, what do we have? We have DuPont, we have General Motors, we have a little of this, well, what do you think would happen to them tomorrow if you have *real* peace? And when they begin to contemplate the consequences of their stock, they don't want peace…until they get out. If they could only know the high point and get out, they could talk all they wanted about peace forever. But they didn't wait for ___(??) to get out...but here was the headline "Peace Scare."

So you watch the market and you see it, it's going this way. And there is not a place in this world where you can put a dollar and get more return for your dollar than in a safety account, a savings account: 4.85%. There is no business. I go to the market in the morning and just watch it. I don't have any stocks here; all I have is in Barbados. I go just for fun. And when you see what they pay in dividends and what they're selling at, it's ridiculous. Let these enormous sums ___(??), must get it up. Today there's no buying on margin, not really. You must get up almost all 100% to buy stock and a stock selling at almost 500, 500-plus, and paying you under three percent. Well, go to the bank and put it in; you get 4.85. And if you don't feel that the government can go beyond $10,000, open a second one at another bank. They're all underwritten by the government. Take your money and go from bank to bank. It's the limit, but they will guarantee $10,000. But you're getting 4.85% return...to come into the world of Caesar, talk this way. Yet they go up this way, up and up and up. It's certainly not paying dividends that you can see in the morning's report. It's nice to have it and say I have a stock that's worth $500 a share. And you say, yes, can you live on it? You got in when it was 300, and maybe you can unload it now, had it long enough. But can you really live on the income from it? No one thinks that way. It just isn't there. But we aren't going to go into business. I'm not a business man. Were I a business man I wouldn't be here.

Well, until Friday. Thank you.

WHAT MUST WE DO? BELIEVE!

1/28/66

Tonight's title is "What Must We Do?" This is asked in scripture, "What must we do to be doing the work of God?" and he answered, "This is the work of God that you believe in him whom he has sent" (John6:29). It all starts with believing; you believe in him whom he has sent. Now, what must I do? Believe that a person called Jesus Christ lived? Just how would I go about believing in him and believing that God sent him? I simply read his story, read all that he tells, all the signs, and then see if I can believe it. For he tells us, "We speak what we know and bear witness to what we have seen, but you do not believe it. If I tell you earthly things and you do not believe it, how can you believe if I tell you heavenly things?" (John3:12).

So what was the earthly thing that he told first? The earliest gospel is that of Mark, and the first words recorded of this central figure we find them, "Repent and believe in the gospel" (Mk.1:15). He encloses within his doctrine the message given to the prophet Jonah, who brought the one message: the message of repentance. So he takes that in, "Repent and believe in the gospel." He knows that man *did* repent. Well, man wants a sign. He calls this now an evil generation; he said, this is the generation, "it's an evil generation, it seeks a sign, but no sign shall be given to it but the sign of the prophet Jonah" (Mt.16:4). And as Jonah was a sign to the men of Nineveh, so will the Son of man be a sign to this generation.

Well, what did he bring? He only brought the message of repentance, and people believed him. He tells us, now they won't believe *his* message; because Jonah's message, you could try it, and if you tried it it would work. The people of Nineveh tried it and saved not only themselves but their city. They repented, and they realized that a change of attitude would result in corresponding changes in the outer aspects of their lives. So he called them an evil generation, but what is an *evil* generation? An evil generation is simply an unrepentant generation, that's all that it is. A man could always repent. If he could change his attitude towards life, he'd change his life; and therefore he could always save himself, or save the environment in which he finds himself by simply repenting. So we are told that they did repent and saved themselves and their city of Nineveh. But he wonders who now will actually believe *his* story, for he brings the final revelation. And here he contrasts the unresponsiveness of the people of this generation to his greater revelation with that response that Jonah got to his lesser revelation.

So here we find, "What must I do?" Well, I could be tending bar tonight and really believe what he told me, and I'll be doing the work of God. Or I could be sitting on the throne in the Vatican, and so busy with my vast portfolio I have no time to believe what is said and not be doing the work of God. So you can't judge a man's profession and think because of his profession—he's a minister, a rabbi, a priest—that he is necessarily doing the work of God. To do the work of God is simply believe in him whom he has sent, and he tells you exactly in the signs. You believe in these signs, because I can't reproduce them for you; they belong to the very depths of your soul. They belong in a region that is outside of the range of one's rational mind, so you can't bring them to the surface that anyone here could experience. You must wait on them.

In the meanwhile, you go and you tell the story of repentance, and play the part of a Jonah. I know in my own case I told it for twenty-one years before I could honestly say, "And now I am a witness to what I have seen." The word seen means "experience." I did not experience salvation, yet I was called and sent. And all that I could actually say I know this from experience. Know what? I know if I change my attitude towards a certain individual and persuade myself of the reality of this change of inner attitude, I would see the day that he will conform to this inner change in me. So I knew that from experience.

So when I took the platform on the 2nd day of February, 1938, here was an actual experience right at my door, my son. I had many before…but I hadn't yet gone out and actually took that platform as a professional. Yes, I would be invited to a platform, always as the amateur. I was dancing, I went from city to city, and they knew of my interest; they gave me their platform. They'd come to my show, invite me to the platform, for some afternoon get-together. But even then I could tell of the story of Jonah, the story of repentance. So this night in question I was speaking at Steinway Hall, my first night. I went to the door, and we almost opened the door together. Here was my son, a boy in his early teens, just about, well, he wasn't yet thirteen. I made every effort that man could make. My mother made every effort, with financial inducement, to his mother to get him. Not one thing worked...and I knew exactly how to apply this law.

So in the month of November I began to assume that he was actually living in my place, even to the point of putting my hand, my imaginary hand, on his head, and feeling his presence at the table, and feeling his presence in my place. And then the week I'm to open, I received a call from his mother saying to me quite casually, "My place isn't big enough for two men, and your son although only twelve, he's a man." I went looking for him...in the meanwhile she had told him that I never wanted him and poisoned him over the years against me and my family. But I ignored it and simply assumed that he was home with me, living in my place. So that very night as I was going out. His friend said I was over there day after day looking for him, and this whole thing was a lie that the mother had told him. So he packed up the little that he had and he arrived at my place as I was going out to give my first lecture. There he remained with me until he joined the Marines after Pearl Harbor. He remained with me through all of his many marriages. It's only now that he is really on his own, at the age of forty-one.

So I know from experience. I could say "we speak what we know," but I couldn't then add "and bear witness to what I have seen." I had not yet experienced salvation...not until '59. So I started in '38 and for twenty-one years I went across the country, all the major cities, telling the story that Jonah would tell. You know what you want in life? Assume that you have it. Fall asleep just as though you had it. Live as though you had it. Act as though you had it, and the world will conform to it. In a way you do not know and you haven't the intelligence to devise the means necessary to produce it, the whole thing will become a fact, and project itself upon the screen of space for you, if you *dare* to apply this story of repentance...that you need not *accept* things if you are willing to repent.

Then came the visions, the series of visions. And that is what *he* brought and called the gospel, the most incredible story that man has ever heard! The story he tells us he meant to be taken literally and to be fulfilled literally. So when you say this is literally so, someone will say, "Oh, no, it couldn't be." That's my problem as I go again across the country. If I go on TV panels or radio panels, if my associates or opponents are ministers, rabbis, priests, they're my most vicious opponents because they can't accept it literally. And then, I tell them I know it from experience, I bear witness to what I have experienced. I'm not theorizing, I'm not speculating.

This burgher of which he speaks when he tells us what I've just quoted in the 3rd chapter of John, he's speaking now to a member of the Sanhedrin, the highest order of the Jewish faith. And Nicodemus cannot understand how a man can be born from above. He intends that Nicodemus accept it literally.

This birth is not from below, from the womb of woman; it's from above, from the skull of man. When he tells you, that as Moses lifted up that serpent in the wilderness, so must the Son of man be lifted up, he means that literally and to be fulfilled literally. You actually are lifted up in the same serpentine manner. Every statement he makes concerning these signs...there aren't too many signs...all told there are four majestic signs. Two are divided into two parts, making it six all told, that's all. These six signs are literally experienced by the individual; they're not things on the outside. Everyone will have it.

Now why do I say everyone will have it? Well now, let me share with you the experience. You're told in scripture, "I am the Lord, the Holy One of Israel, your Savior...and beside me there is no savior" (Is.43:3,11). Is that true? Is that literally true, that my creator and my savior are one? Yes. But more than that, I say "I am," don't I? He said, "That's my name, my name forever, and thus am I to be known throughout all generations" (Ex.3:14). Well, you can't stop me from knowing that I am. Is that his name? Well, then I must be one with the creator and the redeemer. Is that literally true? Am I self-begotten? Do I save and redeem myself? Yes. There is *only* God; there is *nothing* but God.

Can this be taken literally? Is it fulfilled literally? I say yes. The day will come when the third sign of which he speaks appears, and he gives it to us as the splitting of the temple. When you see at the base of that split body that is yours...and you see the golden liquid light that is truly life itself—and the life is in the blood, it's alive, it's liquid—as you look at it you are saying in the depth of your soul, I know *I am it*. But you don't stop there, you have the impulse to say, "O, my divine creator and redeemer." And then you fuse with it. You fuse with what? With your very self that is life, and you know it is the creator, and you know it is the redeemer, and yet one. And up you go, the Son of man, in the form of a serpent. So you know it *literally*, and you can say, I now bear witness to what I have seen, and what I have seen I have experienced.

So you can truly say, yes, I am self-begotten. I did this for a purpose, contracted myself to the limit that is called man, and brought about this contraction, the limit of opacity, the limit of contraction. Then after spending a time, a time interval of a dream, a fantastic horrible dream, the dream of life, then you begin to break it as you would a womb. And you begin to expand, and then there's no limit to expansion, no limit to the translucency as you begin to expand from this limited contracted being called man. Well, who did it? God himself did it. And who is this God? His only name is I AM. Well, who goes up? I am going up. Who beholds this? I am beholding it. Who felt himself being split? I went through the entire experience. And that's his name. He doesn't differ from the creator, and you know it. He doesn't differ from the savior, from the redeemer, and you know it. There aren't three, only one, and his name is one.

So here, what must I do to be doing it? Believe the story. What you do in the outer world that really is not important. So when they brought the first son, he said, "Surely that is he." He was so majestic, so big, so wonderful looking, and the Lord said, That's not he, I have rejected him. Bring me the next. They brought the next, and the next, and none of these were. "Are these all of your sons?" said he. "No, there's one, but he's with the flock." "We will not be seated until he comes. Go and bring him." So they bring him, "That's he. Rise and anoint him" (1Sam.16:6-12). Here was the youngest. Here was the one they put aside to take care of the flock, while these majestic ones came to be picked out by the prophet Samuel as the one that the Lord would announce as *his* choice. "I do not judge from appearances. I judge not as man judges. Man sees the outward appearance." Whether it be your physical form or your social standing or your intellectual accomplishments or something of that nature, he doesn't see that, he sees only the heart. He sees what that one so far has experienced, and here he picks *him* out, this one that is buried in the mind of man, called Olam. Some put the letter Alem—Aleph, Lamed, Mem—the God of the Eternal One, or God the Eternal One. And so, is this the one? Yes. Buried in man? Yes. Is that literally true? Yes. He, too, comes out. He comes out and reveals you to yourself, and calls you "my Father." He comes out...the great and second sign.

So every one of these signs...he said, "Now go and tell it." So I took you this night, apart, and I will say, trust me, believe me, and I speak now from experience. This is going to happen to you, one night when you least expect it. I hope in the meanwhile you have been practicing the art of forgiveness, which is called repentance, changing yourself, changing the world, changing your friends, and making them conform to more idealistic states in your own mind's eye; for they will ultimately conform to it if you remain faithful to your change of concept relative to them. They *will* change, so keep on practicing and practicing, called now, repentance.

And when you least expect it these things will happen to you. And then you tell them. You're going to be born from above. And the story is this...this is the way in which you are going to be born. It will begin with a resurrection and then followed by a birth. Then will come your discovery of God's only begotten Son, who will call you, Father. Then will come the great splitting of the temple and your ascent into heaven, knowing you are the redeemer and the creator. You are self-begotten and self-redeemed, and that very self is the creator and the redeemer. Then you will know the work is finished and this glorious thing is now consummated, it's reached a climax, and it's good and very good. The symbol of the Holy Spirit will seal it with kisses. He comes in the form of a dove. That's literally true, and fulfilled literally.

So you tell that story. What percentage will believe it? You can't tell. So Paul makes the statement, "I should like to depart and be with Christ, that is better by far. But for your sake and because of a better need I stay for awhile in the body." Read it in the 1st chapter of Philippians (verse 23). It is far better to depart and be with Christ, the creative power and the creative wisdom of God raised to the nth degree of creativity. For he is entitled to that now he is one with God. But he has to tell the story, and so he delays it, seemingly for awhile, to tell the story. He's not satisfied with the number who accept it… he turns his back to find they turned away, too. He returns to a city to find they've gone elsewhere…become strict vegetarians now…they believe *that's* the way of salvation. Or, they've become something else and something else, everything *but* believing the story. All you have to do to do the work of God is to believe in him whom he has sent. If you sweep the streets and that's what you really believe while you sweep, you are doing the work of God. If you owned the city and gave everything to charity thinking that is doing the work of God, you are far, far from the point. You're only doing the work of God when you believe the story. And the story is incredible but so simple. It calls upon man to believe something entirely different from anything he could ever envision from this level.

Will he believe that story? That's all you're asked upon to do the work of God. The story of repentance…it's easy. It takes training. It takes practice, daily practice. But it works. And Jonah found people who were responsive; they could believe it. One tried it and it worked, told another and it worked, and the city was saved. But you cannot prove this story of salvation, which is something so deep all you can do is believe it and then let it happen. Then become a voice telling others about it—that's all you can do—in the hope that they will believe you, as they believed concerning repentance. For that makes the great appeal…the whole vast world. You take someone, a child, and you play a game to save the family. That becomes Nineveh, the family, a family of five. The little child comes home and she brings a story of woe concerning the family…they are about to be dispossessed. And you say, "Megan, can you play a little game?" "Yes." "Well now, this is what we're going to do" and you construct a little scene, a few words where she is telling you a story that things are perfect at home, have enough to eat, rent's paid, everything is perfect. She delights in the story as she tells it and you sit and revel with the child because it is so lovely, so altogether lovely, and they are saved.

The next day a friend from out of town calls, finds their predicament, and said to the mother, "Inez, let us forget it. Let us go to the park and get on a boat. I'll take you. You have no money, but we'll have a little fun for an hour." So off they go rowing in Central Park. As they are coming ashore a boat is behind them. He's not a good boats man. He comes with all of his might and she, to protect her boat, sticks her hand out and it's crushed. Not injured seriously but crushed...there was a little blood. It's an obvious injury. So the attendant comes over, examines the hand, takes her name, takes her address, sends her out an adjuster from the city. They're insured against all these things. They're not going to court, no suit, gave her $300 for her little injury. She hadn't seen $300 in years. One time she was big in the theatrical world, she and her husband. They were dancers, went from one show to the other and then came the dive. And here was this little injury, twenty-four hours after we played a little game. She could play it with me and save her little Nineveh, saved the family. They were paying very small rent—I am going back to the Depression days, back in the 30s—and the five of them lived in a small, little unit and still only paid $40 a month, a walk-up, yes. But that story I know.

One exhausts the entire police force of New York City. Lost her furniture...can't find the furniture. She and her two children went to Paris, leaving a maid behind to take care of her apartment. She returned with her children; there is no maid. The apartment is there but no furniture. She investigates. Nobody knows where the maid is or where the furniture is. She seeks the help of the police force, of the detectives of New York City. Calls in a private detective agency; they exhaust all of the suburbs. They can't find where it is stored, if it is stored. One day she comes out of a bank on Madison Avenue, makes the wrong turn, and didn't discover her mistake and she went a block. Then looking down at the pavement she spots a pair of very familiar ankles. She came slowly up to the face...it's her maid. She held the maid and wouldn't let her go until the maid took her in a taxi straight to where she had that furniture. And this happened after she had exhausted all things, and then came home to see me. I said, "Have you forgotten? Don't you know the principle? In the past, how often you worked it...and it worked, it always worked. What are you doing now?" "Well, I haven't tried this. I tried the police force, the detective force and a private detective agency." Well now, I said, "Sit quietly and put yourself among your furniture. You had a grand piano, you used to keep your son's and your daughter's picture framed on the piano. I recall that vividly. Well now, see it on the piano, and see it as near you as you are now to the piano, therefore, make it real, the whole thing all about you." She did, and she lost herself in the reality of what she was imagining, and gave it all the tones of reality, gave it sensory vividness, the whole thing was real. And then she went out, and here came this little incident and she got her furniture back. No court case, no suing, all she wanted was her furniture.

A total stranger heard of me and came to ask to find a friend of hers, but it seemed the height of insanity when I told her what I would do. I would sit quietly and hear her tell me that she had found the friend, that's all that I would do. And she would sit quietly and tell me she found the friend.

She expected some magical something. So at the end of our little mental communion I bid her goodbye. She said, "That's all?" "That's all." Well, she was so, well, disillusioned, for she thought she was going to see some fantastic thing take place in my room, and that's all that she witnessed, something in the Silence, not believing me. But it worked. She took a friend to New Haven where she last heard from her friend. The friend had moved on to Boston. Went on to Boston, yes, they knew the friend, but she left no forwarding address, so she returned, disappointed, to New York City. Coming out of a department store on 14th Street, had she been five seconds earlier or five seconds later, she would have missed her, ran right into her. Then she went all the way to Boston via New Haven trying to find the friend.

So I say, repentance is only an inner change of attitude resulting in a corresponding change in the outer aspects of life. So you practice it until the story told you awakens within you. When you hear the story, believe it. All you're called upon to do is to believe it...the most incredible story in the world...the story that I have been telling you since it happened to me back in '59. So that is the message he brings to the world, expecting everyone to accept it literally...and it will be fulfilled literally. He doesn't depart, though he wants to go now into that creative power and be one with it. As he is one with it he's entitled to it. For all the signs took place in him, no more signs; but he delays it because of the need of those who are always departing, always turning back, always turning away.

So when he was asked, "What must we do?" this is all you do. Then he said, I give you only the sign of the Son of man, and these are the signs of the Son of man. But this is an evil generation...they wouldn't even repent. For the evil generation is only the unrepentant generation, that's all that it is. So how many men today as they succeed even remember how they did it? Now they are surrounded by all the things money can buy they forget these mental attitudes that they adopted to rise to their present state. Completely forget it and turn their backs upon it, and completely ignore that very ladder by which they did ascend. ___(??) repentance. Everyone does it.

So here, as we are coming to a close, I thought I would give you, night after night, from now on, just things that would really fire you in some way to try it. It will prove itself here. And then I hope that you will believe me concerning the message of salvation, for that's the important thing I bring now. For I was sent before I knew the message, the message of salvation; I was called and sent. But all that I knew from experience was that a change of attitude on my part would result in a change of behavior in the outer world. I saw it, I practiced it and it worked. And so, having seen it work I could tell it from experience, but I knew nothing of the message of salvation. Not until that morning of the 20th of July, 1959. That's when it began and it came to its climax on the morning of January 1st, 1963. So three and a half years later the thing was culminated; and I could say with Paul then, I should like to depart and be with Christ. That is better by far, but for your sake and for the need, the far better need, I will stay the morning. But from that morning on, I could...not only could have...but truly desired.

But that's not for me to do, for we are told, "There's a time to be born and a time to die." And when the Psalmist asked, "Show me my end, O Lord, and the measure of my days" (Ps.39:4), he wouldn't respond to that. Wouldn't show him his end or the measure of his days, for no one knows the measure of his days, no one knows his end. You can observe, like our friend Mike Quill tonight is now at the morgue. Just a few weeks ago when he was sentenced, he said---and I saw it on TV, here was a face filled with anger and filled with venom, speaking of the judge---he said, "May he drop dead in his black robes." That night when he was taken to prison he had a heart attack. Took him out, he was taken home this past week, and today he dropped dead—whether he was wearing his black robes or not, I don't know. But here, as a man sows, so does he reap.

I tell you, in the end there aren't others, there's only one, and that one is God. God is the creator and God is the redeemer, and you are he. Actually, God became man, as you see it here now; and when he breaks it, the thing that became it simply expands back to what he was but beyond it. It's his way of expansion, his way of growing...an ever-increasing illumination, that's God. So I say everyone here is going to experience it because we are all one. This is a compound unity, one made up of others, but one.

So tonight you can take it, just like the little girl, and you can set your Nineveh free, if you believe it. It all starts with belief; given that, everything else follows. But how to go about believing? Well, these are the little secrets... the art of believing. If I would believe this night then I would see the world differently. If what I want would change my world, then my world must be seen by me as I *would* see it *after* this thing takes place. So you don't *wait* for it to take place, see it as *though* it were. I saw my little boy, set the table for him, put my hand on his head, felt his presence, and then she found someone. Only they lived in a small place, wasn't big enough for two men. So I sought him a week...I couldn't find him.

I told you a story here, in fact, I told it at Fred Bales years ago. A lady in my audience took great issue with me and complained to Fred that such a story should not be told from his platform. She missed the point completely. I told it to show everyone present that there is no condemnation in God: "Father, forgive them; they know not what they do" (Luke 23:34). Because you are causing the behavior...if you know how to control your Imagination, you are actually causing the behavior of all the people you are meeting. You are in control. When I wanted to get married to the girl who now bears my name, who is now the mother of our daughter, I had all of the entanglements in the world. My dancing partner notified my ex-wife who was not then ex; we had been separated for years but not divorced. Therefore we lived, as you know, in New York City, which has the most archaic rules concerning divorce in the world. And so here, I wasn't divorced. She didn't want me divorced, because she was living very well, and her boyfriend, out of my pocket. So why have him divorced? We're living beautifully by taking his money. So she was notified to make yourself scarce, don't be seen.

Well, I know she left the city, or I was told she left the city, and everyone was very, very happy, they're all very happy, that I am saddled now, can't get divorced. My dancing partner and her boyfriend can live off of me, and the other can go her way. So what I did, no one to be hurt, I simply assumed that I was happily and blissfully married to the girl who bears my name. I went to sleep for one solid week in that assumption, that there she slept and here I am, and I wouldn't be this happy if it was at the expense of someone else. I couldn't hurt someone else. So that's all that I did. And then the phone rang one morning and it's the court. Asked me if I am the Neville who speaks publicly, and if so, they have a case coming up the following Tuesday and it would be to my interest to be in court. Well, I was sleepy, it was early in the morning, and I hung up wondering "What sort of thing is this? I'm not subpoenaed. I have done nothing to warrant this...so I won't go."

Tuesday came, around quarter of ten the phone rang, and here a voice on the wire, "Why aren't you in court?" I thought, "What have I done, I have no reason to be in court?" "Well, we told you you should be here this morning, didn't we?" I said yes. Then said she over the wire: "Your wife is on trial and maybe you can throw a little light on it. You're not subpoenaed, no, you'll not be put under any oath, no, but your presence might be helpful to the judge." I was unshaven, I couldn't...I simply threw some clothes on and grabbed a taxi and got to the court. When I got there, some attendant whispered to the judge, ___(??), said "He's in the court." So they asked me to stand, identify myself, would I take the platform? So I took the platform and then they brought her in between these two policemen. And so, the judge said, "Now, you're not sworn in, but I think you can help me solve this case or bring in a decent judgment on it. Your wife is accused of shoplifting." Then he asked me all the questions. "What's your religion?" I said, "I'm Protestant." "What's your wife's?" "Well, she was born a Catholic." "Is that any difference in your way of living?" I said, "No, it made no difference whatsoever. We just were not compatible from the day we got married, and we've been not divorced, separated, well, for, I should say, fifteen years." I then had my son three years.

And then he read out the charge and I said, "Well, your Honor, I have a son. I'm very proud of him, he lives with me. And if you must sentence her, you have the right as a judge to sentence and then suspend judgment. You can be merciful. So if you must sentence her, sentence her as the law demands, but then exercise your right as a judge and be merciful, for my son's sake." He accepted my recommendation; he sentenced her for six months, suspended it, and then dismissed it. She met me on the outside, waited for me, and she said to me, "That was a very decent thing to do. Give me the papers." I said, "I don't have the papers with me, they're at my home." She said, "Well, I'm coming with you and you're going to give me the papers." So I took her in a taxi, we drove to my place, I got my papers…and this isn't a legal thing to do, to serve your own papers, but I gave her the papers. Then I was granted my divorce in the city of New York.

So I told that story, saying that, "Who made her do what she did? I did." I slept in the assumption that I was free and happily married, and the only way I could be would be to be divorced. She was told by my dancing partner to make herself scarce and she obeyed. They were all living off of me. And all of a sudden she finds herself doing something that she would not normally do. And so, what did it? What was that impulse?—my assumption. So who knows who is treading the winepress? So I told the story to tell people, don't judge anyone. On the record *she* took the clothes. In the depths of the soul that is God I did. Well, did I not write the script? Should you go to a play tonight and you don't like what you see, don't blame the actor. If there's any blame, go to the author. He wrote the script. But he's not there for you to condemn, so you throw eggs at the actor. You dislike the part he is playing, but the author made him play it. And the author doesn't like anyone tampering with his script. Well, if the author here doesn't like it, what do you think God likes?

And so, when you go into the deep and you actually assume the end, and live in the end as though it were true, you set in motion all of these things. Then the actors come. She only played a part, and so playing her part she has to be forgiven. So when I asked the judge to be merciful, he was merciful, he was kind. She was moved by my appeal and asked me for the papers. What other way could it be done? Yet I made every human effort to find her. I made every effort and not a thing could find her. Yet a total stranger calls me from the court, says "You're a public figure and wouldn't want this in the papers. The reporters are here every day to get anything upon someone who is a public figure and they'd love to get you in the paper. And so, I tell you, for your own sake be here in court that you can throw some light on this." It was never in the papers; not one paper in the city carried it. It was simply dismissed. So when I said I took the blame, this lady took issue and thought the story should not be told. Well, she didn't understand. All you can say is, you don't understand. Had you understood you would have understood the words, the words on the cross, "Forgive them; *they* know not what they do." They're moved by compulsion, but who is treading the winepress?

Now, here is a little thought in scripture. He's on the cross and they all reviled him, as told us in the 15th chapter of the Book of Mark. Every one reviles him and someone shouts, "He saved others; himself he cannot save" (15:31). These are the words. That's exactly what no man can do. Man saves himself by, and *only* by, saving his fellow men. So you hear it and you think you're just going to escape? No, you tell the story. You tell it, that the message of salvation may be heard, understood, accepted, lived by, and then grows within them...because there is no other. If one is left behind, who do you think is left behind? You are, I am...for there is no other. So when the unthinking, the un-awakened cried out, "He saved others; himself he cannot save" that is so far from the truth. For man saves himself by, and only by, the saving of his fellow men. So you see someone in distress, apply the first thing quoted that he said: repentance. After that, if you can reach them, tell them the message of salvation. It's incredible. It's the most, well, far-fetched story ever told man. It wasn't conceived by man. It is an eternal message, which is God's way of redeeming himself, not another. There is no other.

So now let us go into the Silence.

*   *   *

We're going to close the end of February, the last lecture night is the 25th. I can't write Dr. Smith until it is official with me from Barbados. I'm waiting for some correspondence. It's a crowded season and we wish to get there when the crowds have departed, so we are waiting for some kind of a green light as to when that date will be best. However, I am planning to close four weeks from tonight and I want to write Dr. Smith as soon as possible to let him know officially that it is so. I can't tell him it will be so until I actually have this letter from Barbados. We want to leave just as soon after we close as we can, maybe a few days later. So, I am still planning to close on the 25th of February. We have exactly four weeks left or eight lectures. I will let him know...he has been very kind to me letting me have this place. So I will let him know just as soon as I hear from Barbados. But we are planning to close...

Q: ___(??) anger of the Lord, could you comment on that?

A: Well, the word translated anger I would think would be better translated "Spirit," for it really means "to breathe hard"; and breath and Spirit are the same in both Hebrew and Greek...the wind, and so, wind or breath. It also defines in the concordance the word anger as "the nose," because that is the orifice through which the breath comes. And because it is on the face, they call it "the face of the Lord." Yet they use the word anger. But our connotation with the word anger is not what the ancients intended. It was "The Spirit of the Lord will not turn back until he has executed and accomplished the intents of his mind. In the latter days you will understand it clearly" (Jer.23:20). The "latter days" being the things I told you this night concerning the message of salvation. These mighty acts, which are four, and yet two are divided, therefore, there are really six. But two happen the same night. The first is a dual act, the third is a dual act; the second and the fourth are single acts.

Q: Then the anger or the Spirit of the Lord is in the wind that occurs at the time in the first act?

A: The very beginning, "And the Lord caused a wind to blow." It's himself. The word translated wind there is the same as Spirit. Tonight, when I quoted the 3rd chapter of the gospel of John, that could be either wind or Spirit. "The wind blows where it wills, and you hear the sound of it, but you cannot tell whence it comes or whither it goes; so it is with every one who is born of the Spirit" (John3:8). The word Spirit and the word wind are the same. Yet they are used in that sentence: the first one is wind and the last one is Spirit, yet the two are the same word. And yet it is wind. It's Spirit, it's a vibration, you can't deny that, but you entertain the thought of wind and wonder "Where is this cyclone, this hurricane?" That's the thought that permeates your whole being when it begins to possess you, as though you're possessed by the wind, but it's Spirit. You're Spirit possessed when you are born that night. Didn't realize it was nine. Well, until...(tape ends).

TIME TO ACT

2/1/66

Tonight's title is "Time to Act." You'll find this a very practical evening and yet it is based upon a mystical experience. If God has spoken, what in the world is more important than to listen to what he's said and what he's telling you?

But first, let me share with you an experience. It happened thirty-odd years ago. When I tell you I was taken in spirit I mean it literally. You may tell me the whole thing took place within me, and I would agree with that, for the whole vast world is contained within the Imagination of man. But you do have the sensation of travel, and so in this I had that sensation of an enormous journey. I was taken into a divine council. The first one that I stood before was infinite might. You may describe him as almightiness, the first word or the first expression of deity in scripture, El Shaddai. Then I was taken into, well, the area, a huge interior, a courtyard. The atmosphere was one of an ancient world, cobblestones, nothing modern about it. Then I saw, well, I called her a lady, like some angelic recorder, a recording angel; and she used a quill pen in an enormous ledger, the kind you see in great museums or art galleries or sometimes even in a private club, where you're called upon to furnish your name. She simply looked at me, looked back at the ledger, and simply wrote.

Then I was taken before infinite love. He asked a very simple question, "What is the greatest thing in the world?" I answered automatically, as though I had no choice; it was simply a response. I said, "Faith, hope and love, these three abide; but the greatest of these is love" (1Cor.13:13). At that moment he embraced me; we became one being. And the words of Paul you can take literally, "He who is united to the Lord becomes one spirit with him" (1Cor.6:17). There were not two of us, just one body, one spirit; yet I did not lose my identity. Here I am one with infinite love. While we were in this embrace, sheer ecstasy, a voice rang out, came from out of space, and it said, "Down with the bluebloods." At that moment I found myself standing before almightiness, the first one that I met when I entered that divine body. I could not find...it spoke, but I couldn't detect any motion in his throat or his lips. He simply looked into my eyes and I heard what he thought, and he said to me, "Time to act!" with emphasis on *act*. With this I was whisked out, and there I found myself back in my room, hotel room on 49th Street.

The 82nd Psalm—considered by some scholars the most difficult of the 150, in fact, they say that they cannot grasp its meaning; they seem to have lost today all that it formerly meant when it was given to the world—"And God has taken his place in the divine council; in the midst of the gods he holds judgment"(Ps.82:1). This is the one where you and I are called gods: "I say, 'You are gods, sons of the Most High, all of you; but you shall die like men and fall like any prince'" (Ps.82:6). They say they can't grasp the significance of this, that God could take his place in the divine council and in the midst of the gods hold judgment. I tell you, that Psalm was intended to be taken literally, for the day will come in the life of *every* man where he will have it fulfilled in himself, literally. He will stand in the presence of the risen Christ, infinite love, and you will know that God does meet among the gods. You will not feel that you are a stranger. You will feel that you not only know him but that you know them. There's a feeling of intimacy as you enter this wonderful gathering, this assemblage.

When you are sent out, it's a message, for the message was "Time to act." That's my message tonight. Many of us think that we have broken, radically broken with old habits of thought and systems of belief, and yet we find that these old things that we thought we left behind still determine our conduct. We haven't left them behind at all. Action tests belief. You try to realize how very severe a test to belief action is. We say, "I believe." That's a statement I use here all the time and I mean it literally, imagining creates reality. I firmly believe—I do not believe that any other cause or force will be discovered in the world— that these unseen imaginal acts are meant in Hebrews when we are told, "And things that are seen are made out of things which do not appear" (Heb.11:3). No one sees the unseen imaginal act, yet they are causative; they are producing the phenomena of life.

I have friends of mine who would say, "Oh, I believe that!" and they'll repeat it day after day, ___(??) but never live by it, never. "Imagining creates reality" ___(??) and so that does it. That doesn't do it at all. The belief that is not strong enough to affect action can hardly be more than a half-belief. And it is always possible to use action to test the force and the genuineness of belief. If I suddenly heard a voice and you heard it, "Fire," and it seemed to be coming from the only exit in this place, there isn't one person present who would not make his exit to that door. We would respond to that; it's part of our training and that's a danger signal. And when we are told it's a fire, everyone...some would even stampede trying to get there first. But nevertheless, we would respond to it.

But now, do we really live by the statement "imagining creates reality"? To the point when whether we are on the subway, whether we are walking the street, whether we are at home and whether it's the morning's mail as we received it, at that very moment when action is called for to resolve a problem, do we act? And by act I mean not going to the telephone and calling or writing a letter, I mean the imaginal act. Do we at that moment act as we would act when someone screams, "Fire!"? Is it automatic that imagining creates reality with us? For that was the message I was given, "Time to act!" "No longer drink water, but take a little wine for your stomach's sake and your many infirmities." Here we have stone, water, wine. And we have those who will go from meeting to meeting, year after year, absorbing more and more water, more and more what they call truth—water being the symbol of psychological truth. And so this one has another...here, we'll do this water...it seems to come through a different land. This one has another flavor...you want to taste all different kinds of waters. He calls upon us to stop drinking water; start now drinking a little wine—put it into practice. *Act* upon what you now know, and don't try absorbing all the more of the water.

So here, we have taken our stone---the stories in the Bible, these literal stories—we have turned them in to water—psychological meaning is given to them—now *act* upon it. Does it really mean that I actually have an opportunity to do something in my Imagination that I do it or that I wait for the most, well, opportune moment? "I am too busy now." You're never too busy to simply act, if you believe in the reality of that unseen imaginal act. All things are possible to God. For we are told by one of the truly great mystics of all time, "God only *acts* and is in existing beings or men" (Blake, *Mem.Fancy*, Plt.15). "Therefore, let us to him who only is give decision." He only is. Where is he?—I AM. Is that he? Well, I believe it. If I believe it and he only is, give all decision to him, and now act. If I act, I have met the test. If I postpone it and I don't act, I go around repeating like a parrot "imagining creates reality," and you're doing everything in the world *but* imagining the solution...but everything in the world.

Here is a lady whose story I have told you. She is now, well, almost seventy...she was beyond sixty-five. Never confessed it, she didn't look it... no reason to confess it. But she never earned more than seventy-eight dollars a week in her life. When I met her she was, and through the years that I've known her, she was a receptionist in a beauty parlor in New York City. Her gross was seventy-eight. What her take home pay was as a single lady, I don't know. But she lived in a small, little dinky dark room in a hotel on Lexington, quite near where she worked. She was the intimate friend of a very, very wealthy man, who was a bachelor. He's now in his eighties. They lived, well, as man and wife, really, but maintained their separate places. He had a palatial home, which he owned on Madison Ave, or rather on Park Avenue, one of those co-ops. Money means nothing to him, has fortunes, and she practically none. So they dined in one of these palatial places every night, night after night. Saw every show that opened, all the musical plays, everything, operas, horse shows, everything. So she saw and heard and did things that many a wealthy person felt they couldn't afford.

But she didn't want that, she wanted security. For he had nephews and there were the businesses, and she knew that eventually he would have to make his exit, and they would come into all if he didn't leave any provision in his Will for her. He always told her he was not giving her a nickel. I said to her, "What are you doing about the law that you know?" "But, Neville, I don't know of anyone who would give me anything." I said, "I'm not asking you to know anyone. This whole vast world is yourself pushed out. That's only response...that's all that it is. 'We love because he *first* loved us.' There is your cue. 'Now be imitators of God as dear children.' That's a response. So what do you want? You want security." Well, you know the story. I've told the story, but there may be a stranger here tonight. When I was in New York a few years ago, on her way to get ready for her job in the morning, she always took her daily tub; and sitting in the tub she simply re-enacted what she thought the lady out here did to get the security for the rest of her days. She couldn't dramatize individual scenes, so she did it in a sort of compulsive manner, "Something wonderful is happening to me now! Not tomorrow, next month, next year, but *now*, right now." Then said she, "I would feel the way I would expect to feel under such circumstances."

This is on Monday. On Saturday of that week, at dinner, he said to her, "You know, on Wednesday, you so disturbed me. I saw you go off from the dinner table and I said to myself---I didn't do it audibly---it's later than you think. And so I got on the train the next day for my factories in Philadelphia, called in my nephews, and then I said, "This is what I want...no questions asked. I want it done and I want it done now, I mean today. I want a certain sum of money set up, where she can't touch it, and you can't touch it, the estate can't touch it, detached from the estate, and all taxes paid on it, free. So free that when she makes her exit from this world, she may give it to a kennel; she doesn't have to return it to the estate. It's hers for the rest of her earthly days, but she can't touch principle." And that principle is paying her $550 a month. She was over sixty-five, so she got her Social Security. All told she is getting well over her $600 a month, and she had never earned or grossed more than seventy-eight dollars a week for any part of her life.

Now with all this, to her it was like a billion, and she said to me, "Well, Neville, I would like to go to Barbados for the winter, but, you know, I haven't had any furniture. When he gave me all this money I didn't have principle, I had just income from it. Well, I had to start from scratch. Although it's one big room, it's a studio room, I needed a carpet, I needed a bed. I needed everything. Well, I went to ___(??) and got the best, and he signed for it. That is, he didn't pay for it, but he underwrote my charge, as it were, but I'm paying it off, and I can't afford to go to Barbados. So I bought the best, and having nothing and all things had to be bought, where would I find the money to go?" And I said to her, "Have you forgotten? Could you forget so soon, where in one week you got it all, and now you're asking me where?"

This is what she did. In Barbados if you come from a northern climate or if you were a Barbadian and went away for quite a while and became acclimated to the northern climate, you would sleep under a net. It doesn't seem to interfere with the local man, he sleeps exposed, no net, and the mosquitoes never touch him. But you come back from America or Canada or Europe, and then you sleep under a net. If she were in Barbados, she would sleep under a net. So that night she simply slept under a net, which would *imply* she's in Barbados. Then she applied this principle, seeing the world *from* Barbados. He gave her the winter in Barbados as his Christmas present. She didn't mention it to him, didn't voice it; it was his gift to her. The second year she did the same thing, she repeated it. Now, she is home, this is the third year...all gifts from him. All she does, she sleeps under the net. The only net she has ever slept under was in Barbados, so she associates it with Barbados. He comes forward giving her her winter in Barbados. She *acted* upon it.

So I ask you not to repeat like a parrot "imagining creates reality," act. Do something about it. It's entirely up to us. If we don't act upon it, we can hear this and what I know is you can forget it just as though you never heard it, and go elsewhere. The phone's been ringing all week. I can't tell you how many dozens have called. Not one will come here, but "Are you closing?" It just got out...he's closing. And so, they're either calling for those who are in the field, or just through sheer curiosity for some columnist, I don't know. You know, it was once said of a very powerful leader in the theatrical field here that when he died he had an enormous funeral. They didn't go out of sympathy and respect; they went to make sure he was dead. So they came back quite pleased because he really was dead. They couldn't conceive such a thing ever died, but he was dead. So they didn't go out of respect.

Yes, I'm closing, closing on the 25th. I'll be back, though. When, I don't know, but I'll be back to still tell the story of "time to act" and tell you what I mean by "time to act," that imagining does create reality; that, "All that you behold, though it appears without, it is within, in your wonderful human Imagination...and that is God himself." We become aware of God in the act of being aware of contents. You can catch him in the act if you can only become aware of these unseen realities, their contents, as she became aware of this net around her. Well, who is doing it?—-her own wonderful human Imagination. Did it produce results? It did. Well, does any other creator live in the universe? No. "By him all things are made and without it there is not anything made that is made." He makes everything, good, bad or indifferent.

Well then, what did it? "Well, I only imagined I was under a net...and a man gives me a vacation in Barbados. Cost him hundreds of dollars; round trip, living in one of the finest hotels, and still living, not just going to a meal, then booking a room, but really enjoying the island." So he didn't just send her with just the ticket in her hand; and he *had* to do it, or someone had to do it. She never thought of him, she thought only of the act. She became aware of God in action by watching, inwardly, content. If I only can assemble the state...the potency is in the assemblage and what it implies. Well, I can get under a net. Well, does it imply anything other than I'm hot? This *implied* something, and *that* was its power.

So here, when almightiness sent me the words were "Time to Act." And he that embraced me, infinite love, he hasn't left me. That form no eye can see, but the form is not out there in space, it's here, it's infinite love... can't describe it. There aren't any words to describe the garment of the risen Christ, none, and no mortal eye can see it. Whether that mortal eye be here, walking this sphere, or now slipping over the veil, it's still mortal. If it hasn't been resurrected, it's still a mortal eye and still can't see it. But those who are resurrected, they could see it, for as they are resurrected they are one with that same body...*one* body and no loss of identity, none whatsoever.

So here tonight, I ask you to please act. At the very moment that the decision is here, act. "Let us to him that only is (walking among us) give decision. For God only is, and exists in all existing beings or men." So when we say, "I am," that's he. Act upon it and believe it. It will work! I promise you it'll work. So if you're called upon, stop drinking water, just use a little wine now. We'll use it in the true sense of the word, not as so many a person used it to plead their cause. When taken before the judge, you're called upon to swear on the Bible, and so, many a judge will scoff at that little bait. So if I had to swear on it because it's the word of God, it's true, it's gospel truth, then you pick me up and I'm intoxicated, I will swear that he told me to drink wine. Many of them have done it. Since the judge never saw that passage in Timothy, he has to let them go. But it didn't mean that. It meant, stop absorbing only the psychological meaning of these fabulous stories and put it in to practice. For it's time to act, that's what the story means.

So here, when I was told it's time to act I really didn't know what the bluebloods meant. Years went by...for that was the voice that rang out in space...and then I discovered it meant church protocol, that's all that it means. No *external* ceremonies, rituals, none of these things are in order: "Down with the blueblood." Man finds it easier to spend a whole hour in church and all this external paraphernalia than to spend one second in actually acting in his Imagination. He'll go to church and sit there and watch it all unfold before him and think he's done God's duty. Go back on Sunday morning after he's done it and really believe he's done something. Spend a whole hour when he could be home actually acting in the true sense of the word.

So when I was told, "Down with the bluebloods," hasn't a thing to do with our association with the word blueblood, those who think themselves important because of the accident of physical birth. Hasn't a thing to do with that. Because in this divine society the only aristocracy that is really admitted, that is recognized, is the aristocracy of the Spirit. No one enters that divine society who has not been called, and you're called according to his purpose. But no one barges in. Everyone there is an *awakened* being. Everyone there has a job to be done in God's fabulous universe. All will be there, eventually. But it hasn't a thing to do with the outer man, for flesh and blood cannot inherit the kingdom of God. That which is born of the flesh is flesh; that which is born of the Spirit is Spirit. And so we are not speaking at any time of the outer man. What you accomplish as an outer being, perfectly alright, do it. I'm all for it, accomplish all the lovely things of the world, and do more and more and more. But it's what the inner man is doing and this inner man in you is Christ Jesus, your own wonderful human Imagination.

So tonight, act, between here and your departure...if someone you know that you could really lift up in your mind's eye. And when he was asked, "How often must I do it? Seventy times seven." Do it until in your own heart you're satisfied, just do it. But it will come back again. Alright, do it. How often must I forgive him when he sins against me?—seventy times seven. Seventy is an Ayin; its symbolical value is that of an eye. It reduces from seventy to its tone, seven, and that's a sword, Zayin: Until the eye is fixed and you can't move from one to the other; you only see what you want to see. When it becomes so fixed you only see what you *want* to see then it's seventy times seven. And so, no matter what rumor I hear *after* I've heard what I want to hear, I hear nothing else. I heard it, I am still hearing it, and I will continue to hear it until what I have heard becomes objectified within my world. So no argument trying to escape it outwardly—if I have done it, I have done it. Having done it I will wait now for the harvest.

And so let everyone take it in that light. You can be anything you want to be if you really believe to the point where you put belief to the test. You need action to test belief, and then you act. It's the most severe test in the world that you can give belief. Did he act? Not yet, he was too tired. Well, he'll wait until tonight; he has a little moment in time just before he goes to bed, that's when he does it. Well then, we go to bed tonight *after* he's been fired. We'll wait, because I intended staying here until nine and it's only…so it's not yet nine, so we aren't going to act now, we'll wait. *Don't* wait! The very moment it's upon you that's the time to act. No matter where you are or what you're doing if the opportunity should come, act upon it. You can always put your belief, what you think is your belief, to the test.

Aren't there many of us who think that we have radically broken with the old habit of, say, numerology or astrology, and the day hasn't gone quite right, and instantly in your mind's eye, that no one may see, you begin to reconstruct your chart. You wonder where the moon is, where the sun is, relative to that fixed chart of birth, and then this motion over the fixed, and you will say to yourself, "That's why." So you haven't broken at all with that old habit. We have a fixed chart in the mind's eye we think we've given up. I speak from experience. It took me time to break it. I can't tell you now where the old chart is. In my mind's eye I smashed it. But even after I proved it was only my *belief* in it that made it work, I was still holding on. So I can sympathize with those who still hold on to these archaic false concepts. They will justify it by saying, "Oh well, we had a little fun with it." How can you have a little fun with something that isn't? You live by *this* and forget all these things in the world. Just live by the simple little statement that "Imagining creates reality." So be careful what you imagine.

I don't know how many of you read the *Los Angeles Times*, but this Dr. Rafferty spoke about the books in our libraries. This librarian said that it doesn't really matter what kind of book that you…we have no evidence that any book ever influenced the behavior of a man. And Dr. Rafferty took one after the other to witness, he said, "Go into any of these homes where they're arrested for some violent crime—mutilation of the bodies of others—and you'll see all this literature in their files. They've done it time and time again. They feed upon it and then they move under compulsion to do it. They can't stop it." He said, "Bluebeard had a library filled with the mutilation of bodies and how to do it. Then he went out and savagely did what he did. He's left his mark in the world, but he was prompted by what he read." Are we not told in the Book of James that the teacher who is false, beware, because it goes so harsh with him, others no. But when a man dares to teach and takes his platform and tells the story in his own biased way, let him beware. What he is bringing upon his own head by daring to claim he's a teacher and then teaching in that manner! For they are all teaching.

Well, that was Dr. Rafferty about, I think, two or three days ago, and he took this librarian to task who doesn't care what books come into his library. He's for them all. No culling of the library, no going through the books, anything at all, not knowing this little mind digging it, drinking it in, is acting. It's putting itself right into the part that it's reading. It becomes emotionally identified with the part, it goes out and acts. And he said that how can librarians rise to that position in the world and not know the influence of a book upon the reader? He gave example after example, all through history, of what people do when they are exposed to these things. You can still get it, for it happened this past...today is Tuesday...I think it came out on a Saturday or a Friday.

So I tell you, in your own quiet moments you are setting the world afire. When James said that faith without works is dead, he didn't imply that we should give up faith and prove it only in works. Works are the evidence whether the faith that we confess is alive or dead. In fact, the word "works" in Greek, especially while it is used in the Book of James, is not used more than, say, eight or nine times, this word. And yet the word "works," you'll find it dozens and dozens of times. But this particular word is only used a few times and it means "an act." That's what it means, as defined by a concordance, an act. So faith without an act, faith without an action, is dead. I say I believe it but I don't act, then that faith is dead. But you can't rub out faith, for by faith the world was made. It seems that faith, hope and love are the virtues out of which our civilization is born...can't rub them out.

So faith is essential. And when you say works, here comes the evidence of our faith. Was it so alive that it prompted action? If it wasn't alive to the point where it could prompt action, well, then it's dead. But if it prompts action *that* faith is alive. And so I go out believing that what I'm imagining is going to become a fact in my world; therefore I become every selective, very discriminating, and only accept as true what I want to be true in my world. If I do it this way, I am acting. So time to act, and down with all outside paraphernalia, all rituals, all ceremonies, everything that would lead you on the outside, forget it, and go on the inside and act. Just as she did with the net and got three wonderful winters in Barbados. Now don't ask who is going to do it for you. The whole vast world is yourself made visible; anyone could be the instrument through which what you have done or imagined done is brought into your world.

So that 82nd Psalm, which is so difficult to the scholars, I have experienced. I stood in the presence of the gods, and I stood in the presence of the risen Christ, known first as El Shaddai, almightiness, and clothed second, as love.

The only being outside that really left the impression was the recording angel, just writing in this enormous ledger…all symbolism yes but taking place within you. The drama unfolds within man. That 82nd Psalm is true, in spite of this great scholar who said that it had lost all meaning…can't grasp anything it could ever have meant. How can he say that God has taken his place in the divine council…how God stands in the midst of the gods and holds judgment?

Well, the judgment is to answer the question and answer it correctly: "What is the greatest thing in the world?" Let that be your guide now, "love." That makes you one with infinite love. You'll actually fuse with it, and he who becomes united with the Lord becomes with him one Spirit. If I am united to him, I'm one Spirit with him, not two. Though you walk the earth as some little person unknown and you have all the afflictions here that flesh is heir to, you still know who you are. And your nights are not the nights that they were before, and your days are not…something entirely different takes place within you.

Now let us go and act. Act with your most glorious dream of what you want in this world.

*   *   *

Now before we have the questions, I want to make an announcement. My friend, Freedom came down about ten days ago and spent a couple of days with us. I persuaded him, oh, maybe eight years ago to go and do this work in San Francisco. He's done a wonderful job…he's still doing it. He doesn't talk on the Promise; he hasn't had the experience. Confines himself to what he has experience which is the law that "imagining creates reality." Undoubtedly in the many years that he has been there now he has found many facets unknown to us. I asked him to come down here once a month, no charge, his own expense, so he's promised to come on the 3rd Sunday in every month. He has taken a small place at the Woman's University Club; it only seats seventy. They tell me that the parking space is more than adequate, it's enormous. There will be no charge for this at all, no taking up for collection. If you want to contribute, you may on your way out. I will remind you that he is now living in Cambria and Cambria is 250-odd miles from here, which means a round trip of over 500 miles. He will come down on Saturday, give this talk on Sunday night at eight, and go back the next day. Then he goes from San Francisco to Sacramento and he'll be doing this once a month. It will be every 3rd Sunday in the month. He won't be advertising. I did something I said I wouldn't do…because he is so close to me, I took the liberty of asking my wife to go through my list of 2,000 and pick out a couple of hundred names, and give him 200 names to send out a card. If you are not among the list, don't be hurt. I haven't seen the list. My wife simply quickly picked out 200 names that are on my live list. You may not be on it. I will ask him to send me a few cards that are unstamped that I may put on the table before I close on the 25th. His first one will be on the 20th and I will introduce him that night.

Q: Do you expect to stay through the summer?

A: I don't know. I'm not making any plans, really. I'm keeping my apartment, if that's any comfort…I'm not going into storage. The only thing in it that I'm taking will be my clothes. My library that I love I'm leaving behind. I can tell you now the only books I will be taking will be my Bible and *The Complete Works of Blake*, that's all I'm going to take, and my entire library will be right there. So everything that I have in that apartment that is moveable belongs to us, it's an unfurnished apartment. So the whole thing will be left behind. Rent will go on. I'm not cutting off the services. The phone will ring, no one will answer, but it's there. Lights and gas, I'm not going to sever. So if at any time to be moved to come back, we can come back and it's waiting for us. But, I'm buying a one-way ticket.

Well, now time is up…until Friday. Thank you.

COMMUNE WITH YOURSELF

2/4/66

Tonight's subject you will find very, very practical. It's "Commune with Yourself"…that is the title. It is my aim from this platform to raise you to a confident faith in imagining. The logical end of this embodiment of faith in imagining is when "to believe" is not distinguishable from "to know." True believing is tantamount to knowing. Reading from the Bible it is faith in God; but man, as he hears the word God, he thinks of something other than self, something in space. The vastness of this enormous universe leads him to believe in something other than self. But I am speaking of the only *true* God. His name revealed to man is I AM. I'm saying Imagination is the divine body in every man, and *that* is God himself. So, when I speak of faith in God, I'm speaking of faith in self. God's actions are the imaginal actions of men; therefore, have faith in these imaginal acts. The basis of all that is is imagining. This world in which we live is a world of Imagination.

Now, in his revealed word to us, does it tell us so? Yes, from beginning to end. Tonight we will take a passage from the 4th chapter, the 4th and 5th verses, of the 4th Psalm. We are told, "Be angry"—that's the Revised Standard Version's translation of this Hebrew message—"Be angry, but sin not." The word translated "angry" is to be enraged when you are opposed by some great authority on this level and there is no way out, but none; he has the authority to impose his will and it's not what you want. You want out, you want the fulfillment of your desire, and here is one endowed with the power to impose his will, and therefore you're told to be enraged, but sin not. To sin is "to miss the mark." Don't give up your goal because he seemingly has the authority to impose his will and say to you, "No, this is final." So to sin is to miss the mark. We're told in scripture, never give up the goal, never give up the intention! So, be enraged, but sin not.

Now, the next statement is, "Commune with your *own* heart on your bed, and be silent." One translation has it, "And be still." I prefer the translation of the Revised Standard Version which is "And be silent." You need not broadcast it, just be silent, having communed with your own heart, you aren't going to sin. What's the next? "Offer right sacrifices." The King James Version, I prefer it, "Offer the sacrifices of righteousness." If I say, offer right sacrifices, you might think there is something on the outside I must take, and take to whom? There is no one on the outside to whom I would take anything. If I take God something, I give him an imaginal act. I don't take anything to any person or organization as a gift to God. He doesn't want a tithe...tithe, if that gives me pleasure, give it. If I want to give to charity, give it in abundance if it gives me any pleasure. If I think I'm doing good, do it. But I'm not tithing with God when I give things. God is Spirit. I bring him an intangible, to him intangible, but to the world an intangible gift is an unseen imaginal act. So, "Offer the sacrifices of righteousness." The *Encyclopedia Britannica* defines the word righteousness as "right thinking." So I offer now the right thought when I'm opposed. That's not what I want to offer him. He's my consciousness, he's my Imagination. Am I going to accept that as final? No. What do I want in place of what I'm hearing, what I'm seeing? I want the fulfillment of my goal; that's righteousness, offer *that* to God.

Now it ends on this note, "And trust in the Lord." The word translated "the Lord" means "I AM." It's Yod He Vau He. When God first reveals his true identity and then caps it by saying, "That is my name forever...by that shall I be known throughout all generations," it's not just for today it's *forever* (Exod.3:14). Where would I go that I'm not aware that I am? I may suffer from amnesia and not know who I am, where I am, what I am, but I can not cease knowing that I am. I can't stop it. So forever that is God, throughout all generations. "Bring me the sacrifice of right thinking and trust in the Lord forever." He has ways no one knows of taking that sacrifice and externalizing it on the screen of space.

Now we learn this through a story. Here is a story told me last Tuesday. I wish I had the child here; she's only nine. I have her father here, and if perchance I'm not telling it as he told me, I wish he would stop me and take the platform and tell you. It's a simple story. Bill, would you like to tell it? Alright, he will one day. It's a very simple thing to talk to self, you know. All of this is myself pushed out. Some oppose me, then I'm opposing it; some agree because I agree, and it's only self pushed out. Well, here is this perfectly wonderful story. My friend is here...he's here every Tuesday, every Friday...he has one child, a little girl, Lynn, nine years old. In their neighborhood there is a little girl, and they are inseparable; they are doing everything together. Well, the parents decided on a trip to San Diego. Naturally, Lynn goes along.

Lynn announced a fact, calling the little girl by name, "She's going too." The mother's reaction was automatic, "She is not going. There is some moment in our lives that we will simply be a family of three, and not always someone else in the family. She is not going." That was final. Mother has the authority to impose that statement. Not a thing that little lady, nine years old, could do to break it.

Lynn comes to the father and begins to complain, "This is what mother has said." The father, very wisely—he comes here, he hasn't forgotten—and he said to the little girl, "Lynn darling, have you forgotten God? He is the final authority. You go to God with everything. You've done it in the past, and hasn't it worked?" "Oh yes." She closes her eyes. He can't read the invisible structure of that mind. She opens her eyes and seems so different, and utters the words, "Thank you" and then turns to the father and said, "It's done. She's going." The mother comes upon the scene and turns to the father, she said, "You know, I've been thinking it over and I don't think it would be bad if really they went along together. They'd be companions, they're down in San Diego, and it would be something always to remember." So she justifies her change of behavior. The father said nothing; the little girl smiles, all done.

Off they go now to San Diego. They check in at a motel. Lynn said, "You know, daddy, we want our own room." Mother hears it, "No!" She's adamant, "You can't have your own room." Well, again, in that little short interval Lynn forgot. Lynn turns complaining to the father. The father reminds her of the presence of God; that she went to God, and God responded for the trip. Oh, suddenly it comes back...only a matter of hours...closes her eyes, she makes her arrangement with God—she's communing with herself—-opens her eyes and says "Thank you." The mother said to the husband, "You know, it may not be bad if they had their own room together. That's something to think about all of their lives, because they have their own room. They can play together, sleep in their own room together, and what a memory when the whole thing is over." The husband agreed with her...and then smiled with the little child.

That night, it was time for dinner. The girl said, "We don't want to go to dinner. We want to stay home and play in our room alone. I promise you we will not leave the room. We will not go on the street, we will not go out, we'll stay right in the room together." "That is completely out! You down here alone...two little children, one nine, one ten, and you're in a room together? You'd have to have dinner with us." Well, again she complains. The father says, "Have you again forgotten God?" How often in the course of a moment man forgets God. She's reminded for the third time in a matter of hours. Alright, she communes with herself, comes out, opens her eyes, ___(??) little bit, "Thank you." The mother said, "I've been thinking this whole thing over, and you know, we haven't dined together in so long. Just imagine, just the two of us dining together, we haven't had that. We've had our Little League or guests, but never in the longest while have we dined together. What a thrill! So, yes, let them have their evening together, and you and I will go to a nice restaurant and dine together, and we'll simply relive a past, just dining together." So the husband agreed with her, "That's very nice"…and Lynn smiled.

Now we are told, "Commune with your own heart on your bed and be silent." She said, "Thank you." We turn the pages over, "Thank you, Father, that thou always hear me." Thank you. He said this at the most, well, you can't conceive of any scene in the scripture that is more impossible to man than the statement I have just quoted, said at the tomb of Lazarus. Thank you. But you always hear me. I said it that they may know that I came from you and that you sent me. Yet, he who sees me sees him who sent me for we are one; I and my Father are one. So when you see me you see my Father. And anyone who sees me sees him who sent me. I can't tell you in better words that I must then be self-begotten. This self is coming out, expanding beyond what it was. And here, I must not forget that eternal self out of which it comes.

Now, what did the little child do? If I could only take her here before you and have her explain exactly how she persuaded self to the point where to believe was to know. It certainly was to know: She persuaded herself it's done and she knew it, and could say to her father, "It's done." Then a change of heart takes place in the mother, and she thinks she initiates it. Yet she didn't originate it. My mother had that secret. She'd want to go to America, but my father was not the kind of person you gave orders to. He had to feel that he thought it, he initiated it. And so, she would mentally pack and mentally get everything ready for America; then he would come home and say, "You know, Wilsey, I've been thinking it over, you should take a trip to America." "Oh no, Joseph" she protested, "Oh, no, no, no, the expense and all of the children." "You've got to go to America, Wilsey, all the more reason why you're going to go to America." She knew exactly how it was going to climax. Then he got the tickets, got everything, and mother went off to America, three or four months at a time. It was all in parceling it out. This one got Neville, that one got Cecil, that one got Victor, and we were all parceled out. And so, she knew it: how to actually imagine a state and so believe it, it was to her tantamount to knowing. She knew it by believing.

If I could only take the little child, Lynn, and have her, in her own childlike manner, explain to the adults just what she does when she's reminded of God…for she forgets him all of the time. It's so easy to look into the face of a father, a mother, who has the authority to impose their will on a minor. She's nine, dependent on her parents for every morsel she eats, every stitch of clothes, where they live, all expenses come out of their pockets. And she knows it, and she knows that until she becomes a major and takes wing and flies from that coop, she still depends upon them for all the things she needs. So their word would be adamant, it would be final, it would be law. On this level, yes it is.

But there is a higher level, a much higher level, and a child can reach it, because a child is endowed with Imagination. Imagination is God, permeating all levels of man's being, and there is no level where it cannot ascend to and, therefore, bring about changes on the level below that seems so fixed. And may I tell you, you don't have to go looking, it's all here all the time. A friend of mine called me last night and asked me to review the first chapter of my book *Out of This World* before I close. I didn't even know what the first chapter was all about. It's been out of print for years. He said, "Use the word dimension, fourth dimensional world," and I thought he meant me to review some book... the reason he came out on the fourth dimension. I have a few at home, like J. W. Dunne, and Ouspensky's works, and things of that sort. He said, "No, your own book *Out of This World.*"

Well, a friend of ours gave us for Christmas the Sunday issue of the *New York Times*. It comes every Wednesday or Thursday...it happened to come yesterday. Well, here on the editorial page at the very back, these scientists just met and concluded their meeting last week, closing it on Saturday at the New York Hilton. All of the great scientists of the land gathered to bring in their theories concerning this world. And here is what he's looking for. We are now training the scientists in the expanding mood of the universe. And it will reach its limit of expansion and reverse itself, and return to a contraction that is unbelievable, unimaginable. Every thing collapses into density that you cannot conceive. And then, maybe it will reverse again, and start, like a breathing process, out to the very limits. In that, energy escapes, and energy would be what is being hatched out as it were...called the sons of God. He doesn't use that terminology, he implies it. He makes a statement that the future exists. That you and I on this level can predict the future, but it is as real now as when it becomes a fact.

Now, here are scientists. I say you *can* predict it now, that, believe me, there are infinite possibilities. That's the future. You can accept the dictate of the mother and make that your future, and then be enraged for the entire weekend. Be enraged, but sin not. Let it off your chest if it will help you any, let it off. Blow your top as it were. But all of a sudden remember your goal... don't forget it. And may I tell you, Lynn, in taking that trivial thing— trivial to us but to her it was a great big thing—but the little trivial act taking her past the facts of life is to God's complete satisfaction. What pleases God?— faith. Without faith it is *impossible* to please him. Suppose tonight I earn all the medals of the world because I was such a strategist. I could protect my land against all ___(??), and my land, to repay me, can only give me, well, honors, and they pile it on. If I didn't have faith, I couldn't please God. If I gave everything in this world to be burned in the hope of pleasing him and had no faith, I didn't please him.

Lynn pleased God. She ignored the fact of the opposition of her mother… went to the source of all phenomena which is her own wonderful human Imagination. What she did to persuade herself to believe, in spite of the opposition of her mother, so that when she came out she could *know* and knowing, she could say to her father, "It's done. We're going." Then comes the change of heart, and being an adult she was convinced *she* had the change of heart, that she initiated it and it didn't originate with her little daughter, nine years old. That's where it started. She had the image, and the mother had to see it three times in just the short interval of a day…a change of heart.

The whole vast world responds, it reflects the activities of man. We're told, "Do not let the sun go down upon your anger," James writes in his one epistle. Don't let it go down on the anger. Be angry, yes. If it is going to release you or in any way help, blow it; but don't let the sun go down upon the anger, for that's the sacrifice that you are making. So offer the sacrifice of right thinking, the sacrifice of righteousness. If man is willing to do *that*, if he wants to spend a few moments with himself in mental argument, all well and good. Now go back to the goal. Don't brag. Lynn didn't brag that she got the better of her mother, she only went to God. And God responded. The mother had to be the instrument in which that response could take place, because unless the mother said yes to it it couldn't take place. So she could thank the mother for the change of heart, knowing that she produced the change of heart. Because, who did it?—she did it.

But if she could only stand here…of if the father…I've asked him to write me this in detail before I forget it. And so, whenever I pick it up again— whether it be months from now or when, I don't know—it's a lovely story, and if not now committed to print, I'll forget it. Yet it means so much as you go along the way telling God's law. Telling how he calls upon every one of us to commune with ourselves, and then be silent about it. Don't brag, just be silent. Then having communed with ourselves to the point of self-satisfaction then put all trust in that imaginal act, for *that* was God acting. So, how to do it? Someday, maybe he will put it on paper for me. Maybe this night when he goes home he can ask Lynn, or tomorrow, just what happened to you, Lynn, when you did it? What do you feel? Did you see anything? At the age of nine sometimes you see. But, when she really sees one day, she's going to see herself. It's going to startle her.

A friend of mine brought me a letter last night. He finally saw almightiness, infinite might. Not one emotion of compassion, no love, infinite might, not a thing he couldn't do. It filled a screen bigger than the biggest screen we have today in these colossal things for the theatre. And whom did he see? It was a steel gray face. He saw himself devoid of compassion, but it was the embodiment and personification of might, sheer might. And it's God. He's called El Shaddai, the first revealing of his power. All through the Book of Exodus it was power that brought them out, not love. No compassion shown at all. Only in the very end he reveals himself as infinite love. All the things that he put us through, all the afflictions, and he took us through the furnaces of affliction, he did it in love…though he did it as you see him as yourself, driving himself through this enormous furnace of experience.

Another friend writes me that here, suddenly, she sees a figure; it's to her right and forward. And looking at it, it turns and looks, and it's herself. As it's looking at her, it begins to collapse, like fainting. She holds it and helps it to the ground. She's looking off into an enormous expanse, there's nothing but the expanse, and a lone figure, herself, looking, collapsing in a faint and she lowers it to the ground. Then it seems like an eternity between that experience and the second, and they happen in one night. The second one, she now sees herself that she had lowered, this time coming out of the earth. The head is free and the arms are free. As these are made free and she looks, seeing herself, it seems to rest the arms on the earth for just a little while to gather the strength necessary to push and push out. What a beautiful vision of what takes place in us. You *do* come out, and when you're out, and this is out, and these are out, and you're up to your loins, then you pull and out you come. She hadn't seen a completed act; she saw what is in store for her, coming out.

A seed must fall into the ground and die before it can be made alive, this great mystery of life through death. "Unless I die, thou can'st not live. But if I die, I shall arise again and thou with me." And so, it dies, God actually dies: complete forgetfulness of self. When we read the story of the prodigal and you read, "He came to his own senses," read it and go to the biblical dictionary and look it up. It is "as one recovering from a faint"—that's the definition of the word—as one recovering from a faint and it differs from waking in the morning…when you recover from a faint. You know what a faint is? Well, when you faint and you come to from a faint it's altogether different from waking when you wake in the morning. This is something entirely different from when she saw the act of the faint. And then, you awake. But now the strength has not yet fully arrived to push and pull it out of that earth into which it was planted. But what's the true earth? This, it's called Adam in scripture, and Adam means "red earth." The seed falls into the ground, Adam, and there it remains seemingly alone. But it brings out the image of the one who sowed it. It was himself, for he was in his seed. It's all one…I and my Father are one.

So here tonight, though you may not know exactly what little Lynn did to persuade self, the story should carry some conviction, some feeling as to *what* she did. And so, you can simply imagine that you can commune with self and try to believe in the reality of your own wonderful Imagination… it's God, it really is God. Now all things are possible to God. With men it may be impossible, but with God all things are possible. And if you can just get beyond this opposition in this world, just beyond it by ignoring it…she ignored it and communed with self, and took it out beyond the facts of life. Took it up where she could say thank you. If you say "thank you" the thing is accomplished. No one but a, well, a cad would say "thank you" in the hope that he's embarrassing you into doing something. When you say "thank you" it's because the act is accomplished, it's done. So when you say "thanks," to you it's done. Now believing is knowing, and you go putting all your trust in that imaginal act; because you are moving it beyond this level into an entirely different level, where all things are. You have this entire sounding board to reflect it.

So here this night, don't give up. What you have today as an objective, as a goal, don't give it up. If you do, you're sinning. Sinning is defined for us in scripture, "Except you believe that I AM he, you die in your sins" (Luke 8:24). It's the fundamental sin, the lack of faith in I AM he. So if you do not believe that I AM he, you die in your sins, because you're going to continue wanting it and not realizing it. You're going to continue forever wanting and not getting. But if you *really* believe, you are *now* the one you want to be to the point of acting in your mind's eye just as though it were true…that you saw it, you gave thanks for it, and go your way.

Then you will know these wonderful words, "Be angry"—-the King James Version takes that passage and translates it "awe", but I can't quite get the feeling that awe conveys to me that enraged does. Awe is something entirely different to me; when I stand awed, startled, I'm not enraged. So the Kg. Jas. Ver. translates it "to be awed, but sin not." Now this one, "to be angry (that is, be enraged), but sin not." "Commune with your own heart upon your bed and be silent." Now comes what you bring, "Offer the sacrifice of righteousness, and trust in the Lord." So I bring my right thinking. What would be my right thinking if things are now, this moment, as I desire them to be? I bring *it* to the Lord.

The whole vast world opposes it, but they all will. And you will know ___(??) that it's this one endowed with power, that one with power. In my own case, here is a man…never saw him until I was drafted. I didn't now who he was, but he was, in Caesar's world, my commanding officer. He was a colonel and I was a private and his word was law. He could order me to do anything, and under the rules I had to do it. When he said no to my request *that* was final. It could not be appealed to any higher echelon in the world of Caesar. To whom did I go? I went to my own wonderful human Imagination. That's the one to whom I went. "I know *whom* I believe in," said Paul. Yes, to me, I personify it because I'm a person, and so I commune with myself. The inner man walked all around the place, but no one present could see him, and walking around all this place dressed not as a soldier on furlough but as a civilian, honorably discharged. Then comes this wonderful confirmation of the screen, the hand, the pen, the writing, and now comes, the vision breaks into speech. When vision breaks into speech, the presence of Deity is confirmed. The voice said, "That which I have done I have done! Do nothing!" I did nothing but wait patiently for nine days. Then the same man had a change of heart, and to this day he knows he had the authority to keep me there, and he believes he initiated that change of heart. He had no choice in the matter.

But our whole vast world...we have the Bible...it remains unopened; and even to those who open it it's a closed book, it's not understood. But here is the message of escape for every being in this world. Every man can be free if he understands God's law. He said, "I delight in the law of God. And blessed is the man who delights in his law...for in *all* that he does he prospers." Not a few things, in *all* that he does. If he delights in it, then he has faith in it, and with faith you please God. And all things are possible to God.

So I say to every one here, have goals, lovely goals. Don't modify them... don't bring them and make it easier for God. The same God that you go to as your Imagination sustains this whole vast universe. So when some people cannot believe in God, perfectly alright. They will one day, because it's the *one* God coming out. And because there is only one, the God that animates the garment she calls "father" is the same God that animates the garment she calls "Lynn." Individualized, yes, you are individualized. And may I tell you, you'll never be absorbed to the point of loss of identity. You're individualized, and you tend forever towards an ever greater and greater individualization. That is the purpose for it all.

A glory...well, I can't describe it, no one here can describe it. I've had these experiences, but what words...words fail me, I can't describe it. It isn't that I don't want to, I can't. I'm not sworn to secrecy; I'm as free as the wind to tell it if I can find words. Even finding words, can I find the word that would be in you that would ring a bell if I use it? And so, it's something entirely different, that thing that you become. Every one, but every one, will one day have this experience where he actually awakens from this earth, comes out of it, and all the grand symbolism of scripture appears before him, and he doesn't raise a finger to do it. Then he knows who he is. He heard about it, but he didn't know. Now he knows. Now his believing in the past has become to him

knowing, knowing now from *actual* experience. Then comes the unfoldment
of the entire picture. And now he waits patiently for the garment, for the last
time now in this age, when he leaves it behind him. And he now is clothed in
an entirely different garment, moving on to ever greater and greater expansion
of his being.

So tonight when you go home dwell on what you've heard. Don't give
it up. It's scripture, yes, but scripture is everlastingly true. Everything has its
date...and my friend goes home tonight to read what I brought him. It was
printed in last Sunday's *Times*, the *New York Times*. That's this age. Blake,
200 years ago, he said, "Eternity exists, and all things in eternity, independent
of creation which was an act of mercy" (*Vis. of Last Judg.*, Pg.614)... and they
called him mad. He never went to school, but he experienced it and told it
beautifully. Now our wise scientists are coming out with these theories, and
they see in theory but they don't know. To them it's the logical conclusion
when they observe an expanding universe, and, therefore, it must reverse itself.

Well, the Bible is reversal from beginning to end. Some scholars believe
in Eve, that John the Baptist was a twin. Some scholars and their research
manuscripts, they come to the conclusion that, here, he comes first, and the
second one will take his place; and the second is Jesus Christ. You start all
through the entire gospels, all through the Bible, here are the first and second,
second taking the first...something coming out. Well, this one cannot inherit
the kingdom of heaven. No matter how perfect he is, "of those born of women
none is as great as John; but I tell you the least in the kingdom is greater than
John." John did violence to himself to achieve it; it doesn't work that way.
Something comes out that is entirely different from this world. A being of love
is brought out of that seeming violence, and then you know that God *is* love.

So you have the prototypes all the way back. You go back and you see the
father saying to the son, and Israel speaks now to Joseph, and he turned to
Joseph and said, "Now let me die, for I have seen thy face and know that you
live." I've seen your face and I know that you live, for it was said though that
the boy was dead. They brought in the coat filled with blood and said your son
Joseph was eaten by the animals and this is his coat. He recognized the coat,
and took for granted his son was murdered and dead. Now comes the word
in the 46th of Genesis, Now that I have seen your face, let me die. Simeon:
I have seen him, he's alive...now let your servant depart in peace...to see the
child and see that he *is* alive. It isn't dead; it comes out and it's something
entirely different. So we see Joseph is the prototype of the bloom that comes
out, called Christ Jesus. Same story told all over the Bible, repeating itself on
different levels and different awareness.

Now let us go into the Silence.

*   *   *

___(??) I'll just take a small ad as I usually do in the *Times*. But in the meanwhile, apply it and put all of your faith in the grace that is coming to you, which is the Promise; where you're completely redeemed from this world of violence and enter an entirely different age, an age of the resurrected. You will. So set your hope fully upon that grace that is coming. In the meanwhile, do what Lynn did...only try to remember more than she did. She forgot three times in the day...and so, don't forget *that* often. Remember *how* you go to God, and always go to God. Lucky for her she had a father who reminded her and they could go together. If you don't have anyone to remind you, try to remember the presence of God by identifying with your own wonderful human Imagination, and close the gap between God and man. As you close the gap, then he's right here. You're always where you should be when you go to God. Don't have to rush into some cathedral, some church, some holy place, wherever *you* are. If you're standing in a bar, that's the place where you can commune with God...no matter *where* you are, that's the place. And he's always present as your own wonderful human Imagination.

Now are there any questions?

Q: (inaudible)
A: In his *Vision of the Last Judgment* he said, "Eternity exists and all things in eternity, independent of creation which was an act of mercy."
Q: Why are there so many differences in intellectual ability? Is it that the child that is closer to God is of higher intellect when it comes out this way and is evolved further than the child that is of lower intellect?
A: I wouldn't say that, my dear. We judge from appearances... and we're called upon *not* to judge from appearances. Someone may have the appearance of a dumbbell in the eyes of the world and be nearer to awakening. For, when he awakens it's a *gift*, and the power and the wisdom of God is a gift. If you're receiving the gift of wisdom that is the wisdom of God, what would be the wisdom of Caesar? All that you read today concerning the latest evolvement, the very latest that man has discovered would be not only not, it would be false to the wisdom of God.

We have this wonderful picture coming back from the moon. It's a marvelous thing for man to contemplate it, but suppose tomorrow you have an experience where the moon is not out there at all. If you want to step on it, you can step on it within yourself. All things exist in the human

Imagination and it isn't out there at all...that the circumference is within. And the circumference is ever expanding, but it is expanding within.

Q: Actually, the child's awareness of a...

A: Don't judge. You know we have in this world of ours...you and I tonight are enjoying the benefits of the gift of a hunchback, Steinmetz. When he came back from Germany, a little tiny fellow with a huge, huge hump on his back, they sent him to Ellis Island. Ellis Island was used in those days for all incoming immigrants who had no money, or who had some defect or had some, well, physical handicap. And we didn't want to take care of him; he was just about to be returned to Germany. Someone heard of his distress, knowing the man's abilities in Germany, and sought him out. They pledged for him, that they would take care of the great Steinmetz, little hunchback, really hunchbacked. He gave us, well, you couldn't number the things he gave us. He was the only one in General Electric that was allowed to smoke in any department. All the departments, no smoking, no smoking, no smoking, and that went from the top down, but not Steinmetz. He was Mr. General Electric.

We have another one...he was considered mad...well, he gave us indirect lighting... came from Yugoslavia. When he said to Edison, "I have it"—"Have what?"—"indirect lighting." I have the model that will do it—Edison, who gave us direct current, said, "You can't do it. Indirect current is insane, you can't think of it. There is no such thing as indirect current." He said, "Well, not only there is, I have the model." He said, "Where is it?" "Here. I can stop it and start it in my Imagination, and I've worked out all of the bugs already in my Imagination. I started it and discovered something was wrong, so I stopped it, corrected it, and started it again." And when he took his model to be put into tangible form in three dimensions, there wasn't one little thing that had to be corrected. You and I enjoy indirect current today.

Well, he lived at the Waldorf Astoria, and he had this peculiar habit of wiping everything with a napkin. Here's a great scientist. He knew you couldn't sterilize by wiping off a fork or a knife with a napkin. He dined alone every night; they gave him a huge stack of napkins, these wonderful napkins. Not any paper napkins, nice linens. Every little thing he took from the table, you see him wiping it off, wipe off a fork, spoon, knife, a plate and throw theses things away. But they tolerated this giant of a man. If you judge people from their habits, I'd say "What sort of a man is this?" His name was Tesla, Nikola Tesla. What a giant!

So if you judge a man because he has a little hunchback...I hope that no one has, for then you become part of the people who don't understand. A man was born blind and he said, "Master, tell me who sinned, his parents or the man, that he was born blind?" He said, "Neither the man nor his parents, but that the works of God may be manifest" (John 9:2). At this moment in time, it is essential to these furnaces that he has this experience. If you read the story, I think it's the 14th of Luke, when the great banquet is given by Messiah really, and he invited all the cultured, all the intellectuals, all the people that mattered, they all had excuses for not coming. He said, "Go into the byways, bring the blind, the lame, the halt, the maimed, the crippled, bring them all, and have them all be seated." They answered, "It is done as you said Lord." He said, "Fill it up."

Do you know that's a true story? It happens in the depth of your soul the night that you're really lifted up and this angelic chorus sings your redemption. They'll call you by name and say, "risen." In my own case, they said, "Neville is risen!" and here I am, twisting up, clothed in this heavenly body of fire and air. I was luminous...I didn't need any sun or stars or moon. I floated...I didn't touch the earth, just off the earth, just gliding. I came upon this enormous sea of human imperfection, and as I walked by, everyone was made perfect. The empty sockets were filled with beautiful eyes that saw; the dumb sang; the men with arms missing, the sockets were filled, everyone was made perfect. When I glided to the very end the last was made perfect. They feasted upon perfection, for at the moment I was lifted up I was perfect. That was the banquet. They had their fill of what they wanted, and they filled until they actually got what they wanted as I walked by. Then this heavenly chorus exulted, "It is finished!" Then it crystallized once more to this.

So I know that story is true and *where* the banquet takes place. So here I gathered all of my imperfections and redeemed them. I was the blind, the halt, the lame and every one there they were, and I took all of these garments that I had worn and turned them back into perfection. Then I came back here to tell this story 'til the end of my present journey. And that's the end, really, nothing more. They'll all be redeemed. Now my time's up.

Until Tuesday.

INVISIBLE THINGS

2/8/66

Tonight's title is "Invisible Things." When one thinks of Jesus, they see a man, or by any other name, maybe they see God, but they see a person, something visible. When we read the words, "We have found him of whom Moses in the law and also the prophets wrote, Jesus," one thinks of a man. It is my hope tonight that you'll find him and you will see he is not a man. "The invisible things of him are clearly seen being understood by the things that are made." You read that in the 1st chapter, the 20th verse, of Romans. They're understood by the things that are made…"even his eternal power and Godhead." "That they may seek the Lord, in the hope they may feel after him and find him." So he's not far from every one of us, "for in him we live and move and have our being." That you find in Acts, the 17th chapter (verse 27).

So we'll take it from here and try to develop it for you. Christ is called the power and wisdom of God. He is referred to in scripture as "the Word of God." We're told he was sent by God. We're told, "My word that goes forth from my mouth shall not return unto me void, but it must accomplish that which I purpose, and prosper in the thing for which I sent it" (Is.55:ll). So he sends his Word. Let us look up the word "word" in Hebrew. It's dabar, d-a-b-a-r. It means "to arrange; figuratively, to arrange words into speech, to commune, to promise." So you sit here and you have a request. You take now a request and you form it into a sentence. You are communing with self, for this that you are doing you are doing it, and yet I and my Father are one. The one forming me is forming out of himself, for *in him* I live and move and have my being.

So I stand here and you tell me a horrible picture, but now I'm trying to arrange in my mind's eye the solution of that problem. If I can extract the solution of the picture you just painted, then I have him. For his name is Jesus, his name is "to save," he is the savior. Can I commune with myself and so trust this feeling that I can actually say to myself, "I promise!" How it is going to be done on this level I do not know, but it *will* be done. I simply take a sentence implying the fulfillment of my dream, my desire, and having arranged it, I have the Word, I have Jesus, I've found him. Now I send it. He will not return unto me void, but he must accomplish that which I purpose, and prosper in the thing for which I sent it.

I am a person, and he and I are one, so I'm not going to deny the right of anyone to think of him in terms of a person. He's person gotten, person sourced, person received, so, I say to them, yes a person...but I then am he. I conceived it all in my own Imagination and trusted completely in this presence, which I am myself, to see some greater way to do it. The whole vast world is myself pushed out; the whole vast world is but response. It can only respond; it does not initiate. So it tells me constantly what I am sending out into being. I'm only sending myself, sending him to accomplish that which I purpose...and he never fails! "His name shall be called the Word of God... thy Word is truth." The word, dabar, is simply to arrange words so they form meaning. When they form the meaning, I commune with myself, and then say to myself, "Is it done?" and actually speak to myself, "It's done." When I can say to myself, "It is done!" and actually believe in this communion, it's a command. So the word dabar means to command, to arrange, arrange words so that they form speech, to commune and to promise. We have all these definitions in your *James Strong Concordance*.

So, this is the Word that was in the beginning, that all of the invisible things of him from the creation of the world were clearly seen being understood by the things that are made. Yes, even his creative and eternal power and Godhead. So I see what I am doing from this invisible reservoir. They're all present, every thing in the world *is*. I simply single out that which I want to form into a meaningful word, and then send it. All I do is wait, wait for the echo, wait for the response...and it *must* come. I am speaking from experience. It will come if you can sit here this night and shut out the obvious, and carry on this conversation within yourself, communing only with self. And then as you commune, you just say, "Is it done? It's done!" and trust it implicitly. For faith is trust in God, holding God trustworthy. It's your own being. But you are seeing this world from a higher level; you're not seeing it here at all. You're seeing it from an entirely different world, a higher level altogether; you're seeing the thing done. It will impinge upon you, upon the whole vast world. Anyone it can use to give birth to the word it will use, without their consent, without their permission, without their knowledge. It doesn't need the knowledge of anyone, for they are all itself pushed out.

Now, all I ask of anyone here is to try it. If this takes from you Jesus, I wouldn't take Jesus from anyone. I'm trying to *give* Jesus to the world. I'm trying to show man how to find him, how to *find* Jesus...far from taking Jesus *from* the world. First of all, I couldn't do it and I wouldn't do it. I am not breaking down idols. I'm not here to break down your ideals but to show you who Jesus really is. So when Philip said, "I've found him. Found him of whom Moses in the law and also the prophets wrote, Jesus." What did you go to see, a man? A man wearing what? a soft garment? Those who wear the soft garment are in the kingdom. They are in king's houses, unseen. Don't go looking for a man called a holy man called Jesus, you'll never find him. If anyone says, "Look, there he is!" don't believe it. You'll never find him not *that* way; but you will find him in yourself, in your own wonderful creative power. And the day will come you will awaken to discover you are the being called God. You and your creative power called Jesus Christ are one. You'll find him.

So here, the Word...you can construct it tonight. You don't realize what you're doing, maybe, but you're actually sending Jesus on his way if it is a saving word. If it's not a *saving* word and you believe in it, he must fulfill your command, and you'll hit him. He takes upon himself all of the blows of the world in man's ignorance. If it is a saving word, you send him. He said, "I've come to do the will of him who sent me...and he who sent me I am one with him" (John 4:34). But you are sending yourself, really, when you send what you have constructed as the word.

So here in scripture, from beginning to end, he brought everything into the world by the Word. "By this Word all things were made, and without it was not anything made that was made" (John1:1). You can ask for something through the human channel, and you may ask in vain. It may *never* come...if you're depending upon this party, that party, the other party. Don't designate *the* party, just commune with self, and let him take all the parties of the world that can best be used to bring about *your* objective. If the one you said must be the one, ___(??) him alone, and he drops before your eyes and you bury him, are you going to give up hoping? Are you going to give up your objective because the channel that you selected is not *the* channel? All these are the channels...and so you simply commune with self and let it go.

So tonight, you will find this most practical, right down to earth. You simply, this night, single out a simple, simple objective. It may be a *fantastic* thing, but you make it simple, because you trust God. Not a thing is *difficult* to God...and yet you and he are one. But you're doing it and seeing it from a higher level. Remember every thing is easy from the higher level; it simply appears on this level. When it appears it seems so natural that you might say to yourself, "Well, it would have happened anyway." But it would not have happened. It couldn't happen without a cause, and the cause was the Word

that you sent. You do all kinds of things, and all of a sudden you turn to him.
Every one of us forgets— not just little Lynn...to be reminded by her father
three times in a day—every one forgets. The teachers forget. No matter how
big they are in the eyes of the world, they forget the one and only God. And
that fundamental sin is lack of faith in "I am he." That's what we're taught.
The moment I forget it I go astray.

Now, the phone rang twice today, many times, really, but two most
important calls, total strangers. I said I'm closing on the 25th, put my affairs
in order and go, get my tickets and go. Only forty-eight hours ago I did what
I'm telling you to do. Instead of trying to arrange them here, seeing that things
are in order here, talking to this one and that one, "Would you do this in my
absence, would you do that?" and all these things, just simply turned within,
not to one person in this world, as though I talked to another but there was
no other, trusting this presence implicitly, knowing all along it was myself,
in self-communion. So, I just simply assumed within myself that the whole
thing was done. This morning the bank called, "We have a draft for you for
a considerable amount." Alright, I ___(??) nothing. This is not the time for
it, but they had it for me. Came home, having put it in my bank, phone rang
again. It's BOAC, "We were notified to notify you that tickets are waiting here
for you at your pleasure. Come in and get them. You can go today, tomorrow,
next month, go when you want." The only one to whom I turned was myself. I
did not turn to anyone to put anything in order. So out of the blue...and one
does not depend upon the other—the most generous dividend is independent
of tickets—that's a gift.

So I say, everyone in this world is serving. All you need do is trust this
inner communion. It's yourself...this whole vast world is yourself pushed out.
So when I say all things exist in the human Imagination, I mean that literally.
All things are going to exist there; they begin and end there, but everything.
And you, you are all Imagination, and you and God are one. And you
gradually move from a God of tradition to a God of experience; moving from
a God of tradition where your fathers taught you of a God on the outside to
find him on the inside. And the Jesus of history is your ability to simply take
the Word and form it into meaning, commune with *it*, and send it on its way
in complete confidence that it's done. And it's done. So the invisible things
of him are clearly seen by the things that are made. I know from what I am
seeing what I must have sent on the way, and somewhere, wisely or unwisely,
I constructed it and then sent it on its way. So I say to every one of you here
tonight, don't let anyone tell you that you are less than someone else, that you
are a young soul, that you are this, that and the other. As you are seated here
and you say "I am," that's God. Believe it.

Now, if you came here this night really believing as you should in Jesus, let me tell you who he is. And if perchance you were raised in another faith and the word offends, it would not offend you after you know who he *really* is. He simply is the Word that God sends into creation, and that Word you send. If you send it, well, then you know who you are. So here, try it tonight. I'll be back on Friday; you should be able to tell me wonderful stories. Yes, between now and Friday. If you *really* believe him, you'll tell me, because it happened. Just have to commune with him, like a friend. We're told, he spoke with him, face to face, just like a friend with a friend. That's all that you do. ___(??). Doesn't take you more than a half minute to do it, just no time at all, if you believe...if you believe in the reality of these unseen states.

Then I thought of Jung, Carl Jung...the last book that came out about him after he was gone. And the day of the funeral of a very dear friend of his, he was in bed, and suddenly he saw in his mind's eye. He said it was not an apparition: "But I saw him clearly, my friend whose funeral I had attended that very day. But trained as I am I said this is an apparition. But why should I, said he, take my friend and treat him this way? Suppose he *is* here. I should give him the benefit of the doubt and say to myself he's real. The moment I credited him with reality, he smiled, turned around, led me to the door, through the garden, up the street to his home several hundred yards away, and there he pointed out a book, one of four. The titles of the four books convinced me of at least survival, for the whole thing was based on they survive. The next day he was so curious he walked up the street to the widow and asked for permission to see the library. As he got in there, just as they were in his vision there were the books. He took a stool and got up, took one away, and there was the title, the title he had seen just the night before when he gave his friend credit for being real. If he had said it's an apparition..."I mustn't treat this as I tell my students not to treat these things as real, therefore, I must not treat them as real." The moment he gave it reality it became real and acted independent of his perception of it, and led him to where confirmation of what he was thinking would be found in tangible book form. That was Jung, Carl Jung's latest book.

So I say, you can't see this?—make it real. He didn't see it with his physical eyes, he saw it in his mind's eye, gave it reality, and it acted as something real. Now *you*, if you don't see it, you're communing. Don't see a face; there is no face to be seen. It's your face and you don't see your face, save you look into a mirror. So you are communing with self and you give to self the power, the creative power, to externalize this communion. And it does.

So tonight, you try it. We have just a few lectures left...five to be exact. Closing on the 25th, and whenever we get back I'll let you know. We have no plans beyond the 25th...close the 25th and take off a few days later. But in the meanwhile, don't forget it. Don't turn to other gods. Don't turn to any *outside* god. Don't turn to any holy man; there aren't any. No holy man on the outside. If anyone should say to you, 'Look, I've found him, there he is!' don't go. No holy man, no little icon, no outside god. The whole thing is taking place within you. You must put him to the test, the extreme test to prove that you too can send the Word and it cannot come back to you void. If it can't come back to you void and you sent it and you knew exactly what you've done, then who are you? Only God speaks the Word! When he speaks it and it fulfills its purpose, then who are you? He said, "My name is in them." His name is "I am."

So you try it tonight, tomorrow night, until it finally becomes a habit and you live by it. If perchance you should forget it, my prayer is that it will not be for long, that you'll come right back to it again. You may not have a father, like little Lynn, to remind us, but you could pick up the book from time to time and be reminded of who you really are. You're here to bear fruit and bear it *abundantly.* Let no one tell you, "Be satisfied, you have enough, that this is alright...just eke out the days and wait." Don't let anyone tell you that. If you have a hunger, satisfy it. Satisfy it in this simple, simple way. No one will be hurt, because when you do it *this* way he isn't going to hurt anyone, for he's not going to hurt himself. So, if you say I want this, that and the other for another, alright, he won't be hurt. If you want it for another, ask a very simple question, "Would I want it for myself? If anyone gave it to me would I want it?" Yes. Well then, do it. And whenever you do it lovingly, you're doing the right thing.

All day long you can create, create lovely wonderful things for every being in the world. Spend a half-minute, just a few seconds rearranging words. When we speak of the ten words of the cross, the shortest is made up of two, "I thirst"; then we have three, "It is finished." We have those that are nine, where each sentence that has meaning is called a word. So there are ten words on the cross, but none is made up of a single word. It's made up of, the very shortest, of two words. But "I thirst" conveys meaning; "It is finished" conveys meaning. And so, these words, though many words, are in scripture, *the* Word, the Word of God. So you are called upon to take all the invisible words and make a word, and speak it into meaning. When you speak it, you give absolute trust to self. Though invisible to mortal eye you're in communion with self, and from that higher level it sees all and can do all.

Now, if you're here for the first time, it may seem strange. I'll give you a chance tonight with your questions to make me clarify the point. If I have not actually given you a concept of Jesus that is true, and you don't think it's true, you hold me here until I clarify it for you. I tell you, *that* what I spoke of this night is the true Jesus. So if you could ever say "I found him, I have found him of whom Moses in the law and also the prophets spoke" and it's not *that* Jesus, you haven't found him. If you found a man, you haven't found him. No matter who you look for, that's not he. You will find Jesus as the creative power of God, the wisdom of God. It is the power to fulfill the purpose for which it was sent and the wisdom to do it. Just send it on its way in confidence that it can't return void.

Today in all of the papers, last week's *Observer*, they said, "The Protestants have reached the crossroad, they will either now become the most radical body in the world or return to Rome. They do not believe in God." That's what the writer [said], filling up two full pages of the weekly paper called the *Observer*...very well written. They write books saying, "God is dead" and then all, similar types, all these professors that are in our great universities teaching our children that God is dead. They haven't the slightest concept of who Jesus is, not the slightest concept who God is. So they want us all then to return to Rome, for we're headed towards being the most radical body in the world, that's what they're saying. But don't believe it.

The Word, the real Word, is that Bible. You read it, extract the word, the meaning, extract all of the messages that it holds for you and then test it. "Come test yourself and see. Do you not realize that Jesus Christ is in thee?—unless of course you fail to meet the test!" That's what we're told in Corinthians (2Cor.13:5). Don't you realize that he's *in* you? The average person would say to that, if he's honest about it, "No, I don't." But if you said to him, "Now come and sit with me...what would you like?" and then he tells you. Then you say, "Don't tell me audibly but close your eyes and talk with yourself, as though you were two; and then say to the unseen one, 'Is it alright? Is it done?' and imagine he said to you, 'Yes. It is done!' And say, 'Thank you' and go your way." You've found Jesus and you've found his Father. Who conceived the words? You say, "I did." Well, you're the father of them, aren't you? You can't deny you're one with him? No, so "I and my Father are one, yet my Father is greater than I." For he conceived it, he rearranged the structure of the mind, and then I asked, "Is it done?" and he said, "Yes." And I believe him implicitly.

Now wait and see. If in twenty-four hours, forty-eight hours, in the not distant future it works, then you've found him. Moses spoke of him; yes Moses spoke of him in the law. No one understood him. They took the law literally on the outside, something external. The prophets, too?—oh yes, they spoke of him. And finally I found him...and to have *found* Jesus...and not let him go. As we are told in the very end of the drama, "Now that you have found me, don't let me go, but let all else go." And they held onto him. They came into the garden and there he was, and when he said, "Whom do you seek?" they said, "Jesus." He said, "I'm Jesus" and they all fell (John18:4). When they regained their composure, he said, "Whom do you seek?" Again they replied, "Jesus." He said, "I've told you I am he; now that you have found *me*, let all else go." It's put into a dramatic form as though a man is speaking to a man. Just as though I'm asking you tonight to commune with self as though there were two, and yet they are one. So in the end, I and my Father are one, and I send my word, and then watch it fulfill itself in my world.

Now let us go into the Silence.

*   *   *

Q: ___(??) recap different ways people have reported to you the way they used the law?

A: Last Friday night, what Lynn did, that's a way. You know what you've done with the trees and you looked beyond the obvious and saw what was not there to be seen. Then you didn't ask him to cut them down, he cut them down, didn't he? That's a way.

Getting out of the army was a way. You know that way. Bringing to me a very big, generous dividend, far in excess of what I even thought, is a way. I simply talked to myself and thanked myself for it. It was cabled... not even by letter. Well, there are as many ways as there are people. What is best for one isn't for the other. How do I simplify it and bring it to a point where it's so simple that a child can do it? Tonight is very simple: communion with self. He doesn't have to be an Einstein, he doesn't have to be a giant, he doesn't have to be some fantastic person, just a child. A child could do what I did if it could believe in the reality of the communion. So I said last Friday it is my aim to raise you to a confident faith in imagining. That's my purpose. If one could only lift himself up to believe in the reality of that unseen imaginal act, it's done. But the average person will say, "What, little me? I couldn't be that powerful. I don't have the background, intellectual, social, the financial, none of these." You don't need any background.

Q: Neville, I'd like to give a testimonial to this wonderful truth. I'm a singer and I wanted to be on the Art Linkletter Show, and you're supposed to have somebody introduce you.

So just in my Imagination I thought, "Well, I don't know who's going to do this," but I imagined I was already on the show, and I'm singing on Art Linkletter's Show. So, today I get a surprise telephone call from a friend and she said, "I didn't tell you but a month ago I wrote a letter...

and you know I borrowed a photograph of you." I said yes. She said, "The 16th of February you have an audition for the Art Linkletter Show."

A: Well, thank you! Now, that's another technique.

Q: I didn't know how...I didn't do a thing but right in here [pointing to head]. My best friend did it and didn't even tell me. And I didn't tell her.

A: All right, that's how it works. You see there is no such thing as two of us, not in the real sense of the word. That's Israel's contribution to the whole vast world, "Hear, O Israel, the Lord our God is *one* Lord." So it seems to be diversity, seems to be, but in the end there is only one. But thank you, Danny, thank you very much.

By the way, the cards of my friend Freedom are at the door if you're interested. We quickly picked out 200 names out of 2000.

Q: I don't know how even to word it...when you speak of Jesus Christ, what is the exception there...?

A: Christ Jesus and Jesus Christ?

Q: Yes,

A: Well, Paul interchanges them. He speaks of Christ Jesus as often as he speaks of Jesus Christ. So he doesn't really mean two when he speaks of Jesus Christ or Christ Jesus.

Christ is really "Messiah." It's the Anglicized form of the Hebrew word Messiah.

Q: Neville, is it possible for you to estimate the time of resurrection to the time of being born from above?

A: It's just a matter of moments, same night. Ascension, that comes nine months later. But resurrection, that comes the same night, comes first. And your exit from the tomb is your birth...as you make your exit from the tomb where you were awakened. To be resurrected is to be awakened from a profound sleep, a sleep that is so deep it appeared to all of the watchers of the world that you were dead. "Awake, you sleeper, and rise from the dead" (Eph.5:14). So when the Lord awakes to find himself entombed, he comes out. The exit from that tomb: he pulls himself out of his own body.

Q: (inaudible)

A: Not if I would analyze it for the gentleman. You awaken in a tomb, it's your skull. You know where to push to get out. At the back of the skull, you push, you start coming out like a child, only you're not a child, you're a fully grown man. You come out, and when you are almost out, you pull from here down, you pull the remaining portion of you out of your own skull. Because, although it's a tomb, the minute your head goes through the opening in what is a skull, you feel it here. The symbolism is a huge, big tomb, a sepulcher. But when you start coming out of the big sepulcher, you actually come out of here. It's out of here that you're coming, the base. And when you are almost out, you pull, and then you turn back and see this out of which you had emerged.

Q: Well, then it isn't a question of "I have power to take it up and put it down," that this is the sheet, and I am outside of the sheet...within the sheet but outside of the sheet. I can lay it down, take it up and put it down. But this is a sheet and I am inside of the sheet

A: You see this is not what certain schools of thought talk about, called an astral projection.

It hasn't a thing to do with an astral projection. I have had those through the years...it's not that at all. This is something entirely different. It is your resurrection from a long, long sleep. Everyone in the world is asleep until resurrected. And who is not resurrected—prior to that moment they are called dead—will be revived, restored to what is called life, in a world just like this to continue the journey until resurrected. Then they enter a new age altogether. They are above the organization of sex. And the children, the little child wrapped in swaddling is there. The witnesses to the event they are there. The story is true.

Q: What's the astral then?

A: Astral? Just like this. I haven't found it any different. When I found myself out of this body, attached by a silver cord, I am moving in a world just like this. It's not heaven. Just as frightening, and you're just as limited and can be hurt as you're hurt here. No transforming power whatsoever in an astral projection.

Q: This is then purely psychic? Is that true?

A: It is.

Q: Well, is that induced by meditation? Is that a preliminary to...

A: My first astral projection was involuntary. My second that took place the same night was deliberate. I was in my room on 49th Street, and I felt this sensation in my head, and then the next thing I knew I was whirled out. There I found myself on a beach. I noticed this cord in my head. Having read and studied over the years about such things, I concluded I am now projected. I didn't know one person on the beach, I knew no one. They didn't seem to know me and I didn't know them. I desired to go back and observe this thing from beginning to end, to go right back into that body and come out this time consciously, deliberately. I no sooner desired to do it than I found myself back in the body, with the same sensation in my head. This time I wanted to control it, so I intensified it by imagining. As I imagined, the thing got more and more powerful, and then out I went. But having decided to control it, as I whirled out, I reminded myself "I want to get right back in that room, not in the body, and observe this thing for myself."

I came back into the room, here is this [body], the face was covered by a cloud. I could see the face through breaks in the cloud. I looked at it, it looked...well, it was Neville, and here is the same room, the same pictures, no change whatsoever. I am in the room but I am out. I walked into another room where my dancing partner's parents slept. We had a three-room suite. I tried to arouse them; they couldn't see me. I talked to them, pushed them, got no reaction. Pushed my dancing partner; got no reaction. Everything was simply as it was, but I, to them, was invisible. I reasoned and I said, "I know I'm out, there's the body; therefore I should be able to go through that wall because I'm not of this substance." So I started; couldn't get through. The wall was as solid as that wall. Couldn't get through. So I said to myself, "I'll rush and jump. You don't seem to have any fear." I was living on the 11th floor and there was no stairway. "I'm going to jump right through and I'm Spirit...wouldn't fall." So I took off and leapt into space, head first, and struck myself so hard I knocked myself out, back into the body.

Then I said, "What's this all about? I should have gone through." And then I realized, it dawned on me I gave solidity to that wall. I gave reality to all these things, and what I gave them they possessed it. So the next time I got up, deliberately, to prove I was right, standing in the room with the door locked, everything locked, I imagined myself elsewhere, and like *that* I was where I had imagined myself to be. And it was real, like this. That astral projection has nothing to do with what I'm talking about on the Promise.

Q: (inaudible)

A: The resurrection is God's mightiest act. The 7th chapter, 2nd Samuel, the 12th verse— skip the 13th, for that's an insertion—12th and 14th. And here, think of God himself bringing forth himself that he had imposed a sleep upon for creative purposes.

Q: In other words, a higher level was revealed to you that you could not possibly induce by yourself.

A: All that happened to me in these four mighty acts were all involuntary, every one. Not one did I deliberately conjure. You can't do it. It's grace. You don't earn it. Just, at a moment in time, the time has been fulfilled, and when the time is fulfilled, it happens, and you unfold.

Q: Is that what the orthodox people call born again?

A: Born again, yes. But they interpret "to be born again" is simply a change of attitude towards life. That's repentance. But it doesn't say that if you repent that you will be able to aid God in bringing in the kingdom. The kingdom is coming whether you repent or not. But you repent to help yourself while you are in this world. For to repent is to change your attitude towards life, and any change of your attitude results in a change of environment. And so, I'm convinced by what has happened to me that fitness for the kingdom is the consequence, not something that man has earned; it's the consequence of the grace of God.

Q: There is nothing that we can do and it is an involuntary thing that happens to us.

Obviously, you are compelled to tell us this story. What good is it going to do us, the hearing of it, if we just have to wait anyway? Why do we need...?

A: Lucy, my dear, tonight's story will aid you in getting anything you want in this world.

But, if I didn't tell you of God's Promise and you owned the earth and all within it, knowing the inevitable is death, wouldn't life be empty? So I tell you of the Promise that's coming, whether you die tonight or not, you won't die; that Promise is going to be fulfilled. And you are coming into an inheritance that is unblemished, unspoiled, that cannot be tarnished, clothed in a garment that is immortal, where you create above the organization of sex. So I tell that to the world. I know of nothing in this world more comforting than that story of the Promise. But to tell the world of this principle, where you can go out and become bedecked with the honors of the world, and then leave them behind to rot, as we must, to become a billionaire and then leave it all behind, so what good would be the law? He said, no one is justified before God by law. So you can use the law wisely—and you should—and do what you want with it, have homes, beautifully furnished, live graciously. In the end, you leave it. Tell you the Promise...when you *sleep* no more, the sleep is behind you.

Q: If this is true, then it's just a matter of time, a matter of just so many experiences, then why are you...you're the only person I know, really, that, or maybe a handful of people, wouldn't you think this would be happening to a lot of people? Because surely there have been lots and lots of people who have gone through all of this?

A: In this audience tonight sits one who has had it, but he's not inclined to tell it from the platform.

Q: Yes, I know, I understand, I know that, but wouldn't you think it would be more common, and when it did happen more people would talk about it? Because most people don't talk about it. This is what I'm...isn't it strange that people wouldn't talk about this thing that has happened to them?

A: You hear it, you accept it on faith and go your way, confidant the Promise will be fulfilled. But to be anxious, "Why did he leave me out, why am I postponed?" No one is postponed...no one is left out.

Q: I didn't mean that. I meant that the people that did experience, because of what it is, wouldn't you think that more people would be telling about it?

A: I don't know who is telling about it.

Q: No...this is...

A: I don't know who's telling about it...I really don't. Not everyone who has it is sent as an apostle.

Q: Then that's it...that's the answer I'm looking for. Not everybody who experiences it has the desire to tell it.

A: He has the different values marked out in his letters. He puts the apostle first. The apostle comes first and to be an apostle there is one outstanding qualification: to have *seen* the risen Christ. He said in the 1st verse, the 9th chapter of 1st Corinthians, "Am I not free? Am I not an apostle? Have I not seen the Lord Jesus Christ?" To have seen him is to become him. You become what you behold. And so, Paul *saw* the freedom that was different, and then he was self-sent. You can have these experiences and not encounter the risen Christ. Experience the birth...you can't take that back. The going up as a serpent...you can't take it back. The discovery of David the Son of God as *your* Son...you can't take it back. But have you been commissioned to be sent? If you aren't sent, you aren't an apostle.

Q: In the part of scripture where it says some are sent as apostle, some as teachers, and so forth, do you know...

A: You have it both in Corinthians and in Romans, I think. The concordance, *Strong's Concordance*...well, then look it up. And he puts the wise man at the very lowest...the one who speaks in tongues. The whole vast country recently was all up in the air about throwing themselves into a trance and speaking in tongues, mumbling, not one word understood. He put that the last of all. The apostle comes first, and then he brings them down. There are teachers, they're down. Until Friday.

YOU FIND JESUS CHRIST IN
YOURSELF AS YOURSELF

2/11/66

Last Tuesday, we tried to share with you what we have discovered about Jesus Christ. As you know from scripture not everyone finds him who sought him. Many found him because friends brought them and showed them Jesus Christ. The story of Philip, he brought Nathaniel; then Andrew brought Peter. So, many find him. And the one who finds him can't keep it to himself he must share it. So having found him, I tried last Tuesday to share him with you. And you saw, if you were here, it's not what the world believes Jesus to be at all…something entirely different…the creative power and wisdom of God (1Cor.1:24). Personified yes, but you are a person and you'll find him in yourself as yourself.

The story of Jesus is an acted parable, an incredible prophecy of what one day will really be the experience of the believer. Everyone will experience the story of Jesus Christ; then you will know from experience who Jesus Christ really is. We are looking for the Father. The world believes that Jesus Christ is the Son. I tell you, Jesus Christ is God the Father. The whole vast world is looking for the Father. We are told in Peter's first epistle, "If we say our Father to the one who judges every man impartially on the record of his deeds, then we must stand in awe before him while we live out the time of our exile" (1Pet.1:17). We're all exiled, not because we have done anything that is wrong. This is a grand play. It is God who exiled himself. It is God in man who animates man. It is that God that you and I are seeking.

This is the tale as told in scripture. As the poet said, "Truth embodied in a tale shall enter in at lowly doors." So we hear the story, and on this journey of ours, exiled as we are, some of us are too busy to stop to listen, some hear it eagerly and then forget it, others hear and it haunts them. They become hungry only for it, and then it steals in at lowly doors. This story…as Paul in his letter to the Galatians, he said, "O foolish Galatians! Who has bewitched you, before whose eyes Jesus Christ was publicly *portrayed* as crucified? Let me ask you only this: Did you receive the Spirit by works of the law, or by hearing with faith? Are you so foolish? Having begun with the Spirit, are you ending with the flesh?" (Gal.3:1). That phrase "hearing with faith" in certain translations they take it and they translate it in this manner: "or hearing the story of faith, hearing the gospel? Did you receive the Spirit in any other way?" You heard it, and you stopped long enough to listen, and it interested you, and you went your way. As you walked your way suddenly within you the story unfolds.

To participate in "the age to come" depends upon God's mighty act of raising the dead, called in scripture the resurrection. It begins there. So while you and I are walking this earth, not at the end of the journey where men call us dead, but within our own personal history it happens. Then the entire story unfolds within us and we go out to tell it. Only a man who has experienced scripture can really understand how perfectly wonderful it really is. Here is this most fantastic prophecy as we are told in Revelation, "The testimony of Jesus is the Spirit of prophecy" (19:10). Listen to the testimony. From whom? Well, then read it. If no one has actually experienced it, read it. And as you read it, believe it. It's all about you.

One day you will know who he is. Why do I say he's the Father? As I search scripture, I find him revealing himself as Father. Go back to the first revelation of the Father. In the 16th chapter of 1st Samuel, here he is discussing with a youth, the youth is called David. Here is David's father Jesse (verse 21). He's talking to both; he knows both, the two. He asks the father of David to let David be his armor bearer…so here he knows him. Yet in the next chapter the promise is made that any man who destroys the enemy of Israel, his father will be set free…the freeing of the Father (1Sam.17:25). Well, here comes the lad, the lad's name is David, and the king is made to act as though he doesn't know him (verse 55). He turns to his lieutenant Abner, he said, "Abner, whose son is that youth?" If I saw the most marvelous person before me and I asked the question, "Whose son is he?" my interest is not in the lad, my interest is in his father. "Whose son is he?" Abner replied, "As your soul liveth, O king, I cannot tell." He said, "Enquire whose son the *stripling* is." No one knows. Then comes David standing before him with the head of the Philistine Goliath, he said, "Whose son are you, young man?" He said, "I am the son of Jesse, your servant Jesse, the Bethlehemite" and the story ends.

The word translated "youth, stripling, young man" is the Hebrew word Olam. The Bible translates it "eternity, the world." In every great city in our land there is a cemetery called Beth Olam. We have one here. Man's eternal home…misinterpreted as something that is final, and there is no return. The word Olam means "eternity" yet it also means "youth, young man, *stripling*. It's the word used in the 3rd chapter of Ecclesiastes, "And God has put Olam…"—it's translated in one Bible as "the world," in another as "eternity." "God has put eternity into the mind of man, yet so that man cannot find out what God has done from the beginning to the end" (verse 11).

What did he put into the mind of man? When he puts eternity, he puts himself— throughout scripture we speak of the eternal God, El Olam, the Eternal One—into the mind of man. And he is the Father. I am waiting and looking for this Father. I put it into the mind of man in the beginning of time, and start man on his journey. But if God the Father is in man, who is exiled? The word we translate God or the Lord, Yod He Vav He, the verb He Vav He, had the original meaning of "to fall or the one who causes to fall; to blow or the one who causes the wind to blow." So the fall was not a mistake. It was a deliberate contraction of infinity to this limit called man. So in the mind of man is God—it's I AM. And he doesn't know it until the very end. And he's on his search, standing in awe in the presence of him while you live the time of your exile.

So I'm calling him "Father" as though he were there. I speak of him as the one all out there. Wait 'til the end of the exile when you're just about to return. At that moment, you'll know what he put into the mind…he put himself right into the mind of man. That self is I AM. And no power in the world can persuade you that *that* is God but the Son of God. Was it Jesus Christ? No, it wasn't Jesus Christ who revealed God to me; it was God's only begotten son, as told in the 2nd Psalm: "Thou art my son, today I have begotten thee" (verse 7). It's said to the same youth, this eternal youth; for if the Father is eternal and the Son is like the Father, the Son is eternal. It's said to David.

I can't explain to anyone here the emotion that possesses you…when you were taught to believe that this character is some historical character that lived a thousand B.C., and here is 1966 and that we are related, that I came before him? For the father must precede the son. Here he stands before you and not a word need be said, yet it is said, he calls you "Father." You know it. Here is this beautiful eternal youth who is calling you "Father," and only then do you know who the Father really is. Only then you know yourself as the Father. Well, who in scripture is the Father? He said God. "And the Lord said unto me, 'Thou art my son; today I have begotten thee." You can't be a father unless there's a son. So in the Book of John, "No one has seen the Father; but the only begotten Son who is in the bosom of the Father, he has made him known" (John 1:18). It takes the Son to reveal the Father. And the Son comes out of nowhere, but he comes out of your Imagination. You actually feel this explosion, right out of your head, and when it all settles, here is this that you can't describe in words, this beauty beyond measure, beyond description, stands before you and calls you "Father."

Now remember this is a story and you've got to take liberties in telling a story, so you take the Father and personify it. Because you are a person, so you've got to personify it. So it becomes a Jesus Christ. It has to be personified. But we can't separate God's eternal power, creative power, from God himself. Well, I'm going to ask you to test it. In scripture when you're asked to test, who do you test? Listen to the words, "Come test *yourself* and see. Do you not know that Jesus Christ is *in thee*?" (2Cor.13:5). It didn't ask you to test Jesus Christ, test yourself to see if he's not in you. Well, how do I go about testing? Is he what? Where is he? He's in me. I just discovered he's the Father. If I ask anything of the Father, he'll do it. Whatever you ask the Father he'll do.

Well, how do I ask the Father? Last Tuesday, we showed you, and last Friday in discussing little Lynn's story. We asked you to try it. I tell you, it works miracles, cannot fail! For if he's in me, I don't have to go any place. I must find out how do I reach him, even though he's within me. What is the core of man? If this very moment, suddenly I don't know who I am, where I am, what I am, I can't stop knowing that I am. So I start there...that's the core of man...I am. So I commune now with myself...and anything in this world...just commune with myself as though there were two. I can then say, "I and my Father are one" (John 10:30). We are one, yet I speak of me *and* my Father. So I now take it like some wonderful exercise and commune with myself, and then I reach an agreement with myself as though it were done, and thank self. But it's thanking another; it makes it easier on this level. If I thank myself, it doesn't carry the same conviction. If I can just actually commune with self as though there were two, and have absolute confidence in the seeming other, and just say, "Thank you, Father"...yet I am the Father. But the Father is on this higher level that sees all, knows all, and can instantly rearrange the entire pattern to objectify that which I asked of myself. And may I tell you, when it comes into our world it comes so easily that you and I will say, "Oh, it would have happened anyway."

So I ask you to try it. If it's money, try it for money. If it's for a home, marriage, I don't care what it is, try it! I'm not going to tell you these things will bring satisfaction, will bring happiness. It hasn't a thing to do...you could have a million, millions, doesn't mean it's going to bring happiness. Night before last, I turned on TV to get the news, and here came Burns, George Burns. He was an intimate of Billy Rose and Sophie Tucker, so he told just a few little stories of the two. Well, he turned to Billy Rose, born in the slums of New York, in the east, raised in poverty, had nothing, very short in stature, he was five foot three, took up shorthand, became an expert and worked for the great financier, Baruch, Bernie Baruch. Then he became a showman. He put on the Aquacade at the World's Fair in '39. In '39 he made his first million. Well, as the years went by he married and remarried, didn't bring him happiness, married five times. One night at dinner, living in this palatial place of his, he said to his wife—which one of the five I don't know—he said, "The most wonderful thing happened to me today!" This is a story told by Billy Rose to George Burns. Well, she didn't seem to be interested, but she listened. He said, "I made one million dollars today!"

He meant it…if you hold what he held in stock and they split. He was the largest single stockholder of A.T. &T. He left 190,000 shares of A.T. &T. Well, if you have any section of that and it splits, you run into millions. On this day he made a million. And he said to Burns, "You know what she said? 'Pass the salt.'" She wanted that salt more than she wanted the millions. So he left an estate of $25 million, he left it as all must do. That's why I told you last Tuesday when the lady asked the question, "Why emphasize the promise?" because without the promise all the success of earth is as nothing. If I didn't have the Promise to support me, that in the end regardless of what I've done with my life, that I will be one with God. That's the Promise: For "I will raise up after you a son that shall come forth from your body. I will be his father and he shall be my son" (2 Sam.7:12)…and yet we are one. He is simply bringing forth himself out of man. And so, without that Promise what would it matter? He is gone tonight, and I hope that those who loved him get the twenty-five million. I know the one person who will get the most of it and that is Uncle Sam. He'll get millions. But there are still millions left for those he will remember in his will. But a generation from now only those to whom he left the money will even know a man called Billy Rose ever existed. No one will know. Well, that's only a mask that God wore while a thing called Billy Rose walked the earth for sixty-six years.

So here, have it if you want it. You can have all the money you want if you really believe in God. God is your own wonderful human Imagination…that's God. So when you sit here, don't look outside. All that you are imagining, that's God in action. But man doesn't believe in the reality of these unseen imaginal acts. If he could only believe in the reality of the unseen imaginal act knowing that it is God in action, nothing would be impossible to that man, but nothing. We're not called upon to devise the means to bring it to pass; all you're asked to do is simply to believe. Having imagined it, just believe. You don't work out anything. He said, "I have ways and means"—speaking now to the mask—"that you know not of. My ways are past finding out" (Rom. 11:33 KJV). And it's not by might, nor by power, but by my Spirit, saith the Lord. So, can I actually believe it? I say, "Father," nothing wrong with that. And the one I now address "our Father" or "my Father" when I stand in his presence I stand in awe as it were. It's a lovely communion, a wonderful feeling between the seeming two who are really one. And you feel it so lightly. No palaver, no special hour, no special holy place to go, just where you are. If tonight you go to a bar from here, that's holy if you're there. Wherever a man is, that's holy, for God occupies man. He actually lost himself in man, he's buried in man. By man I mean generic man—male, female. So in everyone there is God and that is the great mystery. Man searches for him all through space, all through time. And he was nearer than breathing all along: He was his own wonderful human Imagination.

So we have but two weeks left. I do hope you won't forget. I do hope you'll put yourself to the test, and whenever I do return you'll be able to tell me unnumbered wonderful stories of the wise use of this law. My hope for you is that when I do return you will have had the Promise, that's my wish. But for yourself, although that may be your wish too, I do hope you'll apply it towards beautifying your world and getting wonderful things by the use of the law. It's a simple law. As we're told, "Blessed is the man who delights in the law of the Lord. For in all that he does he prospers" (Ps. 1:1-3).

So if you're here for the first time tonight, just let me now address you personally as though you never heard it before. It doesn't matter what you've ever done—you might have been cruel, you might have been a thief, you might be this very night running away from some deed—I will say you are forgiven. Believe now in God: God is your own wonderful human Imagination and with him all things are possible. So regardless of what your background might have been, regardless of what you're doing now, have an object, have a desire, a consuming desire. Believe in the infinite wisdom and power of a presence that is *in* you, and believe that presence to be your Imagination. Don't argue the point. You carry the request to this one within you as though you say, "Is it all right?" He will invariably say, "Yes, it is done!" Invariably! He doesn't argue, he doesn't point to your background, he doesn't point to any restrictions of the past. He played those parts. So whatever you want, go to him, commune with him; bring it to a head as though it were done. Is it done? And get confirmation from this deeper self, "Yes, it's done." And then drop it. Your conscious reasoning mind cannot reach the depth necessary to set in motion all the causes necessary to bring it to pass in this world.

So don't try to analyze it. Leave it just where it is. It will happen in a way you would never suspect. I could tell you unnumbered stories to support this simple, simple tale. But if you labor the point and you think you must know this party, must know that party, you must *do* this, that and the other, well, then you don't trust God. On this level you can do nothing but ask, believing that you have received, and you will receive. As told us in the Book of Mark, "Whatever you ask in prayer, believe you have received it and you will" (11:24). "Whatever" includes everything. You just ask. I give you a little warning: Always ask in love, always. Whenever you ask for another, make sure it is something that you wouldn't mind receiving for yourself. If I'm quite willing to accept it for myself, you can ask it for another. If it is something I wouldn't want, it's distasteful, don't ask it for another.

Now I tell you, the day is coming that you and I will know—this is no little belief on the outside—we will *know* that we aren't two; there is only God. He only has one Son, one name; for in that day, one Lord, one name and one Son. And if my son is your son, then you and I are the same father. I know from experience that everyone in the world will have the same experience of seeing God's only begotten Son call him "Father." Then in the depth of our soul we will understand the unity: He who becomes one becomes united with the Lord, becomes one Spirit with him.

So let me encourage you, the resurrection is taking place. It's not an event that took place once and for all; it's taking place. The one event that took place once and for all is over, and that is the crucifixion. And may I tell you, it's not as the churches of the world paint it. The emotion of the crucifixion is sheer ecstasy. You can't describe the glory, the thrill, the ecstasy of the crucifixion. No blood, no tears, no pain; sheer ecstasy when you are nailed to this garment. These are vortices, these two palms of the hand, and so are the soles of the feet, and so is the side, and so it the head. When you *relive* the experience, if the memory of it brings back such joy, what do you think the original was! So, "If we have been united with him in a death like his, we shall certainly be united with him in a resurrection like his" (Rom. 6:5). So look at the tenses: We *have been* united in a death like his, we *shall be* united in a resurrection like his. So these are two tenses; one is over, one is coming.

Now listen to these words: If you were here, he would not have died. "I am the resurrection. Do you believe that, Martha? Yes Lord. I believe that you are the one who is coming into the world." Read that in the 11th of John (verse 25). You are coming into the world. If you are the resurrection and I am not yet resurrected that I may enter the new age, then I have hope. You are *coming* into the world; you *came* in the crucifixion. In the beginning was the crucifixion…it starts that way…but the new age begins with the resurrection. Entirely different!

So I say to everyone, you will be. And the resurrection is so unlike what the churches teach. Because the whole drama takes place here, the resurrection begins here [pointing to head]. It's not out there at all. "All that you behold, though it appears without, it is within, in your" own wonderful "human Imagination, of which this world of mortality is but a shadow" (Blake, *Jer.*, Plt. 71). You do it all here. If I rearrange the structure of my mind and persuade myself of the reality of this rearrangement, and the outer world then molds itself in harmony with this rearranged structure, where is the cause? If I examine the outside, I might think this one did that, that one did that, and that's why it is as it appears to be. But if I have a memory, I go back to how it started. It all started by my rearranged structure of the mind. I, by changing the inner aspects of my own mind, brought about changes in the outer to conform to the inner changes. So if it always works that way, where is the cause? Is it anything on the outside at all? It isn't!

So I say to every one of you, no matter what you've done, no matter what you've been, no matter what you are doing, believe this story and you'll be completely transformed. No desire to hurt anyone, because there is no other. There is no other; there's only God, and you are he. God became man that man may become God. So don't postpone your good, and wait for something to change on the outside in order to make it easier, don't. Start it now, right here before you leave the room. When you go home tonight do it again. Do it when you go to bed…a little communion with self. For you who were not here, we took the 4th Psalm, the 4th verse, and the words are simple, "Be angry." The day didn't go as you wanted it to go, "Be angry, but sin not." Sinning is "missing the mark." Don't let your anger go with you into the deep of sleep. Stop, be angry, get it off your chest. At that moment having blown your top as it were, now don't sin. Sinning is missing the mark. So you have an objective, a goal, now commune with your own heart on your bed and be still, be silent.

Now you're told what to do, "Bring the right sacrifice." And the word translated "right" in the King James Version is "the sacrifice of righteousness." Righteousness is right thinking. Forget now having blown my top; and then start the right thinking, and commune, and say what I want…not what I didn't get today, what I want. Not the opposition to what I wanted, what I want. Then as I commune with self, reach the point of being thankful, "Thank you." And then we are told, "Trust in the Lord." Bring the sacrifice of righteousness and trust in the Lord. Just go to bed that way and see how it works. The whole thing works quickly. Don't postpone it, and don't try to aid it. It's all within you, and the rearranged structure here rearranges it there; and it's only reflection, it's only response.

So let no one say to you to convince you that because of your background or your limitations of birth you are stuck. No one is stuck save he sticks himself. Billy Rose, there's no one here tonight who was poorer, no one with more limitations. He was sixty-six. Well, a very dear friend of mine, he was born in the same area, on the east side. There were Italians on one side, Jews on the other, and the Jew had to pass the Italian blocks to go to school. My friend Rosy, who today has millions, then he didn't have a nickel, he told me himself, he said, "Neville, I would come out of my home and I would start running…talk about a 100-yeard dash…because everything that they had they threw at us. They threw tomatoes, threw everything. And every day of my life it was the same race to get through that two or three hundred yards to get to school." That's how he started in New York City. So racial problems are not just between white and black, it was the Italian and the Jew, it was the Protestant and the Catholic, and all these stupid little divisions.

So this man Rose, he started as a Jew in a neighborhood where because he was a Jew and one born by the accident of birth a Christian thought himself better…and didn't know the first meaning of the word Christian. But that didn't start sixty years ago; it still is today. Ask all these fellas with all their lovely robes and all their names—now people kiss their hand and think they're kissing a holy man—ask them to really tell you who Jesus Christ really is. They wouldn't know. They really believe he's a man that lived once and for all 2,000 years ago. They don't know that Jesus Christ is God the Father. They don't know he's their own wonderful human Imagination. If you say it, they're shocked. I'm speaking from experience.

They say, "Where do you get that in the Bible?" And may I tell you, when I turn to the Bible…I didn't write it, here it is…what other conclusion can you reach when I read this? They want to close the book right away. They never saw it, but they teach in all the great schools. But they never saw it.

What about these words: "Show us the Father. I have been so long with you and you do not know the Father, Philip? He who sees me has seen the Father. How then can you say, Show us the Father?" (John 14:8). I've been walking and talking with you and you don't know the Father? Bear in mind this is a story and it's a parable. One day it unfolds in man, but it has to be dramatized. As Paul said, as you would on the stage: "O foolish Galatians! Who has bewitched you? Before whose eyes Jesus Christ was publicly *portrayed* as crucified" (Gal.3:1). I can take any life and dramatize it in picture form, put it on the stage, tell it in the form of a story, and so you simply depict it. Well, here is the story of salvation depicted for man, and man forgot the spirit behind the story, and started worshipping the vehicle that conveyed the story. And so they simply worshipped false gods.

Now here, we are closing two weeks from tonight. Another thing I want to tell you, our friend Freedom will be here a week from Sunday…

                    *   *   *

Q: What is the meaning of all the names of generations?

A: Did you hear the question? What's the meaning of the names of all the generations in the Bible? They are states of consciousness, spiritual states, not men, not women. We speak of the great patriarchs Abraham, Isaac and Jacob. You'll find them only in the Bible. Yet we have records that

go back several centuries before what we call A.D. There is no reference
in any book of the name Jesus Christ; you only find it in the Bible. These
characters live in man as eternal spiritual states.

Q: I know that the names mean states of mind, but there are a lot of names
that, uh, like Abraham and Jacob, those are well known names, but there
are others like one was a brother and a cousin...names that at least I don't
know of...

A: Well, my dear, names in the Bible differ from other names in the sense
we name a child after some rich uncle in the hope. That's not how people
are named in the Bible, they're named for their significance. So Abraham,
the father of multitudes, so out of him will come all who have faith, for
he is the foundation of faith. So, many are the children of Abraham after
the flesh, if you want to put it that way, as people claim, but you must be
children of Abraham after the spirit which is faith.

Q: Neville, what do you do when you have a friend who works the law
against you and he thinks he's doing you a favor?

A: My dear, you're giving him a power he does not really possess. Don't give
him the power. If you think you are better than another then you are
better. Do not give to another that which belongs to God.

Q: The law of tithing they talk about, is that man made or from God?

A: The law of tithing...the Bible speaks of tithing. Melchizedek received
a tithe from Abraham. These are states. Melchizedek has no father, no
mother, no ancestors, no beginning, no end. Jesus Christ was called a
priest forever after the order of Melchizedek. If it has no origin and it is
the origin of all, it must be God, would it not? Well then, Abraham tithed.
You tithe with God when you sit quietly, commune with yourself, and
ask for anything in this world in confidence that it's granted. And when
it's given to you it's pressed down, shaken together, and running over. It
always comes back more. You only gave ten percent of what comes back.

Q: It doesn't mean you give ten percent to a church?

A: No. If you want to give to some charity organization and it gives you
pleasure, give it. My wife and I give a few checks based upon our ability
to do it every year. The Red Cross gets one and the different charitable
organizations that depend on gifts. We don't burden ourselves, we simply
give our check. They're doing a good job and it's fun if you have it. I
certainly don't give ten percent of my income to some church. Churches,
whether you believe it or not, they're a big business. They will deny
that they are big business. Last week in Chicago, this man who has his

own consulting…he's a consultant in business, and he addressed all the Lutherans, the head plus those under the head, and he said, "Now, gentlemen, I'm here to tell you that you do not differ from any other business in the world who has my services. They need management, they need management control. And so, you are in big business, and don't deny it." And they'll be the first to deny it.

I don't know what it is, but I'm quite sure if you and I saw the portfolio of the Catholic or the Protestant church—that the Catholic, because they are united, the Protestants are divided in New York City if you took the Episcopal portfolio—it would stagger you. If you took the Catholic portfolio, which is a united body, and that portfolio no one outside of a very small little circle knows that portfolio. Anyone who says he knows it, he lies. And the few who know it won't tell you, because it would be just staggering. That's business. You have no time for God when you have to watch such large sums of money. How could you? How could you devote any time to really deep meditation when you have…I wouldn't be surprised if it ran in excess of, say, fifty billion dollars…a tax exempt organization? You know how it grows in this world. You take the Ford Foundation, it's only the third generation, and the Foundation has in it over two billion dollars. They're giving it away, I think. ___(??), but it grows, you can't stop it. So if you go back now 2,000 years ago, not three generations, it would stagger the mind of man. As far as I am concerned, I don't care. That's part of the play that those who are playing it must play. Let them play it.

Q: How do you work the law for others?

A: Same way. You have someone you love and they are in need, alright, you commune with yourself and you discuss with yourself the good fortune of the other. Just say, "Wasn't that wonderful! It's done, isn't it! I'll assume that you were…yes, it's done."

Q: Without bringing them in your…

A: Yes. Make it easy. He sees all, he knows all. Because you know it and you and he are one, doesn't he know it?

Well, until Tuesday. We have four left, and then we're leaving on the third…as I told you a one-way ticket, but you'll know when I do come back. Thank you.

NAME OF GOD IS KEY TO UNDERSTANDING THE BIBLE

2/15/66

The *name* of God is the key to the understanding of the biblical doctrine of God. In biblical terms, the religious question is not "Does God exist?" but "Who is God?" What is his name? What is his Son's name? And with this riddle you and I wrestle from the beginning of the journey to the end. I will tell you tonight. I am hopeful that you will believe me, but it comes from self-revelation. When it's revealed to you, then there is no argument; you know. Until it's revealed, you search the scriptures and there it is. It is in scripture, but man conditioned as he is hardly ever sees it. When he sees it it's such a surprise he won't believe it...so he goes on, because of his conditioned mind. But, here it's in scripture.

Now we turn to my pal—I call him my pal, for we are separated in time in Caesar's world, but we are closely and very closely woven in the tapestry of life—and that is Blake. Blake had this argument with his friend—I call him a friend—the Rev. Dr. Trussler. Trussler didn't like Blake's interpretation of scripture; and made it very obvious that he didn't care for Blake's work, any of it, and said to Blake that you need someone to elucidate your ideas. Blake answered it...Blake said, "You say that I must have someone to elucidate my ideas? You ought to know that what is grand is necessarily obscure to weak men." He hoped that would put him in his place. Then he said, "What can be made explicit to the idiot isn't worth my care. The ancients considered that what was not too explicit was fittest for instruction because it rouses the faculties to act." Then he asked the question, he said, "Why is the Bible more entertaining and instructive than any other book? Is it not because it is addressed to the Imagination, which is spiritual sensation, and only immediately to the understanding or reason?" To Blake man was all Imagination. He saw the parable…but revealing this revelation of his: That all things existed in the human Imagination. So to him the Bible was the most instructive and the most entertaining book in the world. There was nothing comparable to it.

So tonight, we'll take that book, only sections of it, because how could we cover sixty-six books? The Bible is constructed in three layers. We're told in Ecclesiastes, "A threefold cord is not quickly broken" (4:12). We're told the ark must be constructed with a lower, a second and a third deck (Gen.6:16). The whole Bible is written in that manner. Anyone who can read can read the lower level, the literal level. It's symbolized in scripture as a stone or a rock. Anyone who will dwell upon it, who may be blessed with a vision or some mystical experience, may see that rock (like a Moses) giving water, actually see the inner meaning behind the story. Then one who sees the meaning behind the story, who has the courage to test it, will then find the third symbol and that is wine…so it is stone, water, wine.

So here we are told the shepherds go into the field to water their flock, and when all are gathered together, the shepherd rolls away the stone and waters his flock. After he has watered the flock, he must roll the stone back to the mouth of the well (Gen.29:1-3). You will say that's a very kind act if you took it in that form, for men walking over the field not seeing the well, and there's no protection, could fall into it. But that's not it at all. You always put back…leave it just as it is…don't change the words of God. In other words, you leave it just as the story is told. So then you leave it without an attempt to re-write scripture—and so many are always attempting to re-write it to give it sense—leave it just as it is.. So that well is there forever and it's always covered. If you're a good shepherd and you have a flock and you know how to roll that stone away, then quench their thirst. For man who is sent is the shepherd; or one who has been trained by one who is sent is the shepherd, and he has those who are thirsty for truth. He can read the book, or he can listen to someone who can read the book, and listen to it with understanding. But he will say, what is it all about? Why tell this story in a book called the Book of God? God's Word must never be altered. Why? Here's why.

Here is a story and it has a meaning, and the meaning is symbolized in the form of water. I am thirsty for something more than the facts of life. Because I was born in a certain limited environment, must I accept these facts forever? Must I accept the limitations of birth and go through life with them until the grave? This story is telling me that I need not. The shepherd who comes who knows will show me how to take the stone and convert it—roll it away and draw forth water, psychological meanings, from the stone. So every story has a hidden meaning, a lovely meaning, and it's all to set man free, every story.

So you come to me and you tell me the facts of life, what you're earning, your obligations to life, everything about you, you're giving me the stone. Then I tell you it doesn't really matter. Could you now believe me when I tell you that you can be anything that you want to be, but anything? Could you go that far with me? Well, do you believe you could improve your lot if you can't go that far? Do you really believe you could improve if you can't go that far? Do you really believe that if I told you of a certain trick…call it a trick…and you applied it, that it would work?

Well, this is what the story tells me: I'm going to quench your thirst. If you go away from me thirsting, I haven't helped you; I have left you with the facts. But I'm not going to tell you that you are suffering because of some past karma, that you're reaping the fruit of some past, I forget that. I'm going to tell you right now you can be what you want to be in spite of your past, in spite of your present. In this past Sunday's paper, you might have read it, the science editorial, and he wonders why man has gone all out for psychoanalysis, analyzing the mind of man. For, he said, "The greatest of them all is called Freud, and those who follow him are the fanatics of the world. And so they will say, my neighbor on my right is polite because he has an inferiority complex; my neighbor on my left he is rude because he has an inferiority complex.' So, said he, if I take this theory of complexes and turn it around, I find that the inferiority complex can produce either politeness *or* rudeness. That's not scientific. That's not what I call a theory that proves itself in performance. You tell me that I am rude because of the same thing that the other fellow finds himself being polite.

No, the Bible doesn't teach that. It teaches definite outcome of drinking that water. If you would now in spite of what you told me—you've given me all the facts—if you would dare to assume that you are now what you want to be, and mentally see the world as you would see it were it true, and dare to believe in that imaginal act, in a way that no one knows, and you need not raise a finger to ask the help of anyone, that imaginal act will crystallize and become a fact in your world, a fact that you can share with others. So you come asking for water, I give you the water. You believe it? If you don't have to drink it, you will never turn it into wine. You'll never know the first great mystery as recorded in the gospel of John (2:1-9). He has these signs and the first one is the marriage feast. He turns to the servants—now he is the Lord so they have to obey his command—he said, "Fill the stone jars with water," (the stone). So the servants filled the stone jars with water. He said, "Now withdraw some of it and give it to the steward of the feast." When the steward tasted it, it was the best wine; and all the guests asked of the host, how did you save the best wine for the last? He took the knowledge that he knew… and used it.

So he could write through his servant to his friend called Timothy, he could write, "Do not continue to use water only, but use a little wine for the sake of your stomach and your frequent infirmities" (1Tim.5:6). In other words, this doesn't cure you forever. You come here today with one problem and so I ask you, what do you want in place of what you have? What would be the solution? So you tell me the solution. I ask you to assume that you have it, just as though you had it, and walk the earth just as though you had it. No breaking any blood vessels…just as though you had it. And watch the thing crystallize and become objective fact. But, I'm not saying that that's the final thing. You'll come back tomorrow, another problem. Because man grows in this world, he grows and he outgrows. When I earned eighteen dollars a week, oh, my dream was to earn twenty-five. If I could only earn twenty-five dollars! So I earned the twenty-five. It was not enough. Then I earned the seventy-five…not enough. And I earned the $100…that was not enough. No matter what I earned it's not enough, because new obligations to life. You move out of one environment, you grow, as you grow you outgrow, and as you outgrow, you need more of everything to simply live comfortably in this world. And that's life. You aren't going to simply accumulate and live in your little home; you're going to grow with it in mind, and you're going to grow in your environment. So he said, "Your *frequent* infirmities." Don't use this water only. Use the water, but use a little wine for the sake of your stomach and your frequent infirmities. You'll always have them…up to the very end when the name of God unveils itself and reveals itself in you.

So, all these stories all the way through are on three different levels. The stone is the literal level. And strangely enough, what is literal and stone, the rock, when you experience these stories in depth they are literal. The strange thing about it, you experience it and it's never as you thought that they would be. You always thought that they belonged to the past and that scripture is the record of some past events. One day you are blessed with the unveiling of God within you, and *you* have the experiences—what you always thought when you discover the stone, the water, the wine and you could apply it to this world of Caesar—but you never thought that it was still literally true in depth. Who would have thought that the story of Jesus Christ must be experienced by everyone in this world? And that he himself goes through the experience? That the story is simply an acted parable that every child born of woman will one day actually experience? He will be born from above, he'll be resurrected. And that last question which we proposed the very first moment we took the platform, "Does God exist? You don't ask that question but "Who is our God?"…we ask that. Then we ask, "What is his name?"…we ask that. Then we ask, "What is his Son's name?" and there is the cue. When that comes, everything else is revealed.

When the Son reveals you as God the Father, here is the most, I would say, simple, clear and concise expression of the doctrine of the logos, as we find it in the beginning of the prologue of John: "I and my Father are one" (10:30). Who will take that literally? And yet it is literally true: I and my Father are one. If that is literally true, then I am my Father; and if I am my Father, then I am self-begotten. Well, how on earth can I be my Father? Wait for the Son, and you'll find his name, and then you'll know you are the Father. He reveals you as God the Father. Scripture tells you he did have a Son, but the name of the Father is Jesse. Well, we're not all scholars in the Hebrew tongue. You can look it up...and Jesse is simply "any form of the verb to be." In other words, it's "I am." But scholars added to it to give sense to it and wrote the book called Ruth. So we have a genealogy in Ruth that is not found in the ancient manuscripts. We have a genealogy in other words not found in the ancient manuscripts. So you go back to the earliest known manuscripts and there is no ancestor for Jesse. How can I AM have an ancestor? Because I AM is the name of God (Ex. 3:13-15).

I can tell you I AM is the name of God, but do you know I cannot turn you into love by that knowledge. You can use it as power, real power! As we are told in the 16th of John, "And the hour is coming that they'll put you out of the synagogues" (verse 2). Well, the word synagogue you have associated with only one kind of temple: every church made by man. Well, that was the only church of the day. So today it would be all the churches of the world. "They'll put you out of the churches; and whoever kills you will think he is doing God a service. This they will do because they have not known the Father, nor me"—God believed in, yes, and revealed as I AM. He takes it, I AM, and he works it beautifully, but he doesn't know that that is Father. Until it is revealed as God the Father love doesn't burst through.

I can be I AM and not turn to anyone in this world. As we're told in the Book of Kings, "Why do you walk around all the time limping on two different opinions? If the Lord is God, serve him; if Baal, serve him" (1Kgs. 18:21). Then Joshua comes forth, "Choose this day whom you will serve. We choose the Lord. And then he said to them, 'You are witnesses against yourself that you have chosen the Lord'; and they replied 'We are witnesses.'" Well, the word translated Lord is I AM. I've chosen that and only that to serve; I will not be misled, I will not turn outside. It doesn't make me want to love. And nothing reveals it but God the Father...until I find him as the Father, and not another but myself. Not a power in the world can convince me that I am the Father but the Son who calls me Father. When he stands before me and calls me Father, it is only then that I know how I really am. That comes at the end of the search, the end of the journey.

So here, the name of God is secret in this biblical mystery. Find the name. The name also is his nature, and he unveils, one after the other, his nature. He first unveils it as power, El Shaddai; he unveils himself as infinite power. In the very end what a thrill when he unveils it as love! Here you stand before your very being, a radiant being, and it's infinite love. He embraces you; he has ceased from that moment on to be two, you're one, one with the body of God who is love. You still don't know yet that you're the Father. Then comes the final revelation when he unveils himself again within you, and he stands before you. Who stands before you?—your Son. You had hidden him in you at the beginning of the journey for the purpose of remembering at the end of the journey who you really are, God the Father.

So they will kill you. And why will they do it?—because they have not known the Father, nor me. So God...could believe in; and Father...could ignore. Today, you ask one million Christians of the world about God the Father, they put him out there some place and put his Son out there some place in time and space, and call the Son Jesus Christ, and call his Father by some name, God, some other name, the Lord. Yet there is one who tells you, "The Father and I are one" (John 3:10). How could you say it more clearly or concisely? How can you in eternity find a sentence so short to reveal so much? I and the Father, therefore, I am the Father! Well, don't tell me you're the Father, because then you must have a son...at least, you have a child. What Christian in the world would not think you're blaspheming if you said that Jesus Christ has a Son? What in this world would they do to you if the law allowed them? Why, they would skin you alive for such blasphemy. And he tells you, I am the Father...when you see me you see the Father. Well then, show us the Son.

Now this is the riddle that's propounded in the 30th chapter of Proverbs (verse 4): "Who laid out the foundations of the earth, who did it all? What is his name and what is his son's name, surely you know?" You don't know 'til the end. In the very end you know because he reveals you...when he reveals the Son's name. I'll tell you the Son's name, if you will accept it: The Son's name is David. And David is ___(??) although personified as a youth, an eternal youth, beauty beyond measure, you can't describe the beauty of David, who calls you Father, in fulfillment of scripture; for we are here only to fulfill scripture. In the 89th Psalm (verse 26): "I have found David, he's cried unto me, 'Thou art my Father, my God and the Rock of my salvation.'"

So after he has told them of the two ages—this age where we procreate and are born, and that age where we neither procreate nor are born for we are of the resurrection—we have been raised from this world of procreation and birth. Having explained the difference between the two ages, that a man walking this earth while *in* history he's resurrected and lifted out of this age, out of this section of time; and when he makes his exit, having been raised while he walks the earth his death is a coronation. In that age to which he passes, he is above the organization of sex; he doesn't need a divided image, male-female to create. He is one with himself, wearing the body of God, which is love. So he explains the entire thing…read it in the 20th chapter of Luke (verses 34-44).

Then he raises a question that was not asked, and as you read the entire chapter it's not related …so he raises the question, "What think ye of the Christ? Whose son is he?" repeating the son again. And they answered, "The son of David." Then he replies, "Why then did David in the Spirit call him Lord? If David thus calls him Lord, how can he be David's son?" (Mat. 22:42). And I know that when I was writing the last chapter of *The Law and The Promise*, when I came to that experience of mine I wrestled with it for days. I finally concluded I would say man matures when he becomes his own father's father. I was sticking to scripture, yet he matures when he becomes his own father. But the Bible begins, in the New Testament, "This is the genealogy of Jesus Christ, son of David." But then when David calls *you* Lord—which is the name used by every son of his father, "my lord"—having seen David and David calls *me* Father, and scripture tells me I was his son, well then, I use the expression "I became my father's father." Getting as close as I could get to scripture…and yet I would be quite clear I hope if I said that man matures when he becomes his own father; because David really comes out of humanity. If I took all the generations of humanity, and all of its experiences, and fused them into a single whole, this concentrated time into which all the generations are fused and from which all generations spring, is personified in scripture as "eternity." And eternity is personified as a youth—that youth is David. So you bring forth, after your journey is over, a son that is the quintessence of all generations and all the experiences of humanity. So, in the end you did all and can forgive all, because *your* son is the quintessence of all the experiences of humanity…that's David.

So memory has been taken for a purpose, so that you cannot remember. If man could remember the horrors through which he has passed, if he could remember the horrors to which he lent a hand, he couldn't live with himself. So the veil has been lowered, and memory has been taken for a while. In the end, the whole thing will be unveiled and we well see that everything worked for good, but everything worked for good. There wasn't one little thing that seemed so horrible that when I see it in retrospect and see it at the very end, it was part of the entire unfolding drama…and it all worked for good. In that end, you are God the Father. And it doesn't really matter how your exit is made from this world or what moment, after your resurrection. The other important experiences will come quickly in three and one half years. After the final one, what does it matter? The final one is the descent…where you are sealed with the Holy Spirit…sealed with it as he descends upon you in the form of a dove, and smothers you with kisses. And then you know who you are.

That seal will be broken when they call you dead, and at that very moment no restoration to life. So that's the seal, that's this age, and that death is your coronation. You can say with Paul, "I have fought the good fight, I have finished the race, I have kept the faith; henceforth, there is laid up for me the crown of righteousness" (2Tim. 4:7). "Now I bear on my body the marks of Jesus" (Gal.6:17). Everyone will bear the marks of Jesus, because everyone is going to be God the Father. Not because someone tells him that he is, but he'll know it. Therefore, he knows in the end there's only one Father and *he* is the Father; he only has one son: "Thou art my son, today I have begotten thee" (Ps. 2:7).

So if our priesthoods of the world have misunderstood this mystery, all right, forgive them, they don't know it. Now they're railing all over with this new concept, should the priests marry? Some can't stand the burden of celibacy. And so, I think it's the current *Time* magazine, at some age, I think it's the 14th or 15th Century in a certain town in Italy, these are statistics, half of the illegitimate children in that town were sired by the clergy. They couldn't get married, but they could sire children all over the place. Then who knows the popes that were fathers? Alexander the 6th had four children. Have you ever heard of Caesar Borgia? Lucretia Borgia? Their father was Alexander the 6th, Pope Alexander the 6th. Henry the 2nd was married when he was pope. So what's all the palaver about when his very first command is multiply, replenish the earth. It was never rescinded; it was never taken back. All through the Psalms, the blessing of man is the multiplication of his family. Fill his cradle with these arrows.

So I say, forget all these little isms on the side. Just keep your mind straight and make your choice tonight. We have chosen to serve the Lord. What is his name?—I AM. And I believe he will unveil himself within me, and eventually I will stand in my own presence and know it to be infinite love. I'll know it to be God the Father by revelation, not by persuasion, not by argument. I will know it because he unveils it. Who unveils it? You unveil it…it's all you. You became this for a purpose, and the purpose is hidden until the end. In the end, you see it. So you live by the name of God. Don't turn to the left, don't turn to the right. Become a witness against yourself that you have chosen to serve the Lord, and the Lord's name is I AM, that's his name. He'll take you through all the things, yes, infirmities, yes, but use a little wine. When you come up against these things, use a little wine. I'll also take a bottle of wine…take what you know concerning the psychological truth and use it. As you use it you are turning it into wine.

So his first great marriage feast was jars made of stone filled with water, and the water turns to wine. So here you have the literal truth, the facts of life. So when he said the Father and I are one, they took up stones to stone him (John 10:30). Read it carefully. He said, "For what good works do you stone me? For no *good* works but for blasphemy; for you being a man, make yourself God" (verse 33). We know your background, we know where you came from, and when the Christ comes, no one will know where he comes from. And they're right, because you don't see him; you only see the mask, and you know the history of the mask. You either believe that presence wearing the mask and what he tells you, or you don't believe. So you never see him. When you see Christ, you're going to see yourself. So no one…he said, "Look here, here's Christ! Don't believe him." Why? "It does not yet appear what we shall be, but we know that when he appears we shall be like him, and see him just as he is" (1John 3:2). You shall be like him. Well, if I'm not like him in my own mind's eye, well, then I haven't seen him. But if David called him Father and he called me Father; and if he is the one who is resurrected from the grave, and I was; and if he is the one who is born from above and had witnesses to the birth that came from above, not from below, not the womb of woman but the skull of man, and I was; and if the Son of man who is God himself must rise in the form of a serpent—that's the only way he can rise—and the one who rises must be the one who descended, for no one will ever ascend to heaven but he who first descended, and I did; and if the dove descends only on Christ Jesus, well, then he descended on me, so I know who I am.

Everyone will have these experiences. So if you say it's blasphemy, he's a man, we know his background, we know all about him, and he's blaspheming to say these things, well, go back and read the scriptures. The central figure made the bold assertions, for they were happening in him. And they called it blasphemy; for their concepts of God would not allow this completely startling thing to take place within a man unless their mortal eyes could see it. Can't see it! So they took up stones to stone him, and the stones they threw at him were the facts of his life. We know when you were born, your brothers, your sisters, your neighbors, your father, your mother…we know them all… and you dare to claim what you have claimed? Then he disappeared from their sight.

So this is the story of our great Bible, which Blake claims is the greatest book in the world, and he's right. It's the most entertaining and the most instructive. But bear in mind it's on three levels: the stone level or literal; the water level or the psychological meaning behind the stories; and then the wine level, when you experience scripture and you can take the water and turn it into wine to benefit yourself in the world of Caesar, and wait patiently for the Promise when you're *all* wine. Did they not call him a wine bibber, a glutton and a wine bibber filled with wine? For that's what he gave. He completely fulfilled scripture.

Now let us go into the Silence.

*   *   *

Are there any questions, please?

Q: Have you had para-ocular vision or seeing without the eyes that scientists have been experimenting with?

A: No, I haven't. When I close my eyelids, I see…but not necessarily what the world wants me to see. If I turn my attention in as though I contemplated my brain, I find a world of light, pulsing, living, liquid light. It may lead me anywhere. So it's not ___(??) in the sense of seeing objects in the distance, like deliberately seeing what my family in Barbados is doing now, it's not that. Entirely different form of vision…and it's very easy.

Q: Have you ever seen visions of something that you had memory of about yourself? Have you had a dream about something that …

A: I don't quite understand the question.

Q: Let us say you visualize something that you wanted, that you tried to identify someone else with, then you forgot about it, and then later on you have a vision of the completed thing in a dream at night.

A: That's very possible.

Q: Also, is that an indication of the imminent fulfillment?

A: Well, you see, the book that I talked about tonight, *Out of This World,* that's based upon experience, all my books are. It was printed in '49 and the experience preceded it. You don't have experiences and then go to print the next morning. You dwell upon it, try to write it as well as you can,. So those experiences might have been recorded by me, say, two or three years before. But what started this thought, which I told in the little booklet called *Out of This World,* it was a recent experiment, because I tried it for a year, and being an extremist in all that I do, I tore my body to shreds because I couldn't sleep. I would not let myself sleep. I would be on the surface of my consciousness all the time, so the slightest vision I woke and wrote it down. Then go back to bed, and before I would drop into the deep, I would simply have vision and put it down. Well, I did that, I would say for about a year. I can't tell anyone how tiring that really is.

When my brother arrived in New York City and saw what I looked like, he thought it was death warmed over. But I am and always have been an extremist. If I set out to do something, nothing diverts me.

Well, I was going to test something. It was in the dream, say, I would have many experiences, all beautiful. Told in dream they made sense… the whole thing was just like a dream, a perfect dream. So I would write it down, and then observe the next day if perchance I encountered any episodes of that dream in my waking state. Invariably I did, but they were never in the order that I encountered them here. If I saw you in my dream and you gave me a letter, well, the letter is one event, you are another event, and all these things. Next day, I may meet you and have lunch with you, and you and I may walk the street together into a bar, but someone else gave me the letter. I got the letter but you were not the one who brought it. So every little thing in my dream came to pass, but not in the order I encountered it in the dream.

Well, after one year of this I came to the conclusion that in my dream I am using a different focus, a wider focus that encompasses not just a little moment of time, it encompasses days, weeks, months. And I could take the events and weave a lovely story out of them. But on this lowest of all levels, when I encounter events here, it's like the chromatic scale. I'm forced to move in one direction and hit note after note after note as I move in one direction. When I brought that book out in 1949, I gave a series of lectures in Milwaukee and the head chemist, Professor Imhoff of the Allis-Chalmers place told me that he could not go along with me, that as a chemist they have a law known as entropy. Entropy does not allow going back in time and altering the past. Nobody can take me there and they can't alter it. Memory may project based upon what I know into the future, and I can come to certain conclusions. He said that's how they prophesy. He receives samples from all over the world every day. He has to analyze the chemical content of that water and send his solution to these factories all over the world. Now he said, "If I didn't have the law of entropy and the past *could* be altered, I'm lost. As a scientist we have to go by this law, the law of entropy." So I said, "I don't know, I'm not a scientist, I only know I can alter the past."

Then came this picture…I'm not a musician, but I do know we have ___(??) that that keyboard is fixed. And so I can just hit a note and if I must play the chromatic scale, I go in one direction only. But suppose now in some strange way I could go back and hit a note that I formerly struck, and it sounded very good after hitting this one; and then I could jump forward to a note I haven't yet reached and that sounded very good...and pick out a little theme this way. Now suppose my mind could become split; I hit two events at the same time—you *and* the letter. Why, that's a different picture altogether. Instead of seeing you and then seeing the letter, put them together...it means something entirely different. Then my mind becomes full again, I can see two events, and four events, five events, and finally I can hold in my mind ten events. Then I can move back and forth over this fixed keyboard. And to me creation is finished and we begin to awake and we take from what is, it's all, it's fabulous. All things exist in the human Imagination. Then I become an artist, and I can play by holding in my mind's eye ten events widely separated in time, and seeing them together, strike chords...and they're more beautiful than the chromatic scale.

So it was simply an experiment. Having come to the conclusion that I could do it, I tried it and it worked. All these events I saw, one after the other. At the end of the day, I said, now I did this today and that and that and that. Then I turned to my page for the dream: This is what I dreamt and this is what I encountered today. So every event here was in my dream, but not in the order that I encountered it, and it made an entirely different story.

So man is moving up...and today scientists are agreed that creation is finished, that the entire space-time history is laid out, and we're only becoming aware of increasing portions of that which is. But we're becoming aware of it in one direction only. The day will come man will simply become aware of it in its entirety when he's the great artist. Then you and I, completely awake, with this fabulous keyboard will agree to play in concert. What a symphony! All will agree to play in concert with this fabulous world that we have experienced. Nothing passes away, it's all there. The most horrible discord in the world when we encountered it in this chromatic manner, we can now resolve into harmonies. By then our ears are attuned to appreciate dissonance. And what we'll do when all of us play it in concert!

Well, that's all. Goodnight.

THE ROCK, THE WATER
AND THE WINE

2/18/66

Last Tuesday, we spoke of the three levels of the Bible, the rock, the water and the wine. So much is said in the Bible about the rock. We're told, "Of the Rock that begot you you are unmindful, and you have forgotten the God who gave you birth" (Deut.32:18). So we find the Rock equated with God. Then we are told, "They drank from the supernatural Rock which followed them, and the Rock was Christ" (1Cor.10:4). We are told that the people rejected this Rock and yet it eventually became the chief corner stone. And throughout scripture so much is said about the Rock.

From experience I tell you that truth is literal…although the words used may be figurative. When you experience scripture you will see though before experience they were to you just metaphor and, well, figurative, when you experience scripture you will see how literally true these words are. How could God be a rock? How could Christ be the Rock from which man not only drank but the Rock that gave him birth? How can it be? Well, here is an experience that I will share with you. It was in the thirties. I meditate daily, no special hour, not always to bring about changes, just because I like it. So while sitting in the Silence with my attention turned inward and contemplating nothing in particular, just the brain as it were, and usually after about a minute or so, sometimes it's a matter of seconds, all the dark convolutions of the brain break and they burst into light, golden liquid light that simply pulses and goes all around one's head. Well, honestly, I was thinking of nothing in particular, but suddenly before me came a quartz…I would say about that big. As I looked at it, it broke, became fragmented into numberless pieces; and then quickly it was assembled into a human form and seated in the lotus posture. As I

154

contemplated it I noticed I am looking at myself. Here is the very being that is contemplating and the being contemplated, and they are one. We had only a moment before a rock, and the rock fragmented. The rock was gathered into human form, and a living, breathing being not made of rock. Here it is now living, it's breathing, it's flesh, it's alive. Then as I became interested, it began to glow. It began to glow and increase in intensity, and when what seemed like the apex or limit of such intensity, the whole thing exploded. And here I am, still seated, pondering over this strange, peculiar vision.

I say, God actually achieves his limitless purpose by self-limitation. The word rock is defined as "to compress, to confine, to restrict; to take on the limit of contraction, the very limit of opacity." So we're told in the Book of Philippians, "And being in the form of God, he emptied himself and took upon himself the form of a slave and was born in the likeness of man; and being formed in the image of man, became obedient unto death, even death on the cross" (2:6). Now, the cross, I know from experience, is not outside on a tree or wood, but man himself is the cross, the man himself is the tree of life; that here on *this* cross God is crucified. That I know from experience. I'm not theorizing, I'm not speculating, I know this experience to be fact. This is the limit of contraction that God assumes. As the poet Blake said, "God himself enters death's door and lays down in the grave with those who enter, and shares with them their visions of eternity 'til they awake and see the linen clothes lying that the females had woven for them." Here again is the linen cloth. The word linen means "white as marble, bleached, blanched." That's exactly what you see the very day of your resurrection. You've never seen such a ghastly whiteness on the face of the body out of which you've just emerged. Talk of death…there is really the appearance of death, really bleached.

So here, this is the rock. The occupant is your own wonderful I AM… that's God. Your own wonderful human Imagination, that's God. And he shares with you all these wonderful visions of eternity. Most of them are nightmares, horrible dreams; but to you they aren't dreams, they're objective things, they're facts. But if the day will come that you will awake, then the experiences preceding waking must have been a dream. So he lies down in the grave with them and shares with them their visions of eternity 'til they wake. So when they wake all that preceded it seemed so real, just like the dream of the night. It seemed so real while you're in it, and only on waking and reflecting on it does it seem like a subjective experience, a dream. Well, this whole vast experience of man when God awakes *in* man will be to him a dream. But it had a purpose, an infinite purpose: For man to expand as God. God became man that man may become God. There is only God in the world, there is nothing but God.

So this Rock that begot us…one day you will have the experience of seeing that Rock…beautiful imagery, marvelous symbolism. And yet all through scripture it is all about this Rock, the Rock from which man drank, this supernatural Rock, and the Rock was Christ. You who do not have the concordance will find that in Paul's 1st letter to the Corinthians, the 10th chapter. The Rock was Christ…he equates now the Rock with Christ. As we find in the 32nd chapter of Deuteronomy, the word God being equated with the Rock: "And the Rock that begot you you are unmindful, and you forgot the God who gave you birth." If the Rock begot you and God gave you birth, then Rock and God are one. His name is I AM, in this wonderful unfolding of scripture, for scripture must be fulfilled in me. What is written about me has its fulfillment and everything written about me is in scripture. The whole book is a prophecy of what must be experienced by every child born of woman.

So we are told, call the next witness. Call witness after witness, to do what? To testify to the truth of God's will. So the first witness is external and we reject it. It's to us like myth. It's a rock, so we will not accept that as the building cornerstone on which to build our world. So the more intelligent man becomes, the more he looks upon the Bible as myth. And I tell you it's the only reality. The Hebrew rabbi was uttering the truth when he said, "What is not written in scripture is non-existent." Everything will pass like a dream, but his Word will not pass. This is simply a prophecy of all that man will one day experience. So we take it literally and wait for that day when we are called upon to be the witness to the truth of God's Word. You can't force it. So what one should really believe in is simply the testimony of Jesus. As we are told, "He is the first witness, he is the first born of the dead." Well, listen to his witness, listen to his testimony; for the testimony of Jesus is the spirit of prophecy. What prophecy? The whole Bible is prophetic. Not who's going to win a war, or who's going to become prominent in the world. Hasn't a thing to do with secular history. The Bible is sacred history, brought to climax and fulfillment in the story of Jesus Christ.

You may look upon Jesus Christ—and I take liberties—but in a sense just as though he were a divine reporter giving an account of that which is of infinite concern to man. Well, what is the concern of man other than to tell him his future? His *real* future is to fulfill scripture. I can tell you of a secondary future which is entirely up to you. Anyone can become what he wants to be, that's scripture too, but that belongs to the world of Caesar. If you know what you want to be in this world, it's not difficult to become it. If you dare to assume—in spite of the evidence of the senses to the contrary, if reason denies it and your senses deny it—and yet you dare to assume that you are *now* the man, the woman, that you want to be, and believe in the reality of that assumption, not knowing how it's going to happen, you'll become it.

But that belongs on this level, to this world, and in the end you'll leave behind your record but it will fade…no one will know it in the next few generations.

I only have to look back upon the great stars of forty-odd years ago, when they were so majestic in the eyes of all of us. You mention their names to my daughter, she doesn't know them. I speak of Wallace Reed, she said, "What?" And yet when I was a boy the name Wallace Reed itself was magic. You mention all these names…she knows nothing of them. And then what will be her child's, and her children's children? They will know nothing of the so-called glittering ones of today.

But here is the Bible forever going right through, still remaining contemporary. But I can't tell anyone who has not experienced scripture the thrill that is in store for them when they begin to experience it. Now, if you just read this one simple little statement, you could no longer conceive of Jesus as *a* man. We speak of the universal, cosmic Christ buried in every man, and that cosmic Christ is God. Take the very last verse of the simplest and yet the most profound book in the New Testament, the gospel of John. Read it! Only a few things are recorded, he tells us, that you may believe, but if everything he did and said were recorded, the world itself would not be big enough to contain the books (21:25). Well, can you conceive of a life of a few years doing things that you could not write about in all the volumes, and so many that the world couldn't contain them? But if you see him as a cosmic Christ, from the beginning of history up to the very end, and everyone in the world lives because Christ lives in him, and everyone does what he does because Christ does it in him.

Christ is the slave of man. So you have the most horrible thoughts, he'll execute them, yet he is love, infinite love. But being your Imagination he does not question your right to imagine the unlovely; he will do it. For he laid down the law in the very beginning: "All things bring forth after their kind" (Gen.1:11), everything. So you will know when you reap, don't be surprised that was corn, that's why you're reaping corn; and you're reaping sesamum because it was sesamum when you planted it. So I would say the law…the law of identical harvest. When you reap it it is only the multiplication of the identical seed. So he will actually take upon himself all the sufferings of the world. Who? The cosmic Christ, your Imagination. So he doesn't question your right to want to hurt, he carries the burden, and he is your own wonderful human Imagination. When you know that, you become extremely selective, extremely discriminative. For I tell you, in the end there is no other; there is nothing but yourself made visible, for the self of man is God. As he wakes in man, you know you are the God that begot you…you are self-begotten.

When you have the experience, you read it, how could it be? Out of death came life? Well, here's the mystery of the seed: Except it falls into the ground and dies and rots, it remains alone, but if it falls into the ground and dies, it brings forth much (John 12:24). So we're told, God dies in the most literal sense, and yet it is not death as the world sees death. The Bible equates death with sleep: "Awake, you *sleeper,* and arise from the dead" (Eph.5:14). So when God puts himself into this self-imposed restriction called man, it is, relative to what God is, death. He emptied himself of his glory and took upon himself the form of death, which is man (Phil.2:6). He animates it by being present; he animates it as the dreamer.

Now we're told, "And the voice said, 'Come and I will show you the Bride, the wife of the Lord…the wife of the Lamb" (Rev.21:9). Well, the lamb is a symbol of the Lord. Come and I'll show you the bride, the wife of the lamb. "And so in Spirit he took me,"—always in Spirit—"and there I saw the new Jerusalem descending from heaven"—here, the King James Version translates what he sees now as the most priceless stone—"adorned like a bride." The others, that is, the Revised Standard Version calls it a radiant light. Well, both are correct. It is a stone, but a stone capable of assuming human form, becoming alive and breathing; and then radiating beyond the wildest dream of man…more brilliant than the sun, more brilliant than the stars. And that's *you,* because you're looking at yourself. Here you are contemplating your own being, and it began, as far as you see, a stone, just a quartz. It says, "Come, I'll show you the Bride." Well, what bride? Am I the Bride of God? Yes, I am the Bride of God.

So the story from beginning to end is all about Christ. And man must leave everything and cleave to his wife, cleave to the woman, until they become one. So you see it when you become one. When you become one and not two, a new man is formed, and the new man is Christ (Eph.2:14). So he is being formed in us as it were by cleaving to us. As Blake brought out so beautifully, "His emanation, yet his wife, 'til the sleep of death is past"…his emanation yes and yet his wife. He becomes it and individualizes himself as you. When it happens, we're told, he gives us a new name, and he writes it on a white stone, that luminous, radiant thing, and it's a new name known only to the one who bears it (Rev.2:17). But I'll tell you the name—but you won't believe it until you are called by it—the name is Jesus. In the end, Jesus only…everything disappears and there is Jesus only.

As we are told in Isaiah the 27th, "And I will gather you one by one, O people of Israel" (verse 12)…I know from experience why we are gathered one by one: Because of our uniqueness you can't bring two together. One by one, to unite into a *single* body which is Christ—Christ awake, the risen Christ, is God. And everyone, as we're told…of course, the translation is, "And he will transform or change our lowly bodies to be like his glorious body" (Phil.3:21). But that phrase "to be like" literally means "of one form with" his glorious body. So you will wear the body of love which is the body of God. These experiences are literally true and you'll have them.

So when you're told you must be born again, that's literally true; and you will be, but not in the world of flesh and blood. For God is Spirit and if you're born into the world of God, you're born of Spirit; and you're born from above, not from below from the womb of woman. Everyone will have this experience. If you're here for the first time and just not quite familiar with this teaching, you might say, "Well, suppose I die tonight without having had the experiences?" May I tell you, I know this too from experience, you're instantly restored to life. You're still in this world, this world and this time called "this age." You enter the *new* world through that new birth, which is preceded by a moment by what is called in scripture the resurrection. So we are resurrected one by one, and then as we are resurrected we are born of the Spirit into an entirely new world, wearing the body of God. And in the end, there is only God, nothing but God.

If you are here for the first time, and you're concerned about improving your lot in this world of Caesar, may I tell you, it is very easy to do. It's simple if you could only believe in the reality of your unseen, invisible imaginal acts. If you could sit here right now and contemplate what you would be like were it true that you are already what you want to be. Well, how will I know that I'm doing it correctly? Well, I do the frame of reference—I take a circle of friends, friends so close and so concerned that they would be conscious of the fact of my transformation. If I shared with them my secret, what I wanted to be, when I become it they will know it. So I let them know it…all in my Imagination. I bring them into my mind's eye and let them see me as they would have to see me were I the man that they know I want to be. So should I become that man they'd be aware of it. I let them become aware of it and I believe in the reality of what I've done. Because who did it? Christ did it, and all things are possible to Christ. Did he really do it? Well, he must have done it, because I did it. And we're told, "By him all things were made and without him was not anything made that was made" (John 1:3). If I did it, I made it. It's unseen as yet; it isn't clothed in three-dimensional form, but I did it. And he is the one who does everything, and all things are possible to him.

So my reasoning mind will tell me, well, you don't know how it's going to happen. As far as I am concerned, it *has* happened and I'm only awaiting confirmation. It *has happened*. Like scripture, all this is foretold, as we're told in the 44th of Isaiah, everything is foretold: there isn't a thing that I haven't shown you. But who will believe it? And here, everything is told. Now you become a witness to prove how true all that was hidden comes into your being through experience, and you become the witness. I must have two witnesses if I go to court. The outer witness is the Bible; the inner witness is the Spirit, and so when two agree in testimony, it's conclusive. I have my Bible as a permanent record, and if my experiences parallel the Bible then I am the internal witness; I don't need anyone else. I stand before the one who judges which is myself in the depths of my soul. I can't lie to myself. So if I *know* that I have experienced this, that and the other, I know because I can't fool myself, I can't lie to myself. So when we are told, "God has taken his place in the divine council; in the midst of the gods he holds judgment" (Ps. 82:1, 6 RSV). Bring the next witness...so he comes in, and when he comes in, his very life, his very being testifies to the truth of the fact that he has witnessed and experienced scripture. That's all that we are here for.

But in this wonderful world of Caesar—and it's for a purpose—it's a world of educative darkness. So you and I simply can change our environment regardless of where we were born in this world. Don't complain because you were behind the eight-ball, born on the wrong side of the tracks. It doesn't really matter *if* you know God's law and you're willing to trust God. God acts in you through your imaginal acts. Well then, single out what you want your friend to be, what you want yourself to be, and believe that they are. You can start doing this now with a friend in your office. If you are having any problems with him, treat him as kind, as though he were. Treat him as though he were generous. Treat him as though he had intelligence. Treat him as you would like to see him. Do you know, he'll conform to it. He may be the same rascal to others but to you he wouldn't be. He has to conform to what you actually persuade yourself that he is, and in your presence and in your world he *is* the person. You can take anyone in this room...you're not the same person to any two, far less any twelve. They see you differently, because they see you through their concepts of you; they see you through their assumption of you. Well, what is right?

So tonight, you take yourself, start with self, and try it. See if you do not in the immediate future actually change your world to conform to these changes that take place within your mind. As I change within, I change it without. And how I do it, I don't know. I only know I believe in the reality of the imaginal act, and then if it takes one person or a thousand people to aid the birth of this imaginal act, it will take one or take a thousand. And really it's only an extension of myself...they're all arms of myself. They seem to be detached, but in the end they aren't. So they're going to help...they'll do their part to bring about the birth of what I've assumed I am. And may I tell you, it's all in scripture. They may even intend it to be evil, they may even intend it to hurt me, but time, on reflection, will prove that God intended it for good. Because, I did it and I intended good...but I did it. Their intention may be evil. When the brothers sold Joseph into Egypt into slavery, and they came and they were filled with remorse, he said, you didn't sell me into slavery, it was God. "You intended evil against me; but God intended that it work for good" (Gen.50:20). If you know the story, he became equal with Pharaoh in the ruling of Egypt and he could interpret dreams…the medium through which God speaks to man.

So he interpreted the dream. Without his interpretation of the dream, the world would have starved to death, for it lasted seven years. And this famine was so great that no one remembered any time in history when they ever had anything; that's how intense the famine was. Their very memory faded, they couldn't remember a moment in time when they had anything. So he prepared, from seven years of plenty he prepared and filled the barns. Every year a certain amount had to be put aside. So when the famine came as foretold, it lasted seven years, and he had enough to take care of civilization. His brothers came down and they simply were filled with remorse. But he knew they only played parts…he had a job to do…and getting to Egypt he'd be sold there. And the brothers were moved to play the parts they played.

So someone may want to hurt you, and time will prove their hurt was used…for all things work for good with those who love the Lord. So everything that was done to him moved to work for good, and he became equal to Pharaoh in power, equal to Pharaoh in might, and yet transcending all in his wisdom; for he was in communion with God and could interpret the language of God. So here, don't be concerned. If someone tomorrow on the heels of your assumption that things are perfect, accuses you, well, falsely, you'll prove in time, on reflection, it contributed to what you are, and you're moving towards the fulfillment of your assumption.

I came from a very small, little island. My family is a large family. The day that my father had this terrific blow in business we all despaired and thought this is the end, this really is the end, the whole bottom of the world has fallen out. Here he had these ten children to feed, to educate, to clothe, a wife, mother-in-law, and the usual help that we need in the Indies…and he had no money but none. Total strangers…not strangers but people that we did not entertain at home and who never entertained us…but they, too, came to his aid. One said, "Joe, what can I do?" Well, he said, "All I need is money and I have none, I have no collateral." He said, "Alright,"—he was a commissioned agent—he said, "You want to go back into the same kind of business?" My father said, "I know nothing else but. I know how to be a good grocer, meat vendor, liquor salesman, and so these things I can do." Well, he said, "Find a place, I'll take care of the rent and I'll stock you." He found the place, or we found a place on a little side street. He gave orders to his clerks that every order that came from Mr. Goddard must be filled, no compromise. Fill it without any questions asked, and send no bill until Mr. Goddard pays you. When he feels like paying, he'll pay. So we had what was to us unlimited credit, in that sense, and as the merchandise moved we paid.

Then on reflection, from that little beginning, the greatest day in my family's life in the world of Caesar was the day he was wrongfully accused and eased out of this junior partnership in a grocery shop. Because, had he not been eased out he would have simply gone through the next years of his life doing what he did for the first nineteen in that partnership—working hard and getting nowhere. Then he started just with the help of two friends, who never came home for a cup of tea. And so, on reflection, what day in our life as a family could compare to that day! My brother—not being superstitious, well, he's a very practical, down-to-earth businessman—because this happened on the 13th day of the month, and he opened his new business on the 13th of the month, he got married on the 13th of the month, the new building was bought for him out of nowhere and now he took his signature on the 13th of the month—no one could come to him and tell him thirteen is unlucky. He waits for the day. Thirteen, as far as he is concerned, that's the greatest day of the year, certainly of the month. And so, all the major things in his life fell on the thirteenth. And in spite of his know-how and really a terrific businessman, like so many people of the world they carry one little superstition he carries that.

So here, don't fall for the thirteenth, fourteenth or any other delay. All days are God's days, all equal. The thing you must watch is what you are doing in your Imagination, for your every imaginal act is God in action, and all things are possible to God. It's because of our shortened memory we don't recognize our own harvest when it appears in the world. We don't see it. But here, the whole thing comes up to confront us, to fulfill God's law that all things bring forth after their kind. You can't plant an apple seed and grow something other than the apple. That happens to everyone in this world. Who knows that his partners had to do what they did because he was ambitious for his family, and in his daydream he was dreaming of something bigger, something better, to leave his family, to give his family. He never shared that secret with us, but he could have undoubtedly dreamed these things. So having dreamt these things, they played their part, and so he never condemned them. In the very end, if one wanted help, he helped him. They all went to work for other people, eventually, and he was the only one when he died—of course, the others died before him—when he died he could leave his family financial independence. He had a large family, nine sons and one daughter. He didn't just leave them as a unity, individually they were all independent. It was all from that little beginning where he started behind the eight-ball. So what was the end of the world as a family became the beginning of a glorious future for all the family.

So if tomorrow your world collapsed after you've assumed that you are what you want to be, look upon it as a contributing factor. Time will prove that it is. Don't get on the phone and call someone and say, "I asked you to help me and look what happened! I was fired!" Best thing in the world! The day I was fired I went to my boss and said, "Why did you fire me?" I was making the large sum of twenty-two dollars a week working for J. C. Penney, busboy, putting hats in bins, and all kinds of things. Any moron could have done what I did. I worked for a year, and one day they fired me. When I asked him why, what have I done that's wrong, he said, "Not a thing…but you come from a little island where you don't have the same concept of business that we have, and when business declines we simply let people go." I said, "What am I going to use for rent and food?" "That's not my concern." Well, he must have felt sorry for me and so he gave me a little note to a friend of his who employed people at Macy's, and said, "He's a greenhorn, just in from the West Indies, help him out." I went over to Macy's and so they gave me eighteen dollars a week.

So one day, instead of being fired I quit…and that was the beginning of my world. I had the courage to quit. And when I quit, and didn't depend upon Macy's to feed me or pay my rent, I never worked for another person. Oh yes, I had six Broadway shows, but I never considered myself working for Mr. Schubert. I was an artist and he employed me, and so, when he employed me I never thought that he was my boss. I tore that word completely from my vocabulary and threw it through the window. From then on I was simply on my own. If I starved, no one would know it. I would know it, that's all. And so on reflection, my wonderful day was when J. C. Penney fired me, for I might be today the captain of the elevator operators, could easily be. If I held on just as securely and only securely, then longevity would have given me something there, for that's going all the way back to 1922.

So I say, don't be concerned if tonight you have a blow, a horrible blow, a great disappointment after you've assumed something big and wonderful for yourself; for that assumption is coming into being and has to break up all these things to make way for its birth. When you grow in this world, you outgrow. You can't grow and not outgrow. And so, the growing pains are painful sometimes.

But I tell you, everyone in the world will witness to the truth of God's Word, everyone. And the most impossible statement in scripture will one day be experienced by you, and you'll see how literally true it is. Who would have thought that the statement of "the Rock that begot you you are unmindful, and you forgot the God who gave you birth," that that Rock and God are the same in scripture? And the Rock from which you drank as you went through the wilderness, that supernatural Rock was Christ? Well then, I saw the Rock, a fragmented being gathered together, and it wasn't any picture I'd ever conceived of as Christ. Then I understood the epistle of John, "If anyone said, 'Look, look here...look there, that's the Christ,' don't believe him!" Don't believe him, why? Because, "It does not yet appear what we shall be. We know when he appears we shall know him" (1John3:2). Because why? We shall be just like him. So when you see that Rock which is Christ assembled into human form, it's *you*. And then you know who Christ is, that it's yourself begotten, that God achieves his limitless desires by putting upon himself these self-imposed restrictions and becoming obedient unto death on the cross that is man.

So, when you leave here tonight, don't forget it. Try to remember it every moment of time. As you walk the street, no matter what you're doing, just bear in mind that you are actually creating your future here. Your real future, as I told you earlier, is to fulfill scripture, and that you *will* do. Your secondary future is to use God's law wisely while you are in the world of Caesar. Don't let anyone tell you that you don't have the talent, you don't have this, that and the other. You have all that it takes because you can imagine. If you can imagine, I ask you to imagine the loveliest things in the world. Not only for yourself but for everyone you know, and see how everyone conforms to your Imagination, to what you have imagined them to be. You'll prove it.

Now before we go into the Silence, I want to remind you, if you don't come on Tuesday, this coming Sunday, on the 20th, my friend Freedom Barry...

*   *   *

Q: Neville, would you say that your realization of the light induces a greater acceptance of the wish than the image itself?

A: Ben, I wouldn't say that. We're all differently constituted and some people see easily, see visions; others see this golden liquid light; others hear...they're more attuned to listen; others can touch, but they can't see, and yet feel it so vividly. You can use any medium that will make the thing seem real, but just a simple imaginal act, without see it, without conjuring the light, without even touching it, trusting implicitly in God, knowing that God is doing it. God is your own Imagination. Don't put any barriers in the art of praying. Let no one tell you there's a special place to do it, a special time, special diet, all these things, forget them! Told the story, when Peter said, "I cannot eat the unclean thing," and the voice said, "Peter, slay and eat. For that which I have cleansed I have cleansed" (Acts 10:13). Then he said (Paul is speaking), "I know and I am persuaded by the Lord Christ Jesus that there is nothing unclean in itself; but anyone who sees anything to be unclean, *to him* it is unclean. (Rom. 14:14).

I noticed in today's TV news that after these hundreds and hundreds of years of self-restraint concerning diet, in this month of Lent, and through the year for that matter, they're going to modify it. It's no longer a sin to eat meat, no longer a sin to do the things that were so sinful over the centuries. They should have read the Book of Corinthians before they passed this little silly law, that food will not commend us to God; that you're no worse off if you do not eat and no better off if you do. That's in Corinthians (1 Cor. 8:8). Somebody had an ulcer or something, and he imposed it upon all people. He had the authority to do it. You see, all *man-made* religions—and you can name them by those which have rituals and external ceremonies—they must be superimposed from without. True Christianity must grow from within, must; can't impose it. It unfolds like a flower within you. Then you go back into the ancient scripture for confirmation of the experience that you've had. That's real religion. Christianity is nothing more than the fulfillment of Judaism, and when it's fulfilled by the tree taking on all the blossoms and bearing the fruit, it's the fruit of these experiences.

Q: Neville, you spoke of taking the Bible literally. Is it true that the characters in the Bible, except for Jesus Christ, are states and stages of man's consciousness, not men who lived?

A: They are eternal *spiritual* states of the soul through which the soul must pass. And when you meet them, strangely enough you know them, and you are *before* them.

Q: When you speak in your book of the disciples...

A: Aspects of the mind.

Q: Aspects of the mind, exactly. Well then, the other applies...

A: Also applies to Jesus Christ. The story of Jesus Christ is an acted parable which everyone one day will experience as fact. The first verse of the 3rd chapter of Galatians tells you that: "...before whose eyes Jesus Christ was publically *portrayed* as crucified" (verse 1). ___(??) picture...before whose eyes...the character now is publicly portrayed, do you think he's feeling the pain? He's playing a part, telling a story in the form of a parable. Man has taken the parable and began to make idols of it, and worshipped an outside God. As I said earlier, in a way he is the divine reporter testifying to that which is of infinite concern of men, for the test of a ___(??) Jesus is the Spirit of prophecy. He is called the first witness, the faithful witness, the first born of the dead. But it was not what man thought the Spirit of that stone would be. He brings the Spirit of the stone. The resurrection is not from the sepulcher; resurrection is, while man is walking the street, out of the only stone, which is his skull.

Q: Then he stops working from effects and starts with cause?

A: He simply presents from experience the true interpretation of scripture… and they reject him. So they said he was rejected. That testimony is not what they expected, and there is nothing more difficult in this world than to change a fixed idea. So man has been conditioned from the time he was a child to believe a story as the priesthoods of the world have told it, and that's a false…it's not so at all. But you try to persuade someone to rearrange their concept of this eternal story. The birth is as I have described it. David, the sum of all the generations of men and their experiences, is as I have described it.

That experience of father-son is just as I have described it; I haven't added to it or modified it. But who—believing what they believe concerning David as an historical character who lived a thousand years B.C.—would take my interpretation?

Q: (inaudible)

A: If I understand your question, I would not say that any instrument made by man, the microscope or any instrument, could detect the spiritual side of scripture. I have had people bring me x-rays, trying to convince me that the child is seen in the brain. I saw these x-rays. What are you going to do with a person like that? He's trying to convince you scientifically. It's not so. The child is a *sign* of the birth, just a sign. Read the story carefully, "And this shall be a *sign* unto you, you shall find a babe wrapped in swaddling clothes and lying in a manger" (Luke 2:12). I say, lying on the floor, the very lowest point. He's wrapped in swaddling clothes, the only exposure is arms and his head, neck, and all of this concealed with swaddling clothes. But you're told in scripture, when they asked for a sign, *this* shall be the sign…and you shall find a babe wrapped in swaddling clothes. Well, my Lord, every day thousands of babies are born, and hospitals wrap them in a little cloth, but that's not *the* babe. So the wise men come, and they find exactly what the angel said. It's a true story… but true of everyone when he's born from above.

Q: Have you ever seen the energy in our mind…

A: Don't try to locate it spatially. You actually feel the reality of what you are doing, but don't say it must be here in your skull, for the skull of which I speak isn't this one, and yet it is a skull. If you dropped dead this very moment and you requested cremation, that skull will turn to dust. But I tell you, you will still be in "the skull" and very much the being that you are.

Q: In explaining it to children, you almost have to get down to…

A: I find that they're very easy to reach before others reach them. It's when they're reached by others…(tape ends).

SUMMARY: THE ETERNAL PLAN

2/22/66

___(??) that we may remember what I've tried to say through the months, or years for that matter, because we so quickly forget, and if we aren't constantly reminded, off we go into all kinds of blind alleys.

Since 1959 I have been in the unique position to share with you God's plan of salvation. I did not know it before. I knew his law, taught it, practiced it, tried to live by it, and for years helped hundreds and hundreds to change their world to make it conform to they dreams. But in July, I can say with Paul to me this grace was given: to preach and to make known to all men what is the plan of the mystery hidden for ages in God. But it's such an unusual plan, it's so *unlike* what men expected that from here to the East Coast and north I still find the resistance that has been found throughout the centuries. It's not what man was looking for. He thought of some entirely different savior. He didn't see a *plan* of salvation; he saw a savior outside of himself, not a plan. So I can also say with Paul, to me he has revealed his mystery, "the mystery of his will, according to his purpose, which he set forth in Christ as a plan for the fullness of time" (Eph.1:9, RSV).

Well, Christ of scripture is not a Christ of any little secular history, it's the cosmic Christ. It is the Christ *in you* that has made you alive. Christ in you is the hope of glory (Col.1:26,27). In this Christ the plan is concealed. It is in this Christ that the plan will unfold, and when it unfolds you will stand amazed, awestruck, but there is no other interpretation to the unfolding of the plan. You will see why others resist it, because it's not what you expected. But because you've been here over the months, and some over the years, you are at least witnesses in a sense, because you can say, I heard it said and I trust him. Well, I promise you, you will be able to be a witness from some internal experience, where you can say "I heard of thee with the hearing of the ear"—"I heard him say" that's the lesser revelation—"but now my eye sees thee" (Job42:5)—now I have experienced it. So you will say with Job, "I have heard of thee with the hearing of the ear, but now my eye sees thee." And this comes always at the end of the journey. Then you don't argue the point, you simply tell it, you tell it to everyone. Some will hear it, believe you, and others will reject it. It's so difficult to change man's misunderstanding of scripture and put it back upon track after you have been given the plan. So he said, to me this grace was given—for what purpose?—to preach and to make all men see what is the plan. Here is a *plan* of the mysteries, which has been hidden for ages in God. And then comes the plan unfolding in you, and then you share it with the world.

So here in this last week I want to remind you of this eternal plan. Not to omit his law, his law is perfectly marvelous: you can be anything you want to be in this world by applying his law if you bear in mind that at all times men and women are only in states. A man is in the state of poverty. The being occupying the state of poverty must express poverty; but you need not continue in that state. The man occupying the state of being wealthy must express wealth; he need not continue in that state. But wealth and poverty and all these things are simply states, and men pass through them and leave the state behind, as you and I pass through a city and leave the city behind. To say that the city through which I passed ceases to be because I've gone through it and I'm no longer in it, is just as silly as to say a state through which I have passed has ceased to be because I no longer occupy it. I occupy poverty and pass on if I am so inclined or I know how to do it, but poverty remains forever, it's a state. Foolishness remains forever. Hate remains forever. All these things remain forever. You can hear this law for years and years, and suddenly, if you're not awake, you fall into a state of hate, and it becomes so natural to you. You will find people who actually tell you trying to support their concepts of why you should hate, and use the book of books to support it. Let me remind you the Bible has not a thing to do with secular history; it's *sacred* history, Israel's sacred history which comes to climax and fulfillment in the unfolding of this plan which is hidden in Christ in you. When it begins to unfold, it always unfolds in the very end of the journey.

So tonight you keep in mind the eternal law based purely upon states. Blake could say, "I do not consider the wise or the just or the wicked"—and you could name all the states—"that men falling into these states are in supreme states, but simply states of the sleep which the soul may fall into in its deadly dreams of good and evil when it leaves paradise following the serpent." This serpent is simply God himself. This is the great drama, an eternal drama, of the descent and ascent of one presence and that presence is God. We are told "It has been told us" or rather "It has been taught us from the primal state that he which is was wished until he were." Now put that down, it's a law. Although Shakespeare said it it's based upon an eternal principle. God's first urge was a wish: Let us make man in our image, in our likeness. There's not one word in scripture where he ever changed that plan. So that "Let us make man" man is part of the eternal structure of the universe, and here is a presence now who exchanges his divine form for that of man. So God becomes man that man may become God.

So here, he actually exchanges his divine form. In fact, the word "assume" and the word "form" as used in scripture in this second chapter of Philippians, it means "mode of existence." He exchanged his mode of existence where his creative power was at the nth degree, and he gave it all up to assume the limitations of a man. The same creative power but keyed so low it is as though it were not. And so a mode of existence called man...so in becoming man he isn't pretending he's man, he actually exchanged his infinite power to take upon himself this limitation, and now he is man. But housed within himself called in scripture Jesus Christ is the plan of his own redemption. But when he redeems himself in you, he is individualized *as* you. You are individualized in that unfolding plan, and may I tell you, you tend forever towards ever greater and greater individualization. There is no ultimate absorption in deity; you are individualized, but it is God. In other words, all of us, think of the unnumbered billions all completely individualized and still all God, all exercising this enormous creative power that is God. And it starts with the unfolding plan as described and dramatized for us in the gospel. The gospel is the mystery. Man tries to give it an interpretation that you and I would give the interpretation of *a* man's life on Earth.

Now I say this for a purpose...and I think my friend who is here tonight would allow the use of her conversation with me. No one knows her. I've known her for twenty-odd years in New York City. She would come all the way from her home in Jersey to my lectures in New York City. She knows this law; she's made every effort to live by it. We are close friends. She's now made out here her home. And yet she can be so diverted. I stood startled and amazed after the conversation. She's here tonight. I ask you not to be embarrassed for no one knows you, no one but the speaker and his wife. She could be so carried away because of some person who claims he is teaching what I am teaching. As she said over the phone, "It's just like you, Neville. He uses the Bible and shows in the Bible where all the things that are now taking place are in the Bible." The Bible hasn't a thing to do with this country, with Russia, with China, with the pope, with any of these things whatsoever. The Bible is Israel's *sacred* history. And when they use the Bible, God's word, his plan of salvation, to support a hate campaign...I said the minute you get the hate that's *not* the Bible at all, that's not the plan of salvation. I tell you from experience God is *love*! If anyone tries to show me in scripture that I am called upon to hate a certain ism or a certain race of people or a certain this, then turn your back on them. They don't know, they're blind, blind…if they're leaders they're blind leaders of the blind. But when it comes from one that you love, one that you've known for twenty years.

Seeing how I feel this night when I'm closing to make it so clear to you that no one can divert you, that they can't turn you aside into these blind alleys and throw you into these cesspools (for that's what they are). God wears every garment. It doesn't matter what pigment—the whitest skin, the blackest skin, the yellowest skin—all these are garments that God wears. He actually became man. And may I tell you, these garments, not one is progressive from one to the other, they are eternal parts of the eternal structure of the universe. And God actually buried himself in these garments and he's transforming, individualizing himself. You say "I am," that's God. But when you say "I am" you have a peculiar, wonderful feeling of individuality about it. Even if you have…this very night you suffer from amnesia, there's still that sense of knowing that I am. It is something that's different from any other presence in the world; that's your individual being and it's forever.

Now let us go back and make it clear though I've said it time and time again—and don't think I am repeating it just to repeat it. I repeat it because it's necessary. You can't tell this story too often. I'm speaking this night as I have since July of 1959 from experience. I am one with Paul in that statement, "To me this grace has been given." Grace is God's gift of himself to man. God gave me himself when he unfolded himself in me. When he resurrected, that's the beginning of the New Age. I had no concept of what the resurrection was all about. I was taught it, raised as a Christian what it was, and I thought it meant a *mass* rising of all of us at some future time. The resurrection takes place not at the end but during man's history. While you are seated here, while you sleep this night, while you walk home or walk the street, it could happen then, and you are resurrected. Not the crowd; it's a unique individual act. That's the beginning of the New Age. It's the purpose of the whole Creation, when God completes his wish: Let us make man in our image.

Well now, what is that image? Wait and see. You aren't going to see it with mortal eye; you *can't* see it with mortal eye. Strangely enough, when the resurrection does take place, you see the chrysalis out of which you came. It's this, you see the body, but you the being you don't see any mirror reflecting you. And when those come to witness this event, come into your world as men, they don't see you. They can't see you, because now you are wearing the form of the invisible God. They see the evidence of what has taken place, but they don't see you, for you are wearing a divine body. It's not anything that man as man could ever see, so don't ask for a drawing of it. Don't ask for a picture of it. You remain invisible to all on this level; something entirely different has taken place *in* you. God became you in the true sense of the word, and in this act *you* became God. Yet you return and pick up once more that little garment, and you wear it, and you preach it. As you're told in Ephesians, the grace was given to you to preach, and then to make all men see what is the mystery. This mystery has been hidden for ages in God, but you preach the *plan* of the mystery. The mystery mustn't be kept as a secret; it's simply a truth that is mysterious in character. But in itself, don't hide it, tell it, tell it to the whole vast world. And those who have heard me, whether they believe me or not that's irrelevant, it's entirely up to them. But at least you do hear from one who's speaking from experience, he's not theorizing. I am not speculating. I am telling you the story as recorded in scripture, but not as interpreted by the priesthoods of the world…that's not the story.

So here tonight, for those who want the law, you'll get it. The law is simple. There are infinite states, but infinite states, good, bad and indifferent, and they're all part of the eternal structure of the universe. You are a pilgrim moving. You wittingly or unwittingly go into a state. Someone can get into an argument with you and lead you out into a state, a state of horror. They can present the most wonderful pictures and show you and give you reasons for it and lead you into that cesspool; they can do it. I ask you to remember in every state, it's only a state. You find yourself in it and it's not love, it's not what you want, get out of it, no matter how wise he was or she was who suggested your entrance into that state. They'll do it…they're doing it morning, noon and night. But I ask you who come here, pick out noble states, yes, states of security, nothing wrong with that, states of love, states of dignity, all these wonderful states, and *occupy* them.

How do I know I'm occupying the state? I simply look mentally at my world, and my world that I see mentally should reflect the state I'm occupying. If I don't see it reflected on the screen of my mind, I'm not in it. I always have a frame of reference, so look at my friends, do they see me as they must see me were I the man that I would like to be? Well then, I'm in the state. But bear in mind, you can occupy a state in the twinkle of an eye and get out of that state just as fast. Well, how do I know that I'm in a state that I would call home? How do I know it? That state to which I most constantly return constitutes my home. Like my apartment here, I will go out and remain out for hours, and I'm going to leave it for months, but it's a home to which I can return. When I return, the home is waiting for me; it's home, I'm not putting my things in storage. So that place to which I return most constantly, as I return to my apartment day after day, that constitutes my home.

So the same thing is true of these states. If I find myself returning to a state, it feels comfortable, it feels easy, well, then that's my home, my spiritual home for a moment. I can remain in it as I remain in the apartment. I've been here for six years, I don't like moving around, but I may come back and close it up. But until I come back it remains open, that is, open to me when I return, so that constitutes my home here in the world of Caesar. So what constitutes my home in these wonderful eternal states?—the state to which I most constantly return.

So do I find myself returning, say, to the state of love, the state of teaching, the state of affluence, or the state of feeling sorry for myself? There are those who actually all day long they delight in feeling sorry for themselves. They go out on a job knowing they aren't going to be liked, they know it. So when they are not liked they wonder what's wrong with the people round about me? They're only reflecting that constant state that I have been occupying. If I don't get out of that state, no matter where I go in this world I can't find anything other than what I found when I left the so-called physical thing behind me. I can go from here to the ends of the earth, but I carry the state. I don't leave a state here; these states are ever present. Right standing here, I can throw myself into two dozen states in the twinkle of an eye, one after the other. By entertaining a thought, occupying it and feeling it I'm in the state. But if I'm doing it just to experiment, all well and good. If I don't know and I put myself into a state and remain in it, I'm going to bear its fruit. I am that germ that enters the state as a little germ enters the egg, and I fructify it, and then it has to bear its fruit.

So here we have infinite states. You can select the state you want. Your age hasn't a thing to do with it, your background hasn't a thing to do with it; you're only occupying a state. You will bear the most glorious fruit if it's a lovely state. But even then you don't own the thing, you're simply creating them, pushing them out. They're all yours because you're in the state; when you leave the state they're gone. If I said say to Rose, Billy Rose, if I asked him just before he died if he was conscious, "I've just seen a hundred and seventy thousand shares of A.T.&T. and they are all marked with your name, who owns them?" he would have said to me, "They're mine, they're my 170,000 shares." Ask him the same question today, did he ever own them? While he was in the state he had it all, but he left it behind him, didn't take it with him, his $25 million. But he was in a state in the world of Caesar that could grow $25 million. But you and I don't own anything; we simply are in states.

While we are here we can enjoy the state. So all you do is simply occupy the state. Tonight when you go to bed see that you're in the right state. For you have the unbroken hours of sleep, where before you go into the deep, to occupy the right state. You fructify it in that interval…because in the course of a day you are diverted so often from one state to another. But you can always tell the home you live in as far as states are concerned by the frequency of occupancy. How often do you go back to it? Do you feel comfortable when you are in it? Well then, that's the state.

There is a gentleman in this audience tonight...he told me this story Sunday night when we both heard Freedom Barry. Now here was his technique. He desired to dispose of his home. He and his mother live in this home, and they didn't know where to go...they've been in the home all these years. Inwardly he actually put himself into a state, just a state of having really what he had, and yet he disposed of it and all these things, within his mind. Well, it was an impossible thing, you would say, in this world of Caesar. How could you be in a place that you sold? He loved it, it seemed big for the two of them, and then he tells me his story. He sold the house for $65,000 in cash, and then the sale carries this with it: he and his mother will remain in the house rent free until she makes her exit from this world. The present owner will pay all taxes, all upkeep, all insurance and the gardener. Their only expense while living in this place is to pay their personal insurance on furniture, clothing, jewelry, and so on. $65,000 in cash and still living in the same home with an agreement to remain there to the end of his mother's life, rent free. Everything is possible in God's world. But the average person would have said that couldn't have happened, therefore, I wouldn't occupy such a stupid state...I am putting God to the extreme test. We don't believe that all things are possible to God.

So I say to everyone here, don't put any limitations on the power in you, though he sleeps. For Christ in you is sound asleep until the very end when he begins to awake. The signs set up in the very beginning are all contained within him as the plan of deliverance, the plan of salvation. Let me quickly give you this plan. I've told it to you time and again, but do listen to it carefully; it's going to happen to you. The only way that that story of the gospel will unfold is in this way, there is no other way. You will find yourself at the end of the Book of Luke, and now he's resurrected, and he turns to those who followed him and he said, you are witnesses, you haven't yet received it but you are witnesses. In other words, he's telling that he has dramatized every act of salvation. You are witnesses to that. Now I send the Promise of the Father upon you. I send the promise of the Father upon you, but wait in the city, until you are clothed with power from on high (Luke24:49). Now he departs...the end of his physical presence...wait until you are clothed with the power from on high.

Now, what Promise of the Father is he going to send? It is said of the speaker all the promises of God have their yes in him. He doesn't pick out one and say I'm going to send that or send this, I'm going to send the Promise of the Father. The spokesman was the one who gave yes to all the promises, so he's sending himself. And when he comes, he should come again. When he comes again, he comes in an entirely different way. He came telling a story; now he comes unfolding himself *in you* to whom he told the story. His first act is the resurrection. When it's going to take place—you turn the pages over because Luke and Acts are one book—so you turn over from Luke into Acts, and here you find these words, "And suddenly a sound came from heaven like the rush of a mighty wind and it filled the whole house where they were sitting" (2:2). That's exactly how it happens.

Suddenly, you don't expect it, there's a wind that is unearthly. You can't describe that wind. This mighty wind comes upon you...you know it's a wind...that's all you entertain. Where is this cyclone coming from? Where is the origin of this hurricane? You look over from this little chrysalis out of which you've just emerged and you hear the wind, look back, and the witnesses are there to witness now the great event. The wind starts and awakens you; the awakening is your resurrection. "Awake, you sleeper, and rise from the dead" (Eph.5:14) and suddenly you begin to awake. Even while you are waking, through habit you only think in terms of one kind of waking and that is the kind of waking that you've experienced over the years that you've lived here, to discover it isn't that kind of waking at all. The wind possesses you, your whole head is vibrating...it's a tone...and all of a sudden you are awake. But you aren't on your bed, you aren't where you thought you should be, and here you are in your skull. Your skull is the sepulcher where *you* have been placed, where you have been placed as dead. And God himself entered that death's door with you, and he laid down in the skull with you and shared with you your visions through the long, long journey until you awake. When you awake, you see the linen clothes lying...this [pointing to body] that the females had woven. This was woven by a woman. And so here, this is there and you come out of the sepulcher, and no one knows how you got out. You are invisible, immortal, wearing now the divine body that no mortal eye can see.

Then comes on the heels of this, the sign of your birth into an entirely different world; the sign being the babe wrapped in swaddling clothes. Then comes the only way you will know now that you really are God who became you. There's no way in eternity that you will ever know it save in this one way: "If the son makes you free, you are free indeed" (Jn.8:36). But the *Son* has to set you free. Set who free?—set the Father free. For the Promise is made, that the man who kills the enemy of Israel, his father will be set free. So all of a sudden the Son comes and the Son calls you "Father" and you are set free. Then you really know what the temple is—you thought it was something on the outside, and all of sudden you are split, your whole body is split from top to bottom, every little segment of the spine, that backbone is split. And here you are, you're parted, as told in scripture: one went east, one went west, one moved north and south. The whole thing is split like a valley, and then at the very base of that, the blood of God. You look at it, it isn't red, it's gold, living, pulsing light; and you say within yourself I know it is myself. You also know it's your Creator and your Redeemer; therefore, if it is myself and yet my Creator, then I am myself my own creation. For in becoming me there aren't two anymore. He became me that I may become as he is. In becoming him I am the very being, so I am my own Creator and my own Redeemer. Then you ascend like a serpent; and you know the great mystery then of he who came out and descended into the drama is the same one who goes up. And he ascends as he descended…same wonderful river.

Then the whole thing is sealed at the end and that is sealed with the bodily presence of a dove who descends upon you. And you look up…before he descends he floats and hovers above you. There is no circumference; there's a transparency that has no limit, there's no circumference, infinite. You look into it, and suddenly you look up and you put out your hand, why I don't know. I raised my hand this way and he descended and lit here [pointing to his left index finger], brought him to my face and he smothered me all over my face, kissing, kissing all over my head. Then you go back and read the ancient scripture: "And he put his hand up and the dove took the finger of his hand and he brought him into the ark"

(Gen.8:9). Now you know who the ark is. That's exactly what you do. So man becomes the ark and the ark contains the whole of creation. There is nothing left outside of the ark, so you bring him right in, and he smothers you. The whole thing unfolds in a matter of three and a half years, and then it's done. Then you go and you tell it, tell it to anyone. Even if they reject it, as many will, even if they forget it in the interval and still see it in some strange earthly picture, a little child born of a woman as you and I were. That's not Christ. I'm speaking of the Cosmic Christ who is actually in every man and who awakens in every man.

So, *that* you remember. Try to remember…at least if you think of this platform, think of the one who stands on it for a moment, his words will come back. If you find yourself falling into some ditch that is horrible, think of him and his words will come back and pull you out of it. He'll pull you out, because you'll remember the plan of salvation as I myself have experienced it and then you'll be encouraged to go on; for you *must* experience this salvation. Then "the end" is upon you and you never return to this world. You've completed your journey and God's primal wish: "let us make him in my image" has been completed. You are now in the image and you are the very being. Well, who is the image of God? We're told Christ is the image of the invisible God, he is the likeness of the invisible God, therefore, who are you then? And what did he say? "I and my Father whom you call God are one. Only I know my Father and ye know not your God" (John 10:30). So, who are you then? You are one with God; *you are* God. Then you return to the mode of existence that was God's by divine right before he exchanged it and took upon himself this. But in doing this, he individualized himself as you and made you one with himself with the same creative power.

Now, we can have more time tonight for questions. Let us go into the Silence.

*   *   *

Q: I don't understand "Let us make man in *our* image."

A: Well, the word is Elohim. The first time that the word God appears in scripture in the very first verse, "In the beginning God created the heavens and the earth," that word translated God is plural, it's Elohim. So Israel's great confession of faith, which when asked what is the greatest of all the commandments, he did not mention any one of the ten. He mentioned Israel's great confession which is "Hear, O Israel, the Lord our God is one Lord" (Deut.6:4). If I put it into this language, "Hear, O Israel, the I AM our I AMs is one I AM." The word God, being pure, we use the word "our" image rather than "my." You are God, but so am I. And you do not lose your identity, neither will I, and yet we are one because we have the same Son. So all of us, the billions of us are the same Father having the same Son. So though we're individualized and tend forever towards greater and greater individuality, we still are one because God is one. You understand that?

Q: When we leave the body, where is the dream we left and the astral body?

A: First, I don't even like to use the word astral and things of that sort; that belongs to this same level. When you are out of the body, you are connected to the body by a silver cord, and you can see it pulse, and that keeps it alive.

Q: Then you're actually breathing as you...I mean are you on the bed or is it...?

A: Ina, when you get out of the body, it's only really a shell, and the body that you wear is also a shell, too. They call it desire body and they call it vital body. Call it what you will, that's not what I'm teaching. When you get out of this body and you see this body on the bed on this level, it hasn't a thing to do with that resurrection when you are invisible and see it as something completely detached and dead, something entirely detached and dead...a chrysalis out of which the butterfly has come. But that people get out of the body and go places, I'm not denying that, for

I've done it. It's not so difficult. Hasn't a thing to do with any so-called spiritual advancement, not a thing to do with it. In fact, so many of them who claim they can do it, do it at will, you talk with them and they're filled with hatred, but filled with it. They'll sit down and spend their precious time thinking of some unlovely thing of another, they do. So I don't touch it. But to say it doesn't exist is stupid, because it does exist.

Q: Does it mean anything when you awake in the morning and you have scripture on your mind?

A: To me that would be a very marvelous thing, to awake from the deep bringing back passages of God's Word. I would think it's marvelous. It would show your interest while you are seemingly gone from this sphere.

Q: In one of your books you speak of being smitten through and through. I wondered, since your resurrection from above, ah, …

A: I didn't get it, Ben.

Q: One of your books, I believe it was *The Search*, you said that you were smitten through and through by this being, and I wondered since your birth from above, were you able to have this being permeate you or vibrate through at will?

A: Did you hear the question? Since my resurrection and my birth from above, have I had the same experience that I mentioned in *The Search* where this experience I was smitten through and through by a greater self and yet myself? I have had it time and time since. To say I sit down and do it at will, Ben, no. These things come suddenly upon you. While I'm sitting at home, when I'm on my bed, and sometimes when I'm on the street it comes suddenly. But I'm in the world of Caesar.

Q: Is there some mental setting for it that you…

A: No, there isn't. In my case it always comes so suddenly, comes suddenly.

Q: You don't get any inkling…

A: No, none.

Q: Is it then the grace of God?

A: It is the grace of God! I don't sit down and conjure it, it happens suddenly.

Q: There is a book at the moment on the use of the so-called consciousness expanding drugs, what are your thoughts on these.

A: I'm not familiar with it.

Q: LSD drugs…

A: Oh, LSD drugs? I would shun them. Again, I speak from experience. My friend, a doctor, because I am mystically inclined since I was a child, he said he would like to experiment and take it with me. Aldous Huxley was going to observe the test...our reactions on tapes, but Aldous was sick that night so he couldn't come. So we had two who came with their tapes to observe and we took the maximum dose. May I tell you, it isn't what they say it is at all. It's nothing but distortion, pure distortion, of all your senses. Yes, things become alive, walls become alive, the wallpaper becomes alive. You can share an experience together. He and I shared experiences. If I said, "Look," he could tell me what I'm looking at and we could actually discuss one object as though you both saw it, and you did see it. It didn't do a thing for me other than to just put me in a peculiar state for about forty-eight hours. So I would shun it. I did it to please him.

So driving home that night...when you come out of it, you think you've been in it for days, you've only been in it for a few hours. Took it at 7:30...began to take around 8:15...and I was out by about 11:00, and I would have sworn that I was there for days. Time did differ...everything differs. Driving home every car was coming up, seemed to be going right through my brain, ___(??) ought to go this way to keep them out. Everything is coming right through your head. So the next day when you start to shave there are two of you. Do this with your hand and your hand goes down to the floor. You go this way, it's still going to the ceiling. You're completely set apart and scattered. Didn't do a thing for me that they claim. He went into convulsions; I didn't go into convulsions. Well, he is much thinner than I. I was then many, many pounds heavier than I am today. His "took" half an hour before mine did. When I saw he went back into childhood, he's my age, went right back into childhood, laughed like a child, acted like a child, and became convulsed. His laugh was a peculiar laugh. But I didn't go into that...we are different natures. But we could share similar hallucinations. I can't recommend it. I can't see where it will help anyone. But I'm always happy to ___(??), so I took it only to please him really. He took it again with Aldous. Aldous took it three or four times. I didn't get what they claimed they got. There was nothing lovely in it at all.

Q: (inaudible)

A: Well, the Promise came first and the law was given afterwards.

Q: But then who ___(??) here?

A: It's good for you. It's a creative power and why not in the world of Caesar live well, why not? Why not be creative? But as far as the Promise goes, it's grace...and grace is unearned, unmerited. ___(??) gave in the letter to the Philippians, "He who began a good work in you will bring it to completion at the day of Jesus Christ" (1:6). The plan unfolds in you, for Christ is in you. Therefore, he began it and he'll complete it. It was God's wish, "Let us make man in our image." So you're told in the 8th chapter of Romans that "the creature was made subject unto futility, not willingly but by reason of the will of him who subjected him in hope"—and what was the hope?—"that he would be set free from the bondage to corruption and obtain the glorious liberty of the sons of God" (verse 20). Well, that's going to happen, but it happens in a way no one foresaw. And therefore when it does take place, they don't believe it. It's not what they were looking for. Everyone wants a king on the outside and he doesn't come that way. He unfolds in you and you are he. That's why we are warned, don't look here or look there. If anyone should tell you there he is or here he is, don't look. It isn't there. Your leader is within you and he will unfold within you. That's the only Christ in the world.

Q: I'm not in communication because I have no understanding of "by grace." What function do you mean "by grace"?

A: Well, grace as the scripture uses it means God's gift of himself to man. It's unearned by man, it's unmerited. Men think they can earn it; they can't earn it. So they have all kinds of things they teach…do this, do that to appease God, and then, of course, he will send the Promise upon you sooner.

Q: (inaudible)

A: No, I'm a man just as you are, with all the restrictions and limitations of a man. If I judged myself, I could honestly say I'd never find myself worthy to have received the grace that I have received; for I am still a man and I am in the world of Caesar. I'm very much a man. ___(??), therefore that's one of the ___(??) that differs completely from the world of men in the world of Caesar. But no one can earn it.

Q: (inaudible)

A: We're coming up now to what is called the grand crucifixion. The story on trial…truth stands in the presence of reason. Reason questions the embodiment of truth, and reason tells truth, do you not know and you will not answer me?…"Do you not know I have the power to set you free or to crucify you?" and truth answers, "You have no power over me were it not given to you from above; therefore he who delivered me into your hands has the greater sin" (John19:10). He see's the play. Pilate doesn't see it as a play. He thinks he can exercise his will to set him free or to crucify him; and the one who is dramatizing the part makes known to the wise man, you have no power were it not given to you from above.

This is the most fantastic thing when you see it from on high. Because you come upon a scene just like this and suddenly you know it is taking place here, and you freeze an activity within yourself, and everyone here stands still. They aren't even breathing; they are dead, as though they're made of marble, everyone, no matter how vast the crowd. And then you release that activity which you had arrested in here and they all become active again. Where is the drama taking place? A bird in flight if arrested should fall, shouldn't it? If it's walking on the floor and it stands still, it doesn't go through the floor, but if in flight and the flight is arrested it should fall. I've arrested birds…they didn't fall. A waitress walking and I arrested her, she walked not. Diners dining, I arrested them, they dined not. I did it not by talking to them or persuading them, I did it all in here. I felt it here in my head. I arrested that activity and what I perceived stood still because I just did it in here. It frightens mortal man when he sees the drama as it really is being played…entirely different.

Until Friday.

NEVILLE'S THOUGHTS IF LEAVING PERMANENTLY

2/25/66

___(??) closing night for awhile and I've been thinking through the day, rather days, what should I say were I leaving permanently? What would I like everyone to remember? Well, these are my thoughts to leave with you things I've told you over the years. It is God's purpose to give himself to all of us, to each of us, as if there were no other in the world, just God and you, God and I. Believe this and the most unbelievable story in the world which is the Bible becomes possible and believable.

And it is the Son who makes us sure that it is really true. You dwell upon it: "In many and various ways he spoke to our fathers through the prophets, but in these last days he has spoken through his Son" (Heb.1:1). The fathers spoken of...*we* are the fathers. You didn't begin in the womb of your mother and you are not going to end in the grave. You've been coming a long, long while; it's a long journey. The fathers spoken of are right here this night. And, in many ways he spoke to the fathers. You're told in the Book of Numbers he spoke to us through the medium of a dream, he spoke through the medium of a vision; he is still speaking through the medium of a dream and that of a vision (12:6). The Bible recognizes only one source of dream and vision and that source is God. A daydream does not differ from a night dream save in this one little aspect—in the night dream we are servants of our attention, it leads us anywhere. In the daydream, we should be masters and guide it where we want it. If you remember that in my absence, you can take this world of Caesar and make it conform to your dreams.

A lady wrote me, I got the letter yesterday, and in this letter she said she sat in her dining room and she was reading my book *The Power of Awareness*, the chapter on attention. In it I give her a certain exercise where you take the entire day, just one day, from the last event at night to the first in the day, and you try to hold your attention and put it back, move it back, one event after the other going backwards. It may seem easy but try it. She said, "I failed many times, but finally I succeeded in going back, event after event." You don't change it, this is not revision, this is only an exercise to concentrate the mind where you want it. So she said, "I finally succeeded in taking it all the way back to the first event of the day, when my eyes fell upon spots, ugly spots on this lovely carpet of ours that leads from the kitchen to the dining room. We had tried to remove these spots using all kinds of things, things that were suggested, but they are still there. I closed my eyes and I wondered what it would be like if this carpet today looked just as though it were new when we put it down, and so I just simply imagined it new, clean and said thank you. And that was it…I completely forgot."

In a few days the phone rang. There's a phone upstairs and a phone downstairs. She was downstairs in the bedroom. The phone downstairs unless you are in the bedroom you can't hear it. It's a very, very small bell so as not to disturb, so much so that her husband who was upstairs did not hear it. A total stranger soliciting business over the phone asked if he could come around and give an estimate for cleaning rugs. Well, she said, "These calls come through all the time and at first my impulse was to say no, but on second thought I said why not? I accepted his suggestion. So he came, he cleaned it, and the rug today is just as though it were put down for the first time." So what I want you to remember from that little scene: imagining creates reality. "Man is all Imagination and God is Man and exists in us and we in him; the eternal body of Man is the Imagination, and that is God himself" (Blake, *Annotations to Berkeley*). Every time you exercise your Imagination lovingly or unlovingly that is what you are doing to God. Use it lovingly, for I tell you from experience God is love. These are not idle words.

So this is what I want you to remember. We were told, the day will come the Holy Spirit will come upon you and lead you into all knowledge, and bring to your remembrance all the things that I have told you; and now I tell you *before* it takes place that when it does take place, you may believe that I am he (John14:26). This is not a being on the outside of you talking to you; it's your own, own being. When it takes place it takes place in you, and you will know that you yourself are the being you formerly thought to be God as something on the outside. Now what would he tell you, what would he show you? There is a rabbinical principle that what is not written in scripture is nonexistent. So he leads you into *all* things; he isn't taking you outside of scripture. He isn't showing you what's taking place now in the world of Caesar. This will all vanish as though it never took place. He will not show you any part of human history in this secular world, but he will show you the eternal truth of God's Word. When he shows it to you, he takes you through it as your own personal experience.

Every word of scripture is true and you will experience it. You will know how true it is. You will experience it in the very depths of your soul and it is literally true in depth. On the surface it doesn't make sense. But he will come and when he comes and moves you, he moves you only into truth and truth is scripture. Here is a simple, simple statement: He moved triumphantly into Jerusalem. What a gay, festive occasion! Who would have thought it would end in the crucifixion? That experience you will have. And may I tell you, don't be afraid, it is joy from beginning to end, from the very beginning. Then you will experience the 42nd Psalm, "And I led them in procession, in a gay procession to the house of God" (verse 4). You will lead them. It was the most festive occasion. Everything about it was one of joy. And yet the Psalm itself is one of sadness, "Why is my soul cast down?" He turns to memory, trying to get memory to bring back something to support a joy.

Well, this is what you're going to have. You, too, will lead a crowd. May I tell you, a crowd which you've never seen before, an enormous crowd, as vast as your eye can see; a sea of human beings all clothed in their gay attire and it's festive. A voice will ring out and you will hear the voice and everyone will hear it: "And God walks with them." You will turn to your side and there, if it's a duplicate of my experience, it will be a woman, a very attractive woman in her thirties in Arab robes. She becomes the voice of questioning the voice and she said, "If God walks with us, where is he?" and the voice answered, "At your side." She in the crowd takes it literally so she turns to her left. I am standing at her left and she looks into my face and she becomes hysterical it strikes her so funnily. For the voice said "At your side" and she was questioning the statement "God walks with them." Then she said, "What? Is Neville God?" and the voice rang out that all could hear, "Yes, in the act of waking." Then the same voice heard only by me from the depths of my soul, and this is what it said, "I laid myself down within you to sleep, and as I slept I dreamed a dream. I dreamed…" and then I knew the completed sentence and I became so excited, so emotionally moved that I didn't wait for the completed words, I knew he is dreaming that he's me.

At that moment I experienced a memory of the crucifixion, for I was on the outside of this enormous crowd and then I was sucked into this body. This became a vortex, this a vortex, my head a vortex, my right side a vortex, and my two feet, the soles of my feet, were vortices. Here were these five, these six vortices nailed to this cross and I knew *this* was the crucifixion. And may I tell you, the crucifixion far from being a sad event it is sheer ecstasy! I can't put into words the thrill that was mine that night when I experienced the crucifixion! You and I were all crucified with God. As we are told in scripture, we give all and we bear on our bodies the death of Christ. "If we have been crucified with him, if we have union with him in a death like his, we shall certainly be united with him in a resurrection like his" (Rom.6:5). So the crucifixion is over and was joy beyond measure. The resurrection is taking place. It has begun...the whole thing is in process now...and one by one we are being resurrected. But all have been crucified with God.

So you will experience scripture. When the Holy Spirit comes upon you, he leads you into all truth...and what is not written in scripture is nonexistent, therefore, it's a lie. He's not leading you into what science today knows about the heavens; they will pass away. All we think we know now about outer space it will all pass away, everything we think we know and we've proved it, because imagining creates reality. We can take the lie of lies and prove it, but it isn't true. God's Word is true and when you've experienced it, you know the whole of truth was confined right here. And the purpose of it all is to awaken all of us, every one of us; not one will fail because he became all. God became as we are that we may be as he is. God became man that man may become God. And that is the entire story.

So I tell you this for a reason. Our memories are short and some very wise man will come into your sphere and in no time lead you astray with his wonderful, wonderful words and he knows so much. He can tell you all the things to lead you astray and you go into blind alleys. Try to remember these words. Try to remember that the whole vast Bible is all about you, as told you in the 40th Psalm: "In the volume of the book it is all about me" (verse 7; Heb.10:7). He didn't realize it and so now as he searches scripture, as the Spirit moves him, possesses him, and takes him through these experiences that are recorded in scripture: the final revelation is always by the Son.

So let me repeat, it is his purpose as we are told in Isaiah, "As I have planned it, so shall it be, and as I have purposed, so shall it stand...and my will shall not turn back until I have accomplished and executed the intents of my mind. In the latter days you will understand it clearly" (14:24; Jer.23:20). In the latter days he reveals himself to you through his only Son. Here is a universal language that all can understand. I could tell you from now to the ends of time that you and I are one because God is one and God became us; and when he completes his work in us, there aren't two, there's only one, and it's God. You haven't lost your identity, you haven't lost your individuality, and yet you're God. I can tell you that in words and tell you that I know it, but how to persuade you that you and I are one when you are so completely individualized and I am so completely individualized? There is no way in eternity that anyone will know the unity of being save through the Son, but no one.

So he said, "In many and various ways God spoke of old to our fathers by the prophets, but in these last days he speaks unto us through his Son" (Heb.1:1). So his Son comes; he only has one Son. If he's a father, there's a son somewhere, bring him. What person in this world, 1966, would believe in any way that they are related to David of biblical fame? Yes, Haile Selasie claims he is descended from Solomon, and Solomon of scripture, son of David. But they don't understand these mysteries. Anyone here, would you ever include David in your world, one who is supposed to have lived 1,000 B. C.?" Did it ever occur to you that the day will come you will know you have no beginning, you have no origin, no father, no mother, because you're God, no genealogy? And that David is the very essence, the quintessence of all the generations of humanity and their experiences brought forth and personified as a single youth? That's David...all the generations of humanity, all of man's experiences, fused into a single whole, and that whole personified as the eternal youth that is God's begotten Son (Ps.2:7).

The day will come you will look into the face of David and David will call you Father. Well, I can call you Father but you wouldn't believe it. But when David calls you Father, there is no uncertainty. You don't have to question the honesty of the words of the lad, you know, you've always known. Here he stands before you. I think I know that I am the father of my daughter Vicki. I've never doubted for a second that I am the father of my son that I call Neville, never doubted for a moment. But when it comes to David, there is no uncertainty. You don't have to ask anyone, there is an innate knowing that you are the father and he is your son. In the fulfillment of scripture and the Lord is looking for David, the 89th Psalm, and then the Lord cries out, "I have found David. He has cried unto me, 'Thou art my father, my God, and the Rock of my salvation'" (verses 20, 26). He finds what he sets up in the beginning as a plan, as a purpose. He's brought to climax and fulfillment, and here he finds his Son. He went through all the generations of humanity, all the suffering, as told us in Isaiah: "I've tried you in the furnaces of affliction. For my own sake I did it, for my own sake, for how should my *name* be profaned? My glory I will not give to another" (Is.48:10). And so to come forward as Father and there's only one Father, only one Son. In the 2nd Psalm, "Thou art my son; today I have begotten thee" (verse 7). Now you take the Book of Hebrews, considered next to the Book of John the most profound in the New Testament. Every chapter, almost every verse, he supports by some scriptural passage—by scriptural passage I mean the Old Testament—and asks all these questions, "To what angel did he ever say, 'Thou art my son, today I have begotten thee'" (Heb.1:5). He starts it that way, and all the passages are related to David and he's speaking of the cosmic Christ.

So I tell you, everything in scripture you are going to experience. I don't care who you are; I don't care what you have done. In his infinite mercy he has hidden from us our violence and the horrors to which we have been subjected and the horrors that we ourselves initiated. But in the very end it's all vindicated, everything is forgiven, but everything; for it took all these furnaces of experience to bring out David. And so in the end, I tell you, you, regardless of your present sex...for these are only garments that God wears. He's not a man in the sense not a male, not a female, he's God and God wears these garments. So I say to my own mother who is not in this sphere anymore, I say to my wife, to my daughter, you are the father of David, I know I am the father of David, therefore you and I are one. In the world of Caesar we are three. Here you are my wife, you are my daughter, I am your father and your husband, and yet in the depth of our being we are one. And the only proof of the oneness of us, of the unity of our being, is our one Son...and he calls you Father. There is no uncertainty in you when you see him. He has already called me and there's no uncertainty.

So these things I would have you remember. Dwell upon them. In the world of Caesar you can have exactly what you want. It's based upon this simple, simple principle: "Whatever you desire,"—no limit to that statement—"when you pray believe that you have received it and you will" (Mark 11:24). Well, if I must believe that I've received what at the moment reason denies and my senses deny, how could I come to any other conclusion than that imagining creates reality? I can't reach any other conclusion. You mean, that I want something now intensely and all I need do to bring it to pass as a concrete objective fact is to persuade myself that I have it? The secret then is how to persuade self. But if I find that secret...as the lady sitting at her table just simply closed her eyes, saw the carpet clean, as perfect as it was when she bought it, and she felt so completely relieved she could say "thank you" and then forgot it. A total stranger, drumming up business...then she said to me, "There are two telephone numbers in the book; the one he called is the second one. The second belongs downstairs and the bell is almost, well, you can't hear it." She happened at that moment to be in the room. Were she not there, she wouldn't have heard it, but she was there when it rang. And the impulse would be no, why must I be disturbed? For the phone rings like this all the time, people soliciting some work in your home. Then she said, "Yes, come over and take a little survey of the place and clean the rug" which he did. She said, "The thing is just as new as the day it was put down."

So I say to everyone here, try to remember these words that I have told you. Every one is true. I've been telling you what I *know* from experience; I'm not speculating, I'm not theorizing. I am not an erudite person, I just tell you what I know and my knowledge is based upon what I have experienced. What a man has experienced he knows more thoroughly than he knows anything else in this world, or than he can know that same thing in any other way. If I know it because I trust someone who told me, well, it's hearsay. But when I know it because I've experienced it, well, then I know it. If the whole vast world rose in opposition, it would make no difference to me. I know scripture is true. I know Jesus Christ is the reality of every child born of woman. That he is related—not related, well, like a brother, sister—he is the actual being, the inner being of everyone in the world, but he's asleep. But contained within him is the plan of awakening. When he awakens, you are God, for you are he, regardless of what you have done in this world prior to that awakening.

So in my absence...how long it will be I haven't the slightest idea. I'm going...I did buy a roundtrip ticket but the return is undated. There is no need to date it...I'll come when I feel like it. But in that interval, people get tired, they move away, they hear of some wise, wonderful person and they go to hear him, or go to hear her, and then they lead them into all kinds of strange blind alleys, all in the name of religion. You dwell upon these words. He didn't become the other, so "If anyone says, 'Look, here is Christ!' don't believe him' or 'There he is!' don't believe him" (Mark 13:21)—why?—"For when he does appear we shall be like him" (1John 3:2). Does he look like you? You will never know Christ who is not the Christ who is looking just like you. So his second return is when he unfolds in you all that is recorded of him in scripture so you know *you* are Jesus Christ. Jesus Christ as told in scripture is the Father. He is the father of God's only begotten son, who is David. If you want the scriptural passages, the 14th of John: And one said to him, "O Lord, show us the Father and we'll be satisfied. He said, I have been so long with you and yet you do not know me, Philip? He who has seen me has seen the Father; how then can you say, 'Show us the Father'" (verse 8)?

Now comes a passage, and he has just explained the difference between this age and that age, two entirely different ages, where this age we generate and procreate, we're born, and keep it up over and over. And so those who did not believe that man ever resurrects asked him, to trip him up, he said: "Master, Moses in the law says that if a man marries and he dies leaving no offspring, his brother should marry the widow and raise up children for his brother. Well, there were seven brothers and there was this first one who married her. He died; he left no offspring. The second married her, he died, no offspring. The third, the fourth and finally the seven married her, all died, leaving no children. In the end she died. Tell me, whose wife is she in the resurrection? And he answered, "The sons of this age marry and are given in marriage"—well, that Greek phrase in other Bibles that I have at home reads "the sons of this age procreate, they generate and they are born—"But those who are accounted worthy to attain to *that* age and to the resurrections from the dead"—he looks upon this whole age as "the dead"—"they neither marry nor are they given in marriage, for they cannot die any more" (Luke 20:28-36). Two entirely different ages!

Now he's discussing that and now comes a questions he raises that is not related to anything in that chapter. So he turns to the same crowd who questions, he said, "What think ye of the Christ? Whose son is he?" and they answer, "The son of David." He replies, "Why then does David in the spirit call him Father?" The word is Adonai, translated "my Lord," but in the ancient world every son referred to his father as "my Lord." So he called him, my Lord. "If he calls him my Lord, how then can he be David's son? And they asked him no more questions" (Mat.22:42). He is telling you he is God the Father, and God's only begotten son has called him "my Father" in fulfillment of the 89th Psalm. For he said, "I have come to fulfill scripture; scripture must be fulfilled in me" (Luke22:37). "And beginning with Moses and the law and the prophets and the Psalms, he interpreted to them in all the scriptures the things concerning himself" (Luke24:27). That's all that he came to do.

So your only purpose here while you play the game that you must play is to fulfill scripture. Everyone will fulfill scripture and prove the truth of the Word of God. In the meanwhile, while we are fulfilling scripture let us use God's law wisely, lovingly, and live as graciously as we desire to live in this world. You can be...everyone can do it. I invite you to try it and make it just as simple a thing as my friend did with the rock. As the little girl (whose father is here) what she did with her trip, just simply closed her eyes, communed with self, in harmony with the 4th Psalm (verse 4), and within herself she thanked him for the fulfillment of what she wanted. Then in a matter of moments she got it...and three times, one after the other. Try it! Don't burst a blood vessel, do it lightly, just as easy as she did, and see how it works while you wait patiently for the fulfillment of scripture in you.

As I stand before you, I can honestly say everything recorded in the gospel concerning Jesus Christ, from the birth to the descent of the dove, but everything recorded in those four gospels I, in the Spirit, have experienced... but every one of them. Yet I am a man as you are, with all the weaknesses, all the limitations. Everything that is man and that man is heir to I am. So it happens in the depths of the soul of man that is unblemished, untouched by the world of Caesar. It certainly didn't happen here...this body was on the bed and sound asleep, and yet I, a conscious being, experienced it. So that conscious being animating this is untouched by what this garment is put through.

So don't judge yourself harshly because you've done so and so. You may think you aren't qualified, forget it! You're qualified because God wears you. Every person in this world is a garment that God is wearing, but every person, and not one is better than the other because in the end *all* will be God the Father. And you can't have one greater than the other. No two will be alike save they're individualized and yet they are one. And now we come to the greatest of the great commandments, Master, what is the greatest commandment? "Hear, O Israel: The Lord our God is one Lord" (Deut.6:4). Hear, O Israel: The I AM our I AMs is one I AM. This one I AM fragmented into all of us, and yet together it is a unity. It's one, one made up of others, so that no two will be alike in the sense that you'll be absorbed and I'll be absorbed, and yet one will not be greater than the other. For all will be the father of God's only begotten Son, therefore, God.

Now let us go into the Silence.

*   *   *

If you would like to tell the story as I'm telling it, may I encourage you to start. Start! If you feel that you aren't qualified, forget it. A man or woman who tells me that he feels or she feels qualified to do it, I would suggest to them wait awhile. It's when you feel that you're inadequate...as Paul said, "Why should I?" As Moses said, "Why should I?" He stuttered; the other had a thorn in his side. And no one who does this work when they start really feels that he's qualified. So don't wait until you think you are ready one hundred percent, just start. It will come. All it needs is sincerity on your part. If you really want to do it, do it. Don't ask anyone to ordain you, not in this work. There was no one who ordained Moses or ordained Paul, he simply started. He believed it, he tried it, he proved it, and then he told it. I started on my wife's birthday, the second day of February, 1938. I started on a borrowed five dollar bill to pay the rent. The War was not on and in spite of what you might read in the papers we were still in the Depression, and there was not a job in sight. I rented the place at Steinway Hall for five dollars which sat about seventy. And that's how I started. I didn't charge...didn't have the courage to charge. They either gave it because they loved me or they were embarrassed, and they paid the rent that night. Think six came. So it started from that little, little ___(??).

And may I tell you, again I speak from experience, I had no promotion, no ballyhoo, nothing, no money, completely unknown, but I wanted to tell it. And so, dressed in my best suit which was my tux, I sat in a chair. I think I went as long as fifteen minutes before I gave out, and then we asked questions. Now today, if my voice wouldn't give out, I could go for hours and hours and hours. It never exhausts itself anymore. So I say to you who want to tell it, don't wait until you're prepared. You will never feel prepared. If you don't feel like an artist feels on a first night, don't do it. You must always feel like the artist on first night, always keyed up, always telling the greatest story ever told. So when you are…I've had six first nights on Broadway and I know the feeling, what it is to step before that audience and it's all new. Everything back stage is all afire, all electric, and you are one with it. Well, every time you take this platform you don't take it lightly. You simply ___(??) that same thrill. You're telling the greatest story in the world. So to you who want to do it, and I know many of you want to do it, may I tell you, do it! If you only have one…and the one will grow and grow and grow.

Now are there any questions?

Q: (inaudible)

A: No, my dear, when I go into the Silence not to ask for anything, just to enjoy the Silence, when I come out the hands are parched, my mouth is parched, and it acts almost like a diuretic. In fact, it acts like a diuretic.

Q: And you think that has nothing to do with telling the law?

A: No, I'm just sharing with those who will listen to me my own symptoms when I go into the Silence. But the little child certainly didn't have parched hands and a dry mouth and she didn't rush to the bathroom. She simply closed her eyes, communed with self, felt that she was actually, she was taking her friend with her to San Diego, and so convinced was she she said, "Thank you"; then the mother had a change of heart and said "Yes, you may take her." So don't look upon these as outer symptoms. I told you these things only to share with you should you have them not to be disturbed, not to get excited…it's a natural thing.

Q: When Jesus said, "I felt virtue go out of me" that didn't pertain to that sort of thing, in helping someone? When the woman touched him, she received help. Doesn't that go with giving help?

A: First of all, Ina, whenever you think of Jesus Christ think of Jesus Christ as your own wonderful being, not a "he" out there, walking like a flesh and blood being. It's your own being, your own Imagination, that's Jesus Christ. I will not deny wearing these garments of flesh and blood that we do wear them out, they do tire. And so, I know after a day of interviews I used to be completely pooped. I would give my all…I never took it lightly. So when I would say goodbye to the last one at five thirty in the afternoon, oh, the one thing I wanted was a good double or triple Scotch. I was simply completely gone. I was giving all day, and the body simply is an emotional filter. I would go into the Silence and feel intensely the good that someone asked me to hear for them.

So when I broke the spell and I said goodbye to them, took them to the elevator, that was something going out. At the end of a day of that, if you take it seriously you were tired. That's why I don't have any interviews. I'm pushing a thousand…you can't get that old and just keep on forever.

Q: In reading scripture this morning, I came across "Ask and it shall be given, seek and ye shall find, knock and it shall be opened to you…"

A: Well, the question is, in scripture this morning he is reading the passage, "Ask, seek…" read it for me again.

Q: "Ask and it shall be given, seek and ye shall find, knock and it shall be opened to you." At the spiritual, at the deepest level, why the differentiation between these three directions ask, seek, knock?

A: Well, put…the question is ___(??) ask, seek and knock—he wants to know why the differentiation between asking, seeking and knocking. Really they aren't. If you take the one, knocking…knock and it shall be opened unto you…we go to Revelation now for the interpretation. "Behold, I stand at the door and knock. If anyone will open unto me, I will come in and sup with him and he with me." Well, who is the door? He said, "I am the door." So that we can knock forever, but if I don't open, then I don't admit the solution of my problem. It is there knocking; I have to give acceptance to it. "Seek and ye shall find." Well, you don't go seeking. I'm looking for something and I'm told to assume that I *have* what I seek and I'll find it. So I wouldn't really tear them apart; it's a unity.

Q: (inaudible)

A: Oh, my dear! The question is, would I tell the story of Adam and Eve and God. Well, that's a whole, whole series of lectures. There is *only* God, my dear, in the world…there's nothing but God. There's no room for another. So the fall was not a mistake. It's a plot, it's a plan where God limits himself to the very limit of contraction, of opacity called man; for the purpose of then expanding beyond the translucence that was his prior to that decision to limit himself—because, there's no limit to God's expansion. If we think of a God that is already limitless in all things, then it's not a God that could ever enjoy infinite expansion, infinite wisdom. So think of the infinity without boundaries. And to reach beyond where I am, limitless as I seem to be, I must come down to contraction and wear the garment of opacity; then break through like a seed breaking through. Have you ever seen a little seed coming through granite? I've seen them actually come through granite. You see them come through cement sidewalks…not through the little crevice but actually break the whole thing through. Well, a seed must fall into the ground and die, the seed being God and God being his Word. It's planted in this opacity called man, and it breaks through, and it's God. There's nothing but God! In fact, Yod He Vau He, which we interpret as God, as I AM, which we call it Jehovah, the He Vau He, which is the verb, its original meaning was "to fall, or the one who causes to fall"; or it was "to blow, or the one who causes the wind to blow."

So here, the descent was a *design*. We're told that in the 3rd chapter of John: "No one ascends into heaven but he who first descended" (verse 13). So if the Son of man who is called Jesus Christ ascends, then he had to first descend. Well, that could not have been a mistake. No one can ascend but the one who descended. Well, it was God who descended. It was God who took the fall, in the sense of he limited himself to this [body]; and completely forgetting that he is God he's not *pretending* that he's me, he became me. He's not pretending that he's us. He emptied himself we are told in Philippians, completely emptied himself of his divine life and took upon himself the form of man; and finding himself in the form of a man became obedient unto death even the death on the cross of man (2:5). And from this restriction he's breaking through, and when he actually breaks through he is greater than he was prior to his descent. Truth is an ever-increasing illumination and he said "I am the truth." For you can enjoy ___(??) infinity forever and forever, but it is God's purpose to ever expand. So, as the poet said, "Be patient"... someone asked about these four acts of creation here in this world..."Oh," he said, "Be patient, for the great Master, the Poet, will show us in some fifth act what this wild drama means." Just imagine what the fifth one is going to be.

Q: Neville, as in the physical body where we have some voluntary muscles and organs and other involuntary things, is that the same truth prevalent on a spiritual level as the law is always voluntary and the act of God always involuntary?

A: Bill, I don't know...

Q: In other words, all acts of God are involuntary, there are none induced?

A: As far as I'm concerned, every mystical experience I've ever had was involuntary.

Q: And the law was always voluntary...

A: The law, as far as I'm concerned, it's an act on our part. We are the operant power...unless we operate, it doesn't work. But as far as God's will unfolding in us, it unfolds automatically, it's involuntary. We don't earn it; it's grace, grace, grace and more grace.

Q: (inaudible)

A: Well, Ben, in this case, if you desire you would desire this consciousness only because God has sent the famine upon you. He said "I will send a famine upon the world. It will not be for bread or for the thirst of water, but for the hearing of the word of God" (Amos 8:11). So when that comes upon you, you may think, well now, I voluntarily seek him. No, the time has come upon you and when it's upon you, not a thing in this world can satisfy that hunger but an experience of God.

Q: Does the use of the law have anything to do with the revelations? I mean could a person be unaware of the law and still have a mystical experience?

A: Why certainly, my dear. The law came *after* the Promise. The Promise is in the beginning. Paul personified in scripture, in Galatians, how would you take a book and personify it? Paul said, "Scripture foreseeing that the gentiles would be saved through faith," then he goes on to say "Therefore Abraham…"—the whole thing begins in the loins of Abraham, it all comes out like the sands of the sea. Therefore Abraham was given a sort of preview of the gospel so he could say in the 8th of John "Abraham rejoiced that he was to see my day; he saw it and was glad" (verse 56). Abraham saw your day when he lived 2,000 years before you were born—if you take it in that light. But the whole, all of us, saw the play. We saw it in its detail and then amnesia set in. We had to forget, and then we entered a foreign land which this land and we are slaves. We may have a million dollars, we may have tonight…many a multi-millionaire is a slave of his millions, can't sleep, who is stealing from him, watching all things, he has no rest. If anyone comes near him, he wonders if they want my money? If you take a very, very wealthy young girl who is left, say, a hundred million dollars, beautifully invested—and we have in our land dozens of them, not publicized—but if publicized would they have any assurance at any time that the boy who sought their hand really loved them for themselves? I won't mention names but you have in your mind's eye, you can think of a dozen who have been married seven times and they at all times had to marry say one person with a title, a prince. Of all the silliness in the world, he's a prince, and this one is so and so, this one's a count. What title?—the only aristocracy that I would accept is the aristocracy of the Spirit—an aristocracy of flesh and blood that cannot inherit the kingdom of heaven. We're told that no one born of woman is greater than John, yet I tell you the least in the kingdom is greater than John. Well, take the greatest man who walks the face of the earth because of his stature, his intelligence, his know-how, his everything, he is not comparable to the least in the kingdom because he can't get in with these qualifications. So the only aristocracy is the aristocracy of the Spirit.

Well, I'm away beyond my time, Mr. Fisher ___(??).

Well, thank you so much. And when I return if you're on my mailing list, you will know where I am and all about it. Thanks.

OUR REAL BELIEFS

9/12/66

___(??) I promise you in this series it's going to be the most practical thing that you ever heard. Whether I speak on the law or the Promise, it's all based upon experience. I'm not theorizing, I'm not speculating, I am telling you what I know from experience.

Tonight is the law; Friday night the title, "Behold This Dreamer". But if you've ever known the statement, ever heard the statement, "Christ in you is the hope of glory," you may say what does it mean Christ in me is the hope of glory? Well, on Friday night I hope to show you not only this presence in you but to get you, while you are seated here, to actually experience Christ. Not by looking at the speaker, no, certainly not; in you as you are seated here to experience it in you. I'll show who he really is, as given to us in scripture. You will feel him, and you will exercise all the faculties that are recorded in scripture concerning Christ.

But tonight our subject is on belief, our *real* beliefs. Our real beliefs are what we live by. Our life is the outcome of our beliefs. I do not mean half-beliefs. We either believe or we do not. We're called upon to believe the word of God. If I say to you...and I'm quite sure that almost everyone here believes in God, I hope you do...and so, if I said, "With God all things are possible" and asked for some reaction, everyone would raise the hand, "I believe that with *God* all things are possible." But suppose I spoke from the same scripture, "All things are possible to *him* who believes"—here we have God equated with man. Now, do you believe that with God all things are possible? Yes you say. But do you believe all things are possible to *him* who believes?

Now, here is this little story told in scripture, the 9th of Mark (verse 22). They all who heard the story failed to bring about the results that the father sought, and these are those who are closest to the teacher, the disciples. They

196

could not produce the results that the Father sought. So when the great Master came by, he asked him and said to him, "If thou can, pity us, help us!" and he, in the most surprised reaction said, "*If* thou can! All things are possible to him who believes." Then the request was granted and the son was instantly cured.

Well, why did the father say to him, "I believe; help thou my unbelief"? Now, that is what I am trying to do this night, to help the unbelief. You say, "I believe"—but not to the degree that it will produce that effect. Well, how could I test my degree of belief? There is one supreme test you can give to any belief. If I say to you now and I mean this sincerely, "imagining creates reality," I mean that. If that is true, it's the Word of God. You might not find the words "imagining creates reality" in scripture, but you will find similar words implying the same thought. You will find these words in the Book of Mark, the 11th of Mark, "Whatever you desire, when you pray, *believe* you have received it, and you will" (verse 24). Well, isn't that the same thing? If I believe that I've received what at the moment reason denies and my senses deny isn't that imagining then must create reality? For imagining in my dictionary, and the word imaginary, is defined as "existing only in the Imagination, and, therefore, unreal."

Now I am quoting from a dictionary called the *Encyclopedia Britannica* where the English language is dissected and produced in the most wonderful manner: "existing only in the Imagination, therefore, nonexistent." That's what they say. Well, now, if I am called upon in scripture, and this is the Word of God and "Thy word is truth," and then I'm called upon to believe this statement, whatever—not if it's good for you, not if you consulted others and they thought it came within the I would say the framework of their belief of what is right or wrong, it doesn't say that at all. "Whatever you desire, when you pray, believe that you have received it, and you will." Well, that comes right within the statement and I reduce that now to a simple thought: imagining creates reality. If that is true, then this statement is true.

Now you may go out tonight and say that imagining creates reality, and you could rehearse it so that you will say it in your dream, but do you believe it? If you believe it, this is the test how you believe. Try to realize what a severe test of belief action is. I say I believe, but I don't act upon it. If I really believe, I couldn't restrain the impulse to act, I couldn't. If I believe that imagining creates reality and I'm faced with a problem, it doesn't take me long to conceive the solution of the problem. I don't care what it is, what the problem is. If I have a problem, I need not wait to ask anyone, I could conceive the solution. Well, does imagining create reality? Will I act upon it and simply imagine? Will I? If I don't, then I haven't met the test, and so my so-called belief could only be a half-belief. And so, action tests belief. When I am faced with anything in this world, do I act or do I exhaust all the little channels first before I act? The chances are that man goes through everything that is called a wise channel, everything, and when he exhausts all the channels, maybe, in sheer desperation, finding no other place to turn he might turn back to scripture, and then act. And would he act? If he acts, the promise is this, listen to it carefully, "Whatever you desire, when you pray, *believe* you have received it, and you will receive it." That's the promise. "And thy word is truth." So will we believe?

Now, let me take you aside for a moment. Most of you are familiar with the story. I will not go over the details of it, but you heard me tell a story two years ago of a lady who had nothing, absolutely nothing, and worked as a receptionist in a beauty parlor all her life. She's in her sixties. And here, approaching the time when she had to retire and having nothing but the eighty-seven dollars of Social Security that would come to her, she wondered "What's going to happen to me?" In the interval of twenty-seven years—we're all adults—she lived with a man who was a very, very wealthy man, a single man, but he never wanted to get married. He never married. He was about fifty years her senior...and they simply saw everything in New York City, dined and wined at the finest places. She lived as very, very wealthy people could not live, and do not live. She saw everything, dined everywhere, but no money.

So she said to me two years ago, "What should I do?" and I told her, "You've been coming to my meetings over the years, why don't you apply it?" And so, I said, "Take my book *The Law and the Promise* and you'll find one story that fits you. If you haven't the Imagination to construct a scene which would imply the fulfillment of your dream, then you read this story. There are about forty of them there." And so, sitting in her tub before she went off to work in the morning, she's going to have a tub every morning, she simply re-enacted this little scene, "Something marvelous is happening to me now, not tomorrow, not next month, not next year but now." Then she would feel the way she would expect to feel under these circumstances. At the end of the week, that was Saturday...now every night they went off to dinner...on Saturday night he said to her, "Let us have dinner sent out." Well, he lives in this fabulous co-op apartment on 57th and Park Avenue, so they have their own private restaurant. So they sent out for dinner and he said, "You know, I have done this for you today." And so, to make it short, he had bought an annuity that would pay her $600 a month for the rest of her earthly days, beginning immediately...not tomorrow but now...plus her eight-seven Social Security.

Now, last year when I went back, she said, "Neville, would it be greedy if I wanted to double that?" I said, "I am not sent here to judge people, I am sent to talk about God's law. I am not sent here to tell any story of judgment. But

I stood in the presence of the risen Christ and he embraced me and I became one with the body of Christ, with his infinite love, and then he sent me only to tell the story that man has forgotten. It's all encrusted over with barnacles, all kinds of isms, all kinds of things…this is not the story. So I came only to tell exactly what was told in scripture. If I can find words that would fit today and just tell the same thought, alright, that's what I'm going to do, like imagining creates reality. That's something original. It's not from scripture, yet it tells the same story, and maybe they will pick it up now. But the same thing is in scripture. Not a thing I bring you is new, it's all in scripture. So I said to her, "I don't care what you want." She said, "I want $600 more every month."

Well, as you know, I left here in February. I not only looked like the last run of shad, I felt it. I felt it! And when I took my wife to Barbados, I had no knowledge when I would return. When I got there my family all wept. Here was this strong strapping brother that they knew and here he is like, well, just ready for the grave. And they tried to persuade me day after day to remain in Barbados and retire. They said, "You have all the money that it takes, you don't need any money. You can retire here, with a full complement of servants and live graciously." And if Anthony Eden comes to Barbados… he wants Barbados above all the places of the world where he could live, and they mentioned a score of people who have all the money in the world and just picked Barbados to spend their last years. So they mentioned all these prominent people. I said, "They don't have a mission. So if I die here, then it's my time to die, but the day I feel better I'm going back to tell my story, right where I came from. That's where I'm going to tell it."

And so, in Barbados, this lady came down for six-week's vacation, a Christmas present from this same man who gave her the $600, all expenses paid plus the roundtrip. Well, we had her home to dinner. She didn't know I looked as I did. She took one look at me, she said, "My lord, he is going to die…and then what is going to happen to my extra $600?" She wasn't concerned about my health or my ___(??). But this is what she did. She conceived a scene which would imply the fulfillment of her dream. Her dream was to have $600 more than she now had, which would make it $1200 and $87, $1,287 a month. And this is the scene she constructed, she put me on the platform, like this, in New York City, talking to an audience, just like this, and I'm telling—where she got the $600 more. Well, if I'm going to die in Barbados, then the whole scene that she constructed would fall apart. So after dinner that night she went back to her hotel and she said she went to work on re-creating this scene. "I've got to get him better, because how is he going to tell my story?"

Now, I didn't tell her, because I didn't know, when she left Barbados, I had no urge to go any place. I was enjoying life with the family, enjoying every moment of it, warming in the love that was showered upon me, and you couldn't express in words the affection. We are, really, the clan of clans when it comes to a family. We're more closely tied than fingers on a hand. You hurt one you hurt all. That's the family. And so, the day I felt better, without consulting my wife...the only person I could ever really consult would be my wife, but she might have vetoed it, and that might have put a question in my mind, because I was painfully thin, a way down to a shadow. But I felt better, I turned the corner. And so I went up and booked passage for the two of us back to Los Angeles via New York, to remain in New York, say, for a couple of months to get some wardrobe, because no matter what I would put on would fall off. I dropped from 196 to 138. The only things that fitted me were shoes and handkerchiefs. Everything else fell off. So I gave everything away, including the shoes and the socks...kept the handkerchiefs. And then came to New York and got a new wardrobe.

While I was in New York I gave a series of fourteen lectures. This lady was committed and did not come to my meeting until the thirteenth or the fourteenth that I gave. On the thirteenth night, she got there about ten minutes before I took the platform, and this is her story. She said, "I can't remain too long. At 8:30 please give me some sign it's 8:30 that I may leave because I've got to meet this man at the club and I must pick him up before nine. So at 8:30 please give me a signal. But this is what happened today. My $600 that I told you about comes through the Massachusetts Mutual. Now, today, the same lawyer called me in and said —'I don't mean next year or next month but now, Prudential Life will pay you $600 a month for the rest of your earthly days. That would make it now $1,200 plus your eight-seven dollars beginning now.'"

So she came in just to hear the story. But before that she said to me, "Now, would you think me really greedy if I said to you I want $50,000 in cash?" Well, I said, "Lucille, my dear, I don't give a darn if you want a million. I am still telling the same story over and over that it doesn't really matter, it's all shadows. There aren't any pockets in the shroud that you're going to wear, so if you want it here now, take it. So you want your $50,000 in cash, alright, get $50,000 in cash. What you want it for I don't know, but I'm not going to question your right to want it." She can't spend $1,287 a month. She just can't do it. I know how she lives...she lives well...he's still alive and they dine every night, not on Lucille but on him, in these fabulous restaurants, every night. And so the trips to Barbados are not on Lucille, it's on him. And so, $1,287 a month...but she wants...she said, "Nothing feels secure." You *can't* feel secure until you find God. If you had billions of dollars you will not feel secure in billions; you will feel secure without one nickel in this world if you find God. I don't care what the world will tell you, when you find God you feel secure, and you don't need the symbols of security. They are only symbols; they're shadows that pass off to this world.

So what I'm getting at is this, she didn't know that the structure...you see, God's Word is literally true, but it's conveyed to man in metaphor, in a figure of speech. And so, the words that will convey the Word, that's a figure of speech, that's ___(??). So when she constructed a scene in New York City and put me on the platform to tell her story, alright, I'm telling the story... that whole structure was all figurative. What did it imply? The potency of that structure was in its *implication*, not the structure. She could have taken any structure in the world. But what is the structure? It implies something. It must have meaning. For the Bible is, "In the beginning was the *Word*." Well, the word logos means "meaning." It must have meaning. So there was meaning with God in the very beginning. This is not an afterthought, this is not some emergency thinking. This is something that was prepared before the world was, and this meaning was with God, and this meaning *was* God.

So the whole thing has meaning. So I create the structure. Now, what does the structure imply? Its implication is the word, the truth that God is speaking. So if I am telling that she has $600 now more than she had before, it means she has $1,287. Now, Neville means nothing, the platform means nothing, all these things mean nothing, it's the implication. That's the potency of this structure. So forget structure. It's marvelous because it conveys meaning. And so I have to use words to convey meaning. If I didn't have to use words, I could just think and tell you the most marvelous things in the world. But while I'm limited to this world I've got to find words. And all the words are figures...even a simple little thing like "imagining creates reality." Yet behind the three little words, what am I telling you? It's so much I am telling you in that simple, simple little thing.

So here, we have belief this night. Our beliefs, our real beliefs, are what we live by, and our entire life is the outcome of our beliefs. If, like the father in the story, as related in the 9th of Mark, thought he believed and asked the great one to help his unbelief; then he tells him in a very simple manner "All things are possible to him who believes." Now, throughout scripture, using the word "prayer," "Teach us how to pray," well, there is no reaction to that. There is no statement as to how. He did give us what is called The Lord's Prayer. That's something entirely different...it's the most majestic. But to teach us how to pray...they said he was praying and when he ceased to pray in a certain place, they said to him, "Master, teach us to pray." But no statement is made as to what he said. But if you will take a good concordance and look up the words and see what prayer means, the word prayer means "motion towards, accession to, in the vicinity of"—at or in the very place that you want to be.

Well, she wants to be in that place hearing her story. She got right into it. It's all communion with self; it's not on the outside. You don't really pray here or pray in a church. It's when you actually withdraw from the outer world. and go within, and then get nearer and nearer to the wish fulfilled. Well, I have to get nearer and nearer to the wish fulfilled...so I assume the feeling of the wish fulfilled and give it all sensory vividness, all the tones of reality, everything that would be real were it true. So I am hearing his voice. I hear... and now what is he saying, what does it mean, what does it imply? It implies that I have it. Well, then it awakens in her the reaction of having it. Believe that you have received it—it produces that feeling of having received it. That's the end of the prayer: "Whatever you desire, when you pray, believe that you have received it." Well, how to persuade myself that I have received what at the moment reason is denying and my senses deny? I use all this technique, and the technique is all figurative. Has no power whatsoever. It is what it is implying.

Now, do I believe it to the point of doing it? She did. She doesn't want to hear one word about the Promise. The Promise annoys her. She just can't stand it. We went to dinner one night and it was the night after I gave a lecture on the Promise. The four of us went off, my wife, myself, and the two of them. We always go to these fabulous places and I must confess it's fun. She didn't mean it but she always means these things, they slip out. "Oh," she said, "I was late tonight. I had to go to this damn lecture tonight." I wasn't talking about how to get another million. That night I was talking on the only reality in the world, how God awakes within man and man is God. That God actually became man that man may become God. And there is an actual play recorded in scripture as to how it unfolds, and suggests the audience not to seek new ways to a goal that is already obtained. Follow the *way* that is already laid out in scripture. There's only one way...and there is no other way. So why seek all these ways. They go through the ways of diet. They're going to get good and healthy and find God...and then you read their obituary tomorrow morning. All the new ___(??), they all die just as young as I do. And so they take that and they'll live forever...all about the proteins, the this and the that, and then one morning you open the paper, he wasn't shot, he died, simply died. That's all the people in the world.

My father broke all the health rules of the world. My mother broke none. She died at sixty-one, he at eighty-five. He drank like a fish, to the disgust of my mother, but she loved him dearly. There was only one man in her life and that was Joseph. She couldn't see anyone but her Joseph. If he brought her a rose, which occasionally he would, sometimes as a joke, oh, she thought it was the most marvelous thing that he brought her a rose. She had all the roses in the world in her garden, hundreds of roses. She loved the garden and

she had them, but if he bought her a rose uptown, brought her a little bunch
of roses, that was the most marvelous thing! He didn't go and get them and
cut them from her garden, she brought them in. But when they both came in
at the same time, gloating, alright, he has the roses to give to his sweetheart.
And that was my father, a rugged, rugged individualist if there ever was one.
Eighty-five he closed his eyes. I'm not saying to duplicate him, because maybe
your system couldn't take it. He had a system like iron. Mother was a fragile
person, and having borne twelve of us, and ten of us matured, well, naturally,
it took something out of Mother. So at sixty-one Mother died. She never
drank, never smoked, and lived a very quiet simple wonderful life.

But I tell you, this law that I'm giving you now I was sent to give you.
I didn't hatch it out. I was called and sent. This is not something that man
can sit down and contemplate, and say this is the way that man should be.
The way has already been completely revealed, yet man is always searching
for new ways. He goes off to ___(??), he goes off to this place, he goes to the
other place, searching for a new way to a goal that has *already* been attained.
And the goal is the Father. Everyone is seeking for the Father, which is the
source of authority, the power of the universe. He isn't going to find it through
diet. And that's said quite vividly in scripture, that food will not in any way
accomplish anything, really, the 8th chapter of 1st Corinthians. We are not in
any way brought before God by diet, whether we eat or not eat, whether we
drink or not drink, this will not in any way commend us to God. Whether
we do this or that, these are not...believe in his Word.

Well, now believe in his Word. It's called in scripture, repentance. And
so, she practiced repentance by not accepting the evidence of the senses and
changing, a radical change of mind. So she didn't have it, she's not going to
ask him for it, she's going to try it. So in her mind's eye she sets up a scene
implying the fulfillment of her desire, and then the desire comes to pass. So
that was repentance. She didn't go to church, she didn't go confess to some
priest, she didn't do anything in this world that the world calls repentance.
Repentance means simply a radical change of mind, that's what the word
means. Metanoia is a complete *radical* change, not just a little change, right
down to the root. I don't know how it's going to work, but I'm going to change
radically. I'm not looking and hoping that it comes from this, that or the
other; I just have it. And he's telling my story and so I know. So she began to
apply it. And when she saw me and thought now this whole thing is going to
be simply farcical, it wasn't. She didn't realize that the power was not in the
structure she had done, it was in what the structure implied.

So that is what we have done with the Bible. We take the letter and not
the spirit. The Bible is simply a vehicle that conveys a message, and we have
confused the message that it conveys with the vehicle that conveys it. And so

we worship the vehicle. We worship all these symbols in the world, like the preachers. We have saint this and saint that and saint the other; they don't exist. The whole thing is in man: "Man is all Imagination and God is man and exists in us and we in him. The eternal body of man is the Imagination, and that is *God* himself" (Blake, *Berkeley, Laocoon*). That's God believe it or not.

I hope on Friday I can show you exactly how you prove to your own satisfaction...I'm not going to come out of the clouds here, I'm not going to ride on a white horse and have a golden throne and tell you lovely things. No, while you are seated here, whoever comes, I will have you do a little experiment with me—but in you, not in me. And if I cannot produce in you the consciousness of this presence and prove to you how real this presence is, well, I don't think I'll take the platform again. I'm sure I can do it. I am sure I can make you aware of who Christ is, and with him all things are possible. So, if with him all things are possible, well, now all things are possible to him who believes. If you are the believer, I will now equate you with the one that you're going to feel, when I bring about this demonstration as it were.

But here, in this wonderful world of belief...the whole vast world is nothing more than belief. What evidence had I, unschooled as I was, that I could write a book that really would sell, and sell 70,000 copies un-promoted, no sales effort whatsoever behind the book? I go from New York to California once a year, live here, so I only live, really, in three major cities. Here I live...I go to San Francisco for a series of ten or thirteen lectures; New York for, say, fourteen, fifteen lectures; and then here I live. And I do not promote the book. It hasn't been advertised in papers, not in magazines, not on radio, TV, and the book has sold over 70,000 copies. But I took it in to Scribner's in New York City when I first brought it out. They said to me, "This book will not sell 500 copies in the life of the book." Well, I was such a greenhorn I asked them, "What do you mean by the life of the book?" He said, "As long as you the author lives; for, as long as the author lives he will talk with friends and through sympathy they'll buy a book from him." I said, "Is that what you mean by the life of the book?" He said, "Yes. We speak of the life of a book based upon the life of the author. When authors die, unless it's a classic, the books die. We have a storehouse filled with books where some author was a good salesman and sold us his manuscript against our will, and so, they are unsold by the thousands. So, you aren't going to be one of those salesmen." I said, "No, I know that I have a book that is unique; I do not know of one like it in the field. You tell me one book like this, *Your Faith is Your Fortune*, and I would like very much to ___(??) it. I haven't ___(??) it...there's not anything here that's plagiarized. This whole book came out of me spontaneously. And so I tell you this will sell." Well, it has sold over 70,000 copies and no sales effort.

When I told that to the late Aldous Huxley, he said, "Did you go back to tell the man? Did you write a letter to the chairman of the board or the president?" I said, "No, I'm not given that way." He said, "Well, if I had stock in that company, I would want to know who is passing opinions on such manuscripts, because he's costing me money. Because they have a sales force. If you've done this to a book without the help of any sales effort and they have this enormous sales effort, what would that book have done? And I, with an interest in the stock, I would want to know."

But all I can tell you is, I believe it. We are always believing ahead of our efforts, always. I want something and I believe it. Without any evidence to support that belief I believe it, and walk this earth as though it were true. In a way that I do not know, not consciously, and no one knows, it becomes true. In time, that belief projects itself on the screen of space, and it is to those who cannot see otherwise it's now to them a reality. It's no more imaginary now; it's now a fact. When I first told them, if I did, that was all imaginary, existing only in your Imagination and, therefore, unreal. Now it becomes a fact and they trace it back through the physical being by which it became a fact. And they stop right there. They can't go back to the supernatural origin of the thing. All things go back to supernatural origins, because all things go back to God. Everything goes back to God; there's nothing but God.

So if I can't take you back beyond these physical things here, I will never find the origin of anything in this world. So will I go back far enough to find when I began to believe? Did someone once tell me, "You know, you remind me of someone...you know what he died of?" Now listen to it carefully. All of a sudden I am picking it up, he died of this, he reminds me of you, and then every little symptom that I read in the paper thereafter, I'm picking up the whole thing he died of, and I don't like it. So I go back to somewhere I formed a belief, some stupid belief that I believed in. And all of us...my friend, who's here tonight, he told me this story the other day, that this man said, "I have no superstition. I am so happy I have none whatsoever! Thank God (knocking on wood)!" He was so proud he had none, but he had to knock. Well, that's the whole vast world...we all have them. My wife told me that she was almost, well, a young lady before she could break the habit that her nurse gave her when she was a child that you dare not put on the left shoe first. The right shoe must go on first or it's bad luck. So she dressed every morning, put on the right one first. Then when she began to ___(??), "Oh, I don't believe in it, but I'll take no chance," she puts on the shoe, and for the longest while she would take no chance. Finally, it came that she could really put on the left one first. But that was a habit that was given to her by her nurse when she was just a child and remained with her over the years. We all have these little superstitions.

It all goes back to what do you believe? We're told, believe in the Lord Jesus Christ and you'll be saved. But nobody knows...they repeat that in words. Anyone can repeat that in words, I can take the Christian creed and repeat it over and over and over. What does it matter? What does it do to me? It doesn't change my life at all. So, what have I believed? You say, I believe in Christ and to believe in him I'm saved. Saved from what? Man doesn't know Christ—he doesn't know this infinite being that is housed within him. He doesn't know the God that is completely furled within him. When he begins to believe, that God will unwind himself at the ____(??), and then I am he. But, without belief it doesn't work. We are told, "They heard the good message as we did; but it did not benefit them, because it was not mixed with faith in the hearers." Read it in the Book of Hebrews (4:2). They heard the same message of good news but it did not benefit them. Why?—it was not received with faith in those who heard it. And so, I can tell you...and some will say, well, I think he's silly, I think he's stupid, and go out and completely turn their backs against the story.

I tell you, whether you believe it or not, I stood in the presence of the risen Christ. The risen Christ asked me a very simple question and when I answered it correctly he embraced me. We fused, we became one, and in that oneness he sent me. I am still one; you're never separated from the one with whom you are fused. As you're told, "He who is united to the Lord becomes one spirit with him" (1Cor.6:17). So, "He who sees me sees him who sent me." But you don't see him under this mask. You cannot see the being that I really am through mortal eyes, no man can. To see the being that I really am you have to have the spiritual eye open. And I wear, whether you know it or not, the human from divine, which is the body of God. It's the body of the risen Christ, but no mortal eye can see it. They see this; this is the mask that covers the body that I really wear, and I would have no time between the departure from this when I take it off finally and occupancy of that which I really occupy.

And so, when I was embraced and made one with him, there is no divorce after that. He who God has joined together, let no man put asunder (Mt.19:6). It has nothing to do with my physical relationship with a woman on earth. Not a thing! That's a complete misunderstanding of the scripture. Who God has joined together...God embraced me, and he and I became one. Now, God has joined together...let no man put asunder. Man cannot put asunder, yet they will try to excommunicate me were I a member of a church. How can they excommunicate me and take me away from the body of God when God has joined me to him? I am one with the body of God. So when you meet the risen Christ, there you see infinite love in the human form divine, and he who is embraced and becomes one with him is it. And then he's sent into this world to tell the story.

Until he is called, he is not sent. To be called is to be sent. When you are called and sent, you know it. Not speculating you know your mission. Even though you haven't the intelligence of the world and you are unlettered in the language of the world, he tells you what to say. You go before the learned men of the world and people you call your own and tell them what mortal mind cannot tell them. You'll tell them what they'll never experience by reading books or by speculating, and you tell them exactly what has happened to you. They will look upon you as one, "Isn't he the most wonderful dreamer. Isn't his Imagination vivid." Isn't so at all...you simply are telling exactly what happened to you. But they can't see the being that you are, because on this level when I depart this world, that is, when the world sees this level, they're the same level. They're still clothed in mortal garments that suffer and die... until that one moment in time when, after all the furnaces, they're called into the presence of the living God and embraced, and fused, and then sent to tell the gospel of God. And we come one by one into that state. But, here, we walk the earth unknown, completely unknown, disregarded. You're told in scripture, he reverses the entire thing. The one that he calls and holds the highest rank he ___(??). For he sends him, sends him into the world... no honors, no background, no intellectual, social, financial background whatsoever. He sent him, but he said, I go with him, for he who sees me sees him who sent me. But you can't see him because the eye isn't open to see him.

So I tell you, believe what I've told you this night. It's true you can be exactly what you want to be if you're willing to construct a scene that would imply the fulfillment of your dream. And the power is not in the structure, that's all figurative, that's mental; but the power is in its implication. What does it imply? Remain faithful to its implication and it will come to pass in what the world calls reality.

Now let us go into the Silence.

* * *

Are there any questions?

Q: (inaudible)
A: No, it's the Greek metanoia. Metanoia, it's Greek. You and I aren't Greek scholars, but the word is metanoia, which is translated in our scripture as repentance. So if you look up the word repentance in the concordance, that is, the biblical concordance, it will give you the Greek word metanoia and then give you the definition; and it simply means a *radical* change of mind, that's all that it means. It doesn't mean remorse, it doesn't mean

regret; it means to change your mind radically. And it's something that no one can do on the outside by going to a so-called intermediary between yourself and God, who *is* yourself. You need no intermediary between you and the source of your own being. So, they can't give you so-called... they can't exonerate you. Exonerate what? You go within yourself and then radically change, believing the Word of God, every statement of his. It may take fifteen words to tell a truth, but the truth is called the word, singular; so fifteen words may be used to express it or it may take fifty words to say the word. But the word is what I'm getting at. So the statement is "imagining creates reality"...that is the word of God. If you believe it, something bothers you...assume it now, this very moment, and that's a radical change of attitude. That is metanoia. That's repentance. Now if you believe it, you'll persist in it.

Q: (inaudible)

A: For instance, if I believe a thing, I'd act, wouldn't I? For instance, what if someone came to the door and screamed, "Fire!" Now you believe fire is a dangerous thing, don't you? I do. Well, I hope that no one would stampede and stop the others from getting out, but I hope all would take the hint and start moving toward an exit. I know I would. I believe that if someone screams "Fire!" they mean that the place is on fire and we should all make an effort to get out. I hope we would be kind and considerate and not tear the other one down, but, at least, you begin to smell the smoke and you see the flames, just start moving towards the exit. You believe fire is destructive in certain ways and most constructive in others. Well, if I believe it, I would act, wouldn't I? And if I don't believe, I don't act. So I will say, if you believe what I'm talking about you would act. So you're confronted with a problem, do you believe that all things are possible to him who believes? Well now, learn the art of believing. What must I do to believe? And then act, because if the belief isn't strong enough to affect action, well, then it can only be a half-belief. That's not good enough.

Now do me a favor, even if you have a card take another one. You may displace it with duplicate cards and I printed an abundance of them, knowing that the whole thing was a scrambled series. Like next week, it's Tuesday, but this week we do have Friday. But next week it's going to be Tuesday and Friday. Now what the third week is I haven't slightest idea, because I have to read it every day myself to see what I'm going to talk about. It's a complete scrambled program. And so, I know over the years we came to the Ebell on a Thursday, two nights a week and we never had one missing. We came over to Dr. Smith's place and they were the same two nights a week, but ___(??) ...lovely club. The ladies were very gracious, very kind, allowing me to have it for the time that I wanted it. So I have twenty-three scheduled between tonight, and I'll close for a few months some time in December...I think it's the 16th of December, but I do not know. I mean, it's one of those things, I know that I will be here, as the schedule states, between now and closing the 16th of December. And this coming Friday it is "Behold This Dreamer." This is the night I will show you, those who come, and I'm quite sure I can succeed in getting you to feel the presence of Christ in you. Not some impersonal, intangible something on the outside...I'll show you and you'll experiment with me, you'll feel Christ in you. Now trust him. That's the *only* Christ of scripture. But he hasn't yet resurrected in you. He will. But before he resurrects, I'll show you how to catch him, and then you will touch him.

And the day will come he'll resurrect exactly as described in scripture. The resurrection; then his birth from above; followed by his discovery that he is God the Father. And then comes the grand tearing of the curtain of the temple, and he ascends, using his own blood—not the blood of another, no ox, no cow, his own blood—and ascends like a spiral of lightning, just a bolt of spiral lightning, you could call it that, right into his skull. Then comes the final confirmation of the act when the dove descends upon him. And then you will find the entire story. But you can just feel it before this thing happens.

Well, my time is up. And so, on Friday we'll be here. Do take a card on the way out, even if you have one, and give it to a friend.

BEHOLD THIS DREAMER

9/16/66

As I told you when I opened last Monday, this will be the most practical course you ever heard. It will be the most profoundly spiritual, but whatever is most profoundly spiritual is in reality most directly practical. And the promise I made you on Monday I'll keep tonight. It seems the most extravagant claim in the world. The man who stands before you, who must make the inevitable exit from this world and this little garment be turned into dust, and that I dare to tell you I will this night bring you to the Lord Jesus Christ. I will bring you to him this night. You may not believe him, you may not accept it, that's entirely up to you, but I will bring you to him.

As told in scripture, "And Philip found Nathaniel, and he said to Nathaniel, 'I have found him of whom Moses in the law and the prophets wrote, Jesus of Nazareth, the son of Joseph.'" Now, in this same first chapter of John, John makes the statement, "Among you stands one whom you do not know. I myself did not know him; but he who sent me to baptize with water, he said to me, 'The one on whom you see the Spirit descend and remain, he baptizes with the Holy Spirit.' And I saw the Holy Spirit descend as a dove and it remained upon him. Through him all things were made, and without him was not anything made that was made. In him was life, and the life was the light of men." Now, you listen to it carefully, for I'll bring you to him this night, as we're told in scripture Philip brought Nathaniel. Listen carefully as I unfold these words, because they are so important to you to really follow what I'm going to talk about. I have titled this "Behold This Dreamer." If you are familiar with scripture, it's the 37th chapter of Genesis, and the one spoken of is Joseph. "Behold this dreamer cometh." So he came, his brothers sold him into slavery in the land of Egypt; and Joseph saves the entire civilization from starvation by interpreting the dreams of Pharaoh. Then be bought the entire land of Egypt for Pharaoh, including those who stole the land and made all of them slaves of Pharaoh; and then he was the great power next to Pharaoh.

The Bible begins, the Book of Genesis, "In the beginning God…" and it ends "…in a coffin in Egypt." The one placed in a coffin is Joseph: "In the beginning God…in a coffin in Egypt." And yet, this one placed in the coffin in Egypt, before he's placed there, he extracts from his brothers the promise they would not let him remain there; they would take his bones up and take him back to where his fathers were. That's on the surface.

Here, in scripture you cannot take the characters Abraham, Isaac and Jacob and eliminate them and still have the Bible. They are found in the two genealogies of Jesus Christ, both in Matthew and in Luke. In fact, Matthew begins it with Abraham. Abraham was the father of Isaac, and Isaac the father of Jacob, and Jacob the father of Judah and his brothers, and so on. So here we find these three, the inner core of the patriarchs of scripture. Yet, they have not turned up in any ancient Near East manuscript or record, either as individuals or as tribes. If these are the core, the entire background of that which is now brought to complete fulfillment in Jesus Christ, and that is part of his genealogy, and they are not discovered outside of scripture in any ancient contemporary world, either as individuals or as tribes, why? This whole drama unfolds *within you*. These are the eternal states through which man, the immortal you, must pass. And you begin in the state called Abraham, and you end in the state called Jesus Christ. When you end there you awaken and you are the creator of it all, God himself.

So here, listen carefully as I take these passages, and just try to recall them, try to keep them in mind as I unfold them; for I'm bringing to you this night the great dreamer who dreams everything into being, but everything, good, bad and indifferent. "I have been crucified with Christ; it is not I who live, but Christ who lives in me" (Gal.2:20). Galatians ___(??). "If we have been united with him in a death like his, we shall certainly be united with him in a resurrection like his." Note the difference in tense. "If we have been united with him in a death like his"—that's past; we have all been crucified with him—"we shall be"—now come to the future—"we shall be united with him in a resurrection like his" (Rom.6:5). The identical resurrection! "In him the whole *fullness* of the Godhead dwells bodily" (Col.2:9)—not figuratively, but genuinely in a body. In him the whole fullness of deity dwells bodily. "This is the mystery hid for ages and generations…Christ *in you*, the hope of glory" (Col.1:26,27). Therefore, "I consider the sufferings of this present time not worth comparing with the glory that is to be revealed *in* me" (Rom.8:18). In me! What glory? The whole Godhead dwells bodily in me, and when it's unveiled, I am he.

Now you listen carefully as I bring you now to meet him dwelling bodily in me—not a portion of him, the whole Godhead dwells bodily in me. And I use myself as an example, but I say he dwells in you, the whole, not a portion of him. Can I prove it? Now I'm called upon to test myself, "Test *yourselves* and see. Do you not realize that Jesus Christ is in you?" (2Cor.13:5). Well, ask that of anyone who calls himself a Christian and if they are honest, they would say, "No, I don't realize that at all." And here is Paul in his 2nd letter to the Corinthians, the 13th chapter, "Do you not realize that Jesus Christ is in you? Test yourselves." Now you must make the most daring test in the world of Jesus Christ. Brood upon him, learn to know him better, and then as I am doing this night pass on to our successors what we have found in him. If he dwells in me bodily and I'm called upon to test myself to find him, well, I cannot be indolent about this. I must make every attempt in this world to find him. He dwells in me bodily and the whole, not a little part, the whole Godhead dwells in him bodily, and he dwells in me in his fullness, then I've got to find him. Only the indolent mind would fail to respond to this challenge. Well, I was not ___(??) about him. My whole life has been devoted to finding him; and finding him I have done. I found him.

Let us go back now and get a few words and define them for you. He dwells in me bodily; therefore, like myself he must have organs, he must. On the outward self I have organs—I see, I hear, I smell, I taste. Well, the eye is the organ of vision, the ear the organ of hearing, the nostril the organ of smell, and so on. An organ is any part of an organism that performs some definite function...that is an organ. An organism is an organized or living being, that's an organism. I see here and I can touch this, and I can do all the things here now. But I am looking for something far greater, something in me through whom the entire world was made: "...through which all things were made and without him was not anything made that was made." I've got to find him. He has a body; it must have organs just as I have organs here.

Now I put him to the test. Think of your living room right now, just think of it. You see it with your mind's eye, don't you? If someone changed a piece of furniture or changed a picture, on returning home tonight you'd know it. You'd recognize that someone came in my absence and there's a change, because this is not the way I left it. But right now you remember it as you left it and you can see it in your mind's eye, see it with the eye of Imagination. Alright, can you hear the sound of a voice that is not even in this world? My father made his exit in '59, my mother in '41, I can hear their voices as distinctly as though they were here in the flesh. So I don't have to go back for now some voice that is still being echoed in this world, I go to voices that are gone from this sphere.

I can hear my brother now, who recently departed this world on the 4th of August. We were born and raised like fingers on a hand. No one could feel important in the family, because we all were just simply like one. We all would be pulled right down, all one. And this past summer in Barbados he was making his departure from this world—we all knew it, and they all thought I was, too—but this was his greeting to me in the morning. Called me up one morning and he said—my sister answered the phone—he said, "Is the Lord there? Put him on the wire." He knew exactly who he was calling. And so when I got on he said, "Are you my kid brother?" "Yes, I'm your kid brother, but I'm your Lord." I knew exactly what, because Daphne said, "He wants the Lord." So here I am talking to him and then he said, "Do you feel alright?" I said, "I feel fine, why?" "Well, you sound sober." I can hear him say it now, "Why, you sound sober...you can't be alright." And that was my brother Lawrence to me. But I can hear that voice as distinctly as though he were here.

So I can hear with an organ that is not this ear. I can see with an eye that is not this eye. I can taste with a tongue that is not this tongue. And I can feel with a hand that is not this hand. Try it. Can you feel a baseball? Can you feel a tennis ball? Can you feel a piece of mohair like this? Well, can you feel numberless different objects? Well, who is doing the feeling? You have imagined the object, but the being that is performing the act of the touch and the taste and the sight, do you know who he is? That is Christ Jesus. That is the immortal you who cannot die. No man can die because this presence is not tied to this [body]. It cannot die. But it must completely awaken, and when it awakens it is God the Father.

This is the immortal dreamer in man, dreaming dreams that could save the entire world. As the prototype called Joseph saved the whole vast civilized world from starvation. He could dream and interpret the universal language of dream, and make earthly preparations based upon the dream. He rose to the very heights; and in the very end he could forgive all; forgive those, his brothers, who sold him into slavery. All go into slavery. Now listen to the words carefully, "And the Lord spoke unto Moses and said, 'The time has come for you to sleep with your fathers; and this people will rise up and play the part of the harlot, with strange gods of the land, where they will be going to be alive. And I will in that day hide my face from them because of the evil which they have done, having gone and worshipped strange gods" (Deut.31:16). That's in Deuteronomy, just before he gathers himself together and sleeps with his fathers. Here we find idolatry equated with playing the harlot.

Now, you say, "I believe in God." It's an external God? Well then, you are playing the part of a harlot. I don't care what god you worship that is external to this one that I've just introduced you to. When you put your hand upon the tennis ball and I asked you at the moment, "Who is feeling it?" you would have replied "I am." Well, that's his name. If I say, "What are you hearing?" and then you tell me that you are hearing something, and I say, "Who is hearing?" you would have replied, "I am." Well, that's his name. "That is my name forever...and by this name I shall be known throughout all generations" (Ex.3:14). So, you would have replied "Yes," correctly, "I am." But it's not the God you worship. You go to church and you see these strange, monstrous things that men have created. Images fashioned out of their own hands and they worship them, and think that is God. So I speak to the orthodox of any denomination, whether it be Christian, Jew, Mohammedan, and they have an external god to whom they turn. And they do not know they are playing the part of the harlot, for "Your Maker is your husband, the Lord of hosts is his name" (Is.54:5). If my Maker is my husband and I turn to another other than my Maker, well then, I am playing the part of a harlot. I am serving a strange and false god, and I am now not faithful to my husband who is my Maker.

Well, who is my Maker? "My name is I AM." You will never find God in eternity, not the real one, save in a first-person, singular, present-tense experience. That's when you'll find him. He reveals himself in the first-person, present-tense experience; not plural, singular. And it takes his one only begotten Son to reveal him to yourself. He stands before you and calls you Father. And there is no uncertainty in this moment; you know exactly who he is and exactly who you are. You are the Elohim. You are the God spoken of in the very first verse of scripture, "In the beginning God..."—where?—"in a coffin in Egypt." This is the coffin, this is the sepulcher, the tomb of God. And what was originally only the tomb of God becomes transformed into the womb from which God is born. So the tomb becomes a womb, and out you come, born from above, the being that is God.

By the act of self-limitation he achieves his purpose of expansion: the story of the little seed that falls into the ground—"Unless it falls into the ground and dies, it remains alone; but if it falls into the ground and dies, it brings forth much." It expands beyond the wildest dream of man. So he falls into the ground, like this [body], and dies, complete and utter amnesia. And I don't know who he is, so I play the part of the harlot. And they ask me to worship this god, to worship that god, and I bow down before so-called more important than me. You hear people say, "Who do you think I saw today? I had lunch at a certain place...who do you think was there?" All ears...and they mention some little ___(??), and they're so impressed, so impressed with this peculiar little thing that took place at a lunch. He didn't pick up their check for them. Paid his own check and he couldn't care less if people were there or not. But you're so impressed by his own press agent who is building an image for him to his own satisfaction. And you're impressed...when "Among you stands one whom you do not know." While you were eating whatever you ate, there was one present whom you did not know, and he was Christ Jesus, the hope of glory.

"Christ in you is the hope of glory." This is the one of whom I speak. And when you touch these imaginary objects...the word imaginary in the dictionary is defined as "existing only in the Imagination; unreal," that's what they say. Let me tell you, Imagination is the divine body in every man. "Man is all Imagination, and God is man, and exists in us and we in him. The eternal body of God"—and therefore man—"is the Imagination" (Blake, *Annot. to Lavater*). "God the Creator is like pure imagining in myself. He works in the very depths of my soul, underlying all of my faculties, including perception, but he streams into my surface life least disguised in the form of productive fancy" (Douglas Fawcett). So I sit alone and I perform a certain imaginary act; and I trust this presence implicitly who is performing the act, for all things are possible to him. ___(??) man? Yes, to man it's not possible, but with God all things are possible. And I have found him. He's in me.

So I would say to you this night who are embarrassed financially, or embarrassed in some other way, you could conceive a scene if true would imply the fulfillment of your dream, couldn't you? But, I'm speaking now of the great dreamer, "Behold this dreamer." For can't you conceive a scene and actually take, now, the hand of God and hold it? In him is life, and his life is the light of men. No child could cross the threshold that admits to conscious life were it not that he is in that child, but no child. So God in man is the light of man, and in him there is life, and that life is the light of men. So trust him. Put your hand out on any object that if true would imply you have what you want in this world, just put your hand on it. Now trust the hand of God. See it and trust the eye of God. Hear a conversation with some friend that would imply the fulfillment of that dream, and trust the ear of God, this inner you which you say is all Imagination. I tell you, Imagination is the divine body in every man. It is the eternal vine on which all things grow.

Now, tonight, take it, take the challenge. Test yourself and see. Do you not realize that Jesus Christ is in you? And through him all things were made, and without him was not anything made that was made? Well, now I'll make my world according to my noble dream. If through him all things are made and I've just been introduced to him, and he's not on the outside. I don't have to get up and run to church tomorrow morning early to meet him, I don't have to go tomorrow night to meet him, wherever I am—while standing at a bar having a beer, or a nice good dry Martini which I prefer—wherever I am, there he stands. "Among you stands one whom you do not know." But I've just shown you who he is, and *that* is Christ Jesus.

The day will come, he will stand seemingly on the outside, described in the Book of Daniel, the Ancient of Days. You actually look into the face of this ancient being of infinite love. He embraces you and you are one forever with the Spirit of God...forever one with the Spirit of God. And then you will know what it means, "*He* baptizes with the Holy Spirit." "I came to baptize with water," said John, "but he who sent me said to me 'He on whom you see the Spirit descend and remain, he baptizes with the Holy Spirit.'" When you are embraced and fuse with the body of the living Christ, the risen Christ, you have been baptized with the Holy Spirit, and you are it. You know it beyond all doubt: I am he.

But the work must be done, not yet completed, and you are sent back into this world of death to tell the story of the risen Christ, and to tell them how to find him. You know that you actually saw him as something objective to yourself, and fused with him, and now he's not objective any more. He was your very being...no objective being, your very being. No mortal eye can see it. You now wear forever and forever the human form divine, which is love, nothing but love. But the outer mortal eye cannot see it and the outer senses cannot touch it and hear it and commune with it. But you who wear it know it, and you're communing all day with self, the one being that you are.

So I introduce you this night to Jesus Christ, the *only* savior in the world. In scripture, when we speak of Jehovah, that's Jesus Christ. The name Jesus is the same as Joshua, and Joshua the same as Jehovah, the same root, the same being. And we are told, "I am the Lord your God, the Holy One of Israel, your Savior...and beside me there is no savior. I know not any" (Is.43:3,11). And that is your Savior. I hope I have succeeded in introducing you this night to him of whom Moses, and the law, and the prophets wrote. That you will put your hand upon him, as you're told in the epistle of John: We have seen him with our eyes and handled him with our hands, the very word of life. "I bring you our own information concerning him of whom we have seen with our very eyes and handled with our very hands, the word of life" (1Jhn1:1).

Well, you this night felt him, because you exercised his organs. You exercised his limbs when you spread out your hand to touch a tennis ball, and there was no tennis ball, when you stretched it out to touch a baseball and there is no baseball. So when you actually called upon self to test it, and you could bring in to play organs not known by the scientific world, and they called them imaginary, existing only in the Imagination, and, therefore, unreal. Why he is the only reality, because through him all things were made. There isn't a thing that is now made in this world that it wasn't preceded by an imaginal act. What is any picture in the world that you now see and you call it fact but what it first began in the Imagination of the artist? He caught the thing on canvas...and you call that the reality. It existed first in his Imagination. We are living in a world of Imagination, and that being that is the Lord of it all is housed in you. And the world, they know him not. He comes unto his own and his own receive him not. They can't believe it.

But if someone can take in their imaginary hand, called by the world the unreal hand, and pour out the contents of an imaginary bag and count the contents, and they're bringing out the very pay that they would receive at the end of the week were they now earning a certain sum of money...which was more than twice what they had ever earned before...and doing it over and over until it took on the tones of reality. When it seemed to them to have all the sensory vividness of reality, they dropped it. And then in a matter of two days, that lady was employed by one she had never heard of before and had never seen, paying her *that* sum of money to the penny. She was a combination seamstress and designer in the city of New York. She took in my word, as I hope tonight you will, and she went home either to prove what I said or disprove it. And so she accepted the challenge.

So let me repeat, we must make daring experiments with Jesus Christ. Brood over him. Learn to know him better. And when we have proved his existence as the creative power in ourselves, then share it with others. Pass it on to all the others and tell them what we have found in Jesus...and you will find a *living* God. For I tell you nothing dies. You cannot die, for I have seen the immortal man that cannot die, and he is housed in everyone. When the man is called dead, it's only the departure of the one in whom there is life. The man of Imagination departs a moment from the little garment of flesh. Everything here dies. So, "Awake, O sleepers, and rise from the dead." So try now to exercise him, become familiar with him. And one day when you least expect it, he arrives with such dramatic suddenness that you have no time to observe him. You can't observe his coming he comes so suddenly within you. The wind, just a strange peculiar unearthly wind, and you feel yourself waking, waking, waking. You wake in this grave that was the coffin that was placed in Egypt: "In the beginning God...in a coffin in Egypt." You wake within this tomb and you do not ___(??) know how you got there, who put you there, or when you were put there. Now all of a sudden you awake, and then you come out, and you're born from above, just as told you in scripture.

Until that day comes believe me, that the one that I've just introduced you to is the only true Jesus Christ, the only God of the world. There is no other God. "All that you behold, though it appears without, it is within, in your own wonderful human Imagination of which this world of mortality is but a shadow" (Blake, *Jerusalem*, Plt.71).

Now let us go into the Silence.

*   *   *

Next week were speaking on Tuesday rather than Monday, and you'll notice a few weeks where we only have one lecture. The club is not available that week for a Friday night. So the nights we cannot get the Friday we have no substitute, we simply do not speak more than the one lecture in that week; and it may either be a Monday or a Tuesday. I have no knowledge of the days until I look at the program myself. I happen to know that next week it's going to be Tuesday and Friday. The following week I haven't the slightest idea. Maybe there is no Friday that week, I don't know. So I do not wish you to take a long trip and come here to be disappointed. So please look at the program if you're inclined before you start to attend. Again, let me repeat it's going to be the most profoundly spiritual and at the same time most directly practical. You can transform your earthly life when you know who Christ is., when you find him within you and challenge him to transform your world, knowing you are doing it. You and he are one. Trust in him and do it. I tell you, it cannot fail you, it will not fail you; but remember you are the operant power, it doesn't operate itself. I may know it from now to the ends of time, but knowledge of it is not enough, I must apply it.

So we are told, the world heard it, the same Word that we heard, but the message that they heard did not benefit them because it was not mixed with faith in the hearers. They didn't believe it. So I've asked you now to touch this, but maybe you'll say, "That's stupid. I can tell you that's still my Imagination; that isn't real." And so, maybe you will go out and not put it to the test at all. I am powerless to make you do it. I can't compel you, I can only instruct you, and then tell you what I have found concerning Jesus Christ.

Now are there any questions, please?

Q: (inaudible)
A: My dear, you can do it with all things. Oh, no, take as many as you want. Look at the world, three and a half billion of us, and the one being is doing all. And no two have the same desire. So don't think for one second you're bothering him with multiple desires. Don't think for one moment that you are interfering with the record as it were. It's entirely up to you. God speaks to man through the medium of desire. "Is anything too difficult for me?" he asks. When the man said "If you can!" the exclamation mark caused him to be authority. "If you can!" said he, "All things are possible to him who believes."

Any questions? Now when you get the results that you will, may I ask you to do me a personal favor and share the results with me, that I, in turn, may tell it to those who are here? It increases their faith if I can tell your story… how you heard it, applied it, and then the results that you got.

Q: Neville, I was interested in a point that you made earlier this evening when you said that Eastern philosophies and religions did not have the experience of Christ. Could you say why? In the Western world, in the early times, evidently there were people who had this experience.

A: Now, David, I must correct you. I did not say they did not. If anyone has a tape recorder, they'll know I didn't say that. I said, any orthodox religion, whether it be Jewish, Christian or Mohammedan, are worshipping external gods. I didn't say they did not know of some inner power. But if the teacher who brings it is now picked up...like Mohammed for instance, we have a record that such a man lived as a man...and then millions turn towards what they consider Mecca, his holy place, and several times a day they must go down and bow towards this place, they are worshipping a piece of clay on the outside; they haven't found Christ. For, if on the other hand, the Christian does the same thing by genuflecting as he goes into a church, and bows before the altar, does all these things before the altar, and he's *got* to go to church or else he has some mortal sin or maybe some unforgivable sin, he's worshipping a *false* god. As told me in the 31st chapter of Deuteronomy, he said, "You are about to sleep with your fathers; and this people they will now rise and play the part of the harlot... these strange gods in the land, where they are going to be among. And I will hide my face from them in that land" (Deut.31:16). Well, his face is completely hidden...until man stops worshipping a false god, God's face is hidden. He hides himself while I play the part of the harlot and worship a false god.

Q: What interests me is the fact that the Christian mystic over the centuries has experienced, evidently, the father-son relationship, whereas the Oriental mystic never experienced that in the writings.

A: Well, David, you know I am not familiar with the Oriental literature to the extent that maybe I should be, so I can't say yes or no to that. I'll take your word for it, for you're a scholar and studied much, and so I would go along and say, "Well now, David said so." I, personally, am not familiar with such literature. I've read the *Upanishads*, the *Gita*, and things of that sort, and I love them, as *the Light of Asia*, it's beautiful poetry, I love it. But I do not know of anything outside of the Jewish-Christian faith that is so altogether true based upon my own personal experience. I have experienced Judaism in Christianity; Christianity is the fulfillment of Judaism. All that was foretold and prophesied, recorded in the Old Testament, the New Testament is its fulfillment...like the flower on the tree. And when it happens, it is so unlike what man thinks it ought to be he stands bewildered. It's so different in prospect from what it actually seemed to be in retrospect.

So the Father-Son relationship I have experienced. And that everlasting Son is David: "Thou art my Son; today I have begotten thee," the 2nd Psalm (verse 7). That is literally true. This divine sonship of David is unique, the only one like it, and totally supernatural. It's not the result of generation as we understand it. I go back to the core, the inner core, par excellence of the patriarchs, Abraham, Isaac, Jacob, and they are not discovered in any ancient Near East record. Yet, they are in the genealogy of Jesus Christ. And you can't rub them out, you have no writers...so who are they? I have encountered these various characters in my visions. When I saw Abraham, this majestic...with a look beyond... you can't describe the look of vision. He was not looking into space, he was looking in time. And you're told in the 8th chapter of John, "And Abraham rejoiced that he was to see my day; he saw it and was glad" (John 8:56). As we're told in Galatians, "And the scriptures"—now he takes the scripture and he personifies it—"the scripture, foreseeing that God would justify the heathen through faith, preached the gospel *beforehand* to Abraham" (Gal.3:8); gave him a preview of the entire plan of creation and its fulfillment, a preview. But when I saw him, this majestic being, I didn't have to ask, who are you? You don't ask, you know exactly who the being is. These are eternal states personified. Here is Abraham standing under a tree, the most gnarly oak you've ever seen; not a leaf on it, just gnarled...a gnarly, gnarly oak. His head came almost to the very top of the trunk. And wrapped around that tree was this strange and wonderful, wise, wise serpent, the wisest thing you could ever see, looking right at you. He didn't look at me, he was looking off into the distance, completely oblivious of me, but not the serpent. There was the serpent looking at me but his eye buried upon my eye, the most knowing, knowing look. Here, he was looking into time: "He rejoiced that he was to see my day." And the serpent is looking...for was it not he who said, "you shall not surely die? Oh, yes, you'll die. Did God say you'll die? Well, I tell you, you will not really die" (Gen.3:4). But, you'll die but not really die.

And that's my next subject, which is next Tuesday night, "Where God Only Acts."

Thank you for coming.

GOD ONLY ACTS

9/20/66

Tonight's subject is "God Only Acts." You may ask how could a thoughtful man born as we were born and who will die as we will die know that? Yet I tell you I know it from experience. I told you in the card that I sent you that this is on the Word of God. I have experienced the Word of God, so tonight I will tell you, and I will tell you from my own personal experience how I know that God alone acts. The name of God is the key to understanding the biblical doctrine of God. In biblical terms the question is not does God exist, but *who* is our God? What is his name and what is his Son's name? For Israel, the personal name of God is I AM. You can read that in scripture, as I read it in scripture, but I didn't know it until I experienced it.

Let us go back tonight to an experience of mine that took place in 1929, it was in the summer of '29. Before I quote the passage from the 82nd Psalm, let me say that the editor of the most scholarly of all high criticisms of scripture, his name was Thomas K. Cheyne; he was the editor of the *Encyclopedia Biblica*. You will find this statement concerning the book in both the *Americana* that is the great dictionary, American dictionary, and great British dictionary, called *Britannica*, that it is by far the most scholarly of all higher biblical criticisms. This is what he said of the 82nd Psalm. He said, "It makes the strongest demands on the historical Imagination of the interpreter. The ideas may be perennial, but the outer forms are no longer understood."

Now let me quote the passages in this Psalm that disturbed this great professor. He was the outstanding biblical professor of the day at Oxford University, a master of the Hebrew tongue. He interpreted the entire Old Testament from the original scripture. And here was this master, in his day the giant, and he's still considered...his book of Psalms as we have in our library is still considered tops in translation. When he said, "It's the greatest demand of all Psalms on the historic Imagination of the interpreter." He confesses that the ideas there may be perennial, and still they are, but then he said as far as understanding them they have long been forgotten to man.

Now there are two verses in the very short Psalm that disturbed the great professor, the first and the sixth. The first is this, "God has taken his place in the divine council; in the midst of the gods he holds judgment." That's the first verse. In the sixth, "I say you are gods, sons of the Most High, all of you; nevertheless, you shall die like men, and fall as one man, O princes." You read it in your 82nd Psalm. Now the crux of the interpretation hangs upon the meaning that the interpreters will give to the word Elohim. And may I tell you, I have read so many commentaries, I have many exegeses at home, and they differ widely. Yet the word Elohim is simply stated in scripture as God. It's a plural word. It first appears in the very first verse of Genesis. "In the beginning God…" that's the first time it appears; it's singular, yet the word is plural. In the 26th verse it reappears, and here we find the word now plural, "And God said, 'Let us make man in our image, after our likeness.'" Here we find it now in its *plural* form. In this 82nd Psalm, the word Elohim appears twice, in the first verse and then in the 6th verse. In the 1st verse, "And God has taken his place in the divine council; in the midst of the gods"—that's plural—"he holds judgment." Well, the historic Imagination is concerned only with the facts of secular history. There is no record on earth…even though no history book agrees with another history book on the same event, still they were facts. We know that the Battle of Waterloo was fought, we know the Civil War here was fought, the 1st and 2nd World Wars were fought, and now we're fighting another one. But no historian in telling the story of these events will tell it in the same manner. They will see it through different eyes, but they were recording facts.

I say, in the midst of changing theories and opinions of men in secular history, stands the unchanging Word of God. Secular history is over; it's finished. The time is fulfilled now for it to be fulfilled *in* us. So, secular history is over, secular history a changing thing that will tomorrow fade and vanish like the grass. It will wither like the grass and vanish and fade like the flowers. No matter how big a nation is today it will tomorrow vanish. No matter how big you are you're going to be rubbed out completely like some footstep on the little sand as the waves come in. But *salvation* history is forever. So in the midst of these changing theories and opinions of secular history stands the unchanging salvation history of God. This is literally true. I've just quoted you from the 82nd Psalm. I experienced it in the summer of 1929.

Now here is my experience of this…and I *know* that God only acts. So when Blake wrote that memorable fancy of his, called *The Marriage of Heaven and Hell*, he wasn't exercising his right as the poet when he said, "God only acts and is in existing beings or men." And when he advanced it into *Jerusalem*, in his greatest of all poems, and he said, "Let us to him who only *is*, and who walks among us, give decision." The only actor is God. God alone acts and there is no other actor. Now if you remember what I said when I quoted that passage from the 82nd, "I say you are gods, sons of the Most High, all of you; nevertheless, you will die like men and fall as one man, O princes." Now, "God takes his place in the divine council and in the midst of the gods he holds judgment." Is this literally true? Well, the great scholars up to this day cannot by their scholars' Imagination encompass that statement, they can't. Until it's revealed, they cannot by all of their knowledge of the tongue, called the Hebrew tongue, or the Greek tongue, or any tongue with which this thing was revealed, they cannot grasp it. It is not part of the facts of secular life.

But here is my experience. I was a dancer in that day. It was just before the great financial crash enveloped our country for almost twelve years. We didn't come out of it until the 2nd World War and everything collapsed. But I was a successful dancer, successful about making money and pulling my own. I was sound asleep in my hotel room in New York City when I was taken in Spirit into this divine council. Now the phrase translated "divine council" if you look up the words in the King James Version, they translate that as "the congregation of the mighty, the mighty ones." You go further and it is called "the synagogue, the church." He stands in his church, the synagogue; the synagogue being the assembly of the mighty ones, those who are called by name, the called ones by name; and then ordered and commanded by word. It's the point whence motion proceeds. You are going to be actually sent after you are called. I'm giving you now the definitions of the words as given to us in the biblical concordance, which is *Strong's Concordance*.

The mighty ones...when I entered this wonderful assemblage of mighty ones, I saw one, the personification of infinite might. Others were around, all the assemblage of the gods. I was taken to this heavenly woman, and there she was with an enormous ledger open. She was seated. I stood at her left side. She turned and looked me in the eyes. She didn't say one word; I said nothing. I simply looked and she looked as though she looked for confirmation, for the word is "the called ones by name." She looked, then she looked back at the ledger, and with a long quill pen there she either entered or checked off, I do not know which. I knew she made a motion on the ledger as she looked at me.

Then I was taken before God, the risen Christ, infinite love. As I stood before him I felt nothing but love. He asked the most simple question in the world, "What is the greatest thing in the world?" and I answered in the words of Paul, "Faith, hope and love, these three, but the greatest of these is love." With that he embraced me; we fused and became one body, not two, one, infinite love. I wore the human form divine, which is love, fused with God and no one can put us asunder. At that moment I was one with God, and no power in the world can separate me from the love that is God with which I am fused. We're wearing the same body. As I was embraced, a voice out of space came and the voice said, "Down with the bluebloods." I heard the voice but I saw no face. And then I found myself before the embodiment of might...the mighty ones, now gathered as one. When God first reveals himself to man he reveals himself as God Almighty: He said, "I appeared to Abraham, to Isaac, and to Jacob, as God Almighty, but by my name the Lord (which is I AM) I did not make myself known unto them" (Ex.6:3). So here, I stood before God in his appearance as Almighty God. He didn't commune with me as God in the appearance of love did; didn't ask any questions. Now comes the order, as the word Mighty God is translated in the concordance. He doesn't ask me anything, he commands it, and the words were "Time to act!" Then I was whisked out of that divine assemblage and found myself back in the secular world of man, where I knew I was born here and I will die here. I didn't know then, but I searched the scriptures, that it was the fulfillment of the 82nd Psalm, "I say you are gods, sons of the Most High, all of you; but you will die like men and fall as *one* man, O princes."

So I said earlier that the name of God is the key to the interpretation of the doctrine of God in the Bible and to Israel that name is I AM. So the word "the Lord"—and he reveals himself to the state called Moses—-is "I AM." "Say unto them I AM has sent you." But how do I know I AM has sent me? Well, I saw it. Is this really I AM who sent me? Who did he send? He sent me. Well, who is this mighty one that sent me? He was mighty...and here I am told it contains all the gods...and you and I fell. Listen to the words, "You will fall as one man, O princes." Now the word Yod He Vau He, which we translate I AM, its primary meaning is "to fall, or to cause to fall; or to blow, or to cause the wind to blow." That's the primary meaning of the word Yod He Vau He. We mustn't forget that when we read scripture. Here is one being containing all of us, and the one who fell caused the fall. This is no after-thought, all predetermined...the way that God expands.

So the one God, containing the gods, all of us, sons of the Most High, fell. He fell and caused to fall, confident that he contained the power to rise from this world of sin and death. And the first comes out, then the second comes out, the third comes out. It was one in the beginning; it'll be one in the end. We're gathered one by one, O people of Israel. As we are told in Isaiah, "I gather you one by one, O people of Israel" (27:12). So we are all gathered back into the same oneness that we were before the fall, but enhanced infinitely by the experience of the fall into the world of sin and death. So everyone here when I look at you it seems so insane to tell you this, I say you are gods, all of you, sons of the Most High, yet, nevertheless you shall die like men—who doesn't die here like a man—and fall as one man. The one Rock fragmented into these infinite pieces, and then all are put together again to reform into the one man, this time transcending himself before the fall.

So the word that came to me was "Time to act." So I say, in everyone is the actor; the only actor in this world is God. God is playing all the parts. God is acting. And it seems at moments a horrible part of the drama; at moments it's a pleasant part of the drama. And then you have moments where you are on the wing and nothing is happening. But at every moment God is acting. The most horrible situation in the world, only God is playing the parts. And when I tell you it has sprung from a God that is love it seems incredible. Yet I stood before the God of love, and the God of love embraced me, and I fused with him. We not only became one, we *are* one.

You can't see the body that I wear through mortal eyes; these eyes die. You'll need other eyes to see the garment that I wear, for there's no divorce. Let no man put asunder what God has joined together. And we are brought back one by one and united with him. As we're told in scripture, "He who is united to the Lord becomes one spirit with him" (1Cor.6:17). So when you are united to the Lord you are one spirit with him, and no man or organization can put asunder that which God has joined together. We're joined to the oneness, one by one. When he said, "God only acts and is in existing beings or men," this was not taking liberty as the poet would with words. He saw a vision and he told it in his own wonderful way...as he could really use words. I wish I had the talent in the world of men to use words as Blake did, for I could tell that same vision but no more beautifully than he has told it, "God only acts and is in existing beings or men." He must have heard the identical words, "Time to act."

Now if you are here for the first time, you might wonder what were the words "Down with the bluebloods" and because of your conditioned mind you might think it means down with the social world. Hasn't a thing to do with that. The bluebloods throughout history has been church protocol, the external trappings of the world that is a substitute for religion. All the so-called outward trappings, all the doctrines, the rituals, these, this is called collectively "the blueblood." Down with it! I did not receive my knowledge of scripture from any man in this world, and my authority to preach it is not from any organization in the world. It came, as it did through Paul, by a revelation of Jesus Christ. When he unveiled himself before me, I answered correctly and he embraced me, in fulfillment now of the gospel. "And when they bring you into the synagogue before the rulers, do not be anxious how or what you are to answer or what you are to say; for the Holy Spirit will teach you in that very hour what you *ought* to say" (Luke12:12). You are divinely prompted. I heard no words. It came automatically, as though I'd been so well-rehearsed in what I ought to say that when this moment in time comes for you to answer, like an actor stepping on the stage, he does it automatically. He doesn't take thought as to what he's going to say. So take no thought; do not be anxious how or what you're going to answer and what you're going to say, for the Holy Spirit will in that very hour teach you what you ought to say, and you say it. Divinely prompted you couldn't make a mistake.

So no one is going to falter when they're brought into the great assemblage of the gods. You will see only two, really, there are others, but in the end there are only two: the one who embraces you, the risen Christ, who's infinite love, and then the one who is the same presence, revealed only as might, God Almighty, El Shaddai. And that's all that he is, infinite might without compassion, and the other, infinite love, nothing but compassion, and yet the same being. So "I appeared to Abraham, to Isaac and to Jacob, as God Almighty, but by my name the Lord (which is I AM) I did not make myself known unto them." But, beyond that comes the greatest revelation, when he reveals himself as the Father. God is the Father, with the heart of a father. He could never be envious of a child, for he'd be proud of his son. He couldn't in any way hold back his son from accomplishment; he would simply be proud of his son. So here, we are the sons of the Most High, all of us. Not one will be lost, not one in all my holy mountain.

So now, here on this level, while we are in the world of Caesar, there must be some use I can put to this vision. For here, while I wait to be called into the divine assemblage for no one knows—for he who fell is the one who caused the fall, and he who blew is the one who caused the wind to blow. So he is the wind and the causer of the wind blowing. And that is God's elective love; the secret remains with God. No one knows this night where the wind... the uncertain nature of the wind's course. Who knows how it will come this night and breathe upon you? If it breathes upon you, you awaken. You can't stop it, there's no resistance; you're taken in spirit into the divine assemblage. "And so as the wind blows where it will, and you hear the sound of it, but you cannot know whence it comes or where it goes; so it is with every one who is born of the Spirit" (John3:8). And the very word wind and Spirit are one in both Hebrew and Greek. The same word is used for both wind and Spirit. So no one knows when it's going to happen, and it comes in the same unpredictable manner. You don't know...it's so strange how it comes. Here I was a dancer, sleeping, and then suddenly, of all people, why should I be chosen? I was not a member of a church, not schooled in what is called some religious training, and trying to keep myself afloat without turning to others to help, and suddenly I am chosen. So the secret of God's elective love remains his secret. And so, it is simply a state.

Alright, we are called, as we are told in Romans, we're called according to his purpose. "For those whom he foreknew"—he foreknew us all, then—"he predestined us to be conformed to the image of his Son. And those whom he predestined he called; and those whom he called he justified; and those whom he justified he also glorified" (Rom.8:29). Well, these five terms, foreknew, predestined, called, justified and glorified, add up to a very strong affirmation of predestination. I know of no way you can take the five terms and interpret them to avoid a conclusion of predestination. You try it. Those whom he foreknew he predestined; those whom he predestined he called; those whom he called he justified; those whom he justified he glorified. The implication is a gift of himself to the one that he glorifies. Justification is divine acquittal. No matter what you have done in the world of Caesar, and what haven't we done; no man is without sin, but no man. No man can say that he hasn't violated the commands of God...especially when we read that they must be done psychologically. For "You've heard it said, 'You must not commit adultery. But I say the one who looks lustfully on a woman has already committed the act of adultery with her in his heart'" (Mat.5:27). Well, what man is not guilty? What woman is not guilty? If I take the name man generically, what individual in this world is not guilty of violating that commandment? Yet, he will justify him and in justifying him vindicate him. It's divine vindication. And the minute you are completely vindicated by the embrace of him, you are glorified in his presence; you are one with God. From then on, you aren't two, you're only one.

So on this level, we take that command "Time to act!" and then we read scripture, "Drink no more water; take a little wine for your stomach's sake and your many infirmities" (1Tim.5:23). Well, water is a psychological symbol of psychological knowledge. It's a symbol of psychological knowledge. I come into the field and there's a well, and a stone covers the well. I roll the stone away and draw water and water my flock, then I roll the stone back. The stone is a symbol of literal truth. The water is a symbol of psychological interpretation of the literal fact. Now I turn it into wine, as told us in the 2nd chapter of John. I take the water and I draw forth water, but the water doesn't come out, I draw wine. Wine is the *application* of the truth that I have heard.

So, if I have heard that I must repent...the very first word used "repent"... well, repent is to change my attitude towards life. I change it radically. Well, if I see you and you are not well and I'm going to help you, I've got to actually persuade myself that I have just seen the most wonderful embodiment of health that I've ever encountered concerning you, and so persuade myself that that is fact, when I meet you when I think of you I can only see that. But, I only see this new being in my mind's eye relative to you. Well, then I'm not drinking water any more, I've applied it. I am now drinking wine for the afflictions of my world. So I go through life simply taking wine. I've absorbed all the water that I could take. I have taken all the literal facts of life, turned them into the psychological truths that they represent, and then instead of absorbing more and more of these truths, stop it. Start now drinking a little wine: start applying the little knowledge that you have.

And so you go out to repent. Not to feel remorseful, not to feel regretful for anything you have done, but to see those in need...which is only yourself pushed out, for we are one. We started in the divine assemblage and we all fell as one man, and it became fragmented. When we're all gathered together again it will still be one man and that one man is God. There is *only* God. So while we are fragmented and think there is another, we are at war with self. Now I see an aspect of myself and I heard that he really isn't another, he really is but an aspect. Well, I don't want this little finger to be hurting me all the time. The whole body hurts. If I say, "Well, after all, that doesn't matter, I'll cut it off" I'm just simply chopping off a part of myself. So you need discard no one in this world. We simply change the one that formerly we would have discarded as something that could not be redeemed. Everything is redeemable. So we take every person in this world and change them in our own mind's eye, and change them *in us* radically. We wait for a moment, to find it conforming to the change that took place in us, and the whole vast world only mirrors and echoes the changes taking place in us.

So we stop simply drinking more and more water, by absorbing more and more of the psychological meanings of scripture, and we apply the little that we know. The application is now drinking wine. So we will drink wine from now on, and simply change our world to conform to the ideal that we would like to have in our world, the world in which we want to live. And that is acting; therefore, God only acts and is in existing beings or men. If you don't act upon what you have as knowledge, then God is simply asleep within you. As you're told in scripture, "Rouse thyself! Why sleepest thou, O Lord? Awake! Do not cast us off forever" (Ps.44:23). "Wake, O sleeper, and rise from the dead" (Eph.5:14). If we don't act, we are asleep, and we're likened unto the dead. But to hear what we ought to do and to do it, is to begin to stir and come alive within ourselves.

So I say to everyone, I know this from experience. I am not theorizing, I'm not speculating; I am telling you what I *know* from experience. I have experienced scripture. I have experienced the Word of God. I can't tell anyone in this world what it feels like. Not to the real extent that I would like to tell you what it feels like to have experienced scripture, to see how true it is...that everything here changes, all things fade. There are those who have a billion and they want two billion. One young man is suing his father for a part of a trust fund that is already 300 million, and the father already owns one billion, and he doesn't want to release one penny of it. The boy is thirty-one years old; the father is now seventy-six. He doesn't know how near he is to where he ___(??), but he doesn't want one penny of it taken from him. The son could use some of it...it belongs to the son. He'll have none of it. Money is not for that purpose, he thinks. Money is to hold on to and invest until it grows. And the old story in the Bible, "O foolish man, your soul is required of you this night" (Luke 12:20). But he doesn't know it. So he holds on to a trust fund that his mother left not only to him but to his offspring. So he has offspring. And the three and a half million has grown in thirty-four years to almost $300 million. He's been a very good steward, watching it carefully, protecting it and developing it. In thirty-four years three and a half million has grown to 300 million. Well, now one of the four entitled to his portion of it is asking for a portion, seven million, but seven million out of 300 million when he's entitled to one-fourth of it. And the father...he has to bring suit... sue your own father that you love, at least I hope he does, in order to get him to cough up what is his own, and he is resisting it.

So I say to you, all this will fade. His billions will fade. Our fabulous world that we love so much, it will all fade like the grass. The grass will wither and the flowers fade, but the Word of God will remain true forever. This is the unchanging truth in the midst of these changing things in the secular world. So when they say, "Is God is dead?" or "God is dead" and they make a very affirmative statement, it's so stupid. But you can't blame them, they have not experienced scripture. The very ones who made that bold affirmation are still gods. "I say you are gods," not a few of you who will say God is alive, "I say you are gods, sons of the Most High, *all* of you; nevertheless, you will die like men and you will fall as one man, O princes." If you're a prince, then your father is a king. He is the King of Kings. And collectively we are the King, for the Father and the Son are one.

So when we come back from our fragmented state in this world and all gather together once more, we form the one God. There's only God. So when Blake was asked, "What do you think of Jesus?" he didn't hesitate, he said, "Jesus is the *only* God," but then he quickly added, "But so am I, and so are you." There's no division in God. Although the Elohim is a plural word and, therefore it's a compound unity, one made up of others, it is still one. So when asked, "What is the greatest commandment?" he didn't mention the ten, or any one of the ten. He mentioned the confession of faith of the Israelite, "Hear, O Israel: The Lord our God is one Lord" (Deut.6:4). If you take the word, there are ten words. They are the Ten Commandments: "Hear, O Israel: The Lord our God is one Lord." This is the greatest Commandment. And the second is tied in to the first, "Love thy neighbor as thyself." For there is no other; he's not really another.

So here this night, I tell you from experience that God only acts and is. So the most horrible act this night, it was God asleep; the most loving act is the same God in the act of waking. And the day will come, you and I will leave this world of sin and death and return where we were before, but our translucency is then enhanced. We were expanded beyond what we were prior to our fall into this world, which was a deliberate fall, it wasn't an accident. It was something that was planned in the beginning: God's way of expansion by self-limitation. He achieves his purpose by limiting himself to the limit called man, which is the limit of contraction; and then he breaks the shell and not only returns to what he was but beyond it, by such contraction. So everyone will be saved. And there's only one Savior and he's housed right within you. "God is our salvation. Our God is the God of salvation; and to God the Lord, belongs escape from death"—the 68th Psalm. To God, the Lord, belongs escape from death and this is the world of sin and death. So, "Nevertheless, you shall die like men"—this is the world—"and fall as one man, O princes." But because God is the God of salvation and to God, the Lord, belongs escape from death, and he who fell is within you, then be assured of redemption. You cannot fail. No one can fail. But why not in the world of Caesar use what has been revealed to the nth degree in making for yourself and those you love around you a more beautiful world by acting; and no longer absorbing and drinking the psychological meaning of scripture but putting it in to practice by applying this law that you know.

Now let us go into the Silence.

*   *   *

___(??) scripture from any school or any man. I simply read it now having had the experience only for confirmation of the experience. So my experiences parallel scripture.

Now are there any questions, please?

Q: Neville, would you explain the 12th verse of the 13th chapter of Matthew. Shall I read it?

A: Please do.

Q: ...especially the last part. "To him who hath, to him shall be given, and he shall have more abundance: but whosoever hath not, from him shall be taken away even that he hath"...especially the last part.

A: If you do not know God's law and live by it, you may, like many of the world, think that what I have now I will keep it forever without application of a principle that sustains it. All things come into this world by an imaginal act, they are kept in being by the imaginal act. When that imaginal act for unnumbered reasons ceases to be, it vanishes from their world. So people today who have nothing tomorrow will have much; those who have will have nothing. Not because God is punishing anyone, it's a law: All things bear after their kind. It's one of those laws set up in the beginning. All things bear after their kind. So if I bring something into being and I forget how I did it, and think now *that* is my security and not the law by which I brought the fruit into being the tree stops bearing.

You can take people today who made fortunes in the pools, the football pool of England, which pays off a million dollars for a penny. All their life they had nothing before...came into one million tax free... before he dies he has nothing. It wasn't taxed, all that is tax free money, $1,000,000. And it's been actually investigated...before they go from this world, before they depart, they have nothing because they forgot, if they ever knew, how they brought it in: Some moment of excitement when they lost themselves in the imaginal act of possession, and it became fact. But they couldn't relate the fact to the unseen cause that produced it. So they feed upon this trash, not keeping it alive in their mind's eye. So all things come into this world by imaginal acts; they are sustained by these imaginal acts; and they vanish when the act ceases to be sustained.

So to him that hath it shall be given if he knows how to keep it alive in this world; and the man who has not refuses to believe that he has anything to do with his lack in this world. He thinks it's society. He wants the world to take care of him. And he thinks that the government owes him a living. He thinks that that one owes him a living, and everybody but himself owes him a living. Politicians encourage him to believe that in order to get his vote. Then we have billions being paid out because of people who refuse to pull their own weight, and yet their weight is so simple by using their own wonderful Imaginations. Imagination is the divine body in every man. If he doesn't use it, well, then it doesn't bear fruit, and he sits back and actually believes that everybody owes him a living. And yet the man who will use his Imagination, he brings it in. He may remember the imaginal cause of the physical effect, he may. If he does, he's blessed. As you're told in the 1st Psalm, "Blessed is the man who rejoices in the law of the Lord...for in all that he does he prospers" (verses 2,3). Well, what is the law of the Lord? It's stated so simply in 11th chapter of Mark, "Whatever you desire, when you pray, believe that you have received it, and you will" (verse 24). Just as simple as that...whatever you desire. Don't consult a teacher or a priest or anyone whether it is good or bad. You desired it? Is that what you really want? The story is *whatever* you desire, believe that you have received it, and you will.

Now, do I have that faith to believe that I have what reason and my senses deny? If I do and it becomes a fact, am I going to forget the law by which I made it a fact? If I do, well, then I've gone back to sleep and I don't delight in the law of the Lord. So, if you bring something in… in this meeting of ours I don't see them anymore, but we've had a few others who on the basis of this law went down to Caliente. One fellow made $87,000. He owed a thousand dollars and didn't have anyone to whom he could turn to raise one penny. He had no credit for a thousand dollars. He made $87,000. Well, now he became the wealthy one in his own mind's eye.

Another chap—his hand was as cold as a block of ice—when he heard a man confess from my platform he came back and took my hand and said that he had misspent it; he did not steal it. "Without the consent of the one who loaned me this money, I invested it in business thinking that it would be alright." So he said, "I did not steal it, Neville, only the business failed. Now he wants his money. Do you think I could do what that man tonight said that he did?" I said, "Certainly you can. The same God in you, the same God in me, the same God in him can do it." In one month he made $54,000. But then, both of them made all of this money and they forgot the Word of God. I would be very interested to find out how near they are to the end of the 87,000 and the 54,000. It would be very interesting to find out what they did with all this money.

If you forget God's law and not delight in it, it's not you, you aren't the important one; you are the instrument through which God is acting. This little thing, this little mask, this [body] is a mask, as though I stepped on the stage playing another part, and no one knew me because I wore a mask. And so God is acting. If God stopped acting, the mask can feed on the hay that God has given a moment to produce, and then all of a sudden it comes to an end. A man is carried away with his own little false image of himself, when the greatest is housed within him…it's the God of gods.

Q: You mentioned when you saw Abraham the snake was there. I'm interested in what the snake was doing.

A: I said last week that the characters of scripture are not persons as you and I are persons, they are eternal states through which the immortal you passes. And I quoted from Blake, his *Vision of the Last Judgment*, when he said, "When you read the Bible, it ought to be understood that the persons Moses and Abraham are not here meant, but the states signified by those names, the individuals being representatives or visions of those states as they were revealed to mortal man in a series of divine revelations as they are written in the Bible." Now he makes a confession, he said, "These various states I have seen in my Imagination; when seen at a distance they appear as one man; as you approach they are a multitude of nations" (Pp.76-77).

Well, I have had that similar experience. So I saw the state of Abraham. Abraham was this tall majestic being leaning against the trunk of a very gnarly oak. No leaf is on the oak and the limbs...nothing resembled the human brain more than the branches of this oak. All the convolutions of the brain seemed to be objectified in this tree, and wound around, all around the trunk of the tree was a serpent. Its head was human, its face was human, and there it is looking not at Abraham, looking at me, with the wisest expression you could ever imagine. He seemed to be infinitely wise, as told in scripture, of all God's creatures he was the wisest. Abraham was looking off into the distance, not in space but in time, in keeping with scripture. "Abraham rejoiced that he was to *see* my day; he saw it and was glad" (John 8:56). Abraham was given a preview of God's plan of salvation, as told us in Galatians, "And the scripture, foreseeing that God would justify the heathen by faith, preached the gospel to Abraham beforehand" (3:8). So *beforehand*...if you take it chronologically as though he were a person as you are a person, it would be at least 2,000 years B.C.

Abraham, Isaac, Jacob, Moses, these aren't persons, these are states. They aren't found in any ancient history. There is no record of the Near East where the names are mentioned either as individuals or persons or as their tribes. They appear only in scripture. Scripture is not secular history; it is biblical history of salvation. It's all the history of salvation, God's *plan* of redemption, and these are the eternal states. But when you enter a state, the state becomes personified. So when I entered the state of faith...for Abraham is the state of absolute belief. He heard and believed the most incredible story in the world, and Abraham believed God and it was accounted unto him for righteousness. So you meet the state. But when you meet the state it seems to you a person like yourself.

So when you meet any of these characters of scripture they aren't persons, they are infinite eternal states. God's eternal play *is*, and you can't rub it out. Whether you believe it or not, one day everyone will encounter these states. You are a person; you are the God that fell. But these are states, therefore, you can say honestly, "Before Abraham was, I AM." This is the play; scripture is the play. And you were the God before you fell. And now you fall...not because of any mistake that you made... but by design. You fell by design, and then the one became the many, fragmented. And then you'll pass through these states, and the day will come you will encounter them. At a certain moment of awakening you will encounter all these states and know what they are. I don't have to ask when I meet any of these states, "Who are you?" It's so obvious who they are.

So the serpent, as told in the very beginning of Genesis, and the serpent said to the woman, "Did God say that you would die? You will not surely die." He didn't correct God. He didn't say, "You were lying." He said, "You will not surely die." But he allows the statement, "You will die." So I say, nevertheless, you will die like men...yet you will not really die. Nothing dies. How can God die when God is playing all the parts? Everyone in the world, every child born of woman, well, he couldn't breathe were it not that God the very breath of life is in him. He not only is the one who blows, he's the one who causes the wind to blow. You breathe, well, that's God,

Goodnight.

LOVE ENDURES

9/23/66

Tonight's subject is "Love Endures." I made you a promise when I started that everything I tell you from this platform I know from experience. I am not theorizing. When we are told, "He who does not love does not know God; for God is love" (1John4:8). The apostle John was not speculating. This is not a conclusion that he reached after years of philosophic contemplation. This was an act of God in self-revelation. If God had ever revealed himself as infinite love to man, I doubt that man could ever, with all the philosophy in the world, ever come to the conclusion that God is love. God *is* love, in spite of all the horror of the world. I tell you it is true; I know that from experience.

Another apostle tells us that "Though I speak with the tongues of men and of angels, and have not love, I am as sounding brass or tinkling cymbals" (1Cor13:1). Then he takes all the gifts of God and compares them to love, and if love is not present, I am as nothing. I may have all the wisdom in the world, all the power, everything in the world, if I have not love, it is as nothing. There is no gift of the Spirit comparable to love, and in the end love is the only thing that really will abide. It will abide forever. Faith will be realized, hope will be realized, these are attributes of God, but God is love. He's not an attribute of God; God *is* love. When you stand in the presence of the risen Christ, you have no other emotion in the world, no other feeling, it's simply love. God is love. And when love embraces you, it's only love. And you wear the body, which is the body of the risen Christ, and it's only love. So everything else will pass away, but love will endure forever. So he who does not love does not know God, for God is love.

Now tonight, I will tell you several things that seem incredible, they are all scriptural. ___(??) aren't true. We are told, "Let us be persistent in the race as we run it, looking to Jesus, the pioneer and perfecter of our faith, who for the joy that was to be realized by him endured the cross, despising the shame" (Heb12:2). Embraced the cross and despised the shame. That's true...I know that to be true. When he nailed himself upon this [body], I know that's true, and despised the shame to which he would have to go as the speaker. When he did it on you, embraced it willingly with the joy, and despised the shame which he knew he would have to go through, that was love.

Now tonight the things that I will tell you, all from scripture, you wonder, how could anyone believe it? Here is one, "He who drinks my blood has eternal life and I will raise him up at the last day" (John6:5). Well, I have a very large selection of Bibles at home and commentaries, and many scholarly works, exegeses on all kinds of the sixty-six books. I haven't read one where they can grasp this theme. They cannot believe that it could be taken literally. But may I tell you these statements are expected to be taken literally and fulfilled literally. I will drink the blood of God? "He who drinks my blood has eternal life and I will raise him up at the last day." It doesn't make sense, does it? That's why Myers in that lovely poem she called "St. Paul", "Oh, *could* I tell, ye surely would believe it. Oh, could I only say what I have seen. How *can* I tell, or how can you believe it, how, until he bringeth you where I have been?" Until you see that temple split in two and the liquid golden light at the base of the spine, as though you put a sponge upon it and every drop is absorbed. You look upon it and the word "drink" or to "eat the flesh" or "drink the blood" is defined in the biblical concordance as "to do it with enjoyment." It's the most repulsive quote in the world if you take it on a certain level. May I tell you, the concordance is right. When you look at it there's nothing but joy in your being, because you say within yourself, "I know it is myself, O my Divine Creator and Redeemer." Then coming closer you fuse with it, absorbing it every little drop like a sponge; and then up, like a spiral of lightening into heaven. I will raise you after you have taken my blood: "He who drinks my blood...I will raise him up at the last day."

The last day is not some day in the remote future; it comes every moment of time to the individual. This thing has happened, but it is still in a sense happening. Look to him, the pioneer and perfecter of our faith, who for the *joy* that was to be, I would say, realized by him, embraced the cross, endured the cross and despised the shame. Everyone will simply have that experience. And when you drink it, it's sheer enjoyment. You don't absorb it with the tongue. I don't put it in my mouth and drink it. I look at it and I know with infinite joy that it's my very being, my Creator and Redeemer; and I fuse with it and absorb it as a dry sponge would that pool of golden liquid light. Then he tells you, I will raise you up after you have drunk my blood, and I will raise you up at the last day; and up you go right into heaven. So how to tell it? If one could only tell it, I know there are those who would believe it. But how to tell it that one could receive it?

Here in New York City, this past summer, I always call on my friend who has run this wonderful bookstore over the years. In fact, most of my library I bought from her. She was only interested in money. I would go...she would sell my book because she made a dollar. She had no interest whatsoever in anything I wrote in the books. She had a fabulous library of metaphysical books. She didn't know the contents of one of them, but she knew where every one was and the price of business. If she knew your interest and you started in a certain direction, she could divert you for a moment while she'd take that book out, rub out the price and put another price in. I never corrected her. I caught her doing it with me. She always did it to my wife when my wife went in looking for a certain books for me. She knew she would never question the price if she had the book, and she would do it. I would go in and she would say, "Oh, Neville, you certainly do dream, don't you?" I said, "Mary, these are not dreams, these are visions paralleling scripture." "Oh, Neville!" then she'd turn to something else. If I would talk politics, which I didn't, if I would talk money with her, occasionally I did, then she would have all ears. But when I began to tell her of a vision, of an experience of mine, Mary had no time for it at all. This goes back into the 20s.

So this year, as was my custom, I thought I would go and call on Mary. I said to a friend of mine at the meeting one night, "I haven't had the time as yet to go and see Mary. I think I'll go tomorrow." She said, "Haven't you heard?" I said no. "Mary was killed last month. She ____(??) and there is no more metaphysical library." It used to be called The Gateway. She and her husband had no children, married for 40-odd years and they went their separate ways. They made lots of money. Mary ran the bookstore, and he lived in a home in the country in Bucks County, where so many artists and writers live in Pennsylvania. So they would call each other if someone needed something. If she needed someone to go hunting for certain books, she'd call Bill and Bill would take the train in or ride in and do whatever Mary needed. She would occasionally go out to the house. So they never had any feeling they should call and really inquire. No reason for it, so they thought.

So, many days went by and he called, he wanted some help, and there was no response. He called all through the day, both the shop and her home in the Village, on 18th Street, and there was no response. So he came on in, went to the home first, there was all the uncollected mail. The neighbors said, we haven't seen Mary in five days. He went to the shop, right off Madison Ave. and 60th, and here uncollected mail, and they hadn't seen Mary in five days. It appears that Mary, five days before, needed something from the grocery store and it was late. It was just at the end of the block. So she went out with just a little change purse and no identification at all, nothing on her but her little change purse. Stepped off the curb and a truck moving at tremendous speed...and she was gone instantly.

So Bill went down to the police department and inquired about this missing wife of his. They said, "You know, have you tried the morgue?" He said, "I'm not talking about a dead wife, I'm telling you my wife is missing. She has been missing for five days." The cop said to him, "After all, these things happen all day in New York City. You've just described a woman just like your wife and she's at the morgue. Why don't you go and look." So Bill goes to the morgue and there's Mary, unclaimed for five days. Not one moment could I arrest her attention as I have yours now. Mary made a considerable sum of money on other people. That's all she wanted. And I would have given her any day that I visited...I would say four or five days a week I'd go and browse in her library, the most wonderful metaphysical library. I think that and the one in Long Beach are the two outstanding libraries in this country that I know...the one called Acres of Books in Long Beach. Well, these are the two fantastic libraries.

Mary made this quick departure from this level unprepared, not knowing one word of the great mystery of life. She had every opportunity over the years to hear from one who had experienced scripture, and Mary wouldn't take it at all. So we are told, at the very end of his days Paul turned many and he spent from morning till night trying to persuade all who would listen to him about Jesus, and using as his argument the laws of Moses and the prophets and the psalms. Many were convinced by what he said, while others disbelieved. Well, Mary didn't even give me the chance to disbelieve it. It was simply to her all sheer fantasy, all ____(??).

Yet I tell you every precept in that book, called the Bible, is literally true, and will one day be experienced by you and fulfilled by you literally, even to the drinking of the blood. And it's not blood as I would cut my veins. When you see it you know it's the only living reality in the world. It's that which made you alive while you walked this earth. It was the blood of God, and because God became me that I may become God, when I was severed in two, there was the blood that gave me life. And on that blood I knew it was myself, for in the blood there is life, life is in the blood, golden liquid living light. And you saw it, you become one with it, and then, as you are told, "Then I will raise you up *after* you drink my blood." All that scholars can get out of this statement is, if I would only read his words and assimilate them and begin to understand them, well, then I am eating his flesh and drinking his blood. You will do it literally. I'm not saying you should not understand them and that is the lowest aspect of what is intended. That is intended to be taken literally and experienced literally. "He that drinks my blood has life eternal."

Now he said, "Because I live, you will live also." See the difference in tense? He has completed it. "Because I live"—that's present—"you *will* live also." He's telling everyone that he addresses, and this is in the 14ᵗʰ of John (verse 19), that though you seem to be alive you're really not, not yet...not until you drink my blood. But I have animated you, for I have put my blood within you. "Unless I die thou canst not live; but if I die I shall arise again and thou with me" (Blake, *Jer*.Plt.96). So he dies by crucifying himself on me, on you, on everyone. So his blood is in you. But I did not drink it until he severed me in two. And then after he severed me in two, I absorbed it. Absorbing it was complete drinking of every drop of the blood, and then on the heels of it, you ascend like a serpent, or like a bolt of spiral lightning, just as you're told in scripture. So here, I tell you love endures...it was love. You take the word Jesus in scripture, it means God, it means Jehovah, and it means love, for that is the nature of God. That's the ultimate reality. So every time you read it, you can say love. If the word Jesus offends you, say love...and love said so and so and so...that's alright. And Jesus said so and so, fair enough, same thing. Jesus is love, infinite love.

Now here, I asked you for your case histories. I want to thank you for the six that have come so far. I will use them as the evening permits. One I will use tonight. This lady gave it to me and she said it happened to her on the night of the 4ᵗʰ of September, this month. She said, "As I fell asleep and my body lay asleep on the bed, I found myself looking for something. I didn't know what it was that I should find, but there I am looking and looking for something. I had to find something, but what it was I didn't know until in my left hand appeared three coins. I said, not to anyone, just speaking aloud in the dream, 'Should there not be thirty pieces of silver?' The voice answered and said, 'No, you have the three precious ones.' Then, as the voice spoke, the three were taken out of my hand towards the right, one by one, each separately. As the hand took the first one out, the voice said, 'This is faith'; took the second one out said 'This is hope'; took the last one out said 'This is love.' And then I awoke."

There is the fulfillment of the 13ᵗʰ of Corinthians, 1ˢᵗ Corinthians: "Faith, hope and love, these three abide; but the greatest...is love" (verse 13). Faith will one day be translated into vision and therefore fulfill itself. Hope will be completely realized in this state. But love endures forever. It's something that is basic, you can't analyze it. It's something that's altogether God...there's only God and God is love. So she held the three coins, the three precious ones in her hands, and she thought in terms of the thirty pieces of silver. The voice said, "No, you have the three precious ones." And then came...and the voice...as she relinquished, she didn't have any choice in the matter, it just took one after the other. The voice began to speak. So whenever vision breaks out into speech the presence of Deity is affirmed, as told us in the 3rd chapter of Exodus and the 6th of Isaiah. But it breaks out into speech. When you are in presence of vision and speech takes place, then the presence of Deity is affirmed.

So I say every word of scripture you one day will experience. I have experienced scripture and now, night after night, all the lovely things that come afterwards. Like the 23rd Psalm, who would have thought you took that literally? "The Lord is my shepherd, I shall not want; he maketh me to lie down in green pastures." Would you believe that is literally true for a man to experience? Well, the last two years in New York City we were warned not to walk through the park, Central Park. There were muggings day and night. They said you took your life in your hands if you entered the park. Professors of Columbia were murdered. Bing, the head of the Metropolitan Opera, he was mugged, and stripped, and all of his money gone, right at the very beginning of 59th Street as you entered. And this is where the lights are on, only at ten at night. But I felt regardless of all these rumors I must go through the park. And so, I go for my daily walk and I started through the park. I can't tell you how green the grass was, that luscious, luscious green, and it was so thick. For years New York has suffered from the lack of rain. And they wouldn't give you water in the restaurants; you had to ask for it. They had little signs in the hotels "Please do not keep the water running and only use it when you have to." And they asked you all kinds of pertinent things about "Don't flush the toilet unless you have to" and all these things to save water. It was down to almost fifty percent of capacity. Well, in the last year, for some wonderful reason, the rains came and the grass was so deep. I can't tell you my thrill as I walked through the park and remarked to myself, "How green the grass is."

The following night this is my experience. I saw my earthly father. He looked about fifty years old. He died when he was eighty-five in the year '59. But he looked about fifty and radiant and robust, and I was lying on the grass, right on this wonderful stretch of green luscious grass. I said to him, "Isn't this strange, only yesterday I had a dream, I had a dream that I saw this grass and remarked to myself how green it was, how altogether comforting and wonderful it was, and now here it is an objective reality, it's a fact. Last night in my dream it was subjective, and now here it is objective." He looked at me and smiled. What is objective and what is subjective? Is it not wholly determined by the level on which consciousness is focused? I'm telling him in a dream that this is the reality, and what I experienced only yesterday was the dream. I told him how I dreamed it, and when I woke back here I realized from this level what I told him was the dream. And what I told him *was* the dream was really the fact. Which was the fact and which was the reality?

Now who is my Father? We're told in scripture the whole vast world is seeking the Father, and Christ tells us, "I am the Father. He who sees me has seen the Father." The whole vast world is seeking Christ. They are seeking the authority that is imaged as your earthly father, that seat of authority, that seat of power that you can trust, that you can respect. That power to which you can submit yourself, even if it does, and it does sometimes, chasten. And in doing so, you think it's afflictions, but still you will submit to it if you can trust it. Now what is it? It's the Father in our very selves that we are seeking, that same Father that the Christ of the gospels claims himself to be. So when I met my father, I was only seeing the authority that I had found. He was the image, the symbol of that authority that I loved. I always trusted him. I could always submit myself to him. He was always generous and kind. And here I am, stretched out on the grass, in complete fulfillment of the 23rd Psalm. "He maketh me to lie down in green pastures," who?—the Lord. Well, we're told in scripture Christ is the Lord...and he calls himself the Father. Here's my father. And I'm lying down, not standing on it, lying down in green pastures. It's so green and so luscious. And night after night the entire book unfolds as experiences, after the four major ones take place. Well, they have taken place; that's all behind me now. So I'm sharing with you...and to repeat it, how can I tell and anyone—I wouldn't say anyone—-but the majority receive it? How until he brings them where I have been? He takes them to that same level and then they will know, and they will know all of these precepts are to be taken literally and fulfilled literally.

So I tell you, God who is love endures. Everything is going to pass away. It will simply wither like the grass and simply vanish from the earth, and the earth itself. But God will rise, and then you are he, completely incorporated into the one being who is God. There is nothing but God, and God is all love. Everything else is an attribute of God. Faith will be fulfilled, hope fulfilled, all the attributes fulfilled, but God, who is love, endures forever. It *is* love.

So here, this wonderful story of the three coins...I can't tell you my thrill when someone who comes here will have a vision of that nature and will share it with me. She very sweetly wrote it out in a type written form and gave it to me. Others I have...I have five others and they're perfectly marvelous, and when the night comes that they fit I'll share it with you. So again I'm going to make an appeal to share your experiences with me. They encourage everyone. This sweet lady who wrote it, her message has gone out tonight to everyone who is here. And you will know that you, too, will have a similar experience and know that these three qualities, virtues, they abide. The greatest of these came last, and the last is first, and the first is last. So the last was love, comes out of her hand last. And these, "You have the three precious ones," not the thirty pieces of silver, the price of him who would gore a man by what he said; for that's the price you would pay the owner of the ox. If the ox gored a slave, you pay the owner of the slave, not the slave. You paid the owner of the slave thirty pieces of silver if you had the ox. The ox is the symbol of Christ. And Christ comes to gore man. He simply gores him into...like that ox state called the Lamed or the ___(??) in scripture, an ox goad...and it goads you into moving on to higher and higher levels of awareness. So when he comes he doesn't bring peace, he brings the sword, he brings the ox goad. So when the ox goads someone, the one injured, well then, thirty pieces of silver must be given to the owner of that slave.

So she wonders, "Are there not thirty pieces of silver?" and the voice answers, "No, three...and you have the three precious ones. These are the three." When you stand in the presence of the risen Christ, the only question asked is to name the greatest thing in the world. You do name the three and you also go on to say, "But the greatest of the three, these three, is love." And that's when love embraces you and you become one with love; forever you are one with the body of love and there is no divorcing it. What God has now joined together—you and God are one—no man or organization of men can put asunder. You are one with the body of God, and forever you *are* that body.

So when you leave this sphere in the not distant future after that experience, you awaken as the very being the whole vast world talks about. While you experience it and remain covered in flesh...for the Godhead on this level is simply veiled perfection...and while veiled perfection, no one sees the body that you really wear, and so they have to simply guess at the reality behind what you say. How can I preach God's love? How can God have love, for God is Spirit? How could I see his body? How could I lie down in green pastures? And lying down in green pastures tells me I am protected forever. It's the story of God's protection of his anointed one, his elect. So you are told he actually allows you to lie down in green pastures, for what? He tells me in the very beginning, it's all because ___(??) no concern about where it comes from, no concern about anything in the future, just, I will let you lie in green pastures...an abundance is yours from now on, just for the taking. And then you go on to the fields, "If I were hungry, I would not tell you, for the world is mine and all within it. The cattle on a thousand hills are mine, and so, were I hungry I would slay and eat" (Ps.50:10,12). Why tell anyone of my hunger if the world is mine, when you have an inheritance that is infinite, that is unspoiled, unwavering, when these things begin to happen within you?

And the minute you drink the blood, you are raised. The whole story begins on the resurrection. There would be no Christianity without resurrection, and resurrection without crucifixion is simply sheer nonsense. How could there be resurrection without death? So God dies, and that was his love for you, his love for me: "Unless I die thou canst not live; but if I die I shall arise again and thou with me." Not as two, as one, yet without loss of identity of the one whom I raise. No change of identity, no change of that wonderful specific individuality, the same self, yet now including a far greater self than before, who is none other than God the Father, Jesus Christ. To include him and yet remain the being that I am? Yes. Without change of identity you encompass this infinite presence who is Jesus Christ, and you are he, without change of identity. That's the mystery. And in the end, only Jesus, nothing but Jesus, and you are he.

So I tell you, love endures forever as told us in the 13th chapter of 1st Corinthians. Everything will pass, but love endures always. Someone defined the three virtues, faith, hope and love: faith as believing what is incredible, hope is hoping when all seems hopeless, and love is forgiving what is unforgivable, that's love. But everything that you have ever done is forgiven. If I had to expiate my past as the world teaches one must, I could never be exonerated, not in eternity. But in that embrace of love, though my sins were there at that moment like scarlet, they were, at that very moment, made white as snow. Here was complete divine acquittal of all that I had ever done...and I did everything that man could ever do. I had to. Everything that man was capable of doing I did up to that moment, and he embraced me, and exonerated me. I was divinely acquitted, and my sins that were then like scarlet became white as snow. No one can really save himself. We are saved by the grace of God. It's not your own doing, so there is no way to boast...it's by the grace of God.

Now tonight, take this, we are called upon to imitate God as dear children. Tonight, here is how I would imitate him were I you. It's told us in the 1st Epistle of John, the 4th chapter, "We love, because he first loved us." "Because" implies causation. Our love is response, only response; the cause is God loved me first. Now, that apostolic "we" must now become a personal "I": I love, because God first loved me. Now imitate God as a dear child, as I'm told in Ephesians (5:1). Start to love. I want a response of love? Then I start loving the one I would have respond. If I expect it to come from there and I don't initiate it, I will wait in vain. I'll wait forever, for I must imitate God as a dear child. Well, I'm told because *I* live, you *will* live also...therefore, I must be dead. I live, therefore you *will* live also. See the change in tense? Pygmalion and Galatea: She's dead, the creation of the great artist. She's made of marble. And to whom does he pray to make her alive? He prays to the goddess of love, and asks the goddess to make her animate that he could embrace her, and find affection, and find a companion in his creation. And love responds. When love responds, Galatea utters...her first word is to call her creator's name, and she calls out "Pygmalion."

Well, the first word I ever uttered and you ever uttered is to call our Creator's name. Before I can say anything or see anything, though I couldn't utter the words, I had to be aware of being before I could become aware of being aware of something. I had first to be aware of being before I could be aware of anything. So although I couldn't use words, I was but a tot, you made me. No matter what I could ___(??) my hand moving before my eyes, but I had to be aware of being first before I was aware of a hand, or whatever it was moving before my eyes. And so, a little child is first aware of being before it becomes aware of anything in this world. So here, the first word that the child is really uttering is the name of its Creator. Because, to be aware of being is saying in the depths of one's being, "I am." If I am, then I'm aware. So I must first be before I can be aware of anything. So, as Galatea became aware she calls her creator's name and she calls out, "Pygmalion." Here is simply an aspect of this eternal vision.

So, if I must imitate God, and the initiative is with God, and I am loved because God first loved me, well, then imitate him. Well, then I am aware of being, and I want someone in my world to respond, to appreciate what I do, and to express that appreciation, well, then I must start loving. I must start expecting that appreciation and go beyond it and hear it as though it were true. I must listen just as though I heard what I would hear were it true, then comes the response; for the world is but an echo, the world is only a response of what *you* are doing. So when I am not loved, then I am not imitating God as a dear child. I'm expecting it to originate there, and it can't originate there, it has to originate in you. So the whole vast world is myself pushed out. And if God is love, then I love him *because* he first loved me, and I must imitate him. Well, then I see the whole vast world round about me. Alright, I want the world to respond in what kind?

I once said to my brother Victor, who has made a fortune in this world on the little tiny island called Barbados. You could put four Barbadoses in Los Angeles and still have room. He's made a considerable fortune and he started behind the eight-ball. He said to me, "You know, Neville, nobody will believe it…maybe you will…when they say, 'What is the secret of your success?' they think that because I have money that I love money. I don't love money. Oh, yes, I have it, I have millions, but I don't love money. I love the use of money. But if I told you what I consider my success and the secret of my success, maybe you will believe, maybe you won't…others don't." Because, being a successful businessman they are afraid of him, and they think he's hard. They think he's everything that he's not. And this is what he told me. What do you think he said? He said, "My secret is this: I love people. They're all afraid of me because I have money, but I'm never too busy to see anyone. Regardless of the pigment of their skin, they can sit right down…with anyone coming in. If Churchill came in…when Churchill was alive he came…he would sit in the same seat that my porter would come, if my porter wanted to see me.

And I really love people." And so, he's done it all through believing, by giving. He's always giving, not thinking of himself, just simply giving. But he makes a fortune and he can't stop making it. It pours and pours and pours. And he tells me his secret is because "I love people."

Now he doesn't know the Bible as you do, he certainly doesn't know it as I do; but innately he knew that God is love and I love because he first loved me. How he got that I don't know, but he just loves people. People have to bring him all kinds of information that you can't buy in any other way. He finds all kinds of deals because people love him, and yet they're afraid of him. Just as man not knowing the unknown is afraid of God, who is *in* the flower. If you ever saw the risen Christ, you wonder, how could I ever in eternity have ever been afraid of God when there is not a thing in the risen Christ but infinite love, nothing but love? And yet man fears this unseen. You can't see him until he calls you. He hides his face, because you went astray, and simply served another god, and played the harlot with one who is not God, by worshipping some false power, call it by any name. There's only God, and you go back to him. And one day he will not hide his face any more, he'll unveil it, and you will see infinite love. He embraces you and then you are he. The union is complete and no one can sunder it.

So tonight, you take me at my word. I'm telling you what I've experienced. You start tonight and, alright, fall in love with being successful. And success... you always need, a state always needs a man to express it. And so, a man will express it. He'll come into your world. Fall in love with being successful, and then men will come, and you'll be successful without the effort you think it will take. All these things work almost without effort, if you really believe in God and imitate him as a dear child. So I tell you everything in the world that we now hold so dear will all pass away, but love will not pass away, because love is God himself.

Now let us go into the Silence.

*   *   *

____(??) and I think you will find the story I will tell on Monday a very fascinating story, based upon a letter I received. She doesn't know as yet how perfectly it fits in with the visions, my own personal visions over the past, I would say, twenty years. She may not be here tonight, I don't know if she is here or not, and she may not even come on Monday, doesn't really matter. But what she wrote me this last week...and how perfectly it fits with the visions that I will tell on Monday: is this drama secular or sacred?

Now are there any questions?

Q: Last week, Neville, you said to seek him out and brood over him, would you expand on that?

A: Well, if you took what I said tonight and not just drop it because it's over when you go through the door, brood over what you heard while I'm giving you his words. And when I quote scripture...all prophets were inspired by the same Spirit as told us in the epistle of Peter. So when we read the four gospels...and I quoted tonight from the Book of John, "He who drinks my blood has eternal life and I will raise him up at the last day." Well, these are his words and his Word is himself, so brood over that. Brood over everything that he has said. His precepts are to be taken literally. And he dwells in you, Bill.

So tonight I have explained, taken from my own experience, what it means to actually drink the blood of God. The word translated "drink" means "with enjoyment," not a repulsion. And you can't conceive of anything more repulsive to the orthodox Hebrew mind than the drinking of blood, for the simple reason they are trained in orthodoxy that the animal must be drained of all blood, for life is in the blood. To put blood, why, that's the most repulsive thing. They kill the chicken differently from the way heathens slaughter a chicken, and they would slant the board and drain all the blood from the animal, trying to get all the blood out. Now, raised as I was in a Christian environment, we go in for black sausage and, well, rare goat's meat, and things of that sort, but not to drain the blood. So it hasn't anything to do with that level. It's something entirely different. When they know what that blood is, or when the Christian knows what that blood is, what Christian would take it that he would even entertain the thought of drinking the blood of Jesus? He wouldn't, would he?

Now take this in remembrance of me...people take a little wine... that's not the blood. That is a symbol, a shadow of what will give them real enjoyment when they see that blood and absorb every drop of it. It takes no time at all. You do it willingly, you're so thirsty for it, and you absorb the whole thing, you're it. *Now* there's life in you. He who drinks my blood has now eternal life. Now I'll raise him up. And from this generation you're turned around into regeneration, and you're raised up through the drinking of the blood. So I said brood over it. Brood over that very thought tonight, in the hope that in the not distant future you experience it. And then hope one day will be realized. Have faith in it; that will be realized in the actual experience. But love cannot pass away.

Q: (inaudible)

A: First of all, what man has not departed from the true religion? What man? If we go to the highest level call it by any name, say the pope, if you say the archbishop of Canterbury, if you spoke of the highest in the Presbyterian world—there aren't any bishops or popes but they certainly have heads in that ___(??)—or you go in to any of the great Sanhedrin, they're all departed from the true God, because they don't turn within themselves and see that I am he. The fundamental sin is not to believe that I am he. "Unless you believe that I am he, you die in your sins" (John8:24). And so when they cross themselves with everything on the outside for the benefit of a seeming other, then they've departed from the truth. They're not serving the one true God. Called by any name, I don't care how they justify it they're not serving the one true God. They're playing the part of the harlot.

Another word that's used in scripture for the harlot is called "the sinner." When he became the friend of "the sinner," that was the prostitute in the sense that you and I understand the word. And yet, she was the one who wept and so filled his feet with water she could wash it; when the Pharisee, who was always on the outside—he washed the outside of the cup—that he did not give him water with which to wash his feet when he and the guest came to dine. Yet she came in and with her tears she washed the feet. He did not anoint the head...and she with her little... and he wondered, "How can this man be a prophet? If he were a prophet, surely he would know what sort of woman she is. For he tells me she is a sinner, but he ought to know what sort of a woman." He knew exactly who she was. And he said, if someone owes 500 denarii and someone owes fifty and you forgive both, which shows the greater gratitude? He said, well, I presume the one who was forgiven the 500; it cancelled much. She has sinned much so she is forgiven much. And he who is the holier than thou remains, well, in the same state he was before.

But that is something far deeper than what I've just told you, which we will touch on Monday. You can't stop the flow of tears at a certain level of awakening, can't do it. You just can't do it. And, well, I can't go into it now, it's a long one. But the harlot...to play the part of the harlot, as you're told in the Book of Deuteronomy, "Your time has come to sleep with your fathers"—he's speaking now to Moses—in other words, it's a euphemism for death...time to die now. After you depart, they have no physical leader. They're all allowed to go astray and play the harlot with the strange gods of the land where they go to be among, and they will simply forget my covenants and in that day I will hide my face from them.

He hides his face from everyone who seeks another God. Therefore, the man who has not actually seen the risen Christ is still serving, whether he knows it or not, a false god.

When I turn to the one true God, well then, he will unveil himself and embrace me. I have returned having played the harlot, for we *all* play the harlot. But even to the part of playing that form of sinner, which is called in scripture just the word sinner...but it means one who has gone astray sexually with everyone, and he called it a "sort of woman." But he was a friend of the sinners, he was a friend of the tax collectors, and they called him a winebibber and a glutton. That's why if a man is just like a man they can't believe for one moment that this whole drama has unfolded within him, for they know his history. And he loves the sinners, who else would he help? He came not to serve and to save the righteous; they have no need of saving. They are so righteous in their own mind's eye that they know because they have money and they go before God, they can say, I left fifty million behind in churches, and I gave to charities ___(??). And he said, "I do not know you"...I do not know you. The old story of the temple, I am so grateful that I am not as that sinner while he asks for forgiveness, the sinner. It's an old symbol.

So in the eyes of God all gifts, all things will be forgiven. If you play the part of the prostitute from now to the ends of days, all is forgiven. And those who thought themselves so pure, so altogether good, that they even perform violence among themselves so they could not perform the act, he doesn't know them. But she went astray and played the part because of what? Excessive love, excessive passion. Well, God is *all* love. No condemnation whatsoever, none. So he came among the sinners and the one who saw him at the end was the one who played the part of that kindliness, the prostitute. He appeared to her first and appeared to her last. She came unannounced to the banquet and she washed his feet with her tears. When they complained, no one saw the woman she is. "She washed my feet. You didn't give me any water to wash my feet. Is that not customary?" They thought him just an ordinary man and not really worth his time to give him water; she came in and she watered him with her tears. That's a fact that happens. I'll tell you...tell you on Monday.

Goodnight.

FREE OR SLAVE

10/7/66

First of all, I'll take your letters. I have two tonight that I think should thrill you; one from a gentleman, he's here, and one from a lady, and she is here. His will fit a perfect side of what I want to discuss tonight, and hers will fit the other side perfectly. I asked you to share with me your experiences because they do encourage everyone. I do not need, personally, I do not need encouragement; I've experienced scripture. But everyone who has not experienced scripture needs encouragement.

So we start, first of all, with his. I make the statement that imagining creates reality and I mean that seriously. That man should live *as if* it were true, just as if it were true—I don't care what it is, the most incredible thing in the world—as if it were true. And if he is faithful to that assumption and lives in that state, it will come to pass...of that I'm convinced and I know from personal experience. But to have it shared with me by those who come here when they tell me their stories... So here is his story. He said, "Sitting in an office, I was bored, and I thought there certainly must be a more pleasant way of earning twice what I earn, there must be. So I made the decision right there and then that I would earn twice what I have now. I did it for a few days, and then after a few days there's not a thing changed in my world, I wondered if this thing is right?

"Well, again remembering my decision I stopped it right there and then and re-enacted the scene, not wondering what I would do. I didn't really specify what the job was I would do, simply that I was earning twice what I was at the moment earning. Then, two weeks later, a man that I had known for three years and I have seen him weekly...and suddenly he began to urge upon me to come and work for him. He'd never done that before. He was insistent and when he mentioned a salary it was exactly twice what I was earning. So I worked for him. While working for him, again I said to myself, now this thing has worked...and so, why should I work? Why not have an income equal to all that I need without this so-called work.

"And so, this is what I did. I imagined that I went down to my postal box and I took out the letters...there were the usual things, correspondence and bills and things...but I saw an unidentified envelope. On my way back, I simply stopped and embraced and touched the trees that I so love on my way home. Then I opened it and I found a check for the amount that I thought I would need for a long, long non-working period. Then I saw on my balance sheet from the bank that added to what was there. And that's what I did. But I did it every night as I went to sleep. Well, two weeks later seeing no evidence of this whatsoever, I said to myself, you know, are you going mad? I mean this thing may be completely stupid"— and then he said to me in a little aside—"as I once thought that you were."

Well, he's not the only one who thought that I was mad. He's not the only one that thought that the one who awoke to scripture is mad. You read that in the 10th of John, when one makes the statement that "no one takes my life; I lay it down myself. I have the power to lay it down and the power to lift it up again." Then said those who heard, "What must we listen to him for? Why, he has a devil and is mad; why listen to him (verses 18,19)?" Read it in the 10th of John, "He is mad; why listen to him?" Well, in New York City, in 1939, on 49th Street there was a little bookshop and I would go there daily and browse around and spend hours. I loved the two little ladies who ran it... they were well advanced in years. And they took a huge big picture of me and they sat it in the window. I had no books at the time, but it was a bookstore, so they simply put the picture in the window. There was no reason for it, but they wanted to put the picture in the window. I came...as I came, two ladies were on the street looking into the window, and one said to the other, "Do you know who he is?" This one was a visiting cousin or sister or someone but a relative; and she said no. "Well, he is the mad mystic on 47th Street. You should hear him!" said this one...and I'm right behind them, hearing it. "You should hear him. You know what he tells people? Your consciousness is God. You say 'I am,' he says, 'that's God.' Can you imagine that!" said one to the other. And then she said, "He also tells you that imagining creates reality. Now isn't that the silliest thing in the world? You must go hear him some night." Well, that was it, back in 1939.

So in this little aside he said, "As I once thought you were mad. But, two weeks later, after I did this night after night, and then I dropped it, I kept a date with a friend that I had made months and months ago. It was a dear old friend of mine and I kept this date and went up and spent a few days with him. While I was there, he had just inherited a sum of money from an unknown relative and urged upon me the amount that I had seen, and I took it. Here was the sum of money to the very dollar that I had seen in my account. He urged it upon me, so I took it. Now, here I am doing the things I've wanted to do all of my life, without effort, enjoying every moment...out on the beach, doing all these things...without going to work. And someone calls, one I had never seen, and he asks me to come and work for him. Well, I said that I was so enjoying the kind of a life that I'm living now I don't want to work for anyone. But he was so persistent that he insisted that I would come. He also urged me to bring some of my work. I thought, well, I'll take it... I'll take the work now. So that day I went down to see him with some of my work." What he does, I haven't the slightest idea. I do not know whether he is an artist, in this department, that department or what. But he said in his letter, "He asked me to bring some of my work, so I took it down. He was more enthusiastic than ever in employing me, and said to me, 'I want to show it right now. Not only show your work but I want to show *you* to my chief client.' So we went right away to see the chief client.

"Now, when I walked into that place I instantly knew that I was here before. The wall panel against which I leaned...I had been here before. I know not physically, but I have been here before. The window through which I looked was exactly that same window through which I looked, not in my physical body, but I looked through that. The tree or the plant"—he used the word plant or tree...I think it was tree because undoubtedly he's an artist of some kind, but he said "the plant that I saw was the exact plant that I had seen. Every thing was perfect as I had seen it, but not physically. The man himself was the man that I saw. I took the job, and now I daily talk with *that* man in that office against that paneled room, looking at that same plant through that same window.

"So then, when I came back I remembered—and this is the great lesson that it taught me—I remembered that sitting one day at my desk my mind wandered and in my Imagination I wandered into that office and I looked through that window. I saw that man, I saw that plant, I saw it. Now this is my conclusion: Imagining creates reality in the most determined, definite manner man could ever imagine. It's not only the intentional imaginal act that does it, man is living by this all through the moments of time. Every moment he is living by it whether or not he knows it or cares to know it. Whether or not he believes it or wants to believe it, he can't avoid this principle that imagining is creating reality. And it is not only the intentional imaginal act but *every* imaginal act, for I did not do that intentionally."

Now he said, "I have a plant growing in my living room. It's the most luxurious thing you could see and every nurseryman tells me it just can't, it just cannot thrive under these conditions. Why is it thriving? I simply went forward in my Imagination and saw it thriving, and here is the thing simply taking over the living room, and all the nurserymen telling me it just can't do it." Well now, if there is evidence for a thing, what you or I think about the matter is not important. What does it matter what anyone thinks if I produce the evidence? Well, here we have the evidence.

Well, I can't thank him enough for that letter...these heavenly stories that I can share with you. He doesn't need to encourage me I assure you I know it, I know it from experience. I don't care what a man has done if he knows this wonderful principle of God he can set himself free. God is the forgiving being. If God held things against us, who on earth could escape? God is forgiving—I don't care what a man has done—if you know God's law. But, you have to operate God's law. We are the operant power, because God became man that man might become God. In becoming man he had to forget that he was God. And then as man, the law contained within himself...and then someone comes up who hears it, who experiences it, and then he shares it and tells it. Then the deaf ear and the blind eye know it can't be, but he tells it anyway. He tells it just as he told me. Whether we care to hear it, whether we believe it or not, makes no difference, we're living by it anyway.

So his wonderful conclusion—and you must bear this in mind—it's not only the *intentional* imaginal act, *all* imaginal acts work. So morning, noon and night we are imagining. You can't stop it. Can you stop it? Night after night when I go to bed and suddenly the eye opens from within, I know where I am, I know it, where I see a world that isn't this world. And all I have to do, like someone...I don't drive a car but I know how it must feel like to men who drive cars. I simply press something in my head. I don't put my foot on it or my hand on it. It's all intensity. I simply imagine it, and as I imagine it, off I go where I'm contemplating. And I see it. I step right into it...it's just as real as this...right into it. The whole energy, it's in one's wonderful Imagination. One's Imagination *is* life itself; it animates everything in this world. Suddenly the eye opens. This inner eye is always open when I go to bed. And then world after world after world...and only one thing you want to do. Maybe some nights I don't feel like doing it, so I don't; other nights it's interesting and when I see it I simply, I call it intensifying what I'm seeing. As I intensify it, this peculiar motion and off you go; you shoot like a meteor right into this world that you see. And there you are. Then you explore...the whole thing you explore.

So here, sitting idly at his desk...and what he does I don't know...but he's at his desk...some creative work. Maybe he's a draftsman, maybe he's a painter, maybe he's a designer, I don't know. From what the letter would imply, maybe he designs. But, his mind wandered and he wandered into this place, and while there all of a sudden he's leaning against the wall and looks through the window. He sees the plant and he sees the man. Then two weeks later, this thing is happening. Now he said, "I know that you are teaching the truth, the law, and thank you for having taught me how to use it." Well, I thank him as profusely, if not more so than he thanked me, for having shared with me that I can share with you these wonderful stories.

Now we go to another aspect of this "Free or Slave." We're all slaves. There is one born of woman, the woman called Hagar in the Bible. And every mother...my mother was called Wilhelmina, but she is Hagar. My wife is called...her name is Catherine Willa, she is Hagar; she bore a child. So every womb that brings into this world a child, that's Hagar in the Bible. There is another one called Sarah, and she is from above, and she brings them into freedom; Hagar brings them into slavery. So all who came in through the womb of woman we are enslaved in this world, everyone. While we are in this world as slaves...and let me quote you this passage from scripture, in the Book of Genesis..."Abram fell into a deep sleep. While he slept, there was a great and grave darkness that descended upon him. The Lord said to him, 'Your descendants shall be sojourners in a land that is not theirs, and they will be *slaves* there. They will be enslaved for four hundred years; and then after that, they shall come into a great inheritance'"...after the four hundred years (Gen.15:12).

In Hebrew...it's the greatest tongue in the world, really...but it's not a tongue to use among people; it's a mystery tongue. No language expresses the mysteries like the Hebrew tongue, none. Every letter has not only a numerical value but a symbolical value. He tells Abram, who is disturbed because he doesn't have an heir...he said, "A child born in my household who is born of a slave will be my heir." And the Lord said, "No, your own son will be your heir" and he laughed because he was an hundred years old and Sarah was ninety, and it had ceased to be with her after the manner of women (Gen.17:16). So you take it as a normal story. It isn't that story at all. When we come to the New Testament, I'll show you the passage that interprets this wonderful story of the Old...but for four hundred years.

Now the same story is told in the next book, the Book of Exodus, and he makes it four hundred and thirty. Four hundred and thirty years the children of Israel...and on that very day the Lord watched and brought the entire host out of Egypt, on that very day...four hundred and thirty (Ex.12:40). In the Book of Genesis it's four hundred. Now, four hundred has the symbolical value of the sign of the cross. It's the last letter of the Hebrew alphabet, Toph. You can spell it T-a-u. My old teacher used to call it Toph, but it's T-a-u on ___(??). It's the 22nd letter. He said he was a hundred years old...and it's Qoph. Qoph has the symbol of the back of the Skull. That is the symbol of Qoph. The sign of the cross...we're all on the cross; this is the cross, there is no other cross. No wooden cross, no little tree the world talks about. Forget all this silliness that people talk about Christ on *that* kind of a cross. The universal Christ is on this cross, your body. This is where Messiah, which is God himself, is crucified. I know! I know from experience; I am not speculating. So here, this is the cross, the four hundred years, and as long as I appear in the flesh I wear the cross. At the end of my journey, not four hundred years as you and I measure time, when this is no more; for the glory of my heavenly inheritance cannot become actual, or at least it's not *realized* in us or in me until I take this thing off. Only when this is off can I really realize my heavenly inheritance, as promised in scripture, at the end of the four hundred years.

Well now, why the thirty? Thirty is the price paid for a slave. The unfree person's price was thirty shekels of silver. They paid thirty shekels of silver for him. To whom did they pay it? They paid thirty shekels of silver. We're told in Exodus, if an ox gored an animal—which is the ox the symbol of Christ—should butt, gore or kill a slave, then the owner of the animal must pay to the owner of the slave thirty shekels of silver. That is the price of the unfree person. Everyone here is worth thirty pieces of silver. And when the message of Christ comes into the world and so goads you—for thirty is Lamed in Hebrew, and it's an ox-goad, that's the symbol of thirty. The twelfth letter is Lamed and its symbol is an ox-goad. So, when you are goaded to give up your traditional concepts and move from a God of tradition into the God of experience by the goading of truth as it hits you—for Christ is truth, he said, "I am the truth"—so when the truth comes and hits you and you are shaken loose from your traditional concepts to accept what he is sharing with you, well, then you have been gored, you have been butted by Christ...and thirty pieces are paid (Ex.21:32). Now, he doesn't say to whom it is paid. He took the thirty pieces and no one would receive it...threw it into the temple, into the assemblage. But who took it? They fought yes...the place of blood, whose blood?—the blood of God. That's the price paid for the individual who is so goaded that he is hurt. He has to relinquish his claim to all the past that he believed in and follow now the new concepts, the new interpretation of God's words. So he brings it to man.

Now we are told, "This is an allegory" in Paul's first letter. Now there's no one in scripture that was more Hebraic than Paul. He tells you, "I am of the tribe of Benjamin. I am a son of Abraham, of the tribe of Benjamin. A Roman by citizenship, but I am the Hebrew of Hebrews." He was the one person who persecuted everyone who taught as I speak this night. And then it came to him, and he had the experience, he had the revelation. And there is no one in scripture, and no one throughout the centuries, who has been a greater proselyter of this Way than Paul. He dwarfs everyone. You can't put anyone in the same category with Paul. And so his first letter—which is now a confession, it's really a biography—to the Galatians...and he's now explaining this passage. He said, Abraham had two sons, one by a slave, born according to the flesh—that's you and I—and one by a free woman, born according to the Promise. Now he said, "This is an allegory." It's stated quite clearly in the Bible, "It's an allegory." Well, what is an allegory? Look up the definition. It's simply a story told figuratively or symbolically that needs interpretation, so that when it's told the hearer or the reader of the story must discover the fictitious character of the story and learn its lesson.

Now he tells us, one is from below and one is from above. Well, I've experienced both. I don't recall my birth from my physical mother's womb. I know I called her mother. I'm convinced I did come from the womb of my mother that I loved dearly. I'm convinced that she raised me and nursed me at her own breast. In those days we didn't have other things other than the breast of woman, so I nursed her. And she loved me dearly to the very moment she closed her eyes, and she still does. I meet her. So I came out of her womb. I was a slave; she bore me into slavery, that's Hagar.

I didn't know who the other one was until it happened to me, on the morning of July the 20th, 1959, when I came out of the other womb, and she is from above, right out of my own skull. When I rose within myself, resurrected, and came out as though one who is being born, to find the entire, wonderful symbolism of scripture unfolding before me, and I am the chief actor in the drama. But all the things mentioned they are present—the three men, the babe wrapped in swaddling clothes, everything is present...out of the woman from above. So we're told, the one from above she bears us into freedom; the one from below bears us into slavery. As it was in the days of old so it is today: They are enemies. But what does the scripture say? Cast out the woman, the slave and her offspring; and he shall not inherit with the child that is born free (Gal.4:22-31)...entirely different world altogether.

Now he comes back, and he makes the statement, speaking now of the true Abraham—not a person as you are, as I am—but he said that Abraham has to bring forth Christ. And the promise was made unto Abraham and to his offspring. Not offsprings, referring to many, but to your offspring, referring to one: "To your offspring, which is Christ" (Gal.3:16). So in the same letter he said, "I labor with you until Christ be formed in you" (Gal.4:19). Christ be formed in you? Yes. Well, who is he? He is God the Father. He is forming himself in me *as* me, and when he forms himself in me as me, I bring him forth. Christ as myself, I am he. God laid himself down within me to sleep, and as he slept he dreamed a dream...he dreamed that he is I. And when he woke, he was I. How did I know that *I* am he? Only through the revelation of his Son, David, who in the Spirit called me, Father. When David in the Spirit called me, Father...and he said to David, "Thou art my Son; today I

have begotten thee," so when his only begotten Son called me, Father, I then
knew who I was. There is no other way that I could ever know it. So I tell
you in this way.

Now, the other wonderful letter came to me from this lady. She said, "It
is my habit when I retire I always have a pad at my night table and a pencil.
Well, this morning I got up and got Dusty off to school and then I went back
to make the beds. As I went into the bedroom to make the beds, I looked
and here there was writing on the pad. At the moment I did not recall having
written anything on that pad. Then I read it, and these are the words, ___(??)
quote, 'A voice said, I moved into the womb of woman until it was time.' End
of quote. Now she said, "I don't recall the words, but I do recall after having
read it that I was disturbed in the night to write. But I did not recall the
words until I read them, and I still don't recall having written those words,
but it's my hand, and I wrote them during the night. 'I moved into the womb
of woman until it was time.'" She moved into the woman from above until it
was time. May it not be too long before she is brought forth. She's been having
some marvelous experiences, and may be as far as I'm concerned. But I have
no knowledge when. I wish it could be tonight, but I do not know. He said,
"No one knows. No, not even the Son, only the Father." What Father?—the
Father in her. The fathers sleep in us; the Elohim sleeps in all of us. And then
the Elohim who sleeps in us is forming himself and bringing himself out. That
is called bringing Christ into being.

So, the free or the slave? If you know God's law, as this gentleman does,
you can be as free as the wind. Just imagine the gentleman sitting at his desk,
contemplating doubling his income, and out of the nowhere a man he's seen
weekly for three years is the instrument through which the doubling comes.
Well, in spite of that, he wants something more. He doesn't want to work; just
wants to live, without working. And so he goes and keeps a date made months
before, and the man said, "I've just received an inheritance from an unknown
relative and you must share it with me." In spite of his protests, he urges upon
him, and he accepts it, a check for the amount, the exact amount that he over
a period of two weeks had taken from his letterbox...as he opened up this
unidentified letter, and saw a check in that amount and saw the balance. If
that was added to what he had, that would be the balance.

And now, why work? And so he takes off and doesn't work. Enjoys the
beach and spends the entire summer on the beach, doing nothing, when a
call comes from one he had never seen, urging upon him to, "Please come
and see me...you must work for me." And he said, "I'm enjoying life. I love
what I'm doing. I don't want to work." Well, he kept on urging and urging,
and said, "Please bring some of your work." So, he thought that I'll go. So he
takes down some of his work. Now the man becomes more enthusiastic than

ever, and insists on taking him right away to show not only his work but to show him. He's a handsome fellow, thirty-eight years old, and here he is taken into this place...who is the chief client of this man. The man likes him and he instantly begins to work for him. And day after day he is in communication with this man in that office that he saw when he simply idly moved into while sitting at his desk.

But what he brings out I think that is something that is fantastic. Aside from knowing this law, he said, not only the *intentional* imaginal act produces itself in an experience, the *unintentional*. Every imaginal act is producing itself into this world, whether or not you want to hear it or whether or not you believe it, makes no difference. It is still producing itself in the world, therefore, why not become intentional about it? Why not take the helm and steer the ship like this? We're all at sea as it were; and we are either drifting or we can take hold of that helm and really go towards the port we want to be. It's entirely up to us.

So I repeat that imagining creates reality. The greatest steps forward in this world were made by men and women who imagined *as if* it were. That's what they did. They simply imagined things as if they were. And they rebuilt a world based upon the imaginal acts of these bold spirits that imagined as if it were. When man begins to imagine as if things were as he would like them to be, he breaks the bond. For he's a bond, he's a slave. Until he knows how to imagine and actually lives by it and applies it, he remains a slave in this world until that moment in time comes when that from above is born. Well then, whether he has it or doesn't have it, he is set free. That's the real freedom that comes to man.

But until that fantastic freedom comes to man, let him in the world of the slaves learn God's law; for we are enslaved for four hundred years...as long as we wear the cross, the Toph. Until I take this cross off I cannot really grasp the fantastic inheritance that is mine. I've inherited that which is untarnished, unsoiled, that is forever, a fabulous inheritance that is God himself. But as long as I wear the cross I can't. I have really no desire at the moment to drop it. If it came this night, it's perfectly alright, I move right into my inheritance. But as Paul said, I should desire to be with Christ; that is better by far. But for your sakes the need is far greater that I stay on in the body (Phil.1:23). He had inherited the entire fabulous world, but for the sakes of those he will stay on in the body.

And no one really knows the nature of his end; it isn't recorded in scripture. Tradition in the churches, they have all these messed up things. They have him martyred, they have him murdered, hasn't a thing to do with it. The churches have made such a mess. Now they have Jesus down to five feet, three inches, a little fella...something they found a few hundred years ago, fifteen hundred years after a so-called event. I was on TV one night with a chap just like that, and he brought this strange little picture...and he's an archeologist. Can you see the words of scripture, "It has pleased God to keep these things from the wise and the prudent and revealed them unto babes." For such was his greatest riddle. All of these wise men with all the ___(??) in the world, and he has a vision, a voice of reason, speaks with authority in his church, and now he's got him down to five feet three inches because that's what the shroud, this stupid little thing. What shroud? Christ never walked the earth as the world teaches it. I'm speaking of a *cosmic* Christ...a wholly supernatural being that is buried in man...a *universal* God...not some little thing that came out. A universal Christ, the cosmic Christ, is buried in man, and it's *wholly* supernatural and they're trying to make it a thing of flesh. Paul warned the Galatians against it: "Are you so foolish? Having begun with the Spirit, are you ending with the flesh?" (Gal.3:1). But they read it and they don't see; they have ears and they hear it not. You will never know that you are he until the Son appears and his Son calls you, Father. Then you will know you are he.

So here, this night free or slave? I tell you you can be anything you want to be, I don't care what the world will tell you. Don't ask if it's possible. You may think it's mad. And many think tonight, as he once did, and the little ladies on 49th Street did, "He's mad as a hatter." Well, they haven't put me away so far. No, I'm not mad. I see worlds that no one sees. I see these characters and they are eternal. I commune with these states and I commune with the occupants of those states, like Blake. I commune with Blake. We're separated by two hundred years, but we're so closely woven in the tapestry of time, so closely woven. So that I meet these characters that seemingly are so far in the distant time but they're not. Not to me they are not. Night after night, as I lie on my bed, suddenly I'm seeing what I shouldn't see...not on my bed. All I have to do is actually intensify a rhythm that I am feeling within, intensify it. It's so easy. Off you go, right into what you see, and then you explore. See worlds just like this, solidly real, and you're teaching people.

I go and I teach and teach and teach. Wherever I go I'm always teaching, telling them the Word of God. And they wait for me. I have crowds waiting for me, and I come and I teach them. It's not something that suddenly happens, I go and I teach them, then I return here. So not only teaching here, I am teaching all over. No matter where I go I'm doing the work of God. For when he embraced me and sent me, at that moment of the embrace when I saw the risen Christ and I became one with him; at that moment I was an apostle. So I could say with Paul to whoever would question me, "Am I not free? Am I not an apostle? Have I not seen Jesus our Lord?"—the one qualification for apostleship. Wasn't an apostle one who was first called, embraced, incorporated into the body of the risen Christ and sent. Not only sent here. As you're told in scripture there are others that I must talk to. And the others are not necessarily in New York City or in San Francisco, where I'll be going this coming year, no, there are worlds within worlds within worlds, and they wait for me. And I go and I teach them.

Now that may seem as mad as a hatter, doesn't make any difference to me. I'll show you I am not mad. If this is madness, well, I'm not worried. But I tell you it pays off in *enormous* dividends, if you will know the Word of God and live by it, just live by it. It never fails you. When he faltered twice, the first time he faltered he caught himself and instantly he said, "I made that decision, so I'll go right back to it." And then it worked. The second time he faltered he thought he was mad, thought he was losing his mind, and thought that maybe Neville has lost his, too. And he seemingly forgot it, forgot the whole thing, but a few days later he kept the date made months before. When he made it, the man hadn't come into the inheritance...only a few days before. So he goes and the man urges upon him, presses upon him, a check equal to the amount. He knew then he wasn't mad...and I wasn't...the one who taught him the law, I wasn't either. So he came back, took off for the beach, why work? And while basking in the sun, enjoying every moment of time, the phone from one he had never seen just urging upon him to come and bring some of his work.

Now he knows the law. I hope he will never forget it. And you, who have not experienced it to that degree, I hope you'll start applying it to that degree. No matter what doubts may come into your mind, throw them out, you've done it! Not only the intentional act works; all the unintentional imaginal acts are just as creative. So when the unexpected little annoyances happen, they couldn't happen by themselves. They were brought into being by an imaginal act that is now forgotten. They can remain in being only as long as they are supported by that imaginal act, and when they cease to receive that support they vanish. That's law.

Now let us go into the Silence.

BLOODSHED

10/10/66

Tonight's subject is "Bloodshed." In the Hebrew language, the word bloodshed denotes both murder and humiliation. You can take it in either manner. The Bible takes it both the shedding of the blood and being humiliated.

We're told in the 53rd chapter of Isaiah, "Who has believed our report? And to whom has the arm of the Lord been revealed?" (Is.53:1). Then we read in Ephesians, "Though he was in the form of God...he emptied himself, and took upon himself the form of a slave, and was born in the likeness of men. And being found in human form he humbled himself and became obedient unto death, even death on the cross" (Phil.2:6). Now you read this and you may wonder, "What is it all about?" I am here to tell you every word of scripture is true. It is literally true, and you, individually, will experience scripture...every one of you.

Tonight we will treat this in the form of humiliation. For as you know, as we are told, "He being rich, for your sakes he became poor, that by his poverty you might be rich" (2Cor.8:9). He humbled himself and became obedient unto death, taking upon himself the form of a slave, and was born in the likeness of men. Every man is a slave, born from below. But he who became us will lift us as himself, and we will be God, who created the entire drama.

Now let me tell you a story. It happened to me only this morning, a little after four. Here, I found myself in a room not more than thirty square feet. It was a perfectly square room, not more than thirty, it might have been less, but not more than thirty. I was seated, and the men that I addressed there weren't more than twelve, and I was talking to them about the Word of God, explaining the mystery of salvation. Then, suddenly, one rose quickly and left the room, and I knew that he was going to report what was heard. In no time, a matter of moments after he left came this tall handsome man. He was the authority of authorities. Tall...about six feet four, straight as an arrow, dressed in the clothes of the ancient world; we were all in robes, not as the garb now. And he walked, he came in from my left; there was only one door, the door was here as I'm facing you. He walked rapidly to the end, turned at right angles and walked rapidly to that end, turned at right angles and walked rapidly to the middle, then came and stood before me. Looked into my face and then he took a blunt object and then he started here and he hammered it into my shoulder, right here. I felt every impact as he hammered it in here.

Then when it all went right in, he took a very sharp instrument, and one swirl like this, he severed what I was wearing. Then he held the end of it, pulled it this way, and took off what would have been, like this, a sleeve. But I wasn't wearing a suit like this, I was wearing a robe. And he took it off—and I saw the color, the palest blue, a light, light blue—and he threw it away. Then he stretched his arms out, just like a cross, and he embraced me and kissed me on the right of my neck. I kissed him on the right of his neck. As I kissed him, it dissolved, while I am looking at the discarded robe exposing my right arm. From here to here the whole thing was discarded exposing the arm. The 53rd chapter of the Book of Isaiah, "Who has believed what we have heard? And to whom has the *arm* of the Lord been revealed?"—meaning the might, the *power* of God.

You can talk about the power of God, and tell of the stories of yourself and those who hear you and apply it, and yet in spite of the numberless stories you can tell you still find they don't believe it. They still want a God in some strange way other than themselves. They will not accept *that* God that he who comes to tell you resides within you. The only God in the world resides in man. There is no other God. If anything we need today it is for a new, well, you can't call it Christology. That term is almost abused today. We need, really beyond all measure, a new way of thinking of Jesus as the Infinite God who became man and is man. All the barnacles, all these rituals, all these things on the outside, the ship should be put into dry dock and scraped of all rituals, all external palaver. Take it off completely and throw it away, and start with a new concept of the God who became man that man might become God.

Now let me tell you of a story given me only last Friday night. The lady, she is here, and this is her story. She said, "I have heard you for the last two years and I have benefited from all that you have said, inwardly and outwardly. My world has changed completely from the dreams and the visions that I've had and the application of what you've said. But here, last night I discovered the difference between hearing and experiencing. I heard it and thought I knew it from having heard it, but what a difference between from having heard it and having experienced it. I was aroused out of a profound deep, deep sleep, and as I came out of this profound sleep, I was thinking only of you."

Now let me stop it here for you who may come up to surface when you wake in the morning and you think you haven't had a dream. May I tell you, any thought, but any thought, that occupies your mind is consequent upon a dream. Instead of jumping up and putting cold water on your face and brushing your teeth and getting ready for breakfast as we all do, remain just for a moment and contemplate that thought. It's consequent upon a dream. If you will simply just dwell upon it and wonder, "Why am I thinking what I am thinking?" it will lead you back into the dream, and you will know.

Well, she did this, and this is what she dreamt. Then she said, "I remembered the dream, but it seemed ages ago. Was it last night? This dream seemed so long, so long ago. And I remembered "that man," *that* man Neville, who kept on talking, and he kept on and on and on about the Father and the Son. I remembered that I did not understand him. Then I also remembered, but when I do not know, I do remember that I fell asleep. But I do not remember when I fell asleep, but I fell asleep. But now I am so alerted, so completely awake, I feel as though I were a puzzle and this night a piece of me has been put back into its original place. Now, although it's night, I am sure the morning cannot be afar off." Now here is her story as she gave it to me last Friday. I tell her, no, the morning isn't far off. God is in us. There is nothing but God. God became us that we might become God.

There is nothing but God. So when this morning, a little after four, the arm was revealed, what is the arm?—the power of God and the might of God. The sower...it is called the sower who sows the seed, the sower who returns to reap his harvest. The sower on reaping his harvest sows again. Because who could ever come but Christ? There's nothing but. So here, buried into here, a peg...I felt every impact. May I tell you, it didn't hurt. I only felt the blow, I felt the impulse. Every blow that he gave me I felt it, but it didn't hurt. So when the whole thing was completely embedded, right here, in this shoulder, then he circled, a quick circle, a peculiar motion. Then he took the end of it and made a few little jerks and discarded what he'd pulled off, exposing completely my right arm. When the arm was completely exposed, he went and kissed me here, and I kissed him on his right. Then it dissolved while I'm looking at this lovely pale blue [sleeve] that was torn from my robe. And all these were here. When he entered, we were all seated, but he was so important that all of us stood, stood at attention and looked straight ahead, as you would in the army. Not supposed to turn your head from left to right, you simply look straight ahead; you are at attention. That's what we did as he came, marched this way, marched that way, this way, and then, like this, revealing the *arm* of the Lord.

I say, you are God. To quote the 82nd Psalm, "I say ye are gods, sons of the Most High, all of you; nevertheless, you will die like men, and fall as one man, O princes" (verses 1,6). As she, in her letter to me, she felt as though she were a puzzle that's broken into the multiple parts, and they're all being gathered back together and put back in their place. Well, when you put them back, it's a more luminous being than it was before it fell and broke into these wonderful parts. All fell and scattered, the stone that was shattered, and then each one is found and put back. When it's put back, the whole drama of Jesus Christ unfolds in you.

Now with the 12ᵗʰ of John, this scene that happened this morning, ___(??) end of the ministry of Jesus...the 12ᵗʰ of John. And he quotes that 53ʳᵈ chapter of Isaiah, he said, "While the light is with you, accept it, for the night is coming" (John 12:35). The interval...there are intervals and intervals and intervals. Take the light while you are with the light, for the night of doubt and complete ignorance of the principle of life will descend, always does, and there is night and day, night and day...and take it while it is with you and live by it. And that's the end of the ministry of Jesus Christ, as told in the gospel of John, the most profound book in the Bible, 12ᵗʰ of John. Then he quotes... he doesn't quote it, the evangelist telling the story quotes it of him, and he quotes the first and second verses of the 53ʳᵈ chapter of the Book of Isaiah, "Who has believed our report?" Who has believed what we have heard? "And to whom has the *arm* of the Lord been revealed?"

So I tell you, believe it, it is true. I am speaking from experience. I am not speculating, I am not theorizing. The story of the Bible is true. It unfolds in *us*: "Scripture *must* be fulfilled in *me*." Everyone can use the same statement and say, "Scripture must be fulfilled in me." And this is the end of his journey...the last of his ministry is on this note. And when he departs, who knows? So the plea is urgent, "*While* the light is with you, accept it"; for he identifies himself, and all the titles of God are given to him in this chapter in irony. The Son of man, the light of the world, all these are given to him in this chapter; but they're all given to him in irony, for he's an *ordinary* man. For the 53ʳᵈ chapter tells you, he has no form or comeliness that we should look upon him (verse 2). He's not anything that you really would admire. There's nothing about him that you would think is beautiful, that you should desire...an ordinary man. And how could this ordinary man be what we expected Messiah to be, such an *ordinary* man? Read it carefully, the 53ʳᵈ of Isaiah. He doesn't come through the door like some giant, some fantastic thing, just an ordinary man. And it happens in him. And when he tells this story, who will believe what they have heard?

But in this drama, there was one present and the minute that something was said, I knew exactly as he rose and left he was going to report what he had heard. And then, having reported it, in came this tall, handsome, wonderful looking man, not more than forty, in an ancient robe. But he was the embodiment of majesty, he was the nth degree of thought, and walked rapidly, like a soldier would walk, but straight as an arrow. Then turned at right angles and walked to the end, and turned at right angles and walked to the middle, then turned and came and stood before me. Then hammered into my shoulder this peg, a blunted peg, and I felt every impact as he put it in; and then that circular motion which severed my robe. Then he took the end and just pulled it a little bit and it came off, exposing my entire right arm, then he threw it aside. Then he raised his arms out, embraced me, kissed me, I kissed him, both on the right side of each other's neck. And then, as the scene was dissolving, I was looking at that lovely pale blue that he had taken from me and unveiled my arm. So we can say, "Who has believed it?" You would think, well, then no one has seen him. But, no, they saw him. Those who were standing when he did it, they saw it. "To whom has the arm of the Lord been revealed?" Well, they saw it. It goes on…that same play goes on and on and on.

So I tell you, believe it. Every word of scripture is true. While we're here we are not asked not to apply the law. In fact, we are encouraged to apply the law to cushion all the blows that come our way. Apply it every moment of time and be comfortable in this world by assuming that you are already the one that you want to be. Assume it. I do. I have obligations in the world of Caesar and I've got to live in this world. Rent is due and all the utilities are due and everything is due…and then the unexpected things are due too. They come every month. Not things you can budget, not things that you know about, they simply come. This month an extra $500 is due. Why? Something is needed, out of the nowhere. You didn't budget it. So I have to live in a state of affluence, I have to. I am forced to do it in order to meet the emergencies of life. You can't budget. You're always going to dwell in some fabulous world beyond what life will tell you will be the normal flow towards your direction.

So I tell you, *live* in that state, live in it. Don't let anyone tell you that that is un-Christian. Forget it! What are they talking about? We need today more than ever an entirely new concept of Christology. Scrape all the barnacles from that ship…they're all false, they're all phony. All this palaver of genuflecting before crosses built by man on a wall, and all this ceremony about marriage, and the ceremony about death, and all this junk about being buried in holy ground. When it suits them to plow the whole thing up at a profit, they plow it all up, and then bless the land, so that all the little bones are now blessed because it now suits that purpose to do it. And who is kidding whom? And yet we go blindly on, believing in all this palaver. The time has come for a new concept, a completely new concept of who Jesus *really* is, who that real being is who is God himself who became man. He became *me*, he became *you*…the same God. This cosmic Christ became humanity.

And so the bloodshed spoken of in scripture is humiliation. "Being in the form of God...he *emptied* himself, and took upon himself the form of a slave and was born in the likeness of men. And being found in *human* form humbled himself and became obedient unto death, yes, even death upon a cross." "And Jesus Christ, who was rich, for *your* sakes became poor, that by his poverty you might become rich"...and inherit the same form, the same glory that is his. He isn't *pretending* that he's man, he became man. He's not in disguise; he had to completely forget. As this lady who wrote me forgot. She had to completely forget the story. But who was hearing it? It was the same God in her that now is waking. And the one who spoke to her wasn't better, it's the same God. God is one. And yet she goes back and she says, "It's so far, far away...so far into the past...I heard that man, that man Neville, who kept on and on and on about a father and the son. And I remembered I did not understand it."

Well, may I tell her, I wasn't talking to another, I was talking to myself. Who else can I address? I can't address another, it's all one. We are one. So what I'm telling you today, I tell you because I'm talking to myself. And there is no real freedom for the one who is completely released until all are released... not really. I'll be released in the not distant future; but not really, not until everyone is released, for I am buried in every being that is born of woman. I cannot completely be released until every child born of woman has heard it and has experienced Christ completely unfolding in him, even to the exposure of the power, called the hand. "Who has believed what we have heard? And to whom has the arm of the Lord been revealed?"

So I tell you it is literally true, every word of scripture. So you are warned in the very end of Revelation, the last chapter, "Do not add to or take from the words of the prophecy of this book" (Rev.22:10). Leave it just as it is. It will prove itself in *your* life supernaturally and you will prove it to be literally true. Oh, you may give an interpretation to it. The word does mean power; it does mean "Almighty God's power" when the arm is unveiled. The things you can do after it's unveiled! But even if you did the most miraculous things, as you're told, neither the character nor the number of the miracles that he did evoked faith.

He departed possibly wondering to what extent was he heard. And then he returns to reap the harvest, and to plant again; for the word also means "the sower who sows the seed," and the seed is the Word of God. He comes and he sows the word, returns and reaps the harvest, and then he sows again, one being. Because no matter who comes, his name tomorrow may be by some other name, but he will be simply the same being, for he can't be another. I'm individualized, I know. I will never in eternity be absorbed to the point of loss of individuality, loss of my identity; yet, I am one with anyone who knows that his Son is my Son. There's no one in this world who would look into the face of my Son and know himself to be the father of my Son and not be me. How can he be? He and I are one. It's the only way you would ever know the unity that is God.

So here, bloodshed...I take it this night in the form of humiliation. The word is formed of two words; it forms Adam. Adam is Aleph, Daleth, Mem—and the word is Daleth, Mem, taking Aleph away, and that is bloodshed. So out of him came his two sons; and the first blood to be shed was when Cain slew Abel. So it came out of Adam. So the name for bloodshed is Daleth, Mem, ___(??). Here we find this unfolding within us, the shedding of the blood. But the real shedding of the blood you will experience when that body of yours is torn from top to bottom; and you will see the blood that was in the beginning shed, and it's yourself. For God died for man. But he became man, so when man sees the blood he is so much God it's himself he sees now, it's not another. He doesn't know the sacrifice that was made, because he is *so much* God. When he sees that living pool, that living water, the blood of God, he knows it is himself. He also knows it is his creator, his redeemer, *and* himself. He feels himself self-redeemed, which he is, because God became him. If God did not become him he could not be self-redeemed. He'd be another and still two. There can't be two, God and him; there can only be one. He breaks down that wall of partition between and they become one, instead of two. So he becomes one. And I see it. I am it; then up I go into that heavenly state, which is the throne of God.

So when it happens, it's such a simple thing. This normal, natural room, a bare room, there wasn't a thing in it. And men sitting on the floor...and I'm seated on the floor, and we are dressed in robes, casual things, all of us, ordinary, ordinary men, of no repute whatsoever. But I am telling them what I know from experience: I'm explaining the mystery of God. As I spoke one word, one quickly jumped up and left the room. The minute he left the room I knew he had to report what had been said. Then came this authority of authorities—tall, handsome, wonderful looking man, I would say not more than forty, unusually handsome. And he walked briskly to the end, turned, walked to the end, turned, walked to the middle, and then hammered into my shoulder this blunted peg. And really hammered it...every impulse I felt. Then that quick circle, and then he took off the thing that hung upon me and exposed my entire right arm, from here down. Not just here...just where he made the circle. Just where he hammered it he made the circle with a sharp instrument, one sweeping motion, and pulled it off. A lovely beautiful pale blue...and the cloth was a lovely, lovely cloth. I mean, it was altogether lovely. It seemed like an expensive cloth. To me, looking at it, it seemed so altogether lovely. And there it was. I wondered where had he cast it...just simply threw it away. I was looking at it when the whole scene dissolved...with the arm exposed.

So those that I addressed—minus the one who left, he did not see the arm exposed— the others that I talked to who were still standing, they saw the arm exposed. So when the question is asked, "To whom has the arm of the Lord been revealed?" Revealed to those, and then they would know, and then start their journey, asleep for awhile. For when you come into the world, you have to enter a tremendous depth of sleep, and you only begin to remember. It's all a matter of remembering and remembering and remembering. So this lady who wrote me, "I remembered, I remembered the dream...and as I came out, the one thought that filled my mind was Neville. Well, I was thinking of Neville, and then the dream returned. The dream was 'That man, that man Neville' in the depths that seemed so far, far away and so long in time. And he was talking over and over again, on and on, about a father and a son. And I remembered I did not understand. I also remembered that I went to sleep. *When* I went to sleep that I do not remember, but I do remember I did go to sleep. Now that I am completely alert and awake, it all feels as though I were a puzzle, and now this night a piece of it has been found and put into its original place. And now it's still night, she said, but the morning cannot be far." But it isn't far off...it isn't.

But may I tell you, you can be anything you want to be. You want to be rich? You can be rich. You want to be famous? You can be famous. You can be anything you want to be in this world of Caesar if you apply the principle. The principle is simple: act as if it were true. Just imagine that things are as they would be were it true, and dare to walk the world just as though it were true. And if you do, it will be true. Wouldn't make any difference what the world thinks, because God is in you. The arm has not yet been revealed as mighty power, doesn't matter. Still assume the power is there, and by this mere assumption that things are as you desire them to be they'll become a fact. They'll all become fact, every one of them. Doesn't really matter what the world will tell you. Don't ask anyone anything. Just dare to assume, *I am* the lady, the gentleman that I would like to be, with the comforts, the securities that I would desire in this world. Dare to assume it. And may I tell you, in a way that you will not consciously know you will become it.

As you live by God's law, then in God's own time—he's doing the work within you, which is simply molding you into his own likeness, so that you two become one, not two but one—when it's a perfect likeness they fuse. Not until the likeness is perfect it cannot be. So he tries me in the furnaces of affliction for his own sake, for his own sake he does it. For how should my glory be given to another? Can't give it to another; he has to give it to himself. So he fuses into the perfect likeness; for, I must be perfect as my

Father in heaven is perfect, and when it's a perfect image of himself, we aren't two anymore. He's cleaved to me and now we're one. And then all that is told unfolds within us.

Here, if you go back to the beginning of Isaiah, as we took Isaiah tonight, the very first verse, "The vision of Isaiah"...a vision. These sixty-odd chapters, he tells you, it's a vision and the book, next to the Book of Psalms, is the most quoted in the New Testament. They go back and quote and quote and quote Isaiah, which is a vision. Can't you see it's a vision? The whole thing is completely and wholly supernatural. And so he quotes Isaiah in this end of the ministry of Jesus...he quotes the 53rd, but he begins the Book that it's a vision, "The vision of Isaiah the son of Amoz." It's not spelled like the prophet Amos with an S, it's spelled with a Z, something entirely different. Here is the great...and the word Isaiah means...there are two definitions, "Jehovah is salvation" or "Jehovah will give salvation." Scholars prefer the second one. I have no preference, both ___(??). "Jehovah is salvation" and "Jehovah will give deliverance." Yes, he will. But he gives it only to himself; therefore, he has to become you completely and unfold himself in you as expressed in that New Testament. When the whole thing is unfolded *completely* in you, well, then you and he are one. Then you depart.

But though you depart, don't think for one second, although you reach into your glory and it's a strength beyond the wildest dream of earth, you're not *really* free until *all* depart, because you're still buried in the world of sin and death. So let no one think that because he has simply departed, because the whole drama unfolded within him, that he has escaped. No, not until the whole of you has; he's still buried in all. That's why it's so eager on the part of one who has been sent to tell you that not to turn your back on the light while the light is with you. While he is with you, accept it; he's telling you what he knows from experience. Believe him, and then let it unfold within you. Challenge it and delay, and your delay is really his delay because we are one.

Now, in the practical sense, this night we simply dare to assume that you are the man, the woman that you want to be. Don't ask anyone if they think it is possible. You dare to assume that you are what you want to be. Believe in the reality of that invisible state and just sleep in it just as though it were true. You will enjoy that assumption externalized in this world ___(??). And while we do that, the work is taking place in you of which you are totally unaware, and that work is the unfolding of Christ in you. Everything said of Christ you will experience, and then, and only then, will you really know who Jesus Christ really is. Jesus Christ is God the Father. Whether the world believes it or not, he is God the Father, who became man that man might become God.

Now let us go into the Silence.

*　　　*　　　*

___(??) my father's birthday, Bill's father's birthday and the day that my arm was unveiled. So, ___(??), I can always remember your birthday. Now, are there any questions, please? We have ten minutes. Well, this week we are here on Friday. Next week, I think it's on a Tuesday, but next week there's only one. But look at the card, just ___(??) because I'm not familiar with it. I have to look every week to know when I'm talking. But I do know that this coming Friday I am here, and then next week I know we only have one, and I think it is on Tuesday. But we're still here one more lecture this week and it's on Friday.

Q: Did you recognize any of the people of the twelve that were in that room?

A: No, my dear, they were simply, as I said earlier, ordinary men, just ordinary men, nothing that would cause me to simply be startled or in any way...just ordinary men. I was a very ordinary man among them, very ordinary. We were all simply gathered together, as I was telling the story that I knew from experience. I was as natural and as ordinary as they were. But they were listening.

Q: What about the peg?

A: I do not know, my dear. I only know what happened to me. It was a blunted peg; it wasn't like a sharp nail or a needle. It was a thing that wide. I don't know if wood or metal...I'm inclined to believe it was wood. But it was jagged and wide and ___(??), and he simply stuck it here and he simply hammered it into my shoulder. When it was completely embedded in my shoulder, then with a sharp instrument he made that quick circular motion and severed my robe, up to where he had inserted the peg. Then he took the end of it and pulled it this way and pulled it out, exposing the arm completely, completely bare arm. Everything else was covered, but the right arm was completely exposed. Then he embraced me, kissed me here on my right side of my neck and I kissed him, facing him, on the right side of his neck. And then, while the scene is dissolving I'm looking at that pale lovely blue cloth, which he had taken from my arm, exposing to the view of those ordinary men who were now standing, because we all stood at attention while he entered the room.

Now, you can search scripture to find out where it was. Not everything is written there...(tape ends).

WHAT MUST WE DO?

10/14/66

Tonight's subject is concerning your willingness to accept the one who is sent. "What Must We Do?" is the title of tonight's subject. If you'll believe me and apply it, I promise you, you cannot fail. For all that I have told you since I started has been by a confession of faith in terms of experience, that's all that it has been. I have *experienced* scripture.

So here tonight, what must *we* do to be doing the work of God? And Jesus said to them, "This is the work of God, that you believe in him whom he has sent" (John 6:29). It starts with believing in him whom he has sent. Given that, all parts...but that is the fundamental and foundational thing; you must start on that foundation. It doesn't mean that a man like the speaker is saying to you, believe in me, the speaker. No, "Christ *in you* is the hope of glory" (Col.1:27). He is speaking from *within* you, and the entire story as told in scripture is the God in you telling you to believe in him.

Well, how did he put it in a way that I can really understand it? "You will die in your sins unless you believe that *I am he*" (John 8:24). To sin is to miss your mark in life, I don't care what that mark is. All things are possible to him, all things; no limitation is placed upon this presence within you. All depends upon your willingness to believe in him. Who is he? "You will die in your sins unless you believe that I AM he." That's the name of God. But humanity's tragedy is the tragedy of looking and following, looking for and following after *other* gods. Even when the whole thing is revealed, we find the most perfect born of woman, who had not experienced scripture, making the statement, "Art thou he that should come, or do we look for another?" (Luke 7:19). Still looking for something on the outside, still looking for some being that could save him. There is no Savior but God and God's name is I AM...

all within you...that whole being is God. Either believe in him or don't. If you believe in him, nothing is impossible, but nothing.

So what must we do? All that you do to do the work of God is to believe in him whom he has sent. "If you will not accept my testimony concerning earthly things, how can you accept my testimony concerning heavenly things?" (John 3:12). If I tell you that by assuming that I am wealthy I become wealthy, and you won't believe that, even though I tell you story after story of those who did, what would you believe if I took you out of this world completely and told you of heavenly things? What *would* you believe?

I have the Sunday *Times* from New York every week. It comes usually on a Thursday. In the magazine section of this week, here is a picture of a single cell in the human brain. The scientists claim there are one hundred billion cells in the human brain. They photograph and magnify it 3,400 times, and here is this little cell you could not see with the normal eye. Under the microscopic camera magnified 3,400 times, it's the perfect tree. I have it at home. A perfect tree in winter, winter in the East, or the North, I should say, where every leaf, every blossom, everything is shed, just a skeleton—one hundred billion of those in the human brain. So when Blake saw it, and I saw it, he said, "The gods of the earth and sea sought through nature to find this tree, but their search was all in vain, there grows one in the human brain."

I saw this thing so clearly. And I told it in San Francisco and I've never repeated it since until tonight...I don't think I have. Because a lady rose in the audience and she was most critical, and just most disturbed, so why tell it? But I saw this tree coming out of the human skull. I saw it. Then I saw men on earth who thought themselves important. And this one is now gone from this sphere. He was the third in power in the British labor party about two years ago...he's gone now. He was the one who nationalized all industries and brought England to its knees in an economic collapse. He was going to share everything and take it from everyone who had it and share it because he had nothing to give them, but going to share it. I saw him put from the outside a tree on his head. He tried to jump off and to move with it, and he fell on you know what. Came back again, put it on again, and he jumped again. And again he fell, fell like a piece of lead. Well, I couldn't resist the impulse to smile and to laugh at this trying to put on from the outside what grows from the *inside*. Well, he had the presence of mind to die two years ago, leaving others behind him to make the same stupid effort: All the great effort to give everything to the world and not make them make any effort whatsoever. No attempt to awaken their brain, no attempt. I'll give you all that you'll take. I'll give you all your brains, give you this, give you that...have everything given to you. You don't have to do anything, just stay asleep, remain asleep. Well, that is not life.

I saw it grow so beautifully. One day in San Francisco, I was living at the Palace Hotel. If you're familiar with the Palace, it's a lovely old hotel, enormous ceilings when you enter the lobby. As I came through the door, an artist who was waiting for me by appointment, I came a little bit late and she came early, so she sat in the lobby. When I spotted her—it is a very large lobby—as I came down she started drawing furiously and making a sketch. She wouldn't talk, she wouldn't look at me, she kept on making the sketch. Then she completed it in a quick rough sketch. She said, "This is what I saw as you came through the door. You are human yes, I grant you, but I saw antlers growing from within. Your whole head...you were like a stag coming through the door. Now, the building itself is eight stories tall, it isn't tall enough to hold the antlers that I saw coming through and yet I saw it come straight through the door as you walked through the door."

I tell you, think of it, a hundred billion. If you haven't the *New York Times*, you may still get one, you can write for it. It's in the magazine section. One little cell magnified 3,400 times is the perfect tree, like an oak tree, all gnarled, not a leaf on it, not a bud, nothing, just all the limbs and all the little branches...a single one...and a hundred billion? Can't you conceive of the garden of God, when it is in bloom? Can't you conceive of this wonderful garden and you the gardener, you the shepherd, you the Lord? When the whole thing is in bloom and all the energies turn down that ___(??) into generation and turn now up into regeneration, and they water the garden of God, and a hundred billion in bloom? Well, I tell you that's what is in store for every child born of woman.

But here, on this level, let me now share with you this night...I've asked you for your letters, asked you for your experiences that I may tell them from the platform and encourage the faith of all by telling. Well, I told the story a week ago tonight, the gentleman was here and I told his story, how he believed it to the point where he tried it, and how he moved from one salary to doubling his salary. Then he moved from that to having money without working. And then he moved from that to another, into the growing of a tree that all the nurserymen said could not grow in his living room. Well, a gentleman was present who heard it, and it touched a little memory spot in his mind. And, by the way, what I'm telling you now hasn't a thing to do with this story of the brain that is the article...of what I'm not talking about. They are only concerned with memory—that everyone is a memory point in the brain—therefore the doctors are only concerned with touching this to stimulate a memory.

So, he was present and "As you said it, I remembered" and this is what he remembered. He said, "A few months ago I read in the daily paper a story about a dishonest investment broker. I instantly revised it, changed the entire thing, because I, too, am an investment broker. And I determined that I didn't want anyone with whom I dealt to ever feel anything other than trust towards me. I wanted absolute trust from everyone who came to my office and sought my services, but I mean absolute trust. Having revised that story, I bathed and wallowed in the feeling of trustworthiness. Then I forgot it, completely forgot it. On September the 28th a man called me and he said to me, 'I do not know you, but I'm a friend of a client of yours, and I would like to make an investment.' So he told me what he wanted and I accepted his request and bought a mutual fund, as he requested. This last Friday, when I heard this, that very afternoon before I came here I called my office from Los Angeles and asked if there were any messages for me. They said, Yes, Mr. X wants you to call him. I will not tell you his name, just say Mr. X. So he said I put the call in and this is what he said. Now he's a client as of Sept. the 28th, this is now October, he said, 'I have not seen you, I do not know you, I haven't met you, but friends of mine know you, and I have a feeling that I would trust you'…with emphasis on trust. Now, he said, 'I have many friends, but I have a feeling I can trust you, and I want you to be a co-trustee of my estate. Will you come to see me on Wednesday to discuss the matter?'" With an emphasis on trust…the very thing in which he had bathed himself. How can he bathe himself?—"I am trustworthy."

Throughout scripture…you'll find it beginning in the very beginning of Genesis, the 4th chapter, how we call upon the name. So Seth, who took the place of Abel, brought forth a son whose name was Enos, and men began to call upon the name of God. To call upon the name of God is to call *with* the name of God, that's what it really means. Literally, it's to call with. People say, I will call upon the name of God, and they'll say, "In the name of Jesus Christ"—who is Jesus Christ?—"in the name of Jehovah, in the name of God" all of these phony names on the outside. When you call upon the name, you call *with* the name. If I would be wealthy, I must assume that I *am* wealthy. That's how I conjure it, and bathe in the feeling of being wealthy. If I would be anything in this world, I call *with* the name and bathe in the feeling of being it. *That's* how I call upon the name of God. So, what must I do to be doing the work of God? Believe in him whom he has sent. Believe in his testimony. Well, what did he tell me? He said, "You'll die in your sins"—you'll miss the mark in life—"unless you believe that I am he."

Now we are told he manifested the name of God. I have manifested thy name to the men thou gavest me out of the world. I have made it known and I will make it known that the love by which thou lovest me may be in them and *I* in them (John17:6). So he is in me and he manifests the name; he tells me the name is I AM. So I'm not asking you to believe in Neville, I am asking you to believe in the testimony of Jesus Christ. He testifies to the fact that he's in us and he is sent and the one who sent him is himself: "He who sees me sees him who sent me. I am he." So, "Unless you believe that I am he ___(??)", well, then you continually miss the mark, because you think in this, that or the other. And the tragedy of the world is simply following after other gods. "Art thou he that should come or do we look for another?" Looking for another, for another, for another…there is no other. There is only God. God is one.

When I say I am, do I mean any other being in the world? Do I point any place in the world when I say I am? Well, that's God's name. So when you say, "I am weak," it is God who will suffer with you, for you've made him weak. When you say, "I am strong," it is God who will raise his arm and it will be *you* expressing it. It's entirely up to you. So that's what you do. What must we *do* to be doing the work of God? Just believe in him whom he has sent, that's all that we do. So if this night you would do it, you would be as this chap, who wants to be trustworthy, who wants to be trusted by every client who comes into his world. To feel…a man who hasn't seen him is asking him to be a co-trustee of his estate. Can you imagine that? Last year I went back to Barbados and I spent a few months. I made out a will and I got my brother and two nephews that I knew, I trust them implicitly, and they were co-trustees of my will. But here is a man who lost himself in the feeling of being worthy, being trustworthy, and a man that he's never seen and the man has never seen him, and he felt, "I have many friends, but I feel with you I can trust you." He hasn't seen him. Why, he *had* to come that way. He had to come because he lost himself in the feeling of being trustworthy.

So that's what *you* do to do the work of God, nothing else. To give my body to be burned, to give this to charity, to give that, that is not the work of God. The work of God is simply to honor his name. And do you know that anyone who has received this revelation as you have this night, but *anyone* who receives the revelation, who having received it acts in such a way that he becomes dishonored has actually dishonored the name of God? As you're told all through scripture, he has defiled the name, he's rejected the name; he's done all these things to the name. If anyone who hears it and then turns to any man in this world as the authority, anything as the authority, anything on the outside as the authority, and then acts in a way that he brings about as a result of his actions dishonor, he has profaned the name of God.

You can call God by any name. I can say, "God damn it!"—that isn't profaning the name of God. I can say "Jesus Christ!" I can say anything… that is not profaning the name of God. But let me hear the revelation and not *abide* by it and not *live* in the assumption that I am that which I want to be and that I am hearing from those that I love what I want to hear, I am profaning the name of God. It's just as simple as that. You can get down on your knees and go to all the churches in the world and you can simply pray

from morning to night, there's no God to hear you, none whatsoever. You can
sing all the hallelujahs, all the things in this world, there isn't a thing there to
hear you. "I do not hear them," sayeth the Lord. He hears those who honor
or dishonor his name, and the reward is automatic in this world, automatic.
Like the tree I've just spoken about bearing fruit. And so it's entirely up to
man, will I honor or will I dishonor the name of God?

So what must I do? It's so simple what I should do. I don't care what
a man has done, if I know the true character of God, which is love, I can
redeem him. I can redeem him by simply applying what I know concerning
the revelation of his name. I can assume that I am hearing what I would like
to hear concerning that one, and I don't care what he had done, he can be
redeemed. He can be completely forgiven as though he had not done it. That
is the story that I am trying to bring to everyone in this world. So I ask you
to believe in the name of God. And all you have to do is to *do* it. After the
revelation is given to you, then please do it. Do it in its fullness. Just simply
dwell upon the name of God, and God has revealed himself to us as I AM.
"When you go unto the people of Israel, say unto them, 'I AM has sent you.'
No matter what they ask, 'I AM has sent you. That is my name forever...and
by this name I shall be known throughout all generations'" (Exod.3:14).

So here comes the great revealer of the nature and the character of God,
called Jesus Christ. That's the true revelation of God. You want to see God?
Look at Jesus Christ. There is God in its fullness. Everything that is God is
in Jesus Christ, and he said, "I am he." But he speaks from within you, bear
that in mind, all from within you: "Christ *in you* is the hope of glory. Do you
not realize that Jesus Christ is in you?—unless, of course, you fail to meet
the test!" (Col.1:26; 2 Cor.13:5). If you haven't put him to the test, then you
don't know that he is. He put him to the test...as the gentleman whose story
that I told fired his Imagination to remember. He said, "It was a trivial thing,
because I did it, I revised it; I did what I did, and I dropped it. And then
when you spoke on Friday night, it was right after I received my message that
I called from Los Angeles and they said, Call Mr. X. So I called Mr. X. and
this is what he tells me, and he stressed the word trust—'I can trust you. I
haven't seen you, I do not know you, but I know friends who know you. And
with all my friends it is you that I feel I can trust. Come see me on Wednesday
and let us go over the matter of being a co-trustee of my estate.'" Can you
imagine that? May I tell you, nothing is impossible to God...and God is your
own wonderful I-am-ness. He sets no limit on what he can do, but none. You
say, I am this, I am that, I am the other, if you really believe it and walk in the
assumption that it's true, even though at the moment reason denies it and your
senses deny it, if you dare to assume it and you persist in that assumption, it
will come to pass. You don't need any help from the outside.

All that I am telling you is a confession of faith in terms of my own personal experience. Believe it...everything I'm telling you. I have experienced scripture, from beginning to end, really. All the little pieces...like the arm, the night that I told you...it's a lovely thing. I went back and looked it up, and it's the 22nd chapter of Isaiah. It's a beautiful thing, how he nailed it upon the shoulder, and gave him the key of David as he nailed the peg upon his shoulder. "You shall shut and no one shall open; and ye shall open and no one shall shut" (Is. 22:22-25). And he'll bear the burden for awhile, all the responsibility of being the director, the God of that age; and then in the end the peg will be broken, all will fall from him and the burden will be lifted from his shoulder. You must have the responsibility. You awake as God; you must play the part in its fullness. And the responsibility of simply guiding a certain section of time, a certain age, will be placed upon you. He nails it upon his shoulder and gives him the key of David. He shall shut and none shall open; and he shall open and none shall shut. And then the peg that was nailed into him will be broken off and the burden of Judah and all the inhabitants of Jerusalem and all the utensils of the temple will fall. He will be relieved of the responsibility *after* he has played it for awhile. So that is part of everyone's future in this world.

Not everyone was here who heard the vision. It's a simple, wonderful vision, but those who were here you will understand what I'm talking about concerning the passage that really illustrates it in its fullness. So I have been experiencing, night after night, all the things concerning the awakening of God in man. The awakening of the tree that grows not outside that the gods of the earth and sea are seeking, but grows from the inside in the human brain. And every night is simply another petal, another blossom appears, with another expression of what it represents. If you saw this little thing, one single little cell, a whole tree, and a hundred billion of them? Can you see why Blake said, "All that you behold, though it appears without, it is within, in your Imagination, of which this world of mortality is but a shadow"? The whole vast thing is unfolding from within, that your wonderful human Imagination is the divine body; it is God himself in man, represented as a tree. And now, from our little microscopic thing they actually photograph it and it looks like a tree. You can't see anything but a tree. When magnified 3,400 times, it's an oak tree, without a leaf, without a ___(??), without anything, just the branches, the limbs, but multiple, an enormous thing, a single one, and a hundred billion of them?

And they're only concerned about the memory process concerning the structure of the brain. For man suffers injury to the brain, certain amnesia, he has a partial forgetfulness. I have a friend of mine who is now put away. He made a picture, years ago, with Rita Hayworth and he was shot in this picture in the island of Trinidad. Then a man with whom he's had a feud for years—it is not publicly known, it is implied—they fought through the years for parts, this, that and the other. Others have told me that it was he who struck him. They found him; he was unconscious, and taken to this place, the place of no return. And that absence between that interval and it's about ten years taken out of his life. When I called him and they let me speak to him on the telephone, he would say the same old thing, "I was wounded in Trinidad. I was wounded."

You say we're writing fiction! He played in a picture in which he was wounded and it was in Trinidad. He was struck on the head right there in Hollywood by a man who disliked him. And now his memory goes back, he was wounded in Trinidad…can't remember anything between, things that came before and things that came after, an interval of ten years taken out of his life. So he knows me and takes me back beyond that moment, but he can't remember anything in between. So they're trying to find the great secret of this connection between the little cells of the brain. Yes, it's all there…no question about it. So here this fantastic world in which we live and the whole thing lives in us.

So tonight, you want to know what you should do if you would do the work of God? If it makes you happy to go to church, go to church. If it makes you happy to give to charity, give to charity. If it makes you happy to do all the things that you now do, wonderful, but may I tell you *that* is not doing the work of God. This is the work of God, the 6th chapter of John: "Believe in him whom he has sent" and that alone is doing the work of God. Whom did he send? "I am he." Something on the outside speaking?—no, he is speaking from within me. God became man that man might become God. So he's speaking from within me, and that presence within me is asking me to believe in the reality of my own wonderful human Imagination; that when I assume that I am trustworthy, believe in him, and wait for the results, it will come. They *must* come into my world, tangible proof that what I am doing is true. "And a man that I do not know, I have never seen him, and he has friends, and he calls me, one he has never seen, and tells me that I can trust you, I have a feeling I can trust you. Would you be my co-trustee and come and see me on Wednesday, so we can go into the details of being a trustee of my estate?"

I tell you it never fails. All you have to do is believe in God. Well, the average person will say, I believe in God. The whole vast world will say that I believe in God. All but those few and they will say, I don't believe in God. But may I tell you, the few that stand out in history, the Hitler's, the Stalin's, the Mussolini's, the Fidel Castro's and so on, they will be like a pawn; and one day they'll become the most fantastic promoters of a faith that they tried so long to destroy. When the tree blooms it blooms, and they will make a reversal, just as Paul did. No one was a greater promoter of the faith that he tried to destroy than Paul was. Everyone will. So tonight I ask you to believe in him. Believing in him there isn't a thing in this world that you desire that you cannot realize. You don't have to go out and dig up people to make it so. Leave people alone. He didn't go out and dig people up to prove he was trustworthy...not for one moment. He doesn't ___(??) he just simply bathed himself...having revised the story.

Well, may I tell you as one who speaks from the Word of God, if I read in the paper or hear that one who claims to be a spokesman for God is dishonest and uses his audience to milk them for his own personal gain, I can't tell you my distress, I can't tell you. I wouldn't mention names, but I've seen them across the country. And although they're still acclaimed by others who follow by the thousands to be the great honored things, I know what they've done. I know how they've milked people for personal gain, all under the cloak of spirituality. I never disillusion those who still want to go...let them go, but I know what they did, and I can't tell you how it hurts me. If a dentist hears of a malpractice of a dentist, he is hurt. If a medical man who is a form of doctor, an internist, or a surgeon and he hears of malpractice for personal gain, he is hurt. Well, I can see his hurt when he read of this dishonest investment broker, as I know from my own experience when I heard of those who would take a trusting audience and deceive them for personal gain under the cloak of spirituality. So I say leave them alone; the tree will bloom one day. Revise it, as he did. Revise the story for your own wonderful benefit, revise it, but then leave them alone.

But in your own case this night, would you be...and you name it...well then, believe in his name. What's his name? His name is I AM. You mean, in spite of the lack of evidence I must believe that I am what I now want to be? Yes, that's what you believe. Then bathe yourself and wallow in the feeling of being it. That's all you do. Drop it as he did. And in no time the evidence comes. He said, "A few months ago I read it"—well, a few months to me would be three months...the 28th of September was when the man called him and placed an order, which he executed. Then last Friday—I can't recall the date, was it the 7th, 8th, something like that of this month, which is still October—he's asking him to be a trustee. All an invisible state...the man doesn't know him, he doesn't know the man, save he's a client for whom he's made an investment, bought him a mutual fund.

So I say to you tonight go out believing in God...well, if I know who God is. For the great tragedy of the world is the tragedy of following after *other* gods: "Art thou he that should come, or do we look for another"...still looking for another at the very end. And so he said of the one who asked that question—for he was in jail and he sent his disciples to ask the question, and the one who said it was John the Baptist—he said of John the Baptist, "No one born of woman is greater than John; yet I tell you the least in the kingdom is greater than he" (Mat.11:11). John did violence to his appetites in the hope of gaining the kingdom. He didn't eat, he didn't drink, he wore this, he wore that, all in the hope. You can't *earn* the kingdom of God; it's a gift. You simply apply God's law and live fully in this world, and in God's own good time he singles you out and then you are called. When you are called, there is no stopping. You can't resist him. You're called, called, embraced into his body of love, and sent to tell the story of the risen God. That's all that you're sent to tell. Tell them about what else? Everything will pass away. There isn't a thing in this world today no matter how modern it is but what it will pass away. All the wisdom of man is foolishness in the eyes of God. And the weakness of God is stronger than man. So everything that man thinks so great with his natural, rational mind will all pass away. So go and preach only about the risen God, one who could become the dead and rise from it. Tell that story. No other story.

Now, as we go into the Silence know what you want...just know what you want. As you go in you call not on the name of God, you call *with* the name of God, and the name is I AM. So if you would be free this night of all the things that are pressing upon you then assume that you are it *now*. If it will help you to bring into your mind's eye a friend who would care were it true, bring that friend into your mind's eye and have him rejoice with you because it is you. Then actually accept his congratulations and his joy in your good fortune and bask in the feeling that I am...and you name it now, what it is that you are calling out of the depth with the name of God. Now let us go.

*　　　*　　　*

Q: (inaudible)

A: That entire 3rd of John is on the story of rebirth. A man must be born again, that's the third chapter. "Unless you be born again, you cannot enter the kingdom of God" (John3:3) and "As Moses lifted up the serpent in the wilderness, so must the Son of man be lifted up" (John3:14). That whole chapter is devoted to rebirth. When a man is reborn, although he is strong and healthy, more so than ever before, all the energies that went down into generation are turned up into regeneration. He loves everyone in the world. He sees the beautiful women of the world, he loves them just as much as he's ever loved any woman, he admires them, they're altogether attractive and marvelous, but his energies have turned up right into his skull. The serpent that came down has turned up.

Q: He uses his Imagination creatively for everyone, is that right?

A: His creative power is now all up in Imagination. It's completely turned up. It's something that you can't induce. Some people say they can induce the kundalini fire. Induce what! The thing is an automatic act on the part of the Father in you. When he's put you through all the furnaces, which is himself, then he splits you in two, which is the curtain of the temple of your own flesh, and you behold the blood of God. You know it is yourself that golden, liquid, pulsing, living light; and you fuse with it. As it you move up like a serpent. Your admiration of beauty is still...even more so than ever before. You can admire all the things you always admired. You haven't lost interest in life...not lost interest in people getting children, getting married, getting engaged, all that excites you, it interests you, and you love it all.

But as far as *you* go, you return to a peculiar state without any external operation. You don't do as an early father did, Origin, who castrated himself in order to teach women. He was an early father of the Christian church in the 2nd Century. He was the most influential of all the early fathers. Augustine, who was considered the most, came 100 years after his death, but he laid the foundation for all Christianity. And he purposely and alone simply altered himself that he may teach women without being confused. But you *can't* do it that way. I can castrate a dog...I have one at home, one that was castrated...he still has the impulse. He's not a mule...the impulse is there but he's impotent, but impulse is there. So he castrated himself and so he lost the capacity, but the impulse is there. In the other, you admire completely beyond all measure, but the impulse isn't there. It's turned up, the seed is in him, right into his skull, and he creates from there.

If I could only share with you my visions recently. He simply said, if you will not believe what I tell you concerning here, how would you ever believe when I tell you concerning heavenly things? For when the arm now is unveiled, which is his power and his might, the things you do when you put your head down on that pillow at night! Something that you cannot put into words and have anyone ever believe you, ever, but that's what you do. You are creating now entirely differently. There's nothing impossible when you begin to exercise the power that now springs from within, for his seed remaineth in him. No restraint. All these fellows are restraining themselves. So they become priests and they take their vow of celibacy. What vow? Who is fooling whom? Those who will, by sheer determination, either go into some institution for a little while or they're lying their heads off, or in some other way, they're still filled with the impulse.

And in the 5th chapter of the Book of Matthew, "You have been told, 'You shall not commit adultery.' But I say to you anyone who looks on a woman lustfully has already committed the act with her" (Mat. 5:27). It's all imaginal. So to look with longing is to have committed the act, even though you do not have the courage to execute it. You may contemplate the consequences and restrain the impulse, but the impulse was the act. But here in this state there is no impulse; it's all turned up, completely turned up into the skull, and you're not the same being. On the outside you seem the same being. You're everything that...in fact, you're younger and stronger than you've been in years, everything, but you're not the same being. How to tell that to convince any physiologist in the world? They can't see it. Who can see it?—only you. So I'm telling you, what I tell you I tell from experience. My confession of faith is simply told in terms of experience.

So that whole 3rd chapter of John, which we quoted a portion of...and he tells this to Nicodemus, who was one of the two. For it was Joseph of Arimathea who got the tomb to put him in. He vanishes from the story after the 3rd chapter of John and reappears in it at the end when the body is about to be buried. Then he comes out of hiding as it were and takes the body and puts it into the tomb (Mat.27:57). So it was Nicodemus to whom he told this story, you a master of Israel and you do not know unless you are born from above, you cannot inherit the kingdom of God? And he tells him how it's done: "As Moses lifted up the serpent in the wilderness, so must the Son of man be lifted up" (verses 10-14). When that happens in man, he is born from above in the true sense of the word. He was born before, but he had an interval of time before the true being came out, the living water, that went down in the beginning into generation now, as his very being, turns up. It turns right up into heaven, into Zion, the home, the dwelling place of God.

Q: This is in reference to last week's lecture. You mentioned when you spoke a certain word a man got up and left the room? What was that word? [Occurred in a vision.]

A: My dear, I do not know. I said it when I spoke...I was explaining the
     mystery of God, explaining how God became us that we might become
     God. I was explaining and interpreting scripture, the word of God,
     explaining all these things. And then as I explained it, it seemed arrogant,
     it seemed the nth degree of, well, one could interpret that as almost being
     seditious. For here is an authority who believes himself an authority and
     I'm talking of a greater authority who became man that man may become
     that authority. And so, when I made that statement, which would put
     Caesar and all of his little underlings to naught, this one rose and quickly
     left the room. I knew instantly as he left that room the play's unfolding,
     that he has to report what he had heard. Then comes this handsome, tall,
     six-foot-four, slender man who *embodied* authority. He was the authority...
     if he was not king, he was representative of king. But he came in, thin,
     and walked to the end, turned at right angle, walked to the end, turned
     at right angle, walked to the middle, then came down and he looked
     at me. Then you know the story, how he hammered this peg into my
     shoulder and then cut off my sleeve and then pulled it, and cast it away,
     and exposed my right arm. The whole thing was bare from here down.
     Then he stretched himself out this way and then embraced me and kissed
     me on the right side of my neck and I kissed him on the right side of his
     neck. As the scene is dissolving...the discarded piece of cloth...I saw the
     shade, that lovely pale blue of a wonderful fabric. I could see the fabric,
     it was the best you could find, and the shade was the palest of pale blue.
     And that was the drama.
         Well, then you read the story, "Who has believed our report?" I'm
     telling these people the most fantastic story in the world. They're ordinary
     men—and I am an ordinary man. They're all seated and when he came in,
     because of his position in life, we all stood erect, at attention, like soldiers
     called to attention. And so, the whole drama began to unfold. "Who has
     believed our report and to whom has the *arm* of the Lord been revealed?"
     Then we are told in the 110th Psalm, "The Lord said to my lord, 'Sit at
     my right arm 'til I make thy enemies thy footstool.'" The right arm is the
     power and the wisdom and the strength of God...and it takes everything
     that opposed you in the past and forms a footstool for you. For you come
     into an entirely different power, a different understanding of life, when
     the arm is revealed. You're told in the Psalms when he cries out to have
     his enemies be destroyed, he said, Why keepest thy right power in thy
     bosom, O Lord? It's not yet time to be pulled out and to be redeemed.

So all this symbolism...and then all of a sudden it happens. I never dreamed that it would happen in this manner, but suddenly it unfolded. That tree unfolded and all these are blossoms unfolding. They are all in bud now, and then one after the other they all come out on the tree of life. And everyone has it buried within them. Buried what? God is buried in man and he *is* the tree of life. And that wonderful Garden of Eden... the one that he watered with this water of life that has been turned up, that's been watering this world and now it's watering Eden and all the trees can come into bloom.

Until Tuesday. Thank you.

THE NEW MAN

10/18/66

Tonight's subject is "The New Man." Christ is really the reality that is man, the God that is *in* man. Now, is it all being done on the other side of the veil or is there something that you and I can do on this side of that dividing wall? For we are told the wall is broken down to make of the two one new man.

Now, let me share with you a story told me recently by a very dear friend of mine, one who has had most of my experiences. He wrote me this letter just a few weeks ago. You listen to it carefully because God speaks to man through the medium of dream, and he reveals, he unveils himself through the medium of revelation. That's how he unveils himself. Well here, is his letter. He said, "I awoke at six in the morning. It was too early to get up, so I thought I would simply remain in bed and do some purposeful imagining. As I started, this thunderous voice came from within me declaring 'I am God. I am self-contained. I am self-sufficient' and it kept it over and over and over. And finally I said to it, I know, I know, and I'm trying to do something about it, but you're speaking so loudly I cannot imagine. But it persisted; it kept on repeating 'I am God. I am self-sufficient. I am self-contained' over and over and over. So I said, it seemed to me like ___(??), and so I thought, if you can't prevent it, relax and enjoy it. So I simply lay there in bed and listened and enjoyed it, and fell sound asleep...this proclamation from within that 'I am God. I am self-contained. I am self-sufficient.'"

Now listen to this other dream of his as he calls it. These are real revelations. He said, "I found myself in a desert, a vast desert of nothingness. Not a blade of grass, not a shrub, not a cactus, not a tree, but nothing...just an infinite desert, and here I am in this vast nothingness. But in my hand it seemed that I held some golf balls, and I took one and I threw it. Where a moment before there was nothing, in five seconds, not more than five seconds, boom, a beautiful home and lawn appeared in Technicolor. I threw another, and another lovely home and yard appear in Technicolor with people around it. Then I took another ball and I threw it across the way, and here this wonderful putting green appeared adjacent to this wonderful golf course. A man that I discovered to be at my side said, 'Isn't that terrific! You put the ball right next to the cup.' And he answered, 'Oh, no, no, I don't do it that way, I put the ball down and then I put the hole next to the ball, that's how I play the game.'

"Then I created a huge, great gate, and this friend of mine and I walked through the gate that I had created. As I went through the gate, I came upon the most miserable scene you can imagine. The most dilapidated house, completely gone, but what dilapidation! and next to it, this horrible streetcar in the last very last stages of decay. So I took a ball and I started to throw it and it wouldn't leave my hand. I couldn't get the ball to depart from my hand. I threw it and threw it and it just wouldn't go. But I said to myself, well, maybe I'm not ready for it, maybe it is beyond me. I threw it and threw it... and I said no, I can't, it's beyond me, beyond my power to do it. Then, after a long wait, this that was the dilapidated house suddenly turned into the most modern hotel and what was a dilapidated streetcar into a streamlined bus, which quickly drove off.

"Here, I could not," said he, "change or let go of the past. I couldn't let go. I came upon the past. It was so easy to create out of nothing. Yes, out of nothing I could create anything. But when it comes to something I know to be a fact, I couldn't change it. I couldn't let go of the past. But I persisted and persisted and persisted, and persistency was rewarded. Eventually it turned into this glorious new, very modern hotel and a new streamlined bus, which drove off."

Then he said, "I came upon a scene that resembled the Miracle Mile on Wilshire, with an island up the middle. But it was a strange setting. Here were all these kids, boys and girls...the boys in horrible messy pants and the girls in bikinis. It was so unlike what you should see on the Miracle Mile. So I thought, well, I'll throw another ball there. So I threw another ball and suddenly they were completely transformed into the most beautifully dressed ladies and gentlemen, dining al fresco, under umbrellas, waited on by the most elegantly dressed waiters. I turned to my friend and said, 'You know, maybe I should have left them as they were.'" He's a very humorous man, may I tell you, because his profession is really writing humorous things. So he always ends his letters to me in a very humorous vein. So he had to add that note, "Maybe I should have left them...and I awoke maybe not a moment too soon."

Well, do you know that God speaks to man through the medium of dream? Although there were no golf courses 2,000 years ago, or, say, 4,000 years ago when the great Book of Numbers was written. The word ball appears only once in scripture. Only once would you find it in scripture, it appears in the chapter I quoted, unknowingly, last week, it's the 22nd chapter of Isaiah. And when you read it you'll think that God rejected a man. All of these are states of consciousness, and here is the occupant of the state. He rejects that *state*, not the occupant. And then he turns him into the one that he will accept, the one whose shoulder is going to be hammered in the not distant future with that peg. On him will rest the burden, the responsibility of the house of Judah and the inhabitants of Jerusalem. He doesn't reject anyone in this world, because he's playing all the parts anyway. But we're in states. He rejects the state, not the occupant of the state. As we are told in the 10th chapter of 1st Samuel, when the prophet Samuel speaks to Saul, and he said, "The spirit of the Lord shall come upon you... and you shall be turned into *another* man" (1Sam.10:6). He rejects Saul and chose David, and you think, well, a man could not fit the bill. No, the occupant of that state is God. He rejects the state, not the occupant, and turns him into another man; in other words, occupying an entirely different state. So in this 22nd of Isaiah, the only place where the word ball appears in scripture, he is experiencing that. Here came the moment of the rejection of a state, because he did succeed in transforming the past.

So what can I do on this side of the veil to break down that wall between the two? For, he breaks down the wall of partition between the two, and makes of two, one new man (Eph.2:14).. Let us listen carefully to what I can do, what you can do. And Jesus came into the world preaching the gospel of God, saying, "The time is fulfilled and the kingdom of God is at hand. Repent and believe in the gospel" (John 4:17). Believe my testimony, for I have experienced, "For all the promises of God have found their fulfillment in me," all of them. So believe the news that I bring you, but repent. Repent is what? The glory of Christianity is to conquer by forgiveness, and forgiveness tests man's ability to enter into and partake of the nature of the opposite.

So here, I see you dilapidated...it could be a house, it could be a streetcar, it could be anything in this world, but I see you in that form. Well, that's the past state. That's an old, an ancient and a fixed state. And I throw the ball. The word "throwing the ball" is simply "turning in the same circle" in scripture. It's like a circle...you can't seem to move out of it. It's the past, it seems fixed forever. And so I throw it and I throw it and I can't let it go. I'm still faced with the obvious fact before me. And finally, I do let it go, through what?— my persistency. "How long, Lord? How often must I forgive the brother who sins against me? Seventy times seven" (Mat.18:22). Do it and do it and do it until you succeed in letting it go. Let go of the past completely and see in its place that which you want to see. Do it until you can actually let go. Persist and persist and persist.

Then he tells the parables. The woman comes to the magistrate, and he doesn't fear God and he doesn't respect man, but he says, because of her persistency she bothers me, so I will rise and I will simply vindicate her. He didn't want to, because he didn't fear God and he didn't respect man, but her annoyance by the constant coming forced him to act as she wanted (Luke 18:2). Then the man came at the wee hours of the night, at midnight, and he wanted something to feed a stranger who came suddenly. The man said from above, "It is late; my children are in bed; and I cannot come down and open the door." But the man was insistent, and because he persisted and persisted, he came down and gave him what he wanted (Luke 11:5). And so you say, well, I can't get out of this turmoil. I don't care what the turmoil is, how fixed that seeming past is, you simply persist and persist and persist, and he's got to come down and grant your request.

So you break down the wall that divides the two by your practice of repentance. Repentance is simply practicing *our* part on this side of the veil while the work is going on in a hidden manner on the other side of the veil. Finally the wall is made thinner and thinner, and finally we break the shell, and Christ is born. Who is he? I am he. It's not Christ *and* you after you break the shell, there is only Christ. "And in that day the Lord shall be one and his name one" (Zec.14:9). Not two, only one. So he's breaking and making it thinner and thinner and thinner. But we on this side of the veil must do our part and we practice repentance, which is changing the past. It was so easy for him to create out of nothing. Oh, a vast desert...throws the ball, poof, a wonderful beautiful Technicolor home and a lawn; another ball, another beautiful Technicolor home and a yard with people all around it. Then, another ball, and here comes this wonderful putting green adjacent to this fabulous wonderful golf course. Then he creates a gate, a huge gate, and he and his friend go through. The friend tells him of this fantastic play of his. And he corrects the friend, "I don't do it that way. I don't try to put it into the hole, as you thought, I actually came next to the cup. I put the ball down first and I bring the hole next to it. That's what *I* do."

Then he saw, as he went through the gate, this dilapidated, horrible pictures of the past...a home in absolute decay, beyond repair, and a streetcar, one of the ancient kind. And he thought, I'll change it...but he couldn't let go of the past. He tried and he tried and he tried. But he persisted, because eventually it did go out of his hand. But he waited...the strangest thing in his letter to me...he waited so long. In creating out of nothing, five seconds; in creating, now, and changing the past, revising it completely, he waited and waited. Because nothing happened, he said, well, maybe I'm not equal to it. It's too much for me. The ball did go, but because he waited so long, he thought, well, now it isn't going to work. And while he despaired, suddenly, the home that was so dilapidated becomes this marvelous modern hotel, and the streetcar becomes a streamlined bus, which simply took off. And then comes Wilshire Boulevard, the Miracle Mile, and instantly he transforms it. Now, the power in his hand...it didn't wait now. This thing should not be on Wilshire Blvd., not on the Miracle Mile, bikinis and dirty trousers? And instantly a transformation into beautiful ladies and gentlemen dining al fresco under umbrellas waited on by elegant, wonderful waiters. The whole transforming was easy then, because he had succeeded in taking the most ancient things and transformed it by his persistence.

That's what you and I are called upon to do as we read the words of the earliest gospel, which is Mark. Chronologically, it's placed second, but the first book written of the gospels is Mark. And here we find, that after John was arrested—meaning this conscious, reasoning mind of man—after that is arrested, Jesus comes into Galilee preaching the gospel of God; saying, "The time is fulfilled, and the kingdom of God is at hand; repent and believe in the gospel" (Mk.1:19). Believe my testimony, for all that I tell you is but the fulfillment of scripture, all of his promises are fulfilled in me, that's what he's saying.

And standing before you tonight, I can say, his promises have been fulfilled in me. This normal natural man—unschooled, unlettered, unknown, un-everything by human standards that we call prominent—and everything fulfilled in me. What? Scripture, the only reality in the world, for everything else will pass away; but these words of God will never pass away. They are being fulfilled in everyone, for he's not condemning any man. They're only in states and we must learn to distinguish between the man, the occupant of the state, and the state that he occupies. So when he rejects man it's not man, he rejects the state. That state cannot serve, so he rejects the state.

And then, he puts him into another state, and that state is now the next one, for he has fulfilled it by his practice. And I have known how he's practiced repentance. Since he heard this message years ago, he has been daily practicing revision, and revision is repentance. And revision results in repeal. So I have something that is fixed and I revise it, I've repealed it. He repealed that picture that he saw, the dilapidated home and streetcar. Here, in him is the new annum. I know from his own story to me it's already been born, but it goes through these stages...stage after stage after stage. And this was written to me only this past month. So here he is on that day, the 22nd chapter of Isaiah, the only place in scripture where the word ball appears. So although golf balls were not known, ball was there, turning upon itself, and seeing the same thing over and over and over...and therefore you cannot change it. It's nothing new, you can't change it. Then he persisted by throwing the ball, and he did change it; but he waited a long, long interval between the departure from his hand, for he threw it with his hand. The power and the wisdom of God is symbolized in the hand. You are told in this chapter it is the power of God, so he exercised that power.

You have that power. Bring before your mind's eye any being in this world whose case at the moment seems hopeless, and revise it. Revise it and revise it and revise it until you can let go of that ball and feel satisfied in the revision. When you can feel the breath of relief because it's done, I tell you it is done. If tomorrow will not bring the news or next week will not bring the news, wait. Wait. It is done! And then, in a way that no one on earth could devise, the way by which it *will* be done, it will be done. It will come, and you will see the results of what you did. This is what he did.

So I ask everyone here to practice revision. Revise the past. I don't care what it is, revise it, and the past will conform to your dream of what it ought to have been, and suddenly it will appear before you. Then the new man stands within you: Not two, you *and* Christ, only Christ. So we are told, he goes through the city—this is now in Ezekiel, the 9th chapter—and he said, Everyone follow the man who is now clothed in linen, follow him carefully. He will go through the city and he will leave a mark on the forehead of men, women and children. Then he turned to others and said, Now, you follow him, and everyone who does not bear the mark, whether it be an old man, old woman, a maiden, a young boy, a child, slaughter them; and your eye must have no pity, no pity. Slaughter everyone who doesn't bear the mark on his forehead (Ezek.9:4).

Now, in the 22nd chapter, the last chapter of Revelation, and he turns and he fulfills it. Those who have the mark come before him, and the mark upon their forehead is his own name, and the name is Jesus. Jesus means Jehovah. He only redeems *himself*. Well, let no one think by this strange, peculiar imagery that one is lost. Everyone, at a certain moment in time, is slaughtered because of the *state* he is in, whether it be old, young or infant. He played other parts, other parts, until finally he's playing the part that is the selective part. And then the final part that he plays, the mark is on his forehead, and the name is his own name, and the name is Jesus. So in the end there is only Jesus, nothing but Jesus. There is *only* Jesus. All have been redeemed in the body of Jesus. There's only one being. Infinite mercy steps beyond and redeems man in the body of Jesus. There's only one body, only one God, only *one* being. And so, when you are redeemed, you are he. There aren't two little Christs running around, only the risen God who is Jesus Christ. And everyone is redeemed in that one body.

So I can't thank my friend enough for this letter that he gave me a few weeks ago. I got it in the mail two or three weeks ago and I read it and I was thrilled beyond measure. I wondered, how could I use it and what night would this thing fit? It's so all together marvelous. But it fits this night, the new man. This is the night that it really fits, where the part that you and I must play is redemption; redemption in the sense that we redeem a thing by practicing repentance. Repentance is not to feel remorseful, not to feel regretful. I don't care what someone has done! You don't feel remorseful because you *did* something; the state in which you were caused you to do it. That is not repentance. Repentance is simply practicing the art of moving into the opposite state as though it were *not*. That's repentance.

So I don't wallow in feeling sorry for myself. I don't wallow at some weeping wall that I repent. I simply move right into a state where the thing never really happened. Because "Though your sins be as scarlet, they shall be as white as snow," it doesn't matter what a man has ever done in this world. The most murderous fiend is only a state. In that state he had to murder. In that state he had to steal. In that state he had to do all these things. Don't condemn the occupant of the state, it's the state. We condemn the occupant as though he did it. He is in a state and he entered that state unwittingly. Most of us do. So Blake said, "I do not consider either the just or the wicked to be in a supreme state, but to be every one of them in the states of the sleep which the soul may fall into in its deadly dreams of good and evil when it leaves paradise following the serpent" (*Vis. of Last Judg.*, Pp.91-92).

The two sins that man has done which God finds, as we're told in scripture, impossible to forgive: the eating of the tree of good and evil; but the first thing is our failure to believe that I AM he. Man's unwillingness to believe that I am he is the fundamental sin. God became man that man might become God, and his name is I AM. My unwillingness to believe that I am he who causes me to breathe, to think, to move, is the fundamental sin.

Then I go forward condemning the good and the evil as I see good and evil through life. But then comes this wonderful revelation: I know from the Lord Jesus Christ that there is nothing unclean in itself, but any man who sees anything to be unclean to him it is unclean. Not a thing is unclean in itself. But if any man sees it as unclean, well, to him who sees it it is unclean. And he lives with it in a state that allows it to be seen as unclean. And that's life.

So let us practice on this side of the veil the one part we're called upon to practice. He only gives us one: repent. And repentance is simply to transform completely the past, whatever that past is, unless it is lovely. Let the mind store a past worthy of recall, for eventually everything that is unlovely is going to be destroyed anyway. So if the mind does not store a past worthy of recall, then that mind seemingly vanishes, if the contents vanish. But man will not vanish, for man is God. God became man that man might become God. There is really no death in this world, not in the real sense of the word. Nothing dies, not here. We leave the stage and the actor seems to be gone, but he isn't dead. For the supreme actor is God, playing all the parts. There's only God playing all the parts in the world, all parts. As told us so beautifully in Job, the deceiver and the deceived are his. Oh, I deceive and I am deceived, I'm both. I play all these states.

So in the end, all I'm called upon to do is to believe the testimony of one who has experienced scripture, and then to practice constantly this wonderful art of repentance. Repent and repent and repent. As I walk the earth I see someone in need, I will not feel remorseful for him, sad for him, I'll change it. That's repentance. I don't argue with him and say, "That serves you right. If you hadn't done this you wouldn't have had this." I don't condemn the man for the state into which he's fallen unwittingly. Even if he fell into it knowingly I wouldn't condemn him. He has to reap the results of the state into which he has gone. And so he's only in a state, but the occupant is immortal. You can't rub him out; that's God.

So I don't care what he does in the world, you can't stop him from being; he is this immortal being. And one day he will hear the same words my friend heard, "I am God. I am self-contained. I am self-sufficient." And the words kept repeating over and over and over. He said, "I know, I know, I'm trying to do something about it, but I can't now imagine while I hear your words, they are so loud." And then when he said, "It seemed to me like rape," what a lovely expression. If you can't prevent it, relax and enjoy it. "So I simply lay there on the bed and listened. As I listened to the same repetition, I enjoyed it and fell sound asleep listening to it." Isn't that a marvelous way to go to sleep, to hear the voice coming to the very surface so you can hear it? That same voice is screaming in the depth of everyone's soul. It hasn't stopped from the beginning of time, but the wall is too thick for man to hear it. When it gets very, very thin and just about to break through, man hears it. He heard it as the wall was breaking, making of the two one new man in the place of two, thus bringing peace.

That's what you're told in the 2nd chapter of Ephesians: I bring peace by bringing down the wall that separates the two. So when the wall gets very, very thin...like a house in this wonderful world of ours. Have you lived in apartments where they are so thin that if you whisper they hear you next door without being bugged? Well, suddenly, the wall gets so thin by your practice of repentance you hear God's voice. And God is the eternal I AM in man who is proclaiming what he is. He is the everlasting, he is the eternal, he is self-sufficient, he is self-contained. "I am God," he heard, and could not do a thing about it, because the voice wouldn't sleep. The thing was too thin.

Now he goes out to test the power that is God. And the power is in the hand: he had to take the hand to throw a ball. And the power is called "the hand of God" in that same chapter. He's just about to experience that which I told you about this past week, where he throws and nothing comes quickly; and then he creates a new city; a marvelous city is rising before him. And then he steps through a gate, which he created, and steps into an ancient past, and tries to change it; and thought he didn't have the power, he wasn't ready for it, but his persistency proved that he could change it. Eventually the ball *did* leave his hand and he waited and waited and waited. Even then, because he waited so long, he despaired, it's too long...it couldn't work. And then, suddenly, it worked. So he did not fail. After the ball leaves the hand, it has to work, when you drop that past and hold on to the vision of what you want in place of what appears to be. It doesn't come today, next week, next month, or even this year...but it will come. And then when it appears, he sees that he *has* the power to completely redeem the past. We're told in scripture God requires the past. The whole past will be redeemed as though it were not: "Though your sins be as scarlet, they shall be as white as snow" (Is.1:18).

Now let us go into the Silence.

*   *   *

Now are there any questions, please? By the way, we only have this lecture this week. There's no other lecture this week. Next week we start on Monday, and we'll have two, Monday and Friday. But this is the only lecture this week, as you'll see from your little announcement. If you don't have one, please take one when you leave. There are many of them at the desk.

Now are there any questions, please?

Q: What does it mean in the Book of John where Jesus says, "Salvation is of the Jews"?

A: Salvation is of the Jews. What does it mean in the Book of John, salvation is of the Jews? I have heard thousands of arguments concerning other religions and other things. Christianity is the fulfillment of Judaism. To quote Bishop Pike, that you may not like—I admire the man; I do not look upon him as an outstanding spiritual giant, but I admire the man, like his courage, like his honesty—and he said, "I am a Jew because I am a Christian. Now, I could be a Jew and not be a Christian, but I can't be a Christian and not be a Jew." So the whole thing comes out of Judaism. It was revealed through the prophets, and the Judeo-Christian Bible to me is the only true revelation of God's plan of salvation. All the others are based upon secular history. We know that Mohammed was a man, this one was a man, these were men. The scripture is not secular history; it's salvation history. There is no secular history in scripture. These characters are all eternal states through which man passes.

So salvation *is* of the Jew. Listen to it carefully as revealed in the Old Testament. The New Testament is only the fulfillment of the Old... it's not something new. The New Testament is simply the fulfillment of something as old as that of the faith of Abraham. "Abraham rejoiced that he was to see my day" (John 8:56), "And the scripture...preached the gospel to Abraham beforehand" as you're told in Paul's letter to the Galatians (3:8). Beforehand he had a preview of what the fulfillment would be. But this is a state. So if you enter the state called Abraham, it's only a state, not a person. You can't find Abraham in any book in the world save in the Bible. He doesn't turn up in any ancient manuscript, in any ancient records...mentioned only in the Bible. Yet he is the foundation of it all. So we all enter the state of belief in the most incredible story in the world and believing it, the dream descends upon you. Amnesia possesses us as we enter a deep and profound sleep having seen it, believing it was possible, and we dream the dream of life.

Q: How come we don't hear anything more about the Dead Sea Scrolls?

A: Oh, yes we do. The scholars are studying the scrolls all the time. They haven't found anything to contradict what is said in scripture. Not one thing so far has turned up in the Dead Sea Scrolls that contradicts what is said in scripture. In fact, it only authenticates, it doesn't in any way disturb it. And what is said in the gospels is more beautifully said, may I tell you. I have the translation of the Dead Sea Scrolls at home and I have read them carefully and they're lovely. They only confirm; they don't disturb.

Q: Neville, it would be the walls of Jericho...now this is what you've been talking about tonight, this is the veil?

A: Another symbol of it ___(??) yes.

Q: Joshua being God who...

A: Joshua is another name for Jesus; the Hebraic form of the anglicized word called Jesus the same word. Joshua is Jesus as far as the word goes. Jesus is the anglicized form of the Hebraic word Joshua, and they both mean "Jehovah is salvation." The only savior in the Bible is Jehovah. "I am the Lord your God, the Holy One of Israel, your Savior" (Is.43:3); "And besides me there is no savior" (Is.43:11), so the same word. So when Jesus is born, Jehovah has succeeded in being born in man. So man is no longer something separated from him, he's become man completely, and man is God. God actually became man that man must become God. That is the story...but it's not taught that way. We're taught that the cross and all the things concerning Jesus are objective facts of history. The day will come man will discover them all to be subjective facts of experience.

I have experienced scripture from beginning to end. I am talking from experience, I am not theorizing. And I haven't lost my identity. There's no loss of identity in fulfilling scripture. But everything said in scripture I have fulfilled from beginning to end. So when I hear all this palaver, the arguments between bishops, one trying to unfrock the other, making him confess that he doesn't accept the stupid things that we're called upon to believe. You must believe in this creed and this creed and this ordinance. The most sacred ordinances and all the creeds and all the rituals they are as nothing. When I was sent to do this work, the words were "Down with the bluebloods" which means in scripture all church protocol. But all of it! Not a little piece, but all. It means nothing.

Q: What is the difference between the wall in the Song of Solomon, "I see a wall and not a door," and these walls that we have here?

A: Well, my dear, the wall in any part of scripture, if the wall is a separating wall, as walls are, it's the same wall. In Solomon, those wonderful eight chapters of the Song of Solomon...if you really would understand the book start with the eighth chapter and then go back. You'll find...it's too long a story...it would take me two nights to describe the Song of Solomon.

Q: I heard your lecture...

A: Well, then you know it.

Q: But I thought she had to be a wall and not a door.

A: Well, she is a wall. There are two women in scripture, Hagar from below, the womb of woman; and Sarah from above, which is my eternal mother. I must be born of Sarah if I would be free; I am born, when you see this garment, of Hagar from below. So Paul speaks of the two mothers in his letter to the Galatians. One brings me into slavery where I'm a slave to all the passions of my body, and one brings me into freedom. She who brings me into freedom is the New Jerusalem, which is the Sarah from above. And he tells you it's an allegory. He makes it very, very clear, "This is an allegory." Man reads it as secular history. (End of tape.)

THE PRIMAL WISH

10/24/66

Tonight's subject is "The Primal Wish." And, really, I am so thrilled that you are here tonight. You listen carefully to what I will tell you concerning the primal wish. You read it in the very first chapter of Genesis. God said, "Let us make man in our image, after our likeness" (verse 26). That's the primal wish. And as Shakespeare said, "It has been taught us from the primal state that he which is was wished until he were."

Now this is tonight's subject. We're making an image, said God. Scripture teaches us that the image of the invisible God is Christ, as you read it in Paul's one letter to Colossians, "Christ...the image of the invisible God." In his letter to Corinthians, he speaks of him as the likeness of God, completing this primal wish, the image and the likeness of God. He goes on to tell us, "My little children, with whom I am again in labor until Christ be *formed* in you." The image and the likeness of God must be formed in man. Well, God is invisible. He will never know who he is until God's Son can identify his Father. And he can't identify the invisible; he has to see the face of his Father. So when the image is formed *in* man, God's only Son appears and calls him Father.

Now, let me share with you that which was given to me a few days ago by a dear friend of mine. And you listen carefully to the symbolism in his letter to me. I'll bring it out from scripture. He said, "It was war time. I found myself in a dilapidated farmhouse somewhere in ___(??), and through the window a huge cliff covered with vines, and from it came the bullets of the enemy. They were shooting at me and I was shooting at them. They intended to kill me and I intended to kill them. Then I went into the front room and there to my surprise all the soldiers of my squad were happy, and just about to go out through the front door. I warned them that they would be shot. They told me the enemy was gone. And I said, 'My God, did I shoot them all?' As we walked through the door, they all turned into you. And then you led me to the back of this house and to my surprise what was this cliff covered with vines from which the enemy shot at me and I at them, is now this enormous plain of wheat being harvested.

"In this plain, there were many who gaily harvested the wheat. I looked to the side and here was a mountain of harvested wheat. Then I said to you, 'What are they doing?' and you said to me, 'They are doing the same thing today that they did this time a year ago.' And I sensed a lapse in memory and so I said to you, 'How long have I been here?' You said to me, 'Two years.' In this I sensed symbolism, and so I asked you, 'Did I learn anything?' You nodded and you said, 'Yes, how to move, and discipline.' Then I walked back into the house and it had turned into a palace, and I was led to my quarters." Now you have a dream like that and you will think what a strange interesting dream. But you are told in the Book of Numbers "God speaks to man through the medium of dream."

Well, here is the story. I tell you, you aren't here by accident, not one of you. Everyone is moving towards the fulfillment of that initial wish, the primal wish: Let us make man in our image and give him dominion over everything in the world; things on the earth, below the earth, under water, below the water, and in the heavens and beyond. Infinite power is his after the image is formed in him, for the image is the image of the invisible God. And there's nothing but God. So here, *two* years you've been here. Two is conflict; it's difference, it's enmity. The wall must be broken down, that wall of hostility between the two, and they become one. God cleaves and cleaves to his emanation, his wife, 'til the sleep of death is past. He cleaves to it until they become one. When they become one, that wall of hostility has disappeared and they are one; there is no enmity. But in that interval...not two years (365 days to a year) but two is the important thing. So, while it lasted he had enemies. All the enemies are within him...or they were, I should say. And when the wall is broken down and he goes to the front room and moves through the door, and all of his soldiers forming his squad transform themselves, and they became me. And then I took him to the back of the house.

Now, read the 10th chapter of John. It's the story of the door...and they didn't understand him. Then, said he, "*I* am the door." Those who will come through any other way are thieves and robbers. There is no other way in, but that which I have told you from experience. Listen carefully to my testimony. It's the only way in; there is no other way. My sheep hear my voice and they know me. He knew me when soldiers, just soldiers, are transformed into me. He knew me, he knew my voice; for he asked me questions and he knew exactly who was answering. He said, "I am the door"...and there is no other door into the kingdom. And any attempt to come in by any other way makes you a thief and a robber. And the two years, that's years of conflict.

So here, in this 10th chapter he tells you, I lead you into an abundant life. So he takes his sheep, called all by name, and brings them into life more abundantly when the conflict is over, all within himself. For it was not a cliff covered with vines from which the enemy shot him...the mountains are all within himself. As Blake said, "Great things happen when men and mountains meet." And the only mountains Blake ever climbed were the mountains of his own skull. These were the mountains. And here the harvest is on. What are they doing now? Just what they were doing this time last year...goes on and on and on, forever and forever until the wall is broken down and there is no division between you and he who is forming you into his image.

When he forms you into his image, then his Son can see him, because to look into the face of Christ is to see God, and Christ is the image of the invisible God. Christ *is* the very God, for I and my Father are one now. But God cannot be seen, being invisible, unless he has the image formed. And so his Son cannot find him unless he has an image, for he's invisible. So, let us make man in our image that we may be seen by our Son. So the Son comes, but he can't see you if you're invisible; he can only see you if you have a face. And Jesus Christ is God the Father. Jesus is the invisible God; Christ is the image that he wears. He is forming the image. And when the image is formed, Jesus, who is Jehovah, who is the Lord, can be seen then by his Son.

Here we find the door. We find the shepherd who led him into the back and showed him where instead of being at war there's an *abundant* life. A field covered in the most glorious glow. He said, a golden glow covered the entire scene, both the harvested wheat, a mountain of it, and that which is being harvested. And so, it took a long, long time to harvest that mountain and it was all done in the conflict. Because he wondered, "What are they doing?" Because I knew the war was still on, because I could hear it in the distance. It seemed so far off. But I heard in the distance the heavy guns, and it seemed to come from another country, but the war was still on.

So, during the harvest the war is still on, and then he wakes and he goes through the only door. When he goes through the door, he finds that all who were his protectors, his squad, his soldiers, forming themselves into me. And I lead him to the back. And then he asks me these three questions. The questions are quite simple and the answers simple. What are they doing? What they were doing this time last year. And he sensed in this a certain sign of amnesia, forgetfulness. How long have I been here? Two years. Have I learned anything? Yes, you have learned how to move. The first creative act in the Bible: "And God moved upon the very face of the waters." You learned how to move. Move in what sense?—to move from my present state, which is the conflict, into the state that I desire. When I move into the state desired, I only say, "Let it be. Let there be light. Come, illuminate it. Let there be light." He learned how to move and he learned discipline.

So the very first creative act recorded in scripture, "And the spirit of God moved upon the face of the waters." As he moved, God said, Let there be that into which I have moved; for everything is here, but I have to move. And if I'm going to be his image, I must imitate him. I must imitate this process and learn the art of moving. How to move from one state in which I'm fixed—the conflict is on, the war is on—and to move from it into a state, and rest in it, saying "Let it be!" and it comes into being. For the first thing, "Let there be light," and there was light...no question about it. So I move from one state into another when I learn the art of moving. And so, he said to me, "Did I learn anything?" I nodded and said, "Yes, you learned how to move, and discipline." Well, discipline is simply becoming completely discriminating. Doesn't matter what state is being discussed, what state is now broadcast, what state is in the paper tomorrow morning, all of these things are only states. But I learned how to move. I moved from one state into the state desired and there I remained, saying, Let it be! And the state becomes luminous, becomes real in my world. So I can't tell you my thrill when I got it. Because I know who I am, I know how I've been sent, and sent what to do, to lead my sheep out; for they're all myself, anyway. I hope I know them all by name and they know me by name and they follow no other shepherd. That's the story, in the 10th of John.

Now having received this...first of all, another one in the same letter...he said, "Now this morning (it only came a few days ago) he said, "This morning, it was a shock. I was dreaming I was on my bed and I reached up with my hand and I was feeling the top of my head. The left side was normal. As I moved over and felt...well, the right side was at least one inch higher than the left side. I pressed down on it to discover that my skull had been split, split wide open. So in my dream I called out to my wife, 'Now I know why I've been feeling this way. I cracked my skull.' And then I was wondering how long I would be in the hospital. As I wondered about the time spent in the hospital, I woke." Then said he, "I've never felt more peaceful than I feel now and it started at that moment that I felt the cracked skull. From that moment until now I have never felt more peaceful, as though there is a peculiar reversal of feeling in my life. Instead of being a three-dimensional sense-man using a fourth-dimensional power, I am now identified with a fourth-dimensional power using a three-dimensional sense-man as an instrument.

"And now," he said, "I know that Blake expressed it more beautifully, but after all, it does seem to me that you can't quite ___(??) as Blake, "For hatching ripe he cracked his skull." If you're not familiar with Blake, Blake indicates a parallel statement, and Blake, "For hatching ripe he breaks the shell." So that shell is the skull. But he said it was not as poetic as Blake when he expressed it. And so, in his wonderful way he always has in ending his letters with a humorous note. Whenever the Brothers speak to me they're always, in the most serious manner, they're always humorous, most humorous! For when I meet this infinite body of awakened men, whenever they tell me anything, they always tell it in the most humorous manner. You can tell it from their expression, and yet they're so serious. Yet, it's always a humorous note.

The other night they said to me, "Go, go and write your own concise, condensed paper," and there was a smile on the face of all of them as they were telling me. Well, it so happens that my publisher said to me a few weeks ago that the printing of a book today is prohibitive in a hard cover. He has many copies of mine that are out of print and they all retailed at three dollars. And so he mentioned four of them; he said, "Now these four, would you mind, would you have any objection if I brought out the four under paper cover and sell all under one cover for four dollars, in stead of ___(??) under hard cover for three dollars each?" I said, "None whatsoever." So that night I thought I'd write a last chapter, something entirely different. So I began to dwell upon this last chapter when this night I was one with the Brothers. I mean the Elohim, the gods, and they said quite humorously but in a very serious manner, "Go write your condensed, concentrated paper." But ___(??) they said it, they could have been kidding as my brothers, my earthly brothers, kid me, when they speak of anything that I do in the same intimate family tone. So I finished about 6,000 words and called it "Resurrection: A confession of faith in terms of experience." Telling exactly in detail, all parallels of scripture, what I have experienced, which I know these who spoke to me have experienced. Those who wrote the gospels, they were only relating their own experiences, so I'm telling you exactly what they told that they had experienced. But they tell it in that way.

Sunday morning, in my experiences outside as it were, I was lecturing as I am to you now, but in a more intimate manner. Not standing on a platform, just talking among intimate friends, explaining the Word of God. And I had occasion to look at my watch, it wasn't on my hand, it was somewhere on a table. I looked at my watch—the same one I'm wearing now; I could recognize the watch—and it registered four ten. Well, I kept on explaining the Word of God and it seemed to me at least an hour in the passage of time. Then I looked again, and instead of being an hour later it still is four ten. I said to myself, "Well, my watch has stopped." Then, from then I went into a deeper sleep with no memory beyond that until I woke bringing back this to consciousness.

Well, in that experience God speaks to me through the medium of dream. The outstanding thing in *that* experience is simply four ten. And what I told them, I told them what I'm telling you, it was simply a discussion of the Word of God, interpreting the Word of God. But, four ten, well, what is four ten? You can look up all the commentaries of the world and every great scholar, and they will never understand the four ten. I have so many commentaries at home; they're so far afield. But ever word in scripture, that is, in the Hebrew tongue, every letter has its numerical value, as well as its symbolic value. Well, the fourth letter is Daleth, and it has the numerical value of four, and it has a symbolic value of a door. The tenth letter is Yod; its numerical value is ten; its symbolical value is the creative hand of God, the hand of the Director, the hand of the Creator, the first letter in the sacred name of Yod He Vau He, which we pronounce Jehovah, which is Jesus. Same initials we find in Hebrew.

So here, in this vision, it's the last watch. It's four ten A.M. The 90th Psalm tells us, "A thousand years in thy sight is but as a watch in the night." There are only six watches to the twenty-four-hour day. The day is broken down into the day and then the night. Three watches of the day, of equal hours, three watches in the night. Starts at six and it goes to ten, ten to two, from two to six; then from six to ten, ten to two, from two to six. So this was the morning. I knew this was A.M. from the very start, the atmosphere and the darkness and here is my last watch. And it was four ten. You reach the point of being the door and the creative hand of God. That's what it means. You are now the door, the shepherd and the creative hand of God.

Hasn't a thing to do with all the commentaries, as they do not have the vision. They do not know it. It's the last of the watch. It can't be long delayed when the garment is removed and removed permanently, the garment of sin and death, and join those who now humorously will tell me when I make a mistake just to do so and so. And I communicate with them, and they very humorously said, "Go on and write your nice condensed and concise paper." To join that same body who contemplate on death (this world). As we're told in the works of Blake when he said, "I behold the visions of my deadly sleep of six thousand years." If a watch is a thousand years and there are six watches to a twenty-four-hour day, a watch is a thousand years. "I behold the visions of my deadly sleep of six thousand years, dazzling around thy skirts like a serpent of precious stones and gold. I know it is my Self, O my Divine Creator and Redeemer" (*Jerusalem*, Plt.96).

So here, the watch is over; it's the last of the watch. For if it were the first watch of the day, it would not be the door...certainly not the creative arm of God. It's the last watch, it's four ten in the morning, and that's the last watch of the day. When that is over, you're playing then the part, for a season, of that creative power and the wisdom of God. So I must bring those who he gave me out of this world into the fold of an abundant life. You bring them one by one, and you know them all by name, and they know me by name. You bring every one into the fold—from a conflict where everything is shooting—into a field that is aglow, a golden glow as far as the eye can see. And they're all harvesting. "So I bring you into life more abundant" says the gospel of John. And here is this mountain of already harvested wheat, and yet they're still harvesting. That's how vast the harvest is. And then, we all go one by one through that one door that leads to ___(??).

So this primary wish is simply unfolding in man, as told us in Galatians. "My little children, with whom I am again in travail until Christ be formed in you." It must be. He will remain in labor until every one that was given him is brought out with the image completed and perfect, and brought through the door into the abundant life. When they reentered what was formerly a dilapidated farmhouse in the world of war and conflict, it's now transformed into a palace and they are led into their quarters. And this is this fantastic play, in which all of us are in this.

So the important story tonight, he learned how to move in this conflict, because man in a conflict, if he could only move he wouldn't see it. And so I said to him when he said, What, did I learn anything? I nodded and said, yes, you learned how to move and discipline. No matter where you are in this world...you could be in the most frightful state in this world, if you know how to move. God's first creative act is to move upon the face of the waters and then to let it be. And then wherever he is, it becomes luminous and it simply reveals a state in which he has placed himself. He moved upon the face of the waters. So, he learned how to move. And so tonight if *you* have any dream in this world, if you learn how to move...I've been trying through the years to show you how to move, by bringing into your mind's eye a scene which would imply that you *have* moved from where you were to where you would like to be. For were you now the person that you would like to be, you couldn't see the world as you saw it prior to this motion, you couldn't. Motion can be detected only by a change of position relative to another state. Unless there is some fixed form of reference against which the mover moves, he doesn't know that he moves. If I move with the speed of light but everything moves with me, I haven't moved. If we all move together, I might just as well ___(??) in the whole vast function. But if I can just simply let it be and I move relative to it, then I can by looking at it and seeing a change in position relative to it, I know I've moved. But there is no way of detecting that I have moved unless I have a fixed frame of reference against which I move.

So I start from here and I see all the pictures here and you, and all of a sudden I feel I'm moving, and I find myself in feeling there. Well, then when I look, it's not the same room. I see everything differently; it's a different angle. Well, now in my mind's eye...my friends know me for what I am...my weaknesses, my limitations, whatever I am. If I'm a friend I will share it with them, and they will share their limitations with me. Well, all of a sudden, I want to move from that state. And then I move inwardly, it's all an inward motion. And I move using the same frame of reference; but now I'm seeing that differently, and they see me differently. They see me not as they formerly saw me, one that they pitied, the one now that if they are friends they will rejoice with me, and if they are not they will hate me… whatever they are relative to me. Those who are not fond of me would envy the state into which I have moved, and those who are fond of me and love me sincerely will rejoice with me. So I move, and look at the fixed frame of reference for confirmation of my motion.

So he learned how to move…after he became disciplined in the two years of war. The two years, may I tell you, last for quite a while. It was a long, long conflict, and then he learned how to move. Unless he forgets it, he doesn't have to remain one second in any state today that displeases him, for he's learned how to move. So he can move from one state into another state. And there are infinite states in this world. Man moves into these states either consciously or unconsciously; he falls into them knowingly or unknowingly. But, whether he does it knowingly or unknowingly, he must reap the fruit of the state into which he's entered. That's the law.

So here, in this wonderful experience…and he told it in longhand from three assembled pages, ___(??). It was a fantastic experience of his. The conflict, yes, it begins with the conflict, and then all that would protect him, his soldiers, his squad, the entire squad, and then they ___(??), and they want to go through the front door. There's only one door. He warns them they'll be shot and he questions them, and they said the enemy had all gone, they're gone. He said, "I killed them all"…and instantly as they walked through, the entire squad, the whole company, twos became one man, and I am he. They could not see the conflict. And then beyond the door…I led him around to the back, and to his surprise, not a cliff covered with vines from which the enemy shoots but an infinite field of wheat in harvest, with many women gaily harvesting the wheat, and a mountain of harvested wheat, all in this golden tone.

Then he sensed there's something strange here, there must be. Well, when he asked the question, "What are they doing? Well, they're doing the same thing now that they did this time last year. A wheel within a wheel within a wheel, all over and over and over it goes on. And now he knows I must have had a lapse of memory, some loss of memory: How long have I been here? Two years. Now he senses a certain symbolism in that answer, and he's going to ask a question, "Did I learn anything?" I nodded and said, "Yes, you learned how to move, that's the important part." After all this conflict, this horrible conflict, war within himself where he could not move out of one state, and everything is shooting at him. He gets poorer and poorer and he makes every effort to get out of it, and everything is crowding in on him, but the whole vast world is crowding in on him. And everyone is his enemy. No matter who he is, he is shooting at him. And he's shooting at them; he rubs them all out, all competition. And then, he comes out and he who was trying all the time to lead him out now takes all his protectors and he becomes the one who is invisible to him, until now. He's formed the image, and then you see it, the entire picture. And instead of being a conflict, an enormous field of ripe wheat, bathed in a golden glow. And he learned how to move.

So I tell you tonight, *learn* how to move. The motion is not difficult, may I tell you. But don't go from place to place. Into whatever house you go, you're told in scripture, there remain until I come. Don't go from house to house; into whatever house you enter there remain. And so I go into the house of affluence. Well, it hasn't yet appeared. But I did enter the house of affluence. If I remain there, I'm saying, let there be light. Come illuminate it...make it real. Make it visible to me first and to all of my world. If I know how to move and remain faithful to that motion, my whole vast world will reflect it. And no power in the world can stop it. Man is set free by learning how to move, and he learned discipline at the same time. Now, I look at the same watch...I'm quite sure it is not four ten by mortal time. But it was four ten Sunday morning where it was brought to me so vividly that I am that door and that creative hand of God.

Now, let us go into the Silence.

*   *   *

Q: (inaudible)

A: ___(??) would be division. You're told in scripture, if two different persons agree in testimony, it is conclusive. There must be an agreement. So I want, for instance, to be healthy. Well, if I want to be, I'm confessing I'm not, so we're in conflict, aren't we? We must now agree to be one if our testimony agreed. So if two different states agree in testimony, it's conclusive. So I will now assume that I am healthy and look at my frame of reference, my friends, my relatives, all these, for confirmation. They'll say to me, "I've never seen you look better!" If I can see them all say to me and hear them say, "I've never seen you look better," well then, the conflict has been resolved; that is, the state called health, and I who didn't feel well. So then I cease not to feel well by moving into the state of health.

Well, you do that with anything in this world...the state of wealth. If I am impoverished and I would like to be wealthy or like to be secure, well then, there's a conflict. If I would like to be, it's a confession that I am not, is it not? Then, if I assume that *I am* wealthy, well, then I'm resolving the conflict and the two will agree in testimony, and then it's conclusive. Then I'm saying when I enter that state, Let it be. Let there be light. Let the whole thing become luminous so I can see it, that I may manifest it in my world. Is that clear?

Q: (inaudible)

A: ___(??) I'm not denying that. I would not for one second. Because you are sent in the state of the conflict that my friend spoke of in that letter when he wrote that I was...he began the letter, "The war was on. It was a great world war. Not just a little skirmish, this is a world war, and I was in a dilapidated farmhouse somewhere in Europe." He mentioned no country, because the countries were all within him. But he was at war.

And across the place, this cliff, covered with vines, and men ___(??) they were enemies anyway shooting at him. He admitted the intention to kill each other. That was the conflict. But now he's learned in that interval, while he was trying to get out of it, he learned how to move. How to move from that back room where the conflict was raging through the ___(??) into the front room, to find that his protectors, his soldiers, his great squad were in a gay happy mood about to open the door. Not quite overcoming what he'd just experienced he warned them that they'd be shot. And then, they said, "Well, the enemy's gone." And he wondered, "Have I shot them all?" And then together they went through the door, the only door. There is no other door. Then they all turned themselves into me, and to his surprise I stand before him now as his leader to lead him to the back of the house. Around him he sees this infinite field of a harvest...the conflict is over.

Then comes these many questions. There were three important questions and three answers to these questions. The important one, he learned how to move. So while they are shooting away, I have to move from the state of conflict to the state of peace. But, you learned how to move. If I can move from one state into another which would imply the fulfillment of my dream, well then, remain in it, and say, "Let there be light."

Goodnight.

THE MIRACULOUS CHILD

10/27/66

Tonight's subject is "The Miraculous Child." It may not appeal to the world, because they are so fixed in their misconceptions of scripture, and there is no dead weight so heavy as that which is required to change man's misconception of scripture. So tonight, I ask you to listen carefully, attentively, for "Though Christ a thousand times in Bethlehem be born, if he is not born in thee, thy soul is still forlorn."

God participates in human history and is known in those through whom his timeless purpose is working in time. Right in this world of time his timeless purpose is unfolding. "He who began a good work in you will bring it to completion at the day of Jesus Christ" (Phil.1:6). Jesus Christ appears symbolized as a child. The child is only a sign; he is not the child. When Christ appears, you are he. So you listen to one in whom his timeless purpose has been fulfilled. This promise of a child begins in Genesis, the first book in the Bible. It is given to one called Abraham. If you have been with me through the last few weeks, you know what I have said concerning Abraham, Isaac, Jacob, and all the characters in scripture. They do not appear in any ancient Near Eastern work whatsoever, they're only in scripture. They do not appear either as individuals or as tribes. These are the eternal states through which God passes in you as he unfolds his purpose in you. His purpose is to give himself to you as though there were no other in the world, just God and you, and finally only you. For you are he. That is the purpose.

The whole thing begins with the promise of a child. He promises Abraham to give him a child. Abraham laughed, Sarah laughed, because they were beyond the age of bearing a child. When the child was born, they called him Isaac, which means "he laughs." Now, you think he was born of human stock. No, this child is a prototype of that which *must* be born. For all the ancient prophets were eschatological in their vision; and their visions are only about the end of days, the last days. It's all eschatology; it's all the doctrine of the very, very last things. So the child is a prototype. We next encounter this child in the name of Moses. The word Moses means…it is simply the ancient perfective of the Egyptian verb "to be born." Something is to be born. We think it is a man. So she calls him Moses because he was drawn out of the water. You draw it out of the deep; something is coming out; something is to be born. So we think it's a man.

We find this thing unfolding and unfolding, and we come to the point called David. "Go to my servant David, and you say to him, 'When your days are fulfilled and you lie down with your fathers, I will raise up your son after you, who shall come forth from your body. I will be his father, and he shall be my son'" (2Sam.7:12). You find the unfolding promise of the child. We move into Isaiah: "To us a child is born, a son is given; and the government shall be upon his shoulder, and his name shall be called 'Wonderful Counselor, Mighty God, Everlasting Father, Prince of Peace" (Is.9:6). Here we find this promise unfolding and unfolding.

We find the very last book of the Old Testament still waiting for the son. If I am a father, where is my honor? "For a son honors his father. If then I be a father, where is my honor?" (Mal. 1:6). And now, the very first chapter of the New Testament begins with the fulfillment of the promise. Here he's born, the child is born. And you've been taught to believe that some little child came into the world born of a woman who did not know a man. Hasn't a thing to do with it. The child is born but "born not of blood nor of the will of man nor of the will of the flesh, but of God" (John 1:13)…something entirely different. Now he tells us this shall be a sign unto you. Blessed is she who believed that which she has heard, "that there shall be a fulfillment of those things which were spoken unto her from the Lord" (Luke 1:45). If one could but believe.

And then, they appeared to the shepherds of the field and said to them, "Unto you is born this day in the city of David a Savior, who is Christ the Lord" (Luke 2:11). And the shepherds said one to the other, "Let us go into Bethlehem and see this thing that has happened." And they made haste, went into Bethlehem and found the babe, as they were told, wrapped in swaddling clothes. When you read these words, you think as you've been taught—I was taught it as a Christian—that this thing happened on earth; a little child, born of a woman as you and I were born, with this difference, she didn't have a husband or didn't know a man. Hasn't a thing to do with that. It is a *sign*…"This shall be a sign unto you" that a Savior is born. The only Savior is God. "I am the Lord your God, the Holy One of Israel, your Savior. And beside me there is no savior" (Is. 43:3,11). There's only God. God became man and then he has to be born from man. I am both the root and the offspring of humanity personified as the eternal youth called David. I am the root and the offspring. The creator of humanity, becoming what I created, and bursting the shell; and then coming out transcending what I was prior to my fall into my own creation.

You listen to it carefully…I am telling you what I know from experience. The day will come when you will experience it. My days are at an end, they're all over. My history in the human world is at an end, there's no more. I have finished the race. I can say with Paul, "I have fought the good fight, I have finished the race, I have kept the faith. Henceforth there is laid up for me the crown of righteousness" (2Tim.4:7). There's nothing else to do. All that he promised I have been experiencing within myself, every bit of it.

How would you know? Well, there are signs. Yet when it happens it happens so suddenly and happens without warning. Yet there are signs that come to all of us as we're moving towards the end. I can say to all of you here, you are all at the end. I can't say that to the world. I can say it to you, you are at the end. There isn't a morning's mail or a night that I leave here that doesn't bring confirmation of this motion towards the end. Last lecture night, a lady left a letter, and then in the mail came a letter two days later…and listen to these letters. We have come only to fulfill scripture. The prophecy has not a thing to do with America as the prophets of the modern world will tell you. They are all about what the Bible is telling you what is going to happen to America or Russia or China. It hasn't a thing to do with any secular history, nothing whatsoever. The Bible is simply the history of salvation. It hasn't a thing to do with any land on the face of this earth. It's all to do with you, who walk the lands of the world, that's all that it's about. Not about America, not about Russia, not about Europe, not about China or any other part of the world. So when all these so-called, self-appointed prophets rise and tell you about what they're interpreting in scripture, may I ask you now, don't listen to them. You are at the end.

Well, here are the letters. One lady writes, she said, "I live in Pasadena. I am fifty-nine years old. I did not complete college because I had two little sons and the demands of my family life were such that I could not complete college. ___(??) continue college. I had a dream, a recurrent dream that I must prepare for an exam. Then as the years progressed, the recurrent dream still persisted, only recently it's been so urgent…the sense of immediacy. Then she capitalized the entire great exam—"I must be prepared for a GREAT EXAM." Then she said, "Recently I saw history unfold before me, the whole thing unfolded as I closed my eyes. And then she said, I saw all these faces. There were no eyes in the sockets, just sockets, human faces but no eyes, like the great sculptures and paintings of Michelangelo. Then I saw in the midst of all these bodies an infant, a little babe, and he was smiling at me and he loved me. I felt as though he were in heaven and I here looking at this infant. And then recently I had this vivid dream, I had a son. Now, here I'm fifty-nine, no husband, and no one around, and I have this son, the most beautiful child imaginable. When I woke, I wondered how can this be?" Then she asked me, does it have any biblical significance?

Well, the significance in her dream is the "great exam." If you've ever been on TV—I've never had the occasion to use it because I've always spoken extemporaneously. I have no notes, I don't need notes. I could go on for hours and I don't need one note from any person in this world to tell me what to say. I never lost a thought. Whether I'm on TV or radio, I've gone all through the night on one of these marathons, no notes. So I don't need them. But there is in TV what is known as the "idiot sheet" and you see someone spieling and spieling and spieling so rapidly, and they're looking right before their eyes. Under the camera there is a moving thing like a moving little bit of paper, and bold, bold type, and they're reading off the entire thing. It's called the idiot sheet. All the great commentators and all these profound wise men they're reading the idiot sheet. And you think them so wise. The whole thing has been completely written for them by someone else. They are good readers. Someone wrote the entire news program and they just stand before the camera like some wonderful important individual…and there they are, reading the idiot sheet.

Well, let me say to this lady, I use that analogy only for a purpose. You are facing in the immediate future the great exam. You'll be taken in Spirit right into the presence of the exalted Christ, the risen Christ. He will only ask you one question, "What is the greatest thing in this world?" Well, it's just like reading the idiot sheet. It's so obvious what is the greatest thing in the world because you're looking at him. You're looking at the embodiment of love. Not one thought in eternity could ever enter your mind but what you're seeing, and you're seeing the exalted Christ. Only one emotion permeates you and it is love. You can't fail, my dear.

So you say you must study for it? You can't fail. Right before you stands the exalted Christ who is the embodiment of love, infinite love. And so, when you answer it is automatic…you cannot fail. So put your heart at rest, you don't have to study any more for the great exam. It will be automatic. When you look into the face of the risen Christ, you can't think of anything but love. At that moment he embraces you, at that moment you are one with the body of Christ. And then the prophecy, "He will change our lowly bodies to be of one form with his glorious body" (Phil.3:21). Our translators cannot bring themselves to believe the literal words of scripture, so they translate it this way, "He will change our lowly bodies to be *like*…" It isn't "like" at all. The literal meaning of the word, that Greek phrase, is "to be of one form with," that's what it is. You aren't like him, you *become* him. In the end, there's only one body, one God, one man…and you are he. So your lowly body is completely refashioned to be of one form with, not like, his glorious body. So I tell you, put your mind at rest. Your great exam has been answered. You will stand in his presence and you couldn't in eternity think of anything but the right answer because you're looking at him. You're looking at the greatest thing in the world, the body of the risen Christ, the human form divine which is love.

Now another letter came in the mail and this from a gentleman. He said, "I came home on Monday night, I threw myself on the bed to relax for awhile, and I closed my eyes. I felt a little bit in a daze—not unconscious, but quite relaxed, in a daze, in a lovely dream. And while in this state, a blaze of light appeared before me. I forced myself not to open my eyes to see the cause of the light. The light persisted. Right before me, here is this light, with my eyes closed. I noticed in the middle of this light a pool of golden, *liquid* light is beginning to form. It's pulsating, the whole thing pulsating. I noticed that it's taking a form and the form it takes is that of a beautiful rose. It forms itself into a rose, and then the rose expands and expands and almost reaches the periphery of this vast area. I'm looking at the rose and then the rose itself begins to pulsate. Here's a pulsing, living rose that came out of this golden, liquid light. And just as I'm looking at it, wondering what is next, I was called to dinner." And he asks, "What does it mean?"

Well, in the 2nd chapter of the Songs of Solomon, "I am the rose of Sharon, the lily of the valleys" (verse 1). The 5th chapter implies…now in your letter you said it was a golden rose…the 5th chapter implies, because it likens it unto the lips—it doesn't state that the rose must be red but lips usually are red. Nevertheless, it's a rose. One translator can't bring himself to believe it's a rose, he calls it a crocus. Alright, a crocus is a lovely flower, beautiful flower, but it's a rose, just as he saw it. So here is scripture unfolding in you. "I am the rose of Sharon"…who is I AM…well, that's God. There's nothing but God. So, I'm looking at it…he said, "Strangely enough the rose was not simply something put upon the golden, liquid light. It was not separate and it was not superimposed. The light just now formed into the rose."

Now listen to the words, "I am the light of the world" (John 8:12); also, "I am the rose of Sharon." Well, Sharon means "prosperity; the straight, straight pathway, the right way." But it means "prosperity"…and abundance when that rose appears in the consciousness of man, that's what it means. Here is real, real abundance in the consciousness of man. Now abundance need not be measured in dollars and cents, although in the world of Caesar it will be, too, but in a sense of well-being that you've never known before, a sense of peace, a sense of rest, a sense of importance that you've never known before… all that is Sharon. The rose is God—he said, "I am the rose of Sharon, the lily of the valleys."

So, I tell you everyone here is waking. To repeat, God participates in the history of man, actually participates, and is known in those through whom this working is taking place. God is working in you. That's why the whole scripture is unfolding in you: "Scripture must be fulfilled in me...for all that is said about me has its fulfillment" (Luke22:37). "And beginning with Moses in the law and the prophets and the psalms, he interpreted to them in all the scriptures the things concerning himself" (Luke 24:27), not speaking of anything else. What does it matter if you were the king of kings on earth, lord of lords, and all these of the world, what would it matter?

I was sitting around yesterday around four. I had a seven o'clock dinner date, and so I had lots of time, and as is my custom I was reading the Bible. My wife, knowing we had a 7:00 date she goes to take a little rest prior to the dinner date. So, she was in the bedroom resting and I sat in my leather chair reading the Bible. I expected no one and suddenly I heard footsteps coming up the stairs. I was sitting in my underpants and my little sports jacket. Not knowing who it was—it could be some delivery man or something, I expected no one—I went to the door and to my surprise when I opened the door here stood a nun before me...at least she was dressed as one. So I apologize for my appearance, I said, "I'm awfully sorry that I am like this, but I wasn't expecting anyone."

She had a Bible in her hand, black robes all the way down to the ankles, white veil over her head, and all these beads around her neck, and all the things...and then papers in the Bible. She said, "I am a witness sent by God to you." I said, "A message for me?" "Yes, a message for you." "And what did God tell me or wants you to tell me?" Well, "the world is gone...it's the devil, the devil is loose. There are millions of devils in the world, all by the great devil." I said, "He could not have told me that because I stood in the presence of the risen Christ and he's all love. And he plays all the parts. The only devil in the world is that God allows man such freedom that he can create the most horrible things in the world and God allows it. He will adjust it. As we reach certain imbalance he will bring it back into balance. But, he allows everything in this world, and you and I are simply creating; and God is not deceived—as you sow you reap. So you believe in devils? I don't! There is no room in my world for the God that I know for a devil."

"Oh," she said, "Brother, brother, you must listen, you must listen, brother." I said, "Alright" and she started giving me all this baloney about this devil and all the minions who are working for him to dethrone God. So I said to her...I told her a little anecdote that Frank Lloyd Wright always liked to pull on friends of his, and that is about two clerics. One said to the other, "There's no need for us to quarrel. We're both doing the Lord's work, you in your way and I in his." She looked at me. I don't think she understood one word that I said. She wasn't listening. She wanted me to listen, "Listen, brother, listen." She didn't hear one word. I could tell from her face there wasn't any registration whatsoever of what I said to her.

And so, I said, "I'm awfully busy. You interrupted me reading the Word of God. I was reading the Word of God when you came and now I must go back and complete my study." She went, mumbling down, "Listen, brother, listen." You've got to listen, brother…listen to all of her junk about this awful, awful evil world of the devil in control, and poor God is helpless. He just can't do a thing about it, and so she is going to get me on her side by fighting devils. And that thought came to me of Shelley's, "He has awakened from the dream of life. 'Tis we, who lost in stormy visions, keep with phantoms an unprofitable strife." You fight devils, so you make more devils because you recognize them. What you recognize you perpetuate, you make it real in your world.

So here, all I can tell you is what I have experienced concerning scripture. This miraculous child is a fact. The day will come that everything said about this child you are going to experience. No one sees you…that moment when those who watch their flocks at night made a hasty journey to see the thing that had happened in Bethlehem. For they come…they come and they find the child. They know exactly whose child it is, and they call you by name. They will say, if your name is John, "Its John's baby." The others are amazed that you have a baby. Then they'll pick it up and put it on the bed. You will raise that in your own arms and look into its lovely, heavenly face and speak some endearing term. Like Isaac, the word "he laughs," the child will laugh. He laughs right into your face, the most heavenly laugh. And then the whole thing comes to an end. And you will know the reality of the child that was given to man as a *sign* that the Savior was born. And there's only one Savior and the Savior is God. So, if the Savior is born, it is God who is born. He came down into man, and now he raises man by being reborn himself from man. So, I am the root *and* the offspring of David.

Now, this will drive it home for you. About a month ago…in fact last night the lady with whom we were out for dinner, she and her sister, and this lady was the one in the dream. And my friend, who is here tonight, his name is Jimmy…he does not know this lady. Her name is Vera. I've known her for years, back in New York City, when she was a dancer. She came to all of my meetings. She was born in Russia, came here at the age of thirteen, having trained as a ballerina in Russia then completed her training here, and was a dancer in New York City. Being a dancer myself ___(??) befriended, she came to all my meetings, she and her mother, and her two sisters. So she moved west. She so loved all that I told her that when she opened a shop here on Wilshire Boulevard, she called it after my sister's name. My sister's name is Daphne, so she called it The Daphne Shop. Here she ran it for several years and then she sold it and moved into the Wilshire Hotel in Beverly. She had the most wonderful shop right at the entrance as you enter the hotel. She gave it up, she sold it out this past February, and now she's opened a new one, or will open next month at the Disneyland Hotel in Disneyland. So we were out last night for dinner and I had to tell her, because I haven't told it to anyone but my wife. So she does not know my friend Jimmy. He was born in Italy; she was born in Russia. I have had them both home but not together. I've gone to their homes, but I did not meet them there. They do not know each other.

But in my dream, here is Vera, a lady, she's quite small, about fifty years old in my dream and he is about fifty years old, handsome, wonderful, well put together as he is always. She is his mother in my dream. She has her arms around me and she's holding me and hugging me in a nice friendly way. But he is disturbed and he scolds her for showing such feeling towards me. She's still holding me and holding me tightly and with great affection. It annoys him because she is his mother. And so, when he scolds her for showing such obvious affection, she turned to him and said, "And why shouldn't I?" in a very Russian accent… English but all very Russian, "And why shouldn't I? He is your father." Well, the bewilderment on his face when he heard that I am his father. You have never seen such utter bewilderment.

Well, looking at him I started to laugh. I laughed so loudly in my dream, I kept on laughing, and woke myself up laughing. I was still laughing so loudly I woke my wife. It's now 3:30 in the morning and she said, "What on earth is wrong with you?" I said, "I had a dream. I'll tell you tomorrow…can't tell you now." But I couldn't go back to sleep, because I had to really complete that laughter. So I went to the living room and sat down in my chair and chuckled and chuckled when I thought of that face. If anyone could have photographed that face and painted it…like a Blake. If Blake had seen that face, he would have painted the expression of utter bewilderment as no one ever could have done it, and all of the museums of the world would be bidding for it now. You've never seen such utter confusion.

But, it was a true revelation. If I am the father of David, and that I know that I am, and David is the personification of all the generations of men and their experiences and Jimmy is a man, am I not his father? Am I not the father of humanity if I am the father of the essence of humanity which is David? David is the sum total of all the generations of men and their experiences, and he called me "Father" in fulfillment of scripture, the 89th Psalm (verse 26). If I am David's father and he is but the personification of all the generations of men and their experiences, am I not Jimmy's father if he be human, if he be man? So he thought in a secular level and he was so bewildered. He always thought some other person was his father and now he's stunned beyond measure when he hears from his own mother I am his father.

It's all the unfolding of scripture. There is nothing but God in this world. And when he unfolds himself in you, you will know it. Those who have not experienced scripture will think you are stark mad, mad as a hatter, because they haven't experienced scripture. But I tell every one of you, the day will come you will experience it, and you will know you, too, are the father of humanity. Because you are going to be the father of the sum total of all the generations of men personified as a single youth whose name is David. And so, when he calls you "Father" and he's only the essence, the quintessence of humanity, are you not then the father of humanity?

So in the very last chapter of the Bible, the 22nd of Revelation, "I am the root and the offspring of David." The creator entered his own creation and then emerged from it, therefore he is now the offspring of it. But by creating it is he not the root, the father of it? And by entering it, not pretending but actually becoming it, with all the limitations of the human flesh and playing all the parts, you don't come out 'til the very end has been played. It's all concerning the end of the drama, and when the end has been played and you've played it all, you emerge. Then the essence of the whole vast creative world stands before you as a son called David, and he calls you "Father." So, you must have now an experience to prove that the creation itself is your son. And the earthly woman states, "He is your father." Then comes that surprise, because he interprets the statement in terms of a secular world and he always believed another was his father, and "now she tells me that he is my father." You get it? All this wonderful symbolism unfolds within man.

So here the child comes. It is the most wonderful child. Now listen to his name, "Wonderful Counselor" (Is. 9:6). First of all, the government shall be upon his shoulders, the 22nd chapter, the 22nd verse of Isaiah. The full responsibility, all the authority will now be on his shoulder. He will lock, none shall open; he shall open, and none shall lock. No one can shut it if he opens; no one can open if he shuts it. That's the responsibility placed upon his shoulder—the government shall be upon his shoulder as told you in the 22nd chapter of Isaiah. Now the names: "Wonderful Counselor"…infinite wisdom now. And what is wisdom? "Christ the wisdom of God." What is the next one? "Christ the power of God," so the next name is "Mighty God." Here Divine Might is now one of his names. Divine Wisdom, Divine Might. Then comes the third name, "Everlasting Father"…Father forever. He is the eternal Father of humanity and the essence of humanity summarized in the eternal youth called David.

Then comes the final title "Prince of Peace." Not just a cessation of war— it means that too—there's no more conflict within him. Like my friend the other night who had this wonderful experience, the war is over now. He's been here with the conflict lasting, and now the war is over. "How long have

I been here?" "Two years." "What have I learned?" "Well, you learned how to move." Ah, then the war is over. Then I can move from a state of conflict into a state of peace and joy. So here now, the "Prince of Peace" is his name, a full, complete enjoyment of everything in this world, no conflict, none whatsoever. And these are his four names. Then you are told, "Of his reign there shall be no end...none whatsoever."

So all of this takes place in the individual. God actually participates in the history of man and is known in those through whom this work is unfolding. And in you I say it is unfolding. His divine purpose, his timeless purpose is working in time. So while walking in time, his timeless purpose is unfolding within you. Everyone will experience it and no one will fail, because God became us, each of us, that we, each of us, may become God.

No let us go into the Silence.

*   *   *

___(??) "I am the rose of Sharon" and then a great exam. And then the answer is so obvious that no one need prompt you. There's no idiot's box, no prompter. The answer stands before you in the form of the risen Christ. The greatest thing in the world is love, and he *is* that very rose of Sharon, the lily of the valleys. And his was a golden rose.

Now, we only have one lecture next week and I think it's on Tuesday. You can check me, I think it's Tuesday. There'll just be one lecture, that's all. Then we start...I think we have two the following week...but you have a little program and you'll know. Do check so you will not come here, as some have come, nights that we're not here. Now are there any questions, please?

Q: Neville, could you relate how you discovered___(??) before you went to Barbados, when you were traveling in your imaginative body, and you were in an undesirable situation, and you felt your way back on the bed. You felt the sheets and instantly you were returned to your body. You said that in the event that this happens to you, the way back is to *feel* your way back. And so I had this experience of being on a battlefield and there were dogs and serpents plus men with guns. And I wondered what I was doing there? Then I remembered that my body was on my bed, the garment that I wore, so I began to get the message of what you had once said. So I said I'll try it. I tried it and sure enough I felt the sheet under me. I couldn't understand how you came upon this revelation of feeling as your way back.

A: Well, thank you, Ben. I'm so glad that in the very depth of your soul you
     remembered the teaching. That was revealed to me one night, oh, many
     years ago, when I found myself on the beach in some…oh, it wasn't the
     West Indies because we aren't that primitive. We have far more cultivated
     land then the things of the far Pacific, the little islands. The West Indies
     are really…they've been under a certain governmental rule of the Western
     world for over 300-odd years. In fact, they were discovered before this
     land, and so, little Barbados has had the same flag since 1605. Never had
     a change of government and we had the same parliamentary system since
     1625. We had the same thing that England has only on a miniature scale,
     and ___(??) law and order. So I knew it was not in the West Indies. I've
     gone to all the islands in the West Indies. So I thought it was somewhere
     in a far more primitive area, where they were up on stilts, the houses were
     on stilts.

          I saw this strange animal approaching and as it approached me I was
     wading in water. I put my hands around a pillar. The bridge was already
     gone, and only the pillars remained. There were piles down to the…to
     support a bridge. I felt that I was dreaming about this ___(??). I felt that
     if I could hold on to it and not let go and force myself to wake, I either
     would wake in the dream or I would wake. But, the funny part about it,
     I woke in the dream, and now the whole thing is just like this. I am right
     in the dream. So waking in the dream to this dream, and this strange,
     peculiar monster, an animal, is coming towards me, but we're separated
     by water. And then the emotion of fear in some strange way brought me
     back to my body on the bed.

          Well, then when this other thing happened that I recorded in the
     book, I was not really in an unpleasant situation, but I had unfinished
     business on earth. I had an unfinished schooling for my child; she was in
     high school and she had desires to go through college, and I hadn't left
     the proper sums of money invested well for my wife. That's my obligation
     in life…to cushion my wife. That was my responsibility when I married
     her. And so, I felt these were unfinished things. I must come back and
     do this. I cannot make my exit now, because of these two outstanding
     unfinished pieces of business in my life. I remembered that holding on
     to the pillar and as I held on to it I awoke in the water, completely awake
     like this. So when I did, I imagined I was holding on to a pillow…this
     time not a cement pillar but a pillow under my head. And I could feel
     that feeling that I would feel were I waking on a pillow. Then I actually

came back to find myself cataleptic. In a little while…and you know the story…I could open my eye after several seconds and then a little while later…I came back. So I discovered that feeling *is* the secret. One can feel something even though it's not visible to the mortal eye, and if you can feel it and accept its reality based upon what you are feeling, you'll get it. It will come to pass. Everything is here: "Eternity exists and all things in eternity independent of creation." So you simply move into a state where you can feel. You can feel anything. As you feel it, if you accept it as fact, though to you it's only a subjective fact, it will in time become in an objective fact.

So in your case thank you Ben for telling me that you had the experience, and you remembered. The one thing all through scripture is the constant call to remember. Son, remember when he called upon Abraham to send someone and ___(??) is his son. And he asked him to remember what he did, just remember. Well, they notified my brothers… for if they were not listening to Moses, why should they listen to me? If one rose from the dead, they wouldn't believe. So he's called upon to remember. If man could only remember…like my friend the other night. He had a feeling that there must have been a lapse of time somewhere, because I told him they're doing the same now that they were doing this time last year. Well, he couldn't remember, therefore, he must have had a lapse of memory…so, again the call to remember.

Oh, could man but remember, for this whole thing was shown man in the beginning before he started the journey. "Everything was shown me, naught could I foresee"—but in the very end of the drama—"I learned how the wind would sound after these things should be."

So until next week, thank you!

THE CONGREGATION OF GOD

11/1/66

Tonight's subject is "The Congregation of God." The Bible speaks of the assembly of God, the gathering of God, the congregation of God. If I say to you, you are the body of Christ and individually members of it, would you believe it? Well, I've only quoted Paul's letter to the Corinthians, "partakers of the same body, partakers of the promise" (1Cor.12:12).

Now, in scripture only one set—they're given two names—is excluded from the assembly of God. We are told that they all gathered as one man in the square before the watergate, and they said to the scribe, Ezra, "Bring the book, the law, the law of Moses that the Lord gave to Israel." Ezra brought it and read from the 23rd chapter of Deuteronomy, "No Ammonite or Moabite shall enter the assembly of the Lord forever" (Deut.23:3). Now why this exclusion? Who are the Moabites and who are the Ammonites? As Blake said, "That which can be made explicit to the idiot isn't worth my time" and the ancients felt that what was not too explicit was fittest for instruction because it rouses the faculties to act.

So you look up the word Moab or Moabite and look up the word Ammon or Ammonite, it gives you no light, none whatsoever. But you read the story... just read it...and you will see they are the offspring of incest, the offspring of Lot's sons and daughters. Is that wrong? The child was born; nothing wrong in that. It's not saying that the child born of incest is not born of God. But that shows you segregation. We have segregation not only in races, we have it in society, we have it in every walk of life. You are completely out of the social register if you marry outside of what *they* consider the proper people. We have race against race; we have religion against religion. In the Protestant world, the Catholic world, all Christians, they do not sanction inter-marriage. I have three brothers married to Catholics. They couldn't get married in the regular church, married on the side. So they had to go into some little chapel to get married because they weren't blessed and their wives were. But they're good providers and wonderful fathers. One sired five and the other two sired four each. The children have all gone to college, sent not by their mothers, who didn't have one penny to rub against the other, but sent by their fathers who had the money to send them to college. So here, they couldn't come into the regular church. That was taboo. You find it in the social world, the racial world, all over. "They shall not enter the assembly of God."

Well, how will I go about it if I am of that world? Man is redeemed through the death of his delusions. You wait...everyone will be redeemed, because he'll be put into situations where these delusions created in this false manner will all disappear. I have watched it. I have watched men who hated certain races, certain nations, and their salvation came through that race and that nation. Right here, he told me...this chap born of Irish background, Catholic. They came from Ireland. He was born in Boston and raised in that very limited environment, where nothing was right but a good Irish Catholic. He said, "I hated two people in the world: I hated the Jew and I hated the Negro. Then came the 2nd World War and I was a sergeant in the Pacific. The Japanese had us pinned down. I couldn't move, I just couldn't move... my entire company pinned down. The slightest motion and the machine guns simply swept us. On my left was a Jew. Because he was a Jew, I gave him all the dirty work in the company. I was a Catholic and he a Jew, and I threw everything I should not have, because he was really not worthy of that treatment.

"Then he said to me when we were pinned down, he said, 'Sarge, do you have a grenade?' I said yes. He said, 'Let me have them.' So, he said, I unpinned a couple and the very motion caused fire, and he took them. He stretched his hand out and took them. Then he jumped up like lightning and threw, pins pulled, threw them right into that nest and blew the entire nest apart. He was wounded, seriously wounded, but he saved the company. From that day on, no matter who he was, if he was a Jew, he was tops in my world. That delusion died when I saw the bravery of a man. I always thought that they were cowards, and I, the great Catholic, and I wouldn't budge to get up to give my life, but he jumped up to save others, and he saved the entire company.

"I came back to America. I hadn't yet gotten over my prejudice of the Negro. Now, I'm a builder, bricks, all the things that go into building buildings. In San Francisco...I didn't return to Boston, I went to see my family, then I came back to the West Coast. Having spent a little time here, I liked it." So he came back, another job in San Francisco, producing materials for all construction. "One day, an explosion took place in a factory and I'm afire. My whole body is blazing. And all the Caucasians around just simply are afraid, not one came towards me. This Negro rushed towards me, picked me up bodily, and threw me down, and laid on me, smothered every little spark on my body with his body. He was burned, yes, really burned, but he saved my life and smothered it. And now, as the employer of all the work in building, if you are a Negro or a Jew, you get the first choice."

Man dies through the death of his delusions. He's no longer, then, an Ammonite or a Moabite. He breaks down the wall of partition between himself and the world. For you are the *body* of Christ and, individually, members of it. But as long as you have the little membrane tying you alone and you can't meet this one because they are a different world, they are an entirely different world, they belong to a different strata altogether, well, then you'll never break down the wall and you'll never join the assembly of God.

Now we are told, "There is only one body, one Spirit, one hope, one Lord, one faith, one baptism, one God and father of us all, who is above all, and through all, and in all." Read it in Paul's letter to the Ephesians, the fourth chapter (verse 4). He repeats the word one seven times, each time attached to a noun. One body, one Spirit, one hope, one Lord, one faith, one baptism, one God and Father of us all, who is above all, through all and in all... until one sees the oneness of it all.

Let us now illustrate it with a letter that came to me this past week. She said, "On the night of October the 18th you spoke of the new man, the breaking down of the wall of partition between two and making the two one new man. I can't tell you what it did to me. It stirred something in me; and it's all that you talk about, but this particular night it stirred something. The whole thing simply galvanized me. So I went back to what I call my records." She writes all of her dreams down...most of them are done unconsciously. She writes not even knowing what she's written until the next day. "And on the 10th of September I wrote this." She had this strange dream. There was a frightful explosion. She thought a bomb had dropped and she felt her ears pierced. Then she remained still and when all things seemed alright, then she stirred. "From then on," she said, "the piercing of the ear and the explosion from within—because it wasn't from without, that whole explosion took place within me—I began to have clearer communion with God. It's no longer like a dream. It's like talking with and I ask him questions. I quote scripture, he explains scripture, and it's simply an intimate communion with God.

"So the night of the 18th, having heard your lecture on the new man, I felt myself in communion with God and I said to God, 'Why do certain desires take so long and others so short and still others never? Why so long for some to be fulfilled and others short and others are never fulfilled?' God said to me, 'All your desires will be granted. The difference in the time between your desire and its fulfillment is this.'" Now, here is what God said to her and she had it all written down on paper as she had that night communed with God and the words came back audibly, as you are hearing my words. And these are the words, "It depends upon the state you were in when you desired and the state you are now in because you have not practiced revision." Can you imagine that? It depends on the state you were in when you desired plus the state you are *now* in *because* you haven't practiced revision.

Are we not told in scripture, "Whatever you desire, believe that you *have* received it, and you will" (Mark 11:24). Well now, if I desire something, it's a confession that I don't have it. So I know the state that I am in when I desire, that's obvious. But now, I must move from the state desiring to the state where the desire has been granted. And that brings about the state called revision. I must revise it. How would I feel were it true? How *would* I feel were it true? Well, then I assume that *feeling*. Then I have moved from the state when I desired it to the state of fulfillment. That shortens the interval. If I still remain in the state desiring, I have not practiced revision. I have not put into effect the teachings of scripture. So God said to her, "The difference is this: the state you were in when you desire plus the state you are *now* in because you haven't practiced revision." So, I say to everyone, listen to it carefully. These are revelations coming rapidly, coming, oh, one on top of the other through everyone who is here.

That drove me to the 17th chapter of John when I read that letter. It's the greatest prayer uttered ever. The entire 17th is simply a meditation within oneself. It's called the high priestly prayer. The Christ has finished the work that God gave him to do. He tells you he is God himself: "I and my Father are one." But he came into the world of limitation, sent from the Father, who is himself, so he sent himself: "For he who sees me sees him who sent me." He comes into the world having abdicated his glorious form and having taken upon himself the limitations of the flesh—not pretending but completely absorbing all the limitations and the weaknesses of the flesh—and then finished the work that he came to do.

Now he said, "Glorify thou me…glorify thou me with thine own *self* with the glory which I *had* with thee before that the world was" (John 17:5). So the first part is devoted to the prayer for self. It's broken into three parts. The second part is his prayer for the disciples, "Those whom thou gavest me." Those in whom I can plant the seed knowing that it will grow, and they'll carry on and spread it. And finally, he prays for the entire universal assembly. So in three parts he breaks it. First, for himself, to return to glory that he abdicated when he came out, when he became man. Becoming man, he completed it, and he has found those who dared to believe the most unbelievable story in the world. They dared to believe him and he prayed for those who dared to believe him in a world of scoffing unbelievers. And then he prayed at the end for the whole vast universal family, the whole vast world that one day will be assembled when all these little membranes are broken down, the little delusions of life.

So you take the revelation that came to this lady. It's a true one. God speaks to man through the medium of dream and revealed to her why some things take long and some things are short. Long because of the state you were in when you desired it makes a difference, and then you didn't practice revision. You could have shortened that distance instantly had you actually practiced revision and believed what you're told, to assume the feeling of the wish fulfilled. If I believe that I *have* what I am desiring, haven't I assumed the feeling of the wish fulfilled? And an assumption though false—because scripture teaches this—if I persist in it, remaining faithful to that state, it will harden into fact.

And so the only excluded one is the one who is drawing a little circle around himself. As the poet said, "He drew a circle that shut me out, infidel, scoundrel, a thing to flout; but love and I had the wit to win, and we drew a circle that took him in." So the circle expands and expands while they still remain within their little drawn circle that "I am better than, I am holier than." Like my friend from Boston, he was born and raised a good Irish Catholic thinking he was better than any Protestant in the world and infinitely better than a Jew and infinitely better than a Negro. So he went blindly on in his state believing all these silly things, sheer nonsense. And then, he died to these delusions in a way that he could never have planned it. How could he plan to set himself afire and find all the Caucasians afraid to come to his help because he set himself afire? And the Negro comes and throws him on the floor and douses himself with his own body, and smothered it, using himself as a blanket. And when all the others in his company that he did not give latrine duty to, but he gave it to the Jew, and the Jew said, "Give me a grenade, Sarge." He undid two from his belt and passed them quietly. He pulled the pins and the Jew—they all thought because he was a Jew he was a coward, the only brave one in the company—and he jumped up and threw them right into the Japanese nest and blew them to smithereens. So here we find all these little divisions in the world.

So how would I enter the assembly of God? There's only one body, only one Spirit, only one hope, only one Lord, only one faith. Now, does that mean I must accept the so-called Catholic doctrine, the Protestant doctrine with its many divisions, or this doctrine? No, only *one* faith, what faith? The fundamental sin is lack of faith in *I am He.* That's the fundamental sin. If I don't believe that I am he, I die in my sins: I keep on missing the mark. But if I am he, is there anything outside of me? There is nothing outside of me if

I am he. So that "All that I behold, though it *appears* without, it is within, in my Imagination of which this world of mortality is but a shadow" (Blake).

So you have these wonderful experiences and you wonder, what is objective, what is subjective? And it's wholly dependent on the level on which consciousness at the moment is focused. Tonight, I would find a world so real—not this world—and to me it seems the only world, it's objective to my perception; and if I can remember this that I shut out in so-called dream, it would seem to me subjective. Then I will wake with the memory of what I have done and it will be subjective and the world to which I've returned will seem objective. So what is objective and what is subjective? The whole is taking place within me.

So when I come back with the memory that I met Abdullah last night, I met my father, I met my brother, I met all these people and they're not here in this world any more, but they were so real and so wonderful. I embraced them, kissed them, felt them, and we had the most heavenly time and then I returned. Any modern psychiatrist would say, "Well, Neville, you know they are only images of the Imagination." I would say to him, "They're just as solidly real as you are. When I touched them my hand didn't go through them. When I talked with them they did not seem to be some little thing on the outside. But I will grant you they are images of the Imagination. But what do you think you are now?" He'd be mortified if I told him that he doesn't differ now from what he calls the *real* world from that world that he calls the unreal world, because that was as real, when I experienced it, as this that I now experience. So what is reality? So here, the whole vast world is unfolding within man. And God is man. "Man is God...and that eternal body of man is the Imagination and that is God himself" (Blake).

So when I desire something, how long will it take, how long, O Lord? Well, the measure is where you are as against what you desire. But, if you revise you're present state so that you are one with the state desired, so you're basking in the feeling of the wish fulfilled, it will take no time, no time. It will simply come because you're dwelling in the present, in the now. When I say "I am", is that past? Is it future? Is it not present? And what is his name? Is it not I AM? "And that is my name forever...and by this name I'll be known throughout all generations" (Ex. 3:14). Well, it isn't something that is past. I didn't say I was, or I will be, I said I am. That is my name forever.

Man desires, though the reason tells him that it's impossible or it's going to take time; the time is only measured, by this revelation to my friend, by revision. To what degree have you revised your present state? You can come closer if you want to. But don't come closer, come right into the state...that when you desire and whatever you desire, when you pray, believe that you have received it, and you will. So, how could I reach out for something that I *already* have? How could I pursue the goal that I *have* obtained? So men who have not accepted this, you find them running from pillar to post, seeking, seeking, seeking, and you wonder why are they seeking a new access to a goal already attained, why?

I have friends of mine, and like all people, it's the old story, familiarity breeds contempt. They know you as a man, your weaknesses...they know you intimately as a man...and they don't want that. They want something called a holy man; something that has an odor, that comes unwashed, you know that's a holy man. They'll follow him all over because he is so holy. He tells them he is. They'll go all over the world after this holy man, and finally they find he, too, has clay feet. Disillusioned they go elsewhere...they keep on seeking and seeking. They will not accept the *only* way. There's only one way, only one faith, only one hope. Well, what is the hope? You and I will endure all the burdens in the world patiently if we think it's inevitable, but that same burden becomes intolerable as soon as there is hope of escape. And so, you and I are given hope of escaping every burden in the world through the teachings of the Christ. The minute there is *hope* that I could escape this restriction, then whatever that restriction is it becomes to me intolerable, I can't stand it any longer. But while I thought it was inevitable and no escape, I patiently endured. And that's the world. So you give a man hope...only one hope. The Bible speaks of the hope: faith, hope and love, these three. These are the great virtues out of which the whole vast civilization is made. Give him hope to escape the limitations of birth. Give him faith in the only reality, faith that I AM HE. And finally you'll find that that being is infinite love. These are the three.

So he begins in this 4th chapter, "only one body." That I know from experience. You're gathered one by one into this assembly, and when you're gathered, one body. You go into the body and as Paul states in the 12th chapter of Corinthians, "You are the body of Christ." You are, when you are brought and assembled into the body of Christ...only one body. One Spirit, "For he who is united to the Lord becomes one spirit with him," one spirit. Only one hope tending the law of God as interpreted by the risen Christ. You've heard it said you should not commit so and so, but I say to you, when you do it in your mind alone you've done it (Mat.5:27). You committed the act the minute you had the impulse to do it, so physical restraint means nothing. You've done it therefore the whole thing must be now psychological. The whole drama of life must be all imaginal. If I have committed the act of adultery by wanting to have an affair with another even though I didn't, the restraint because I contemplated the consequences of my actions were I caught, the embarrassment, or the this, that or the other, and so I restrain the impulse, well, the impulse was the act he tells us. Therefore, if the impulse is the act, then I must begin to become disciplined and learn how to actually become discriminating in all of my choices in this world.

So here, if I know that I could just do it by simply shortening the interval between desiring and assuming that it's done just as though it were, then that's the hope, I've escaped. One Lord, what's his name? I AM. The word Lord in the Bible is always translated I AM. Now, one faith: faith in I AM. One baptism: that's when you stand before the risen Christ, and after your confession of faith that the greatest thing in the world is love, he embraces you, and you mingle with his body, and you become one. That's baptism with the Holy Spirit. And what God has joined together let no man put asunder. You who was his emanation, you were the emanation, now he brings it back and he cleaves to it, and they become one…so one baptism.

Now he comes to the last: "One God and Father of us all, who is above all, and through all, and in all." Then the fatherhood reveals itself in you and you stand and see the "only begotten," which is the result of your passage through all of these states. For he who stands before you personifying all the generations of men is the eternal youth David. Because you went through it all and broke all the little membranes that would put you into one little circle after the other, and finally you come through, and there is only one God and the Father of us all, and you are he. So in the end there's only one. We live as one man, contracting our infinite senses we behold multitude, multitude of nations; or expanding we behold one, as one man containing the universal family. And that one man we call Jesus the Christ. So when you are now one with the body of Jesus the Christ, you *are* Jesus the Christ. Only one Spirit, for now you are untied with him, one Spirit. And now you know exactly what the one faith is, what the one Lord is, what everything is. There's only one. One, one, one, seven ones, each attached to a noun as you read it.

I want to thank this lady for her perfectly wonderful communion with God and sharing it with us, so that I in turn could share it with those who are here.

So in this wonderful prayer, the very end, read it, there are only twenty-six verses; try to commit it to memory, twenty-six verses, the greatest prayer ever recorded, the prayer of the high priest. And he is the high priest after the order of Melchizadek, who had no father, no mother, no beginning, no end, no genealogy, because he's the source of all that is. So now he radiates a prayer…breaks it into three parts…his return. I am no longer in the world, he said. "Holy Father, keep them in thy name that thou gavest me that they may be one as we are one. I have made known unto them thy name and I will make it known that the love with which thou hast loved me may be in them, and I in them," so he ends it. The same love that will what? "The love with which thou loved me may be in them and I in them." He precedes it by saying, "O

Righteous Father, the world has not known thee, but I have known thee. And I have made known to them thy name."

I can't conceive of anything more beautiful than that 17th of John. When you read it and you get lost in it, I defy you to just restrain the tears. It's the one chapter that old Ab, my friend Abdullah, insisted that we commit to memory. Everyone had to know it. No reading of books. You rise and together we would say…"the 17th chapter of John," he would say. And then he would close always with "Praise be unto that unity that is our unity, one in all and all in one." We all had to simply rise at the close of the meeting and recite the 17th of John. It was driven into the mind of everyone who was present. You read it, if you do not know it, you read it when you go home.

Now let us go into the Silence.

*   *   *

Q: I still don't quite get what it means by being sealed in Revelation, sealed in this and sealed in that.

A: First of all, you have to give me not just the word sealed but the context. In the Book of Daniel he was told to seal it, the time was not yet; in the Book of Revelation, do not seal it, for the time is fulfilled, and therefore let the filthy be filthy still (22:10). Do not for one moment raise a finger; let them be as they are. For they've heard the story and from now on just let them all move in their own respective ways. Do not seal it anymore, for this is not a mystery to be kept as a mystery. For now the mysteries of God, although they are great mysteries, they're not matters to be kept secret, but they are mysterious in character. But now we have broken the seal. The seal is broken in the story of the gospel. And I am trying my best to tell you from experience what that breaking of the seal is. It's broken in me. I have experienced the entire story of the gospel. I do not know of one little part of it that I haven't experienced. And yet, you're told in the end of John, there are many things not enclosed in this book. If they were all written, the world itself couldn't contain the books. So the visions go on and on that are not now recorded in scripture. But the outstanding sections of scripture concerning the one who is to come have taken place in me. All the other things are not recorded in scripture, but they follow on the heels of what is recorded. So John tells you, I have recorded these that you may know, but if I took all the things that he did, I would say, the world itself would not be large enough to contain the books that would be written. So there's no limit to the unfolding of the power and the wisdom of God.

Q: (inaudible)

A: Alright, all sins are forgiven but blasphemy against the Holy Spirit. You are told in the Book of Luke...that same quote is made in Luke that it's made elsewhere, but Luke adds something to it. That the sin against the Holy Spirit is not forgiven; but he adds, "When they bring you into the synagogue, that is the assembly, before the authorities, do not take thought concerning what you are to answer or what you are to say; for the Spirit will, in that very hour, teach you what you ought to say" (Luke 12:11). So he qualifies it. There is no such thing as an ultimate sin that cannot be forgiven. So you've gone through and all of a sudden you are prompted now. You stand in the presence of the risen Christ, who is the embodiment of love, and you cannot fail in the answer. So do not be concerned as to what you're going to say, how you will answer; for the Holy Spirit will teach you in that very hour what you ought to say. So Luke goes beyond Mark, who quotes it, and shows you something far beyond it, that you won't fail anyway.

I know it's been called a sin against sex, a sin against this...that's all speculation. Blasphemy against the Holy Spirit is not forgiven. No, you will blaspheme. Until that moment maybe you did. And I am convinced that when you are brought into the presence of the risen Christ that fitness for the kingdom, which is just about to take place when he embraces you, is the *consequence*, not the condition of his grace. So you are brought in when you are still a simple being. And you stand before him and you answer correctly, because you can't...it's so obvious, the answer is so obvious. So he embraces you. And so I say fitness for the kingdom of God, which comes with that embrace, which is baptism by the Holy Spirit, is the consequence of that baptism; it is not the condition of his grace. For grace is the gift of God himself to the one that he embraces; he gives you his very Spirit by fusion with him. And I am quite sure that no one is brought in who has not blasphemed, who hasn't denied that I AM HE. Who hasn't with all of their idols on the outside and worshipped false idols?

Q: Neville, your story about the Catholic sergeant and the ___(??), is there any place in the Bible that gives guidance on this factor? When, regardless of what factors went into the making of the war, when this man threw the hand grenade he did destroy some other people who were, after all,

God too. Is there anything in the Bible that would counsel one in how to face the facts like this we meet in life?

A: I haven't found any part of the Bible where such violence is frowned upon or condoned. When we are told, "You say that when the tower fell and eighteen were killed, were they more sinful than others in Jerusalem?" He said, "I tell you, not; but unless you repent you shall perish as they did" (Luke 13:4,5). So he didn't liken this eighteen who died as the result of the tower falling to any sin on their part. We're living in a world of sin and death. This is sin and death. He said, "If I were hungry I wouldn't tell you; for the world is mine and all within it. The cattle on a thousand hills are mine" (Ps.50:10,12). So why would I tell anyone that I'm hungry? If they're mine, I'd take it, I'd slay and eat, he said. And when Peter said, I cannot eat the unclean thing, and the sheet came down from heaven covered with all manner of flesh; the voice said, Peter, that which I have cleansed I have cleansed; slay and eat (Acts 10:13-15). It's all God.

That's the great division that takes place in the 6th chapter of John: Eat my flesh and drink my blood. "For except you eat my flesh and drink my blood, you have no life within you, your body." This is a hard saying, they said, and many left never to walk with him again. He said, "No man comes unto me save my Father calls him, no man"

(John 6:52;44). Can't come. My Father knows exactly which one will fit right now into the pattern. So in my world as I am assembling the one being, think of it as the fragmented Rock. The Rock that begot you, you are unmindful, and you've forgotten the Rock [God] that gave you birth (Deut. 32:18). So here comes the fragmented Rock and every little fragment of the Rock contains the core. From that center in the fragment it must gather the whole together into the Rock which is Christ. Everyone is a fragment of the Rock and each contains the core, the heart, the center. And from that center it gathers all the fragments and rebuilds that vast Rock, and *it* is the Rock that begot the universe.

So what man could I kill? In the end this whole thing will be simply the greatest dream. Believe me, nothing dies, there's nothing to kill, even though they seem to be. So in the end, one being, one Spirit, one body, one hope, one faith, just one. And the fragments become the center and from each center the whole mass is gathered. And so night after night I have to be gathering all those within my world and they fit into the pattern as the Rock is re-established, and I am he.

I saw that so clearly one night when I saw this quartz smashed, fragmented. Then quickly all the little fragments were gathered together into a form, and the form was that of a meditating Buddha. Here was this being sitting in a lotus posture. As I looked, I'm looking at myself. But I had never seen myself so glorious. I can't describe the beauty, the handsomeness, the majesty, the strength of character in that face. Everything you could think of in the superlative that face contained...in deep meditation. And as I looked at it, it became flesh, it became alive, and it began to glow and it glowed and glowed and glowed. When it reached the apex of intensity—here I am glued to it—it all exploded. And then I woke here. I had gathered the fragments together and formed them into *one* form, and I was it.

Everyone will gather all the fragments together and form it into the one form, and he is it. And these living stones become gathered together into *one* form that is the risen Christ. As Paul tells you, "You are the body of Christ and, individually, members of it." All, without loss of identity; yet you are the one. No loss of identity. You're wonderful definite individuality is still in tact and yet you are he. (Tape ends.)

LIFE IS FOR ACTING

11/7/66

Life really is for acting. Time to act! "God only acts and is in existing beings or men" (Blake). God is not some passive spectator observing the great passage of life. He is the supreme actor. Now, to play a part an actor must to some extent *feel* the part and imagine himself as the character he is depicting. Now God became man that man might become God. He is not pretending that he's you, he became you. He so feels that he *is* you that there is no separation. He *is* you. That's God. Therefore, we conclude that life is for action.

How do we act? If I tell you that an assumption, a mere assumption— which is God's way of creating—though at the moment that you've assumed it, reason denies it, your senses deny it, if you persist in it, it will harden into fact. If you demand from me proof before you dare to assume, you will never come to action. To act I really must assume, and the assumption is the act of faith; and without faith it is impossible to please him, as told us in the unknown author's letter to the Hebrews. Without faith it is impossible to please him, and faith is simply this bold assumption. I dare to assume that I am the one that I would like to be. If I would dare to assume, then I have proven to my own satisfaction that I have made the great act of faith.

Now we are told in Ephesians, Paul's letter to the Ephesians, "Be imitators of God as beloved children"...if this is how God creates (Eph.5:1). He became me and made me alive. And then becoming me, now he plays all the parts that I would ever play—the rich man, the poor man, the beggar man, the thief— whatever I dare to assume that I am. If I judge from appearances and then from appearances I accept what it suggests and then play its part, well then, he'll play the part. He plays every part in the world; there's nothing but God.

Now we are told in scripture, "Commune with your own heart and be silent"—the 4th chapter, the 4th verse of Psalms, commune with your own heart. Well, the word heart, the word mind, and the word self is really the same in scripture. So commune with your own self, for the self is God. Now you commune with self, dissect every little action of the mind, dissect it. If you do, you *will* find the very fount of the primal truth. And who is the truth? "I AM the truth." "I AM the way." What way?—commune with self. If I dare to commune with myself and dissect every little action of the mind as I commune with self, I will find the fount of truth. And finding it, I find myself...and I am he. Now we are told, he comes to us through the gate of dream. Yes, God comes through the gate of dream and he builds in our mortal thought *immortal* dreams to haunt us. He paints the entire picture within us through the gate of dream; that we can't let go, we must find this that was painted on the inside as it were. But he comes through the gate of dream.

Now let me share with you tonight a couple of letters. One gentleman, I know he is here; the other, undoubtedly because of weather could not make it. But his is equally lovely. I'll take the one who is here first. Quite a while ago, I'm going back quite awhile, a year or more, he wrote me a letter and he said it's not for publication. But that's a year ago and he'll forgive me, because I'm not going to reveal the entire letter. Much of it is very personal. There's no need to share it with anyone but the two of us. But, the first part of it, he will love this. He said, "In my dream I was a spectator observing a lecturer. He was a little small unpretentious man, unusually homely...little tiny, very, very homely man. Not a thing about him was, I would say, desirable. Yet his subject was this, he was speaking of the necessity of transforming one's own self by one's own Imagination. Then the lecture ended, and as it ended, he left the stage and as he walked he grew and grew in stature and his face became completely transformed into the most incredible beauty. Then, with his head held high in pride of what he had become, he departed, and then I woke."

The Bible only recognizes one source of dreams: All dreams proceed from God. He's telling me his experience, but who's having the experience? Would he not say to me if I asked him, "I am having it." Well, his name is I AM. Here was this marvelous revelation. Here, this little tiny almost dwarf-like creature, not a thing was ___(??) save his pity for it, yet he's talking about the necessity of transforming oneself by one's own power of Imagination. And then, as he departed, he grew and grew and grew in stature; and the face that was so homely became completely transformed into the most incredible beauty. But that's what I'm talking about every time I take the platform. God became man, every child born of woman, that every child born of woman may become this incredible beauty that is God. And how does he do it? Just like the actor; to play the part the actor must believe to some extent and *feel* to some extent that he is the character that he's depicting. As he loses himself in it, he *becomes* it. So that is the story.

Now, from the same letter came this one...and this only happened this past week. He said, "I found myself driving down Beverly Boulevard. And strangely enough although I was seated correctly I was looking backwards and holding my car in the proper lane. My wife is telling me that I should simply turn around and I told her it was much easier to drive this way, looking back and down, once I kept my car in the lane, perfectly alright. Along side of me was a police car and he kept on gesturing that I should turn my head around and look where I'm going. Well, I knew I wasn't breaking any rules. As long as I kept the car within the proper lane, I wasn't breaking a rule. And so, I simply aloofly ignored him.

"Then I found as I turned around, which I occasionally turned around, at this junction I turned and as I looked forward, here was a crisis. I found myself on La Cienega and I had to make a turn. Well, I made a wide turn and came into the wrong lane. The police car drove up along side and then the policeman said to me, 'Do not mind looking where you have been, look where you are going.' Then he gave me, or rather, he had the ticket all written out and before he could give me the ticket, I woke." So it didn't cost me a nickel, he said. Then he said, "I learned a great principle from this: Sleep may bring counsel, but waking saves you money." Now he's a very wonderful humorous writer, a very successful writer. But even in that closing remark he revealed to me in this, "Rouse thyself! Why sleepest thou, O Lord? Awake! Awake, O sleeper, and arise from the dead." If I awake...yes, I realize the whole vast world is mine. And if I were hungry then, why should I tell you? I would slay and eat, for it's all mine...if I awake. If I'm not awake, well then, I play the part of the rich man, the poor man, the beggar man, the thief. If I awake, I am the supreme actor playing all the parts. And so, he said, "I learned this principle, and the principle is: Sleep may bring counsel (and it does), but waking saves you money." You dwell upon it. It's a humorous tagline for the end of his letter to me. But I got so much out of his letter. Don't look back and down.

Now, I must bring this out, whenever a vision breaks forth into speech, the presence of God is affirmed...as the Bible teaches in the 3rd chapter of Exodus and the 6th of Isaiah, whenever it breaks forth in speech. Well, the policeman is law. Here is the embodiment of law; secular law yes but law. And he's warning him not to look back where he's been, look forward to where he's going. But the voice broke forth in speech and wherever in dream the voice breaks forth in speech then the presence of Deity is established. And God is speaking to him: No matter what he has accomplished, forget it. There is infinity before him; that nothing in this world that he's ever accomplished compares to what is before him. Leave everything behind and start moving on.

Now the other chap, who undoubtedly because of the weather isn't here, he wrote this story. May I tell you, his hunger to have an experience of God is all possessing. I never met anyone more hungry, more desirous of experiencing God. He's successful in his work, doing very well...but that hunger for God. And he said, "In my dream I found myself in the presence of friends. Strangely enough I thought they were my brothers, but I cannot really remember that they were my brothers. But I know they were my friends. And one said to me, 'The silver serpent is here. The most powerful of the serpents is here.' Another one said, 'And when he strikes, he strikes suddenly.' Now they take me in this house. When I went into my room, they all entered, and the one who first spoke, spoke again, and he said, 'The all-powerful silver serpent is in this room.' I started looking all over to find the serpent. I was lifting the blankets from my bed, looked under the bed, looked all over. Another one said to me, 'Looking here and there you will never find him. When he appears you will see him, but he will find you. He comes suddenly, but he finds you.'"

Well, the serpent is the symbol of Christ awake. That's the symbol of Christ, the great serpent who fell, bringing with him all of us. "I have been crucified with Christ; nevertheless, I live, yet not I, but Christ who lives in me" (Gal.2:20). The name of God, the primary name, Yod He Vau He, the verb He Vau He means "to fall or to cause to fall; or to blow, or the one who causes the wind to blow." So here, the serpent fell taking with him all of us. It is Christ, it is God who became man that man might become God. And here this power, the greatest power of all, he was told, is right in this room. And he started looking, he's so eager to find him. "When he appears you will see him, but he will find you" as told us in the end of Job, after all the trials are over, "I have heard of thee with the hearing of the ear, but now my eye sees thee" (Job 42:5). You'll see him.

Now here, we are told...but how would I go about doing this? I want to change my life. I want to become something greater, something better in my own eyes. The world reflects it. Doesn't matter what they think at the moment. If I change myself, the world is only an echo. It only responds to all that I am and it will mirror me, just like a mirror, whatever I am. I will see reflected in their behavior the man that I am. Well, how do I do it? You're told, "Commune with yourself upon your bed and then be silent" (Ps.4:4)... commune with myself.

Well, a lady gave me a book last week. You know, people seldom read a book given to them? If I ___(??) read the book that I buy, I will pay a nickel for it. I've paid $100 for a book. But when I buy a book I read it. And I have paid a hundred dollars for, say, three volumes that I wouldn't even give room to after I read them. But I was hungry to find out what it contained because of the promotion behind it. There are others that I've bought only for a nickel...

and what I got out of it! When she gave the book to my wife to give me, she said to my wife, "I bought it at a rummage sale. I only paid a dime."

Well, when I went home after the last lecture, I read the letters first, and after we had discussed, and I just talked for a while with the chap who brought me home, when he left and I closed the door and relaxed in my chair, I simply took up the book and started to thumb through it. As I turned over and started to read it, I couldn't put it down. Couldn't put it down until I finished the entire book...one of the most beautiful things I've ever read. She said she only paid a dime at a rummage sale. You know, people have a library, they don't know the value of the library—I don't mean in dollars, I mean in the actual content of books—and then a church comes by, they want something to sell at a rummage sale, and they give the book.

Well, this is called—I never heard of the author's name before, T. Howard Wilson, whoever he is, printed here in this city—it's *The Quest Everlasting*. That's the title. It's all about Lancelot and Guinevere, that's the cycle. Every page is something that we should drive right into the brain. But here, concerning now "Commune with yourself upon your bed." You want to help someone in this world? As Job said, when he prayed for his friends, forgetting himself, all of his limitations were lifted; and then all that seemingly was taken from him, all came back a thousand-fold. Every thing he lost came back multiplied and multiplied when he prayed for his friends; and in the praying for himself he forgot himself.

Now this is the love story. One who unnumbered ages ago saw this face, and then after unnumbered years he encountered it, and now he knows "I have looked upon this face before." So when she heard his name after he heard her name...and this one little thought, it's so altogether lovely, "His name upon her lips was like a prayer breathed by some holy nun at vesper hour." Have you ever gone to church at the vesper hour, when you sit at sunset and everything is so quiet? The organ may be playing, but it's always that eventide lovely music, soft, it isn't blaring. No one talks, no one speaks audibly, it's all communion within self, and you sit in the silence. These are the best I've ever gone to. You walk in just at sunset into St. Thomas' church in New York City, where I live only two blocks away. And I just pop into that lovely church at vesper hour. Just a few people coming from work, before they go home they drop into it, and the organ is simply playing that lovely soft wonderful music. You sit alone.

But just imagine that you have someone that you want to really see lifted up in this world. And you can call it her or can call it him, depending upon who you are. But in this, it was his name, Lancelot. His name upon her lips was like a prayer breathed by some holy nun at vesper hour. Well, can't you imagine that? Well, who is breathing it? In the Bible, when God calls man, the first recorded calling is "Moses, Moses." God called him. So what is his name, if he called Moses? He said, "I AM." Well, if I sit in the Silence and I call your name, who's calling? Am I not calling? Is it not God calling? If I sit in the Silence and then I actually call your name, and then feel that you are all that I would love you to be, that I want you to be, and with complete acceptance of this assumption, breathe like a holy nun at this vesper hour, wouldn't it work? I tell you, it works.

But, I can't tell you my thrill in reading this book, page after page after page. I can't begin to tell you the beauty in the book. She got it for a dime. *Quest Everlasting* is the title. Now, if they're still in print, I don't know. It's a beautiful job, lovely printing, nice binding. But maybe no one fully appreciates it, so they'll open the book and go, "Silly," and throw it away. And then came the rummage sale, get them together, give it to the church, and if they sell it for a dime, they get a dime. Luckily she got it and fortunately for me she gave it to me.

So here, I tell you this is how we commune. "Commune with your own self upon your bed and be silent." To commune is simply to inwardly call the name of the one you love, your husband, your child, your friend, anyone, and as you call him, who's calling him? *God* is calling him. Well, are *you* not calling him? Well, his name is I AM. As we said earlier, God is not pretending that he's man; God became man. For to play a part, the actor, the supreme actor, as all other actors, must first of all to some extent feel the part and then imagine himself *as* the character he is depicting. Well, he has imagined that he is the being that is talking to you. And gradually he actually steals through my dreams, my visions, for he comes to me through the gate of dream, and then he builds in my mortal thought immortal dreams. The immortal dreams are recorded in scripture. So he builds in my mortal thought these immortal dreams and then when I am *haunted* by them and I experience these immortal dreams, I know he wakes in me…he wakes and wakes and wakes, having first built in me these immortal dreams.

So I say to every one of you it is time to act. The act is not getting out and ranting all over the world trying to change the world; we change it from within. "God only acts and is *in* existing beings or men." Now we are told in the 4th chapter, the 17th verse of Romans—there are many translations of this but I like the one from the Catholic Bible; there are many and they're all lovely—in the Catholic Bible, "He calls a thing that is not now seen as though it were seen, and the unseen becomes seen." Now, my Bible, what I call the Protestant Bible, the Revised Standard Version, "He calls a thing that does not exist, and that which does not exist as he calls it comes into existence." Well, that's alright, it's lovely, but I'd rather have the other: He calls a thing that is not seen by mortal eye and that which is not seen as he calls it becomes seen.

So his name upon her lips is like a prayer, nobody hears it. She just simply comes from within herself the name of her lover, the one she's known through the ages, and she hears that response. And to her, though she is a person come back from Macy's after a hard, hard day's work, she is like some holy nun at that vesper hour. For that vesper hour need not be sunset in a church, it can be when you are on your bed. That's the vesper hour, that's the eventide.

So Christ wakes in us. But he comes through us through the gates of sleep first, and then upon our mortal thought he simply paints these immortal dreams and you and I experience them. And the immortal dream painted you...find it right in the Bible; it's everlasting. Having painted it, it haunts us, like my friend with the silver serpent. He's haunted by it. He's not here to hear the interpretation, but he knows it because it happened to him. So whether he hears it from me or not, it doesn't really matter, he knows now. But here, in his own house and in his own room...but he can't find it by searching for it; his hunger brings it. And when he comes he'll see him. But he will find you; you don't find him. It strikes suddenly, one said. So in his case, too, the vision broke forth in speech and whenever vision breaks forth in speech Deity is affirmed.

So here this lovely thing: it's always time to act. So to every one of us, now is the time to act. Don't wait for tomorrow, now. And that vision that I told earlier of my friend's, this little man, very, very homely, not a thing to look at, in fact, you would pity him. Yet his subject was to transform oneself by the power of one's own Imagination. And when he got through telling it and he started to depart, he grew and grew and grew in stature. As he grew, his face became completely transformed into the most incredible beauty. Here was a complete demonstration of what he was talking about.

So here, I act, time to act. It is time to act, time for everyone, because God is not something on the outside. God became man that man might become God. And God is not some passive spectator observing the great pageantry as it unfolds, he is the supreme actor in man. But it takes a tremendous actor to play the part of the buffoon, the fool, the poor man, the this. But maybe you don't like playing that part. Alright, the supreme actor can change it over night and play another part, and the world—it's all a stage anyway—will reflect the change in you.

The story is "transform *oneself* by the power of one's own Imagination." Well, I will simply assume. For the assumption is the act of faith and without faith it is impossible to please him, you can't please him. So I will simply assume that I am...and then I name it. Then I take those that I love and then call their name, and let it be to me like some lovely breath as I call it at this vesper hour. I tell you, who is calling him? I am calling him. But what's his name?—I AM. Therefore, what is impossible to God? Nothing is impossible to God. So you call it and you feel the reality of it, and then it's done. All you do is simply wait in confidence that it cannot return unto you void. For you've spoken; and "My word cannot return unto me void, but it must accomplish that which I purposed, and prosper in the thing for which I sent it" (Is. 55:11). And here you stand, completely in control of transforming self, and by it, the world transforms itself relative to you. So, no screaming on the outside. And this goes for every one of us. There is nothing but God, but God is in man. Where else would you find him? He became man in the most literal sense that man might become God.

Now let us go into the Silence.

*   *   *

Q: Neville, in John 17, you said that this was a prayer by one who had already experienced it, as yourself, and been lifted out of the world. Why then is he saying "Glorify thou me with thine own self" because, has he not been given that self?

A: Natalie, that begins the entire chapter, "the hour has come"...he begins it, "My hour for departure is come." Now, he wants returned to him the same glory that he had before that the world was. And what was the glory? The glory that was mine, now, "Glorify thou me with thine *own* self." That was the self he gave up; he gave up divinity. He abdicated his divine form to become man. He's asking now for the return. And then how can you find in mortal words, words better than that to express it? It's only expressed for us on this level. It's all a communion within self. Because, who would have known it? How could any writer have recorded it? For this is all communion of the risen Christ. What evangelist was present to hear this communion with self? So then what could be the revelation but the evangelist's own experience of the Christ in him? For, who was present? No one was present. The hour has come and now, "Father, glorify thou me with thine own self with the glory that I had with thee before that the world was." And then, he simply goes through "I have kept them in thy name." And he gave..."everything that he gave me I have given to them that they may be one as we are one." It goes through the entire oneness...all through the entire 17th, the most glorious prayer that one could ever conceive: "I in them and thou in me that they may be one as we are one."

Q: Are you speaking then of something that is coming to you in fullness after you leave this body?

A: You are told it before you leave this body, but you remain in this body to complete the story. It is all done within you. And you know it, you have experienced it all, and although you hunger…as Paul said, "It is my desire to depart and be with Christ, but for your sakes it is better, the need is greater, that I stay on in the body." And so he has to stay on until he tells it and tells it 'til the body can't take it any more. When the body can take it no longer, then he has to depart. At that moment, he is one with what he was when he walked the earth as he experienced it. So God actually became us and in each one he awakes and awakes and awakes and awakes.

And then the same story, it is all within us, and it all came through that wonderful gate of dream. So I ask you for your dreams, to let me know at the moment where you are in the unfolding dream. Because, the dream is so important, for he comes through the gate of dream and then he builds in mortal thought immortal images. It's all there. In the mortal thought?—yes in my mortal mind. But I am haunted by what he's done in the immortal state. Can't rub them out; they are there forever. And when you have experienced them, then the whole thing is over. And you really hope to depart, but the work isn't finished as far as telling it and telling it, so that everyone will know that he should not despair. No matter what happens in the world, don't despair, for the very one who created the whole vast universe is in you. You're not some little puppet on the outside. And this goes for every child born of woman regardless of race, regardless of nationality, regardless of anything. But every child born of woman, God is housed in that child when he says "I am."

Q: When you're on your bed in the Silence and you mention this person's name, do you just ___(??) or do you try to focus on some of their problems?

A: No, not problems. For instance, when I call one that I love dearly and call her name because I'm separated, say, in space or I may be a thousand miles away, and your heart longs for the comrade, and you call, hoping in your own heart first that she's right, that everything is perfect, and then you just simply call the name. When you call the name, it's God calling the name, because *I am* calling it. But you whisper it from within. Call the name…for in the beginning of Genesis, and "he named everything and it was as he named it."

Q: When you call is it her name, the first name, or as you know her?

A: By whatever. If you call her "Sweet", let her know what you mean by Sweet. Her name may be Joan, but you call her Sweet if you can call her

Sweet. It wouldn't make any difference because it's all something within. You know what you mean when you use a certain endearing term. I call my wife Bill and every time I speak publicly about Bill and I went to bed, I have to stop and explain it because the association is a man. Well, she's always been to me Bill. And so I speak of her and I call her Bill, but I rarely call her Bill. I mean, every day I have occasion to call her and it's always either the word Sweet or Darling or Dear. She knows what I'm talking about. These are terms that I use in calling her. Occasionally I might call her Bill. I've never called her by the name given to her at birth, which is Willa. When others call her Willa, I don't know who they're talking about, because to me she's either Bill or she is the names that I always speak when I speak of her as Dear or Sweet or Darling, and she knows exactly what I'm talking about.

So if tonight in the Silence were I separated, say, across the country 3,000 miles, and I naturally think of her, I wouldn't call her Bill. I might use the word Sweet, but there are millions of things that are sweet in the world, but I don't mean many ___(??) of things, I mean only one. And I would know exactly what I am calling. It's all in me. "For all that you behold, though it appears without, it is within, in your Imagination of which this world of mortality is but a shadow." All objective reality is produced through imagining. The whole vast world comes out of God and God is your own wonderful human Imagination. And so, I would call her, and then commune, embrace her, do anything, hold her, kiss her, and then see her as I would like to see her, and go to sleep. Well, God called her when I did that. Am I not calling her? What is his name? I AM.

TAKE MY YOKE

11/11/66

Tonight's subject is "Take My Yoke." This is a common rabbinical expression for the study of scriptures. So when someone offers you his yoke, he offers you his understanding of scripture based upon experience, for others who offer you their yoke based upon scholarship, based upon some analysis, based upon speculation and theory. So here, he offers you what he knows from experience, for he has experienced scripture.

Now, to yoke is "to cover, to join, to bear." You take a wooden frame and you put it over their necks, the necks of, say, two oxen or other draft animals, and you yoke them. And we also ___(??) yoke, as we're told in the 27th of Genesis, that Jacob...it was predicted that Jacob would yoke Esau. Now, Esau is this...as you look at me you're seeing Esau, this outer body is Esau, covered with hair. I am normally quite a hairless person, outside of my head and beard; nevertheless, if you could actually see it under a microscope, you still would see the entire body covered with lots of hair. I don't see it, because to me I'm a hairless person as it were, but the body itself is covered, like Esau. And it's predicted that he would yoke Esau. Who? Jacob...and Jacob is the one that the Lord loved. He said, "Is not Esau Jacob's brother? Yet I have loved Jacob, but I have hated Esau" for he yokes them.

Now, Christ in scripture offers me his yoke. So if I would yoke Esau... and there are two of us, because you always yoke two, it's a coupling, it's a pairing. Well, if Christ offers me his yoke, he not only offers me his knowledge of scripture but he's going to yoke me if I take it. If I will take what he gives me, well, then he will yoke me and we'll move together. And the ultimate end is we become one if I will take it. So he offers you his knowledge of scripture based upon his own personal experience of scripture.

Now this past week I received two letters. Strangely enough both were written on the 3rd of November, or the events happened on the 3rd of November. I'll give the shorter of the two first. She's here tonight. The other lady can only make it once in a very long while. She lives very far away and it's not convenient for her to come, so she's only been here once since I opened, but she wrote this as an experience of the 3rd of November. But I'll give you the shorter of the two. She said, "I sat up in bed and wrote these words as I heard them come from the depths, 'Like a handkerchief you *absorb* the truth, rather than accept it.'" Then, she said, "I addressed the voice who was speaking and I said, I do not know what you mean...and I do not remember what we were talking about. And then I lay back on my bed and again I fell asleep. Instantly, in my dream now, I found myself holding a handkerchief in my hand and my nose was filled with mucous. So I put the handkerchief to my nose and I blew; and I looked, and the handkerchief had absorbed all the moisture. Then I found another handkerchief in my hand; it was clean and dry. I opened it. As I opened it, a marble was dropped into the handkerchief. The handkerchief *accepted* the marble, but it couldn't absorb it. Then the voice said to me, 'This is the will of God.'"

So, I can tell you night after night after night and you may accept it and go out and repeat it word for word, like a parrot, such as "Imagining creates reality," no ___(??), like people say the Lord's Prayer...you go to church on Sunday and the average orthodox churches, they all repeat the Lord's Prayer. They all know it, from little tiny children up. It's a marble... they have not absorbed the Lord's Prayer. You can take all the statements, "Whatever you desire, believe that you have received it and you will." That's a marble that most of the people who will believe it, if they do believe it, haven't absorbed. You take these fantastic profound statements and you ponder them, you dwell upon them, and then you gradually absorb them. They become part...really, you breathe them, you live them, and you cannot think in any other terms. You simply become it.

So like a handkerchief you *absorb* the truth, rather than accept it and do not know what you mean, "I don't remember what we were talking about." And then comes the vision to explain exactly the difference between absorption of the truth and acceptance of the truth, one who accepts and keeps it like some little toy and worships it as something on the outside. I put food into my mouth, and not everything that I take into my mouth can I assimilate. My system will assimilate what it can, build into my structure, and then expel what it can't. There are certain little things that will not help me any, but I eat them. Take a banana, I peel a banana...I love a banana, so I eat it. I am told the tiny little threads that go down the middle they do not harm me but they do not help me. But my system cannot absorb them. No system can absorb it. It's like a little fiber, and you simply expel it by some orifice of the body...to expel that which it cannot absorb. So here we eat all kinds of food. And this is now mental food: You take it in, you think you do, but then if you don't absorb it, you don't assimilate it, and you expel it, and cast it off into the trough.

So I can tell you night after night that you can be anything that you want to be in this world, and that I mean, if you will take my yoke upon you. "Take my yoke." He's made to say, "Thank you, Father, that thou hast hid these things from the wise and the prudent, and has revealed them unto babes; for such was thy gracious will" (Mt.11:25). Then he makes this statement, and you wonder what prompted this statement: "No one knows the Son except the Father, and no one knows the Father except the Son, and any one to whom the Son chooses to reveal him" (Mt.11:27). On the heels of this, he now gives the information, "Take my yoke upon you and learn from me," and he tells us, "The yoke is easy, it's so easy, and the burden is light." That's the 11th chapter of the Book of Matthew, the very end. Here he invites us all to accept it. Will I allow myself this night to be yoked to Christ? This is an *easy* yoke to bear, for he tells me that the keeping of this law externally is a frightful waste. I must go to church regardless of the weather, regardless of this, regardless of that, or else I am now committing a sin. If I eat meat on Friday, it's a sin. If I do this...if I marry outside of my faith, physically, that's a sin. If I have to actually be yoked to all these laws, what a horrible burden! So he tells me now, "*My* yoke is easy."

Then he says, anything you do in love is right. That's his yoke. No matter what you do, if it's done in love it's right. I can marry anyone in this world if I love him. I can do anything forever if I do it in love. That's easy; take my yoke. And he gives me all these wonderful laws to set me free. "Whatever you desire, just believe that you have received it, and you will" (Mk.11:24). That's easy, isn't it? You mean regardless of my educational background, regardless of my social, my political, my financial, all these backgrounds, if I dare to assume that I am that which I would like to be, is it true that I will become it? Yes, if you take my yoke upon you. I will yoke you to me, for I am he, and with me nothing is impossible.

So here, he yokes me, just as we're told Jacob yoked Esau. He yoked him. And this outer man, moved by reason, reason tells me it can't be true, my senses tell me it isn't true, and so, here is the outer man, but I'll yoke him. I'll put my yoke upon him and join him to me, because Christ can't get away from me if I accept his yoke. Christ is God, the only God. So I take his yoke, then he's as much joined to me as I am to you. I am joined to you and he is joined to me. He can't get away from me if I take his yoke. If I take his yoke, then all things are possible to God, and he is God. So I walk the earth yoked, and completely abandon myself in every dream in this world that I desire. If I do, I am promised it will come to pass. I will realize everything that I dreamed of if I believe it.

Now the other letter…bear in mind what I just told you about the first, about complete absorption, rather than simply accepting it but not absorbing it. The world accepts a creed, ___(??) a creed but they don't absorb it. It's not something that drives them forward to act upon it. They simply accept and put it aside when it pleases them, but they don't really absorb it, and completely absorb it and live by it every moment of time.

Now the other letter, it's a very long one, so I have to somewhat condense it, long, page after page of typewritten ___(??) so this is the essence of it…the same 3rd of November. She said, "I had a dream, and in my dream I was in my house, and there was the most wonderful man present." She doesn't describe the man beyond "a man with every noble characteristic of a ___(??), kindness, gentleness, generosity, every conceivable attribute that you would admire. He was dignified, everything. And I found myself on several occasions coming back to the house." She doesn't know when she departed, but she found herself returning with an empty heart, hoping that he would be there. He was always there, and she felt so relieved when she got back to the house.

This past time, she was more than anxious if you could describe it, hoping that he really would be there. She came back and she was relieved to find him there. But this time he was packing and she knew he was going to leave. She knew that not a thing she could say would persuade him to remain, that he would do as he pleased, the same kind, gentle, wonderful man of love. She said, "I can't describe the love. There's not an emotional state in the sense of a physical emotion, there was no word past simply a love that you cannot, that is, I cannot find words to describe the emotion of love that I felt in his presence. But, he had laid out for me presents. The first one I noticed, a beautiful bottle of champagne all wrapped up that we would drink. And then, many little packages, beautifully wrapped. Above them I noticed a glass of water from which he had been drinking, and I fished it out, knowing that he drank from that glass. Then I drank from it too. It amused him, but he was happy that I took the drink.

"Then I took one of the presents and I opened it. It was a little sliver of beautiful precious crystal and the insignia was a star. It was carved into the form of a star." Now, she didn't tell me whether it was the five-pointed star, the six-pointed star, the eight, or what. That would have been significant had she brought that number back, but it was a star. "But although he said to me, "it's a very precious thing and it's sweet to the taste." She said, "But even though it was precious and sweet to the taste, the mere fact that he was leaving I found no interest in the others. But, they were so beautifully wrapped, and there was a hole in each wrapping paper that I could see below each with a little nugget of the same crystal. And I could see portions of the design of the star in each little piece of crystal with the star on it. And then, my last time back, I'm in a market place. I never knew that I departed from his presence. But I always knew when I came back that I did it because for some unknown reason I felt that what I went out to seek was in some strange way important, and I left the presence of this infinite love in the search for what at the moment seemed so very important that I was distracted by the ways of the world.

"Now this last month I'm in a market place...and, Neville, I can't explain to you, it was like a ___(??). I can only describe it and equate it to the story you told years ago, when you were a child you went through the obstacle race, where every conceivable obstacle was placed in your path, and the prize was a way beyond after you went through all the obstacles. And this is where I found myself in a market place. I had a stick in my hand, my right hand. It was a big heavy round stick, and I fought every being, every condition, everything. I struck the street with that stick so hard that the reverberation, the sound, scattered every one in my sight. I pushed and I pulled and I ran and I did everything. No one could stop me from returning to "that man." I just kept on moving and moving, and not a thing in this world...it seemed that every conceivable ___(??) force rose to distract me, to draw me, to stop me; and I kept on striking and striking and striking with this stick to go back to that man." Now she said, "I do not know...because I began to wake, and knowing that I had awakened, I wished I were dead if I didn't get back. I didn't want to wake; not a thing in this world could hold me. But in spite of my desire to prolong this state and not wake upon this level, I said to myself, Return! Finally I woke, and I do not know if I got back, but I can tell you, since then I am ___(??), and night after night I sleep in the hope I will go back and find that presence of love, that man."

Well, that's scripture. "Your Maker is your husband, the Lord of hosts is his name" (Is.54:5). And now we are told, "You will depart from me and play the harlot" (Hos.4:12). The harlot need not be what the world calls a harlot, because really in the true sense that makes no difference whatsoever. I don't want to encourage men and women going out and doing all kinds of things, but that said, it doesn't mean what it means in the eyes of God. That hasn't a thing to do with reality. It is to depart from the true love which is God, and find interest in the things of the world: fame, wealth, recognition. And all these things seem so *more* important than to find him. For she was distracted time after time after time, and she went in search for the ___(??). Even while she was doing it, she knew what she was doing, and yet she kept on doing it, knowing the trouble she would have when she started returning. Every time she did it, she knew while she was preparing to depart that it would be a sorry time and the anxiety would be hers upon her return, hoping he would still be there. Well, that's the other letter.

So I ask everyone to take my yoke upon you. I have experienced scripture; I know what I'm talking about. No, I'm not a scholar to take it apart and analyze it. Listen to the words, "Thank you Father that you hid these things from the wise and the prudent, and revealed them unto babes" (Mt.11:25). So it was said of him, how did he know these things, he has no learning; we know him, we know his parents, we know everything about him. He has no learning, how can he know these things? No, you can't know them by any scholarly work in the world; you know them only by revelation. And because you return and become faithful to the love, he unveils himself to you, veil after veil after veil. After he unveils himself completely the yoke is now taken off, and you aren't two, you're one. I am his emanation, yet his wife 'til the great sleep of death is past.

And so, "Take my yoke upon you and learn from me. For my yoke is easy, it's so very easy, and the burden is light." There's no burden whatsoever. You don't have to say, well, I am not qualified for this. How could I be successful, I'm not qualified? I know no one, I have no social background, I have no intellectual background, I have no financial support, none whatsoever. How can I venture and dare to assume that I am the man that I would like to be without this support, without one to whom I could turn? There isn't anyone but *that* one to whom you are yoked. Who is he?—I AM. "Except you believe that I am he, you die in your sins" (John 8:24). And there's no other name; this is my name forever and forever. So you say, "I am," well, that's he. It is this one that is asking you to really accept him, to trust him, and then go forward, believing that you are everything in this world that you would like to be. Not only what *you* would like to be, but what you would like another to be, for they're the same. The whole vast world then becomes yourself pushed out. There's nothing but God, and God is your own wonderful human Imagination. That's God; there is no other God. When you believe that, then you are completely free and there is no curtain. It's all light ___(??). And this is hidden from all the wise men of the world.

May I tell you, we will reach...tonight we are going to the moon, and circle the moon, and we sent back these lovely pictures. We will know more about the moon on this secular level than we possibly ever knew before. That's not enough; we will land on the moon. We'll land on the moon and do all kinds of fantastic things long, long before we know the mystery of Bethlehem, oh, long before, because he's going to hide that mystery from the wise and prudent. Oh yes, they'll show me how to get to the moon...[interruption, noisy feedback, loss of some words].

So here, when the yoke is offered...unlike what the world thinks the yoke to be, and it is, it's true, you put this wooden frame over the necks of oxen. I was born in the environment where such things exist and still do, where you put it over oxen and you plow the field. But this yoke is a coupling, it's a pair, and there must be two. For if he offered me his yoke—I look around, there's no one that he ___(??) offered me that I can see—therefore, he has to be yoked with me. And so, Christ is yoked with me if I completely accept it to the point of absorption. To give lip service to his words, it means nothing.

I was so surprised the other day when I heard a minister of one of our most prominent churches in this city, one of the most prominent. I will not mention it, because it will be embarrassing. Most of them write their sermons out and just read it as you read from a book. He not only does not write his sermons, he subscribes to these sermons. They come from the East. And he's not a good reader at that, so he mouths the whole thing as he reads it Sunday morning. And he's the minister to this very prominent church, right here in our city, where so many of the social and the so-called intellectual and the wealthy members of our community attend,...because they all come. And he is the honored person and here is a man who can't even write his own sermon. But if he wrote his own he'd have to read it anyway. He subscribes to a service that writes sermons for him. And when it comes, because he didn't write it, he knows nothing of what is there. And he's not a good reader so he can't read it very well. So he mouths the thing Sunday after Sunday when he's allowed to take the pulpit...and he's the head of the church. People go and he puts his hand on them, they think they're blessed. He touches the head of the child and the child is told by the parent, "The great holy person touched you, my dear, you're blessed." What nonsense! Nothing is absorbed. Not one thing is absorbed. He is like the handkerchief with the marble in it, not a thing absorbed. What a revelation!

You who may not have been here when I told the story, some came a bit late, and she sat up in bed, and it's her custom to carry a pad and pencil to bed with her, put it on the night table, and she wrote out, "Like a handkerchief you absorb the truth, rather than accept it." So she spoke to the one who had dictated this to her, she said, "I do not know what you mean...nor do I remember what we were talking about." Then she fell asleep and dreamed that she had in her hand a handkerchief and her nose was filled with mucous. She put it to her nose and she blew. As she looked at the handkerchief it had absorbed all the moisture. Then she found another handkerchief. It was dry and clean and folded. She opened it. As she opened it a marble was dropped into it. It accepted the marble but couldn't absorb it. And then the voice said to her, "This is the will of God."

So I ask you this night not to accept what I have told you as a marble dropping into your mind, which would be like the handkerchief, but ponder it, dwell upon it and then try to absorb it so that it becomes one with you and you live according to it. So every moment of time you realize it is not what I simply sit down to imagine that comes to pass, as a friend of mine, who is here tonight, told the story two weeks ago, that the unintentional imaginal acts are just as effective. If imagining creates reality, it can't deliberately ___(??) the conscious deliberate imaginal act, but *every* imaginal act is as effective as a deliberate conscious imaginal act. You and I are called upon to become more alert, more aware, more discriminating, more selective in the imaginal acts that we would entertain. But whether we are or not, the unintentional imaginal acts are just as effective in producing results as the intentional imaginal acts. So, when I say imagining creates reality, I mean it literally. So you can repeat "imagining creates reality" and walk, saying "He's no good, she's no good, and I don't care for them" and do all these things, and people say, now that doesn't matter, because I didn't sit down to imagine deliberately. These are just as effective as the moment that you employ when you think that you are in meditation and doing something deliberately, yes, they will work, but all the other imaginal acts they are just as effective.

So when I say take my yoke upon you and learn from me, I am telling you what I know from experience. I will take you night after night into deeper and deeper and deeper levels. When I tell you that the entire story of scripture has unfolded in me, I mean that literally. That my divine heavenly inheritance, this glorious inheritance is mine, I know, but it cannot become *actual* as long as I still remain in this body. It is mine and I know it and share in it; but while I remain in this body I use it not only for this purpose, to teach you and offer you the yoke that is my yoke, but night after night I find myself in other levels, levels that are called in scripture "he goes into hell." They know who you are. No one hurts you; they can't hurt you. They know exactly who you are and all the ___(??) forces in the world, and you still teach the story of God. You'll find everyone quoting that level, but you still plant the seed. You still teach it, you still tell it, because you know that you are completely impervious to any blow, any hurt that they would intend.

You're perfectly conscious as I am now. I work night after night. Go into all these levels, all within myself, for I have infinite levels within myself. I walk into these levels and these strange characters will come, and they know exactly who I am. But in that level you don't care as far as they're concerned. But they can't hurt you and they don't frighten you. Not here they don't frighten you and they are completely harmless to you, although they are vicious in the extreme. But you walk through and you are simply telling the story of God. Strangely enough, you went to bed at one in the morning and think the time hasn't passed because you're so conscious, and then the sun is up and it's six and here you've been five hours in the worlds talking and telling the story. You think you've been completely awake, and you have been awake, but anyone who would hear your body would have heard the deep breathing. But you are not unconscious. And you wonder, well, I must have remained awake completely. It was one o'clock and here it is six, and in five hours I've been awake? No, you've been sound asleep physically. You're refreshed when you get up, but you haven't had any break in consciousness. There you are in the deep. And you go through the strangest characters in the world and you go through just simply telling them the word of God, offering the same yoke, quite willing to yoke yourself to these aspects of yourself because every one must be redeemed. "Nothing is lost in all my holy mountain" and every one is salvaged in the end.

So here, you take it this night, and learn the lesson from that lovely short letter, the difference between saying "I believe that" and absorbing it. Like the handkerchief, you absorb the truth, rather than accepting it. Paul was so fond of using the body as an analogy. Well, the body can be used...and I put food in my stomach and I assimilate what I can build into my tissues, into my bones, into my blood; what I can't, I expel. So you hear the word of God and you take it in and the body makes some food; and then you ponder it, you dwell upon it, and you try to absorb as much as you can. Alright, you take it again, you take it again, and finally the whole Word becomes you. And the Word begins to unfold within you and every little aspect of it unfolds within you.

So I tell you, everyone here, everyone in the world, but I think you, because you know more, you can be this night what you want to be. Regardless of your limitations, seeming limitations, based upon your educational, social, financial or other backgrounds, there is no limit save the limit we place on ourselves. You either believe that "I am he" or you don't. I say that advisedly, because I go back now twenty-odd years into New York City, and there's a large crowd in this country—possibly it's become now almost international— they will get up and affirm, I am...this, that and the other. Well, this lady used to come home, and my mother, er, my mother-in-law, pardon me, my sweetheart, she'd have a fit calling her my mother—but she would say, "You know, you must stop her coming here. I can't take it any longer." I said, "Alright, I'll tell her not to come. But she must still come. I'm drawing her. For some reason or other she's coming, so I've got to accept her. I can't turn her away." She would come and she was willing to pay any price in the world. I didn't charge anything, but she was quite willing to put down a hundred dollars, a thousand dollars. She had money, lots of money. But she couldn't do what she thought she could do at home. She'd come and she'd say, "Neville, close the door. Close the door, close the windows." She could do now what she couldn't do in her own hotel room, what she's now about to do. And she would stand in my living room and affirm, hold her hands down, and affirm, "I am" and she'd name it. Didn't believe one word of it, not one word!

When we were leaving for California for three months, I invited a friend of mine to take my home, rent free. She was an elderly lady...I said, "Move in and take my place and in an emergency my neighbors will come twice a week to clean while I'm gone, and the whole thing is yours, and it's rent free. Use the phone, I won't cut it off, and if you go beyond the normal, you can pay it. The lights and the gas, all these normal things, I will pay. Everything is yours. If you go beyond the normal use of the phone, well then, pay that. Outside of that, pay nothing." So she moved in. And this lady, affirming all these things, she came one day, about a week before we left, and she gave me a grip. She said, "I have my papers, all my stocks and bonds, and my..." oh, she mentioned all kinds of things in her Will. I said, "Why should I keep it here, I'm going away?" She was afraid to leave it in her room in the hotel, so I put it in the closet and told her where it was. I begged her to take it out before I left, telling her that my friend was a sweet, dear, elderly lady, who was coming to live there, and I didn't want her responsible for this little grip. Well, she didn't come, and we went on to California for three months. In the interval she came, my friend answered the door, and here was the lady at the door. She came for the grip. I had told my friend about this little thing. She said, "Well, please come and get it, because Neville told me not to touch it." ___(??). She wouldn't come into the place. She could have taken my little friend and torn her in two she was so strong, but she was afraid. Then my friend said, "Alright, if you will trust me I'll bring it just this way and put it in the door." "Bring it." She was afraid if she came in and went to get it out of the closet—it's a big walk-in closet—that my sweet little old lady, my friend, would close the door on her. And here, she's affirming, "I am strength, I am ___(??), I am power," quoting all these things. And all she had was a marble. There was no absorption whatsoever of all these so-called declarations.

So stop all this affirmation orally and simply ponder it. Am I really he? Am I *really* the presence that created the universe? Did he really yoke himself to me? Did he become me? Are we yoked? Are we eventually destined to be one? And just dwell upon it. Then test it. Test it and test it and test it by assuming that you are what at the moment reason denies...dare to believe it and walk in that assumption just as though it were true. And when it becomes true in a way you could never devise, then you begin to suspect that it *is* true. And then more and more you absorb the truth.

Now let us to into the Silence.

*   *   *

Q: (inaudible)

A: ___(??) and you went through every conceivable obstacle. They were
    obstacles. And you were both under a top ___(??) where all the boys and
    men would sit at the other end leaving you practically no room. You
    could almost stifle going through. You could lift the thing and speed
    yourself through and creep on your belly like a snake to get to the other
    end. When you came out, you went through a barrel. There was a barrel,
    a very narrow barrel. You had to go through it to pull yourself together
    to the second stage.

    Then you would climb a pole, and the pole often they would grease it.
    Then you'd climb the pole and take from the top when you had climbed
    it whatever they placed there, like a little flag. Then you drop down to
    earth, and all these things, after all these things you're exhausted, being
    able to run the remaining distance, to try to make seventy-five to 100
    yards. And you were simply completely done-in by the time you got to the
    end, because it was tremendous work moving through the obstacles. This
    was an obstacle race. Who conceived it I don't know. But, I mean, that is
    what we did as children. But when you're a child it's fun, and you think it's
    fun though your parents are bewildered because they're on the other side
    of this madness. Because, boys are boys, and they'd just a soon squeeze
    you inside if you were there, by pulling it tighter and tighter and try to
    make you...you try to get through. They aren't going to give one inch.
    They'll get off and pull it in to hold you down, because they don't see the
    consequences. They think of fun. And so, you went through these things.

    So when I told that story she must have been present. For we did all
    these crazy things when we were children. My mother said, "Why we
    were not all killed, I don't know." Because what to do with nine boys?
    She couldn't find us all at the same time and we played these crazy, crazy
    games. We'd go off...and no boy thinks when you're a child...you would
    go a way out to sea, but you didn't swim out you went out in a little,
    tiny boat. Then you started playing around the sunken ships—we had
    sunken ships in the harbor and fish all around—and the little boat goes
    back. You've played and you're exhausted and there's no boat to take you
    back, so you've got to swim back. So why you wouldn't drown, I don't
    know. And how could you dive from the top of these masts, I really don't
    know. I wouldn't do it today. But I can see a ship now. It came in and it
    floundered, a four-masted ship ___(??). The ship itself was as tall as this
    building, went down, and then we would climb the mast. And how do

you dive from that height and not break your neck, I don't know, but we did it. And all the fish and they're all swimming, sharks too...never occurred to us that they would really attack. We only read about that when we came in. And so, this is what we did as boys. Boys will do it all over the world, the same boys, haven't changed, you'll never change them. They have to grow up to realize these things *could* be dangerous, but they don't know it. If you don't know it, well then, it doesn't exist.

One morning, I went way out on a Sunday morning. I shouldn't have done it but I went out and these two friends of mine and we went way out to catch...to bring up a pot, a fish pot. We used to take these huge big pots and then sink them; and then mark them against objects that were stationary on the island. You'd always take a V-shape. Here is a plant that is stationary, like a coconut tree and beyond it another tree, that's a straight line and here a house and a tree then you've got the two and here at the apex you'd drop the pot. The pot went a way down, fathoms down, and you had to mark it with a broken plate or something so you could see it if the water was clear. But not every day the water was clear, so we'd fish for it. You'd put yourself within the area of this apex, then you'd fish for the pot, with this three-pronged thing you'd go down and find these fish, pot fish.

Well, this morning we go for a pot, another pot, another pot, and there are three of us. One fellow wouldn't so anything. He was the biggest of the three, so the two of us said to each other, let's put him over. He wouldn't do any thing, so we got ___(??), reset the pot, put all the moss and the dead fish back into it, and reset it. Then because he was still lazy, do nothing except sleep, we just simply got on one side of the boat, and then together we ___(??), and then we jumped. All of a sudden he went over and when he came up, his nose was simply like a whale blowing. He could have drowned. But he couldn't beat the two of us. He could beat one of us but not two, and we knew it. He went all the way down and we had to fish him out, because he wasn't working, a lazy ___(??). So when he came up, he had to get in himself. And if one of us had been present, he would have really murdered us, but he couldn't do it with two. And so, we brought him back and it's been a joke ever since. Now they're both gone from this world. Both were named Joe.

Q: Do you think that God and ___(??) have a running battle for consciousness?
A: Why certainly. These are demons...these great visions of the great masters. When you read any inspired poetry like Daniel, Blake, and some of the

horrors that Blake has said it's all based upon fact. But when you are awake and you walk into these worlds the worlds are real, they're horrible, but really horrible. But it's all part of the unfolding picture of one being, one God. But when you walk into it *after* you're awake you're unafraid, doesn't matter. And strangely enough, they will call you, Son of Man.

Q: (inaudible)

A: ___(??), and they're always here, and they will speak to you, as you're told in scripture, "Son of David, what have I to do with thee?" They recognize who you are, for they see what other eyes cannot see. You're now wearing the human form divine. It's impervious because they can't hurt you, and they know it. But they ___(??), for all must be redeemed. Every thing in this world must be redeemed. Nothing can be lost, "Not one in all my holy mountain." God can't have one little atom of his being lost. Everything must be redeemed, and because it must be, it will be.

Thank you.

THE RETURN OF JESUS

11/15/66

It may seem insane, but I tell you it is true! I'm speaking this night, as always, from experience, I'm not speculating. So in the beginning it is stated the truest return of Jesus is when the story of Jesus is recreated in you. Everything said of Jesus in the gospels *you* experience.

We are told in Acts, "Men of Galilee, why stand gazing into heaven? This Jesus, who was taken up from you into heaven, will come in the same way as he went up into heaven" (1:11). This is a bold statement, and the world will think they are looking into heaven for him to come. If I left the platform now and walked through the door and I told you will return in the same manner I departed, wouldn't you expect me to come from that door back into here? I didn't go that way. I didn't come from that door into here when I left the room. When I left the room, I left it from here.

Well now, let me show you a story and I know it from experience. The characters of scripture are the eternal states of the soul; they are not persons as you and I are. When I think of Abraham, Isaac, Jacob and Moses these are the eternal states through which the immortal soul passes; from a state of innocence to the state of being God and the passage is through experience. This world is the world of experience, a world of educative darkness. And we leave a state called Eden, of complete innocence, and we enter the state of experience, move through it, and awake a completely awakened Imagination where all things are subject to our creative power. *There* we are God himself.

In the beginning, we are told, when man in the state of innocence was addressed by a serpent, and the serpent said to the woman, "Did God say you should not eat of the fruit of the garden?" and she answered and said "No. God said we may eat of the fruit of the garden, but not the fruit of the tree in the midst of the garden. We should neither eat it nor touch it lest we die." The serpent said, "God said you would die?" She replied yes. Then the serpent said, "God knows that you will not surely die, but your eyes will be opened and you will become as the gods knowing good and evil" (Gen. 3:1-6 KJV). And it seemed good to her to taste of that that would make her wise…it seemed so good to become wise and so she ate and shared it with the man. Then we are told they were expelled, and told to bring forth everything in pain.

Now, this seems like a myth, doesn't it? The world treats it as such. But now let me give you my visions of this beginning. I said they were eternal states, and man starts in the state called Abraham "the friend of God." When you meet Abraham you see faith, just infinite faith. This is a state as I came upon it. There was an oak tree, the trunk was about seven feet, and the branches, not a leaf on them, that resembled the human brain, all gnarled and curled, just like the convolutions of the human brain. Standing against the trunk of the tree was a giant of a man, six foot six. I didn't have to ask, "Who are you?" It is so obvious to you when you come upon these states who they represent. They are only representations of states, but they are all personified because God is man; and every attribute of God is personified, so you see man. I knew exactly who he was. He is looking into the distance, for there is distance in his eyes, not just of space but of time. He is seeing the distance in time…that's all that concerns him.

Coiled around the trunk of the tree is a serpent with a human face. When you see that face, you have never seen anything before so wise. You see in that face not only the wisdom of the moment, of the past, of the future…it knows everything. It doesn't look at Abraham; it has just whispered into the ear of Abraham. Abraham is hearing what is said and he is seeing its fulfillment in time. But the serpent looks at *you* who entered that state. In my case it was the return to the beginning, for I have returned now to the state that I entered in my innocence. So, at the end of the road you return and see where you really started the journey. He is looking at me, not a word is said, but, oh, what an expression! You can't describe wisdom…that there is nothing unknown to this face, and yet it is a serpent coiled around the tree trunk with a human head, resting on the trunk but looking over the head of Abraham.

Alright, how do you think the word serpent is defined in Hebrew and Greek? The word is "to whisper; to prognosticate, i.e., to tell future events by indication, signs, by omens; to learn by experience"…Hebraic. Greek, "to gaze with wide open eyes as at something remarkable in contrast to the ordinary, mechanical, passive observation of facts." You are looking in innocence at the complete transformation of man into God. The story is being told you. What story? Told in the 3rd chapter of Galatians, "And God preached the gospel beforehand to Abraham" (verse 8). *Beforehand* the entire gospel was told *you*… that's the distance in his eyes. Here, he's looking in the distance and seeing the complete transformation of man into God. Who is the one who told him? We're told God told him. I saw the serpent...well, Christ is called in scripture "the wisdom and power of God" (1Cor.1:24). So, is not the serpent called God's wisest God himself?

Now we go to the Book of Proverbs, chapter 8: "The Lord possessed me at the beginning of his way, the very first, before the creation was." Here is God and God's wisdom personified. The Revised Standard Version says, "God created me" but that's not the word; it's not "bara." The first verse of Genesis is "bara," which is "created"—"In the beginning God created the heavens and earth." It is not that word at all. It is "to own, to possess"..."qanah." There never was a time that I as wisdom was not. Here, God possessed me in the beginning before he brought forth the universe. Now we're told, "I stood beside him like a little child." Before he brought forth anything, I was just like a little child beside him, delighting before him always, rejoicing in the affairs of men. Now he invites all to listen to him, "Listen to me, my sons, learn from me: he who finds me, finds life; he who misses me, injures himself; he who hates me, loves death" (verse 36)...all who are in love with the world...this is the world of death. They want to leave their name behind them, want to pile up fortunes, be better known...everything is such a struggle and everything dies...they are in love with death. So when you bring this message, they want no part of it. If in your search you miss me, you injure yourself. If you find me, you find life and receive favor from God. Then life begins to stir within you, and you are not an animated being anymore, you are a life-giving Spirit.

Here, we have the return of Jesus. How will he? First of all, he is called the great serpent and he whispers into my ear "disobedience." *He* caused me to disobey the command of God and to eat of the tree of the knowledge of good and evil that I may have my eyes opened and become *as God*...one with God (Gen. 3:5 RSV). The same word Elohim, the same word used in the very first verse: "In the beginning *God*...before the heavens and earth"—that word is Elohim. Well, "Did *God* tell you..."—that's Elohim. "God knows you will not surely die"—that's Elohim. "And *God* knows you will become as the gods"— that's Elohim. You become as he is; that is the story. Who told me? Wisdom told me and wisdom was one with God before he created the universe, so God told me. Do I have any statement in scripture to support this? Yes, the 11th chapter of Romans: "And God consigned all men to disobedience, that he may have mercy upon all" (verse 32). So who then is God? He consigned me to disobedience by whispering in my ear to disobey his order. I would have my eyes opened and become as he, knowing good and evil.

Any other passage to support it? Yes, when he comes to the world, he calls himself—and the words are only found upon his lips—calls himself by the title "Son of man." Others call him by other names, but no one calls him Son

of man. He refers to himself constantly as Son of man. He identifies himself
as the serpent: "As Moses lifted up the serpent in the wilderness so must the
Son of man be lifted up" (John 3:14). That's exactly how it's done—lifted as
a serpent...no other way for me to enter heaven. Who then fell? He says "No
one ascends but he who first descended" (John 3:13). Well, if the Son of man
ascends as a serpent, then the serpent must have descended.

Have you ever seen the spermatozoa under a microscope? If you have ever
seen a serpent...look upon it. I don't need a microscope, I can see it right now.
They are unnumbered...as you are told in scripture, "More numerous than
the stars of heaven, than the sands of the sea." You can see them all the time.
When the eye is open, you can always see them...this wonderful, brilliant
diamond-head, just like a diamond, and a long spinal column trailing behind
them. You see them actually in motion—a long spinal column, every little
segment, bone, and the top is a luminous, brilliant diamond in triangular
shape.

So God himself in the form of the tempter betrayed me into taking what
he told me not to take, that I would actually eat of it so that my eyes would
become opened; and through the world of experience—and it is a horrible
experience—I would then awaken as God. So who descended?—God, in the
form of a serpent. When he ascends, he ascends just like a serpent, and yet
it is your own wonderful human identity, no change in your own wonderful
I-am-ness. Same being, same identity...only you include a far greater self and
that self is God the Father.

So the return of Jesus in the truest sense is when the return of Jesus Christ
is *recreated* in you, and everything said of him you will experience. You are the
star in the entire drama and everyone has it. You begin with resurrection—it
comes suddenly out of nowhere—and you find yourself waking and waking.
Where you entered in the beginning, there you find yourself waking, and you
wake from this profound sleep, something you've never experienced before. It's
been a long dream. "As you are told, "In the beginning...having heard it...a
profound sleep fell upon Abram, a dread sleep, a horrible dream possessed
him." He was told, "All of your descendants will go into a land that is not
theirs and they will be enslaved for 400 years. Then they will come out with
signs and wonders and great possessions" (Gen. 15:12). Possessions beyond the
wildest dreams of man will be theirs. Things?—no, but the *power*, the creative
power to create things, to create anything in the world. I don't need a thing
if I have the creative power to create what I want. What then do I need with
things? Give me the creative power to create what I want and you have given
me the greatest gift in the world. You will come out with signs and wonders
into an inheritance that transcends anything known to man. If you give me
the earth and then it could be rubbed out, but you give me not the earth,

rather the power to create the earth, and never took from me that power, then you can rub it out as often as you like and I will recreate it. Give me the power to create and make things! For I have the power to create things.

So here, who is actually the Christ returning? He can't return; he is *in you*. So he is telling you in the story, when I come again I will come as I left you… in the same way that I was lifted up from you; in that same way I will come again. Well, he is lifted up this way [gestures an upward spiral motion]… that's how he comes. He doesn't come down this way [gestures a downward motion]…he's already down…I'm already crucified with Christ. But now, I am ready for the resurrection with Christ. Everyone has been crucified with Christ or you wouldn't be here. "I am crucified with Christ, nevertheless Christ lives *in* me"—so we're told in Paul's letter to the Galatians—"Henceforth I see no one from the human point of view; even though I once regarded Christ from a human point of view, I regard him thus no longer" (2Cor.5:16). This is something entirely different, a purely supernatural experience. When you move up, you move right into heaven, and you move up in the same manner that Christ was lifted up. So why look into the so-called heavens? "O men of Galilee, why stand gazing into the heavens? Jesus who was lifted up from you will come in the same way that he was taken up"…the same manner. That's how he went up as told in the 3rd of John: "Just as Moses lifted up the serpent in the wilderness on the rod, so must the Son of man be lifted up." So when Jesus comes again, he comes *in* you. And like the story in the Bible, no one will believe it…I say no one, I mean others will not believe it. You will tell your story and it will seem like an idle tale, and they will not believe it. But may I tell you from experience, every word recorded in scripture that is said that Jesus says you are going to say, even those that are repeated by seeming others. You will live long enough to hear them come back as echoes by others.

Let me give you this story. My friend and publisher, Grace, two years ago she wasn't feeling well—this is after he had returned in me, it couldn't have happened before, for these are the words of the risen Christ—she sat at home looking at a travelogue on TV and dozed for a few moments. As she returned to this level she said audibly, "I must remember what Neville said." Her husband Jack asked, "What did Neville say?" "I am with you always to the end of the age." Well, these are the words of the risen Christ. Anyone in whom he rises will repeat these words, and in scripture they are said to those who *believe*. He first appears to women, as he appears in this world. It is the women first…three of them who will come forward bearing witness, using the words of scripture and putting them into your mouth as he rises in you.

Now another letter came this week: "A year ago last October, I found myself in a crowd at the base of an enormous mountain. There was no pathway up the mountain, yet we all desired to climb it. I knew that if I climbed that mountain I would find the Father. I began to dig a little pathway, started making steps to climb on a very difficult road, not a straight road it was winding peculiarly up the mountain. When I got to the top I thought I should find the Father. Surely the Father should be here waiting for me, but there was no one. I was on the very top of what I had built. I thought I could rest here awhile or wait awhile, for I knew the Father would come. Suddenly the entire mountain disappeared, and all the people down below who could not find the pathway disappeared. Only my crooked pathway winding up to the top remained and myself. I realized I had been building blocks, one square and one a triangle, a square and a triangle up to the top, and the top on which I rested was a triangle. Then the voice said to me, 'Be.' All I heard was just 'Be.' And I woke crying and couldn't restrain the tears, yet there was no emotion concerning the climb, just tears.

"Many months later, in March of 1966, I heard the same voice. I went to bed saying, "I and the Father are one." I fell asleep and the voice said, "I am the Father." Again I awoke crying, tears poured out like a flood, and again no emotion to prompt the tears. Then, months later, I heard the voice, last September, say: 'Do you not know that you are a priestess after the order of Melchizadek? Act like it!' Then I woke and I don't understand it." Well, scripture only mentions the name in the 14th of Genesis, the 110th Psalm and Hebrews. Melchizedek, as told in scripture, is the only one to whom Abraham submitted himself, the one to whom Abraham gave tithes. You are told, "Tithe with the Lord." Well, he tithed only with Melchizedek; that is the Lord, the king of righteousness and king of peace. That's what Melchizedek means. Jesus is called a priest after the order of Melchizedek, a priest forever. Abraham, in coming into the presence of Melchizedek, it is stated Melchizedek has no origin, no father, or mother, no beginning of days, no end of days, no genealogy, he is forever. Who could he be but God! Here is a prototype of the priest spoken of when Christ comes into the world, unfolding himself *in* man.

I tell her, if she's here tonight, whether it be priest or priestess it is the same thing. As you very sweetly said, in searching the scriptures there is only the 28th verse of 3rd Galatians that throws any light on it for her. That's right. But go back and read the 27th verse: "And you were baptized into Christ, have put on Christ...and there is no bond or free, no Greek or Jew, no male or female in Christ." All are one in that body. When you are incorporated in that body, whether you are male or female, you are the priest—call it priestess if you want—after the order of Melchizedek. You have your beginning there because he has no beginning. He was in the beginning with God, God's possession—didn't create him as the Revised Standard Version mistranslates the word. It is not "created." Here, I am one with God in the beginning: I am his creative power. He buries his creative power in the limitation called man, and then lifts it up, transcending what it was before. It is an *ever*-expanding creative power that is Christ, the wisdom of God and the power of God.

So I say to you, you are it. But the voice told you, "Act like it!" If you act like it, you start to create. How do you create? Out of nothing...you ask self what you want and then *assume* that you have it. The world denies that you have it. Alright, assume that you have it thereby creating out of nothing. Don't get little pieces around and try to remold them; create out of nothing. What is it that you really desire in the world? You say to find the Father and to know you are the Father? You will never know you are the Father unless his Son reveals him to you. The Son [David] tells you who you are when he calls you Father; and you know exactly who he is for he is the only begotten Son of God. If he calls you Father, well then, you are the Father. So you are seeking the Father and you are now being told *you are* the Father...priestess of the order of Melchizedek. And then the voice says, "Act like it." Well, act like it. Assume that you have found the only being in the world who can reveal you as the Father; for if you are the order of Melchizedek, you *are* the Father. But you aren't acting like it, because it hasn't actually happened, that the Son came into your world. Begin now to act like it.

Then she said, "In July, I was fully awake, not a dream. I sat down to rest after dinner and thought of you. I knew when you left here in March on the way to Barbados, and that you said you wouldn't return 'til the fall of the year. So I took it for granted you were still in Barbados and wondered how you were. Suddenly you are standing before me. You seemed in excellent health, dressed in a grey business suit. You stood for a moment and then said to me, 'There is no time' and vanished." Well, there is no time save in the secular world. Time has a stop when resurrection takes place. It does...it belongs only in the secular world where things appear, they wax, wane and vanish, to reappear, wax, wane and vanish, and the cycle goes on and on in the secular world. But there is no time. In the Lord and with the Lord, a day is as a thousand years, and a thousand years is as a day. Really, there is no time after the resurrection. But you are told you will enter this state and be enslaved for 400 years. 400 years is not as we would measure time; 400 is the numerical value of the last letter of the Hebrew alphabet which is Tau, whose symbol is that of a cross. As long as I wear this cross I am now in the journey of 400 years. I am a slave while I wear this cross, a slave to the passions of this body—whether it be for a cigarette where I will do anything to get one if I smoke. If it is for a drink and I'd give anything to buy one, steal to buy one. I have ambition to be great, to be known, and I'd do anything...sell my mother toward that ambition. And I'm a slave to all the passions of this cross, the passions of the flesh. So, as long as I wear this cross I am a slave, with all the weaknesses of the human flesh, all the limitations of the flesh.

But when I take off the cross and all that he foretold me has come to pass in me—for he whispered the future into my ear, like Abraham—because I am now one with him. We all saw exactly what was going to happen, for everyone is a descendant of Abraham, not after the flesh…for he is not a being of flesh but after the Spirit, and all men of faith are children of Abraham. So I saw exactly what he spoke into my ear, "I heard of thee with the hearing of the ear but now my eye *sees* thee," and now I experience everything that was foretold (Job 42:5). He foretold everything and gave me the sign by which I would know when they are accomplished. The first is that I should be raised from the dead. That seems a crazy thing, and the world thinks you come out of little graveyards. No graveyards. You weren't put in a graveyard. No person in this world ever went into a graveyard. That's big business. If you bought the stock when it first started, you'd be a millionaire today. But not one person was ever taken to that place…just the little skin it wore.

Well now, who is the one that said, "You will not surely die?"—the serpent. How does the serpent grow? It grows and out grows by shedding its skin. Does it die? No, simply sheds its skin and finds itself clothed in a new skin. It grows and outgrows. You can't grow and not outgrow. So man goes through the gate called death, and he has merely outgrown that part. He is re-clothed instantly, like the serpent, in an entirely different skin but the same serpent. And he keeps on growing and outgrowing 'til the very end when he ascends vertically. Instead of moving horizontally as a serpent does on the land, he moves up the tree of life. Then man completely awakes from the dream of life.

So the return of Jesus is when the story of Jesus is recreated in us and then we know who we are and can truly say, "I and my Father are one"; for he said, "I am the Father." Well, then I and my Father are one, for I became the Father. You know exactly who you are and everything said of him, the words recorded of him will be in your mouth and someone will hear it. Whether they write you or tell you about it, know that when the whole thing starts, beginning with the resurrection, somewhere in this world you have appeared to someone who is distressed and you have said, "Be not afraid. I am with you always, to the very end of the age." Where else could you go? If "all that you behold, tho' it appears without, it is within," then where could anyone you know including the speaker go? Where could he go?

So the whole of you begins to resurrect. But, you the central being, you must resurrect. And when you do, you find all of these, the brothers, called the Elohim—a plural word, translated both in singular and plural, a compound unity of one made up of others. So it takes all of these to form the one called

in scripture the Lord. We are called the Elohim. The Elohim rises in man and
then becomes one with the risen body...there's only one. So when I said in *He
Breaks the Shell* I meant every word of it from experience, that we are gathered
one by one to unite into a single body who is God. I meant that literally! God
is man—not just an impersonal force, an over- or under-soul, the unconscious
or subjective, forget it. When you see the risen Christ, you see man, infinite
love, that's what you see...nothing but love. But every attribute of God is
personified. When you see faith personified, you see Abraham, a state. You
enter the state called Abraham and start your journey through darkness, but
it is from darkness to light, for he "is the light of the world" (John 8:12). Well,
you pass through the darkness of sin and death. Everyone does.

I am convinced from your dreams and visions and letters that those who
are here are on the verge of waking...of that I am convinced. I wouldn't fool
you. There is no reason to fool anyone. It is so easy to go out and feed the huge
multitude with the law and show them how to get more and more shadows
of the same thing as wealth, so easy. No problem, no gimmicks to it at all.
Don't try to know the better people, don't try to know the rich people, just
apply the law. If that's what you want, well, you can go across the country and
have enormous crowds by appealing to that, but that's not what I was sent
to tell. I was sent to tell you of the *last things*, all eschatology—the doctrine
of the last things. These things you will see, and when these things begin to
appear, know that the kingdom of God is at hand. When you see now...the
resurrection appears and someone describes it, remember he is describing it in
your presence, and you would not be in his presence to hear the description of
it, you couldn't be, were it not brushing off onto you. And all are beginning to
awaken, for we are all one, and not one person can be lost, not one in eternity,
for then the body of God would lack something.

So everyone is being gathered into the one body, and that body is God.
So we are told, "He who is united with the Lord becomes one spirit with
him" (1Cor.6:17). And you who are now baptized into Christ have put on
Christ, and therefore there is no Greek among you, no Jew. The word Greek
translated from the Hebrew is the same as gentile or heathen or nations, so all
the nations are brought into it. The same word goy...you hear me speak of the
goyim, "something strange, foreign, of another world," as against the Hebraic
concept of "the chosen." All are brought in; therefore, there is no Greek, no
Jew, no bond nor free, no male nor female, for in the resurrection we are above
the organization of sex. It only belongs in this dream world of a divided image
of male and female. In the resurrection there is none. Yet the creative power
transcends the wildest sex thrill on earth when you are united. If you think
on this level that that is a fantastic, exciting experience, and undoubtedly it
is when you see three and a half billion people in this world, and everything

in advertising is catering to sex—if you don't use this or you lose your teeth then you won't be loved by someone else—everything is catering to sex. So it is a terrific power, but it fades into nothing compared to the creative power when you are one with the body of God. Speak of an emotion! Well, you can't describe it in any terms known to man when you create from on high. So I must say, you must *not* bottle up this sphere; while you are in this world live it fully. The day will come when the energy will be reversed within you, and the serpent instead of crawling on his belly will turn up as he was in the beginning when he whispered in your ear. The word serpent means Jesus Christ. He is called the great serpent, for he is the wisdom of God. The wisest of all of God's creations is called the serpent. It was he who betrayed man into coming into the world of experience that man may awake as God. And it was God, as we are told in Romans, who consigned all men to disobedience that he may have mercy upon all (11:32).

So, to come back to that statement concerning the lady…well, in the 4th of Zechariah the shouts of joy went up when the last stone, called the headstone, was placed in place. Amidst shouts of "grace, grace" they placed the stone there. So you built it up in a serpentine form, a crooked way you call it. Well, that's the way. As the poet said, "Does the road wind uphill all the way? Yes, to the very end! Will the day's journey take the whole long day? From morn to night, my friend." You went all the way up to the very last, and it was the triangular stone. You are right…on that you stand. For when you see that, you see that it is the most brilliant diamond-head trailing the stones you left below, that's the spinal chord. The whole drama took place within you. All the mountains disappeared and the crowd below disappeared, for they couldn't find the pathway. "Only one way, only one truth: I am the truth, I am the way" (John 14:6).

If I say Jesus departed…truth never departs. It is man who forsakes the truth, therefore it is man who comes back to the truth. Truth can't depart, so "I am with you always, even to the end of the age" (Mat. 28:20). How can he go any place? It is man who forsakes, man who plays the harlot and goes in search of other gods. They will hear this from morning to night and then call you up and ask you about some medium who has just arrived in town and knows all the answers reading cards, tea leaves, etc. And they go in search of other gods.

The serpent is the only prophesier. He prophesies events to be, but tells you they will come after you see these signs which appear in you. He is the great prognosticator…the word means "to whisper; to prognosticate; to learn by experience." And when he whispers into your ear, your eyes open wide as though you are looking at something remarkable. Well, can you imagine looking at a worm—what man would look like if you saw the semen of a man, nothing more than a small serpent—and see it transformed into God? Suppose you would look off into the distance and see that transformation taking place. That which groveled through the 400 years, groveling on its belly, feeling like a slave, for that's what a slave does, gets down on its belly and spreads itself out before anything it thinks more important than itself. Everything is more important than itself. We don't get down and do it, but some say, "Who do you think I saw today lunching at the Brown Derby?" and they mention some nut, a "star." They are so impressed they saw something special. Well, that's how a slave acts. So you go home and play the part of a slave in the presence of your wife, or wife to husband, and they don't know they are flat on their belly and eating dust. The day will come and you will turn up and Christ will be lifted up in you. Then you will know who you are. Your eyes will be opened and you will be as the gods, one with God. That's what Abraham saw with his eyes wide open: a state of utter awe and complete wonder in his eye as he saw the transformation of the worm into God.

*　　　　*　　　　*

Q: Regarding John 17, who is the son of perdition (verse 12)?

A: The son of perdition is the belief in loss. Perditio is loss. Only the idea of loss will ever be lost; nothing else can be lost in all God's holy mountain. One day we will understand who Judas really is. The word Judas means "praise." Who could really betray me in this world but one who knows my secret? Who knows the secret of a man but the spirit of the man? No one knows the secret of God but God himself. So if I have a friend who knows enough about me to betray my identity, then he must be my very Spirit.

OCCUPANT OR INMATE

11/22/66

(This lecture was slightly abbreviated and originally typed by someone else. Tape?)

Tonight's subject is Occupant or Inmate. An occupant dwells in; one who establishes title to unknown property by dwelling in it. An inmate is confined, as in a prison or asylum. An occupant is free to come and go; chances are he doesn't really move and remains just where he is. The inmate feels he can't move, feels he's retrained by law. He doesn't know he's just as free as the occupant and vice versa. The occupant is free by our standards, the inmate is not free; but by this law both are free. Christ is what God means by man. If you know who Christ is, then Christ is what "man" means to God. "Christ in you is the hope of glory" (Col. 1:27); "Let us make man in our image" (Gen. 1:26); "Christ is the very image of the invisible God" (Col. 1:15). So I say, Christ is what God means by man. If you know who Christ is…I tell you he is your own wonderful human Imagination…then that is what you should mean by God. So, you tie God and man together. God is man and man is God. God is infinite man and man confined to his senses is finite God.

So tonight I am going to try to show the difference between the two and how both really are free, though they don't know it. In the beginning of John they asked him, "Where do you live?" He said, "Come and see, follow me" (1:38). Well, to follow him is to move, isn't it? If you said to me, "Where do you dwell?" and I said, "Come and see, follow me," and then I start and you follow me, aren't you moving from where you are to where I'm going to take you? So here we find *motion*. Come with me, I'll show you where I dwell. Where do we dwell? That state to which we constantly return constitutes our dwelling place. It is a state. For example, a lady called to say people don't like her where she

works. This same pattern has happened many times, one job after another…
she knows they don't like her. When I tell her, do you realize the whole vast
world is all Imagination? No, not for a moment can she grasp it. The world of
reality is the world of Imagination, and you imagine they are talking against
you and don't like you time after time? Then where are you dwelling?

Well, tonight I want to show you all how to move. Because if you move
from one state where you are into any state in this world, that state is waiting
for occupancy. And the great fallacy of the world is perpetual construction and
deferred occupancy. I don't occupy it. If I would only occupy the state I have
constructed in my mind's eye—wouldn't it be wonderful to be and name it in
my mind's eye. But then I say, "Oh, it couldn't be. I'm not born to it, I don't
have the social, educational, etc." So because I believe I can't, I remain in my
present state. Now listen to these words, "Do not think that I came to bring
peace upon the earth. I came not to bring peace, but a sword; to set a man
against his father and a daughter against her mother…and a man's enemies
will be those of his own household" (Mat.10:34). No other enemies! These
words are everlastingly true; you have no other enemies but those of your own
household…my physical wife, son, etc.? No, they aren't my household. My
household is all within my own wonderful human Imagination. These are my
intimates, and all my enemies are in my Imagination, personified in what I
think is this one or that one whether it be when I go to work and think they
are ganging up to get me out of this job though my record is good. I am my
only enemy, for the whole vast world is within myself. If it really is so, and all
the states are really waiting for occupancy, how do I move into another state?

(Neville repeats the dream in a letter from R. Crutcher regarding conflict.
Enemies were shooting at him from a hill covered by vines. Neville appears to
take him to the back of the house where the hill is *now* a field with men and
women gaily harvesting the wheat. To the side was a mountain of harvested
wheat. Neville says, "They are doing the same thing now they were doing a
year ago!" Crutcher sensed in this some little amnesia, for he didn't remember
they were doing this a year ago and he asked Neville, "How long have I been
here?" Neville replied, "Two years." Two is conflict. The division of two is
opposition; they must become one in agreement to have peace. Crutcher said,
"Did I learn anything?" Neville answered, "Yes, how to move and discipline."
How to move! The first statement in Genesis: "And the Lord God moved…"
and creation began. Without a motion there could be no creation. And God
moved and something happened…as the Spirit of the Lord God moved upon
the face of the deep. So how to move? A lady wrote, "The story of the harvest
meant so much to me." Her letter relates a dream. Upon going to bed, feeling
insecure after a long illness she alone caused, she assumed "I am secure, really
secure." "There was a little child and an elderly woman. The little child was

complaining that certain things were going to cost so much, $250,000. I told the little child, 'What does that mean? That's only a pittance against the multi-millions that you have!' Then I said to them, 'We will go into another place... we are going to move now." It was dark outside and the old lady was reluctant to go. I said to both, 'I have a light.' At that moment the wall where we were contained parted and beyond it in another room appeared this wonderful fireplace, all blazing. Then a few days later this dream occurred, I was in a field of wheat and it was all harvested, but there were a few stalks, and I saw the grain in the stalks, and I knew from what I saw they were matured beyond reaping. Then I saw a buffalo and as the buffalo appeared I wasn't afraid of it, I knew that he couldn't see me. Then another and another buffalo, making three altogether."

Now we are told not to harvest the whole thing, leave it. Don't muzzle the ox that plows the field. You are told, if you harvest the field, do not return to take the grapes you didn't bring in; leave it for the sojourner, the fatherless, the widow. If you have beaten the olive tree, do not beat it again...leave it for the sojourner, the fatherless, the widow. Don't harvest to the end. Leave it for those who will come, for remember always you were once a slave in Egypt.

Now three in scripture is representative of resurrection: "On the third day the earth rose up out of the deep." Eight is the perfect resurrection, but three is also significant of resurrection. And the buffalo, you can all it the ox, though it's not in the Bible, but it is also used in symbolism as "the long arm of the law" and it reaches and sees and knows everything...to what extent you are willing to leave behind you the stalks and let the buffalo feed upon it. Let the stranger who is coming by feed upon it, the fatherless, the widow feed upon it, don't take everything. My earthly father carried that story to such an extent he'd always leave a large portion on his plate, saying, "The servants have to eat too." He had to leave it for the sojourner.

But here in her dream, she brought it back, she didn't take the stalks, she left them for the fatherless, widow, sojourner, remembering "You were once a slave in Egypt." So I can say to her, you are having biblical dreams, and when these dreams begin to appear within you, you are near the unfolding of God within you. For Christ is what God means by man, and Christ is what man, if he knows him, means by God. So he is stirring within you. And I can't tell anyone when Christ begins to stir within him of this almost intolerable tension that takes place within us when the whole thing within us, called Imagination, begins to be stirred. What it means to man when it begins to be stirred! You can't pass the buck anymore. You are either with me or against me. He who is not with me is against me. And you go all out, burn all bridges and completely abandon yourself to a state. You either sink or swim. You move from one state into another.

Another letter came and this is really a lovely one to show you how to move. I told you a few years ago when I met Blake—but perhaps it didn't impress you, maybe he didn't quite move you, all these things are true—and he showed me how to move, how to see infinite man as one, the whole vast humanity gathered into one body that was man—and he showed me exactly how to do it, and I did it. And then I saw it…I saw man. I saw the heart of that man like a flaming ruby as I approached it. It wasn't just the heart, here was infinite humanity…all the nations of the world contained in that heart… and here is only one man. Well, he showed me how to see it.

The lady writes, "In my dream I came upon scene after scene, and every scene presented I revised, and before my eyes, the whole thing became what I had imagined, and I knew I was the cause of the change for it was changing as I saw it." So she remembered the principle of revision in her dream and so what she heard has become a part of her picture, whether it be waking or sleeping it is part of her feeling. Through the night she was doing it and when she woke she was filled with joy concerning what had happened in the night. Sitting down dwelling upon what she had done, she began communing with self, and suddenly self took over and said, "Move into the state of love." Then she felt the entire room receding, and "I felt myself falling backwards and down. As I feel this, I open my eyes and break it, returning. I regret I did that, but now I know how to move."

That's exactly what Blake told me. He said, "Let yourself go, Nev, fall backwards, just fall backwards and you will see what I have told you, the infinite man, one man, and you will see it contains the whole vast world of humanity. Now, let yourself fall." I turned backwards and fell, as though I'm taking a deep dive as I have done from a high-diving board, backwards. This time I am falling through interstellar space. I'm not just diving into a pool, I am falling backwards into interstellar space, and when I came to a rest and looked, here is a heavenly being in the distance, one man. Then on approaching him the heart was aflame like a ruby blazing. I came closer and closer, and here it isn't…it simply contains all humanity, all the nations, all races, every being in the world contained in the heart of one man. But I fell backwards.

So, how to move into any state from another? The story is fall backwards; let yourself go into another state—from one of not being wanted into one of being wanted. So when my friend said to me, "I have been here two years, but did I learn anything?" I said, "Yes, you learned how to move and discipline." Well, the man knows how to move. And I would not have told him that in the depths of his soul, or he wouldn't have conjured me in the depths of his soul, were it not true. For God speaks to man through the medium of dream. So I told him the conflict is over, that hill that shot at you is no longer an enemy. It is now a field, a harvest of golden wheat with all gaily harvesting…already a mountain of harvested wheat. Conflict is over because you have learned how to move." For the one I am speaking of now has had the three outstanding events: the birth of the child; the discovery of David; and the splitting of the temple of his body from top to bottom, and ascent of himself up into his skull like a serpent. He now only awaits the descent of the dove. So he is the one that I took at the door and led him to the back of the house. The back of the house is where Moses led the sheep. He was the great shepherd and led the sheep to the back of the mountain when he saw the mountain. So Crutcher saw this, and when he walked into the house, it wasn't what it was before, a simple drab thing but a palace.

So are we occupants or inmates? Am I an occupant? Then I should be able to move wherever I want to. But I usually go back to the same place night after night. But suppose tonight I desire to be other than what I am. Will I sleep as though I am what reason tells me I am, or will I sleep this night as though I am the man I would like to be? If I dare to fall into that state and sleep, and then carry it into dream so that it is the natural state, and then day after day that's where I dwell in consciousness, well then, the whole vast world must take on the atmosphere of that state, it must. There is no power in the world that can stop it! I don't have to ask anyone to help me. I simply fall into the state, but this time I do it knowingly, not unwittingly as we all do. So Blake could say, "I do not consider either the just or the wicked to be in a supreme state but to be every one of them states of the sleep the soul may fall into in its deadly dreams of good and evil" (*Vis. of Last Judg.*, Pp.91-92). He uses the word fall advisedly. Blake never used a word in some loose way. He'd give certain words enlarged meanings but never a word loosely. In his *Vision of the Last Judgment*, "that they may *fall* into it" and falling into it if you fall—he told me this when he told me to see the only man containing all the races, all nations, all as one man—then he said, "Fall *backwards*—not just fall, but backwards. This lady said the room began to disappear and she found herself falling backwards and down.

Now, everyone can do it. No one is less than the other! Christ in *you* is the hope of glory, not the Christ in that one or that one, Christ in all man. Let me repeat: Christ is what God means by man. "Let us make man..." Are we not told in Galatians we bring forth Christ. Then in Timothy, how he remains with us in labor until Christ be formed *in you*. Is he not forming his perfect image, and *that* is Christ? So he is saying, let us make man...who is Christ...Christ is man. And when man knows who Christ is, that's what he means when he speaks of God; for we are one. God became man that man may become God. We are not some little thing to be cast off, no, we're not. We can be anything in this world that we want to be if we know how to move from one state into another.

Here in this past week, the November 18 issue of *Time* magazine, a statement from the official press reporter for the Vatican. Now they are changing a radical thing that has taken place for 1100 years. This is official: The teachings of the Catholic Church must be considered as certain; and whenever they change it is only a change from one state of certainty to another state of certainty. Well, aren't you living in an Alice in Wonderland? For 1100 years ___(??) false to eat meat on Friday. May I tell you, truth cannot contradict itself! If it was not true then, it was never true. In 1st Corinthians, chapter 8, "Food will not commend you to God" (verse 8). You are no better if you eat or don't eat. Here it's a rule for 1100 years and now not expedient. When it was inaugurated 1100 years ago that doctrine was a certainty inspired by someone with whom possibly meat disagreed, but he spoke as though he had it from on high. Now the present one probably likes his meat on Friday so he's going to change it. The Mad Hatter said, "Words mean what I want them to mean." So he gives these meanings to words. But Truth can't contradict itself. If it was true then, it would always be true.

So Christ defines himself as the Truth. Christ is your own wonderful human Imagination, that's Christ, and with him all things are possible, all things. I don't care what the world will tell you there is no reason for a man to feel insecure if he knows who Christ is. You're only in a state when you feel insecure or secure, loved or unloved. These are only states that's all that they are; and the occupant is the same being and that being is Christ. He takes upon himself all these things. When one knows it, he wears the universal garment. He wears it when he knows exactly what he's doing. He's wearing the whole universe, just like a garment. But he has this individual choice to move from one state into the other and become the real occupant who can simply decide tonight I will not live here anymore and I'll go elsewhere. I will go into a state of affluence, a state of being known, a state of this or that, and he'll do it by just falling into it deliberately, not unwittingly. He'll *fall* right into it...actually clothe himself with that state. And that is Christ. There is nothing in this world but God...and God is man.

God is man, and then he makes the statement speaking of Christ, that's what God means by man; so he has made *you* in the image, and the image of God is Christ. Now the churches speak of Christ and make images of him. Does he look like you? Then that's not Christ. All kinds of images are made... and now they're suffering because some little thing was injured by the flood in Florence. I do love these lovely things that people have made, but do you think that little thing is Christ? Does it look like you when you look at it? Well, if anyone should ever say, look here or there he is, don't believe it. If he doesn't look just like you, you haven't seen him. When you see Christ, you are looking right at yourself...there is nothing but you. One day you will see who you really are, and you will not lose your identity, but you will see a face so beautiful, such majesty, such greatness, such strength, every noble characteristic in the world embodied in that face, and you know it is *your* face. Something you could never on this level ever hope to attain, yet there it is, and you know exactly who you are looking at. You are looking at yourself and you know it could only be Christ himself. You are going to see it. I tell you from my own experience exactly what you are going to see. Everything here on earth is but a caricature of the being that you really are.

While we are here on earth wearing these masks that hide us, we can apply this marvelous principle, not only for ourselves but for everyone. So like the lady who calls me all the time that they don't like her, when I hang up I still must do what she asks of me...to have them like her. "Lord, how long, how long?" "Seventy times seven," until you do it. That's all there is to it. Until you so put her into the state of being wanted and loved that she remains and occupies that state, you just keep on doing it. That's what I'm told. Never give up and turn and discard it as something hopeless. It is not hopeless...only if you give up. How long, my Lord, must I do it? If some brother sins against me, how often must I forgive him? "Seventy times seven." Four hundred and ninety times? No, until I actually do it, that's what he means. When I really succeed in putting him into the state where it is his dwelling place, he occupies it, and the world reflects it. He dwells in that state and the world sees him as that being and now he is happy in that state. Only then can you relax. He turned to you, didn't he? Well, if he turned to you, is there another in the world? There can't be another: God is one. So the one who turns to you, is it not yourself? Is it not yourself made visible? It is yourself extended, and *you* want that changed, all right, and you do it—if the phone rings forever—until that one occupies the state they desire.

Yes, we are human enough to say, oh, my Lord, when Lord, when will they remain in the state into which I have put them? So they get a job right after they have been fired, a marvelous job, and they all love me. You relax, and the phone rings a week later, "They're all talking about me." No matter what you say, "It is all in your Imagination," they go right back into it. All you can do is not to complain..."Lord, how often? Seventy times seven"...keep on doing it...it's good for you. You do it over and over and all of a sudden it jells, and then they remain in that state. It is yourself made visible and you can't discard any being in this world. It is not your Father's pleasure that one be lost, why?—because he's in everyone. Because he's in me, he can't lose me. Were he not in me and only in you, then he could discard me...but he can't because he dwells in me and you. Therefore, he can't discard any being in the world. But because he's one, then bear one another's burdens. And everyone who is asking for help, do it even if they can't see immediate results and it seems hopeless. There is *nothing* hopeless…it is only a state…everything is a state in this world. And when you see the state, you stand amazed. They are all human. Strangely enough every state I've ever seen is personified—hope, love, faith—all personified.

If I tell you this night…people speak of hell and heaven. If I told you that you and I are rooted in hell, and hell is the region of fear; we aspire to heaven and heaven is the realm of hope. Supposing I marry these two, synchronize them, they produce vision…simultaneous, same place at same time. Fear plus hope results in vision. Every child born in this world is rooted in fear, hell. That's where we fell and while here we aspire to heaven and we flower upon earth. While I walk the earth, the drama unfolds within me. I flower upon earth while I'm in this garment of death, flesh and blood, for it dies. It is here that I rooted in hell, aspiring to heaven, flower, and unfold the entire drama of God within me. Then the garment is taken off and the whole thing removed, and I am no longer here. I walk in the world knowing I'm here, yet I can say I am in the world but not of it. I can say to all, be of good cheer, I've overcome the world. In the world you have tribulation for you are rooted in fear, hell, the region of fear; but you aspire to heaven, you have hope that the dream of God that he'll make you into his image, you hope he will succeed. So you aspire to heaven, the realm of hope. While you are rooted in one, walking the earth aspiring to the other, you flower and it all unfolds within you. When fear and hope are blended, vision results…you will see.

So everything is states…the whole vast world. No one can brag…it doesn't matter who he is, wise or fool, so what, only states. If the wise man falls into the state…Emerson died as an insane person. So when he died he was not in the state of extreme wisdom, and they all said, how can a man so great fall into that state? They don't realize that when Imagination is stirred within man that enormous tensions take place in man. Sure he fell into a state of insanity, so what? He left behind him for us all the lovely things that he is. Only for a moment…when he went completely out in the last few days or months, so what does it matter? At sixty-two, I wouldn't care what my exit looked like. I wouldn't care and I wouldn't know anybody if I did. To those who loved me dearly I hope they'd understand what I'm talking about and not really care; and think what I said prior to the so-called fall into another state where I blow the brain that what I said was wrong. Because at one moment you get to the point of exploding, and the whole thing is simply getting so much within you, you can't stop it, and the body can't take it. You've reached the point of complete flower and you have flowered in the world, but no one sees it. They can't see the garment that I wear. What man looking at me knows the garment I wear? No mortal eye can see it, for I am wearing the garment of the risen Christ. I am one with Christ, and Christ is God. And there is nothing but God; there is nothing but Christ. When you are fused with that body, you are forever that body, yet you walk the earth until every little bud unfolds. And so you are rooted in hell, aspire to heaven and flower upon earth. Every little bud must unfold within you. What does it matter when the one unfolds what happens to the garment?

So tonight learn how to move. Move from one state into another state. And it takes no time, just the willingness to let go completely. You cannot serve two masters; you either believe me or you don't. He who is with me then he is not against me. He said, you are either with me or against me. And so burn your bridges and completely abandon yourself to a state. It seems mad, doesn't it? Sleep this night as though you were exactly the person you want to be. I have seen David...reason tells you it cannot be? Reason can't answer these things at all. It is not a thing reason can answer at all concerning this wonderful story of Christ. It can't. You go to the very depths in science and what do you meet? You confront mystery. They thought they were going to find and weigh and measure the whole universe. Then they got to the core and it opens out into another whole fabulous universe and they confront mystery again...can't reach a core. They think they do and it becomes like an onion once more, layer after layer. You find it only within yourself. It comes only by revelation, only by vision. So don't be afraid that you are fearful. Who isn't fearful in this world? What man can tell me he hasn't been afraid? We are rooted in fear because we're rooted in hell. Are we not told Christ went down into hell? All right, he's rooted in hell but aspires to heaven, and heaven is the realm of hope. So the three great virtues of the world: Faith, hope and love. The greatest is love, for when the whole thing flowers there's nothing but love. In spite of all the horror in the world it is love guiding everything in the world. So in the end not one will be greater than the other, because there is no other, only one, all one.

So tonight try it. Try this simple little technique, a falling. You can feel it. Sit quietly, so you won't physically fall and hurt yourself, get on the bed and try to get the feeling of falling backwards, knowing where you're going to go. Don't fall into just *any* state...you are going to fall into security. Let yourself go. Don't open your eyes because you feel yourself falling, let yourself go. You won't die, no, not really die. Weren't you told that by the serpent, not really die? So you fall and fall right into a state and you'll find it natural to get into it, natural to be in that state. And then from then on you'll find yourself returning to it more constantly, and the state to which we most constantly return constitutes our dwelling place.

So "Where do you dwell Lord? Come and see." And you move. If I say come and see, you're going to move. Everything remains just as it is unless man moves. This world will remain completely what it is until I move. If I move the slightest little way and look at the same room, I see it from a different angle, so I see it differently. So don't hail anyone as a great important person and don't put anyone down. They are only in states, though they don't know it. The majority knows nothing of what you've heard. But as you are told, "Thank you, Father, that you hid these things from the wise and prudent and revealed them unto babes; for such was thy gracious pleasure" (Mat.11:25). You aren't going to find it in books or by scientific research. You hear it right from one who experienced it, and you either believe it or you don't believe it. If you believe it, you can test it. As Lord Lindsay of Oxford University said to some ministers: "You ministers are making a mistake. In your pulpits you are arguing for Christianity and no one wants to hear your arguments. You ought to be witnessing, does this thing really work, then share it with the rest of us." He was speaking on this level of moving from state to state, not the Promise. The Promise comes as the tree begins to flower. Flower on earth, that's the Promise. But until the Promise unfolds, then share what you have discovered in this mystery. Share it with us so we can all enjoy it afterwards, all enjoy freedom, all the lovely things in the world.

Tonight I hope you have heard enough to want to test it. Test falling into the state desired, and remain in it long enough to make it natural. If you make it feel natural, it's like you will go home tonight, it will seem natural to go home and you feel so relaxed when you do get home. It's been home for several years, so you go in and take off your clothes, shoes, socks, and simply feel so good, so relaxed, and you're at home. No matter what home is, it's accompanied by a certain feeling. Now make something else that is a far more lovely place or more marvelous state so you feel comfortable in it. The average person, if you take them into some palatial place tonight wouldn't feel at home. They'd feel ill at ease, because they aren't accustomed to it. You can feel at ease in any place in the world and it is yours…it's entirely up to you.

*   *   *

Q: How do you get around the fear of height and falling?
A: Lie on your bed and know you are there. Then you can induce a sensation of falling while you can't physically. If the garment is secure—you don't want to fall and be injured—then in your Imagination have the feeling of falling into the most glorious state.

Reason will tell you your body is secure, it won't fall, then let yourself go. What can go but your wonderful immortal, eternal Imagination, that's all. Just let yourself go.

THE ETERNAL FATHER

11/25/66

____(??) one may not know it, but he really is seeking for the eternal Father. He is seeking for power, he thinks, for fame, for health, all these things in the world; but what he is really seeking for is the core, the cause of it all. The fatherhood of God is the central doctrine of the Bible. The individual will one day transform this doctrine into a first-person, present-tense experience. And so long as it is taken from experience a doctrine is valid and defendable. I tell you from experience it is true. One day you will discover the core, the cause of the whole vast world and all within it, with all of its horrors. And that core, believe it or not, is not only God the everlasting Father, but God the everlasting Father is infinite love. How could you conceive of it now when you see such horrors in the world? And God the Father is infinite love.

When I search the scriptures, we start in the early passages. He first presents himself as Almighty. To Abraham, Isaac and to Jacob I made myself known unto them as El Shaddai, God Almighty, but by my name—which is called Jehovah, which is translated I AM, and we speak of it as the Lord—I did not make myself known. That begins with the revelation to what is known as Moses. As we told you, these characters are not persons; these are eternal states, Abraham, Isaac, Jacob, Moses, all of them, eternal states. When one reaches a state called Moses...and the word means "to be born." It's the old perfective of the Egyptian verb "to be born." Men and scholars have played upon the word and because it is made up of Mem Shin He, they call it "to draw out." You can turn it around and get the word "name" out of it, Heshem. You can take the middle letter, put it in the front, Shema, you get "heaven." But heaven is within you (Luke 17:21). There is something to be drawn out from *in* man. And from within man is heaven; and you're drawing out a name.

Take the name Moses and turn it around, it spells name, Heshem. What is being drawn out?

The word [Moses] means "to be born." There is something to be born that comes out of the depths of man...a name...the fulfillment of that which is coming out. It comes out in detail, but it comes out in sections. First: Almighty. Then it comes out as I AM. Finally it comes out as Father. We find that all through the gospel of John. He does not omit I AM, but he tells you "I AM the Father. He who sees me has seen the Father. How can you ask me to show you the Father? I have been so long with you and yet you do not know me, Philip? He who has seen me has seen the Father" (John 14:9). No one understood it, no one grasped it. For, if you are a father, well then, there *must* be a son. You can't be a father unless there's a child. And he speaks about a son from the beginning. He promises a son to the first being to whom he reveals himself as might; that's Abraham, the state called Abraham, which is faith.

You enter the state of faith and you hear the most fantastic, the most incredible story in the world: God's plan of salvation. To this state he promises a son and that son is called Isaac, it's also a state. Here is now the beginning, the shaping of the unbegotten. You must not see Isaac as the product of generation but the shaping of the unbegotten. So here, the formation begins; it's a prototype of what is finally coming out. You meet him now in Isaiah, "Unto us a *child* is born, to us a son is *given*; and the government shall be upon his shoulder, and his name shall be called"—and now we have four— "Wonderful Counselor, Mighty God, Everlasting Father, Prince of Peace" (Is.9:6). Here are four names given. In Isaiah, in Ezekiel, we find all these four-fold. The great poets, like a Blake, he speaks of the four-fold man. But in Ezekiel so much is said of the four-fold man, the four faces of man. Here we find in Isaiah the four *names* of a presence that is being born.

How do I know that this one is coming out? Well, these are now signs, these are signs and portents. A child is born and that a son is given, two entirely different things. Not the child becomes the son; a child is born. It's only a signal of something taking place in the individual as he moves towards the discovery of the fatherhood of God...for it's a child. Now comes, a son is given. It's entirely different from the child. Here, when I see the son, I know myself the Father. When I see the child, I only know I went through the strangest experience of being awakened from a long, long imposed sleep. It's the resurrection of man, and it's followed instantly by the birth of the *man* from above, symbolized in that of a little child that is born, wrapped in swaddling clothes. It's only a *sign*...that's all that it is.

Now comes, as he unfolds, he finds a son is standing before him, that given. The little one is born, he comes out. He *is* born in the same way that a child is born. But *he* [the individual] is being born, and the child symbolizes it.

But when it comes to the son, it's entirely different, it's now given: And "God so loved the world he *gave* his only begotten Son" (John 3:16). Well, who is God's only begotten Son? The 2ⁿᵈ Psalm tells us, "I shall tell of the decree of the Lord: He said unto me, 'Thou art my son, today I have begotten thee'" (verse 7). He brings forth a son. Well, David is not a person as you are a person, as I am a person. David is the sum total of all the generations of men and all of their experiences fused into one great whole; and that concentrated time into which all the generations are fused, and from which they all spring, the ancients personified as eternity, and called it David. David is the Olam, "And whose son are you, young man?" Young man, Olam. "Inquire whose son the stripling is" (1Sam.17:56). Stripling: Olam. "Whose son is that youth, Abner?" "As your soul liveth, O king, I do not know." Young man, youth, and, here, stripling, all the same word meaning eternity, the word Olam. "I have put eternity into the minds of men, yet so that they cannot find out what I have done from the beginning to the end" (Eccles.3:11). And that word translated "eternity in the minds of men" is Olam.

So what did he put into the mind of man? God himself entered death's door, the human skull. And because the Son is with the Father, he took the Son with him. And so, in the beginning the story begins, "Father, I see the fire and I see everything, but where is the lamb for the gift offering?" "I have the wood, here is the fire, but where is the lamb?" He said, "The Lord will provide *himself* the lamb, my Son" (Gen.22:7). The Lord gives himself as the burnt offering. He enters death's door, the human skull, and lays down in the grave of man with his Son in his bosom, and shares with man—who is dead, who he's now going to stir into a living being, an animated body, and share with him—all of his visions of eternity, the horrors of the world. And then, when he brings him forth and he awakens from that dream, by then he is God. And if God is a father when he entered, taking with him his Son within his bosom, well then, he in whom he awakens is the father. If he is a father, then there's a son.

So now John begins with these words—not the beginning but the first chapter—"No one has ever seen God; but the only Son, who is in the bosom of the Father, he has made him known" (John 1:18). No one has ever seen God, and yet the same Book of John makes the statement, "No one has seen him but he who is *from* God" (John 6:46). He was born of God. He who is *from* God, he has seen God. His form you have never seen, but I have seen him. His face you have never seen, said he, but I have seen him, for I am from him. He sent me and sent me into the world. He who sent me is with me, so if you see me, you see him who sent me. Here you find the most profound teaching in the Book of John. When you see me you see him who sent me, for he and I are one. I and the Father are one. I dwell in him and he dwells in me, and we are one.

Well, how do I know that? You wait. You know it in this manner, "No one, but no one, knows who the Son is except the Father, and no one knows who the Father is except Son and any one to whom the Son chooses to reveal him" (Mat.11:27). So, "What think ye of the Christ? Whose son is he?" "The son of David," they said. And he replied, "Why then did David in the spirit call him Father? If David in the spirit called him Father—the word is called the Lord, but the Lord is Father, it's Adonai in script. But you do not always use the sacred name of Yod He Vau He, and we speak of the Adonai meaning "my Lord." My Lord is the name used for the Lord, the Father, and a son always referred to his father as "my Lord" or Adonai. So, "Why then does David call him Lord? If then David thus calls him Lord, how can he be David's son?" (Mat.22:42).

So, here he declares, David called me Father, in fulfillment of the 89th Psalm. "I have found David...and he has cried unto me, 'Thou art my Father, my God, and the Rock of my salvation'" (Ps.89:20,26). For, he comes now only to fulfill the prophetic word. One day you experience this and you boldly proclaim the prophetic word, and then leave entirely into his hands your fate. If they stone you with the literal truth of the world...for they know who your earthly father is. So in the 8th of John they said, "Who is your Father? Where is your Father?" He said, "You know neither me nor my Father, if you had known me you would have known my Father also" (John 8:19). But you do not know me, or you would not ask that question. For had you really known me you would have known God, for he and I are inseparable. He didn't send me as another; he who sent me is with me. He has never left me, for we are fused, and we cannot be separated. We are one.

Limited, yes, to a garment of flesh and blood while I tell the story, but you can't separate me, he said, from the one with whom I am fused. I am fused with the Father and share with the Father everything the Father is. He's a father and he has one son, and that son is the sum total of all the generations of men brought into one solid wonderful externalized person, and it is David, "a man after my own heart." I brought forth everything. A man after my own heart...I found him...he is David my Son. Everyone contains in himself first the Father, but he doesn't know it; and the Father contains the Son, for the Son is in the bosom of the Father. And it takes the Son to reveal the Father. That's a real explosion when it takes place. The whole brain seems to explode, and standing before you, what you brought forth now, "Today I have begotten you," I've brought you forth, the same David. "Thou art my son" and you see your son. The relationship is so altogether unique, there's nothing like it. But you bring forth that which was buried in the very bosom of your being, and that being was the Father. By then you and he are one.

Now I tell you, how do you know this? Well, if I tell you other important, very, well, fantastic things and you try it and it works, are you not inclined then to believe this? So he tells this story, and then he tells other stories. "This is my body"... he takes a piece of bread and breaks it, and he offers them bread. He said, "Eat it; it is my body." Then he offered them a cup and he said, "Drink of it, all of you; this is my blood" (Mat.26:26). "Except you eat my body and drink my blood, you have no life in you; but if you eat my body and drink my blood then you have life in you" (John 6:53). Is that true? He tells you, whatever you believe, if you really believe it, your Father in heaven will do it for you; that your Father in heaven sees in secret and rewards you openly. He sees in secret and rewards you openly if you believe it (Mat.6:6). "If you don't believe that *I am he*, then you die in your sins," you don't believe it (John 8:24). If you believe that I am he, meaning the Father, and he sees in secret what he sees he'll reward you openly. Now don't be deceived, he isn't deceived, whatever you believe you're going to reap, *whatever*. It's called planting. Whatever you sow, so shall you reap (Gal.6:7).

Can I prove this? You can prove it in the immediate present. A lady writes, and here I have her letter, "My dream began...we are three, all dressed in a pale, pale baby blue. There are three plates, on each plate there are three pieces of food. And a voice said, 'You're eating break food' and I said, 'You mean, breakfast.' The voice answered, 'No, break food. That's what you're eating, you're eating break food.' Then Bud, she called him by name, Bud gave the blessing. 'And there is a time'...I can't quite quote it, it's a prayer that is his...'a time to work and a time to play, a time to go and a time to stay.' At that, after the blessing was over, I reached with my right hand for the food, the break food. I reached so far that I was falling off the bed physically and woke, startled, and so much so I woke my husband."

Eating what? The doctrine of Christ, that's what you're eating. People go to church and they take the little what's called communion, the bread and the wine. Do you know what communion really is? Listen to it carefully, for if you eat it, if you eat this bread and drink this wine, your Father is seeing it, and what he sees you do, he'll reward you openly in the immediate present, if you actually take communion. What is communion? Imagination is the *means* of communion; it is the soul's bread and wine. So I stand here and think of a friend, and my friend all of his dreams have collapsed, can't see any daylight, not a thing. But I see him now completely reaping every dream of his, and he's radiant in all the things that I see. Haven't I resurrected him from what he seemed to be, a dead person with all of his dreams failing, like the Pharaoh?

Well, do I really believe it? Can I say I'm seeing someone in my mind's eye; don't tell anyone, for my Father is seeing in secret? And so I see him in secret, well, who is seeing it? Well, I am. Well, what's the Father's name? I AM. So my Father is seeing exactly what I am imagining, and so this is the means of communion. This is eating the doctrine, this is drinking his blood, make it alive. And as I actually lose myself in this state and see the fulfillment, the resurrection of my friend before my mind's eye, in absolute confidence now I go.

Where did he do it? At the tomb of Lazarus, right at the tomb, he actually called him forth from the dead. If you would but believe, you would see the resurrection. Oh, I know in the end, they took it on this level. No. Now, "For I am the resurrection and the life." At that very moment when he collapsed and is but nothing, you simply, in the Silence... standing at a bar I would do it, standing any place. You don't need a church, don't need a synagogue, don't need some so-called holy place; wherever *you* stand that's the holy place, for you are the temple of the living God. And so, you're always in temple *wherever* you are, for you are the temple. And you bring before your mind's eye a friend, and you know his request, and you see him the embodiment of that which he would like to be. See it clearly in your mind's eye and rejoice, as though you could say "Thank you, Father, that thou has heard me. But I know thou *always* hear me" (John 11:42). Didn't I hear myself? Didn't I see what I was doing? Well, who is seeing it? If I am seeing what I am doing and he who watches it is I AM, am I not seeing it? Can I fool myself? Well, did I believe it? Unless you believe that I am he, the one who is perceiving it, well, then you die in your sins. If you really believe that I am he, the one perceiving it is the God, the Father of all, well then, what I am seeing all things being possible to him he'll resurrect it.

Now in the same letter comes this. She said, "I sell real estate. And in the Valley, this family of five, father, mother, and three little children, he was transferred to San Francisco, and, naturally, they put the house on the market, and it was given to me to sell. I had the listing. A month went by, she's more than anxious to join her husband and take her children to San Francisco, and no sale, not even an offer. So every day she called me. I said to her, would you do something for me? She said, 'What?' I said, would you go to bed tonight... first of all, let me ask you a question, were you in San Francisco what would you do? Well, she said, 'I'd go horseback riding.' She said, when you retire tonight, would you simply start riding, in your Imagination, riding a horse, and remember when you were in Los Angeles, as you mount the horse, ride the horse, and you are in San Francisco. To prove that you are in San Francisco, remember *when* you were in Los Angeles.

"Two weeks later, she called up to say that she had this offer, and to come on over." The next day was Sunday. When she went over and saw the terms, it was exactly the price she wanted, exactly the terms, and the length of escrow, the period of escrow. My friend, who made the sale, said, "Isn't that wonderful!" to this lady who had sold the house, and she replied concerning the wonder of it all, "You do not know, really...you've changed my entire way of thinking, everything about it." And she wondered how, how could I change your thinking? And then that's when she was reminded of what she had done. And my friend said to her, "Isn't it wonderful, tomorrow morning when you get up you don't have to, unless you want to, you don't have to make the beds." She said, "That is not the wonderful part; I don't have to ride that darned horse through the night, for I have saddle sores from riding."

And then she said, "She went to San Francisco with her family. There they are, and then she called me, only two weeks later"—this all happened between October the 1ˢᵗ and writing the letter to me on the 21ˢᵗ of this month—"she called me two weeks later to tell me that she is now buying this lovely home of her dreams, and described the home, exactly what she wanted." And then told her, "You have no idea how you changed my thinking." She said, "This is where my cup today really is running over, for she said to me, 'I now know that imagining creates reality.'"

So here, someone has proven beyond all doubt at least the doctrine is true based upon this level...even if she can't quite grasp this peculiar mystery of the fatherhood of God, who is buried in every child born of woman. Being a father he has a son; I tell you who that son is, the son is David. One day, to prove that you really are the father you're going to bring him forward, but you can't bring him forward until you've played all the parts in the world. Not one can you fail to play, you can't. You've played them all. I have played every conceivable thing in this world, the bum, the royal person, scavenger, the outcast, the judge and the judged, the jailer and the jailed, but everything. And having played all, it all adds up, and then you bring forth a son, which is the quintessence, the result of all the generations of men, because you played them all. Having played them all, then you bring him forth. He is the result of your journey through this world of sin and death. Then you will know the Everlasting Father.

There is only one savior in the world. Now we have divided Jesus Christ from the one we speak of in the Old Testament as Jehovah. That's a strange, peculiar concept, a completely false concept, as though there were two Gods. There aren't two Gods. The word Jesus, the word Jehovah, the word Joshua, means the same thing. The root is Yod He Vau, the same in all, and it means "to save; Jehovah is Savior." The whole story say now of Job is the story of man, and the word Job means "Where is my father, O God?" Where is my father?

We're told that David took the city of Zion and renamed it the city of David. Now, the one who really took it, his name is Joab, if you read the 2nd Samuel carefully. Joab took it and the word Joab means "Jehovah is Father." That's what it means, Joab, "Jehovah is Father." Job is "Where is my Father, O God?" So he's asking, with all the tribulations around him, "Where is my Father?" If I could only find the cause, the source, of all these things in my world!

Well, here if you read the story of Joab, he very kindly set himself apart when the city was about to fall. He conquered, but then put himself apart and allowed King David to enter and take the credit, and name it after himself. That's the sacrifice of the Father for the Son. He gave all credit to the Son and called the Son his glory. So Joab conquered the city and then as it was about to fall, it was inevitable, imminent, he stepped aside and invites the king to enter victoriously and then name it after himself...the everlasting sacrifice of the Father. So here, the Father is buried in every man, and is playing all the parts. Again, he brings out his only begotten son, David.

But you can take it on this level and you can actually this night eat the bread and drink the wine; for Imagination is the means of communion. You can sit right here or when you're riding home, you bring one before your mind's eye...as you bring him and you see him transformed into the man that he would like to be, you're eating the doctrine, you're eating the bread and you're drinking the blood, you're drinking the wine. For in the blood is life, and you're making it alive, the whole thing is alive before you. But do you believe it? For, except you believe that I am he...and I'm seeing in secret...I am seeing exactly what I'm doing, I can't fool myself. So I'm actually seeing in secret, I'm communing. I'm communing with God, but God is I AM so I am communing with myself.

Now if you put it to the test and it works, does it really matter what others think? What does it matter what the whole vast world would think if you test it and in the testing it proves itself? What would it matter what the world would think? So you can take all the little pieces of wafer in the world and drink all the wine in the world; that is not communion. Communion means, well, communion with God, and, therefore, forgiveness of sin. Well, you forgive the man all of the missing of the mark in his world. He was missing it, you became aware of it, and then you did it. Did it to whom? You did it to yourself, because he's yourself pushed out. There is nothing but yourself. So you became aware of someone in this world who was in need... well, there is no other but God. So you take every aspect of yourself and by communion you free him, you forgive him. So the supreme test of this doctrine is the forgiveness of sin. And only God can forgive sin. It tests your ability to enter into and partake of the nature of the opposite. So a man doesn't look well, then you put yourself right into the state where he does look well, and persuade yourself that he has never been healthier, or that he has never looked healthier. And to the degree that you are self-persuaded of what you are imagining to that degree he becomes *it*. If he becomes it, then what could anyone tell you?

So, "Thank thee, Father, Lord of heaven and earth, that thou hast hid these things from the wise and the prudent and revealed them unto babes" (Mat.11:25). The scholars have searched and searched and they cannot find the Christ of whom the scriptures wrote, and whose coming they foretold, they can't find him. They have searched...and every day you find some confirmation in the press by the so-called wise scholars of the world. They'll take every word and analyze it, tear it apart, but they can't find him, because he comes only by revelation. He reveals himself to the babes, the unlearned of the world, not to the scholars. We have volumes after volumes, they are trying so hard to unravel him from the script, and they can't find him there at all. He's not in the dead letter, won't find him there. He comes from within. And you take this external testimony and see how it parallels it, but it's not there, it's in you. The whole thing is in you, the scripture is in you. The very words you're going to hear, you're going to hear them from within you. So no man sat down to compose the scripture; it's not of human composition. The whole thing is something springing from the depths of one's soul...the whole thing comes out. This is the eternal Father unfolding in man. So every child born of woman will awaken as God the Father; and God the Father personified in scripture we speak of as Jesus Christ.

Now, we're reading it in the gospel...you ask, well, who are they, who are these evangelists called Matthew, Mark, Luke and John? Nobody knows. Anonymous names...all of these names are anonymous; no one knows who they are. What story were they telling? They were telling their own experience, and they told it in the third-person, singular, and called it Jesus. Well, Jesus means Jehovah. But they were telling their own experience and signed the anonymous names, Matthew, Mark, Luke and John. But no one knows who Matthew, Mark, Luke and John are, any more than they know the authors of the five books called the law of Moses. They only go by initials. We have the J manuscript, the E manuscript and the P manuscript, but nobody knows who signed J, E and P. There is no book signed Genesis, or signed Exodus, or Leviticus, or Numbers, or Deuteronomy. They signed three little letters: there is the J manuscript, E manuscript and the P manuscript. You bring out these manuscripts and nobody knows these unknown authors. They're all called Moses, but Moses is not a person. It's an eternal state through which the great revelation of the name comes and the law is given.

But who knows who they are who wrote it? Who knows who these evangelists are? They were telling and relating their own experience, that's what they were doing. But they told it in the third-person...man would then accept it. If you could tell it in the third-person, well, then they would think you aren't bragging; therefore, he's telling it because he saw it, it was someone else. And man then builds this third-person into some strange idol and they call it Jesus Christ, and make all kinds of things about him. But these unknown authors are telling their own experience; that's Jesus Christ. The whole story that was foretold in the Old Testament unfolds in man. And the men in whom the story unfolded, they told it, but wrote it in the third-person, singular, and then put into the mouth of one they called Jesus all these things. Called him Jesus, why?—for he will save his people from their sins.

Well, who is the savior? Read it in the 43rd chapter of Isaiah, "I am the Lord your God, the Holy One of Israel, your savior...and besides me there is no savior" (Is. 43:3,11). And read what the one they called Mary said in the beginning of Luke when she gave this grand praise to her Savior, the Lord Jehovah...just, "My Savior." There is no other Savior. Well, who is he? He reveals himself as I AM..."that's my name forever, and by this name I must be known throughout all generations" (Exod. 3:15). But today man has put a little tag on it, and they do not know the word Jesus means Jehovah. When these evangelists write, they're writing their own experience. But they didn't call themselves and say, well now, they addressed me as Mark or Matthew or Luke or John. They told it all in the third-person, singular, and, here, they called him Jesus. Then the churches organized around this state and make an idol out of him.

I tell you, the whole drama unfolds in you, and it's Jehovah, the only Lord, unfolding in man. And he only has one Son and that Son is David. David is _____(??), it's unique, the only one of its kind; brought forth *not* of the flesh, brought forth *not* of the blood of man, nor the will of man, but of God. God plays all the parts and then at the end brings forth the result, and the result of playing it all is personified as a child, his heart himself, that's the essence of it all, "My Son in whom I am well pleased." So I have found David. I have found a man in whom I am well pleased, he said, a man who will do all my will. Therefore, it was God's will doing it all, and then it came forth personified as this eternal youth called David. And so, if in the end, and it will be you bring him forth as I have brought him forth, and a friend of mine present he has brought him forth, and we all bring him forth the same David, not another, are we then not one? Is not then the confession of faith of Israel the greatest confession ever made? "Hear, O Israel, the Lord our God is one Lord" (Deut.6:4). Are we not the *one* Lord with the *one* begotten Son, and in the end, the Elohim, which is plural, the compound unity, one made up of others, all gathered together and brought back into the *one* state? And then, what happens then?—another great drama, for another expansion.

So, what is his name? Almighty God. These are his names, and his name shall be Wonderful Counselor. Well, who is the Wonderful Counselor? We're told the Holy Spirit. "I will send the Counselor." So who is the Holy Spirit then, if the same one now becomes Mighty God? Mighty God is El Shaddai, and that was called Jehovah's first revelation to man, but he's not the same then as the Holy Spirit. There aren't two. And what is his third name? Everlasting Father. And who said that? He said, Holy Father, I have made manifest thy name and the name thou gavest me I have revealed to them (John 17:6,11). Well, he gave me the name of Father by giving me his Son. And so, "Keep them in thy name, that thou gavest me, that they may be one as we are one." So now, keep them in the same love, the love with which thou lovest me, that we are one.

But he called himself, now, the Holy Father. But the Holy Father now we've seen is the Mighty God, and he is the Holy Spirit over the Wonderful Counselor. Here he comes now to this wonderful state of the Everlasting Father, the Father forever. And his final one is Prince of Peace. There is no peace until you find him. That comes at the very *end*, the Prince of Peace, and of his reign there shall be no end. That peace is broken only when to transcend this fabulous drama a new drama is conceived. So the poet said, "Be patient. Our playwright will show in some fifth act what this wild drama means"... then a *new* act. So we have the four acts and then when the curtain comes down on the last scene of the last act, it's only for a moment to enjoy that seeming infinite peace—it's all over and it came out just as foretold only to transcend it. And who wouldn't want to transcend it even though the drama may put this one to shame? So be patient and our playwright will show in some fifth act what this wild drama means.

So I tell you, what I've told you this night is true. I've experienced it. I've experienced every bit of scripture. The whole thing has unfolded right within me, just like a tree. And you can't stop it, the time has come, the time is fulfilled and the kingdom of heaven is at hand, and not a thing, seemingly, that you're doing consciously about it. It was simply planted in you. As we're told in Habakkuk, "The vision has its own appointed hour; it ripens, it shall flower. If it be long, wait; for it is sure and it will not be late" (2:3). Not late for itself, the whole thing comes on time. No one knows that moment in time when the first thing appears. It just comes so suddenly upon you.

But tonight you can partake of communion without going to any church. Without taking any cup of wine, without taking any wafer, you can eat the body and drink the blood. You do it simply by bringing into your mind's eye a friend, and seeing that friend as he would like to be seen. Just see it. Now, do you believe it? You're eating it...you're actually drinking the blood, which is the doctrine, that's what it means. Take my doctrine, take my teaching:

"Take my yoke upon you and learn from me." If you take my yoke upon you and learn from me, then you are eating what I am teaching, and that is the wafer, that is the wine. It is Imagination that is the means to commune, can't commune without it. If you believe in what you are doing, what should happen? The whole thing will happen, come to pass, just like the lady in the selling of the house.

Though I have many others...but they didn't fit tonight. Many of them are marvelous. One is called "The Maverick," which I'll take one night. Another one...a gentleman who made an effort to turn this thing off for me, he wrote me a fantastic one. It will fit before I close. I thought this one would fit tonight, in showing you the Father *does* dwell within us and he reveals himself on different levels. And he told you how to eat his body, how to drink his blood, and told you what would happen, for he sees you in secret, sees what you are *doing* in secret, and he rewards you *openly*. So you do it, eat it, drink it, and then you're assimilating, and now before your eyes will come the answer to what you've done. In her case, one month went by, nothing happened. And she asked the lady to do something for her, "Go to bed and do what you would do were you in San Francisco." "Well, I'd ride a horse." "Then ride the horse." At the end, she was so happy that it happened because she got tired of the saddle sores from riding her horse.

So I ask you to do the same thing, no matter what it is. What would you do *if* it were true? Well then, do it. And you have no room for boasting, because your Father's doing it. You do it in your mind's eye, and then it happens in a way that you do not know. This lady didn't go out and pull the buyer in. It was there for one solid month and no one came, not even an offer. But by doing the end, then it pulls all things into place. How can you boast? Who pulled the buyer in? Who pulled the terms in, exactly what she wanted as to price, exactly the terms and exactly the period of escrow? All came, just as they should come.

Now let us do the same thing here. And there isn't one that you should turn away, because you can't meet one stranger in this world. There is no stranger; it's all God. So turn no one away, no matter what he wants. How easy it is to imagine that the thing is done, and then let it be done.

Now let us go into the Silence.

*   *   *

Q: (inaudible)

A: I was quoting Tennyson. My dear, when David is revealed to you, you're the most startled person in the world. See, I have in this world two children. At least, they were born by separate women and they told me I sired the child. I believe it implicitly. I really believe that I am the father of my daughter, Victoria, and my son, Joseph Neville, I do, but I have to take that on faith. They know that they are the mothers, and I believe I am the father. Well, when you meet David you don't take anything on faith. It's so obvious this is something started in the beginning. It's a knowledge that not a thing could disturb. There is no argument that you could conceive that could disturb this relationship. It's entirely different.

I look into my daughter's eyes and I am so thrilled that she is my daughter. I'm so happy whenever she comes home. I could never be too tired to welcome her, and she could never stay late enough for me. So, that feeling about, my feeling towards my daughter…and I believe I am the father in a physical sense. But I don't have to believe in the sense that I believe in this when I meet David. This is a relationship that seems to be in the very beginning, but wasn't brought forth to confirm my journey until the end. For he was in the bosom of the Father before the Father entered me; and when the Father became me and shared fatherhood with me, making us one, then he had to come out to prove that I am the Father. And that is a relationship that you cannot in any way disturb. Yet, here I am one of ten children that survived, there were twelve of us, and my father…I know, that is I believe, how would I know that he is my father? How would I know that my mother is my mother? My mother knows and my father believed. And so, here was this lovely feeling…and I loved him, in fact, I don't question the fact that he is my father. But my father had a very lovely expression when he toasted when he wanted a drink, and he said, "Here's to the man that rocks his child, and rocks his child alone, for there's many a man who rocks another man's child and thinks he's rocking his own." That was my father…having sired, or thought he did, twelve of us. And so, in this new relationship of David and yourself as the eternal Father, there is no doubt, none whatsoever. Not that I've ever doubted or the average man has ever doubted. I don't think that the average man…in fact, he's so proud that he could report the child, he's thrilled beyond measure. I know I was. When I was told that my wife was pregnant it was nothing but joy. And when you first see the child and you take him in your arms, what a thrill to hold him! And to actually see your son do a fist, that's a tremendous thrill. But it's not the same feeling as when you see David. David is something entirely different. And every person, including every woman, is going to be the father of David.

Because in the resurrection there is no sex; we are *above* the organization of sex. And we speak of him as Father. You dwell upon it, my dear.

In the meanwhile, commune. Commune and take that wafer called the food that is broken. As this lady had the experience, it was break food. Not breakfast, it was break food. He took the bread and broke it, and then gave it. There were three that were present and there were three pieces of food on each plate. Three is associated with resurrection. So here, she knows the three and they were friends of hers, all three, she and the two. And so, she actually in the dream felt, "Well, isn't that wonderful! This means resurrection." But the whole drama begins with resurrection—that's where the man awakens and comes out of the tomb. So, she had inward, I would say, inwardly a biblical suggestion the time is near for waking. All these signs...when these signs appear, then you will know the kingdom of heaven is at hand.

Well, we were late in starting, but it is still late...and they may want to push us out. So thank you for coming. And the next one is on Monday. Thank you. Goodnight.

AN APOSTLE

11/28/66

Tonight's subject is "An Apostle." I really should have said The Apostle, but we let it go. In the epistle to the Hebrews we have this statement...and here Hebrews is completely anonymous, no one knows who wrote it. Scholars have speculated and thought it was Paul, and yet Paul is just as anonymous as Matthew, Mark, Luke and John...the whole Bible is anonymous. But in the epistle to the Hebrews, the 3rd chapter, he said, "Holy brethren, who share in a heavenly call, consider Jesus, *the* apostle and high priest of our confession" (3:1). In this epistle the word apostle is applied only to Jesus, as if there were no other apostles. May I tell you, he's right...whoever wrote it, he's right. The word apostle means "one who is sent, not as a mere envoy but as one who is authorized to speak in the name of him who has sent him." So throughout the gospel of John you read, "He who sees me sees him who has sent me" (John12:45). Here we find *the* apostle. Without explaining why, we say just Paul, as though he were a person. Paul is a state as much as Abraham is a state. Well, we say Paul, and he lays it down as an indispensable qualification for apostleship, that is, to have seen the risen Christ. He said, "Am I not free? Am I not an apostle? Have I not seen Jesus our Lord?" (1Cor.9:1). That is the indispensable prerequisite for apostleship, to have seen the *risen* Christ.

So we read in the 52nd of Isaiah, "How beautiful are the mountains...how beautiful upon the mountains are the feet of him who brings good news, who publishes salvation, who says to Zion, 'Your God reigns'" (verse 7), because he speaks with authority. He stood in the presence of the risen Christ, and he was embraced and incorporated into the body of the risen Christ, who is Jehovah, and sent to tell the story of the risen Christ, called the gospel. The gospel is the Word of the risen Christ.

Here, this is the perspective in which the whole of life is understood. That you become a king, a financial giant, a brilliant person, a great scientist? These things mean nothing compared to standing in the presence of the risen Christ and having him embrace you and incorporate you. And although you come to earth clothed in a garment of flesh, no one sees you, but no one. There is no human eye that can see the thing that your really are. Because when you are once incorporated into his body let no man put us asunder. He who is joined to the Lord no man can put asunder. We are called, one by one, to be incorporated into this glorious body, and our lowly bodies are changed to be of one form with that wonderful, glorious body (Mark 10:9; Mat.19:6; Phil.3:21). You can talk about it and say all kinds of things, but who can see it?

So here, the apostle is simply the one man; and so in Hebrews it is only given to Jesus. It's so difficult for man to believe that all could fit into one man, that we're gathered one by one to be incorporated into one man, and that one man is Christ the Lord, and one man, Jesus. This is a strange, peculiar thing, but I'm telling you what I know from experience. I'm not speculating, I'm not theorizing...I tell you exactly what happened to me. Thirty years before the birth [from above], it was 1929, and we are told, two were in the field and one is taken, one is left. Two women in the mill and one is taken and one is left (Mat.24:40). Do not return to ask why. No one knows the secret of God's elective love. All will be called, but the order in which they are called remains his secret. No one knows why we are called as we are called, in the order in which we are called.

And so here it was in the summer of 1929, I was called, taken in Spirit into the presence of the risen Christ, answering a very simple question—because the answer was before you, you couldn't fail—and having answered his simple question he embraced me. As he embraced me we fused. I was no longer this body; I am this body, this human form divine, the body of love. From it I can't be sundered. There is no power in the world...I wouldn't limit it to the earth...there's no power in eternity that can sunder me from the body of Christ, for I have been incorporated into this body. Then he sent me into this world with the words, "Time to act!" It took thirty years and then the whole drama began to unfold within me. So we are told in the end of the 3rd chapter of Luke, "Jesus, when he began his ministry, was about thirty years of age" (verse 23)...after the baptism with the Holy Spirit. For you are told, "I baptize with water, but there will come one who will baptize with the Holy Spirit. He is the one on whom the dove will descend, that is, the Holy Spirit will descend. And I saw the Spirit descend upon him as a dove, and it remained upon him. He will baptize you with the holy Spirit" (verse 16-22). In other words, he will baptize you with himself. Just as you are baptized in water, but you come out of the water, you're not part of it. But when you are baptized with the Holy Spirit, you are actually absorbed into the body of the risen Christ. You don't come out of it. So he who sees me sees him who sent me. But you don't see me you see the mask I wear.

So that moment on...but I wasn't yet born from above. Yet I was baptized into it. And so it takes thirty years between the baptismal by the Holy Spirit and the beginning. It takes three and a half years for the unfolding of the drama. It begins with the resurrection. So we are told, "I, Paul, an apostle, not from men, nor through man, but through Jesus Christ and God the Father, who raised me from the dead." That's the first book. Not chronologically speaking, but by all judgment, all scholars agree this is the first book written in the New Testament: It is Paul's letter to the Galatians. He begins it, "Paul an apostle—not from men nor through man, but through Jesus Christ and God the Father, who raised him from the dead" (1:1). So he raises every one of us, because Jesus Christ is *in* man. If he were not in us, we couldn't breathe, you'd have no life, for in him is life. Are you alive? Well, then you couldn't possibly be alive were he not in you. So he raises you into the presence of the risen Christ and embraces, really, himself, for there is nothing but Jesus Christ buried in all these garments of flesh.

Now here this past week I received a lovely letter. She isn't here tonight, but you can tell her. No, she is here, pardon me. She had this experience. This is all in a dream but remember, God speaks to man through the medium of dream. She's in her home, the house is lit, and someone announces, "Come." And she wonders, "Why should I come?" and he gave some vague explanation why she should come. So she went out into the street and the whole street is dark, not a light in sight, all the houses were dark. There's not a street light. So she goes to the intersection. All the houses now begin to be empty of people, and they all look like puppets. Their eyes are closed, and she could see behind and here was the emptiness behind the closed eyes. It was a cold night, she had no hat or coat and she felt comfortably warm. They came out completely bundled up, hats, scarves, coats, everything, and all in gray, and they themselves seemed gray. They looked just like puppets. And so at the intersection where she remained they all began to move up what she called a hill, really a steep street, from what she described in her letter. At the top of the hill, she began to separate herself from them, and she felt sorry for them, these strange, peculiar dead-like people. At the top was a man that she remembered in a previous dream. There was a light over his head and he spoke with tremendous authority. He had a head of hair that resembled a mane of a lion only the top was cropped, very shortly cropped across the top. But it was cut in something like a lion's mane.

He said to all these people, "I will call each person's name three times. If you cannot answer when I ask you for your name, you must remain with the group." Well, it seemed like the height of nonsense. So he called the name of each and no one could answer. They were bewildered. And she tried her best to tell them; she couldn't voice it and she tried her very best. She said, "It' so simple, only two little words." But she couldn't in any way convey to them what they should say, she couldn't, and she knew she couldn't. But she felt so sorry for all these puppets. They could not give voice to their name, and he called it three times to each one. And then, as the scene faded, feeling sorry for the entire bunch, she went up the street to the first house, and she entered it...and here was a receptionist, she was busy about something. And she was terribly concerned about these people and she wondered, "Where are they?" The receptionist, in the most cold, indifferent manner said, "Oh, they're in that house up the street asleep." She asked, "If they are asleep, why did you call them out? Why were they called out?" and the receptionist said, "It's not their house. They are only in it, but it's not their house"...a complete cold indifference about this. She knew that they were sound asleep in this place, and not a thing she could do about it. So she came out of this house, returned to her own home, and here was the light lit in her house. It was the only house lit in the entire street...and not a street light.

What a wonderful experience! It's so difficult to tell man in whom the light is not yet lit; but everyone here, Christ is sleeping in us, everyone. So you are not quite the puppet that she saw. Well, that is life. But in everyone here he's waking, waking, waking...on the verge of waking where the light is lit. One will come out and see the entire world round about and it's dead. It's a strange thing to say, but it really is. "Eternity exists and all things in eternity independent of Creation, which was an act of mercy." No reason in the world why this thing here should be awakened as God, none. Only an act of mercy could do it. And to do it, God buried himself within me and took upon himself this form, the form of a slave. He slept and shared with me then as he made me alive horrible dreams, nightmares, horrors, the wars, the conflicts of the world. Then one day he awakes and calls me into his risen state, and embraces me, and sends me back to experience thirty years later the drama as foretold in the gospel: The resurrection, the birth; the discovery of the fatherhood of God through his son calling me Father; then the tearing of the curtain of the temple, which is my body, and lifting me up into Zion; and then the descent of the dove upon me. But in the meanwhile, surrounding me with all kinds of signs and wonders, all kinds of heavenly visions, wonderful visions, and all related to scripture. Not necessarily part of these great four... these great four stand out of them all...but there are others not recoded in scripture that will come to you, and you'll experience them.

So when you are sent, you are in the eyes of the world if they will accept it, an apostle. And yet, there is only *the* apostle. God only sends himself, he can't send another. After you are incorporated into his body and sent, how could he send another when you cannot be sundered from that body of love? You can't be separated from the body of the risen Christ after you have been called and embraced and incorporated into the body of Christ. So, "How beautiful upon the mountain are the feet of him who brings good news, good tidings, publishes salvation, and says to Zion, 'Your God reigns.'" So I can say to Zion, the whole vast world: Your God reigns, he is raised, he's resurrected, and he is gathering us all, one by one, into his body. So in the end, "There is only one body, one Spirit, one hope, one Lord, one faith, one baptism, one God and Father of us all, who is above all and through all and in all" (Eph. 4:4). So in the end, there is only one God, one name, one king, all gathered, and you are he. Not some little thing down on the lower level, but one. There is no one who is outcast…but we are gathered.

The secret remains the secret of the risen Christ. When this little garment is taken off for the last time, which is the next time I take it off, I will know the secret of the call, because I am one then, not veiled, but unveiled with the risen Christ. But that secret remains his secret. No one here while he still remains veiled though he's been called and incorporated, he does not know the secret of the order in which we are called. So I can't tell anyone that you're going to be called next or you are next. I can only tell you from your visions and your experiences.

Now another friend of mine who is here tonight, he said that many, many years ago, approximately ten years ago, he was driving a car and suddenly there was nothing but light. He said, "I can't say there was light and myself, no, just light…and infinity falling in little, little kinds of light, all light falling. What I saw falling…the other night when you spoke of the serpent, of these diamond-headed serpents and trailing the little vertebrae, I didn't see that. To me the head was a grain and then a tadpole like tail. But everything was light, nothing but light. I heard and knew within me, "All is one." Then I became aware that, after all, I am driving a car…and there's going to be a ditch…and how will I turn off? By some reflex action I simply stopped the car, and the light subsided. As the cars went by, angry looks on the people as they passed me. Then I said to them, whether I shouted it audibly or not, I did say to them, everything's all right! and I knew everything was all right, in spite of their angry looks as they looked at me. By some reflex action I stopped it, stopped the car. But everything was light."

May I tell him, he's here tonight, you can, you can do it now, but it's better during the day. I can do it any time, day or night. But tomorrow go to the window and don't look at the building across, don't look at the sky, just look into space. Not an object in space but something in space and you'll see infinity falling, these little, as you called them, tadpoles. They do look like tadpoles until you arrest one. You can arrest it. You arrest one and you'll see exactly what I've told you, a diamond head trailing a perfect vertebra. You can hold him as long as you want. And you say they were not liquid. No, they are not liquid but they're moving, or they appear to move in a fluid. They appear to be in a fluid, just like little tiny fish in a bowl, and you see their motion. They move in the same way. You say tadpole? It is just like a tadpole moving. But you can arrest one or you can arrest a dozen. So pick one...follow him quickly. Because he makes a peculiar dart, you think you can't follow him but you can. He goes in all directions. Well, pick one and hold him. Leave all the other millions alone. There are millions. You can't count them. Take one and follow him. He seems to go out of sight for a moment, don't let him go. Hold him in your mind's eye. He'll stop, as you arrest him he'll stop, and you'll see exactly what I tell you, a little diamond head, brilliant diamond, and he's actually trailing a vertebrae.

So I say to you, you said you were partly illumined, you feel you were, I tell you you were. That happened to me and it came through light back in 1926 in the city of Larchmont in New York. I retired early. It was Prohibition days...I wasn't drinking in those days...I went to bed quite early. I was reading a book, *The Life of Buddha,* and as I read *The Life of Buddha* I must have fallen asleep, and the book fell on my chest. A thing I rarely do is read in bed. When I go to bed, I go to bed for the purpose of sleeping. But this night I was told by my host, who was the manager of the club, that he didn't think it wise for me, his guest, to join the members and the children of the members of the club; that they did not like it because after all he was employed by the club, and I was his guest, and I should not mingle with the members of the club. And so I did not go down. I remained upstairs in my room and took this book and I was reading it. In 1926 I was twenty-one years of age. I had the bed light on, and the whole thing fell upon my chest, because when I woke the next morning it was nine. I was in a trance from possible nine at night to nine in the morning. I hadn't moved. Usually when I sleep I turn side to side as we all do in the course of the night.

But this night, the bed was completely, I would say, unwrinkled twelve hours later. I hadn't moved. I was reading...at some moment it fell upon my chest, and as it fell there I went into a trance. In this trance there was nothing but light, infinite light—no stars, no moon, nothing but light, and I am light. I am all there is in the entire universe, and I am light. So when you read in John, "I am the light of the world" (8:12), that is not conjured through reasoning, it is not the result of some philosophic contemplation, it's revelation. It happened. So I can say to him, you were at that moment illumined...driving down, and suddenly everything is light. And when you told the passersby, "Everything is alright...all is light...and all is one" you're right. All is one. So don't be concerned, you actually saw it.

Now he asked me, "Please," said he, "I used to be called one of the most responsible men imaginable. I was brought up to do things and to hold my own, and to do and be responsible. I think I am a doer and I am responsible, but recently I think I've become a little bit irresponsible, because all of my values with which I was raised have crumbled. You said in one of your books that when all of the things you held so precious and so dear collapse around you...then you led them to the scriptures." Which you can, you can find it, the 13th chapter, I think it's the 13th of Mark, which shows you the whole thing crumbled about you (verse 2). And he said, "Here, I feel myself irresponsible, because today I don't think I have to do anything to achieve my objective. Now that is not something I was raised to do. I had to work, I had to do, I had to actually do things. Now here all of a sudden having proved this law I feel that I don't have to do as I was raised to do. I don't feel that I have to work as I was raised to work. I feel I can actually bring these things to pass, and it's the most cleansing feeling, so free," he tells me in this letter. "Please explain some night when it suits you, what is man's duty, what is his responsibility; and is this something more than you've said in the past, that whenever you use your Imagination lovingly on behalf of another you are mediating God to man, and that is what we should do? And please, if it is something other than that explain it, and if there isn't, well, then let it go."

May I tell you, you know the law. I'm speaking to him; I'm speaking to all of you. What must I do to be doing the will of God? That question is asked and the answer is, "Believe in him whom he has sent" (John 6:29). Believe in him. Believe in Neville? No, believe in him whom he has sent. You read it in the gospel. What do I read in the gospel? "Whatever you desire, believe that you have received it and you will" (Mark 11:24). That's doing the will of God if you believe it and apply it. You mean I do nothing? Well, just try it. That's doing the will of God. If today someone gets a fortune and it comes out of the nowhere, not one person knowing the source of the fortune because he had the fortune says, "Oh, you know who we saw today? ___(??) very rich person, and so and so." So they go through the world looking upon all these people who have things and they don't trace it as to where they got it.

Our present governor of...is it Arkansas...Winthrop Rockefeller, and someone said in the campaign against him he was born rich and he does not understand the poor, doesn't know anything about the poor. He said in rebuttal, "I have had nothing to do with either of them. I was born rich. I didn't know a thing about it. I've never known poverty. I've had nothing to do with that either. So are you going to condemn me because I was born rich and because I have never really known poverty?" So they elected him to the governorship. He never knew it...so he is born rich. But may I tell you, that pales into insignificance compared to what *you* inherit: You inherit the creative power of God! Not a billion dollars or the city of Los Angeles, that's nothing! Or the earth itself, that's nothing. You inherit the creative power and the wisdom of God. That's your inheritance.

Well now, God speaks to me objectively through his written Word. And no one knows the authors, really, it is all God. Whatever you desire, believe you have received it and you will. Now must I go about the old training, saying I've got to do something and work for it? The money that I have today, did I really work for it? I earn, the little that I do earn, and it's barely expenses compared to my expenses. Every night I come here that it rains and just a few people come, the club doesn't tell me, "You know, only a few came last night, therefore, we're going to give you a refund." I pay my rent in advance, and, may I tell you, it's a considerable rent. It's all paid in advance. I put it out. The *L. A. Times* when they send me the bill they give me an ad, but they send me a bill and I must pay it. I send out notices, 1500 notices. I go to the post office and buy the envelopes and the stamps. That's all paid for whether you come or not. But the money that I have, may I tell you, I didn't do anything to earn, didn't raise a finger. My father gave it to me, and it grows and grows like a lovely, wonderful fortune. My only satisfaction is that I have a little family to whom I would willingly tomorrow give it. If I go this night, I go relieved that they don't have any pressure, none whatsoever. It's adequate, more than adequate to take care of all of their earthly needs that money can supply.

Money can't supply everything in this world. It can't buy friendship, can't buy understanding. It can't buy all the *real* things in this world...it can't buy them at all. How can it buy artistry? How can it buy all the lovely things in the world? If all the Rockefellers in the world came together, and put them in the forts, and put them in all the wealth of the world, and put them into a composite picture, and you stand in here, they could not together buy what I have received standing in the presence of the risen Christ. What money in this world would you need to buy the embrace of Christ and to be incorporated into his body, forever and forever, never again to be sundered from it? Is there any wealth in this world that could actually come near? You can't buy that. So you see there's so much that money cannot buy.

Now, they would not be interested in what I'm telling you tonight. They would be so far removed from what I tell you concerning this night, the real realm. And yet on the earthly realm I didn't raise one finger to get it. I had it. I did not work another hour in my life to live and live graciously, with any home I want, in any part of the Sterling area, with a full complement of servants. I can afford it and not in any way reduce my way of living, in fact, augmenting it. But I don't touch it. I live normally in this world from here.

So I say to this gentleman, what is one's duty? What is one's responsibility? "Believe in him whom he has sent"...that is your duty. To go out in one grand manner and dare to *assume* that you are the man that you want to be... just let it happen. Just let it happen. It will happen if you dare to live in the assumption that things are as you desire them to be. So that is my advice to all. If it seems insane, may I tell you it isn't. The greatest...or one of the great visionaries of the world, William Blake, they thought him insane, too. He wasn't insane. The other day I was reading one of his...some little comment on him, and they thought the man insane because of his pictures. I have a lovely collection of his pictures at home, so I was going through these pictures what they called the insane ones and, oh, if they only knew how true they are!

I told you the other day that we're all rooted in hell, the region of fear, and we aspire to heaven, the realm of hope, and when these two are synchronized it results in vision. Well, Blake in his *Gates of Paradise,* the 13th plate, here is obviously someone that's dead. You don't see the face. You see the feet and you see what, undoubtedly, is the body on the bed and there are two figures at the head, concealing the face, you can't see the face. One is fear and one is just full of hope on the two sides next to the head. Then at the foot of the bed but rising is the Ancient of Days. He calls it, *Fear and Hope Equals Vision.* But in the actual words that he uses to describe this particular plate, he uses just two little lines of twelve words: "But when once I did descry the Immortal Man that cannot die." The same man rises out of that, so he hid the face, because you will think your father died, your mother died, your child died, you're going to see that image. No, you're going to see Christ rise...there's only Christ. There's nothing but Jesus Christ and Jesus Christ is God.

So you think you're going to find some little thing there rising out just like him? No. So he conceals the face of the dead little garment. But who is the one? He comes nearer than anything that I have seen, for when I stood in the presence of the risen Christ, it's not like that...it's more glorious. Because you can't paint it and you can't draw it but he comes very close. But it's not like that. And here rising from this dead garment is the Ancient of Days. When anyone dies, who rises?—the Ancient of Days. It was God who became man that man may become God, and his name is I AM. So you say, "Well, I am" and you drop all the other little garments because I AM is rising. Nothing dies, but nothing in eternity dies. But it has to be *awakened.* He's sound asleep in all, and wakes one after the other, in this one, that one, the other one, and he awakens in all.

So the apostle is the one who has been embraced by him, incorporated into his body and sent. To be called implies to be sent. And you're called one by one. I hadn't the slightest idea in 1929, unschooled, unknown, uneducated, and sleeping in that little tiny room, not knowing where the next week's rent would come from, not knowing anything…and to be called. Called out of the nowhere and there are billions in the world and I am called. So no one knows the actual secret of his elective love, it remains his secret. Read the 15ᵗʰ chapter of Corinthians—the order no one knows. But we are called in our own order.

So here, I thank the gentleman for his wonderful letter; and the lady for hers, a wonderful dream, it's a true dream, and the experience is true. I can't tell you what my thrill is to get your letters, for they're all, really, coming to the surface of the awakening God. I can't conceive of anyone coming here and coming over the months who is not on the verge of waking. I was not sent by some man, I wasn't sent by some organization. When you read in the papers that these people call themselves apostles…an apostle, as someone said in a certain …I would not call the name of the church, it's a large church, almost three million members, and they have their twelve appointed by men. If you want to become president to that large group, all you have to do is live long enough to outlive the others. They call that apostles. And they actually claim that no one else but that very small little group of less than three million are eligible for the kingdom, and all converts are simply to much lower strata. What nonsense! And here they aspire to the highest secular office in our world…the strangest, peculiar thing. But what peculiar visions they seem to have…so unlike the gospel.

May I tell you, when he's sent you will know it. He will come for one purpose: An apostle is sent to witness to the Word of God. He can only witness if he *experiences* the Word of God. So he is sent, and he is bewildered. As you're told in scripture, Paul was bewildered because he thought himself so unworthy…he persecuted. So he and everyone in the world you go berserk, you don't believe in him, and then you turn completely around. You're an atheist, you're agnostic, you're everything, and finally you're called. Then everything you tried to rub out you will now protect with your life, and willingly sacrifice your life to not only protect what formerly you would have destroyed but to promote it. His whole life was devoted to the promotion of the very faith that he would have destroyed. Having gone through all the states of the world you reach that point…all of a sudden you're called.

So don't condemn anyone who tonight might think they are agnostic or they are atheist or they are this, forget it. They may be called tomorrow. After you're called, what can you do? You're bewildered. You never once believed that the risen Christ was a fact; that Christ is God, and God is man. You stand in the presence of the risen Christ and it's man. It's not some impersonal force, it's man, and it's nothing but love. He embraces you, then sends you. And you know that you cannot in eternity be sundered from that body of the risen Christ; it's your body now. At that moment of the embrace your lowly body was changed to be one form with his glorious body. No mortal eye can see him, so the longing is always, as Paul said, I long to depart and be with Christ—that wonderful form into which he was incorporated—but for your sakes, said he, the need is far greater that I stay on in the body. And when you stay on in the body, you only talk about the risen Christ and the gospel.

Now let us go into the Silence.

*   *   *

___(??) on Friday. I think we have four left before we close on the 16th of December. We'll be closed until the 13th of February, and then we go through to the end, or the last week, I would say, of April; and then we are off until September. So we have four lectures left. Friday is the next, then we have two the following week, and then one our last week. So I hope I'll be able to send out cards when I come back during the Christmas holiday, but remember the date if you are going to come between now and closing. We are reopening on the 13th of February; we're closing here on the 16 of December.

Good night. Thank you.

GOD PLAYS ALL THE PARTS

12/2/66

God plays all the parts...I mean that literally. Moses said, "When I go to the people of Israel and they ask me who sent me, what shall I say?" The Lord answered, 'Say I AM has sent me unto you. This is my name forever and thus I am to be known throughout all generations'" (Ex.3:13-15).

So just imagine my return home and I said to my wife, "You know the play we saw last week?" and she remembered vividly. I said, "I have invited the entire cast to supper, so let's get ready to receive them." So we made ourselves busy and we got all the things ready for a lovely party after the theater is closed tonight. But as they arrive, I take it for granted that my wife knows them. She doesn't know them and so she will say, being the perfect hostess, "I am Mrs. Goddard and now tell me who you are?" He replies, "I am the author of the play." "I am the hero of the play." "And who are you?" "I am the villain." "And who are you?" I am the accused in the play." "And you?" "I am the accuser...I am the judge...I am the maid...this, that and the other." She then turns and says, "I have seen you all and loved you. But I don't recall having seen *you*, who are you?" "I am the stagehand." "You?" "I am behind the scenes, too, I'm the carpenter...I am the light man...I am the soundman." Everyone declared himself to be God before he gave the name of the mask that he is wearing. He played all the parts. The author and everything conceived was himself... everything he conceived was himself.

Tonight when you go home, do me a favor. I presume you have a Bible— read the 12th chapter of Job, the deceiver and the deceived are his. He takes the king and tears down all that he has, and then wraps a loincloth around him. He strips the priest. He brings the lowly down. He builds up the nation and tears it down. *He* does *everything*! And Job is wondering what have I done to deserve this? Would you number my iniquities? I ask you to number my iniquities. Why do you hide your face from me? He says, this is my salvation; for he knows that the ungodly man cannot stand before God and he doesn't feel himself guilty of anything of which he is accused. So he knows, I will come before the Lord and this is my salvation. Why do you hide your face as though I were an enemy? Because he knows that when he comes before God and God looks into his face, God can see no other than himself, he can't.

So let me share with you a wonderful experience that came to me through the mail. In fact, I have many to share with you tonight. This lady writes— and God speaks to man, by the way, through the medium of dream and through the medium of vision—"I heard the lecture on the 22nd day of November, and that was on motion, "Are You an Occupant or Inmate?" Then you told the story of your friend who had learned how to move. So that night I assumed as I went to sleep that I am fully awake. That was exactly what I want to experience...I am completely awake. So I moved into that state and as I fell asleep I heard these words: 'You are the apple of my eye.' and it kept on over and over. I replied, yes I know that is scripture. I heard Neville talk about that, oh, a long, long time ago. And the voice continued, 'You are the apple of my eye.' So I awoke and wrote it down; that is my custom to do that. I said to myself as I wrote it down, 'Maybe that is not quite the thing.' So I went back to sleep, trying to gather it together."

The word apple in Hebrew means "the little man reflected in the pupil of the eye." Look into the pupil of any person's eye in this world and whom do you see? You can only see *yourself.* If I ever came before the face of God— that is what he's asking for—this is my exoneration. Why do you hide your face? If I could only come before your face, you would know how innocent I am. You will look into my eye and you will see only yourself. So in this 12th chapter he said, all power, all wisdom are his. The deceived and the deceiver are his, there is no other; so I look into the eye of the deceiver and whom do I see?—myself. I look into the eye of the deceived and who do I see?—I see only myself. There is no one in this world, if you see clearly, other then your self. There is no one. God plays all the parts.

Then she said, "Two nights later, as I fell asleep I heard these words, 'In God there is no black or white, Jew or Christian' and it kept on repeating it over and over. So I got up and wrote it down. Again I said, "That is scripture, but it is not quoted accurately"...but I could not recall the accurate quote. So I went back to bed, struggling to find out the right quotation. As I did so, the same voice came, 'In God there is no black or white, no Jew or Christian' and suddenly our Ben appeared." Now I'm going to ask Ben to rise. "Our Ben appeared and Ben said to me, 'I am not this black skin that you see, I am God.' Then he vanished and my next door neighbor"—she calls her Frieda—"she appeared. She said, 'I was born into the Jewish faith but I am God.'" And then she woke. Here, I AM not black or white, I am not Christian or Jew, I AM.

Well, next day came another letter...I will not go through the entire thing. This friend writes, "In my dream I had this experience concerning the black. I saw this black, black young Negro, the blackest Negro you could ever see, and he was so scared, so frightened. Then came a woman, she looked to me like a Spanish woman. She had on a leather riding skirt, a black hat and a quirt fastened to the wrist. A quirt is simply a whip and you fasten it to the wrist. It's really braided leather, that's really what it is, a whip. And she walked over towards this man who was so scared and so frightened, and without emotion she flayed him. I protested. I rose from where I was and went forward to protest this awful unmerciful beating and a voice said to me, 'That is how we move from darkness to light.'" She knew that it was all symbolism! Not a Negro becoming a white person or vice versa...but from darkness to light. In the same 12th chapter of Job, the 16th verse, I think, you will see it: "the deep darkness to light." You read it in the 26th chapter of Acts, when the risen Christ appears, "Why do you persecute me?" Paul answered, "Who are you?" "I am Jesus whom thou persecutest." And then he sends him to open the eye of those who are in darkness and lead them from darkness to light (verse 18).

Then comes another letter, all in the same week, and in her letter she said, "I came to a rummage sale and all kinds of gifts where there, jewelry and watches, and I wanted a watch. I looked over all the watches, but they were old and ugly, so I wasn't interested. Then I saw one, and it was an odd watch, and I thought that would be all right...but I declined it, put that back. Then I walked upstairs to a higher level, and there I found a watch, a blue enamel watch, a lovely watch. I thought I'd take it. I came downstairs with it and then I decided that I wouldn't take it. Then the clerk said to me, 'I found many other gifts that came in when I went upstairs, other new gifts came and they were lovely gifts, much lovelier than the other gifts.' The clerk said to me, 'Look at these perfumes' and then she said, 'Neville donated this one.' She said, 'Well, if Neville donated that one I'll take it!' And then she looked me right in the eye and said, 'If you look into it, it will heal your eyes.' I woke, hoping that Neville's perfume would open my spiritual eye."

Well, the word perfume in Hebrew is simply "a fragrance that is produced by fire...like burning incense. It's burned in a very close room which then empties the room of its occupants." So if blindness occupies your world and this is lit by the fire of the Spirit, it empties the darkness of that room. Whatever is now possessing you that shouldn't, any limitation, any poverty, anything, if you look into it, it will simply act like that fragrant perfume in the closed room and empty the occupant that should not be there. So he opens up the eye and leads them from darkness to light.

So here, I say God plays all the parts. No Negro becomes a white man or white man a Negro, because God is playing *both* parts. Everything in a dream is a symbol. But in this world, this is a waking dream…and this is a waking dream and this is a symbol, too. Everything is a symbol, so that no one is moving from a little worm into manhood as evolutionists teach. Evolution belongs only in, I would say, in the affairs of man. Instead of shooting a man with an arrow we now blow up a million with a hydrogen bomb, so he has evolved the means of mass destruction. That is evolution in the affairs of man. Instead of simply plowing it with a hoe, he now plows it with a tractor that is now driven, and tomorrow it will be with some nuclear energy. The means of transportation, instead of walking across the country and then riding a horse across the country, he now flies, and tomorrow he'll go by almost the speed of light. That's all evolution in the affairs of man. But the little bird builds its nest today as it did in the beginning of time. In God's creation there is no evolution. Everything is but a symbol of God *awakening*.

So when in your wonderful dream…and God speaks to you every moment of time, either in the dream of the night or the waking dream. And so when Ben grows—and "Ben" is "the child of fortune," that's what Ben means. We find throughout the Bible the benediction, the descent of the Spirit upon man, which is the descent of the dove. That is the benediction of the dove, at last, when it comes upon the individual. When man, being the ark of God containing everything, but nothing is outside of the ark, and when the dove returns and Noah sticks his hand out and the dove descends upon the hand; and he brings it in, and the dove smothers him with kisses, and he takes it into himself, the Spirit enters. Having been sent out, he returns, the flood being over. What flood?—the flood of illusion. Buried in all the illusions round about us, and we think them so real, they are all symbols screaming at us, trying to tell us to awake. And when man begins to awake, and the flood begins to subside, the dove returns and the dove comes and lights upon his hand; then he takes him into himself, the ark of God.

So I tell you the little story concerning the play is a true story. This one, who are you? I am the author. And who are you? I am the hero, I am the villain, I am the accused, I am the accuser, I am the judge, I am the warden, I am the jailor. Every one called God's name first before he put the mask upon him. Everything in the world is God, nothing but God.

My old friend, Abdullah, years ago, one night—we never had more than fifteen, sixteen at any one time; if we got twenty we were most fortunate—he said, "Suppose now your mother, the one you love dearly, (who doesn't love their mother), and if your mother now, and you could actually see her eyes, the real mother wearing the mask that you love, you embrace that mask and you love it. But suppose now that she was the fairest, blue-eyed, blonde in the world…" and Ab looked at me, for in the class most of us were Negroes, not more than four of us who were Caucasian. He looked at me and said, "Suppose now the mother you love so dearly, and she is blonde and blue-eyed and very fair of skin, suppose you saw her rise and then she went over and you saw her buried in that very dark, black person. Could you embrace that black, black person knowing the occupant of it is the one you so dearly loved?" Well, I must confess it was a shock to the entire class. Abdullah taught that way. He taught by shocking. He always demonstrated everything, which I don't do from the platform because it would embarrass many of you. Everything he did, he did it with a physical gesture that would really shock. But you can do it in words without using your hands and other members of the body to demonstrate. But he would use all parts of the body to demonstrate passages of scripture to show the unity and oneness of God. He always began the meeting, "Praise be unto that unity that is our unity" Always, the oneness of us all! No matter what we appear to be on the surface, we are all one.

And so, I tell you, God *is* one…there is nothing but God. He is playing all the parts in the world. So when this lady had the experience "you are the apple of my eye," you find it first in the 32nd of Deuteronomy (verse 10). He is speaking to Jacob whom he found in the wilderness and he surrounded him and cared for him and then said, "You are the apple of my eye," for when God looked into his eye, he could only see himself. So when the eye is open so that it can reflect and really reflect the beholder, then he sees himself…and he always embraces himself.

So Job is crying out, do not hide your face from me. Let me see your face, number my iniquities, tell me what I have done that is wrong. What have I done to warrant this? Why do you hide your face as though I were an enemy? Show me your face. If I could see the face of God I would have my salvation, for he would not look upon the ungodly. We are told in the Sermon on the Mount, "And who shall see his face—who but the pure in heart will see his face?" May I tell you, the pure in heart is not something you and I must work for and cry for. I am convinced from my own personal experience that this coming before God—I can't understand why I was drawn there—so my fitness for the kingdom of God is the *consequence* not the condition of his grace. I certainly was not pure in heart. I certainly was not anything I would say worthy of that call, but I knew as I came before him and stood in his presence, of the risen Christ, when he looked into me he could see no one but himself. I returned…the prodigal son had returned.

But, I returned because he called me. Everything springs from God: We love because he first loved us. We come because he first called us. Everything comes from God. So I in my distress, playing the part of the prodigal son, I certainly did not earn the right to come into the presence of God. But in a way not yet explained he opened the eye so it reflected. And I came into the presence by his call and so when he looked into my eye and asked a simple question, it was so obvious, the answer, for I am looking at the answer…that God is love. Then he embraced me and we fused and became one; and he raised my lowly body, at that moment, to be one with his wonderful, glorious body. But certainly I did not earn it. So I can't say to anyone that you can *earn* it. Paul asked a question, "Did you earn it? Then why do you brag and why do you boast?" If you earned it, you could boast, but you didn't earn it. Only hope that the grace of God will come upon you soon! So you can just simply hope.

And no one can tell you how close you are to it. But from my experience and from the visions that are coming, I'd say that so many of us are so close. And I personally am waiting eagerly for this benediction of a dove on a friend of mine, who has already had three [of the visions]. He feels he isn't so near, but I feel it is so near, and I think we have both forgotten the time interval between the last and the coming dove. He didn't date his letter and I didn't date it when I received it. Should have, but that's also scripture, "He comes like a thief." Had I dated it, I'd be calling to tell him it is tonight…and you don't do that. I will come in my own good time and no one will know…it will come so suddenly. But I have a feeling it is not far off, it is almost upon us. I eagerly await the benediction of the dove. When it returns and the flood is over, all the illusions are gone, and then the eye is completely open.

And when the eye is open, you sleep but you don't sleep. I woke on Dec. 1st from an experience I was having in San Francisco, entertaining a small group which I always do when I go there and which I will be in January, and I was explaining that you are not really seeing the being that I *really* am. They said, "Well, I'm seeing the being that I know." I said, "No, you're not. Even now, this very moment the mask that I wear you know, and it resembles the one you touched last year, but this is not the same mask. It's a different mask, but resembles that mask." And then this lady, her name is Jo Craig, said, "Neville, whenever I think that I understand you, you lose me. Just as I think that I really understand you off you go and now you lost me. Here you stand before us and tell me that what I'm seeing is not what I saw last year. I understand it is something that covers you and the being that you really are I don't see. But don't tell me this is not the same being that I saw last year." I said, "No, it's not the same being. The being you saw last year I left on a bed at home in Los Angeles." She said, "No, that's altogether silly." I said, "All right. Good night" and vanished and I woke on my bed in Los Angeles. I was as awake as I am here now, just as awake. I knew exactly what I was doing. I could see Jo before me and she was simply the same lovely, gracious lady that she is, and she said, "I think I have got him now, exactly where I had him, I now understand him completely. Now he tells me this is not what I saw last year, that I didn't touch this body last year."

So I tell you, God plays all the parts. There is nothing but God. So whether he be a thief, a murderer, the judge who judges and condemns them, the jailor who will put them in, the warden who will watch, everything is God. Do me a favor and don't sleep before you read the 12th chapter of Job. In fact, the whole Book of Job is the book of man. But from the 13th verse to the 25th, read it from the 13th through. And then, of course, you'll get so excited that you'll read the 13th chapter. And the whole thing is so altogether fantastic…his plea to see the face of God, because he knows the ungodly can't stand in his presence. Because the moment you stand, though you *were* ungodly, the minute he can see himself reflected in your eye, the apple of his eye, then he embraces you. He embraces himself and therefore you cease to be the ungodly at that moment, and you are one with the risen Christ who is God. You dwell upon it.

Everything in this world is yours for the taking. You take it by a mere assumption. A mere assumption, that's all that you do. You dare to assume that you are the man that you would like to be and sleep in the assumption that it is really so, and see what happens. Because every being in the world is yourself, and they all play the parts that you are now enacting, and everyone who will aid the birth of this assumption will aid it, you don't have to ask them because you are playing all the parts. If it takes a thief to do it, the thief will do it. What man can actually look back at his fortune and know in his heart that only so-called honest men did it? Do you think any great wealth in this world could actually stand the shock if they knew how it happened…the wealth that he has? Start with the kings and emperors of the world. If they knew what went into the fortunes which they now enjoy…and coming down to the great financial barons of the world. Of course, we justify it by putting on blinkers. We say that it is marvelous to have all this money. We become so holy. But God isn't fooled. So in the end he calls us one by one. And then one can look back upon their past and see the whole vast world as their play… and the horrors of it all. But in the end all is forgiven: "Father, forgive them; they know not what they do" (Luke 23:34).

So these wonderful experiences that have been coming in for the past two weeks, I can't thank you enough for sharing them with me that I in turn may share them with everyone who is here…for we are all waking. And in the end, all the wisdom of the world will be as nothing. So Job in this chapter makes the statement, "The power and the wisdom are his." Well, who is the power and wisdom? Paul tells us in his letter to the Corinthians, "Christ is the power of God and the wisdom of God" (1Cor.1:24). So then what is this power and wisdom Job speaks of? Then he tells us the deceived and deceiver are his—the same creative power created the deceiver as the author does and created the deceived as the author does. And God the author is playing all the parts!

My very dear friend who is my partner, Grace Griffith, she and Jack were home a few years ago when this series appeared on TV on Sunday afternoon. It was simply the great ages of man, the kings of England. I can't recall if it was Richard III…and lovely words would come out of his mouth as Gielgud would now explain them. And Grace said to me quite innocently, "You see, they were not really that evil at all." I said, "Grace, my darling, Shakespeare said that." "Oh, yes, yes, Neville." One second later, "You see, they were not so bad at all." I said, "Grace, dear, Shakespeare said it." "Yes, yes, yes." And so it went on and on and on, and she forgot one second later, she forgot it was Shakespeare doing the whole thing. So Hamlet said to his mother, "Assume a virtue if you have it not." Who said it? Shakespeare said that. What Hamlet? Was Shakespeare present to hear what the Dane said? Was he present to hear what Caesar said? Everything is in the mind of whoever the Shakespeare is.

So you want to blame someone, blame God—he played all the parts—because he gave me Christ, gave me his creative power, to use or misuse. He gave me the wisdom to either use or misuse, for he gave me Christ and Christ is the power and wisdom of God. Christ *is* and he lies as in a seed in the soul of every man. And that little seed unfolds and it is called "being formed in man." So "I will labor with you until Christ be formed *in* you" (Gal.4:19). So here he is, he lies as in a seed in the soul of every man in the world so man can breathe. Man can actually create, but what? He doesn't write a letter or maybe he can't even write, but he can imagine and he creates. He creates all the strange things, fantastic gods, and does it whether he be in this form or that form or the other form. One day, having played all and suffered all, the risen Christ calls him and sees reflected in his eye himself. Then he has played it all. What more can he play? And he embraces him…the return of the prodigal son. Whether he is black when he comes back or whether he is white when he comes back or whether he is Oriental when he comes back, when he is embraced he is one with the risen Christ. Don't ask me to describe or define the being that is the risen Christ. It defies description…can't tell… yet it is human but all love embracing everyone.

So no black man is moving from the black to the white, and white to some other color. It's all symbols; everything here is a symbol. So your dream is a symbol and the waking dream is a symbol, too. Ab used to tell us, "You know, if you only understood. You can get on a bus and you can count them…"—he and I would sit in the park together and he would watch people go by, counting, a lady and two gentlemen or maybe two ladies and a gentleman…and maybe three birds flying by…and it all meant something. He tried to explain to me the symbology of what is passing by, that two ladies and a gentleman would differ from two gentlemen and a lady. Get into a bus and as you enter you can tell the future of the ride by the people who entered. The whole thing to him was simply the language of God, and not one of them entered by accident or departed by accident. The whole thing was God unfolding, screaming his language to everyone, but he has ears but they are not yet opened and he has eyes but cannot yet see. Everything in the world is talking to man and there is only God.

So the greatest commandment…just imagine 613 commandments. The rabbis have calculated 365 prohibitions and 248 positive plans. And Jesus reduced it to two, quoting the 6th chapter of Deuteronomy and the 19th of Leviticus, and put these two into one command. He did say there were two, for he said this is the first when he as asked, "Hear, O Israel, the Lord our God, the Lord is *one*" (verse 4). The ___(??) of the word Lord is I AM. "Hear, O Israel"—and the word Israel means "to rule as God." That's what the word means, to rule as God. Jacob, who was the apple of his eye, was called Israel after he succeeded in wrestling with God. He renamed him from Jacob to Israel. So here, "Hear, O Israel, the Lord"—that is, the I AM—"our God"—it's a plural word, Elohim, our I AMs—"is *one* I AM"…this compound unity. So all of us gathered together form one I AM. That's the first command.

Now love it with all your heart, with all your soul, with all your mind, with all your strength. This is the second: Love your neighbor *as* yourself. There is no other commandment greater than these. He takes 613 commands and reduced to two, and tells us there is no need for any other. And always remember that all the I AM's—the blacks and the whites, the yellows, the thieves, those who are stolen from and those who stole, those who sell and those who buy—all the I AM's are one I AM. Always remember it! I am looking into my world and seeing the whole vast world pushed out, it is myself pushed out. Now love this center being, my own I AM—it's all one—with all of my heart, with all of my soul, with all of my mind, with all of my strength. Now the second is this: Love your neighbor *as* yourself. Well, why?—he *is* yourself!

When something happens…like this simple little story. In New York City, this man came ___(??) into my apartment and said he came from San Francisco and that he was here and a paycheck wouldn't come for another two weeks and he couldn't pay the rent. He was only paying four dollars a week and he said, could I help him out to pay the rent? I said, "How much do you need?" He said, "Just ten dollars." I said, "Could you use twenty dollars?" He said yes, so I gave him twenty and off he went. Well, he is one of the phonies. I was deceived and he was the deceiver. So the next lecture night he came to my meeting and my wife was there. He didn't know who she was and said, "What does a nice lady like you…what are you doing here?" I had described the man to my wife and she said to him quite innocently, "I'm here to protect my husband. He happens to be on the platform." He ran down that stairway like a dart. He had faced the wife of the one that he had deceived. I know what happened…well, what show on Broadway could have given one more amusement than this fellow, all this to get twenty dollars? He only wanted ten; I gave him twenty. He only really wanted ten. He spent one hour of his time and my time to get ten dollars. With that intelligence he could have put it to work and made a fortune. But no, so that's how it is. He came in just as my wife said to "case the joint" to see what lady he could touch. ___(??) the entire field to see if he could now get another for ten or twenty or fifty dollars. Well, that's his life. Who is playing it? I am playing it. When I realized the humor of it all, what would be twenty dollars? It's so funny. So you kiss the twenty dollars goodbye and you had an experience. Then you must learn, forgive him, Father, he knows not what he does because you made him play it. Because he is our very being playing it and he is playing it. One day when you become the Father and know who the Father is, he's playing it, played all these things, haven't you played it? You haven't asked someone for ten dollars that you didn't pay back, but you've deceived, you've deceived unnumbered times. So you are the deceiver and the deceived, and the whole vast world is yourself pushed out.

So I say and I say it advisedly and I mean it literally, God plays all the parts. In the end the Elohim, the compound unity, all of us, are gathered together and then the Lord, the I AM, explains in detail the meaning of it all. And then from then on we go into a far, far greater, I would say, breaking of the primal rock into a greater play. That's the challenge, that's the joy. We don't want to simply return and last forever having played the play. We don't want that, we want a more marvelous play, following this that we may be more translucent ___(??), more expansive, and greater and greater. That's how God ___(??). So the One is ever increasing, expanding beyond the wildest dreams, by condensing and fragmenting himself; then gathering all together into the same One. And no one has lost his identity. I know from my own experience you do not lose your identity, yet you include the far greater Self, which is none other than God the Father.

Now let us go into the Silence.

*   *   *

___(??) plus something that I hadn't printed before called *The Resurrection*. That forms the fifth book of the five. You have four that were formerly out of print, and then *Resurrection*. And I do hope that you will read that *Resurrection* over and over. I'm not saying that it is the easiest thing to grasp the first time.

Every word of it is true. It's all true. I've only told you my own experience and you read it and let it seep in. For what they told in the gospels, they are relating their own experience. I stand to witness with them...the same experience.

Any questions?

Q: Would you elaborate on that statement, "Love thy neighbor as thyself." When you're in a state of irritation or you enjoy provoking, what should be your attitude in order to love him as yourself?

A: Love him as yourself and start practicing. As we are told in the very first words of the earliest gospel, which is the gospel of Mark, the earliest words of the Bible are these, "The kingdom of heaven is at hand. Repent and believe the gospel." The word repent is a radical change of mind. So he is unlovely...a radical change is going to change him into loveliness...a radical change. So someone is really a bore, you turn him around radically. You go right down to the roots, not just a little pruning of the tree. Suppose he were or she were the most wonderful being in the world.

You know, some people don't even want that. One fellow in New York City during the last war, he hated Roosevelt, hated him. I said why? Well, he said, "I can't tell you...he thinks he's a king and we don't want any kings in this country. He makes his son Elliott a general when other boys far better qualified are privates...he's a general." I said, "So what? Forget it. You know the law, don't you? This is a principle." And so, he said, "No. You know what I do in the morning? I get before the mirror, while I am shaving I'm telling him off, and do I tell Roosevelt off!" I said, "Who are you hurting? So you are looking into the mirror and you're telling Roosevelt off, what he is, that he's a bum, he's a this, he's a that, and he thinks he's a king." I said, "Why do you do it?" He said, "Neville, there isn't a play on Broadway that I can get into for under ten dollars— oh, in a morning I spend, say, five minutes on my face and in five minutes telling him off I have such fun—there's no play on Broadway running two hours that's going to amuse me to the extent that this does for five minutes." So he wouldn't give it up. He didn't want to see Mr. Roosevelt as a noble person, he didn't want to. He just hated him. He was the only child of devoted parents and he had lots of money himself, but he didn't want any part of Mr. Roosevelt. And no matter what I would say, he would agree with me in words but not in practice. And so I'd say so-and-so is really is a lovely person and you hated him because of some reason you haven't explained...you don't want to know he's a lovely person. And you encounter that all the time.

We had someone home last night, we went off to dinner, went to a lovely dinner and there were four of us. So when we came home, the chap in the party of four—we went over to this place called Scam on top of this building, and had a lovely meal, lovely atmosphere. So when I came back I was...she's the aunt of this boy, but I didn't have the pleasure of meeting his father and his father is her brother; he's gone from this world and the mother of his boy is gone too. I said I only had the pleasure of meeting his mother. Now she doesn't like the mother and the mother is gone, vanished from this world. So I told her what a lovely, gracious lady she always had been in my world, and I didn't want any disturbance. I don't care what you think of her, as far as I'm concerned she's a gracious lady. I could only see her in my mind's eye as the loveliest, loveliest, tender, kind lady and mother of my friend. Well now, he was totally intrigued because he loved his mother dearly. He admired his father, but the father is the brother of this aunt, and he doesn't want to offend the aunt, yet he knows that he loves his mother. I didn't care what the aunt thought or what he thought, I'm simply talking about the lovely lady I met. I always said I wish I had met his father, but he died. Yet she could not be reconciled. She had an opinion of this dead sister-in-law that is not pleasant and to her she couldn't see the need for overcoming that dislike. The woman's dead, but she couldn't falsify an opinion. Here are two opinions of the same person and radically different.

So I say fall in love. God loved us, that's why we love. I couldn't love unless he first gave me the gift of love. Every time I love it's a gift. He gave me every passion in the world so I can exercise it. He gave me hate, he gave me violence, he gave me everything. Then he gave me the greatest gift of all, himself which is love. And I can exercise it. What could I get that God didn't give me? He's giving me himself and he's everything. Yes, he's the thief and he's the one from whom he stole. You read it carefully in scripture. What a book! It's the Book of Books; it's the Word of God. You want to find out who he is? You read it, read the Book of Job. He doesn't understand why these things are happening to me, the innocent victim of this horrible experiment. But it's worth it: "Let us make man in our image." Man didn't request it. Everything is dead and it's dead, it can't be right or wrong, and it can't feel anything. Now he's going to endow it with the capacity to feel, and put it through hell that it may receive the gift of God which is himself. And he puts him through all the things. But Job doesn't understand until the end of the last chapter: "I heard of thee with the hearing of the ear, but now my eye sees thee." The eye is open, all now can be understood; and if you understand all, you see it all.

What author would condemn the actors for playing the parts beautifully that he conceived? Would he rave about the thief if he conceived the thief if he played it well? He'd ball him out if he didn't. If the thief came off that stage without getting the sneer and the hate of people, then he didn't play the part well, and the author is disgusted with that actor and would fire him. I would. "Play it my way ___(??)...you're not telling the part as I conceived it." Therefore, when the audience hisses the one on the stage, who should they hiss? He's unseen: the author. He's in the wings, can't see him, yet he's written the whole thing. So you go and replace the actors. They're all puppets wearing masks; and you want to blame something you call that author out. And he's always unseen. Well, God is unseen and he's playing all the parts in the world. There's nothing but God!

Someone writes a great symphony and you get the 150 to play it. Well, the one who composed it and he hears all these strange things that he didn't intend, he' isn't satisfied. He's going to replace that musician. He just cannot bring out what I want to hear. That's what I intended and he's not bringing it out. So the one who composed it, he wants to hear it as he is hearing it. He wants the perfect actors, the perfect players. And in the end, if there's any praise for the symphony...yes, you will praise the players, they did a beautiful job of interpreting what one man conceived... well, one: "Hear, O Israel"—this is the First Commandment—"the Lord, our God, the Lord is one."

So you start practicing revision. It's called in the Bible repentance. And here in the modern day, here we understand today what revision means; but repentance has become so barnacled that it doesn't convey anything to man but remorse and regret, and that's not what it is at all. So today the churches speak of repentance and you have to repent and do your penance and do all these things. That hasn't a thing to do with repentance. So in my writing I have ___(??) it out and I have changed the name from repentance to revision, because today we understand what revision means. Maybe a year from now or ten years from now it will have barnacles on it too, and somebody will come and change it again, and scrape off the barnacles again, and give it a new name.

We have words that have changed their meanings. In fact, today we almost hate to say...now I have brought in a lovely bouquet of flowers and I say, "Darling, I have brought you a bunch of pansies." Well, my wife understands what I mean; the average person raises the eyebrows. The word pansy has changed its meaning. Pansy used to be a girl's name. All these change over a period of time. So you go back in the Bible and the translator has to get the original meaning. That is all that it means. If I could get the original meaning in the language that I am using that's all that I need. But if I am using the same word that has changed its meaning over the years, I am going to confuse people. And so giving a good translation is as accurate a meaning of the author as possible, and so that is what we need. We need revisions all the time because words change meanings.

Now, our next meeting is on a Tuesday of next week. Thank you.

THE WORD

12/6/66

First let me answer a friend's question. Just a few moments ago this lady asked me, "What does this mean? My daughter..." and I must explain this background. She became a Catholic, a convert, and like all converts they are more of what they become than anyone else, and always resented and opposed her mother attending, well, this. It's so foreign to anything that she believes truth to be. Well, in this dream—and God speaks to man through the medium of dream—she appeared to her mother and she said, 'Mother, tell me about Lazarus.'" Well, I think everyone is familiar with the story of Lazarus, the one who was dead, the one whom he loved, and then Christ came and awoke him from this profound sleep which was likened unto death... he was dead.

So may I tell you that the resurrection of man and the coming of Jesus Christ are one. There is no question of the dead being raised prior to his coming, or independently of it. And his coming is when he comes *in us* and repeats *in us* all that is recorded in scripture concerning himself. It's not a man taking another by the hand and waking him. You've got to tell the story and you tell it in a certain manner. But the resurrection of man and the coming of Jesus Christ are one. He comes *in* us and that's how he *raises* man. There is no possibility of anyone being raised from the dead—and this world is the world of death—prior to his coming or independently of it. So let everyone dwell upon it. He comes to all. Because he *is* risen all will rise. But we call death in this world...it isn't death at all, it's simply continuity. Man continues just as he is, believing himself alive, but he isn't until the coming of Jesus Christ. And Christ rises in us, ___(??) us through his life.

Now tonight's subject is "The Word." We are told, "In the beginning was the Word, and the Word was with God, and the Word was God" (John1:1).

Now it becomes a person. "He was in the beginning with God; all things were made through him, and without him there was not anything made that was made. In him was life, and the life was the light of men. The light shines in the darkness, and the darkness has not overcome it." But I have been reading for forty years, forty-odd for that matter. I became fired with reading at the age of twenty. Prior to that, nothing interested me but sports—cricket, soccer, football, everything athletic—but not anything of the mind. I was in London when a Mr. Bacon(?), a Scotsman, interested me in literature. I returned at the age of twenty to the States, simply hungry beyond measure, and I had to overcome the hunger, so I put in six, seven, eight hours a day reading and meditating. But I have never read any book that has crowded so much into so few words—the first five little verses of the 1st chapter of John—I have never. I have read and read away, but I cannot find anything that is crowded as this is crowded.

If you obtain it, it would take a life time to unravel it. "In the beginning was the Word." Well, the Word both in Hebrew and in Greek means "the meaning." The Word in Hebrew is dabar; the Word in Greek is logos. But it means in Hebrew, the root meaning is "back; that is, something that is behind the thing, the meaning behind." Whatever it is, that is the Word. Someone comes here and makes an announcement or he asks something. What is the purpose of his visit? He may be deceiving in his words…but that's not the Word. Get behind his action. What is the purpose of his visit? Someone calls on some bereaved relative who has just lost a friend, or a husband, or a wife, who is fabulously wealthy, what is the purpose of the call when they haven't seen them in years? What is the purpose? What is the Word? So the Word is purpose, it's meaning, that's really what it means. So in the beginning was meaning, and that meaning was with God, and the meaning *was* God. He can't send any other than himself now. He was in the *beginning* with himself, his whole plan. In him was life, and the life was the light of men. And the light shines in this darkness, and the darkness has not overcome it.

Now, I am told, "And his name shall be called the Word of God," whose name? We're told in the 19th chapter of Revelation it is Christ (verse 13). Christ is all the Word. He's called, then, "the meaning of God." He said, "I am the truth." The Word is the truth. He said, "I am the life," so he is the life (John14:6). He also tells us that the Word is the seed; the seed is the Word (Luke8:11). And God buried his seed in man: he buries his Word. He buries Christ in man, just as a man would bury his seed in the womb of woman; for man is the offspring, the wife of God, "his emanation, yet his wife 'til the sleep of death is past."

Now man is the emanation of God—by man I mean generic man, male, female—and the only husband is God. He buries himself as seed, and the seed is called Christ, called the Word. So Christ is the image of the invisible God, as the seed of man is the image of the one who buries it, mixed somewhat with the soil in which it is buried. So it's not a complete duplicate, but it is as close as you could get to the one who buried the seed. Here we find the Word of God is God's seed. "The promise was made unto Abraham and to his seed," God's seed. "It did not say 'unto his seeds,' referring to many; but 'to his seed,' referring to one, which is Christ," as we're told in Paul's letter to the Galatians, the 3rd chapter (verse 16). To his seed—only one seed buried in man—-the same seed which is the image of the one who buries it.

So here, I find this Word before it is awakened completely in me, it stirs, and tells me all kinds of things to prove that it is true. It tells me all kinds of things, how to test that this thing really is power. "In him is life," is that true (John1:4)? Well, before he was born *in* me, before Christ awoke *in* me, just as described in the gospel, I discovered that there was life in me. I came upon a scene, just like this, objective to me and seemingly independent of my perception of what I was perceiving; and then I knew innately that it wasn't, that if I could arrest what I was feeling *in* me, not in things I saw, they all would stand still. Well, I did. Everything stood still, not a thing could move. So I know life was in me, not in the thing perceived. The objects were there and seemingly independent of my perception of them, but the life in them was not. "And the life in him was the light of men." And so, "As the Father has life in himself, so he has granted the Son also to have life in himself" (John 5:26).

So before the Son is actually born who is one with the Father, he reveals that there is life in him as there is in the Father. Then, he knows the Father and the Son are one. He sees him animate and start things in motion, turn it off, and let them all remain as they were. They were dead. And not one could actually rise until the coming of Jesus Christ. ___(??). So our hope...as the Bible ends with the hope, "Come, Lord Jesus!" Come, because until he comes, we, who *seem* to be animate and alive, are really dead until he comes...and there is no rising independently of the coming of Jesus Christ.

Now, so he comes into the life of all just as recorded in the gospels, as he comes...but prior to it, signs begin to appear, and the signs are life in himself. He stops and he starts the whole clock as it were. The whole thing, he can stop it at will, and start it at will. He realizes where the life is. And the life in him is the light, the consciousness, of those round about him. They're all eating and carrying on and talking and animated, the birds are flying, the leaves are falling; everything is happening and so completely alive and independent of his perception. Then he knows it isn't so at all; all in him...that in him is life. That the Father has life in himself, so he has granted the Son *also* to have life in himself.

"Everyone who hears my Word," as we are told, "and believes will have everlasting life." He is buried in man, but until it is actually quickened by belief it doesn't grow. So he tells the story of the sower that goes forth to sow seed, and the seed is the Word of God, and the Word is God. He sows himself in man. Now, he likens four soils (Mat.13:18). The first soil is the highway, and people tread upon the Word, the seed, and the birds of the air came and devoured it. Then another one, they receive it with joy, but there was no root, no moisture, and then it was withered, in no time it was withered. And then came the third, among the thorns and the thistles of the waste, and they grew together, and the thorns choked the Word. And then came the fourth, on good soil, and it brought forth an hundred-fold.

The same seed planted on the four different soils. Not different seeds, there's only one seed, not *many* seeds. We're told in Galatians, referring not to many, but to one, which is Christ, which is the image of God. He plants himself, his own image in man. And then, from time to time he sends into the world one in whom he has awakened to quicken the seed that it may fall now; the same seed…it's already planted…that it may quicken and the soil be fertilized…in some wonderful way be ready so that it will come out. Because the tears and the trials of the world will choke it, they will be completely forgetful of what they heard.

The first one, they aren't interested at all, not at all. They're interested in all the glamour of the world. If you want to see a modern picture of it, read this current *Time* magazine with the great Truman Capote and his party at ___(??). All the Who's Who were there. Some paid $600 even for a little mask over their face. They couldn't be disguised, but they don't want anyone to know they're not who they really are. Their disguise?—a little mask. Others paid forty cents and publicized it too. Others paid thirty cents and they saw it was really publicized, they only wanted to make the next ten. And all the so-called Who's Who…they couldn't care less. Oh, they'll give millions to the churches. They'll give millions to all kinds of charity. And the Word is trampled on the ground. They haven't the slightest concept of Christ.

In the same picture, there's a little cartoon. This couple is dining in a restaurant, and she said to him, "If the Catholics *don't* have to eat fish on Friday, how can we tell who are Catholics?" ___(??), "How do we tell who are Catholics?" And then, in the *New Yorker*, a delightful one, the devil is sitting on his throne with his pitchfork, and here is one next to him, a little devil, his messenger, and he asks the king of the world—for the devil is only disbelief in all things; the devil really is complete disbelief in the *Word* of God. Not disbelief in other things, only concerning the *Word* of God, the Promise of God. And so the little one turns to the great king of the world and asks a very simple question, "What must we do with those who ate meat on Friday?"

For 1100 years their concern ___(??), burning and doing all kinds of things because they disbelieved, and now they're being burned, what must we do with them? Proclaim amnesty and let them go free? You can't let any more in because it's not a sin anymore. So here, what must we do?" It's in the current *New Yorker.* I think it's a delightful magazine. They bring all these things out...it takes courage to face 500 million people with something just like that, even if you lose a subscription or two. What must we do with them? We've had them there for 1100 years, and every one who ate meat on Friday we got him and brought him in, put him in the furnaces. And here, this thing goes on and on and on, all trivia. So we're living in a world of death.

Now the question is, what must I do? Believe the Word. So let me show you who Christ Jesus really is. In the beginning was the Word, and the Word was with Christ, and the Word was Christ. I use the word Christ instead of God, because they're the same. "In the beginning was the Word, the Word was with God, and the Word was God." Now, the next one it becomes a person, "*He* was in the beginning with God." So the Word now becomes a person. Now comes the revelation of Jesus Christ, if you follow it, "All things were made through him, and without him was not anything made that was made." So I stand here and I bring before my mind's eye two friends of mine, and see them vividly. Sometimes I see them as vividly as I'm seeing you now, not always, but sometimes they become that objective. But they must do what I am going to make them do, and they embrace each other, and one is congratulating the other upon his good fortune.

Well, who did it? Is that a creative act? Why certainly that is a creative act. I can't draw a straight line, ___(??), yet here I can create what Michelangelo couldn't do. Could he make it as vivid and as real as that? He couldn't. Could Leonardo do that? He couldn't, not what *I'm* seeing. This is flesh and blood, this is real...and I'm doing it. Now what does it mean? Well, I can't deny all things were made through him and I am doing it now, then I've found him. I have found him of whom Moses and the law and the prophets spoke. They wrote about him? Yes. All that was written in the book, it's all about me, he said in the 40th Psalm. Everything, it's all about me. So I see what I'm doing. So what does that matter? Now watch...what does it imply? For its potency is in its *implication.* For the Word is not just the arrangement of words to form a sentence, it does mean that, but it also is the arrangement of objects. These are all words of God too, all symbols. And so I arrange objects in space into a certain frame. Now, the Word means "back"; that's the meaning of the Word. Meaning in this sense "that which is *behind* the thing observed or heard; the meaning, the sense," is the Word.

Now, what does this embrace imply? Well, one is congratulating the other on his good fortune. And the Word is power...its potency is its implication.

Well now, does it work? Alright, wait patiently and see. All of a sudden I am confronted with the fact; and one is telling me of the good news, the good fortune of his friend, who happens to be my friend, and I witness. Then, where is Christ? "All things were made through him, and without him was not anything made that was made." Well now, who is he? Did I not do it? Is not that Word now growing within me? Long before it actually unfolds—in the form of the child, and David, and the tearing of the curtain of my body from top to bottom, and my ascent into the heaven of heavens, and then the dove—long before, I was sensing the power that was rising within me. Sensing it by actually applying this principle toward these things in this world, and it worked.

A man looks up and he sees across the street a sign reading his family's name...just he reads the name. He does it patiently two years. Costs him nothing and he delighted in doing it. Two years later the building is for sale, a stranger buys it for him, and he has no collateral, just a piece of paper with his name on it. And that day, that family owned it. One boy for two years began to stir the Christ within. He hadn't had the experience of the birth; he's only had the experience of a power that is latent within. He still believes that Christ is on the outside, that doesn't matter. No matter what I will say to him, and he's my brother, my physical, earthly brother, I can't persuade him that Christ *is* his own wonderful human Imagination. No, he wants to feel otherwise, even though he is making this wonderful, I would say ___(??) miracle come to pass.

In 1922 when he started, he didn't have a nickel and the family was stone cold broke. And today, I don't think, I don't think you could buy the family out for $25 million. I don't think you could...unless I'm misled. It grows and grows and grows. There he is, he started from scratch, by looking and seeing what he *wanted* to see, all in his Imagination. Well, if all things were made through him and without him was not anything made that was made, hasn't he found Christ? He's exercised it but he hasn't found him, not yet. He's exercising Christ, but he hasn't found him. And so, in the world of death he remains. And he said to me when I was home last year, "I'm not interested in anything beyond. When I make my exit from this world, I will find myself in the world wherever I go, if I survive, as I did here. I didn't know. I started from scratch and made a living, did what I've done; and when I find myself there, whoever directed me here will direct me there. And I will simply...I'm not interested in finding out about the world into which I will go."

"So, when I tell you in spite of all the things you have made, not only for yourself but for us, all of us, you aren't interested?" I said, "Alright, perfectly alright. May I tell you what will happen to you? You'll die as all will die to find yourself in a world just like this. It wouldn't be the year in which you died, it seldom is. It's in a year best suited for the work still to be done to awaken you. It may be the year 3,000 and you die in the year 1960-something—for he's my senior by two years—or it may be in the year 2,000, or it may be the year 1,000. You don't have to go this time, you can go into a world...it's all taking place. It's a play and the whole play is *taking* place, and it hasn't stopped. Queen Elizabeth is still dumping her teeth that no one knew how to correct in the day that she lived, when they were all rotted and there was no way of repairing them. She's still hiding behind her handkerchief. That era is still with us. And Shakespeare is still with us in that marvelous age, where they didn't know what a bath was all about, so they drowned themselves in perfume. For they didn't know what it was to really clean the body as we do today. But the whole play is taking place *now*. So then he goes into a world best suited for the work still to be done...for "He who began a good work in you will bring it to completion at the day of Jesus Christ" (Phil.1:6).

So when Christ comes...there is no rising from the grave apart from the coming of Jesus Christ. When my friend asked the question concerning her daughter's request, "Tell me about Lazarus, the one who is raised," Jesus had to come to the grave, didn't he? Then he said, "And he wept"; shortest verse in the Bible, "Jesus wept." So he came to the one he loved who is dead. But, it's the coming of Jesus Christ that coincides with the rising of man. So the resurrection of man and the coming of Jesus Christ are one; but he comes in us, he rises in us.

But before he rises, the signs begin to appear, and all these signs...life in man. He comes upon a scene and he knows that life is but an activity of his own Imagination. Well, what did he stop? He stopped his Imagination. He stops it, he turns off the light, and they're all dead. They aren't conscious. They're still objects, objects in space, but not living. He's drinking his soup, he's dead. There's no life there, there's no consciousness. And so the waitress, walking, and she is not conscious, she's dead. The bird is flying, it's still in space but it doesn't fall. A leaf that's falling, it doesn't fall. Everything is still and there is no life in them because I turned it off by arresting the activity in myself. So I know from actual experience that life is an activity of imagining. You stop it in time and it just stands still. They don't vanish from the world. So Blake said, "Eternity exists, and all things in eternity, *independent* of Creation which was an act of mercy" (*Vis. of Last.Judgment.*, Pp91-92).

So all these are objects of creation; they are forever, they are in space, but they aren't alive; you animate them. And something is taking place in you. This is the soil where God is buried, and he comes out and comes out, and it's God, leaving behind him the play...the whole play. But something entirely different comes out, and it's *all* God. He's bringing out himself. He buried his Word, his seed, in man, and then he brings it out. What he brings out is himself; it's God. "So the Word that goes forth from my mouth shall not return unto me void. It must accomplish that which I purpose and prosper in the thing for which I sent it" (Is.55:11). So the Word has gone out and it's fallen into man. So no matter what man does, in the meanwhile, the Word is still there. But one took it and he didn't believe it. He said, "The Word that came to them also came to us, but the message"—now the word message is translated from the Greek word logos, which means Word; this is now in the 4th of Hebrews—"and the message which they heard did not benefit them because it did not meet with faith in the hearers" (verse 2). So the same Word that we heard and we got benefit from it, they heard, but they got no benefit, for it was not mixed with faith in the hearer.

So the Word is the gospel. The Word is the promise made to Abraham. And the whole gospel summarized is now personified and it's called Christ Jesus. Now it has become a person...so the gospel is Jesus Christ. So, what must I do? Believe him. Believe him whom he has sent, believe him. He's only telling one story, he's telling the story of God's Promise to man, and the story summarized in what is called the gospel is the seed of God. You hear it, you didn't manifest it because you didn't believe it, but it's still within you. It's in you, and you can't get out of it, it's in you.

Now he sends his apostle from time to time to stir it. Not a crowd will come, not a crowd, but those who have allowed it to rise for a moment, and then the cares of the world snuffed it out, go. And then he goes and he sends another one. And then finally the Word is served, for the Word is buried in everyone, in everyone. Not one is going to fail, for he will send his messengers over and over until all awake, because it's God, and he can't lose himself. His seed is buried in humanity. And everyone must awake. When they awake and rise from the dead, it's only because of the coming of Jesus Christ in them, in the same series of events as recorded in what is called the gospel or the Word of God.

So Christ Jesus, this eternal being, is your own wonderful human Imagination, that's Christ. Tonight, try it, test it. Test it...arrange structures of the mind implying the fulfillment of some desire of your heart. It need not be for yourself, it could be for another, but just simply hold it in your mind's eye and get the thrill of seeing what you're seeing. What does it imply? Its implication is its potency. Now just watch it, in your mind's eye, and believe it. Let it go. If you can remain faithful to what you have heard—I heard it, I saw it—well now, remain faithful. It may put him through hell in the immediate present to bring it out. It'll come out, and he'll forget the tribulation and all the horrors that preceded this moment when he becomes healthy or wealthy or whatever it is you want for him, perfectly all right. And he'll be completely oblivious to the fact that you did it, that's perfectly all right, too. He may go sound asleep and ignore anything you are telling him about Jesus Christ, and become one of the great givers to the churches of the world, that's all right, too. God is patient, and he'll send you back to get him once more on another time level.

And all are being called and then awakened. One is awake in the time he is awake, because we are awakened in this world. This is where we flower, and while we're here we're sent. After that we aren't sent. We become the watchers from on high, those that Blake describes as "Those in great eternity who contemplate on death and they said thus: 'What seems to be, *is*, to those to whom it seems to be, and is productive of the most dreadful consequences to those to whom it seems to be, even of torments, despair, and eternal death; but Divine Mercy steps beyond and redeems man in the body of Jesus'" (*Jer.*, Plt.36). Jesus is Jehovah. Jehovah is Jesus, same word.

So one after one after one we're gathered, all into one body. And in the end, may I tell you from my own personal experience, we are one, one body, and yet no loss of individuality, none. I will know you in eternity; and you're not only individualized in my world, but you will tend forever towards ever greater and greater individualization. No melding into a oneness where the whole thing is lost, no. Yet one God, one king, one name, one, and not one of us lost individuality. I'll know you and love you beyond the wildest dream of anything on earth. For the closest relationship on earth is like standing at arm's length, really it is.

I know what it is to love a woman, to love a child, to hold a child in your arms and smother it with kisses and smell it. Nothing is sweeter than the odor that comes from a baby, as far as I'm concerned. To put your nose next to the neck of a little baby and just this sweet...oh, I can't...there's no perfume like it as far as I'm concerned. And to put your hand on the flesh of the woman you love just to touch it. But it doesn't compare to this level of which I speak, can't compare, because not a thing separates you when you embrace in this world. It's the mingling that you can't describe in this world when we're so separated by these garments of flesh and blood. And all are destined towards that one body...that all are gathered without loss of individuality, not one. I'll know you all. Not only do I know you all, I'll know everyone. Though there be billions, my consciousness will encompass all; for I am one with my Father, and he knows all, and not one will be lost.

So the Word of God which is called externally the Bible is really his message of salvation, which is buried in every man. For it was told to Abraham in the beginning, the state called Abraham—Abraham is an eternal state where the journey begins. "And he told the gospel beforehand to Abraham... and Abraham rejoiced that he was to see my day" (Gal.3:8; John 8:56). And then came the story. So we are really heirs not only to this promise of a child but to a presence. We are heirs to the presence of God. God becomes man, in his seed, that man may become God. So I'm heir to a presence *and* to the Promise of his Son. His Son is David. So he gives me himself as the Father; and to prove it he gives me his Son who calls me, Father. Then I know that the drama has been completed in me. And there's no other way that I could have moved from the world of sin and death. And all will...everyone will.

So here, "The Word was with God, the Word was God." He was in the beginning. God was a person, am I not a person? Alright, "He was in the beginning with God." So there I am a person. "All things were made through him and without him was not anything made that was made." And then I try it. No one ever told me I was ever destined to be God. My mother never told me. My father never told me. My minister never told me. No one told me. Like Paul, it came through revelation. So I never heard it from a man, they never told me, and suddenly I tried it. Well, it worked. But, all things are made through him? Well, then I have found him. Well, how could I do it?—I imagined it. Then Imagination must be he. It is. The divine body Jesus is the human Imagination; that is God himself.

And then, you see that you assemble not only words to convey meaning, you assemble objects in space to convey them. And what do they convey when you assemble them? In my brother's scene, the name of the family on a building that we did not own and could not have paid a dollar towards it, here it takes in a whole block, and he is seeing the family's name on it, and persists day after day for two solid years. Then a stranger buys it and takes only a piece of paper from us as collateral, and no money. Paid him back with a six percent interest over a period of ten years, and then the building is completely ours. When he died, he left my brother another $150,000 in cash, several homes, and all personal effects, saying it was the best investment he ever made.

That was something on the side...like extra food on the tree, as it were. He started from there and started...and not a thing has stopped him. Yet, in spite of his physical success he's not interested in knowing anything concerning... but he will give generously to churches, generously to all things. When I go, they tell me what to do as they told me here when I came, which is perfectly alright, it's a healthy condition, but I wasn't giving back. I came to do something different. And he and I, loving each other as we do, we know we have one little bone of contention. He never liked the drinking of my father. My father drank heavily, and he loved my father dearly but disliked his excessive drinking. And so, I am not an excessive drinker but I drink, and that's our only bone of contention. He almost said, "How can you be a man of the Spirit and drink?" I said, "You manufacture it, don't you? You make a lot of money manufacturing rum, don't you? Will you sell your stock or give it away? Give it away if you are opposed to it. Give it away." No, no, he makes money. Well then, I will have to make more by drinking. So I drink and enjoy every drink that I take...unless I take too much...and I do sometimes, occasionally.

But nevertheless, our only bone is simply my martinis. Outside of that, he thinks Neville has done very well—hasn't any money. I remind him I haven't any money...but for my stock in your so-called business. "It's not yours, you know. Don't you dare touch it, it's all mine," and, I have always to remind him. Because I don't *earn* money from what I do, he thinks you don't have it. I said, I have as much as any member of the family and don't you dare forget it. You might have made it, but you didn't give it to me. My father was the means through which it seemingly came, but I gave it to myself. That's why I came through Joseph and Wilhelmina Goddard. So I knew you could be replaced and you were going to make it, so I came through so that you may make it and give me the freedom that I now enjoy. To him that's complete madness. I was shown all the parts I could play and said now give me this one, in this little tiny island, where no one knows you, you're completely unknown, unwanted. But I know that you're going to come before me and I know exactly what you're going to do in this world: You're going to make an awful lot of money for me! So I came right through. ___(??). And so when it came my father's turn to give it away though I was not present he didn't discriminate. I was a thousand of miles away when he made his Will, but each shared equally, no discrimination.

No one could dare raise any questions concerning me to my father, because he'd slap them right across their face. None of us was old enough for him not to whack us, never...even though we're grandfathers. And so, I told him, I said, I came in and I know exactly what, because the whole thing was shown me before I came. Here is your part now take your choice. You're coming in to awaken this time, in this little island, completely unknown. This morning's paper said they'd just become independent in Barbados, and how the first act of theirs was to make a sand___(??). And now the first act after they make a sand___(??) is to find a place big enough to spread it out to dry. ___(??). Hard to find any place in the little tiny thing called Barbados to spread the sand out to dry it. That's where I came in, that little point in space, unknown family, unknown everything. But I knew what the family would produce, and it would give me then the cushion to do the work of telling the Word of God. So I took it. Oh, you have a choice, in time.

So the Word of God is buried in you. It is God himself. And if you question it, put to the test what I've told you this night. I tell you that the human Imagination is the divine body of God, and God is Jesus himself. It is your human Imagination. Now test it. You too can speak the word that can't return void—assemble imagery implying the fulfillment of your dream. Believe in the reality of what you've done, what it implies, believe its implication, that's its potency. Then drop it. Do nothing about it, and see how it molds itself in this world of ours. Then you find who he is. Then patiently wait for him to come. He will come. "Come, Lord Jesus!" is the end of the Bible, the very last chapter of Revelation: "Come, Lord Jesus!"

Now let us go into the Silence.

*   *   *

___(??) then we close the following Friday for a couple of months. We're looking at two lectures left. So next Friday we'll be here and then we have but one lecture the following week. That would be the following Friday, the 16ᵗʰ. Then we are closing and reopening here on the 13ᵗʰ of February. Just for a couple of months...and then we'll be gone until September. Are there any questions, please?

Q: Who is Solomon?

A: Who is Solomon? As much a state as his father David. Solomon is the beginning to awaken; that is, when I play the part of David, then comes the Solomon. So I am Solomon, I am David, I am every character in the story as I begin to unfold. David is the *central* character of the entire Old Testament. Well, I would say Abraham is the beginning, but there are more things written about David than any other character in the Bible, because he is the essence coming through. Well, the promise is made to David his son would inherit. And so, we say, is it really Nathan or is it really Solomon? It is neither: "I am the root and the offspring of David, the morning star" (Rev. 22:16). So I am the Father, I am Jesse, I AM, and I am the offspring. And I am the Word of Christ. So I pass through... Solomon is simply a state of wisdom through which man passes. He is called the wisest of all the kings and the richest of all the kings. So man passes through the state of being extremely wise and just and kind and merciful. It's a state through which he passes. So it's not a person as you are a person or I am a person, but it's a state of wisdom. Even though you may not be considered by others today to be wise, you pass through that state.

   And like all of us, I know many of my dear friends who were great educators who died enslaved, for they were not wise when they died even here. A very dear friend of mine, in fact, the father-in-law of my sister-in-law, he was the headmaster of all the Friend's(?) schools in the

East, a great educator, a brilliant Greek and Latin scholar. He read Greek and Latin as easily as you read English, a brilliant scholar. The last two years of his life he knew no one, not even his wife. So here was wisdom turned into imbecility. Edison, who was his idol, died insane...a wise, wise philosopher, he died insane. What causes that? If the wisdom of man is foolishness in the eyes of God, it doesn't really matter. It doesn't *really* matter. All that we must think to be altogether wise and wonderful will prove, in the end, it isn't so at all. It's all foolishness in the eyes of God.

So all of our wise, wise men...I wouldn't say all, but many of them...of course, we've had others who were mad from the beginning, like a Hitler and a Stalin. They were mad from the beginning, but no one knew it, and they worshipped and followed these mad beings. That they were stark mad, who knew it? Now the generals are writing their books and they are confessing now that they knew he was mad but late in their knowing of it. They should have known in the beginning. Khrushchev came out and said that he always knew that Stalin was mad, but he didn't do a thing to stop him and he killed millions of people. Khrushchev himself said he never knew if he ever went to see Stalin if he'd ever come out alive. And he ruled all of Russia. We have the same mad states of mind all over the world, who would follow him and try to impose his concept of life right here.

So here we have these people who are not violently mad, brilliant minds, like the Edisons and people of that sort, who in their declining years the body wears out, they went mad. So let them be now. Once I do not become violent and injure anyone in this world, it wouldn't matter what they said of me, plus they called me mad for years, anyway. ___(??) it's the Spirit.

Q: Neville, you said that Ab talked to you about symbolism and you used an example two women and a man as opposed to two men and a woman. Would you explain what you meant by that?

A: To him everything was simply a symbol, that everything in the world was a symbol. And he tried to awaken in you some intuitive faculty to interpret symbols as they went by.

Two men and one woman would differ from two women and one man. He never explained it; he just would tell you it differs, try to understand. But what he would make me do is skry, and he would say, I want you to skry for me. Well then, I would skry and then tell him what I am seeing. Skrying is looking not at but through. You look through the lamp shade and see what you are seeing as you look through it, rather than at it. Don't look at the lampshade, look through it, and then tell me what you are seeing. And so, he would then begin to interpret my skrying. And so, he would have me skry...all to awaken the intuitive faculty. But he said, "Everything here is screaming at us, but it's God's alphabet and we don't understand it." If you could read the unfolding symbols, I doubt that you'd be walking the earth. You could know exactly what's going to take place by reading the symbols, because every letter in the Hebrew has a numerical value.

Q: I'm trying to think of the statement that you made about Dr. Albert Schweitzer. The ___(??) the resurrection. He made some statement about Jesus...and ___(??) he experienced something.

A: What Schweitzer said in his *Quest of the Historical Jesus* was that although he wants to believe in the historical Jesus, he has not unearthed any evidence to support an historical Jesus. That is Schweitzer's final comment on the subject. It's called *In Quest of the Historical Jesus.* He made a serious effort to find proof to support his belief that a person called Jesus walked the earth. I tell you there is no evidence to support it. That the story of the Bible concerning Jesus Christ written by our unknown authors, called the gospels—Matthew, Mark, Luke and John—they're completely anonymous. No one knows who they are. They were relating their *own* experience. And because only God could rise...well, God is the only Savior. For the Lord, our God, is the only Savior. We call him Jehovah, the Yod He Vau He, or the Lord. It's the *only* Savior. Therefore, when they felt themselves passing through these experiences, they interpreted the Old Testament based upon what they were experiencing. It was so unlike what they had foreseen in prospect. And so, when they could now see what *actually* happens as against what they thought would happen, that some savior would come from without, and he's coming from within, the seed is unfolding from within the man, and *they* are the Lord. So then they named and personified the experience as Jesus Christ, Christ being the anglicized name for Messiah. There comes the blessed one. There comes something that *really* is taking place. But they didn't realize it until it happened. They told their own experience. Jesus Christ is in man, as the seed, as the Word.

So, Schweitzer made every effort. He wanted to believe in the historical Jesus Christ and sought and searched. As much as any man could he made a sincere effort, and came to the conclusion that there is no evidence to support the historicity of a person called Jesus Christ. And yet, it is more true than were it an individual. It's a *cosmic* Christ buried in all as the seed of the Creator, and wakens *in us*, and *we* are the very one formerly we worshipped as without, and hoped someday to see him coming from without…and all the churches are still expecting him to come from without.

So when we read in scripture, there is a mingling of both the present, which is the realized state, and futuristic, that's the gospel. He *comes* and *will* come. You're told that in the fifth chapter of John. He is speaking now of those who will hear and believe the Word of God. Now he speaks of this presence who not only *will* come but who *has* come. "Truly, truly I say unto you…" and he tells them that this presence has come and will come. So here is realized and futuristic, eschatology, mingled together as one. So he's always coming in everyone, individually, and, therefore, still to come in those in whom he hasn't come. The Bible is a mystery. It's not secular history at all.

Q: The baptism of the Holy Spirit more or less stops ___(??).

A: The baptism of the Holy Spirit comes thirty years before the drama of Jesus Christ begins to unfold in man. You are taken in Spirit into the presence of the *one* body, the glorified body of Jesus Christ, who embraces you and you are incorporated into his body. At that moment, your lowly body is completely changed to be of one form with his glorious body. Then you are sent. From that moment, you are sent. It takes thirty years telling the law…and you're telling the law for thirty years. As you're told in scripture, "And Jesus when he began his ministry was about thirty years of age." Not a man thirty years old, but thirty years from that moment of being baptized with the Holy Spirit. For when you're embraced, that's the baptism of the Spirit. At that moment you're baptized and made one with God and no one can sever you from that union. And now you become a spokesman for him in your own way. Whether you articulate it for others or not, you're only telling one story, not trying to give any solutions to the problems of the world. I wasn't sent here to plant any opinions on what America should do or Russia should do or races should do, only to tell the story that Christ has risen and, therefore, *all* will be saved.

That's my only story. And thirty years comes to an end, it comes so suddenly you don't observe its coming; it comes as the resurrection. Then, you're resurrected from the dead. So I say that no man can rise from the dead apart from the coming of Jesus Christ in him. And the whole thing begins to unfold—that takes three and a half years, or as Revelation calls it, 1260 days (12:6). ___(??) speaks of it as a time, a times and half a time (Rev.12:14). A time is a year, two times, and then a half a time, which would be six months, and three and a half years would be 1260 days. Christ's ministry lasted three and a half years. And that end comes with the dove descending upon you and the voice said, he loves you. And the drama is over. And like Paul, you linger in the flesh for awhile, still trying to stir the Word in others. For he said, "It is my desire to be gone and be with Christ, for that is better by far, but for your sakes the need is far greater that I stay on in the body." And you stay on in the body while you can still stir the Word that is buried in man. Not everyone will take it, but they aren't ready for it. The soil must still be plowed and then ___(??).

The time is not right for, I would say, 99.99 percent of the people in the world. Today they are far more interested...in London in 1925, this wonderful lad—he was six months my junior; in '25 I was twenty, well, he was twenty-plus—I said, "Are you interested in these things?" He said, "No, certainly not. I'm young, I have to live first." No matter what I would say to him...I said, "Well, your father gave me this *Light of Asia* and he gave me all these lovely books, and I can't tell you, I just can't tear myself away from them." "I'm not interested," he said, "My father is an old man." The man was fifty years old, but he was an old man. His father was an opera singer, who had retired, and they lived in a small, lovely little home in Alastead(?) And they were a delightful family, called the Baileys(?). Well, Matthew, that was his name, and he would not have anything that was ___(??). So when we came back to America four months later, next thing I heard that he'd gone off to India as a tea taster, and contracted some kind of tropical disease and died...wasn't interested. He had so many things to do in this world that he couldn't possibly be interested. So he made his exit at the age of twenty-one, unprepared, uninterested, not a thing could interest him. He had to live it up, because he had all this before him. He left what he called the old father and the old mother. Well, they lived to be in their eighties without their son. So he wasn't interested.

And today, if I saw that crowd over at the Plaza Hotel who attended ___(??) for the party, do you think that one would attend this meeting? First of all, it would not be socially correct. What, to be seen among certain riffraff when they're all wearing thousands of dollars on their backs and tens of thousands on their necks and their hands. And that is glamour. Well, all tomorrow will go to the undertaker, and he will not know one body from the other. Take all their rings off, and their sons and their daughters-in-law could not care less, into the auction room it will go...all the things that have been so precious, all that goes to the auction room. And the little garment means no more to the undertaker than an undergarment.

But they're not interested. The Word fell upon the highways. It's in *them*, but they are the highway where the birds eat it. All they are is simply the rock where there is no water: Nothing there to give it life—no psychological interpretation of it—so it can't take deep root; and then the cares, the prejudices, and all the glamour of the world, the thorns and the thistles of the way, they choke them. Very few have the soil prepared to receive it, where Christ can come into his life and unfold in him. I say to you, he *has* to come. You can't rise from the dead independently of the coming of Jesus Christ.

Goodnight.

WE ARE WITNESSES

12/9/66

___(??) I found it. It's "We are Witnesses." Everyone is a witness to God's Promise. We're told in the 44th chapter of Isaiah...in fact, it starts with a question, "Who has announced from of old the things to come? Let them tell us what is yet to be. Fear not, nor be afraid; have I not told you from of old? And you are my witnesses! Is there a God besides me? There is no Rock, I know not any" (Is.44:7). So he tells every one of us, you and I were all in God in the beginning. This is not an accident—we're all contained within him—it's a purpose, it's a plan. We saw exactly what God's purpose was, every one of us, no one left out.

Now, what is a witness? A witness is one who has first-hand information of a fact or an event. We're told in scripture that the evidence of two or three, if they should agree, it is conclusive. If two or three witnesses agree in testimony, it is conclusive, but you cannot on the testimony of one man. There must be two or more. Now we are told that scripture is God's testimony. This is what man must testify to. And he testifies to it by telling the story not as hearsay but of his *own* personal experience. Here we find the words, "That which was from the beginning, that which we have heard, that which we have seen with our eyes, that which we have actually seen and touched with our hand, of the word of life, *that* declare we unto you" (1 John 1:1). There now are the witnesses.

Now, "Call the next witness." May I tell you, everyone in this world will be called to testify to the truth of God's Word as revealed in scripture. According to some rabbinical principle, and it really stands forever, what is not written in scripture is nonexistent. That seems stupid, doesn't it? This room is not written in scripture and we're told it's nonexistent. My name is not in scripture, your name is not in scripture, a marriage is not in scripture, the whole vast world is not in scripture, and what is not written in scripture

429

is nonexistent. And we're called to testify not to anything here in any court we know, but only to the truth of scripture, to the Word of God. That's all that we're called upon to do. There isn't a pope's name in scripture; there isn't a rabbi's name in scripture, no one. Rockefeller's name isn't in scripture; our presidents are not in scripture; the kings aren't in scripture; none of these things are in scripture, and we're told they're nonexistent. We're only called upon to testify to the Word of scripture. And God's play unfolds in us. How? The whole plan is contained in what is called Jesus Christ. Jesus Christ in us fulfills scripture. And said he to them, "All that is written in the law of Moses and the prophets and the psalms *must* be fulfilled...scripture *must* be fulfilled in me...and Christ *in you* is the hope of glory" (Luke24:44, 22:37; Col.1:27). So Christ in man slowly unwinds himself, unfolds in man, and fulfills scripture; for no man can enter that state of glory until he fulfills scripture. And every word is fulfilled in us, in every child born of woman.

Now here, in the 20th chapter of Luke, we're coming to the end, and he asks a question. He looked at them, having looked at all of them, he said, "What does this text of scripture mean: 'The stone which the builders rejected has become the chief corner stone? If anyone falls on it they are broken into pieces; if it falls on anyone it will crush him'" (Luke 20:18). This is the Lord's doing and it is glorious in our eyes. No one had it, no one understood it. But I have at home...I wouldn't want to exaggerate...at least a dozen different commentary works on scripture. There isn't an exegesis that touches it, no commentary title. Any attempt goes so far, far away from it; they do not know what it is all about.

Now let me tell you from my own personal experience, God is your own wonderful human Imagination, that's God, and God and Christ are one. He speaks of a rock, "Of the Rock that begot you you are unmindful, and have forgotten the God who gave you birth" (Deut. 32:18). He equates the Rock with God. In the letters of Paul, the 10th chapter of 1st Corinthians, he speaks of this Rock, "And we all drank from this supernatural Rock which followed us, and the Rock was Christ" (verse 4). So he equates now Christ with the Rock, and the two with God: God is Christ.

Now, what does he mean "If I fall upon this Rock that I will be broken into pieces, and if the Rock falls upon me I'm crushed"? Listen carefully. I tell you your own wonderful human Imagination is God. That is Christ in you that one day will awake, and you'll have life in *it*: The whole vast world will become alive in you. There's nothing but Christ. There is nothing but God. Now, what does it mean, if I fall upon it? The word fall is "to light upon," as you read it in scripture, just to light upon. The word stone or rock means "that which is steadfast, that which endures, that which abides, that which seems so secure, that is so *sure* in this world."

Now, here in this room right now, here we are and we all agreed to dream in concert. Same room...our reactions differ...but the same room. The mountain is the same mountain. We all see it and our reactions differ. In the mountains of life, the problems to overcome, and I know what your father did, you know my father, and they all seem so real and so abiding and so solid you can't overcome it when we are what *we* call awake. So in this state of consciousness we all agreed to dream in concert and see the same thing and play the part, all in concert. But by night, by dream, we are hurled each into a separate world, completely broken, as we fall asleep. Let man fall asleep and he is hurled by his dreams into a separate world. And then he conjures from the depth of his soul what he may expect when he returns to this that is so solidly real and so unmovable and so abiding. And I tell you, all this world that is so real and so abiding and so unmovable is just as much Imagination as that into which we fall when we are fragmented at night, every one hurled by a dream into a separate world. And we bring it back, all of our broken self; and we bring back all these pieces into a picture, and try to unravel it, try to interpret it. We'll be confronted with this...and here is the rock that now crushes. If the rock falls upon us we are crushed; we are crushed by this seeming immovable object, round about. And we fall at night into sleep and we are broken into pieces, each into his separate world.

Now, you need not accept this *huge* rock and dream anymore in conflict. You can change it without altering for others the seed, without altering and destroying the great conflict. You need not accept as fact anything in this world; then you begin to awaken. No matter where you are born in the world, no matter what a person is doing in this world, you don't accept it as final. You simply will not. And then you take it up in your mind's eye and rearrange it. When you rearrange it in the depth of your soul, then you are broken at night. Until you become conscious you don't rearrange it to your own satisfaction, but it tells you so much when you come back to this awful rock that crushes you when you see it.

So, the witness..."You are my witnesses! Who has announced from of old the things to come? Let them tell us what is yet to be. Fear not, nor be afraid; have I not told you from of old, have I not declared it? And you are my witnesses!" Now, if I am a witness then I must experience. You told it to me, but now I must experience it. You told it to me and executed it in the written Word. For the Bible is now personified as a person. Everything written about me is in that book; everything written about *you* is in that book. So you are told, now that I know that all that is written here is all about me. So everything written in the scripture must be fulfilled in me. And then scripture becomes a person and it speaks. As we're told in the 3rd chapter of Galatians, "And scripture, foreseeing that God would justify the heathen..." It's translated the gentile, but the word gentile in Hebrew, which is goyim, and the word nation and the word heathen are the same. So you can translate the word goyim as "nation, gentile or heathen." So they choose to use the word gentile, but there was no gentile in that day. Either you were a heathen or you were simply one who accepted the law of God.

So here we find, "The scripture, foreseeing that God would justify the heathen by faith, preached the gospel beforehand." The scripture is preaching. So the scripture is telling, it's become a person and is preaching the gospel beforehand to Abraham. Now we're told that all of us are collected in Abraham, the father of the multitudes, the father of the nations. We all entered that state of faith and we heard this story, everyone heard it. And everyone must become eventually the witness to the truth of what God foretold. What did he foretell? Not a thing about your position in this world or my position. If I became the biggest aspidistra in the world, it's only a big shadow, meaning nothing. People pay billions to publicize their name and build monuments to themselves, and then they vanish leaving not a trace behind. But something in them will come out and one day witness to the eternal Word of God. So only as we witness the truth of God's Word have we really done anything in this entire wonderful universe of ours.

So I tell you, these are the things you will witness. You will witness a drama in four acts. It will have a prologue and an epilogue. The prologue will last, well, up until the embrace of the risen Christ. When he embraces you and you're baptized with the Holy Spirit, you will answer only from scripture. You will not answer any word of Shakespeare, no word of the great giants of this world in literature; not one word will you utter of theirs, you will answer from scripture. Every question that's asked of you the response is scripture. From then, for thirty years, it is the intensified prologue. It comes to an end so suddenly you have no time to observe it. And then, four wonderful scenes, the great plan, and that takes three and a half years. It culminates with the great descent of the Spirit upon you, that which comes in the bodily form of a dove.

Then after that is an epilogue. The epilogue is simply fulfilling scripture. Night after night, passage after passage after passage unfolds within you. But the drama is over with the descent of the dove. And then the epilogue...and played based upon the need of those who are about to awaken. And he sends you still locked in your physical garment because of the need of those who are breaking the shell. And this is the witness of God. We are all witnesses, and everyone eventually will witness the truth of God's Word. It doesn't matter what a man does physically in the world, he plays all the parts. There isn't a part he doesn't play...be it the thief or the one from whom it was stolen, be it the billionaire or the pauper, not a thing.

But bear in mind if...and no one answered. Because they couldn't answer it, the Sanhedrin plotted to trap him and then sent spies in upon what he said. He would say something and it would seem to be an offense against the secular world, then they would trap him. But he had to play the part. But of what they heard, or what they thought they heard...and they accused him of being king. "So you are the king?" He said, "You said it, I didn't." But if I am delivered into your hands, he said, he who delivered me is the guilty one. "You could do nothing to me were it not given to you from above." The whole drama is being played from above. He said, I am not in this world. "You are from below, I am from above; you are of this world, I am not of this world. And if you do not believe that I am he, you will die in your sins" (John 8:24). You'll hit that rock and it will crush. You'll fall night after night, as you will, and it will simply break you into pieces. Every night we fall asleep, and we're scattered into pieces, and form our personal drama in our separate worlds; and bring it back with the hope that he, in the depth of our own self who is Jesus Christ, has spoken to us in this wonderful symbolism and given us the ability to interpret. Sometimes it needs interpretation; it seldom comes in a simple, simple manner.

But I will tell you everything recorded you are going to experience. Will you experience the crucifixion? Yes, and may I tell you, there is no pain attached to it...that the triumphant entry into Jerusalem, which is followed by the crucifixion in the gospel...and he moves triumphantly into Jerusalem, into the City of God. It was *there* that he was crucified. And may I tell you, the night that you move fulfilling scripture into Jerusalem means in fulfillment of the 42nd Psalm: And I led them in a triumphant march into the city, the Holy City, and they were all in this gay procession. Then as you move into this marvelous city, this crowd that is so gay and so marvelous...and someone next to you will hear a voice. The voice will come out of space, and the voice will say, "And God walks within them." Who else could walk with you? I couldn't be animated were it not that God animates me: He's my breath. And God walks with them and the woman asked the question, "Where is he? If God walks with us, where is he?" and the voice answers, "At your side." And turning to her side, she looked into your face, and she will call you by name, and she'll be hysterical because she knows you on this level, and knows all of your weaknesses, all of your limitations. Because she knows you so intimately, she'll become hysterical in her laughter. Then as she calls you by name and asks the voice, "Do you mean that"—calls you by name—"is God?" Then will come the voice, but not for her ears or for the ears of the tens of thousands that you're leading in this gay procession, only for you; and it comes from the depths of your soul. What a voice. And the voice will say to you, "I laid myself down within you to sleep, as I slept I dreamed a dream, I dreamed..."

and then, maybe you will not break it as I did. I became so ecstatically happy that I couldn't resist responding and reacting to the emotion. For he's sleeping within *me*! That God laid himself down within *me* to sleep! "And as I slept I dreamed a dream, I dreamed..." and I knew what he was dreaming: He is dreaming that he's I, and when he wakes, he *is* I. But before I could hear the final sentence that I knew, I now was able to describe in that fantastic height or depth, call it what you will.

Finally, I returned here and I am a sea of vortices. A vortex, a vortex, a vortex, a vortex and my two soles of the feet are vortices, six vortices. But what ecstasy! What joy! You can't describe the thrill that is yours when you are nailed to this cross. And you wake on the bed, pondering this fantastic experience in the fulfillment of scripture. Now you are a witness to this story, that God became man—you are man, generic man, we're all man—so God became man that man may become God. So he actually becomes man in the most literal sense and nails himself upon this cross. And then he wakes in us. Then he gives us the most wonderful way of knowing: Only through his Son, the 2nd Psalm, "Thou art my Son; today I have begotten thee" (verse 7). And so the Son [David] stands before you and calls you, Father. You know you are his Father and you know he is God's only begotten Son. So now you know exactly how God did it. Nailed himself upon you and awoke within you and brought forth his Son who calls *you* on whom he's nailed, calls you, Father.

Now, a friend of mine, in the audience tonight, she wrote me a letter this past week. She said, "I had this wonderful experience. I woke at three in the morning and I can only remember the last part of my dream. I knew my dream came in three parts, but I could only remember the last part. The last part, when I woke at three, was preparing fruit, all kinds of wonderful ripened fruit, and I was preparing to eat. I woke. I took a pad, I took a pencil, I thought I must remember the first two parts but I couldn't. I thought if I go back to sleep in the feeling that I could remember them, well, then I will. So I went back to sleep, and suddenly I woke. It was seven in the morning. I couldn't believe my eyes when I saw the clock. It was only a matter of moments that I fell asleep, how could it be seven? It was three when I awoke and fell back to sleep, how could it be seven? However, I had not a thing written on the pad. The pad was on the bed, the pencil on the bed, and not one word written on it.

"So I went about my duties for the day and at 9:30 the phone rang and my dear friend Jan called, who holds this group where we all discuss only the Bible and our visions and our dreams. So she called, as she often does, it was 9:30, and she was discussing with me the Book of Job. And something she said...I can't for the life of me remember what she said...but it triggered the memory of the dream. Quickly, I recalled the entire parts, the first and second part. It was, in my dream, I was actually on a cross, a wooden cross. And then, suddenly, I am observing the cross. I am not on it, I am looking at it; but while I was on it there was no pain, none whatsoever. I am on a wooden cross; then I am looking at a cross. And before my eyes the cross seems rooted and it begins to grow, and takes on branches. The whole thing becomes the most wonderful living tree filled with ripened fruit. Here I am now from this ripened tree upon which I was crucified I am gathering fruit... when I awoke at ten."

So here, another aspect...all these are similar. I'm not going to say that you and I must have the identical...we have the same experience, but it must not be a duplicate in the sense that it's a copy. The birth of the child may come differently from my own case. Someone reaches up to his head, holding it from the forehead, and it falls into his arms. That's different, but it doesn't mean that it is not the birth. One is severed from top to bottom and it's a gentle thing. It was not so in my case. Mine was a violent act, but without pain. It was so quick. If I took a sharp, sharp knife now and slit your throat so that you ___(??), you wouldn't feel it. If I really made a quick incision you wouldn't feel it, the impact is so great. But in my own case it was terrific, but not any pain. In my friend's case, he said, it was a gentle motion, like a hot knife through butter, and the ascent was a gentle ascent. It wasn't so in my case. But I will not go out and say it *must* happen in the way that mine. No. One woman is in labor for twenty-four hours and one opens her mouth and the child is born.

The grandmother called me tonight and thanked me for whatever happened. What did I do but assume that she called me that the thing was perfectly done and the child was perfect. The child was three weeks overdue. The little mother...it's typical of this day or that day...for the boy was born, 8 lbs. 4 oz., ___(??), and three weeks overdue. Still she got the feeling of going to the hospital. She went and before she could almost get on the bed the child was born. No problem whatsoever. And so, in her case the child was born that way. I know of others in my own circle who labored for twenty-four hours and forty-eight hours to bring forth a child that was only five months. So I can't say that because in my own case that it happened the way I recorded it that *that* is the way it's going to happen in every case. But, I do say the *sequence* is the same. I do say the child follows on the heels of resurrection. I do say all these things just as I have recorded. I am a witness to the truth of God's Word. That's all I can tell you.

But to tell you that it must be a *duplicate* of the way that I have told it would be stupid. Matthew doesn't tell it as Luke does. Matthew speaks of three kings who came, and Luke of three shepherds. Shepherds...he didn't say three...but he said shepherds. In my own case they were normal ordinary men and there were three. But, in Matthew he named them as kings, and they were brothers who came as kings. Tradition has it that they were kings, and all were brothers. In my own case they were not kings but they were brothers. They were my brothers, but they were normal ordinary men that I played with and wrestled with and fought with...and loved dearly. But they were my brothers. They certainly were not kings, but they were brothers. So, Matthew claimed by tradition that they were brothers, and Luke doesn't claim that they were kings at all or brothers, just ordinary men.

So I will not go out and say it must happen just as it happened to me. But I promise you you're a witness. Everything I have told you you have heard. "Who has announced from of old the things to come"—didn't say a word about Russia or America or any president or any king or any queen or any person in the world. He's only speaking of his Word must unfold in man. So, "Who of old announced the things to come? Let them tell us what is yet to be. Do not fear, be not afraid; have I not told you from of old and declared it? And you are my witnesses! Is there a God besides me? There is no Rock, I know not any." When I unfold in you, I do not need any secular world to actually aid it. I will do it while you walk in the secular world, but I am doing it *in you*.

So here, the rock will fall upon you, like this world it will crush you. But learn from scripture how to live even though it frightens you. You can get out of that state. And you dare to assume that you are the man, or the woman, that you want to be, and that rock, even though it's a mountain, it will change and conform to an easier way for you in this world. If it falls again into another state, dare to apply God's law. Day after day...as Paul said, "I die daily"...I will die to this and assume that I am that. And when that becomes a mountainous state, I will die to it and assume this. I keep on assuming day after day, and changing my fabulous world to make it conform to my ideal, what I want it to be in my world. But night after night we fall. So when we fall upon it—what?—our Imagination. That's what we fall upon, for we're only Imagination. So I fall into my Imagination. And here I am fragmented and each falls into a separate world. So by day we agree to dream in concert; by night we are hurled by our dreams into a separate world. Everyone will experience it.

Now, some will take this challenge. One lady wrote me, she made a nice design, made a circle, and wrote on the outside of the outer circle "Imagination is the true man." Then the other, 'Man is God." In a faint red ___(??) is "I am." Then she drew another circle, and then a still smaller circle. And that inner circle she divided into six parts of sixty degrees to the section, making 360 degrees for the circle. But at the very center she said, "The Father within us, he does the works." And then in each section she's written, as she conceives it, six virtues: "Faith to do nothing," "Persistence to do nothing"...and she mentions these wonderful six virtues, where if she had the courage to do nothing. "If the Father within me is doing the work, then let me have the faith to do nothing." And so, he's bringing forth a witness to his Word. But in the meanwhile, I will assume that I am that which I want to be, and let the Father within me do *that* while he's working in the depths of my soul, producing a witness to the truth of his Word.

So, faith in the deeper sense is the acceptance of the witness. Can you believe the witness who is a friend? For your own sake I hope that you do, for you're not going to hurt the witness when he departs by not believing in his testimony. For you're told in scripture they did not believe him. But he covers the earth anyway. In the 3rd chapter of John you'll find many verses, and he came bearing witness to what he had seen and heard, and they did not believe him. "If," said he, "you will not believe that which I have seen and heard of these things of life, how could you believe if I tell you of heavenly things?" How could man asleep in the secular world believe for one moment what one could tell him concerning the heavenly things? It wouldn't make sense. And then they would turn completely away from him, so he did not tell them. ___(??). You'd become completely disturbed if you told of the heavenly things, because you have no symbols on earth to relate them. How are you going to relate them if there's not a thing on earth that you could use to relate what you see that hasn't a thing here to relate it?

I know even in these four scenes, as the drama unfolds, it frightens one the minute you get to the state called "the serpent." The child is alright, that doesn't frighten. Awaking in your skull doesn't frighten, or your skull, but you never thought of yourself as a serpent. Never thought of that symbol in any relationship to self, and it scares. Right there one is scared. So if these things that must happen to all frightens one, then what are you going to do when other things begin to happen? You have to lock them within and asleep. He said, "It is not yet. I have many things to tell you, but you cannot bear them."

So here, I tell you everyone is going to be a witness, to what?—to God's Word. The Word is already printed for us and you're going to actually duplicate it. The whole thing will unfold within you and you will be a witness before God. No one can fool him. When you are called it's because you have done it. And you're called right into his presence and you are once more the Elohim that you were before you *deliberately* fell for expansion of the whole. Everyone will once more rise to that state.

So if I would suggest anything, just read that Bible. Don't understand it? Read it anyway...read it and read it and read it in the hope. As Paul said in his letter to Timothy—he's about to depart and he wants to make it very, very clear to Timothy, for he said, my departure is at hand. "The time of my departure is here. I have fought the good fight, I have finished the race, I have kept the faith. Henceforth there is laid up for me the crown"—definitive, not *a* crown, *the* crown, there's only one prize—"the crown of righteousness." Here in this he's explaining the ___(??) letter by ___(??) "Paul, an apostle of Christ Jesus by the command of God our Savior"—he pinpoints the Savior of the world as God—"and of Christ Jesus our hope" (1Tim.1:1). Christ Jesus is the *image* of the invisible God. So our hope is *to be* that image. For if I only become that image he will resurrect me, for only Christ is resurrected. Man is saved through the resurrection of Christ *in him*. Remember that Jesus Christ in man is resurrected. There is nothing but Jesus Christ, and he's in every man, and raises himself in man at that appointed hour.

But the one who raises him is God the Father, who is looking at his own image. He that is seen is one with the one who beholds him. So, I and the Father then are one. So Christ in man is raised, and when he's raised then this world is left behind. But Christ himself is still buried—that seed of God—in everyone in the world. In everyone he'll be raised and he'll witness; as he's raised he'll witness to everything said in scripture. So let the nations rub it out. Can't buy the Bible, I'm told, in, well, maybe more than half the world. If you take Russia and China together they would represent more than half of the world, or maybe half the world in population and the Bible is not available. They look upon it as an opiate that keeps man enslaved, so let them keep it away. All will come to it eventually.

Now let us go into the Silence.

*   *   *

Q: The thirty years, how is that explained? I know it isn't thirty years ___(??).

A: Well, my dear, strangely enough, it is. It is thirty in multiple ways. But you're told in the end of the 3rd chapter of Luke, "And Jesus, when he began his ministry, was about thirty years of age." That's the end of the 3rd chapter and then you go right in to the seeming genealogy, but he had no genealogy, really. This is an insertion to give it some standing in the secular world, for he's a wholly supernatural being. Jesus Christ is supernatural. It's not some little man walking the earth; it is in you, that makes you breathe. Christ allows everyone to breathe. Because without Christ *in* man, you couldn't breathe, you'd be simply, well, dead. And when he begins to breathe in you, you are still, until he awakes in you, an automaton. In many respects one is. When you experience it, it's disturbing, but I can't deny the experience.

So when he was about thirty he began it. Well, I know from my own experience from that moment when Christ, the risen Christ...which is only one man, Christ is God. Believe it or not, there is only one God, and that's the risen Christ. You and I are but members of that one body. And he's gathering back his fragmented world into the one body; but this time instead of being made of dead stones we are living stones. It's the *new* Jerusalem, the *new* body, each a *living* stone with life in himself to make things alive in this world. Everything you will make alive tomorrow, but everything. And so, we're gathered one by one into one body, and that one body is Christ Jesus. As we're told, "One body, one Spirit, one Lord, one faith, one baptism, one God and Father of us all, who is above all, through all and in all" (Eph.4:5). And that is the risen Christ.

So I say to everyone, I know Christ is risen therefore humanity is saved. I don't care what they go through. Let the bomb fall—I hope it doesn't—but you're saved. Why?—because Christ is risen. And that doesn't come when someone calls you dead, no, that's continuity; it's not discontinuity, which you must get to the point of discontinuity. For instead of moving horizontally you then rise vertically, and I, if I be lifted up from this horizontal motion, I'll draw all men up. One being is drawing all. All are coming into the one body and you're his body. His body is your body. He's changed your lowly body to be of one form with his glorious one. That is the most fantastic thing! How can one body contain *all*? But it does. It was all there to begin with anyway; one Lord who fragmented himself into this "more than the sands of the sea and the stars of heaven." You can gather altogether. It is not the will of your Father that one be lost, so not one is going to be lost. I don't care what he's done. The most violent...well, I don't have to go into the morning's paper to find someone who kills six people. Just look at Stalin or a Hitler...that these things in the world...who deliberately took the seeming innocent by the millions and gassed them or shot them or even buried them alive, they still will not be lost. That's the love of God. God is all love; that's all love. And everyone is going to be drawn back into his body as a witness to all that he foretold in the beginning, and then we're all the risen Christ. There's only Christ.

Q: (inaudible)

A: We're told that salvation is of the Jew. Alright, here, by divine knowledge... put it this way, there are some who are organized by this divine wisdom to be instruments for his pronouncements. So he makes from his own scattered body a selection through which he speaks, and it's recorded. They haven't grown in numbers throughout the centuries. We in this country have grown to 200 million people. The little place of England, they were only a few wild men, they grew to 55 million and ruled almost a billion people in the world before they became broken and had to give up India, it 400 million, and this other place with 60 million, and that other million. But that little group of wild men, they would grow that enormous crowd. We have grown to 200 million; Russia grew to 220 million; China to 700 million. And yet, a little Hebrew remains that little Hebrew and only 11 million. The world always points it out, trying to kill it. They can't kill it. Not in eternity will they kill it. And when they feel that something is wrong again, it's the Jew that's at fault. I think you could completely overcome it and can't overcome it at all. The minute something goes wrong, it's the Jew. ___(??) all day long. Always the Jew... he points at the Jew and blames the Jew for everything in the world. He has all the money in the world, they'd say. Why else would ___(??) ask him for a five-dollar bill? I'm not saying there aren't wealthy Jews and that there are very wealthy Americans who are not Jews. Is Mr. Rockefeller a Jew? Are the Mellons Jews? Are the Fords Jews? And so, you point these up and they just don't like to talk of that, because you pointed this fabulous billions in the hands of ___(??). Are the Kennedys Jews? In two generations they made 400 million. Ask them how?

Yet they point to the Jew, because someone can afford a better house and wants to have a better house. Well, you say, he always wants to get into a profession. Well, he has to. The Jew was forced into developing this because there were so few of them and he couldn't develop this. So he had to ___(??) on them. And the world still goes wild trying to...you'll never in eternity rub him out. This is God's Word: "Salvation is of the Jew." The wandering man, he wanders the world. They think they have a home? That's no home. That'll be scattered too. Little Israel, all will be scattered. That's no home...not *intended* to have a home. So they think they're home. ___. That's not Israel, that's not Jerusalem. Jerusalem is here [pointing to skull]. Jerusalem from above is called Sarah and she's our mother who brings us into freedom; and Hagar is from below, the loins, who brings us into slavery, ___(??). So they think that is their home...that's no home. They'll be wiped out. And this Israel...certainly wiped out. It was never intended. They were carrying the Word of God; wherever they go they have it, even in a little place like this, and keep the Word alive. And out of this wonderful Word will come all. All that comes out other than that, they're called the nations of the world, the goyim, the heathen. So we think that we really understand Christ as we worship Christ? What priest have I ever met who really understands the mystery of life?

Q: I'm not talking about the literal meaning...I'm talking about when they say the Jews crucified Christ. Now, in your meaning what is meant by the Jew when they crucified Christ?

A: That's what the churches teach...

Q: But the Bible...

A: No it doesn't. May I tell you, read the 10ᵗʰ chapter of the gospel of John: "No one takes away my life, I lay it down myself. I have the power to lay it down, and the power to lift it up again" (verse 18). And then they began to stone him with the literal facts, because they did not know what was speaking. This is all a mystery. Did not Paul say, "Great indeed is the *mystery* of our religion"? If it's a mystery, then it is a mystery. A mystery is not a mystery ___(??) the facts, but not a mystery. He said, "Great indeed"—and he's speaking now as he's taking his departure from the world, he's writing his letter to Timothy, the 3ʳᵈ chapter, the 16ᵗʰ verse— "Great indeed is the mystery of our religion." He didn't know it at first, and he went off to destroy everyone who would talk about this. And man began to awaken as God. He thought it was history until Christ appeared in him. The whole thing is simply God unfolding; there is nothing but God. So no one takes away my life, I lay it down myself. I have the power to lay it down and the power to lift it up again. I spoke earlier tonight from experience of the crucifixion that was ecstatic, no pain whatsoever. No Jew took my life. I willingly contracted to this limit of contraction and opacity that I, after reaching the limit of confinement, would burst the shell and begin to expand beyond the wildest dream into translucency.

Goodnight.

GLOSSARY

Affliction - Experienced for the purpose of fashioning man into the image of God which when completed the individual is inwardly awakened and shown to be God (one's own I-am-ness).

Awakening - The soul of man awakens from a profound sleep of "6,000" years to his true divine identity (the return of long memory). Man experiences a series of six visions: resurrection/birth from above; David and the father- hood of God; splitting of the temple of the body/ascension into Zion; the descent of the dove, over a period of three and a half years—all are signs of your transformation from limited man back into God.

Bible - All parable. Not secular history but salvation history. Man's spiritual autobiography. The Old Testament is adumbration and prophecy, while the New Testament is fulfillment of the prophecies: the events depicted in the story of Jesus Christ which man experiences.

Bible Characters - Personifications of eternal states of consciousness (not historical beings). Two lines of personifications run through scripture: the inner man and outer man; e.g. Eve (inner) culminating in Jesus; Adam (outer) culminating in John the Baptist.

David - The symbol of humanity—all of its generations, experiences, and the concentrated time in which they spring, fused into a grand whole, and personified as a glorious youth who (in vision) calls you "Father." God's only son (Ps.2:7); the anointed, the first born from the dead, the Christ. Also, eternity, a lad, a stripling; personification of the resultant state; symbol of man's creative power that overcomes all challenges. Only David reveals the Father.

Egypt - This age of illusion; the state of ignorance that I AM is he, as opposed to "that" age, the awakened state.

Enemy of Israel - All false gods and beliefs in causation other than the only God which is I AM (your I-am-ness or awareness of being).

Faith - Response to revelation rather than discovery of new knowledge. An assumption persisted in; an experiment that ends in experience. Loyalty to unseen reality. Opposite of faith is worry. To determine a thing.

Glory - God's gift of himself to each individual soul, ultimately. Achieved by an internal transformation of man into God by God (man's inner being) (2 Cor. 3:18). The state of awareness man enjoyed prior to the descent into man (John 17:5). Man's true identity returned, greatly expanded having experienced and overcome death.

Imagination - The eternal body of man; God himself. Man's awareness of being; the inner five senses; God's/man's creative power; the I AM (called God, Lord, Jehovah, Jesse, Jesus, the Dreamer, the Father). Man's creative power keyed low is human Imagination, the son— but the same in essence.

Imagining - Picturing a scene that implies the wish fulfilled, feeling the present reality of it, drenching self with that feeling, believing it is done, and remaining faithful to the imaginal act until it manifests.

Israel - "He who shall rule as God" (all of humanity at the end of his/her journey as man); a man in whom there is no guile.

Jesse - Any form of the verb "to be" (hence I AM; God the father of David, Ps.2:7).

Jesus - The I AM (Exod.3:14); the Father. Also called Jehovah, Lord, Jesse. Means "Jehovah is salvation." Anglicized Hebrew word Joshua. God individualized is when you say "I am." Universal humanity.

Christ - (See David above) The power and wisdom of God personified (1Cor.1:24)

Jesus Christ - Personification of awakened Imagination and man's creative power. God awake in man (two having been transformed into one, Ehp.2:14). Personification of man's soul; the animating principle of a being. Bifurcated term: "Jesus and his Christ" (Rev.11:15; 12:10). Father/Son.

Man - God (Imagination) is man, the son, the creative power keyed low. Destined to be awakened as God. Man's power is greatly expanded by overcoming this world of the senses, of extreme limitation, opacity and contraction.

Old Testament - Series of permanent states of consciousness through which man must pass, personified as characters; New Testament is Old Testament's fulfillment.

Parable - A story told as if it were true, leaving the hearer to discover its fictitious surface character and learn its hidden meaning. (See Mat.13:3 and 13:18 for instruction on how to solve the riddle of parable.)

Paul - To find the I AM; to desist in seeking (as opposed to Saul, one who seeks; also humanity still suffering from amnesia). Paul is the symbol of anyone who awakens; one in whom the six visions has occurred.

Potter - The Imagination personified (Jeremiah 18:1). Also teaches revision of facts in order to get new results. Lord (Imagination) and Potter linked (Is. 64:8).

Power - One's ability to create by use of Imagination. The inner five senses used to to assume the wish fulfilled, which contains the way to bring it into being.

Pray/Prayer - To imagine. Defined as: motion toward, accession to, in the vicinity of, nearness at. A mental-emotional movement into a new state of consciousness by assuming the feeling of the wish already fulfilled, along with gratitude therefore. Not supplication.

Primal Form - A being of fire in a body of air.—not flesh and blood.

Purpose of Life - To learn to create imaginatively and to exercise the power of love to overcome this limitation called man. Eventually, to regain the exalted state of God, without loss of identity...a gift to man (Luke 12:32).

Repentance - A deliberate radical change of attitude towards life, called revision by Neville (called repentance in scripture). Not contrition or remorse.

Time - Two times exist simultaneously: Eternity or big time; and sidereal time or man's view of a past, present and future (temporary and part of this dream's illusion).

Transformation - The inner process conducted entirely by the Inner Being (God) on the individual to change man into himself. Man cannot earn it, nor do anything to shortcut the process or the time required to accomplish it. A loving result of the journey of the soul through fires of experience as man.

Vision - Revelation. Contains three elements: the supernatural, parallels stories in scripture and quite vivid. Issues from the only source, God (Num.12:6; Job33:14).

Visions of The End (Six) - Signs to man that the internal transformation into God (by God, your "I am") has been completed and the promises to man have been fulfilled. (For a list see above "Awakening")

World - A dream dreamed in concert for the purpose of sentient experience and expanding our creative power. The world is dead if not animated by Imagination (as is man). Also, the individual (aka, nations, cities, rivers, mountains, etc., all man).

A few sources of the quotes used by Neville:
James Strong's *Exhaustive Concordance of the Bible* (with Hebrew and Greek dictionaries, containing the original meanings of words); Bayley's *Lost Language of Symbolism; The Complete Writings of William Blake; The Bible— Revised Standard Version* (most used).

PRODUCTION NOTES

1. The word Imagination is capitalized because it is synonymous with Lord, God, I AM, Jehovah.

2. The set of figures ___(??) is used to indicate a missing word, words, even a phrase, inaudible on the tape from which it is typed.

3. Parentheses are used at the end of a sentence to indicate book, chapter or verse of a biblical quote or other source used in the lecture but not identified by the speaker.

4. Italicizing of a word usually indicates voice emphasis made by Neville. Also used to indicate a book, magazine, newspaper and sometimes reference to a chapter within them.